WRITER:
DANIEL WAY

PENCILS:
CARLO BARBERI (#50), ALÉ GARZA (#51-54 & #61-62), SALVA ESPIN (#58-60) SHAWN CRYSTAL (#55-57), & FILIPE ANDRADE (#63) with MATTEO LOLLI (#62)

INKS:
WALDEN WONG (#50), SEAN PARSONS (#51-54 & #61-63), SHAWN CRYSTAL (#55-57) & SALVA ESPIN (#58-60) with DON HO (#62) & JEFF HUET (#63)

COLORS:
DOMMO SANCHEZ AYMARA (#50-54 & #58-59), JOHN RAUCH (#55-57), GURU-eFX (#60-63) & VERONICA GANDINI (#49.1)

LETTERS:
VC'S JOE SABINO

COVER ART:
DAVE JOHNSON

EDITOR:
JORDAN D. WHITE

SENIOR EDITOR:
NICK LOWE

DEADPOOL CREATED BY ROB LIEFELD & FABIAN NICIEZA

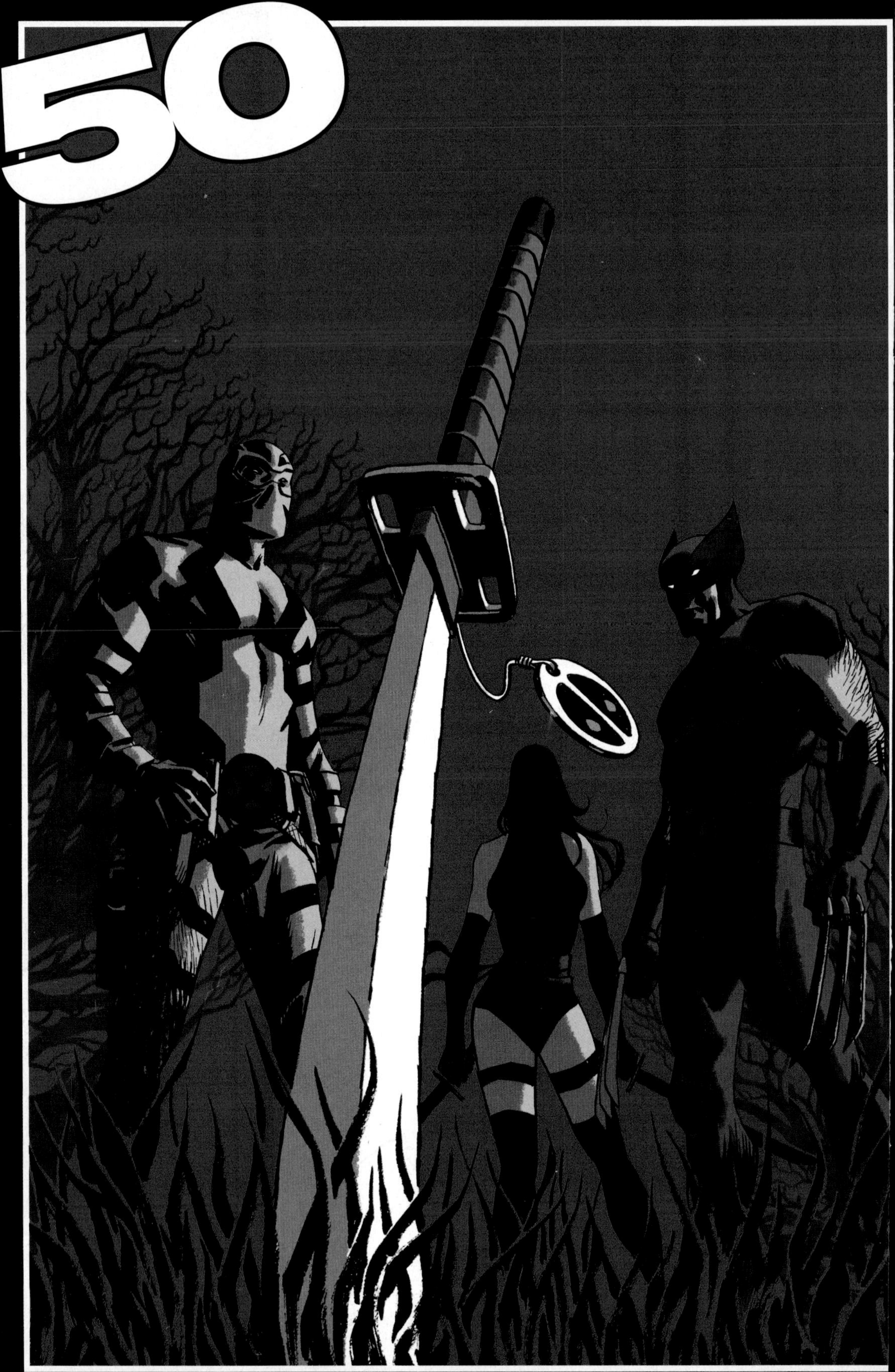
50

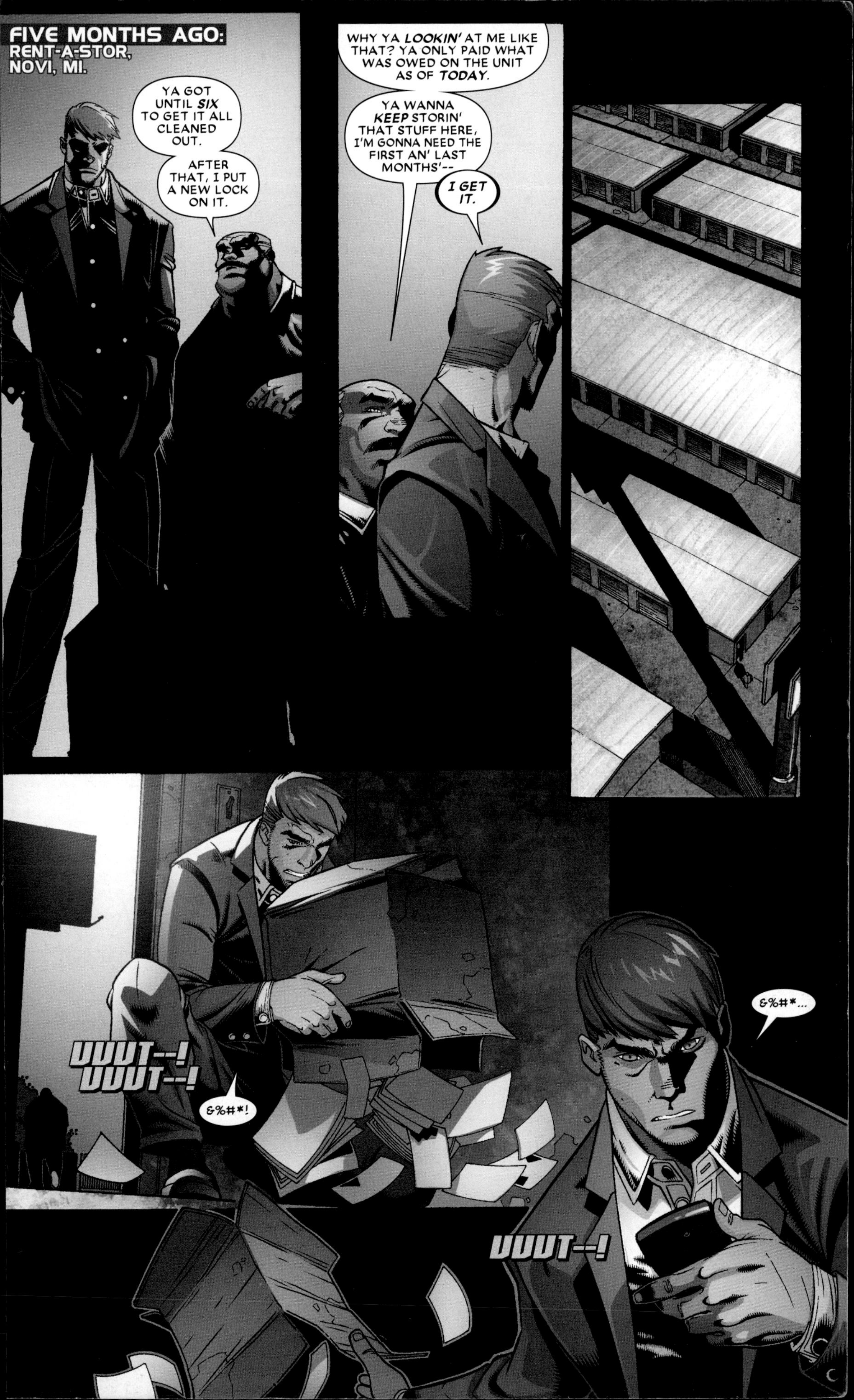
FIVE MONTHS AGO:
RENT-A-STOR, NOVI, MI.
YA GOT UNTIL SIX TO GET IT ALL CLEANED OUT.
AFTER THAT, I PUT A NEW LOCK ON IT.
WHY YA LOOKIN' AT ME LIKE THAT? YA ONLY PAID WHAT WAS OWED ON THE UNIT AS OF TODAY.
YA WANNA KEEP STORIN' THAT STUFF HERE, I'M GONNA NEED THE FIRST AN' LAST MONTHS'--
I GET IT.
VVVT--! VVVT--!
&%#*!
&%#*...
VVVT--!

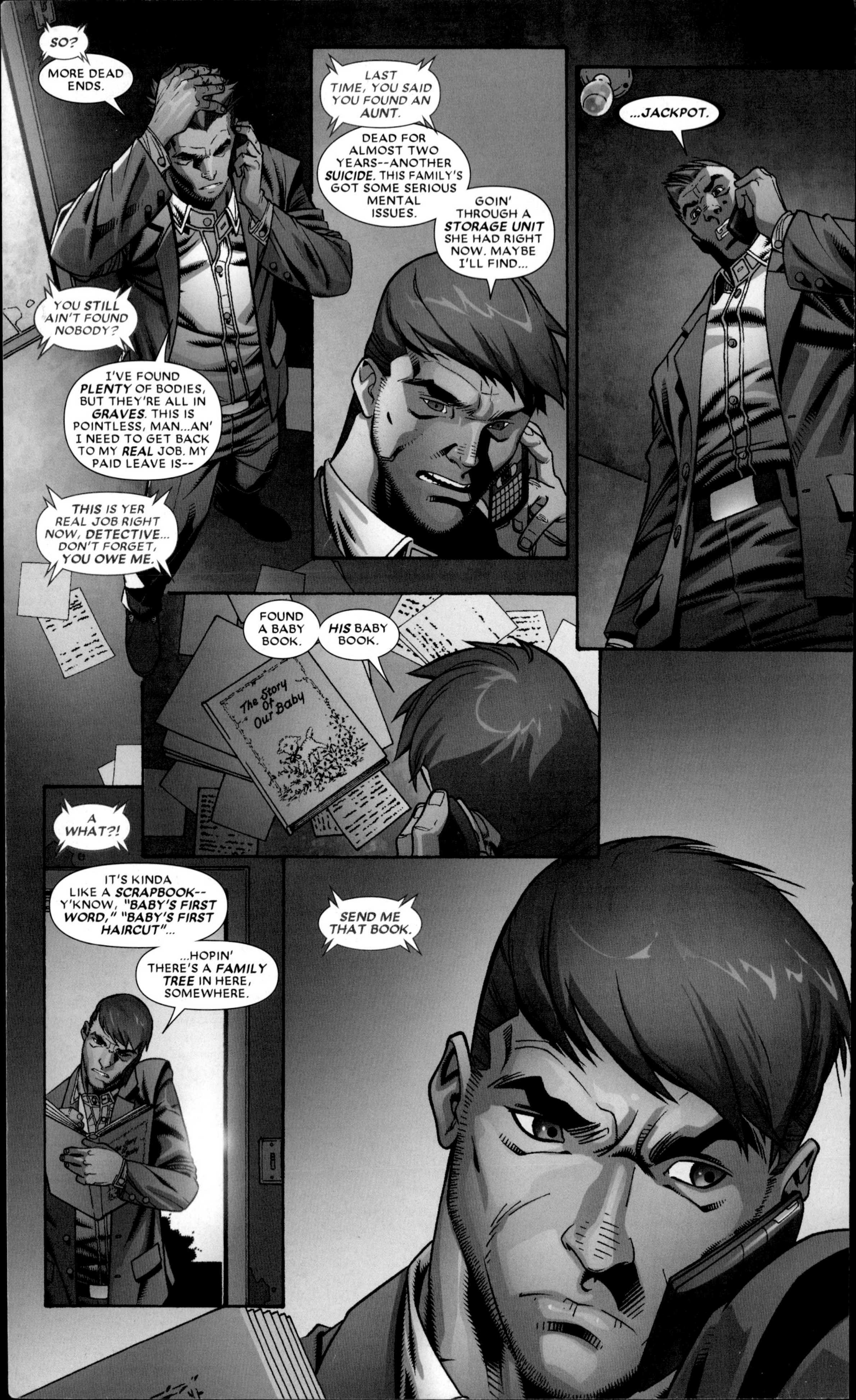
SO?
MORE DEAD ENDS.
LAST TIME, YOU SAID YOU FOUND AN AUNT.
DEAD FOR ALMOST TWO YEARS--ANOTHER SUICIDE. THIS FAMILY'S GOT SOME SERIOUS MENTAL ISSUES.
GOIN' THROUGH A STORAGE UNIT SHE HAD RIGHT NOW. MAYBE I'LL FIND...
...JACKPOT.
YOU STILL AIN'T FOUND NOBODY?
I'VE FOUND PLENTY OF BODIES, BUT THEY'RE ALL IN GRAVES. THIS IS POINTLESS, MAN...AN' I NEED TO GET BACK TO MY REAL JOB. MY PAID LEAVE IS--
THIS IS YER REAL JOB RIGHT NOW, DETECTIVE... DON'T FORGET, YOU OWE ME.
FOUND A BABY BOOK.
HIS BABY BOOK.
The Story Of Our Baby
A WHAT?!
IT'S KINDA LIKE A SCRAPBOOK-- Y'KNOW, "BABY'S FIRST WORD," "BABY'S FIRST HAIRCUT"...
...HOPIN' THERE'S A FAMILY TREE IN HERE, SOMEWHERE.
SEND ME THAT BOOK.

Some jobs are just too tough for your average fast-talkin'
high-tech gun-for-hire. Sometimes...to get the job done
right...you need someone crazier than a sack'a ferrets. You
need Wade Wilson. The Crimson Comedian. The Regeneratin'
Degenerate. The Merc with a Mouth...

It's no secret that Deadpool has a healing factor. It's that certain special
something that allows him to heal from all wounds, take any and all
damage and bounce back without a scratch. It's also made it impossible
for him to achieve his heart's desire—to slip off once and for all into
the cold embrace of Death. But wait! Wade was recently fighting Evil
Deadpool, an evil duplicate with that same power, when evil Deadpool
was shot with a dart that negated his healing factor! And he died! Like,
DEAD dead! So...there IS a way to kill Deadpool!

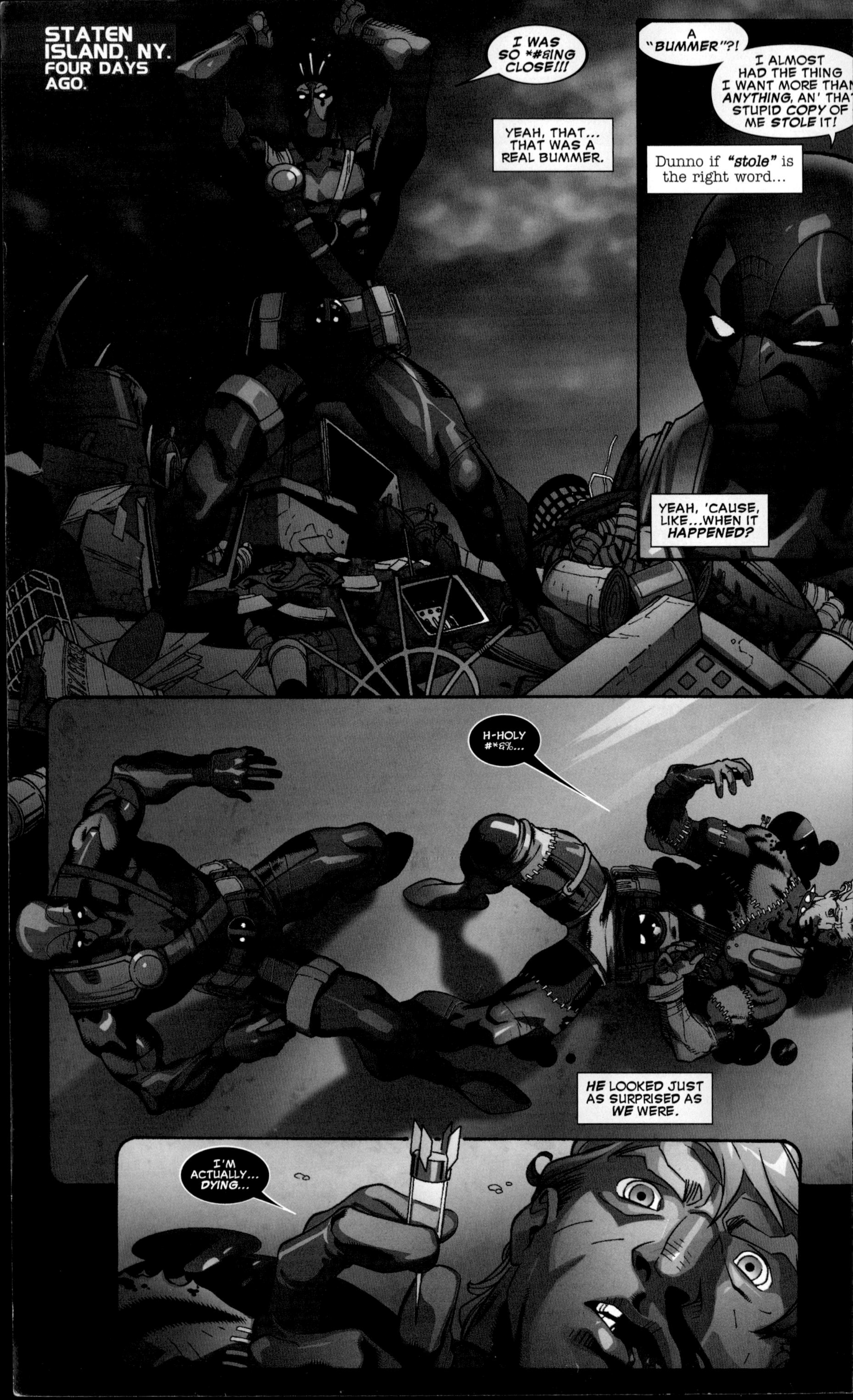
STATEN ISLAND, NY. FOUR DAYS AGO.
I WAS SO *#&!NG CLOSE!!!
YEAH, THAT... THAT WAS A REAL BUMMER.
A "BUMMER"?!
I ALMOST HAD THE THING I WANT MORE THAN ANYTHING, AN' THAT STUPID COPY OF ME STOLE IT!
Dunno if "stole" is the right word...
YEAH, 'CAUSE, LIKE... WHEN IT HAPPENED?
H-HOLY #*&%...
HE LOOKED JUST AS SURPRISED AS WE WERE.
I'M ACTUALLY... DYING...

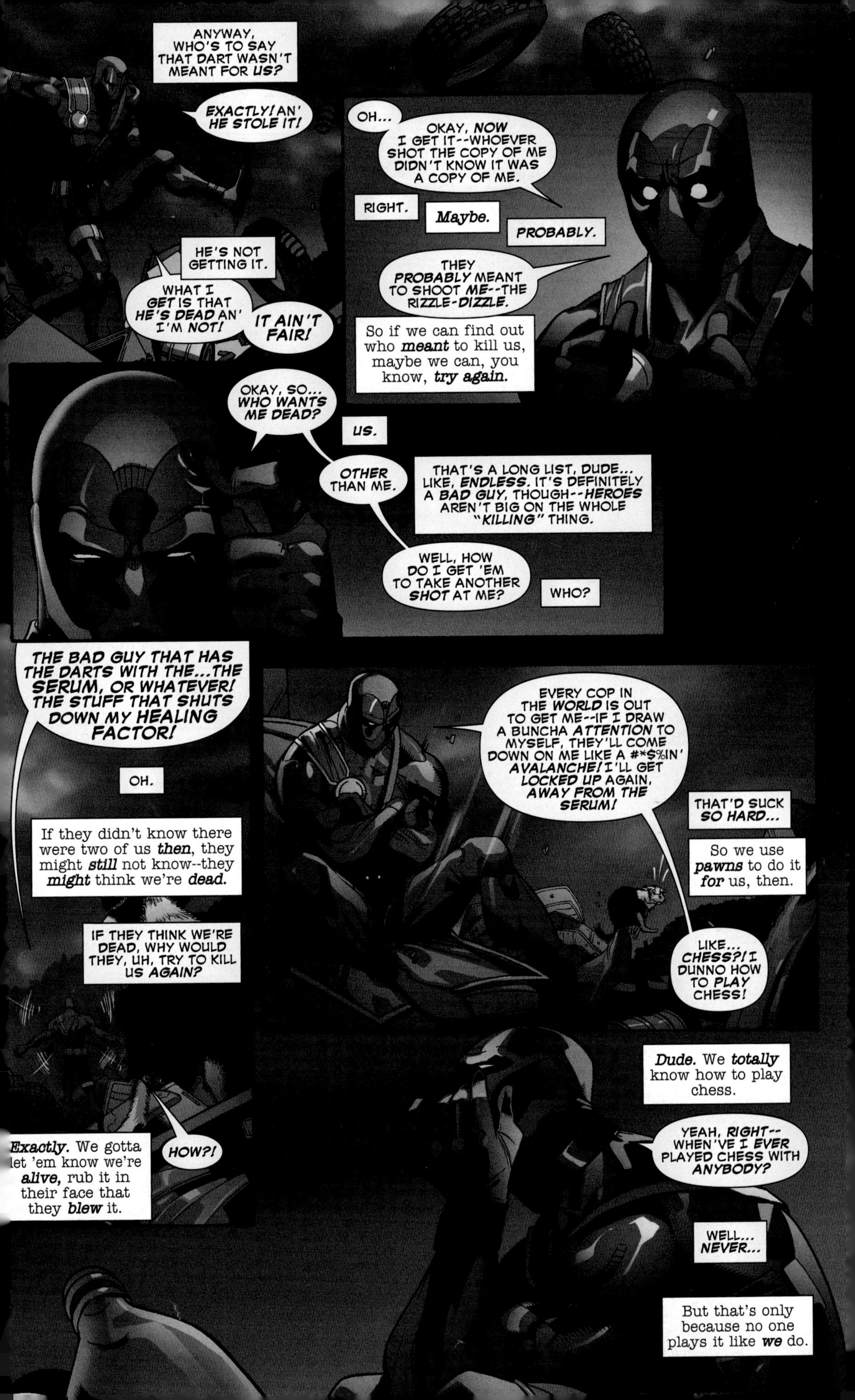
ANYWAY, WHO'S TO SAY THAT DART WASN'T MEANT FOR US?
EXACTLY! AN' HE STOLE IT!
OH...
OKAY, NOW I GET IT--WHOEVER SHOT THE COPY OF ME DIDN'T KNOW IT WAS A COPY OF ME.
RIGHT.
Maybe.
PROBABLY.
HE'S NOT GETTING IT.
WHAT I GET IS THAT HE'S DEAD AN' I'M NOT!
IT AIN'T FAIR!
THEY PROBABLY MEANT TO SHOOT ME--THE RIZZLE-DIZZLE.
So if we can find out who meant to kill us, maybe we can, you know, try again.
OKAY, SO... WHO WANTS ME DEAD?
US.
OTHER THAN ME.
THAT'S A LONG LIST, DUDE... LIKE, ENDLESS. IT'S DEFINITELY A BAD GUY, THOUGH--HEROES AREN'T BIG ON THE WHOLE "KILLING" THING.
WELL, HOW DO I GET 'EM TO TAKE ANOTHER SHOT AT ME?
WHO?
THE BAD GUY THAT HAS THE DARTS WITH THE...THE SERUM, OR WHATEVER! THE STUFF THAT SHUTS DOWN MY HEALING FACTOR!
OH.
If they didn't know there were two of us then, they might still not know--they might think we're dead.
IF THEY THINK WE'RE DEAD, WHY WOULD THEY, UH, TRY TO KILL US AGAIN?
EVERY COP IN THE WORLD IS OUT TO GET ME--IF I DRAW A BUNCHA ATTENTION TO MYSELF, THEY'LL COME DOWN ON ME LIKE A #*$%IN' AVALANCHE! I'LL GET LOCKED UP AGAIN, AWAY FROM THE SERUM!
THAT'D SUCK SO HARD...
So we use pawns to do it for us, then.
LIKE... CHESS?! I DUNNO HOW TO PLAY CHESS!
Exactly. We gotta let 'em know we're alive, rub it in their face that they blew it.
HOW?!
Dude. We totally know how to play chess.
YEAH, RIGHT--WHEN'VE I EVER PLAYED CHESS WITH ANYBODY?
WELL... NEVER...
But that's only because no one plays it like we do.

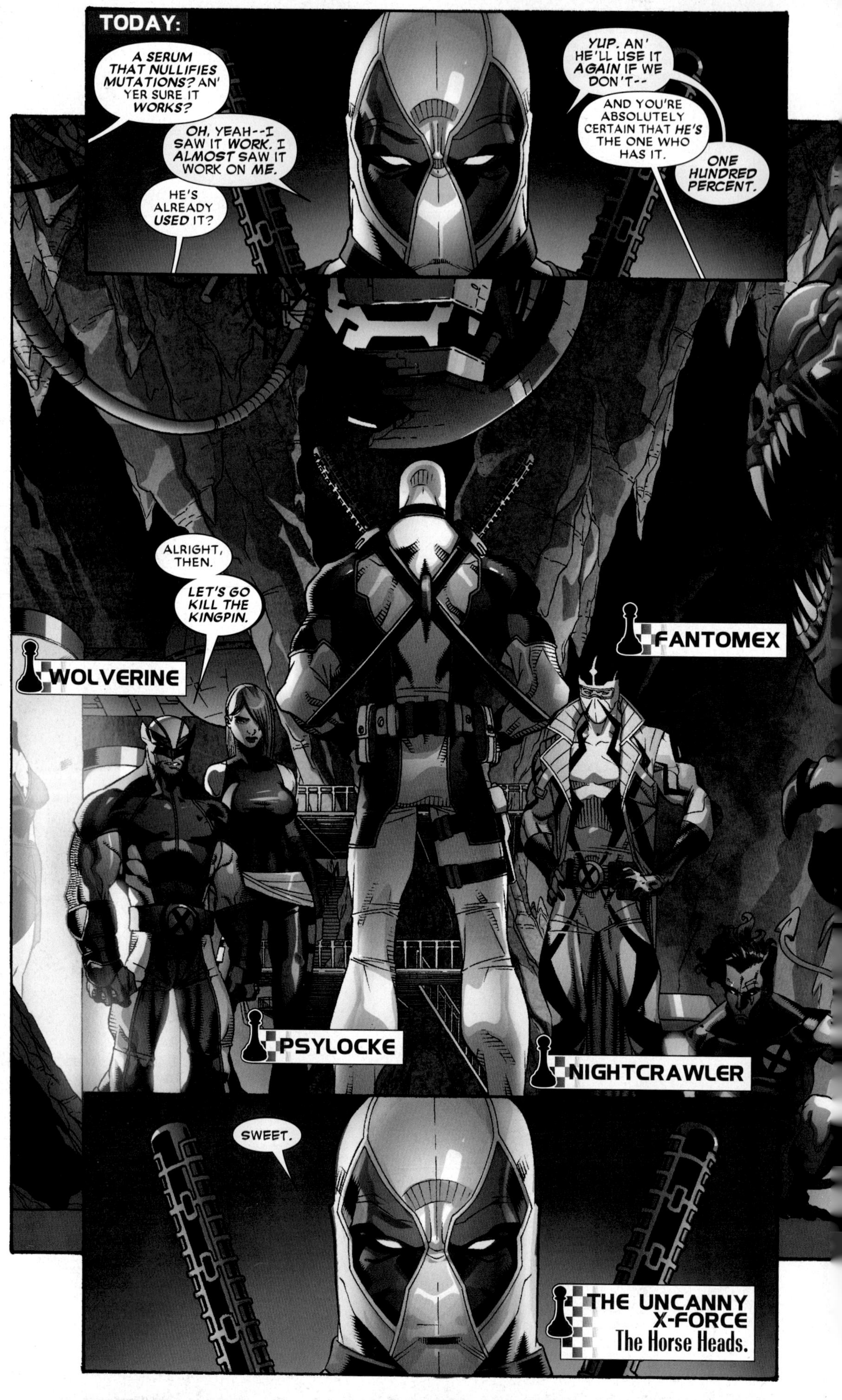
TODAY:
A SERUM THAT NULLIFIES MUTATIONS? AN' YER SURE IT WORKS?
OH, YEAH--I SAW IT WORK. I ALMOST SAW IT WORK ON ME.
HE'S ALREADY USED IT?
YUP. AN' HE'LL USE IT AGAIN IF WE DON'T--
AND YOU'RE ABSOLUTELY CERTAIN THAT HE'S THE ONE WHO HAS IT.
ONE HUNDRED PERCENT.
ALRIGHT, THEN.
LET'S GO KILL THE KINGPIN.
WOLVERINE
FANTOMEX
PSYLOCKE
NIGHTCRAWLER
SWEET.
THE UNCANNY X-FORCE
The Horse Heads.

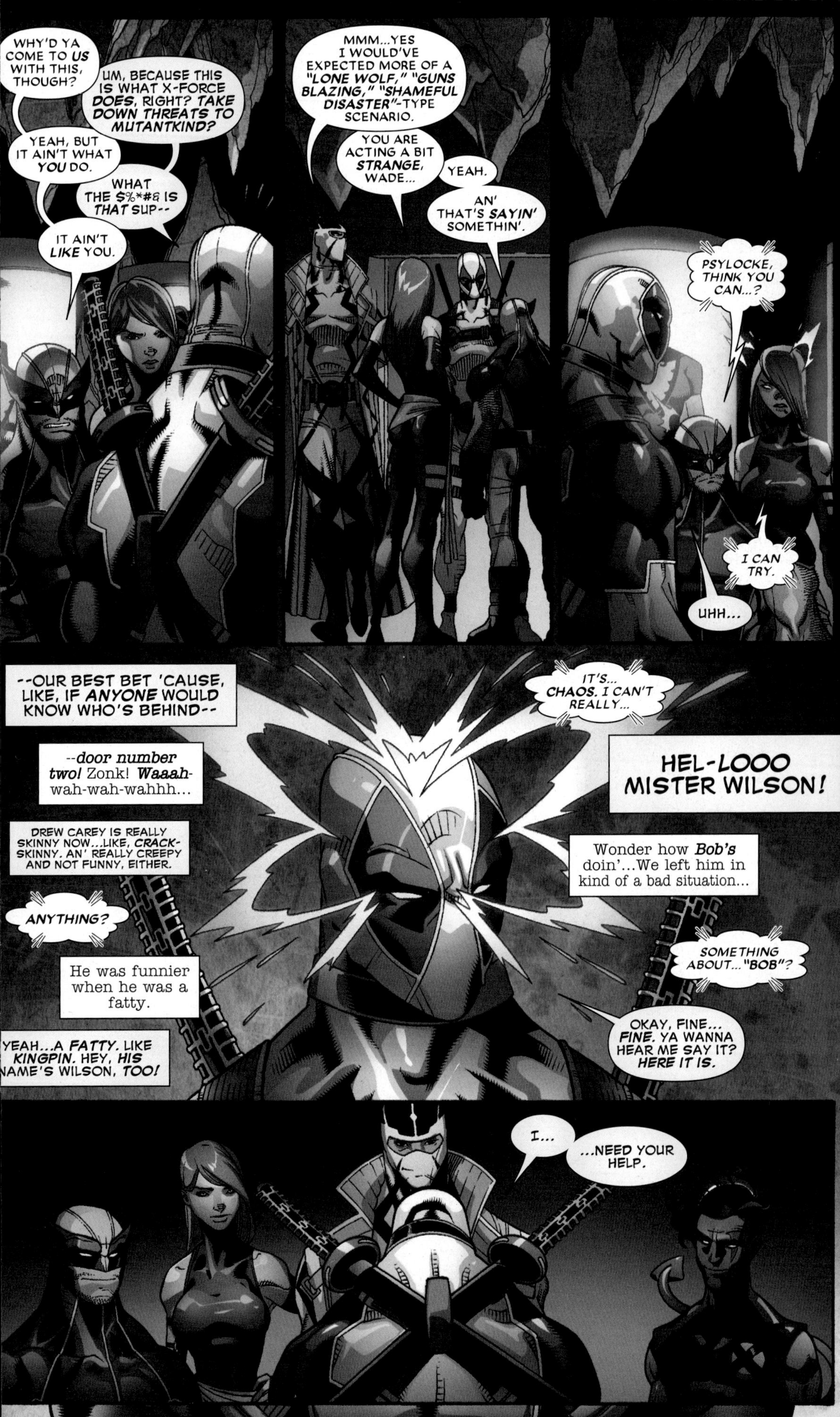
WHY'D YA COME TO US WITH THIS, THOUGH?
UM, BECAUSE THIS IS WHAT X-FORCE DOES, RIGHT? TAKE DOWN THREATS TO MUTANTKIND?
YEAH, BUT IT AIN'T WHAT YOU DO.
WHAT THE $%*#& IS THAT SUP--
IT AIN'T LIKE YOU.
MMM...YES I WOULD'VE EXPECTED MORE OF A "LONE WOLF," "GUNS BLAZING," "SHAMEFUL DISASTER"-TYPE SCENARIO.
YOU ARE ACTING A BIT STRANGE, WADE...
YEAH.
AN' THAT'S SAYIN' SOMETHIN'.
PSYLOCKE, THINK YOU CAN...?
I CAN TRY.
UHH...
--OUR BEST BET 'CAUSE, LIKE, IF ANYONE WOULD KNOW WHO'S BEHIND--
IT'S... CHAOS. I CAN'T REALLY...
--door number two! Zonk! Waaah-wah-wah-wahhh...
HEL-LOOO MISTER WILSON!
DREW CAREY IS REALLY SKINNY NOW...LIKE, CRACK-SKINNY. AN' REALLY CREEPY AND NOT FUNNY, EITHER.
Wonder how Bob's doin'...We left him in kind of a bad situation...
ANYTHING?
SOMETHING ABOUT..."BOB"?
He was funnier when he was a fatty.
YEAH...A FATTY. LIKE KINGPIN. HEY, HIS NAME'S WILSON, TOO!
OKAY, FINE... FINE. YA WANNA HEAR ME SAY IT? HERE IT IS.
I...
...NEED YOUR HELP.

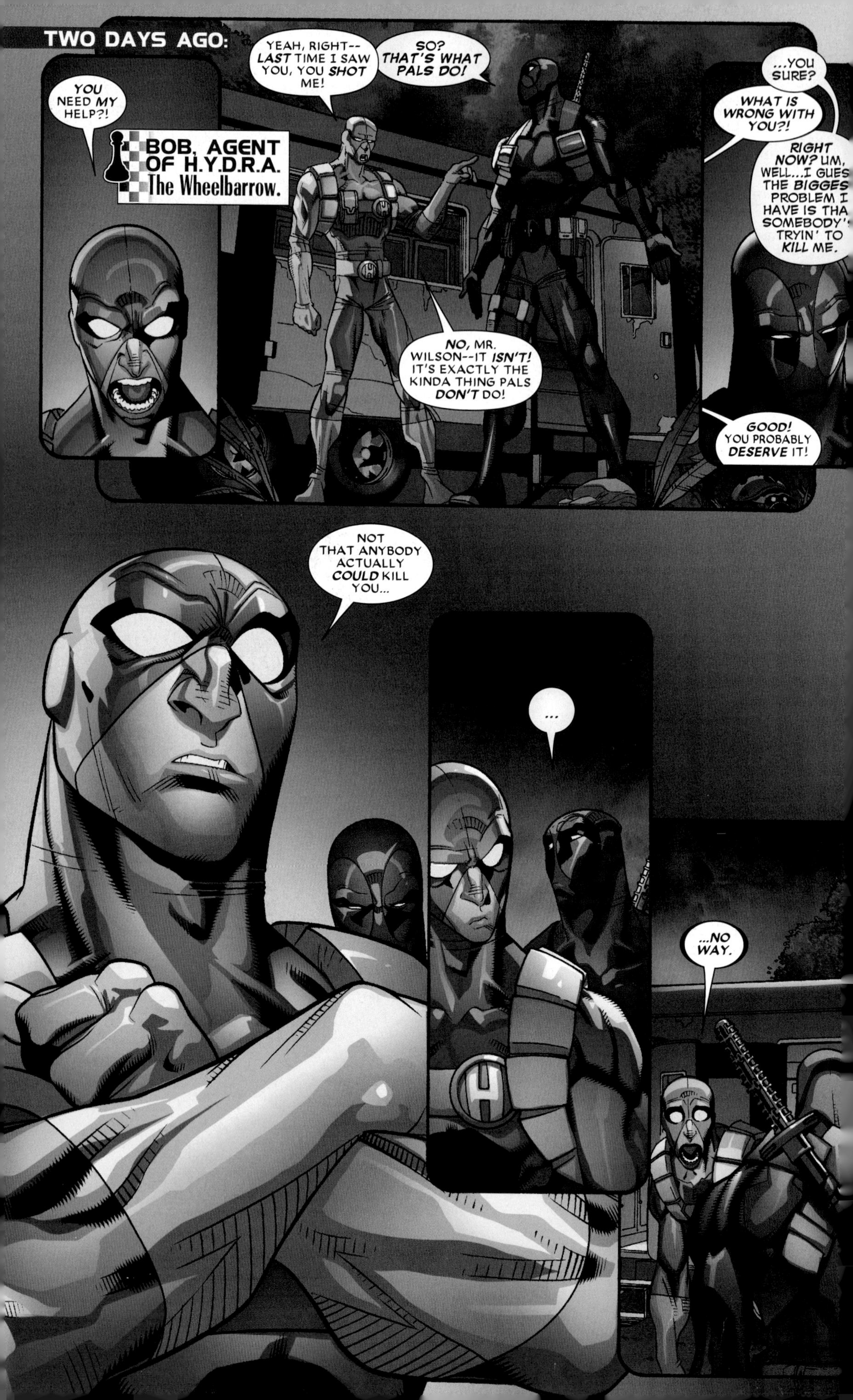
TWO DAYS AGO:
YOU NEED MY HELP?!
BOB, AGENT OF H.Y.D.R.A.
The Wheelbarrow.
YEAH, RIGHT-- LAST TIME I SAW YOU, YOU SHOT ME!
SO? THAT'S WHAT PALS DO!
NO, MR. WILSON--IT ISN'T! IT'S EXACTLY THE KINDA THING PALS DON'T DO!
...YOU SURE?
WHAT IS WRONG WITH YOU?!
RIGHT NOW? UM, WELL...I GUES THE BIGGES PROBLEM I HAVE IS THA SOMEBODY' TRYIN' TO KILL ME.
GOOD! YOU PROBABLY DESERVE IT!
NOT THAT ANYBODY ACTUALLY COULD KILL YOU...
...
...NO WAY.

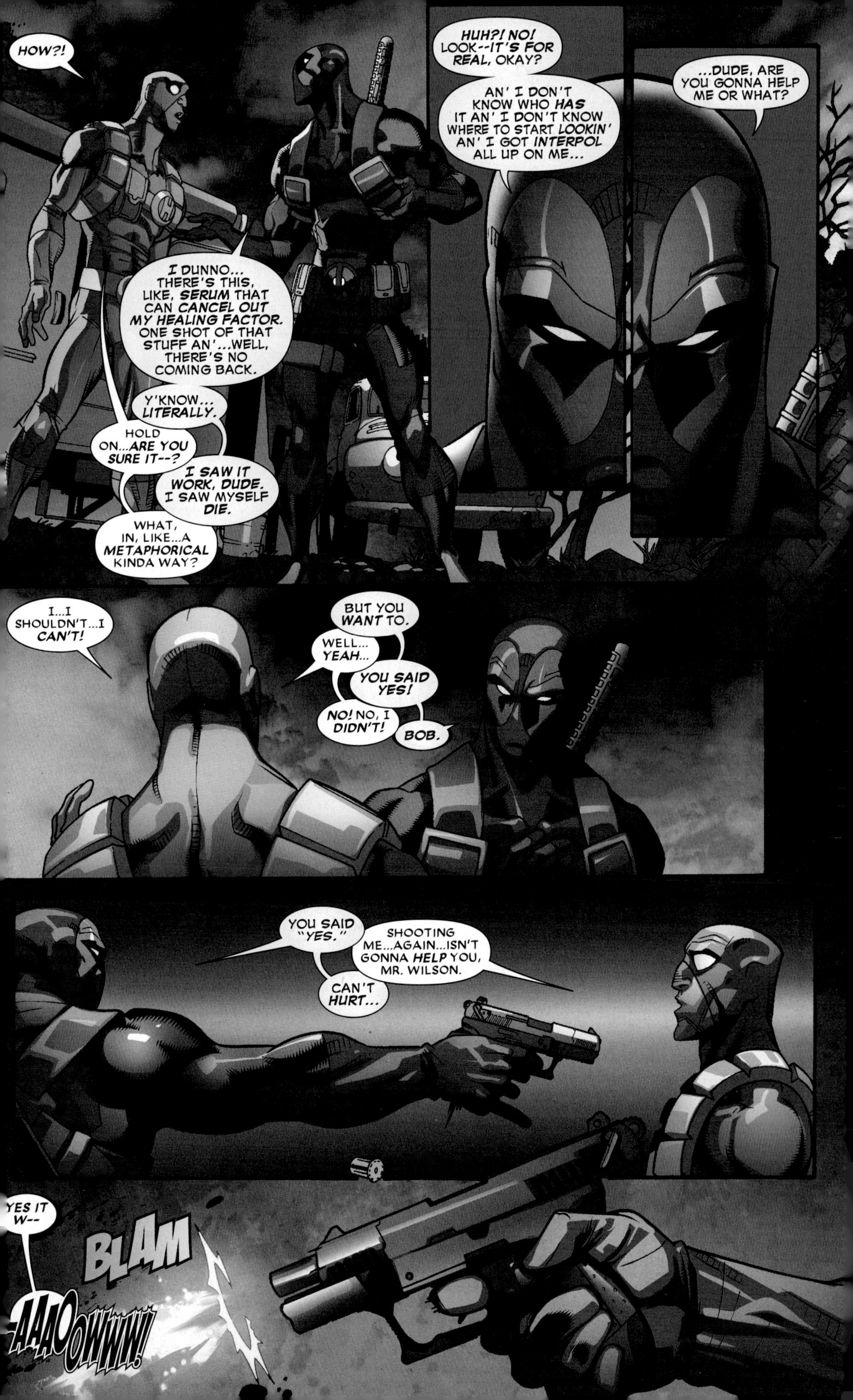
HOW?!
I DUNNO... THERE'S THIS, LIKE, SERUM THAT CAN CANCEL OUT MY HEALING FACTOR. ONE SHOT OF THAT STUFF AN'...WELL, THERE'S NO COMING BACK.
Y'KNOW... LITERALLY.
HOLD ON...ARE YOU SURE IT--?
I SAW IT WORK, DUDE. I SAW MYSELF DIE.
WHAT, IN, LIKE...A METAPHORICAL KINDA WAY?
HUH?! NO! LOOK--IT'S FOR REAL, OKAY?
AN' I DON'T KNOW WHO HAS IT AN' I DON'T KNOW WHERE TO START LOOKIN' AN' I GOT INTERPOL ALL UP ON ME...
...DUDE, ARE YOU GONNA HELP ME OR WHAT?
I...I SHOULDN'T...I CAN'T!
BUT YOU WANT TO.
WELL... YEAH...
YOU SAID YES!
NO! NO, I DIDN'T!
BOB.
YOU SAID "YES."
SHOOTING ME...AGAIN...ISN'T GONNA HELP YOU, MR. WILSON.
CAN'T HURT...
YES IT W--
BLAM
AAAOOWWW!

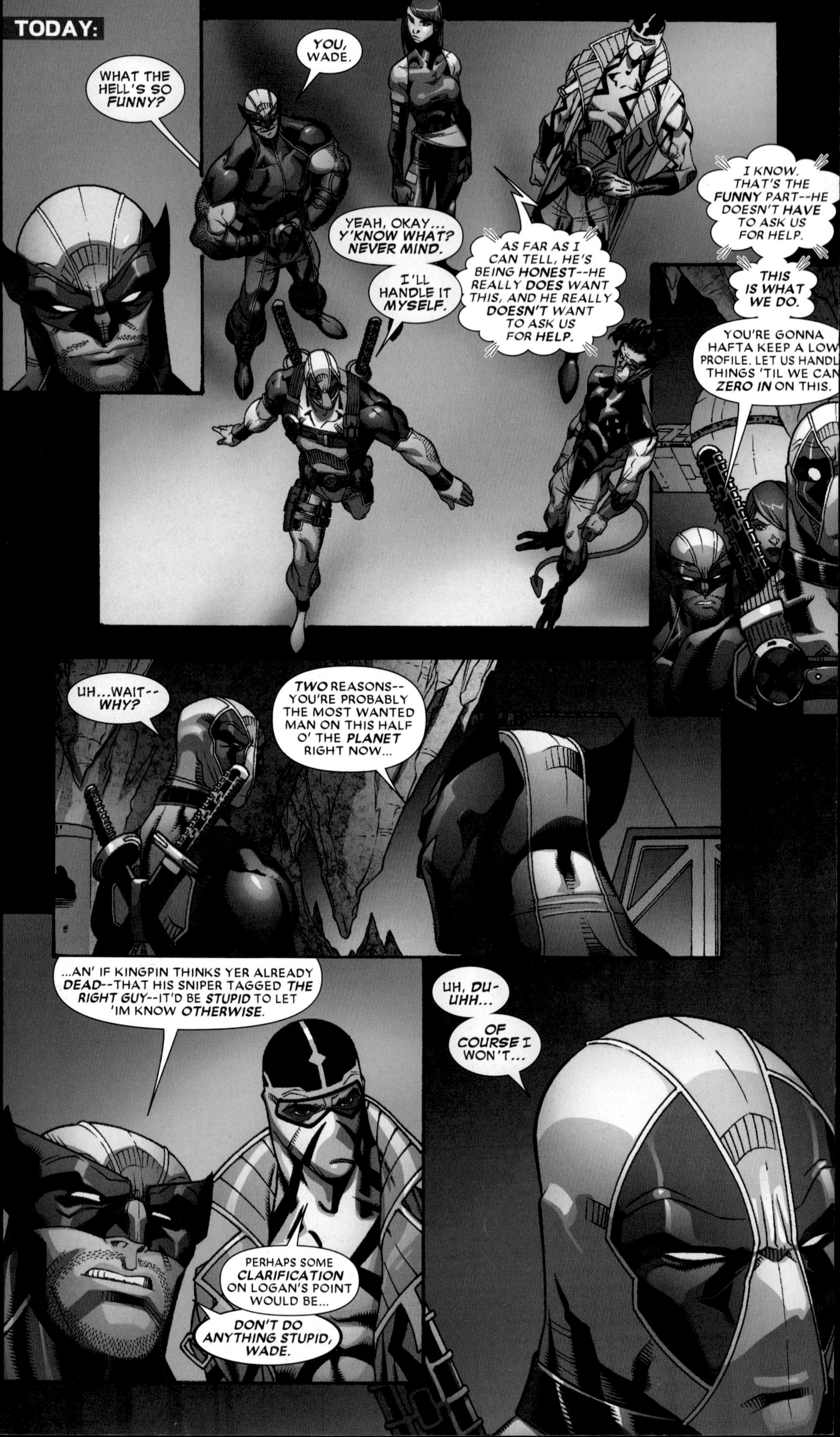
TODAY:
WHAT THE HELL'S SO FUNNY?
YOU, WADE.
YEAH, OKAY... Y'KNOW WHAT? NEVER MIND.
I'LL HANDLE IT MYSELF.
AS FAR AS I CAN TELL, HE'S BEING HONEST--HE REALLY DOES WANT THIS, AND HE REALLY DOESN'T WANT TO ASK US FOR HELP.
I KNOW. THAT'S THE FUNNY PART--HE DOESN'T HAVE TO ASK US FOR HELP.
THIS IS WHAT WE DO.
YOU'RE GONNA HAFTA KEEP A LOW PROFILE. LET US HANDL THINGS 'TIL WE CAN ZERO IN ON THIS.
UH...WAIT-- WHY?
TWO REASONS-- YOU'RE PROBABLY THE MOST WANTED MAN ON THIS HALF O' THE PLANET RIGHT NOW...
...AN' IF KINGPIN THINKS YER ALREADY DEAD--THAT HIS SNIPER TAGGED THE RIGHT GUY--IT'D BE STUPID TO LET 'IM KNOW OTHERWISE.
UH, DU-UHH...
OF COURSE I WON'T...
PERHAPS SOME CLARIFICATION ON LOGAN'S POINT WOULD BE...
DON'T DO ANYTHING STUPID, WADE.

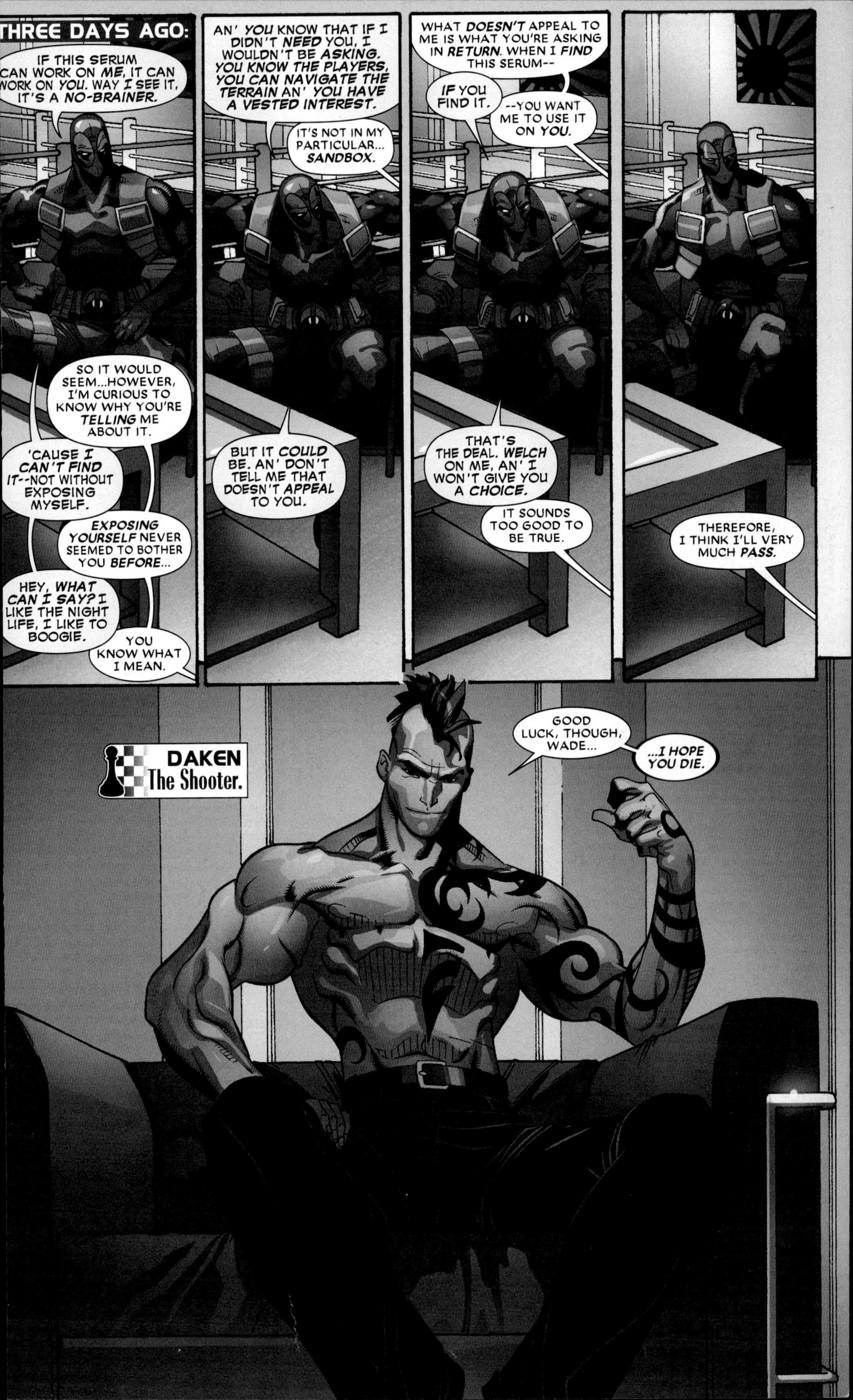
THREE DAYS AGO:
IF THIS SERUM CAN WORK ON ME, IT CAN WORK ON YOU. WAY I SEE IT, IT'S A NO-BRAINER.
SO IT WOULD SEEM...HOWEVER, I'M CURIOUS TO KNOW WHY YOU'RE TELLING ME ABOUT IT.
'CAUSE I CAN'T FIND IT--NOT WITHOUT EXPOSING MYSELF.
EXPOSING YOURSELF NEVER SEEMED TO BOTHER YOU BEFORE...
HEY, WHAT CAN I SAY? I LIKE THE NIGHT LIFE, I LIKE TO BOOGIE.
YOU KNOW WHAT I MEAN.
AN' YOU KNOW THAT IF I DIDN'T NEED YOU, I WOULDN'T BE ASKING. YOU KNOW THE PLAYERS, YOU CAN NAVIGATE THE TERRAIN AN' YOU HAVE A VESTED INTEREST.
IT'S NOT IN MY PARTICULAR... SANDBOX.
BUT IT COULD BE. AN' DON'T TELL ME THAT DOESN'T APPEAL TO YOU.
WHAT DOESN'T APPEAL TO ME IS WHAT YOU'RE ASKING IN RETURN. WHEN I FIND THIS SERUM--
IF YOU FIND IT.
--YOU WANT ME TO USE IT ON YOU.
THAT'S THE DEAL. WELCH ON ME, AN' I WON'T GIVE YOU A CHOICE.
IT SOUNDS TOO GOOD TO BE TRUE.
THEREFORE, I THINK I'LL VERY MUCH PASS.
DAKEN
The Shooter.
GOOD LUCK, THOUGH, WADE...
...I HOPE YOU DIE.

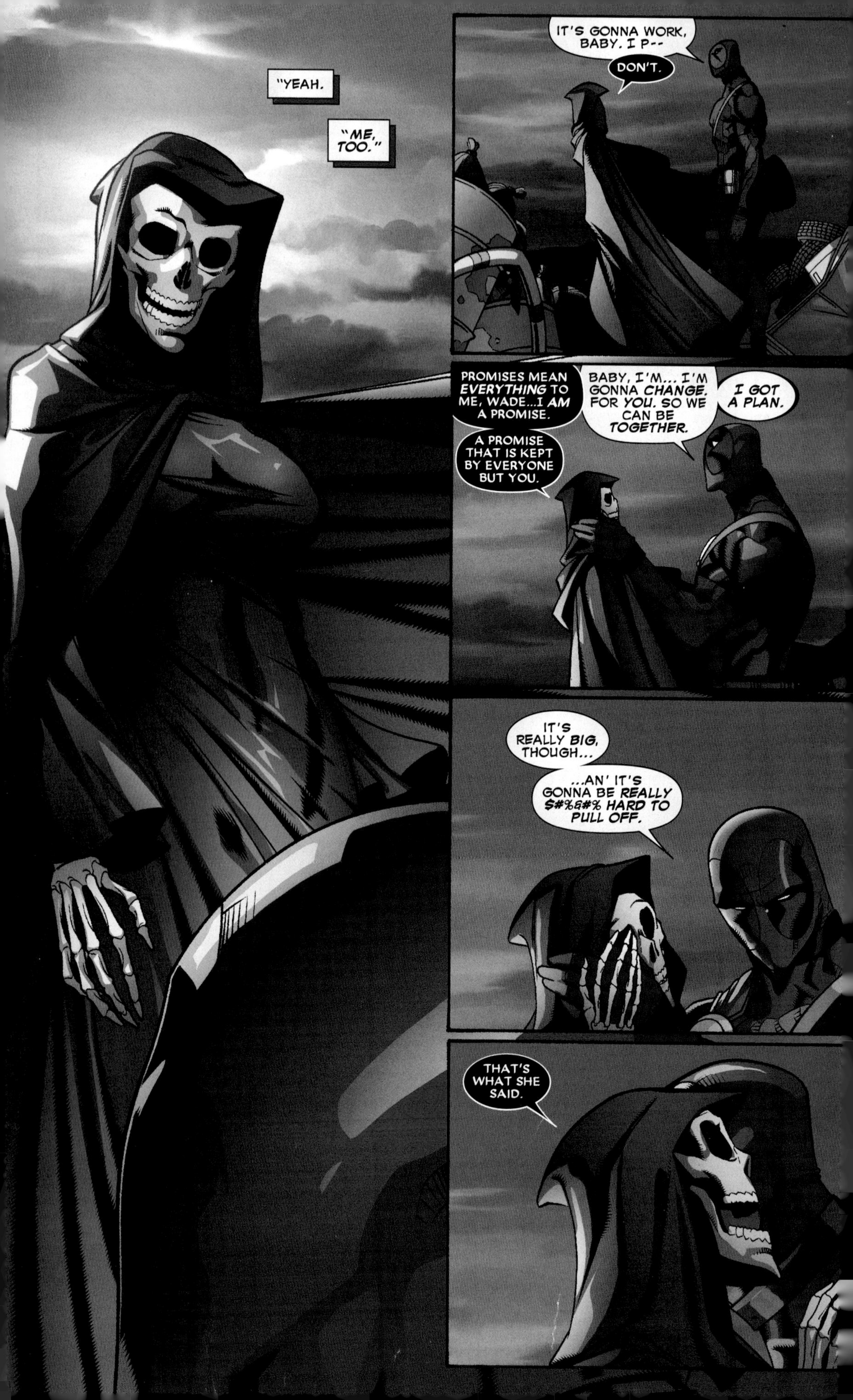
"YEAH.
"ME, TOO."
IT'S GONNA WORK, BABY. I P--
DON'T.
PROMISES MEAN EVERYTHING TO ME, WADE...I AM A PROMISE.
A PROMISE THAT IS KEPT BY EVERYONE BUT YOU.
BABY, I'M... I'M GONNA CHANGE. FOR YOU. SO WE CAN BE TOGETHER.
I GOT A PLAN.
IT'S REALLY BIG, THOUGH...
...AN' IT'S GONNA BE REALLY $#%&#% HARD TO PULL OFF.
THAT'S WHAT SHE SAID.

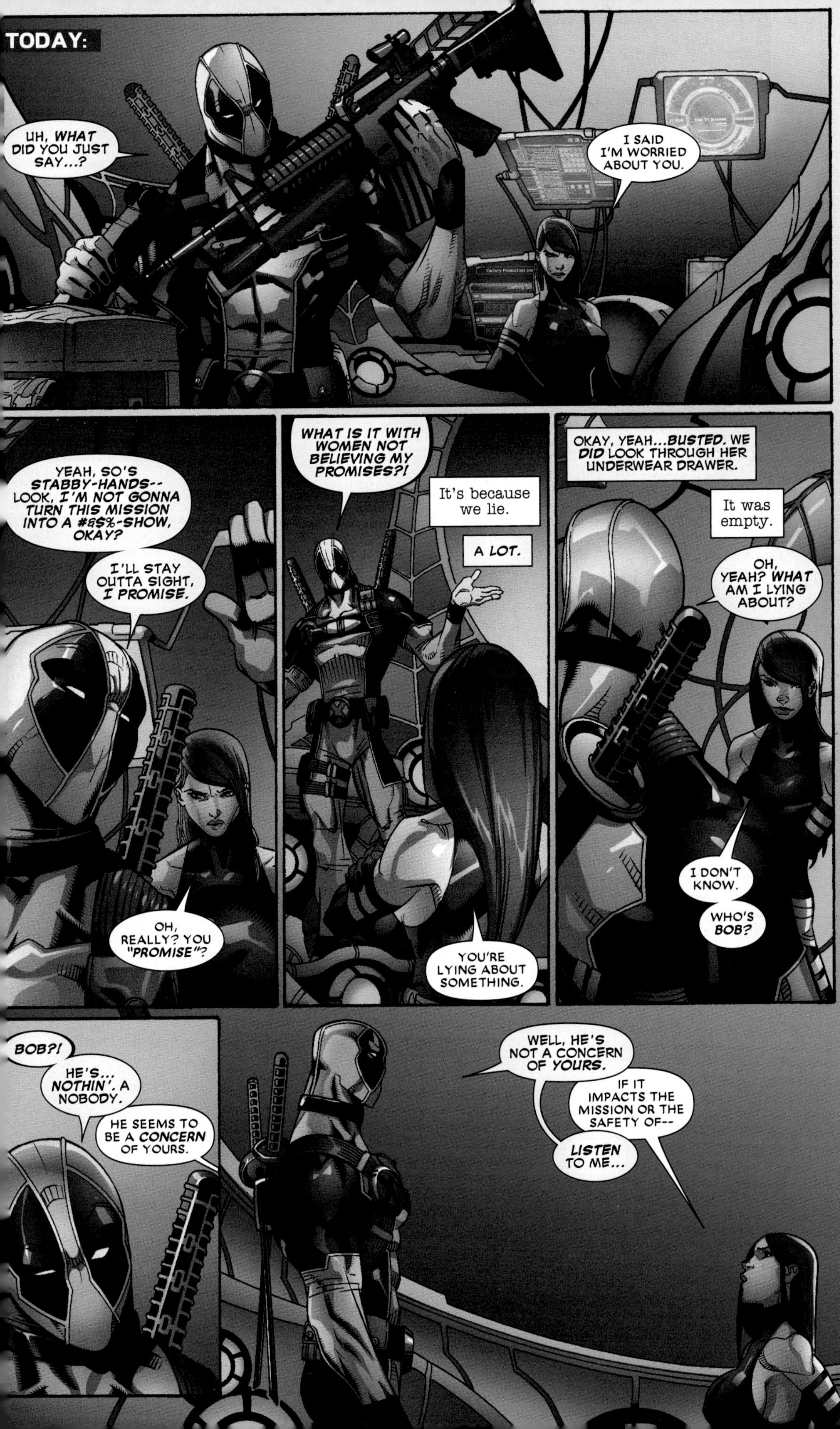
TODAY:
UH, WHAT DID YOU JUST SAY...?
I SAID I'M WORRIED ABOUT YOU.
YEAH, SO'S STABBY-HANDS-- LOOK, I'M NOT GONNA TURN THIS MISSION INTO A #&$%-SHOW, OKAY?
I'LL STAY OUTTA SIGHT, I PROMISE.
OH, REALLY? YOU "PROMISE"?
WHAT IS IT WITH WOMEN NOT BELIEVING MY PROMISES?!
It's because we lie.
A LOT.
YOU'RE LYING ABOUT SOMETHING.
OKAY, YEAH...BUSTED. WE DID LOOK THROUGH HER UNDERWEAR DRAWER.
It was empty.
OH, YEAH? WHAT AM I LYING ABOUT?
I DON'T KNOW.
WHO'S BOB?
BOB?!
HE'S... NOTHIN'. A NOBODY.
HE SEEMS TO BE A CONCERN OF YOURS.
WELL, HE'S NOT A CONCERN OF YOURS.
IF IT IMPACTS THE MISSION OR THE SAFETY OF--
LISTEN TO ME...

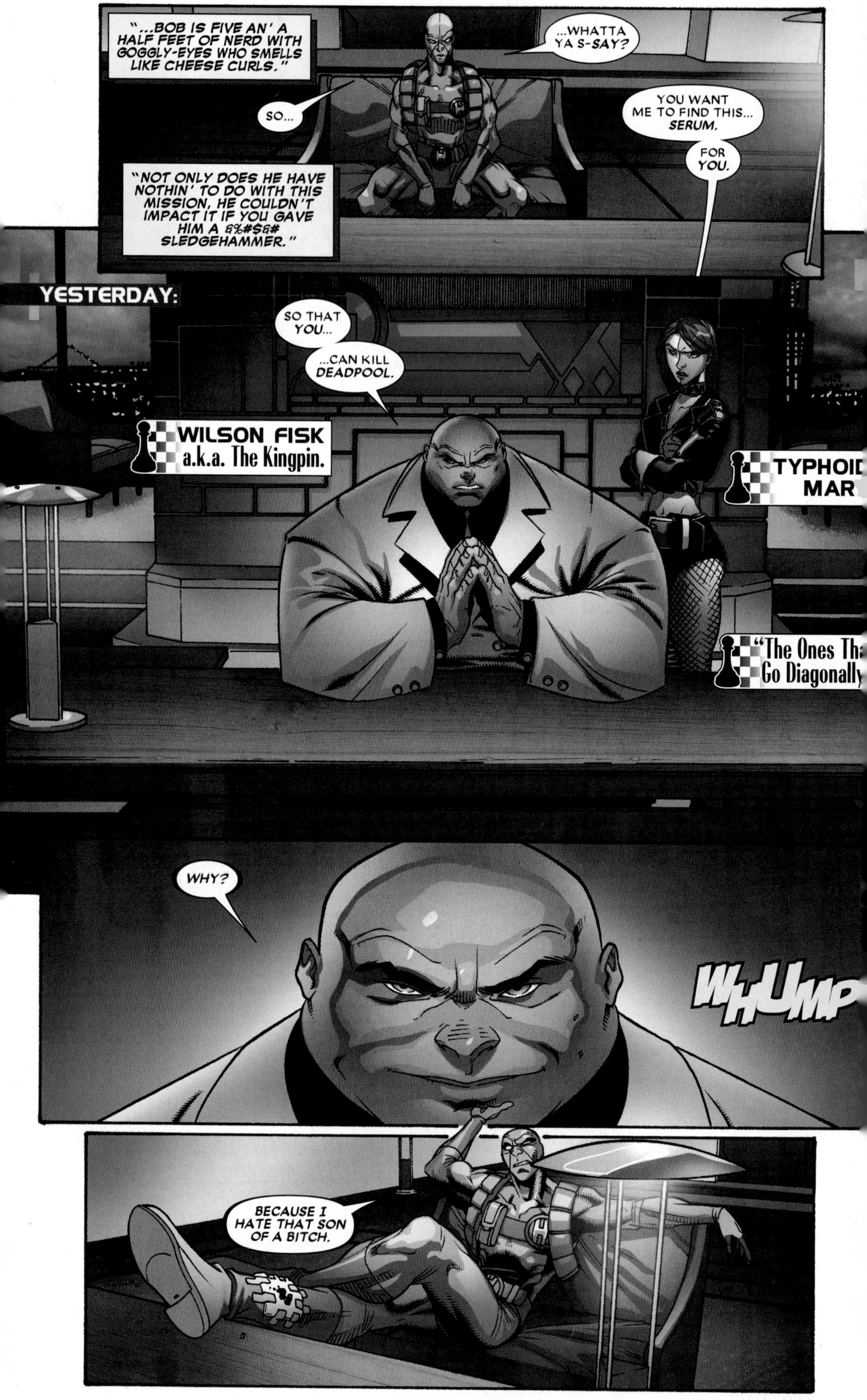
"...BOB IS FIVE AN' A HALF FEET OF NERD WITH GOGGLY-EYES WHO SMELLS LIKE CHEESE CURLS."
...WHATTA YA S-SAY?
SO...
YOU WANT ME TO FIND THIS... SERUM.
FOR YOU.
"NOT ONLY DOES HE HAVE NOTHIN' TO DO WITH THIS MISSION, HE COULDN'T IMPACT IT IF YOU GAVE HIM A &%#$&# SLEDGEHAMMER."
YESTERDAY:
SO THAT YOU...
...CAN KILL DEADPOOL.
WILSON FISK a.k.a. The Kingpin.
TYPHOID MAR
"The Ones Th Go Diagonally
WHY?
WHUMP
BECAUSE I HATE THAT SON OF A BITCH.

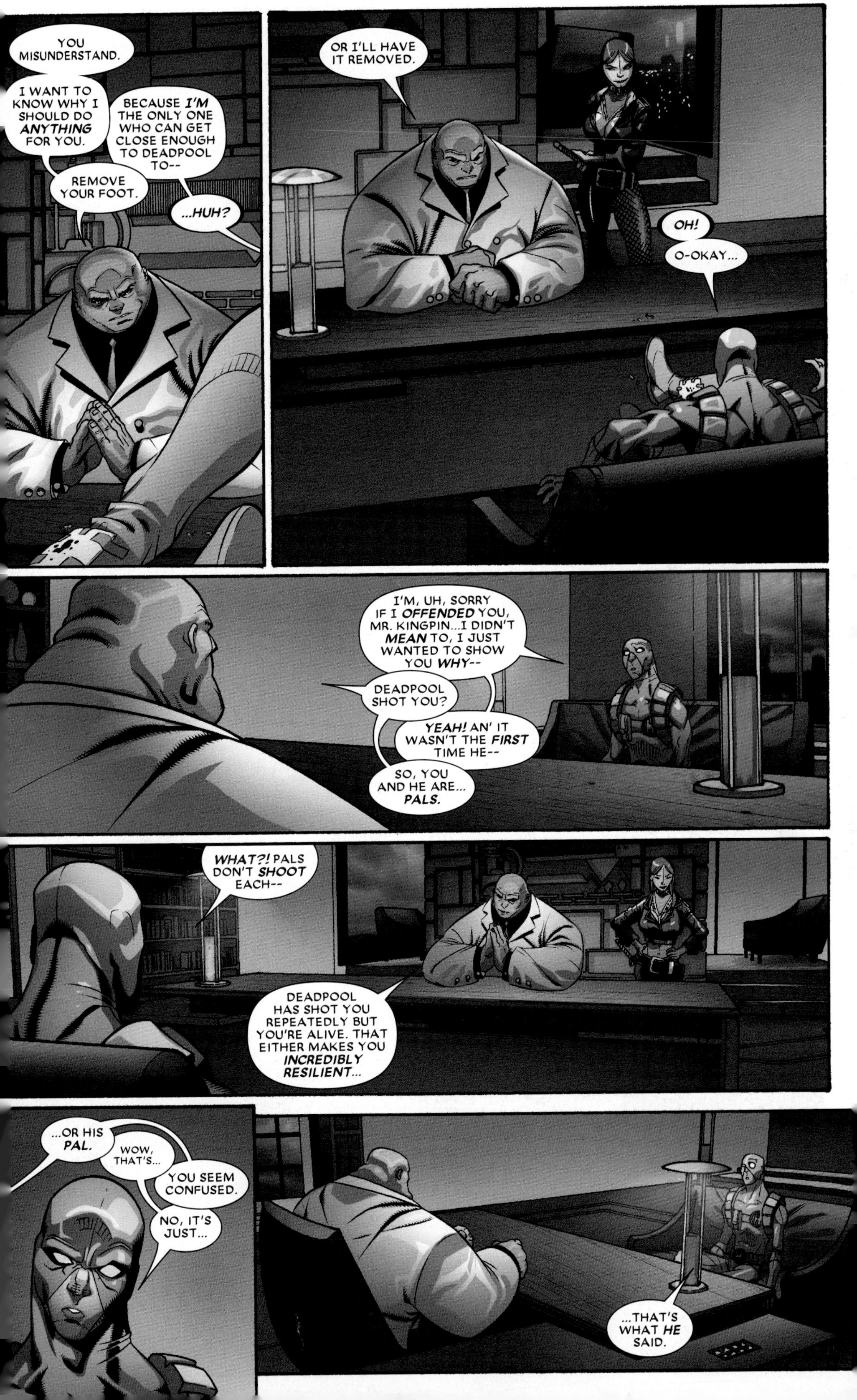

YOU MISUNDERSTAND.
I WANT TO KNOW WHY I SHOULD DO ANYTHING FOR YOU.
BECAUSE I'M THE ONLY ONE WHO CAN GET CLOSE ENOUGH TO DEADPOOL TO--
REMOVE YOUR FOOT.
...HUH?
OR I'LL HAVE IT REMOVED.
OH!
O-OKAY...
I'M, UH, SORRY IF I OFFENDED YOU, MR. KINGPIN...I DIDN'T MEAN TO, I JUST WANTED TO SHOW YOU WHY--
DEADPOOL SHOT YOU?
YEAH! AN' IT WASN'T THE FIRST TIME HE--
SO, YOU AND HE ARE... PALS.
WHAT?! PALS DON'T SHOOT EACH--
DEADPOOL HAS SHOT YOU REPEATEDLY BUT YOU'RE ALIVE. THAT EITHER MAKES YOU INCREDIBLY RESILIENT...
...OR HIS PAL.
WOW, THAT'S...
YOU SEEM CONFUSED.
NO, IT'S JUST...
...THAT'S WHAT HE SAID.

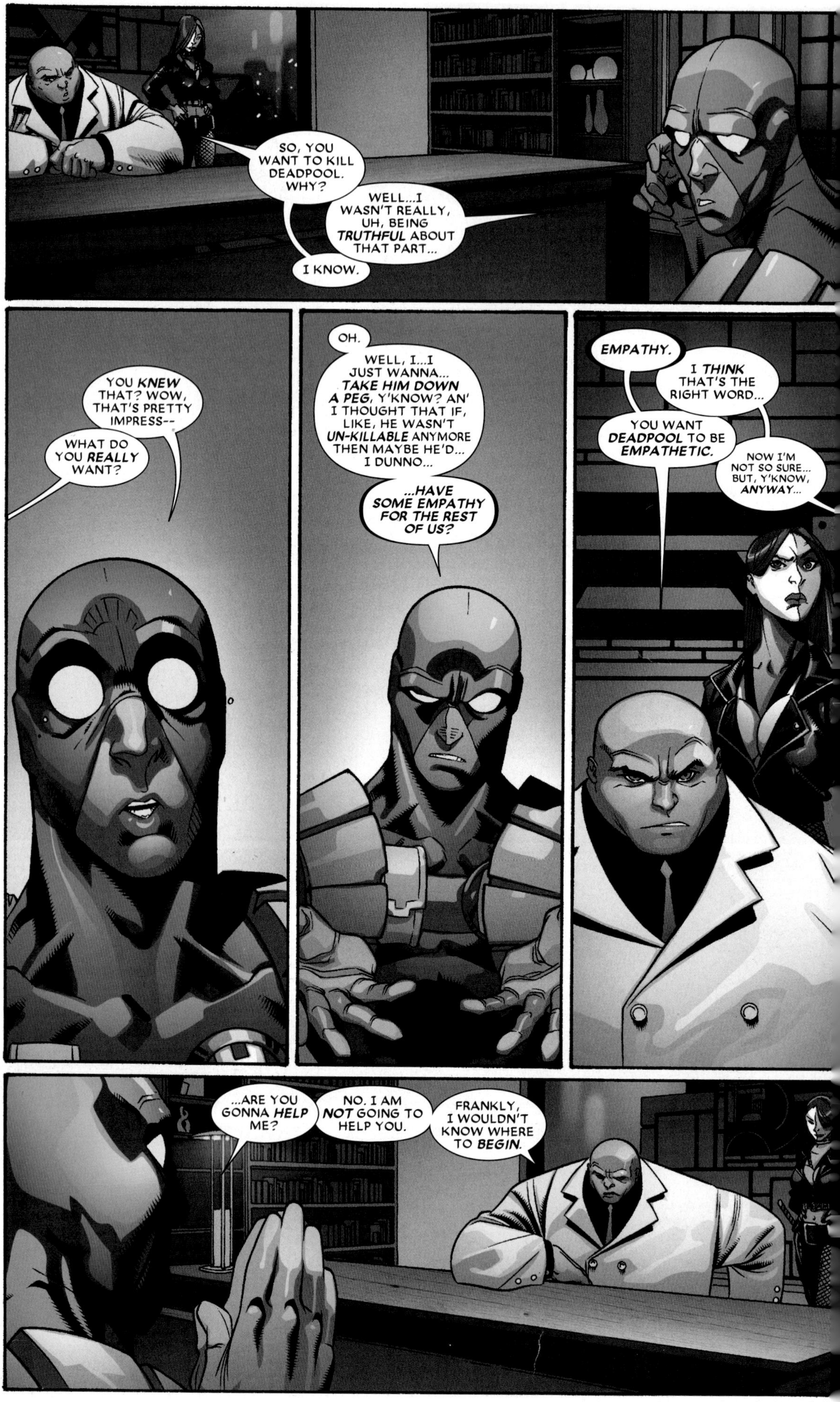
SO, YOU WANT TO KILL DEADPOOL. WHY?
WELL...I WASN'T REALLY, UH, BEING TRUTHFUL ABOUT THAT PART...
I KNOW.
YOU KNEW THAT? WOW, THAT'S PRETTY IMPRESS--
WHAT DO YOU REALLY WANT?
OH.
WELL, I...I JUST WANNA... TAKE HIM DOWN A PEG, Y'KNOW? AN' I THOUGHT THAT IF, LIKE, HE WASN'T UN-KILLABLE ANYMORE THEN MAYBE HE'D... I DUNNO...
...HAVE SOME EMPATHY FOR THE REST OF US?
EMPATHY.
I THINK THAT'S THE RIGHT WORD...
YOU WANT DEADPOOL TO BE EMPATHETIC.
NOW I'M NOT SO SURE... BUT, Y'KNOW, ANYWAY...
...ARE YOU GONNA HELP ME?
NO. I AM NOT GOING TO HELP YOU.
FRANKLY, I WOULDN'T KNOW WHERE TO BEGIN.

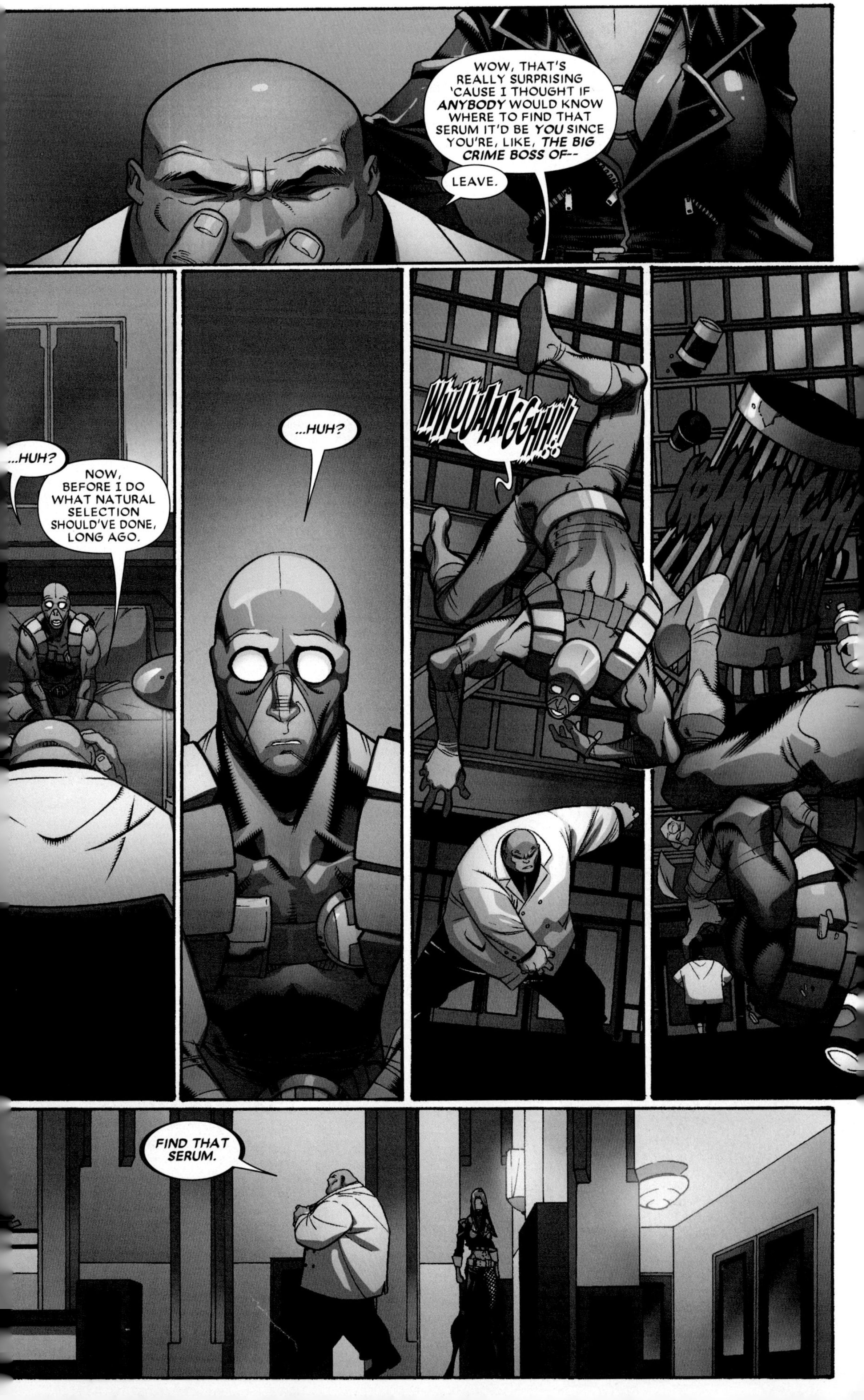
WOW, THAT'S REALLY SURPRISING 'CAUSE I THOUGHT IF ANYBODY WOULD KNOW WHERE TO FIND THAT SERUM IT'D BE YOU SINCE YOU'RE, LIKE, THE BIG CRIME BOSS OF--
LEAVE.
...HUH?
NOW, BEFORE I DO WHAT NATURAL SELECTION SHOULD'VE DONE, LONG AGO.
...HUH?
WWUUAAAGGHH!!
FIND THAT SERUM.

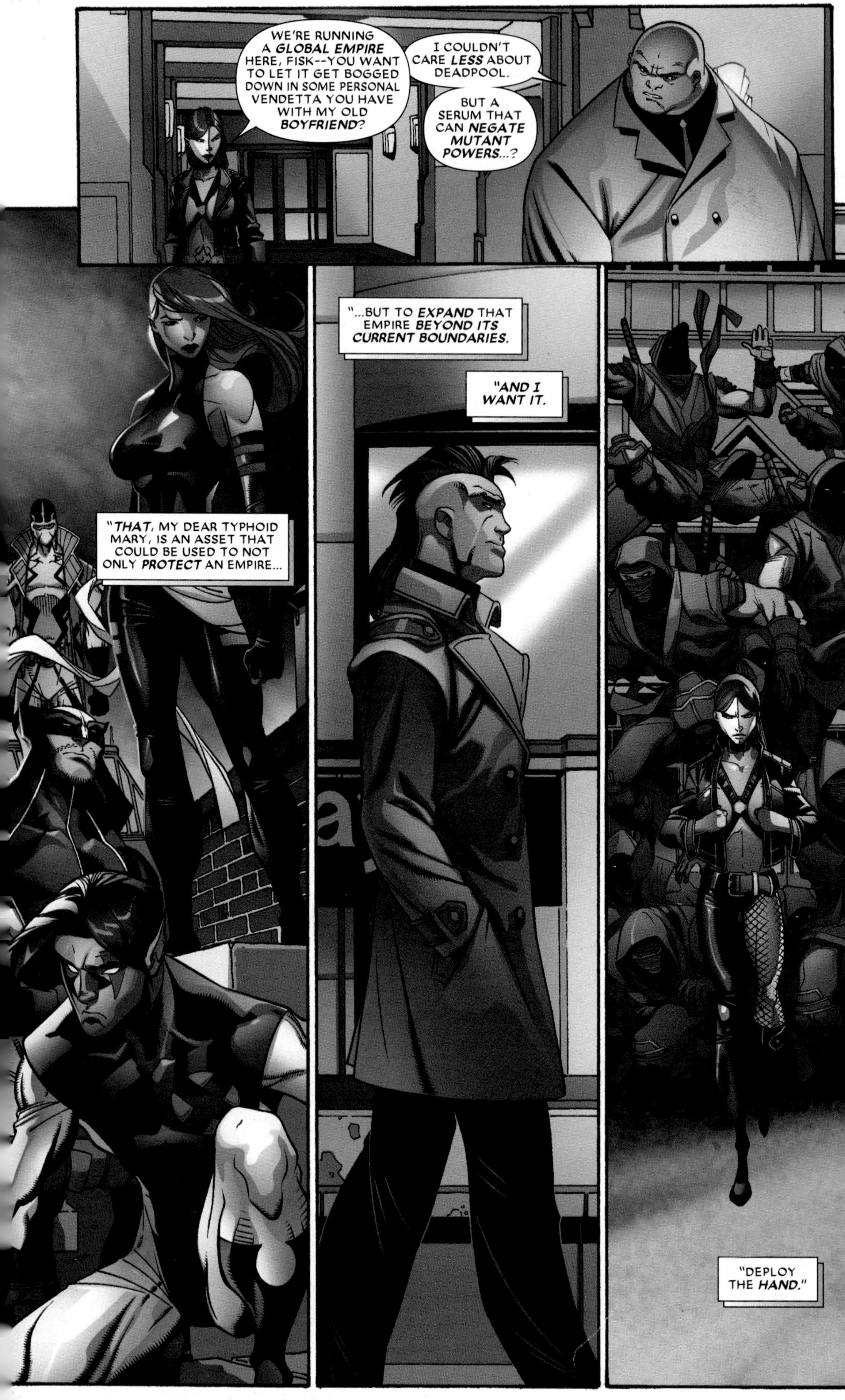
WE'RE RUNNING A GLOBAL EMPIRE HERE, FISK--YOU WANT TO LET IT GET BOGGED DOWN IN SOME PERSONAL VENDETTA YOU HAVE WITH MY OLD BOYFRIEND?
I COULDN'T CARE LESS ABOUT DEADPOOL.
BUT A SERUM THAT CAN NEGATE MUTANT POWERS...?
"THAT, MY DEAR TYPHOID MARY, IS AN ASSET THAT COULD BE USED TO NOT ONLY PROTECT AN EMPIRE...
"...BUT TO EXPAND THAT EMPIRE BEYOND ITS CURRENT BOUNDARIES.
"AND I WANT IT.
"DEPLOY THE HAND."

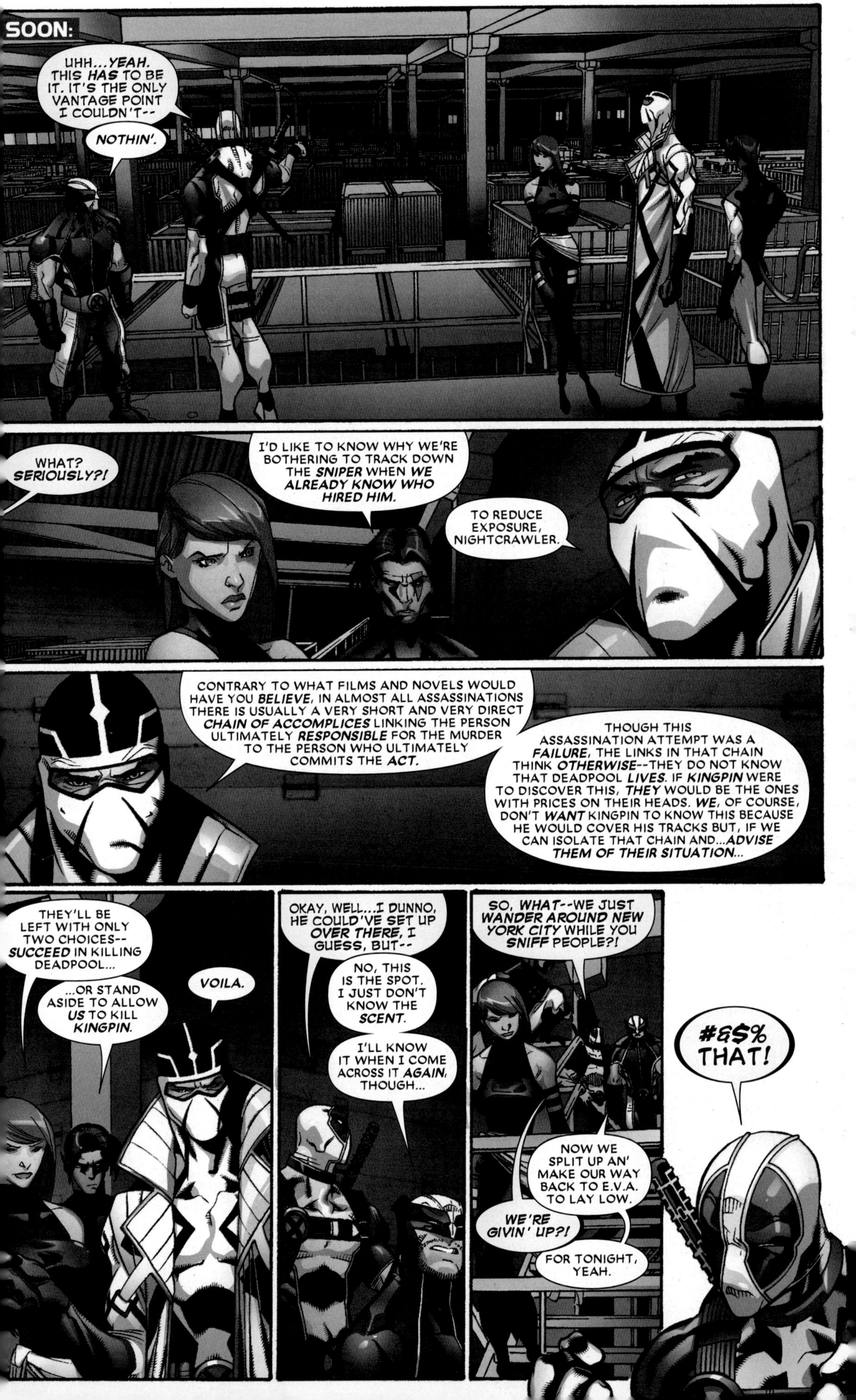
SOON:
UHH...YEAH. THIS HAS TO BE IT. IT'S THE ONLY VANTAGE POINT I COULDN'T--
NOTHIN'.
WHAT? SERIOUSLY?!
I'D LIKE TO KNOW WHY WE'RE BOTHERING TO TRACK DOWN THE SNIPER WHEN WE ALREADY KNOW WHO HIRED HIM.
TO REDUCE EXPOSURE, NIGHTCRAWLER.
CONTRARY TO WHAT FILMS AND NOVELS WOULD HAVE YOU BELIEVE, IN ALMOST ALL ASSASSINATIONS THERE IS USUALLY A VERY SHORT AND VERY DIRECT CHAIN OF ACCOMPLICES LINKING THE PERSON ULTIMATELY RESPONSIBLE FOR THE MURDER TO THE PERSON WHO ULTIMATELY COMMITS THE ACT.
THOUGH THIS ASSASSINATION ATTEMPT WAS A FAILURE, THE LINKS IN THAT CHAIN THINK OTHERWISE--THEY DO NOT KNOW THAT DEADPOOL LIVES. IF KINGPIN WERE TO DISCOVER THIS, THEY WOULD BE THE ONES WITH PRICES ON THEIR HEADS. WE, OF COURSE, DON'T WANT KINGPIN TO KNOW THIS BECAUSE HE WOULD COVER HIS TRACKS BUT, IF WE CAN ISOLATE THAT CHAIN AND...ADVISE THEM OF THEIR SITUATION...
THEY'LL BE LEFT WITH ONLY TWO CHOICES--SUCCEED IN KILLING DEADPOOL...
...OR STAND ASIDE TO ALLOW US TO KILL KINGPIN.
VOILA.
OKAY, WELL...I DUNNO, HE COULD'VE SET UP OVER THERE, I GUESS, BUT--
NO, THIS IS THE SPOT. I JUST DON'T KNOW THE SCENT.
I'LL KNOW IT WHEN I COME ACROSS IT AGAIN, THOUGH...
SO, WHAT--WE JUST WANDER AROUND NEW YORK CITY WHILE YOU SNIFF PEOPLE?!
NOW WE SPLIT UP AN' MAKE OUR WAY BACK TO E.V.A. TO LAY LOW.
WE'RE GIVIN' UP?!
FOR TONIGHT, YEAH.
#&$% THAT!

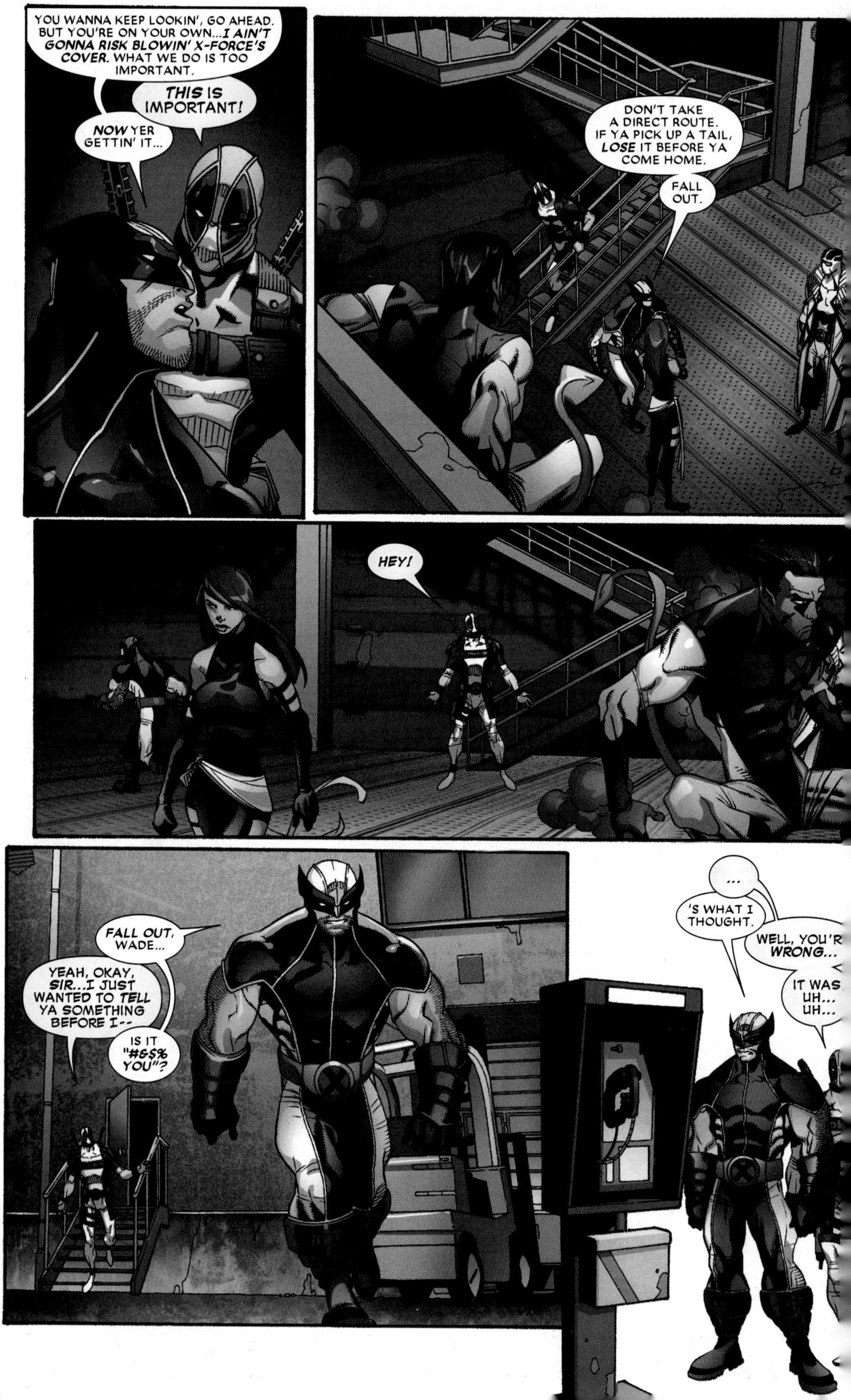
YOU WANNA KEEP LOOKIN', GO AHEAD. BUT YOU'RE ON YOUR OWN...I AIN'T GONNA RISK BLOWIN' X-FORCE'S COVER. WHAT WE DO IS TOO IMPORTANT.
THIS IS IMPORTANT!
NOW YER GETTIN' IT...
DON'T TAKE A DIRECT ROUTE. IF YA PICK UP A TAIL, LOSE IT BEFORE YA COME HOME.
FALL OUT.
HEY!
FALL OUT, WADE...
YEAH, OKAY, SIR...I JUST WANTED TO TELL YA SOMETHING BEFORE I--
IS IT "#&$% YOU"?
...
'S WHAT I THOUGHT.
WELL, YOU'R WRONG...
IT WAS UH... UH...

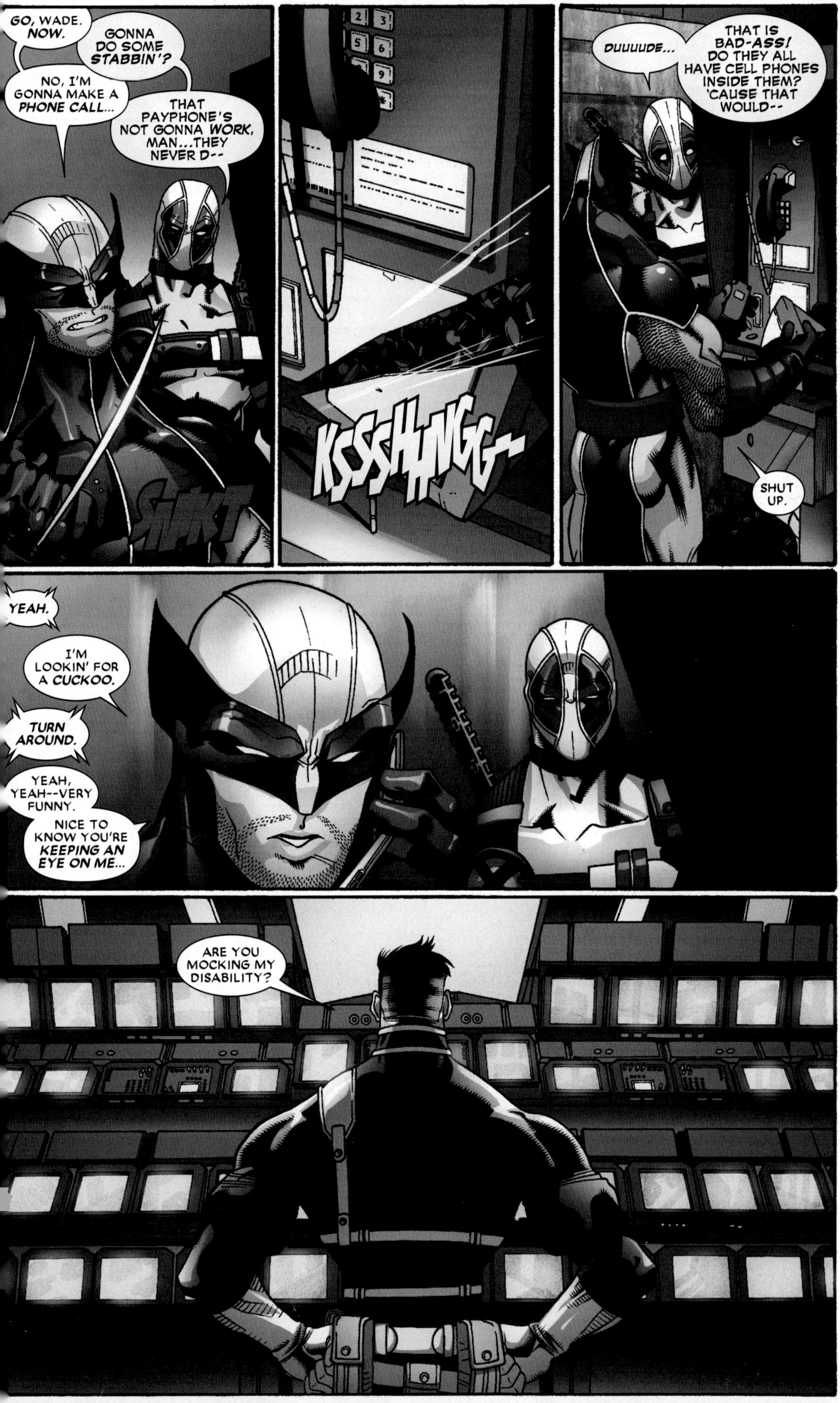

GO, WADE. NOW.
GONNA DO SOME STABBIN'?
NO, I'M GONNA MAKE A PHONE CALL...
THAT PAYPHONE'S NOT GONNA WORK, MAN...THEY NEVER D--
SNIKT
KSSSHNGG--
DUUUUDE...
THAT IS BAD-ASS! DO THEY ALL HAVE CELL PHONES INSIDE THEM? 'CAUSE THAT WOULD--
SHUT UP.
YEAH.
I'M LOOKIN' FOR A CUCKOO.
TURN AROUND.
YEAH, YEAH--VERY FUNNY.
NICE TO KNOW YOU'RE KEEPING AN EYE ON ME...
ARE YOU MOCKING MY DISABILITY?

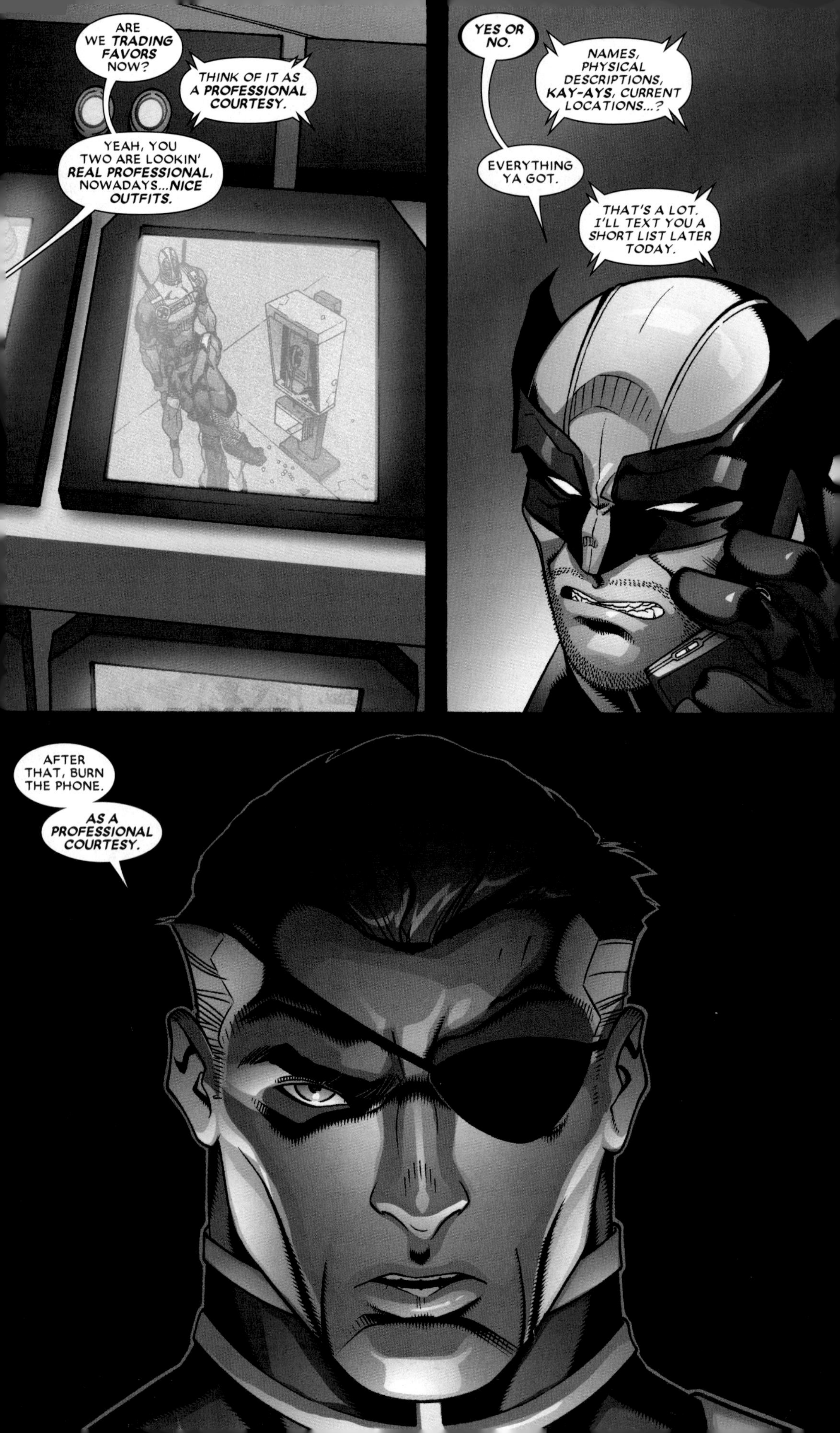
ARE WE TRADING FAVORS NOW?
THINK OF IT AS A PROFESSIONAL COURTESY.
YEAH, YOU TWO ARE LOOKIN' REAL PROFESSIONAL, NOWADAYS...NICE OUTFITS.
YES OR NO.
NAMES, PHYSICAL DESCRIPTIONS, KAY-AYS, CURRENT LOCATIONS...?
EVERYTHING YA GOT.
THAT'S A LOT. I'LL TEXT YOU A SHORT LIST LATER TODAY.
AFTER THAT, BURN THE PHONE.
AS A PROFESSIONAL COURTESY.

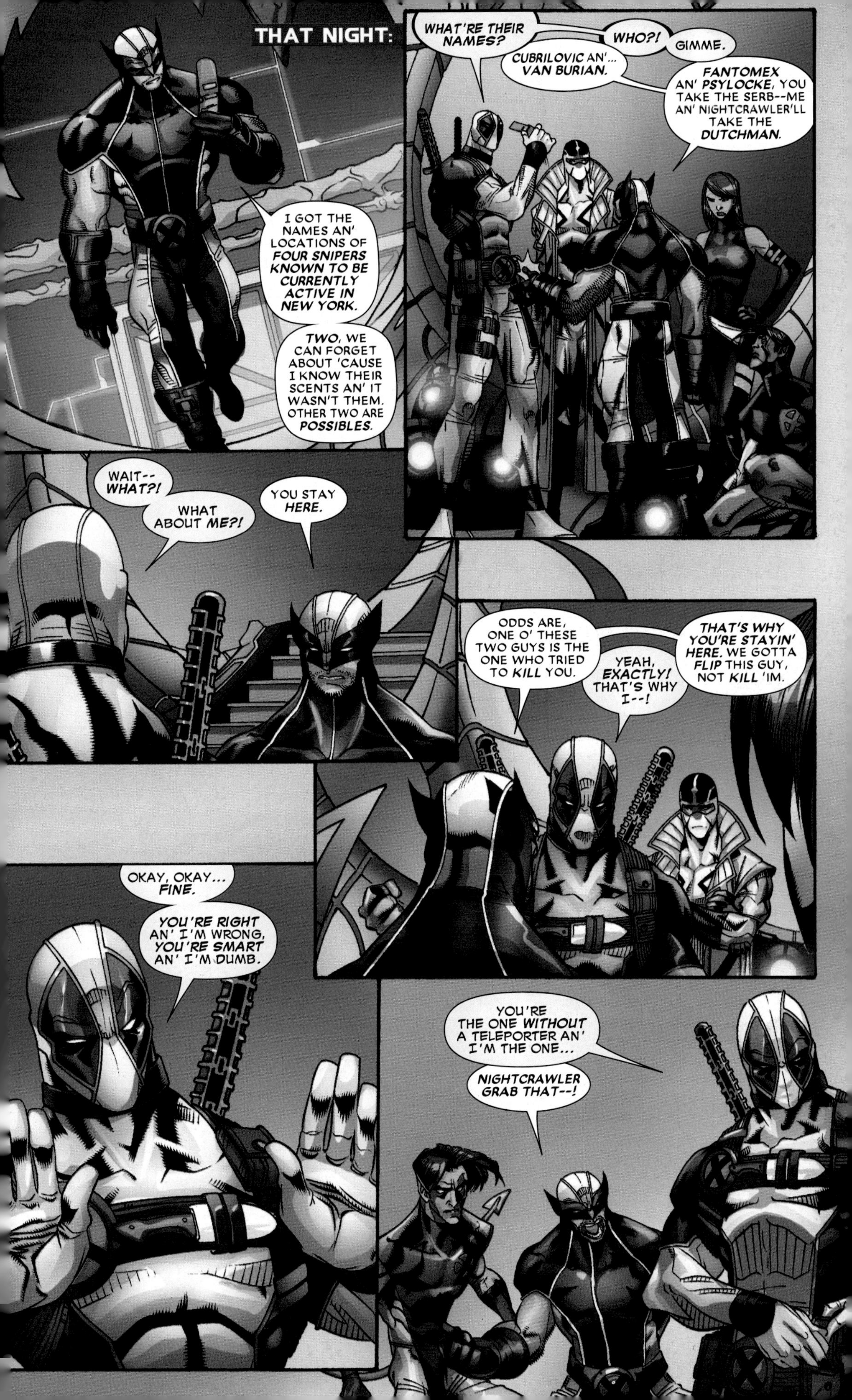
THAT NIGHT:
I GOT THE NAMES AN' LOCATIONS OF FOUR SNIPERS KNOWN TO BE CURRENTLY ACTIVE IN NEW YORK.
TWO, WE CAN FORGET ABOUT 'CAUSE I KNOW THEIR SCENTS AN' IT WASN'T THEM. OTHER TWO ARE POSSIBLES.
WHAT'RE THEIR NAMES?
WHO?!
GIMME.
CUBRILOVIC AN'... VAN BURIAN.
FANTOMEX AN' PSYLOCKE, YOU TAKE THE SERB--ME AN' NIGHTCRAWLER'LL TAKE THE DUTCHMAN.
WAIT-- WHAT?!
WHAT ABOUT ME?!
YOU STAY HERE.
ODDS ARE, ONE O' THESE TWO GUYS IS THE ONE WHO TRIED TO KILL YOU.
YEAH, EXACTLY! THAT'S WHY I--!
THAT'S WHY YOU'RE STAYIN' HERE. WE GOTTA FLIP THIS GUY, NOT KILL 'IM.
OKAY, OKAY... FINE.
YOU'RE RIGHT AN' I'M WRONG, YOU'RE SMART AN' I'M DUMB.
YOU'RE THE ONE WITHOUT A TELEPORTER AN' I'M THE ONE...
NIGHTCRAWLER GRAB THAT--!

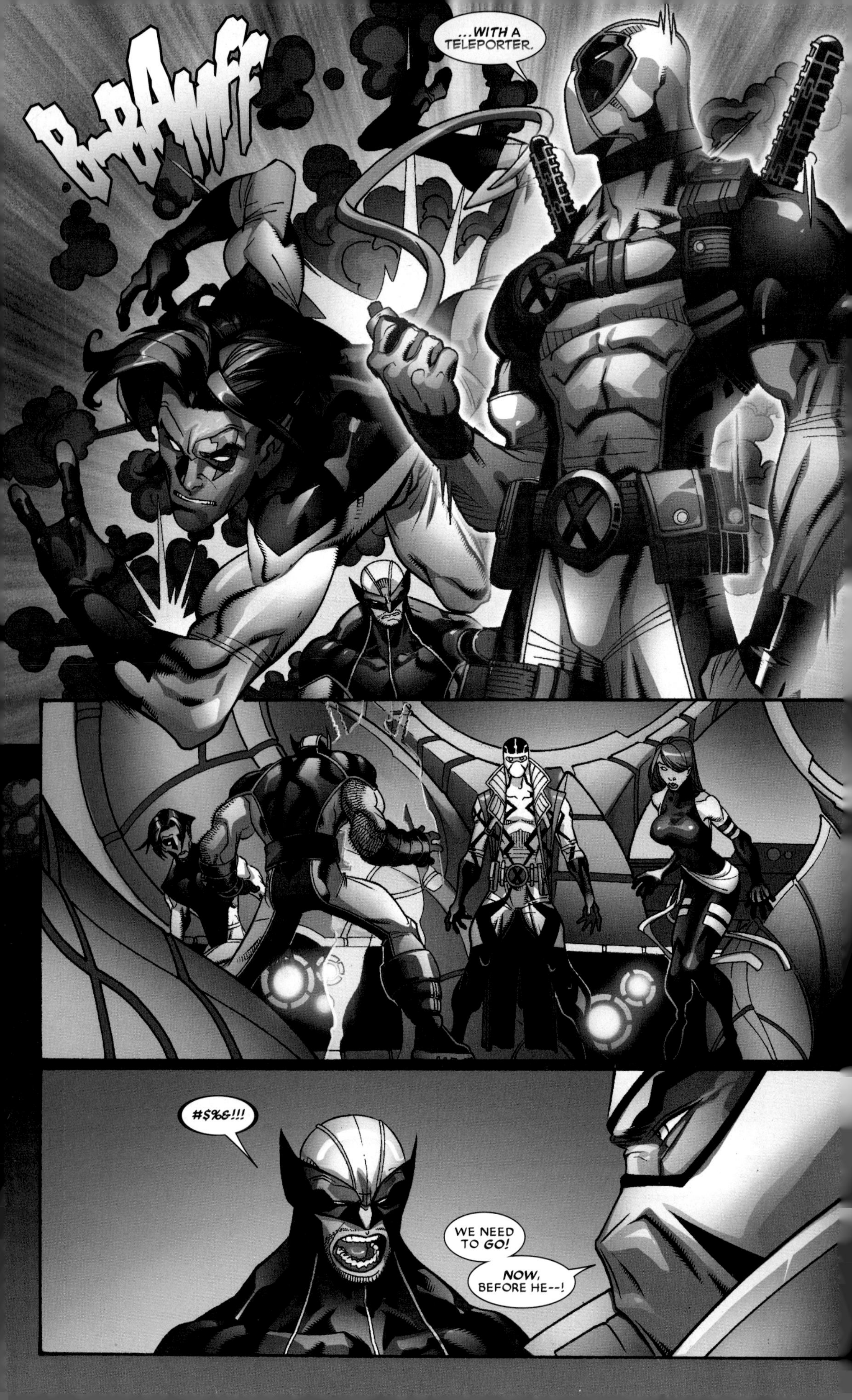

B-BAMF
...WITH A TELEPORTER.
#$%&!!!
WE NEED TO GO!
NOW, BEFORE HE--!

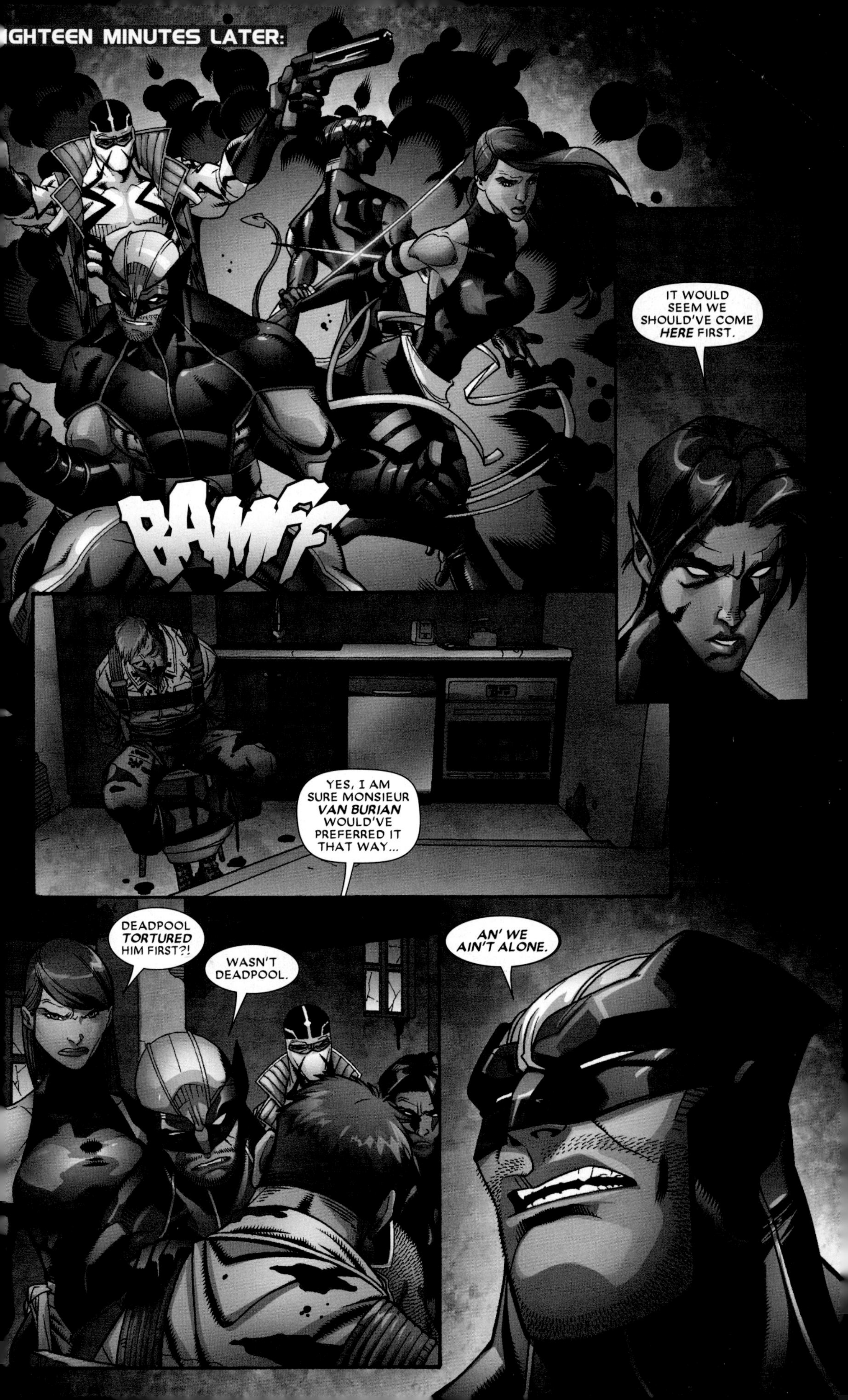
IGHTEEN MINUTES LATER:
BAMF
IT WOULD SEEM WE SHOULD'VE COME HERE FIRST.
YES, I AM SURE MONSIEUR VAN BURIAN WOULD'VE PREFERRED IT THAT WAY...
DEADPOOL TORTURED HIM FIRST?!
WASN'T DEADPOOL.
AN' WE AIN'T ALONE.

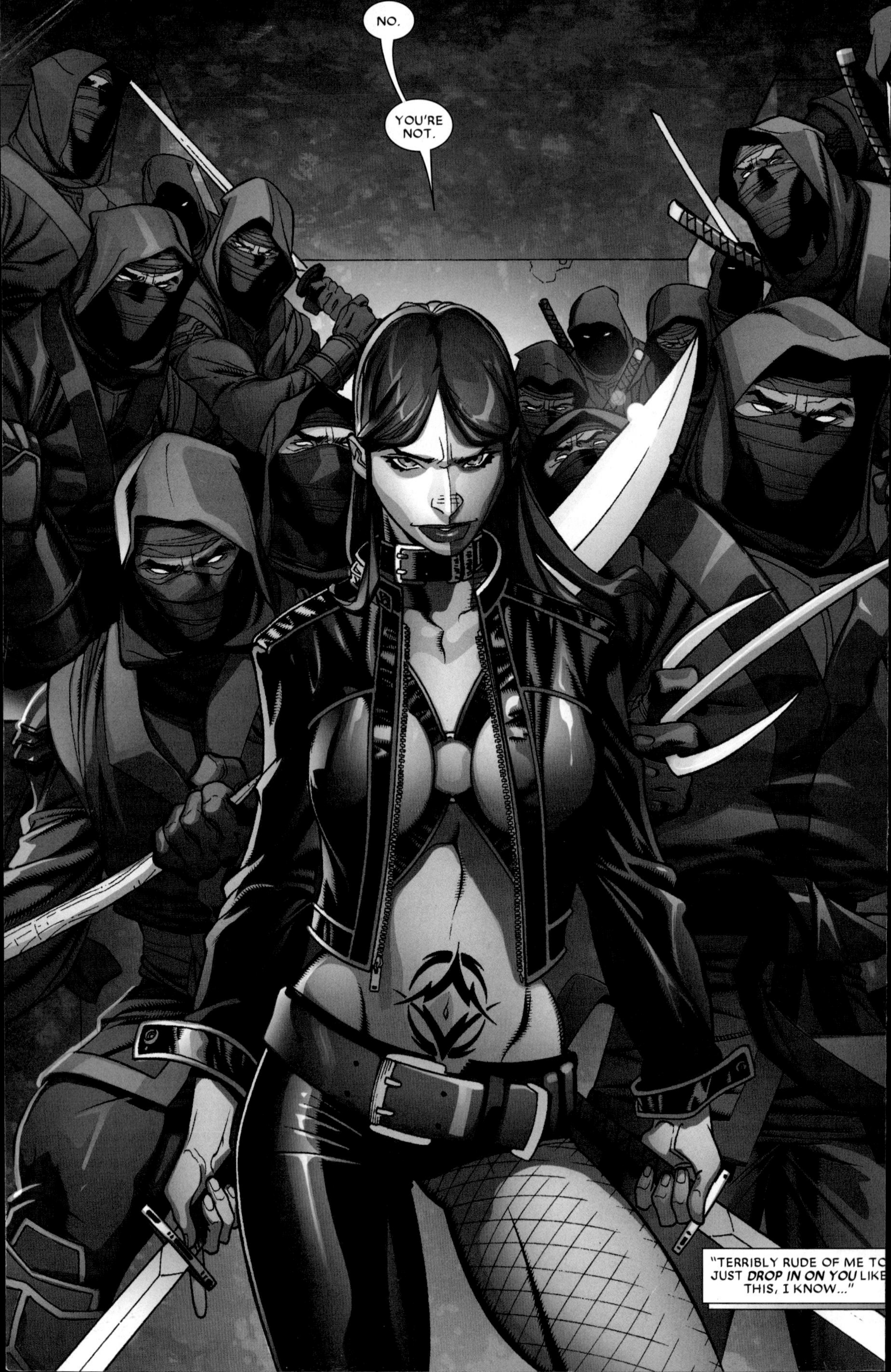
NO.
YOU'RE NOT.
"TERRIBLY RUDE OF ME TO JUST DROP IN ON YOU LIKE THIS, I KNOW..."

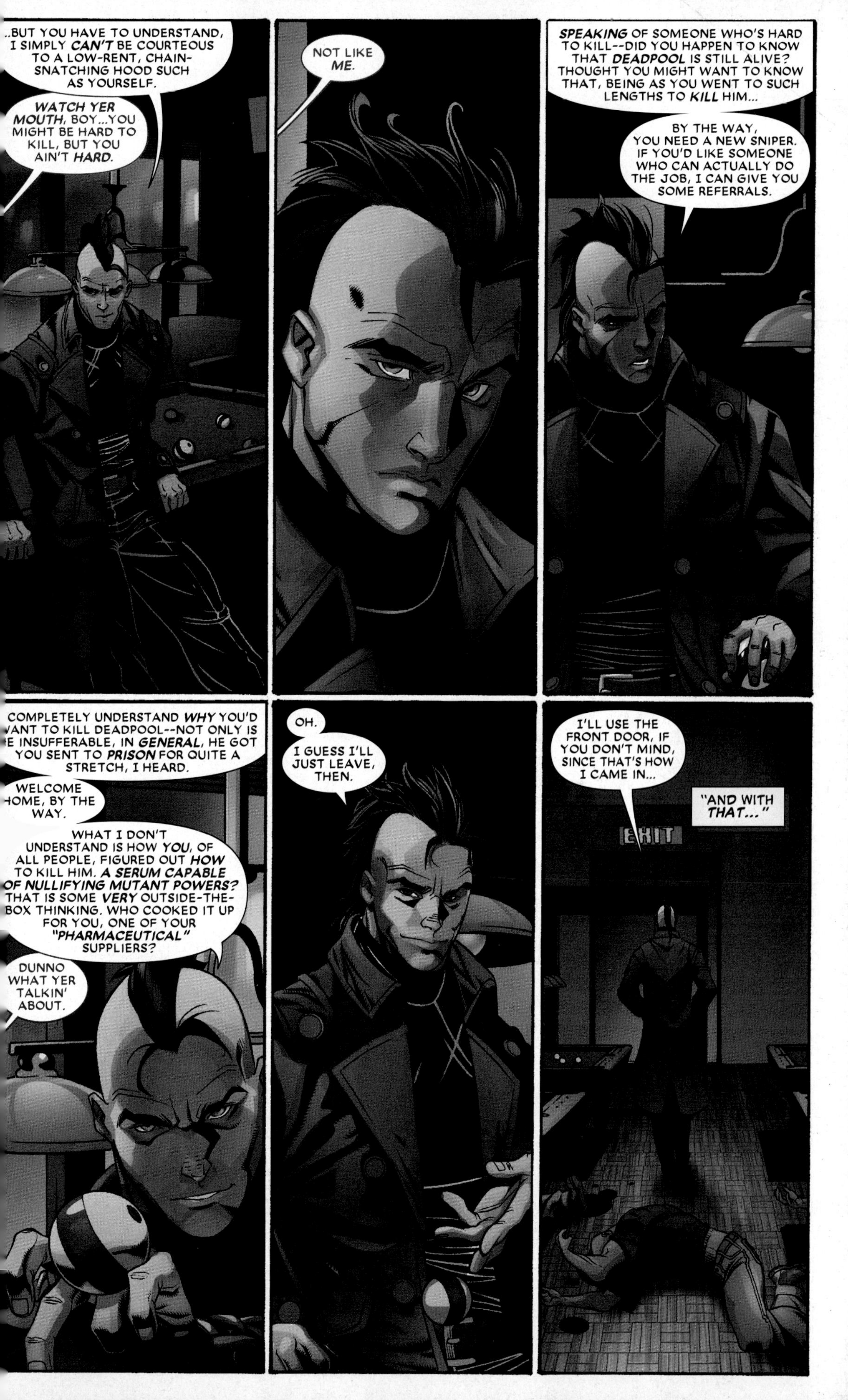
..BUT YOU HAVE TO UNDERSTAND, I SIMPLY CAN'T BE COURTEOUS TO A LOW-RENT, CHAIN-SNATCHING HOOD SUCH AS YOURSELF.
WATCH YER MOUTH, BOY...YOU MIGHT BE HARD TO KILL, BUT YOU AIN'T HARD.
NOT LIKE ME.
SPEAKING OF SOMEONE WHO'S HARD TO KILL--DID YOU HAPPEN TO KNOW THAT DEADPOOL IS STILL ALIVE? THOUGHT YOU MIGHT WANT TO KNOW THAT, BEING AS YOU WENT TO SUCH LENGTHS TO KILL HIM...
BY THE WAY, YOU NEED A NEW SNIPER. IF YOU'D LIKE SOMEONE WHO CAN ACTUALLY DO THE JOB, I CAN GIVE YOU SOME REFERRALS.
COMPLETELY UNDERSTAND WHY YOU'D VANT TO KILL DEADPOOL--NOT ONLY IS E INSUFFERABLE, IN GENERAL, HE GOT YOU SENT TO PRISON FOR QUITE A STRETCH, I HEARD.
WELCOME HOME, BY THE WAY.
WHAT I DON'T UNDERSTAND IS HOW YOU, OF ALL PEOPLE, FIGURED OUT HOW TO KILL HIM. A SERUM CAPABLE OF NULLIFYING MUTANT POWERS? THAT IS SOME VERY OUTSIDE-THE-BOX THINKING. WHO COOKED IT UP FOR YOU, ONE OF YOUR "PHARMACEUTICAL" SUPPLIERS?
DUNNO WHAT YER TALKIN' ABOUT.
OH.
I GUESS I'LL JUST LEAVE, THEN.
I'LL USE THE FRONT DOOR, IF YOU DON'T MIND, SINCE THAT'S HOW I CAME IN...
"AND WITH THAT..."
EXIT

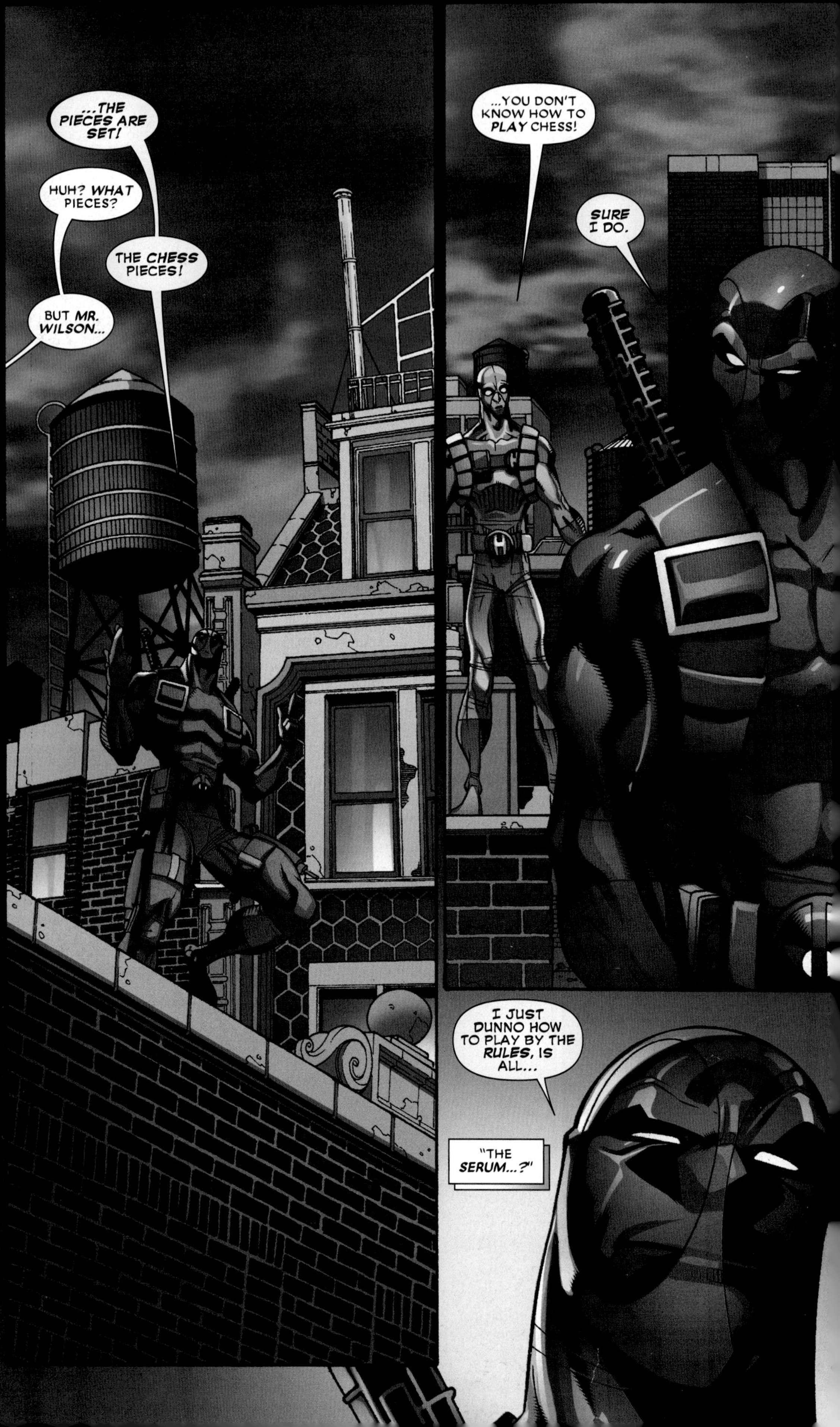
...THE PIECES ARE SET!
HUH? WHAT PIECES?
THE CHESS PIECES!
BUT MR. WILSON...
...YOU DON'T KNOW HOW TO PLAY CHESS!
SURE I DO.
I JUST DUNNO HOW TO PLAY BY THE RULES, IS ALL...
"THE SERUM...?"

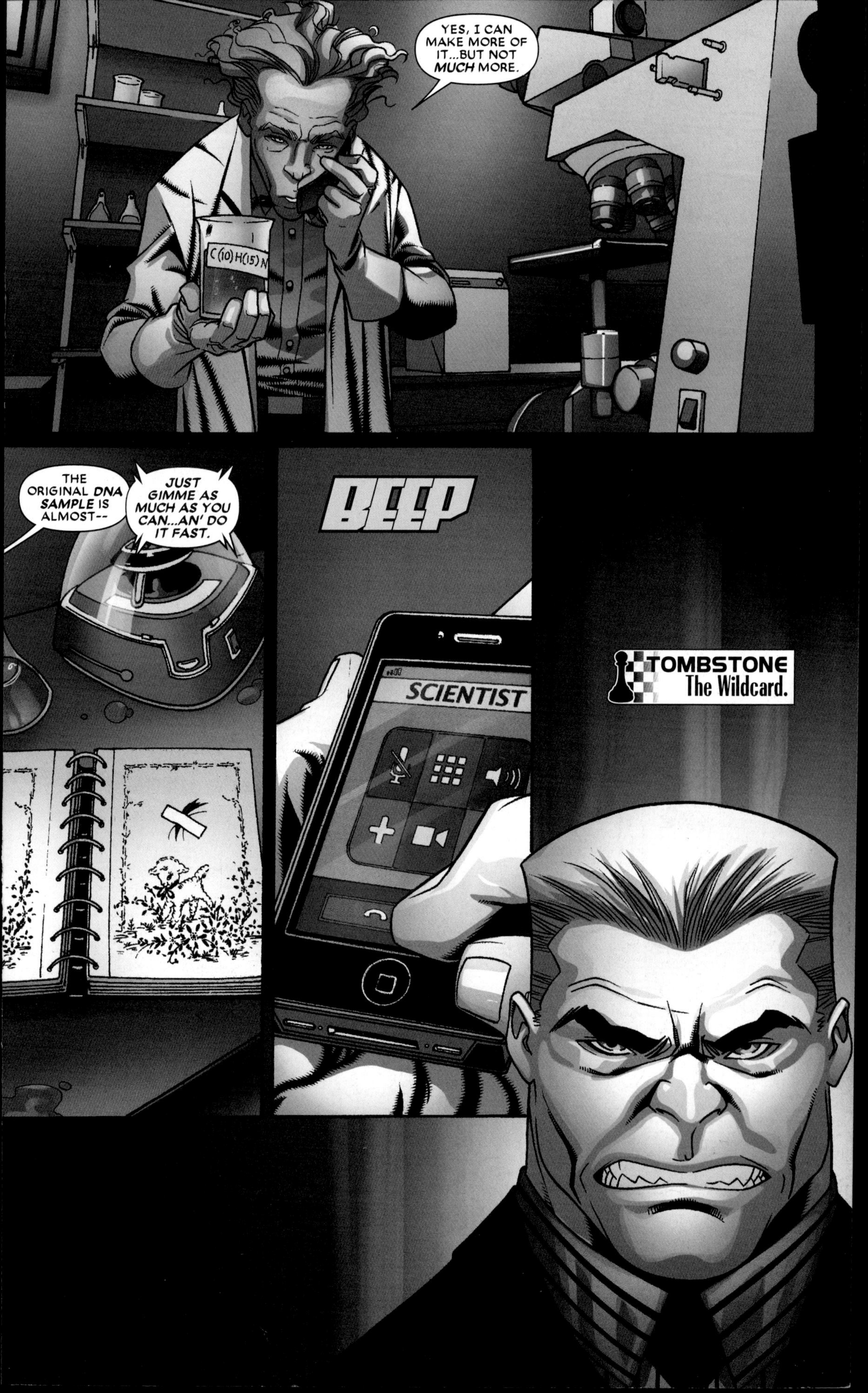
YES, I CAN MAKE MORE OF IT...BUT NOT MUCH MORE.
C(10)H(15)N
THE ORIGINAL DNA SAMPLE IS ALMOST--
JUST GIMME AS MUCH AS YOU CAN...AN' DO IT FAST.
BEEP
SCIENTIST
TOMBSTONE
The Wildcard.

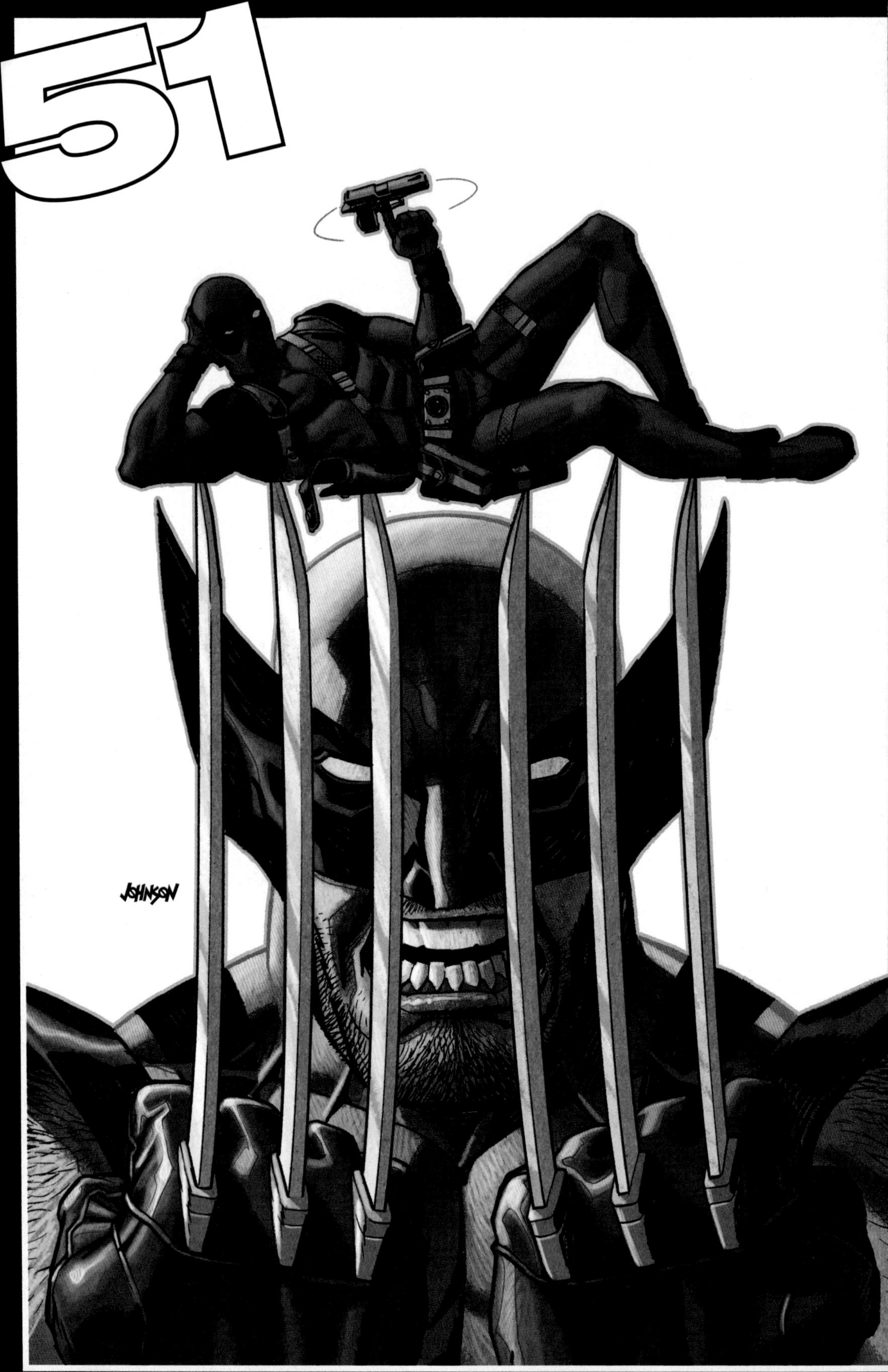
51
JOHNSON

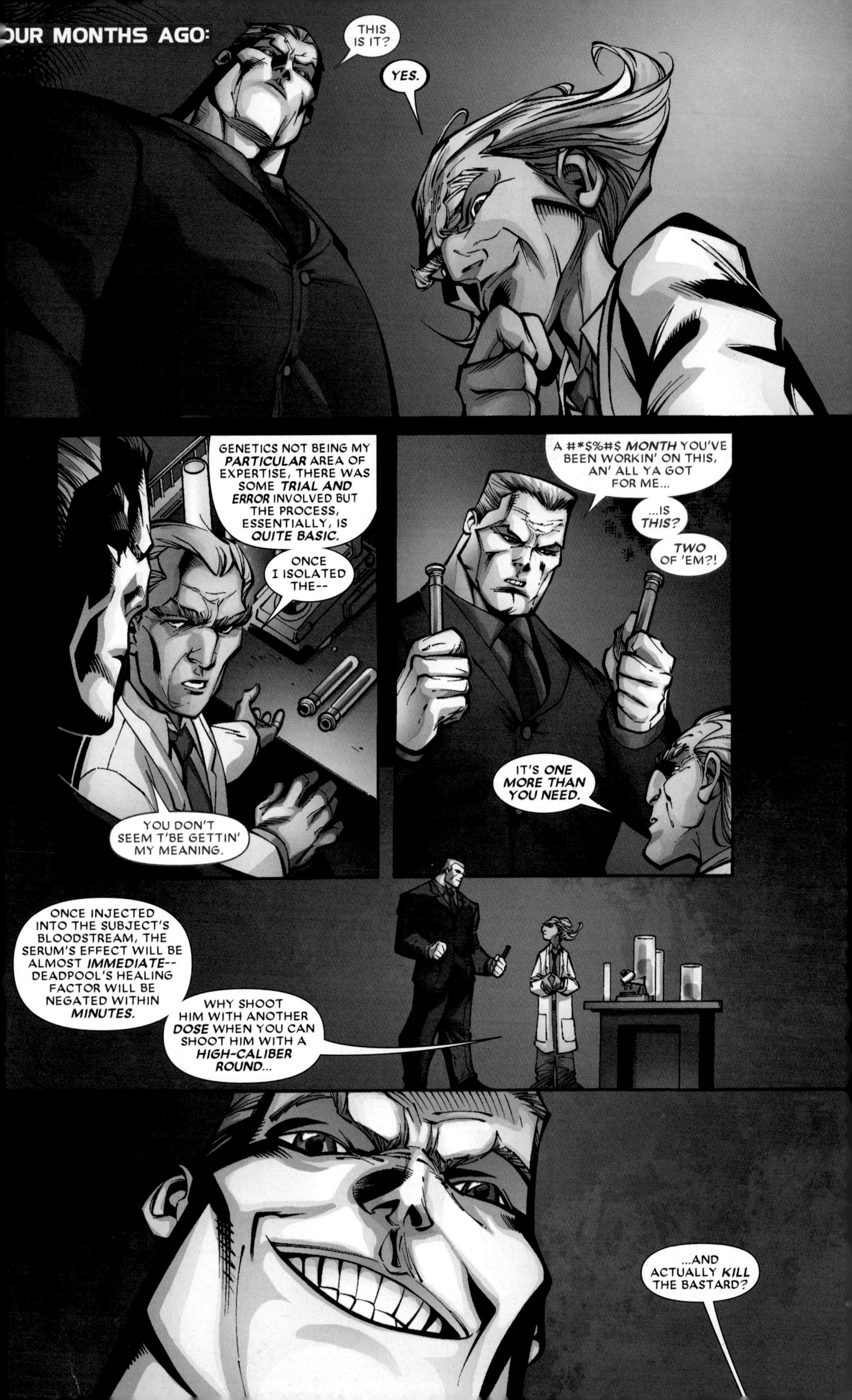
OUR MONTHS AGO:
THIS IS IT?
YES.
GENETICS NOT BEING MY PARTICULAR AREA OF EXPERTISE, THERE WAS SOME TRIAL AND ERROR INVOLVED BUT THE PROCESS, ESSENTIALLY, IS QUITE BASIC.
ONCE I ISOLATED THE--
YOU DON'T SEEM T'BE GETTIN' MY MEANING.
A #*$%#$ MONTH YOU'VE BEEN WORKIN' ON THIS, AN' ALL YA GOT FOR ME...
...IS THIS?
TWO OF 'EM?!
IT'S ONE MORE THAN YOU NEED.
ONCE INJECTED INTO THE SUBJECT'S BLOODSTREAM, THE SERUM'S EFFECT WILL BE ALMOST IMMEDIATE-- DEADPOOL'S HEALING FACTOR WILL BE NEGATED WITHIN MINUTES.
WHY SHOOT HIM WITH ANOTHER DOSE WHEN YOU CAN SHOOT HIM WITH A HIGH-CALIBER ROUND...
...AND ACTUALLY KILL THE BASTARD?

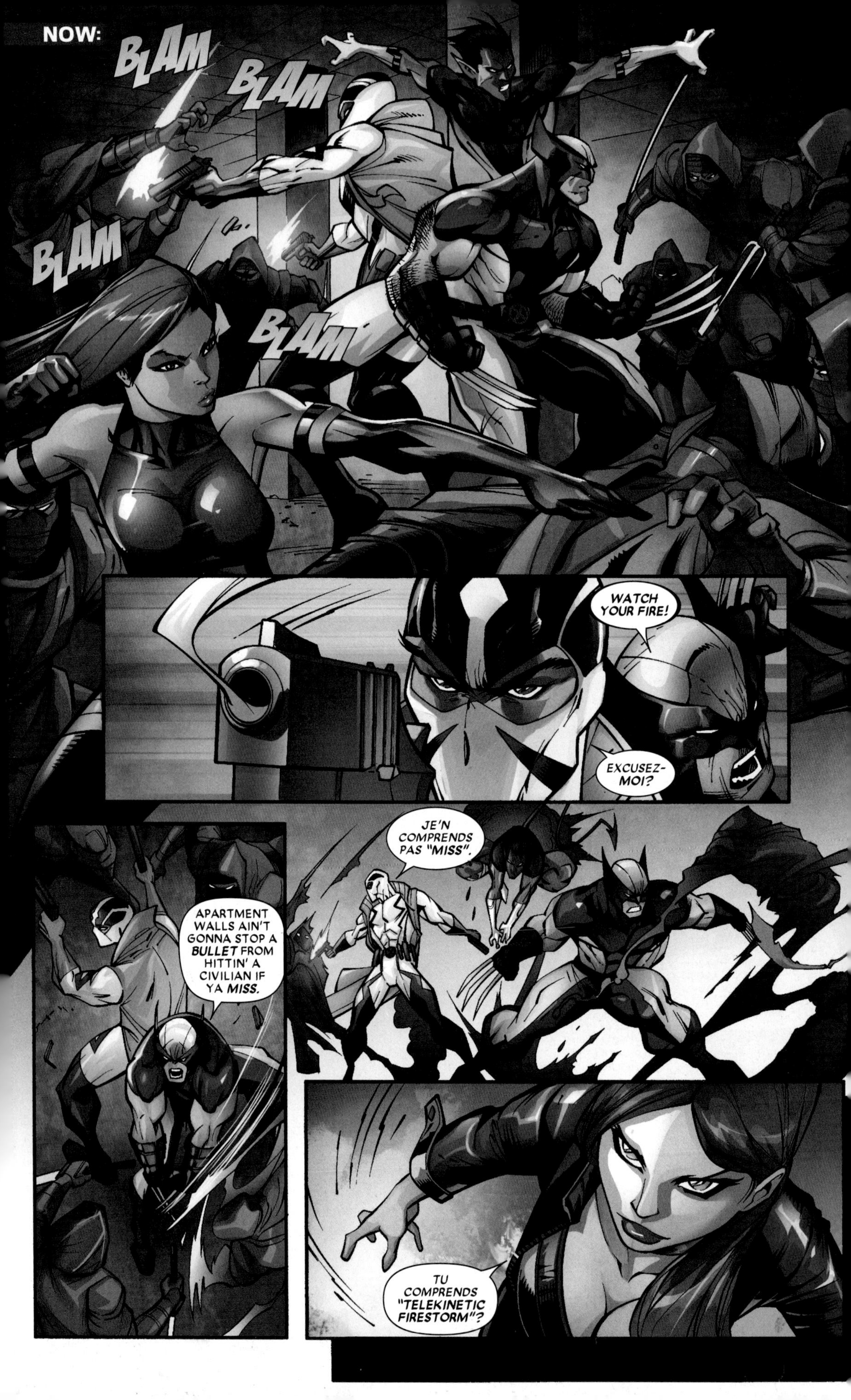
NOW:
BLAM
BLAM
BLAM
BLAM
WATCH YOUR FIRE!
EXCUSEZ-MOI?
APARTMENT WALLS AIN'T GONNA STOP A BULLET FROM HITTIN' A CIVILIAN IF YA MISS.
JE'N COMPRENDS PAS "MISS".
TU COMPRENDS "TELEKINETIC FIRESTORM"?

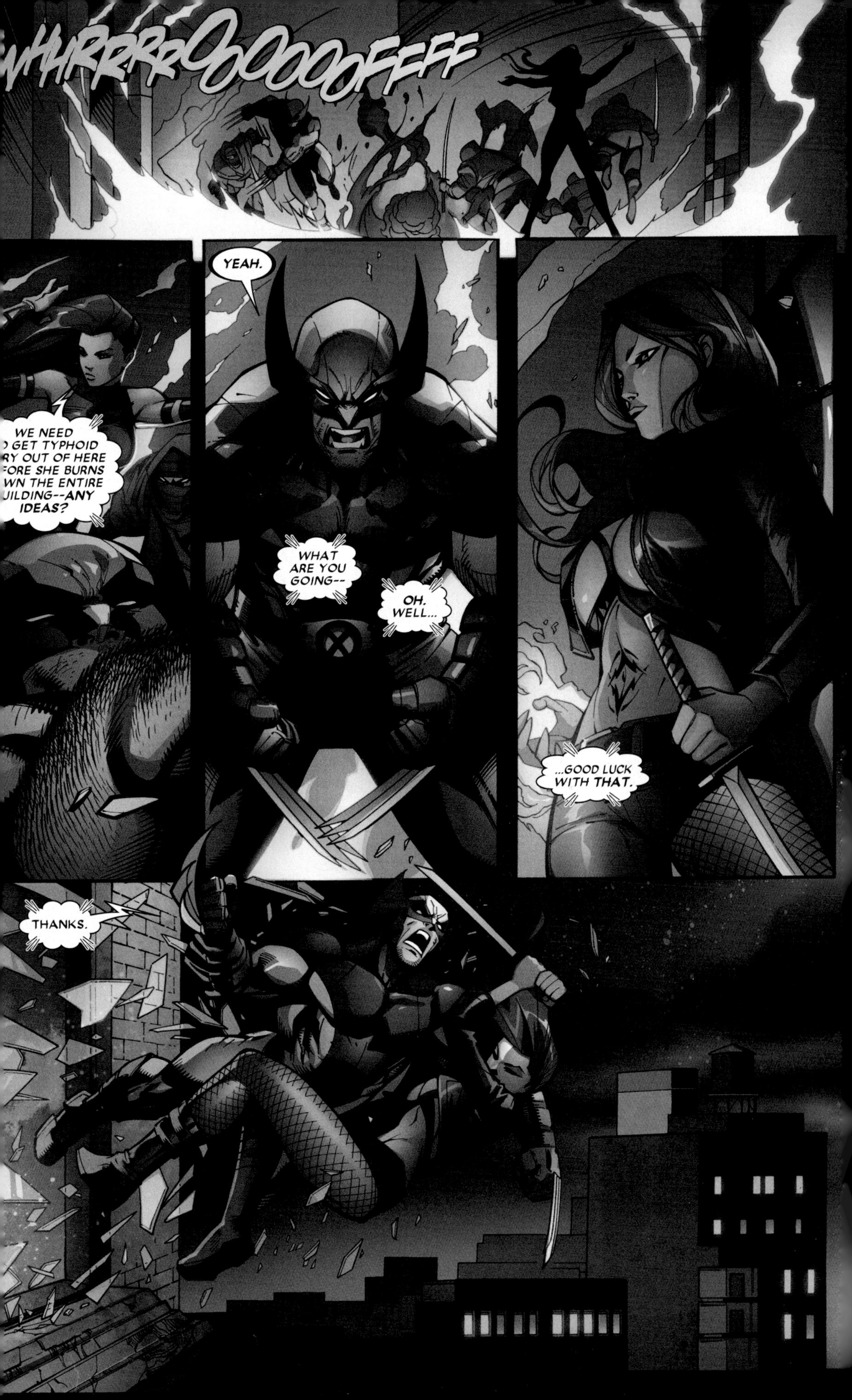
WHURRRROOOOOOFFFFF
WE NEED
O GET TYPHOID
RY OUT OF HERE
FORE SHE BURNS
WN THE ENTIRE
UILDING--ANY
IDEAS?
YEAH.
WHAT ARE YOU GOING--
OH. WELL...
...GOOD LUCK WITH THAT.
THANKS.

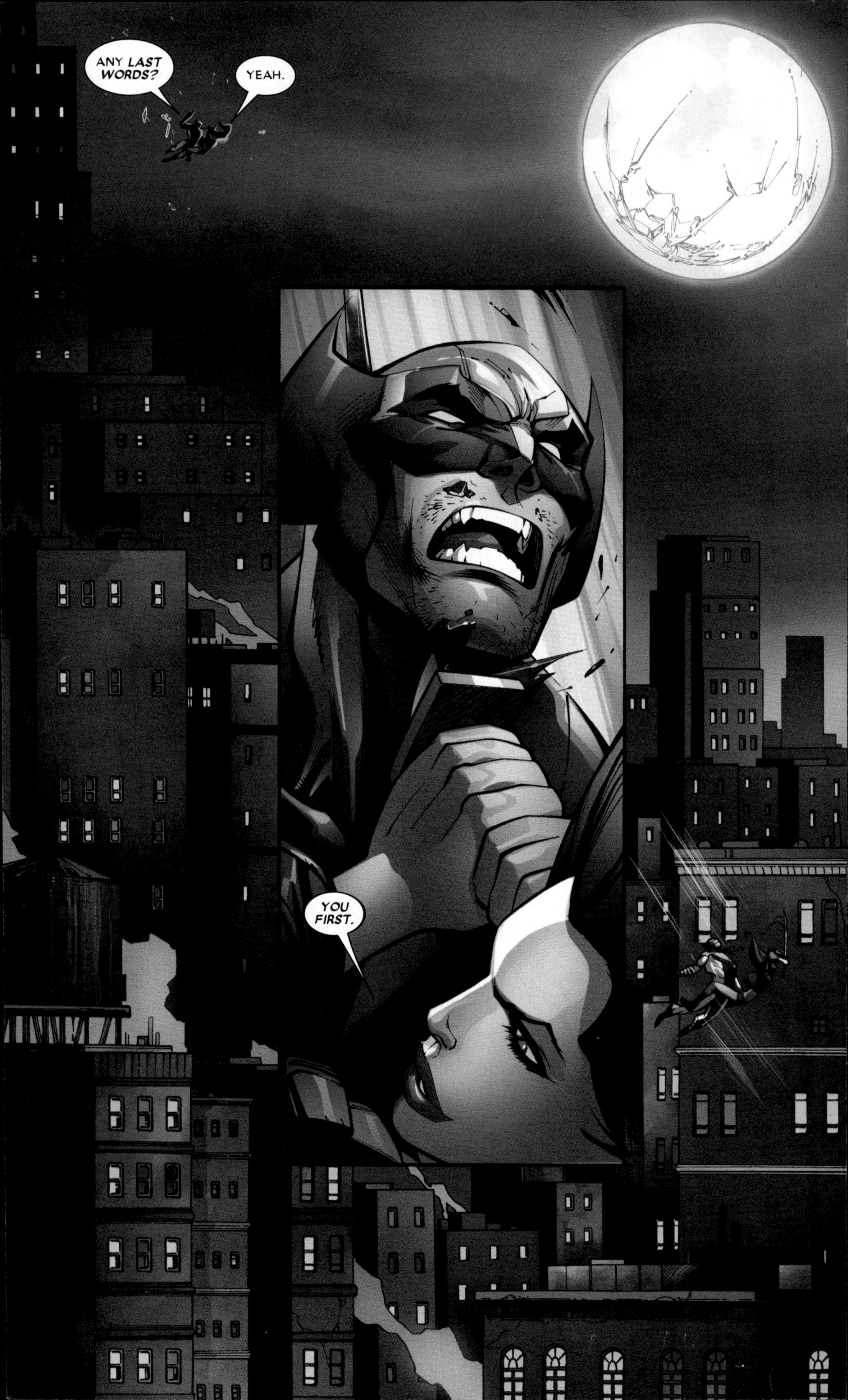
ANY LAST WORDS?
YEAH.
YOU FIRST.

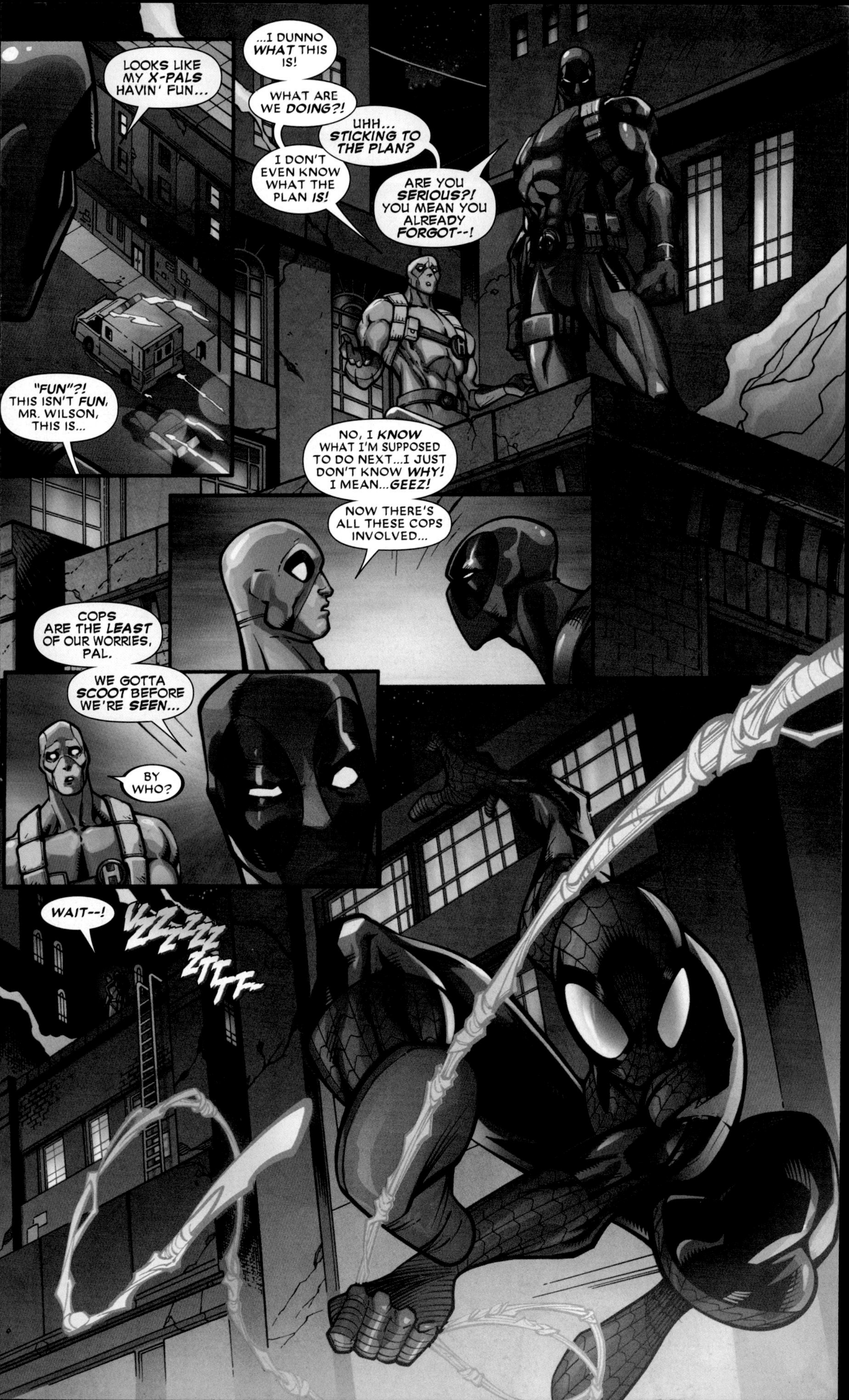
LOOKS LIKE MY X-PALS HAVIN' FUN...
"FUN"?! THIS ISN'T FUN, MR. WILSON, THIS IS...
...I DUNNO WHAT THIS IS!
WHAT ARE WE DOING?!
I DON'T EVEN KNOW WHAT THE PLAN IS!
UHH... STICKING TO THE PLAN?
ARE YOU SERIOUS?! YOU MEAN YOU ALREADY FORGOT--!
NO, I KNOW WHAT I'M SUPPOSED TO DO NEXT...I JUST DON'T KNOW WHY! I MEAN...GEEZ!
NOW THERE'S ALL THESE COPS INVOLVED...
COPS ARE THE LEAST OF OUR WORRIES, PAL.
WE GOTTA SCOOT BEFORE WE'RE SEEN...
BY WHO?
WAIT--!
VZZZZZZZTTTFF

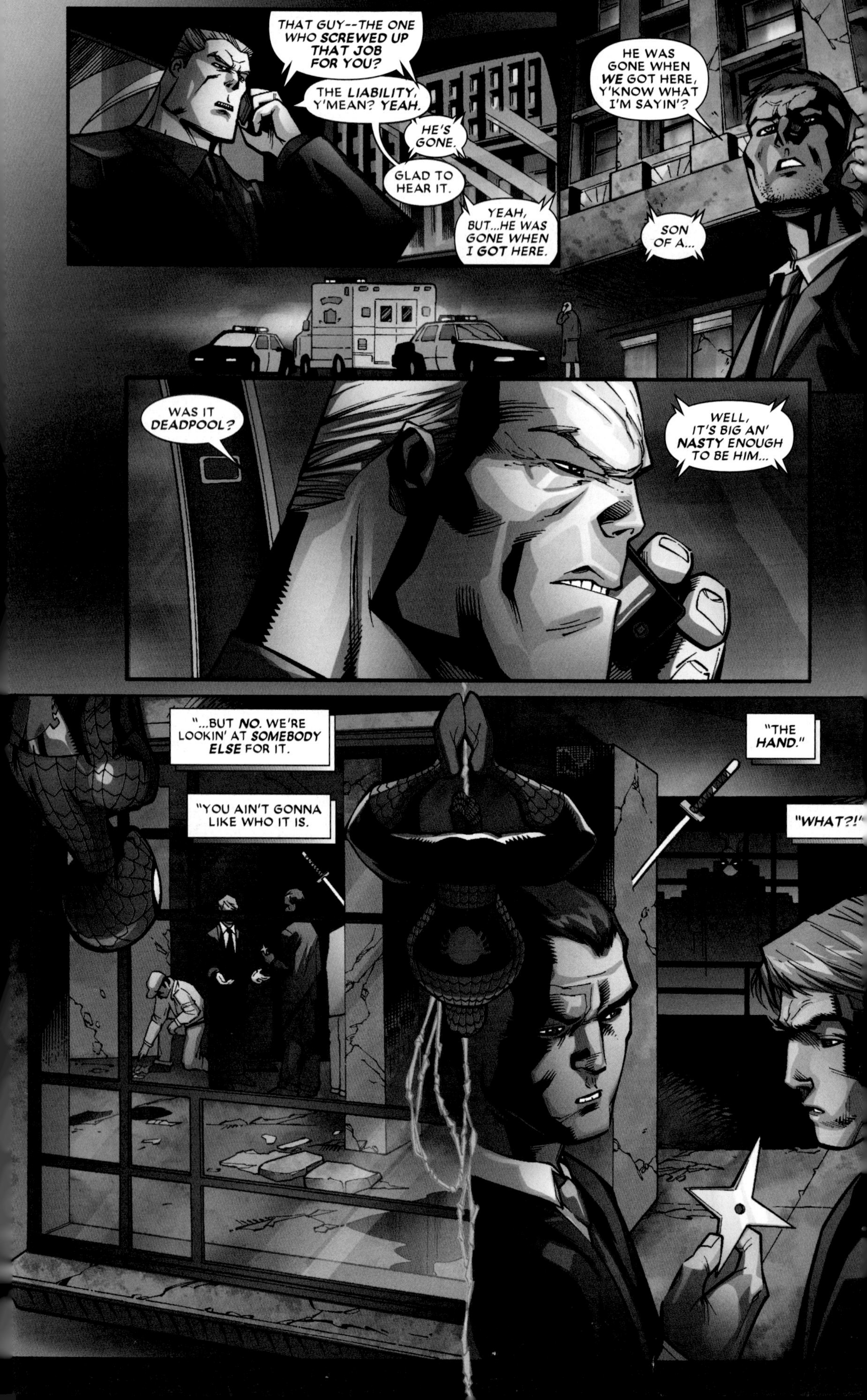

THAT GUY--THE ONE WHO SCREWED UP THAT JOB FOR YOU?
THE LIABILITY, Y'MEAN? YEAH.
HE'S GONE.
GLAD TO HEAR IT.
YEAH, BUT...HE WAS GONE WHEN I GOT HERE.
HE WAS GONE WHEN WE GOT HERE, Y'KNOW WHAT I'M SAYIN'?
SON OF A...
WAS IT DEADPOOL?
WELL, IT'S BIG AN' NASTY ENOUGH TO BE HIM...
"...BUT NO. WE'RE LOOKIN' AT SOMEBODY ELSE FOR IT.
"YOU AIN'T GONNA LIKE WHO IT IS.
"THE HAND."
"WHAT?!"

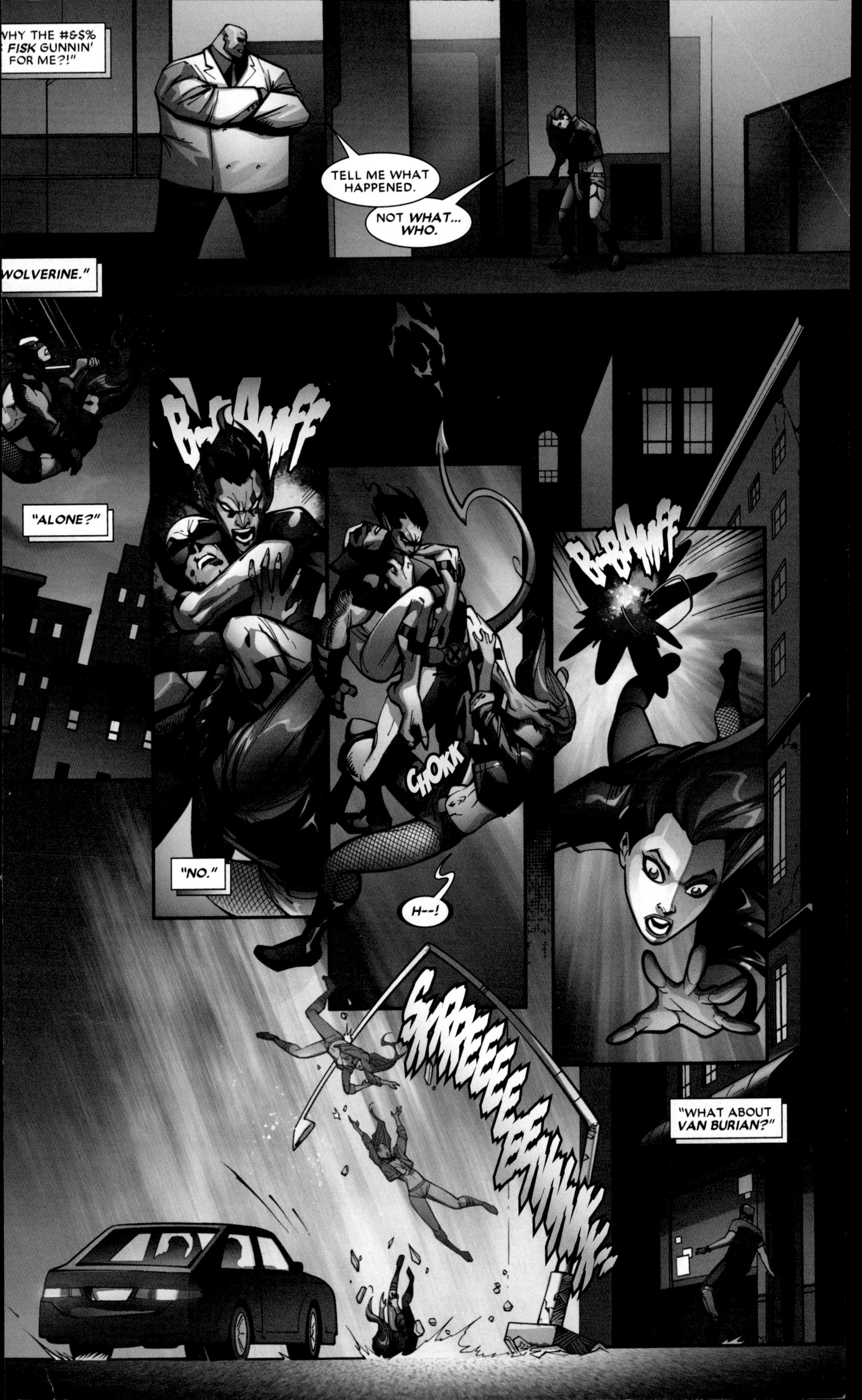
"WHY THE #&$% 'S FISK GUNNIN' FOR ME?!"
TELL ME WHAT HAPPENED.
NOT WHAT... WHO.
"WOLVERINE."
"ALONE?"
B-BAMFF
"NO."
CHOKK
H--!
B-BAMFF
SKREEEEEEEENNKK
"WHAT ABOUT VAN BURIAN?"

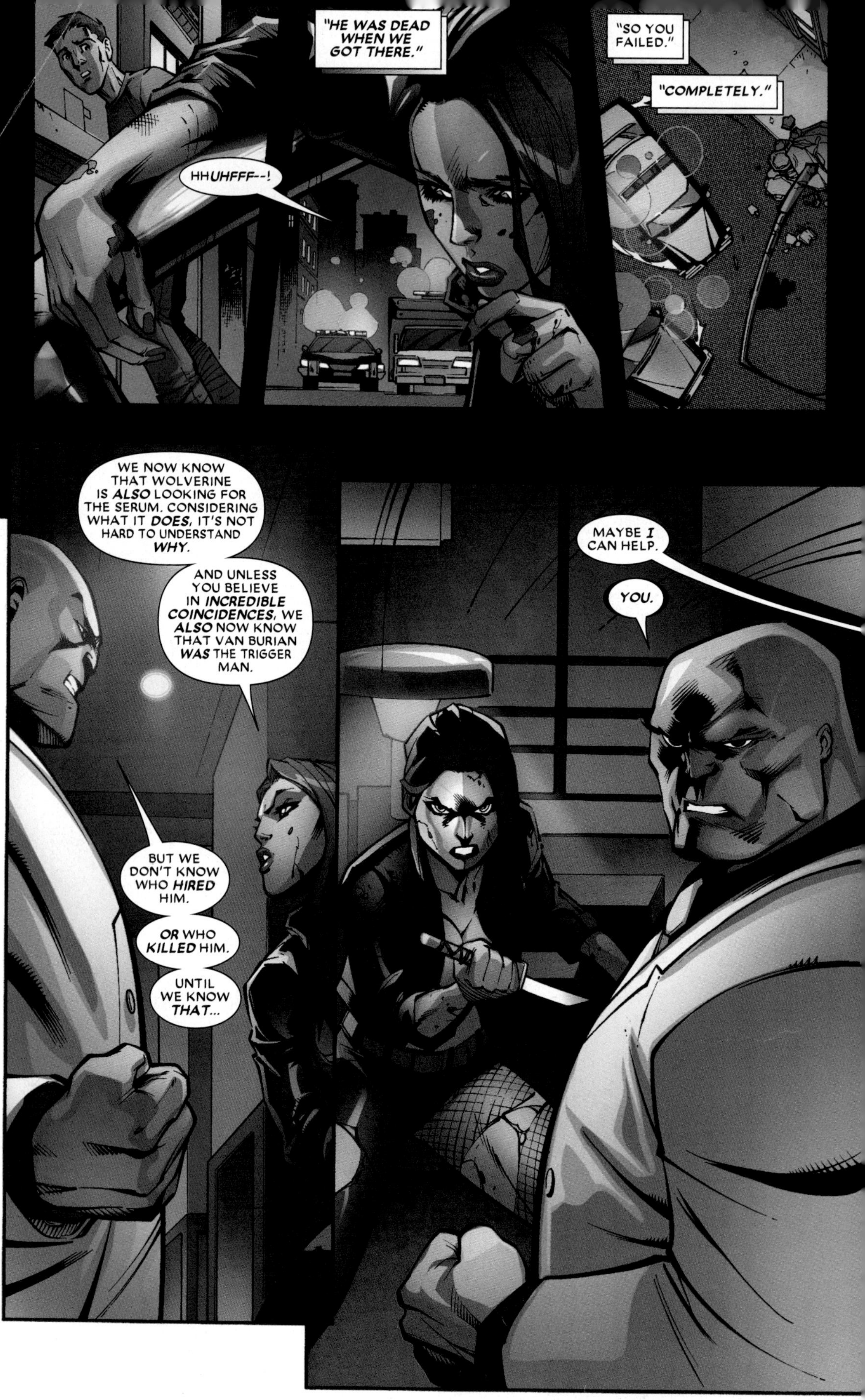
"HE WAS DEAD WHEN WE GOT THERE."
HHUHFFF--!
"SO YOU FAILED."
"COMPLETELY."
WE NOW KNOW THAT WOLVERINE IS ALSO LOOKING FOR THE SERUM. CONSIDERING WHAT IT DOES, IT'S NOT HARD TO UNDERSTAND WHY.
AND UNLESS YOU BELIEVE IN INCREDIBLE COINCIDENCES, WE ALSO NOW KNOW THAT VAN BURIAN WAS THE TRIGGER MAN.
BUT WE DON'T KNOW WHO HIRED HIM.
OR WHO KILLED HIM.
UNTIL WE KNOW THAT...
MAYBE I CAN HELP.
YOU.

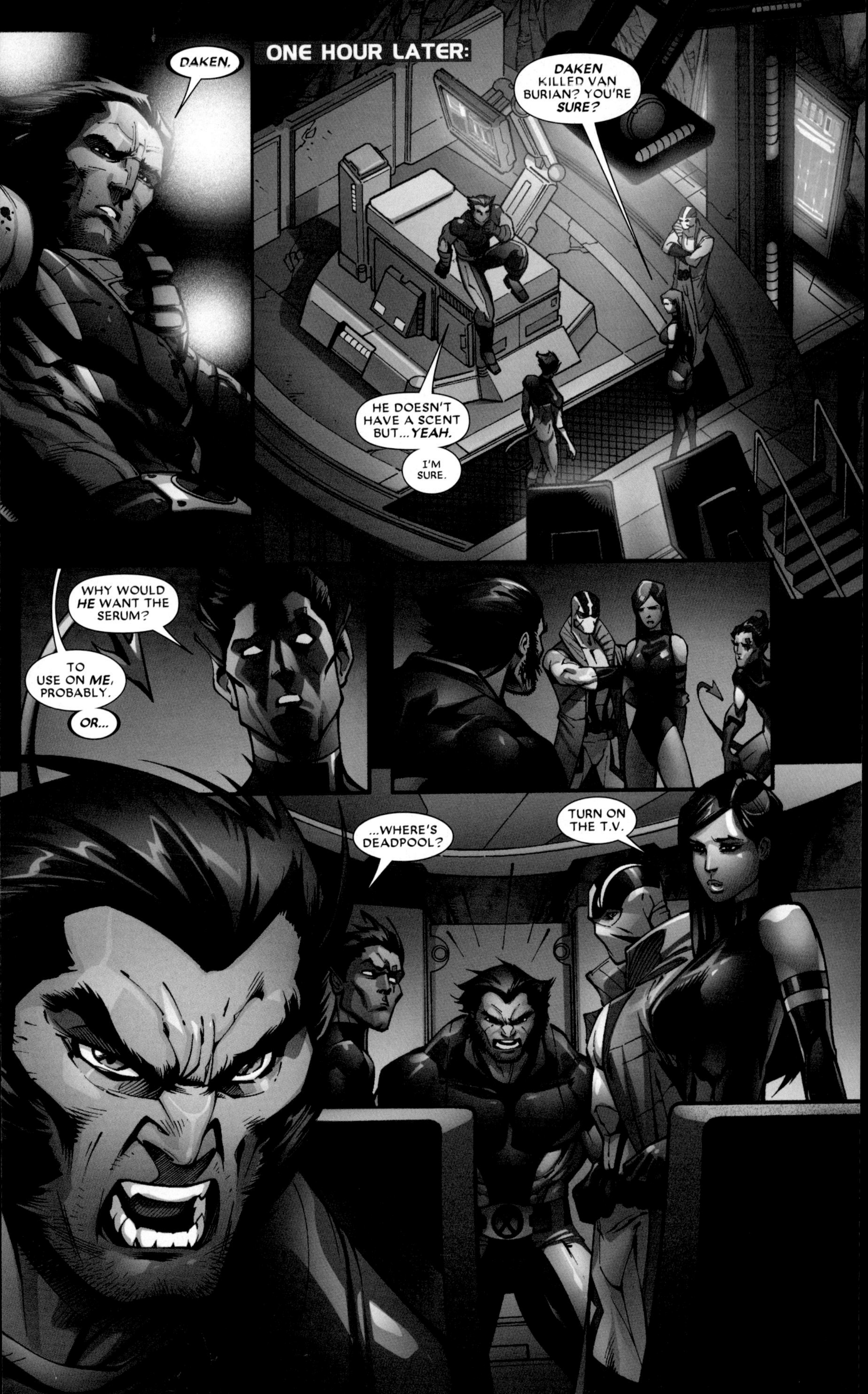
DAKEN.
ONE HOUR LATER:
DAKEN KILLED VAN BURIAN? YOU'RE SURE?
HE DOESN'T HAVE A SCENT BUT...YEAH.
I'M SURE.
WHY WOULD HE WANT THE SERUM?
TO USE ON ME, PROBABLY.
OR...
...WHERE'S DEADPOOL?
TURN ON THE T.V.

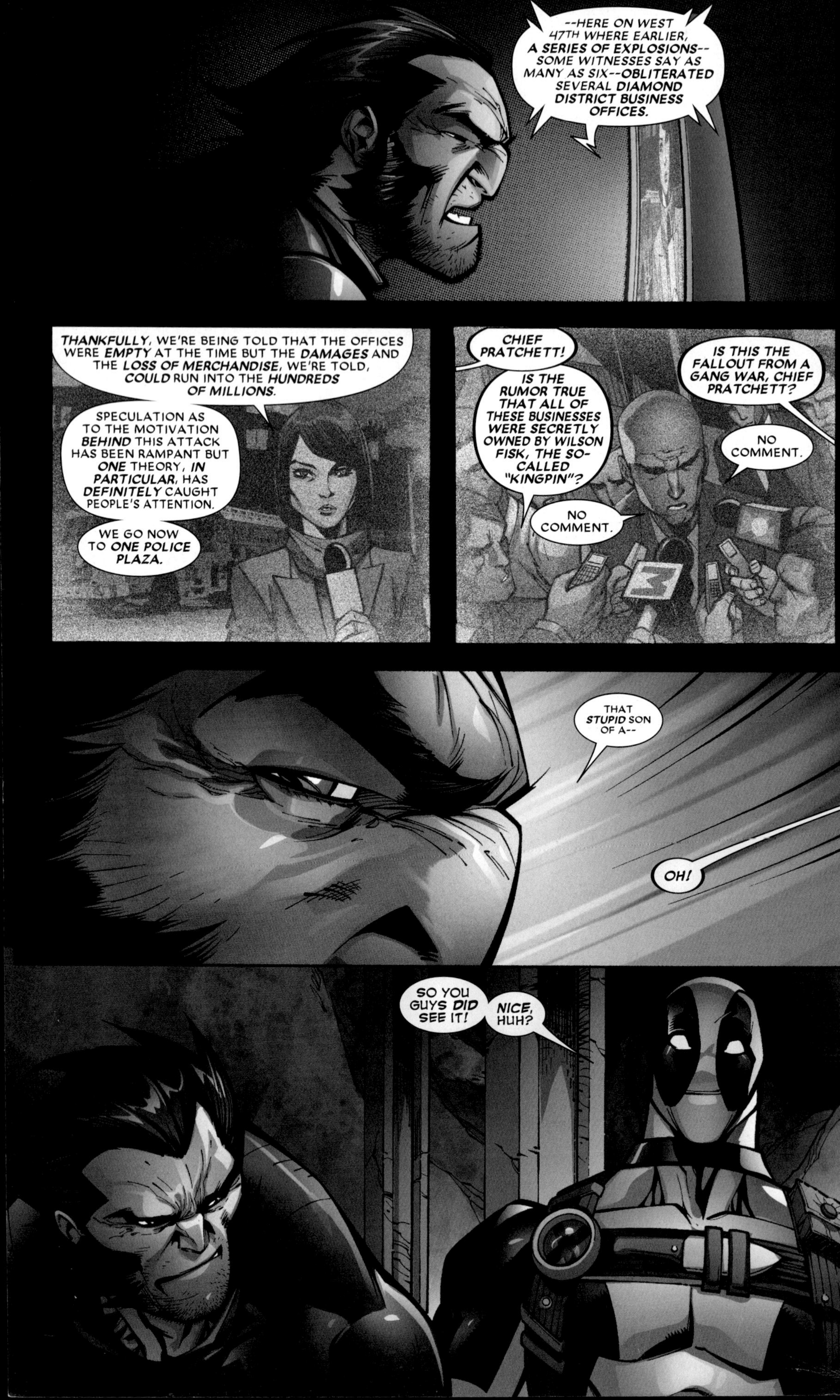

--HERE ON WEST 47TH WHERE EARLIER, A SERIES OF EXPLOSIONS-- SOME WITNESSES SAY AS MANY AS SIX--OBLITERATED SEVERAL DIAMOND DISTRICT BUSINESS OFFICES.
THANKFULLY, WE'RE BEING TOLD THAT THE OFFICES WERE EMPTY AT THE TIME BUT THE DAMAGES AND THE LOSS OF MERCHANDISE, WE'RE TOLD, COULD RUN INTO THE HUNDREDS OF MILLIONS.
SPECULATION AS TO THE MOTIVATION BEHIND THIS ATTACK HAS BEEN RAMPANT BUT ONE THEORY, IN PARTICULAR, HAS DEFINITELY CAUGHT PEOPLE'S ATTENTION.
WE GO NOW TO ONE POLICE PLAZA.
CHIEF PRATCHETT!
IS THE RUMOR TRUE THAT ALL OF THESE BUSINESSES WERE SECRETLY OWNED BY WILSON FISK, THE SO-CALLED "KINGPIN"?
NO COMMENT.
IS THIS THE FALLOUT FROM A GANG WAR, CHIEF PRATCHETT?
NO COMMENT.
THAT STUPID SON OF A--
OH!
SO YOU GUYS DID SEE IT!
NICE, HUH?

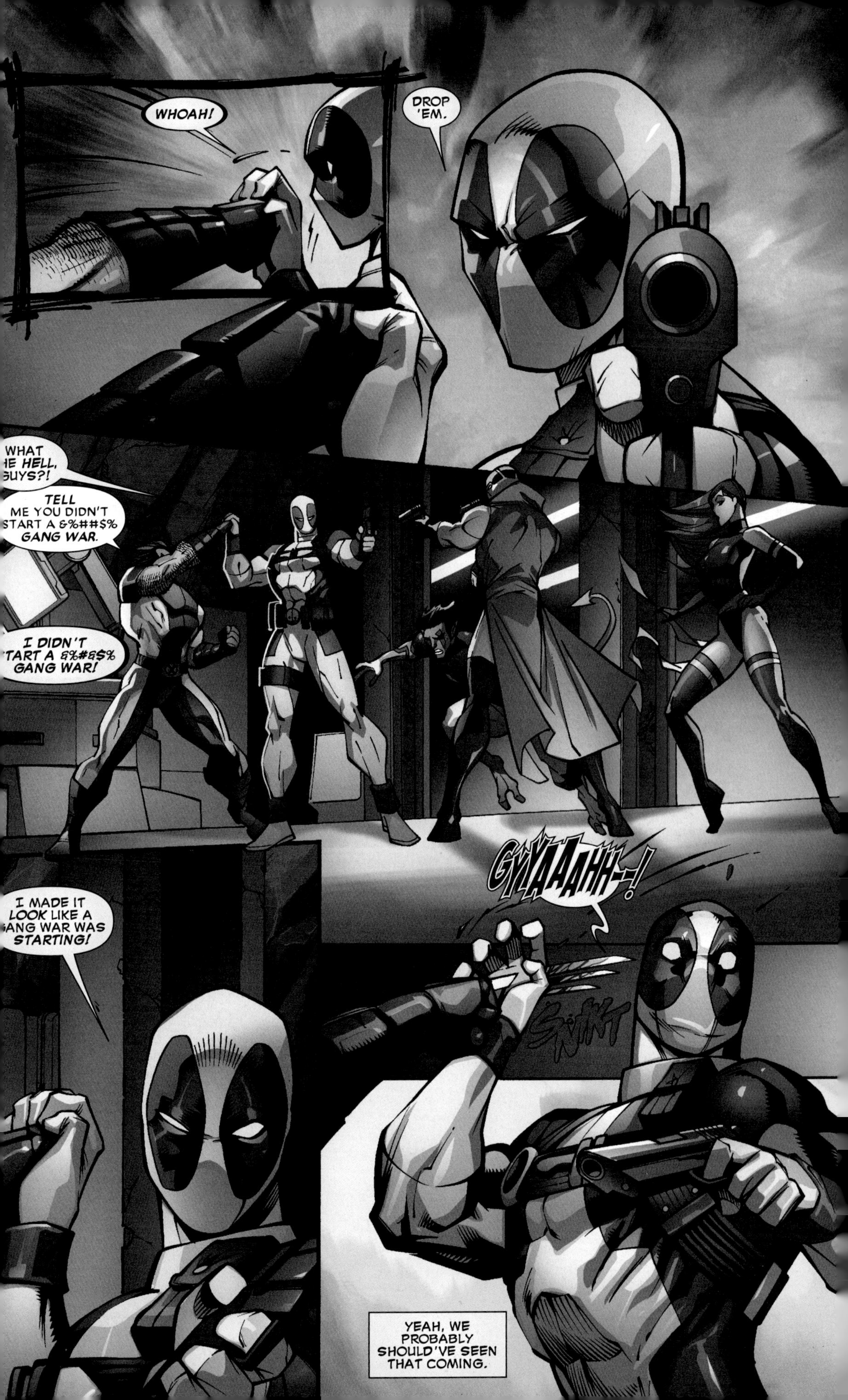
WHOAH!
DROP 'EM.
WHAT HE HELL, UYS?!
TELL ME YOU DIDN'T TART A &%#&$% GANG WAR.
I DIDN'T TART A &%#&$% GANG WAR!
I MADE IT LOOK LIKE A ANG WAR WAS STARTING!
GYYAAAHH--!
SNIKT
YEAH, WE PROBABLY SHOULD'VE SEEN THAT COMING.

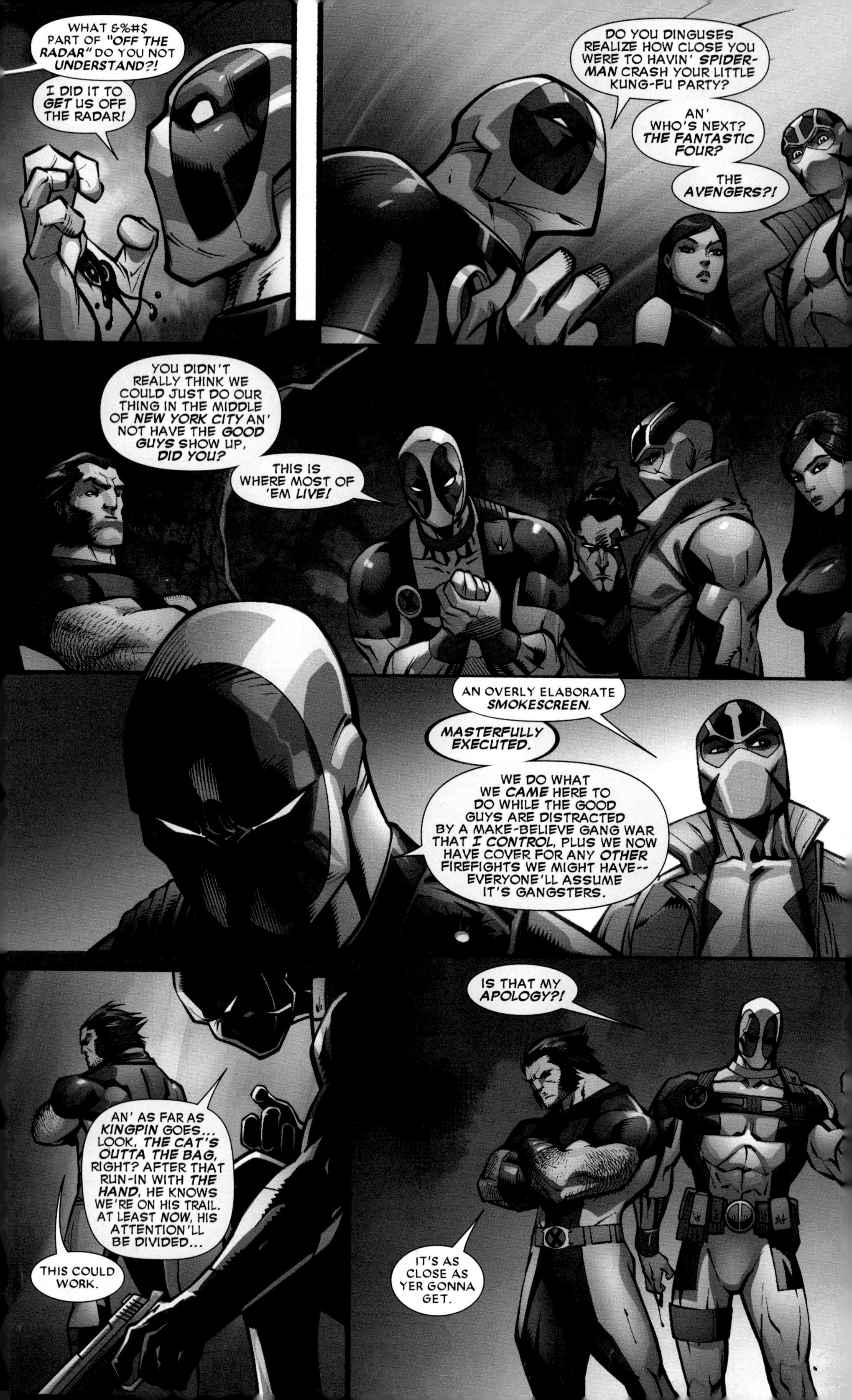
WHAT &%#$ PART OF "OFF THE RADAR" DO YOU NOT UNDERSTAND?!
I DID IT TO GET US OFF THE RADAR!
DO YOU DINGUSES REALIZE HOW CLOSE YOU WERE TO HAVIN' SPIDER-MAN CRASH YOUR LITTLE KUNG-FU PARTY?
AN' WHO'S NEXT? THE FANTASTIC FOUR?
THE AVENGERS?!
YOU DIDN'T REALLY THINK WE COULD JUST DO OUR THING IN THE MIDDLE OF NEW YORK CITY AN' NOT HAVE THE GOOD GUYS SHOW UP, DID YOU?
THIS IS WHERE MOST OF 'EM LIVE!
AN OVERLY ELABORATE SMOKESCREEN.
MASTERFULLY EXECUTED.
WE DO WHAT WE CAME HERE TO DO WHILE THE GOOD GUYS ARE DISTRACTED BY A MAKE-BELIEVE GANG WAR THAT I CONTROL, PLUS WE NOW HAVE COVER FOR ANY OTHER FIREFIGHTS WE MIGHT HAVE-- EVERYONE'LL ASSUME IT'S GANGSTERS.
AN' AS FAR AS KINGPIN GOES... LOOK, THE CAT'S OUTTA THE BAG, RIGHT? AFTER THAT RUN-IN WITH THE HAND, HE KNOWS WE'RE ON HIS TRAIL. AT LEAST NOW, HIS ATTENTION'LL BE DIVIDED...
THIS COULD WORK.
IS THAT MY APOLOGY?!
IT'S AS CLOSE AS YER GONNA GET.

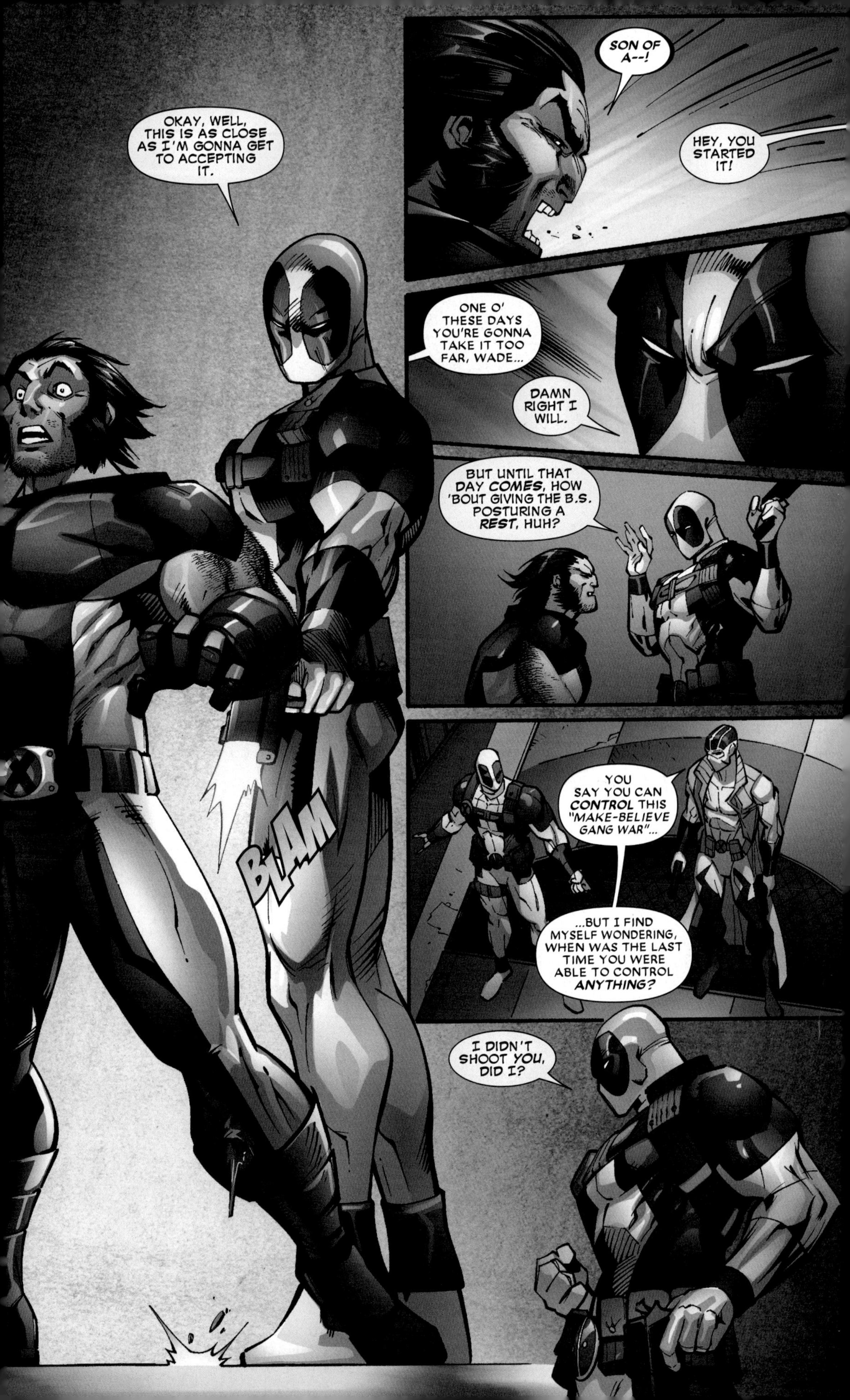
OKAY, WELL, THIS IS AS CLOSE AS I'M GONNA GET TO ACCEPTING IT.
BLAM
SON OF A--!
HEY, YOU STARTED IT!
ONE O' THESE DAYS YOU'RE GONNA TAKE IT TOO FAR, WADE...
DAMN RIGHT I WILL.
BUT UNTIL THAT DAY COMES, HOW 'BOUT GIVING THE B.S. POSTURING A REST, HUH?
YOU SAY YOU CAN CONTROL THIS "MAKE-BELIEVE GANG WAR"...
...BUT I FIND MYSELF WONDERING, WHEN WAS THE LAST TIME YOU WERE ABLE TO CONTROL ANYTHING?
I DIDN'T SHOOT YOU, DID I?

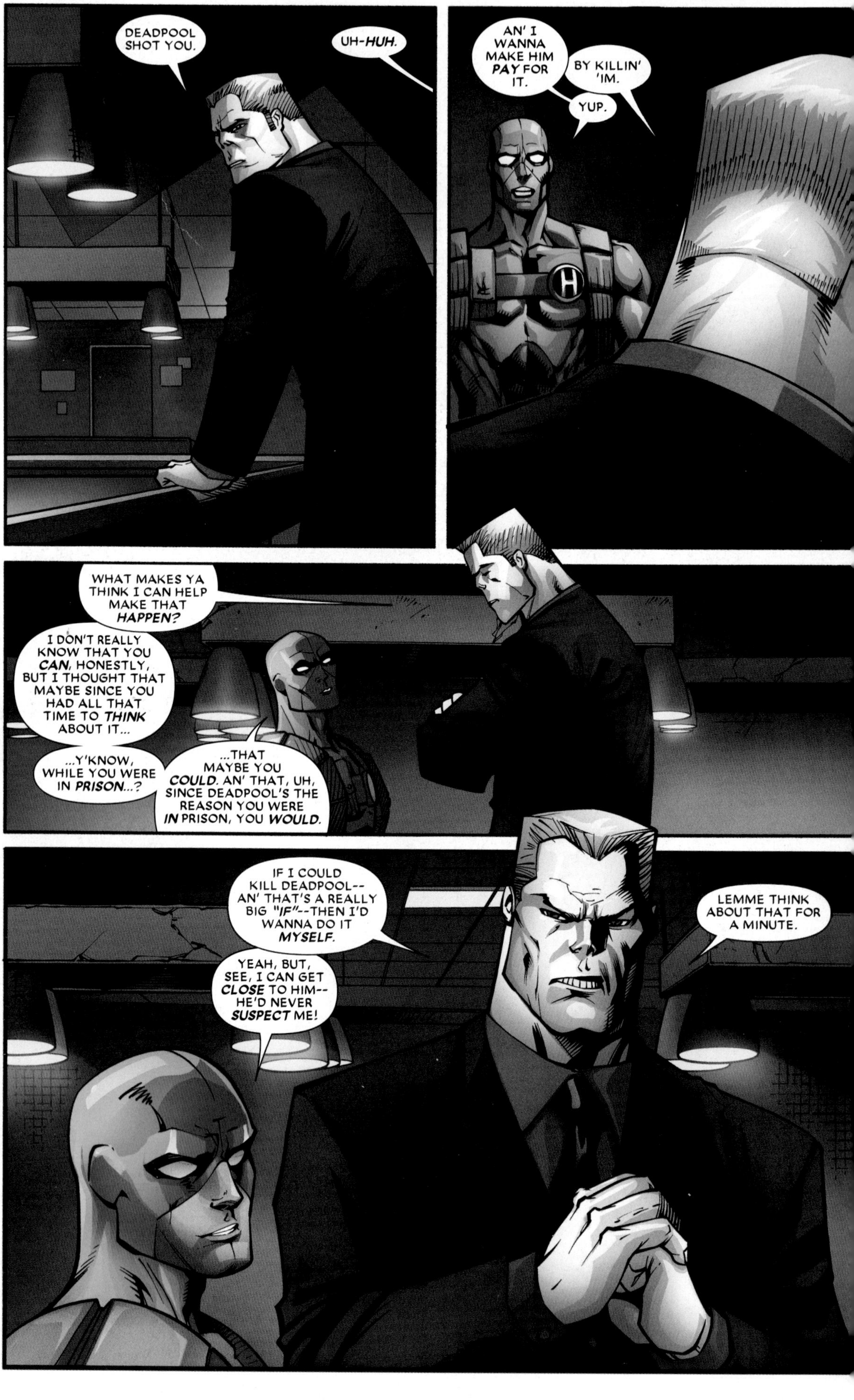
DEADPOOL SHOT YOU.
UH-*HUH*.
AN' I WANNA MAKE HIM *PAY* FOR IT.
BY KILLIN' 'IM.
YUP.
WHAT MAKES YA THINK I CAN HELP MAKE THAT *HAPPEN?*
I DON'T REALLY KNOW THAT YOU *CAN*, HONESTLY, BUT I THOUGHT THAT MAYBE SINCE YOU HAD ALL THAT TIME TO *THINK* ABOUT IT...
...Y'KNOW, WHILE YOU WERE IN *PRISON*...?
...THAT MAYBE YOU *COULD*. AN' THAT, UH, SINCE DEADPOOL'S THE REASON YOU WERE *IN* PRISON, YOU *WOULD*.
IF I COULD KILL DEADPOOL-- AN' THAT'S A REALLY BIG *"IF"*--THEN I'D WANNA DO IT *MYSELF*.
YEAH, BUT, SEE, I CAN GET *CLOSE* TO HIM-- HE'D NEVER *SUSPECT* ME!
LEMME THINK ABOUT THAT FOR A MINUTE.

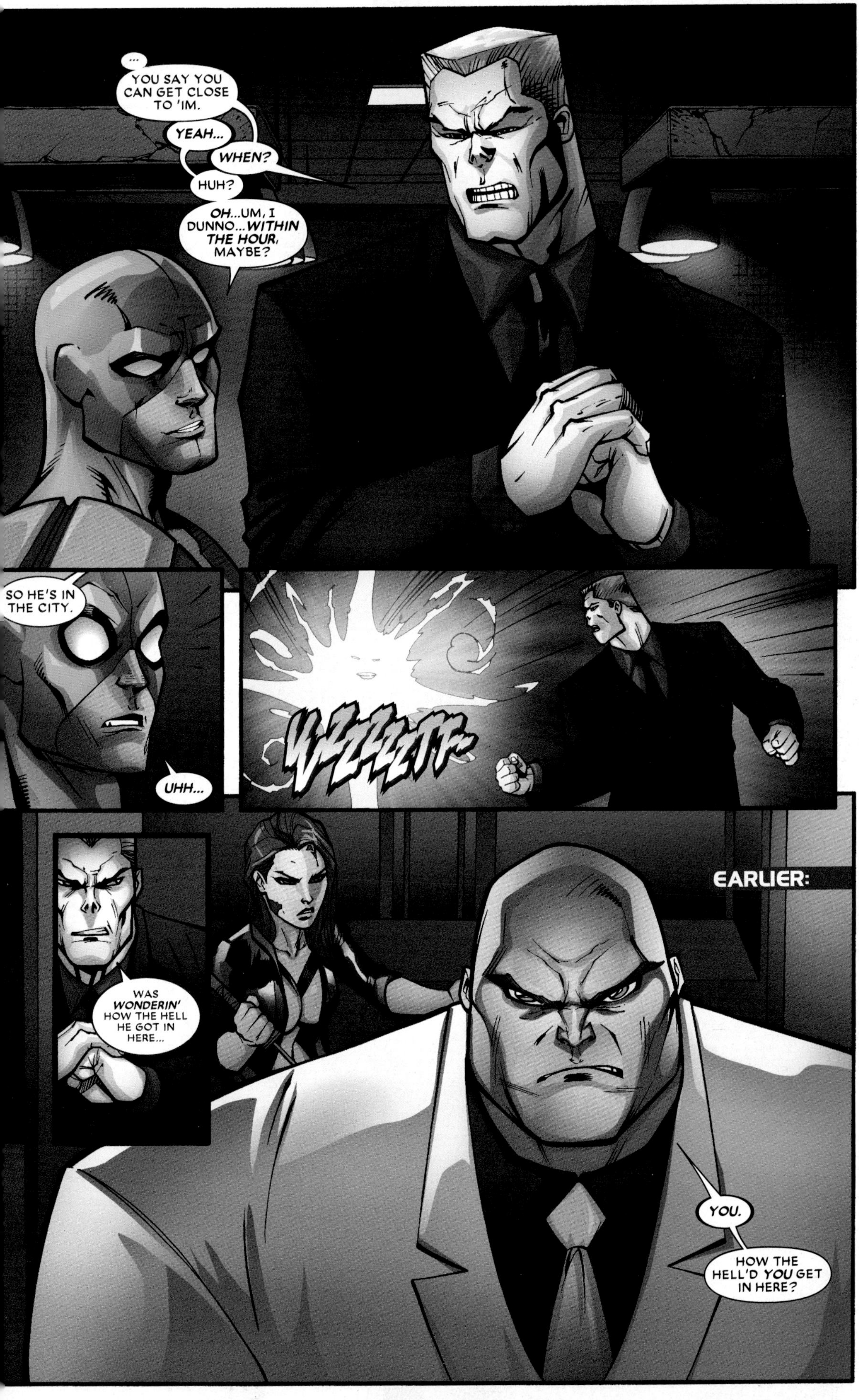
...
YOU SAY YOU CAN GET CLOSE TO 'IM.
YEAH...
WHEN?
HUH?
OH...UM, I DUNNO...WITHIN THE HOUR, MAYBE?
SO HE'S IN THE CITY.
UHH...
VZZZZZTT
EARLIER:
WAS WONDERIN' HOW THE HELL HE GOT IN HERE...
YOU.
HOW THE HELL'D YOU GET IN HERE?

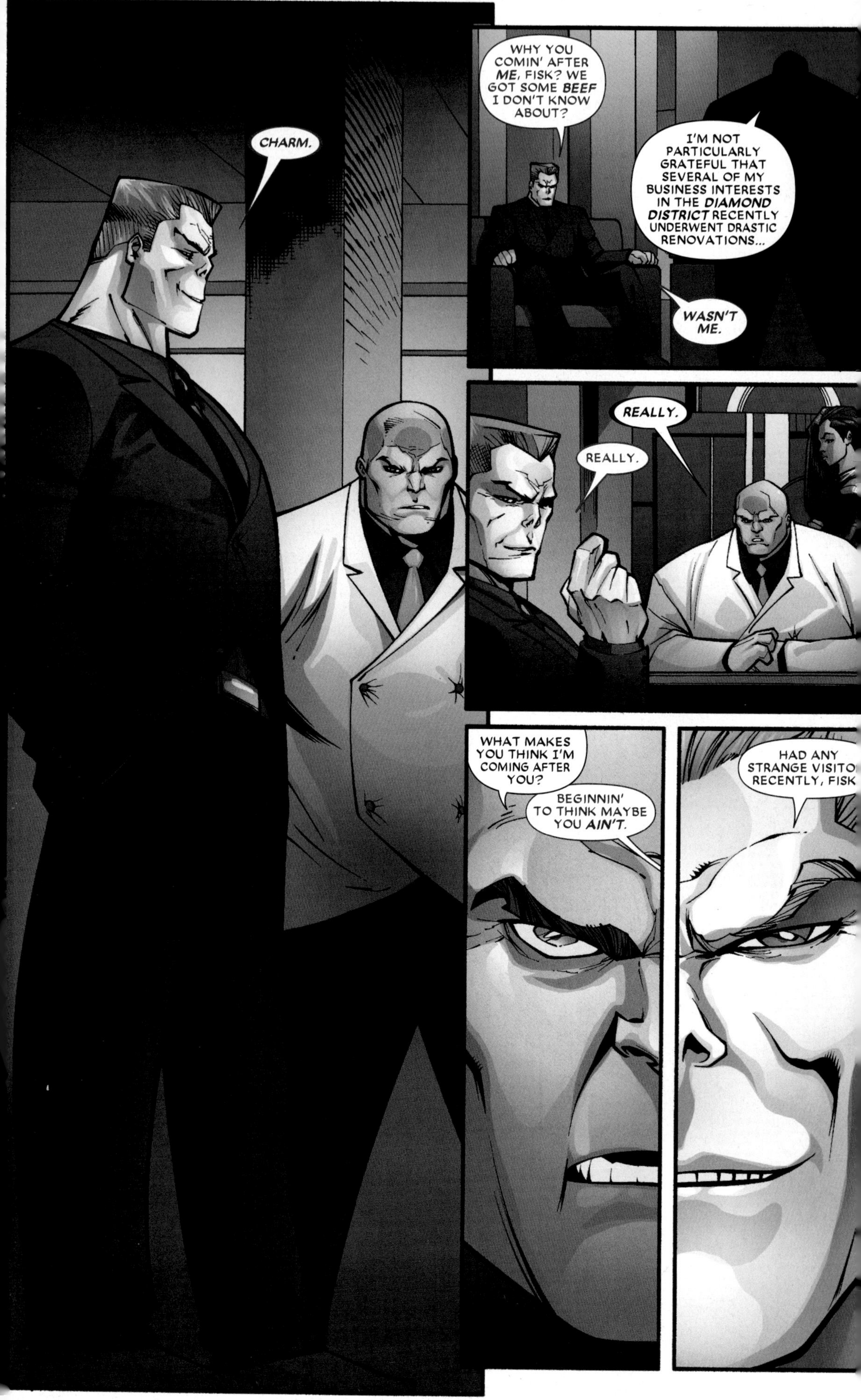
CHARM.
WHY YOU COMIN' AFTER ME, FISK? WE GOT SOME BEEF I DON'T KNOW ABOUT?
I'M NOT PARTICULARLY GRATEFUL THAT SEVERAL OF MY BUSINESS INTERESTS IN THE DIAMOND DISTRICT RECENTLY UNDERWENT DRASTIC RENOVATIONS...
WASN'T ME.
REALLY.
REALLY.
WHAT MAKES YOU THINK I'M COMING AFTER YOU?
BEGINNIN' TO THINK MAYBE YOU AIN'T.
HAD ANY STRANGE VISITO
RECENTLY, FISK

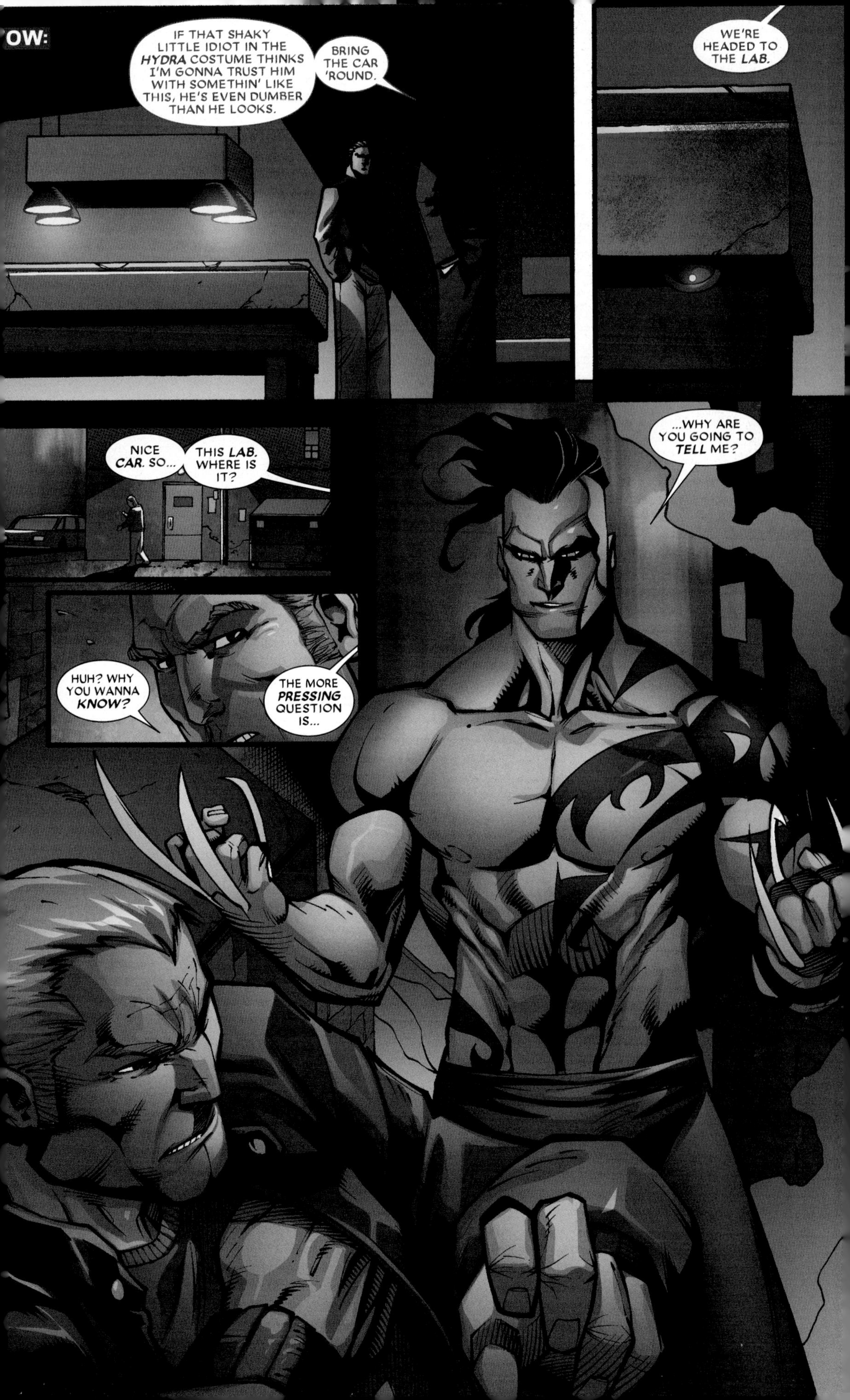
OW:
IF THAT SHAKY LITTLE IDIOT IN THE HYDRA COSTUME THINKS I'M GONNA TRUST HIM WITH SOMETHIN' LIKE THIS, HE'S EVEN DUMBER THAN HE LOOKS.
BRING THE CAR 'ROUND.
WE'RE HEADED TO THE LAB.
NICE CAR. SO...
THIS LAB. WHERE IS IT?
HUH? WHY YOU WANNA KNOW?
THE MORE PRESSING QUESTION IS...
...WHY ARE YOU GOING TO TELL ME?

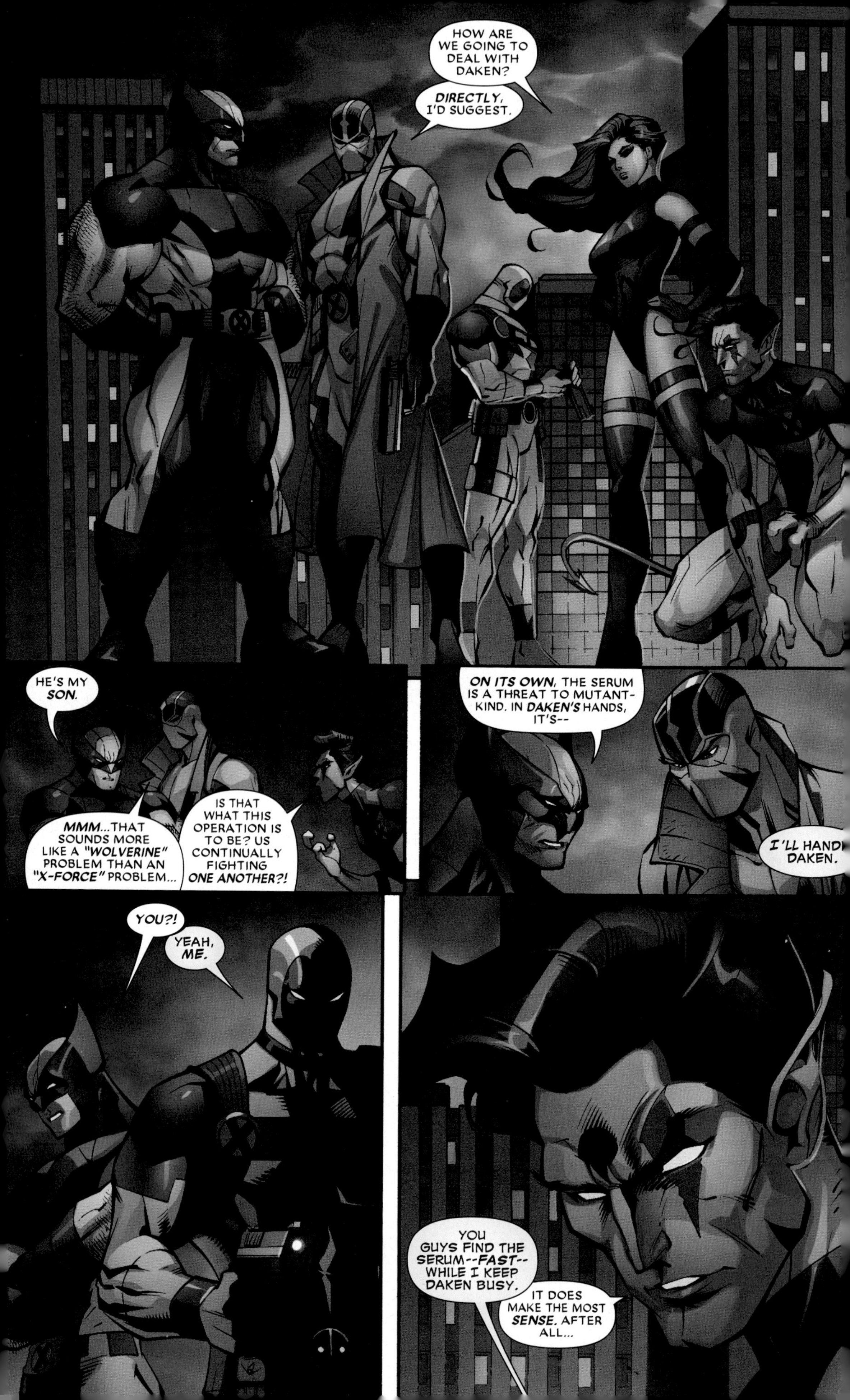
HOW ARE WE GOING TO DEAL WITH DAKEN?
DIRECTLY, I'D SUGGEST.
HE'S MY SON.
MMM...THAT SOUNDS MORE LIKE A "WOLVERINE" PROBLEM THAN AN "X-FORCE" PROBLEM...
IS THAT WHAT THIS OPERATION IS TO BE? US CONTINUALLY FIGHTING ONE ANOTHER?!
ON ITS OWN, THE SERUM IS A THREAT TO MUTANT-KIND. IN DAKEN'S HANDS, IT'S--
DAKEN.
YOU?!
YEAH, ME.
YOU GUYS FIND THE SERUM--FAST--WHILE I KEEP DAKEN BUSY.
IT DOES MAKE THE MOST SENSE. AFTER ALL...

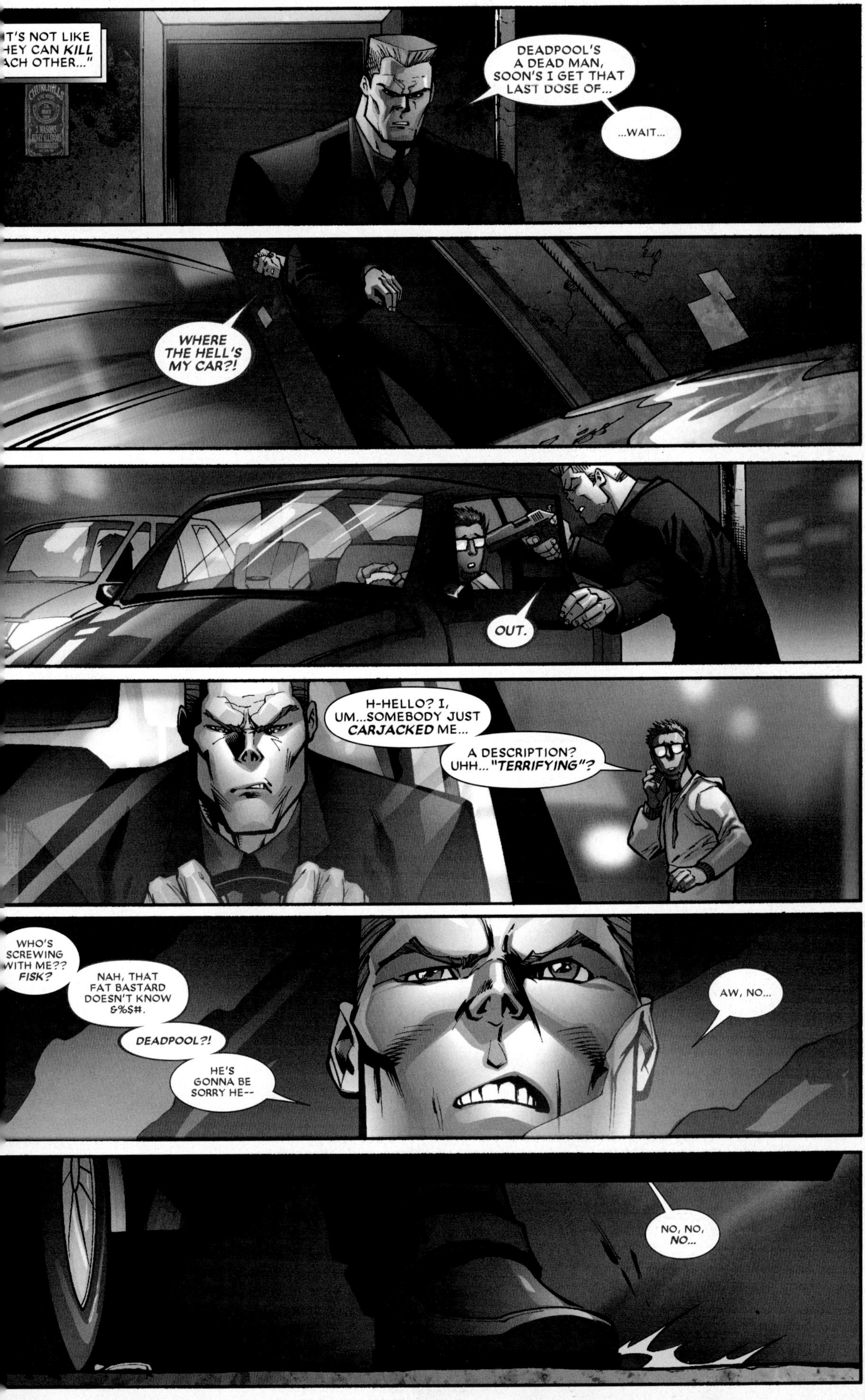

IT'S NOT LIKE THEY CAN KILL EACH OTHER..."
DEADPOOL'S A DEAD MAN, SOON'S I GET THAT LAST DOSE OF...
...WAIT...
WHERE THE HELL'S MY CAR?!
OUT.
H-HELLO? I, UM...SOMEBODY JUST CARJACKED ME...
A DESCRIPTION? UHH... "TERRIFYING"?
WHO'S SCREWING WITH ME?? FISK?
NAH, THAT FAT BASTARD DOESN'T KNOW &%$#.
DEADPOOL?!
HE'S GONNA BE SORRY HE--
AW, NO...
NO, NO, NO...

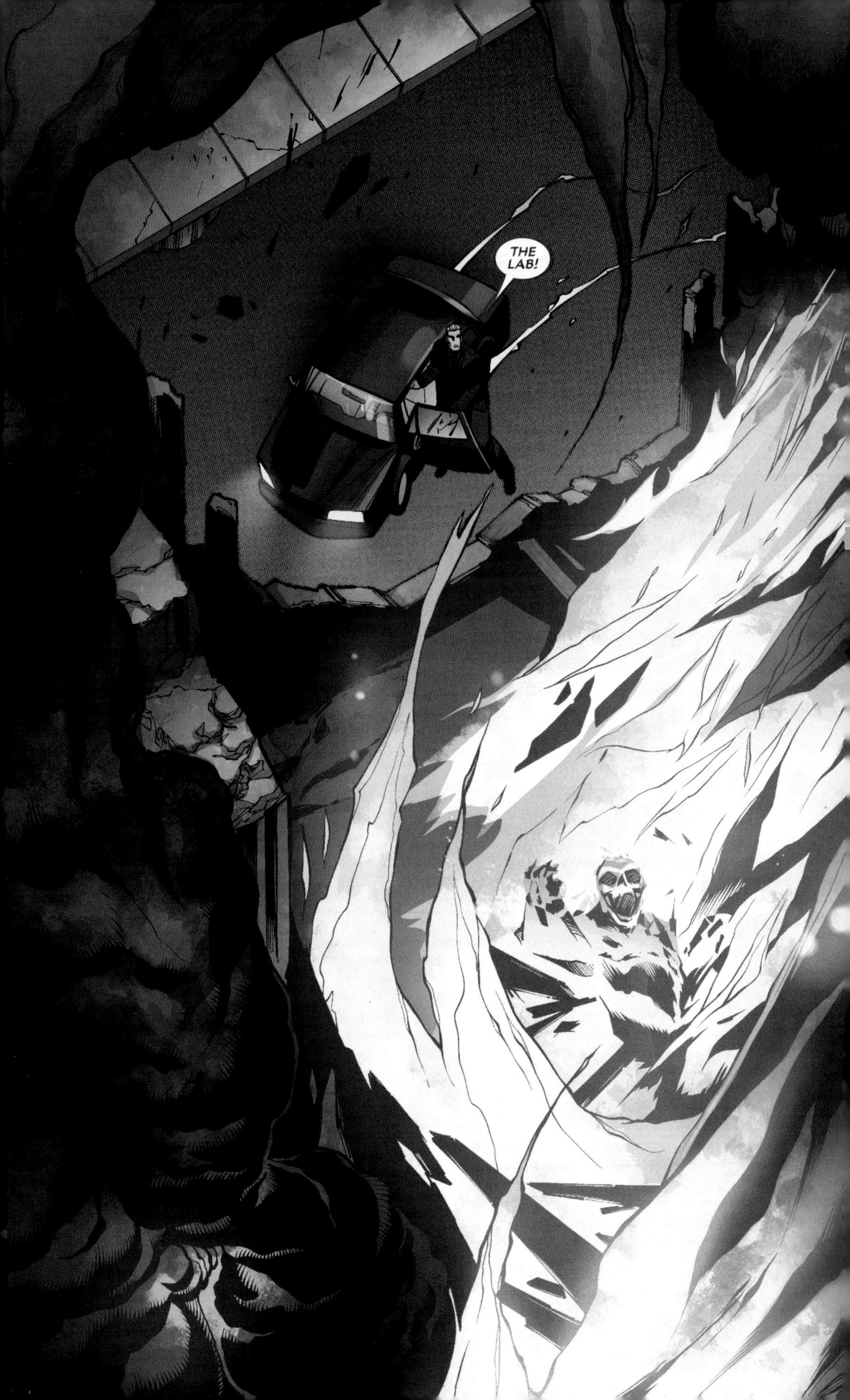
THE LAB!

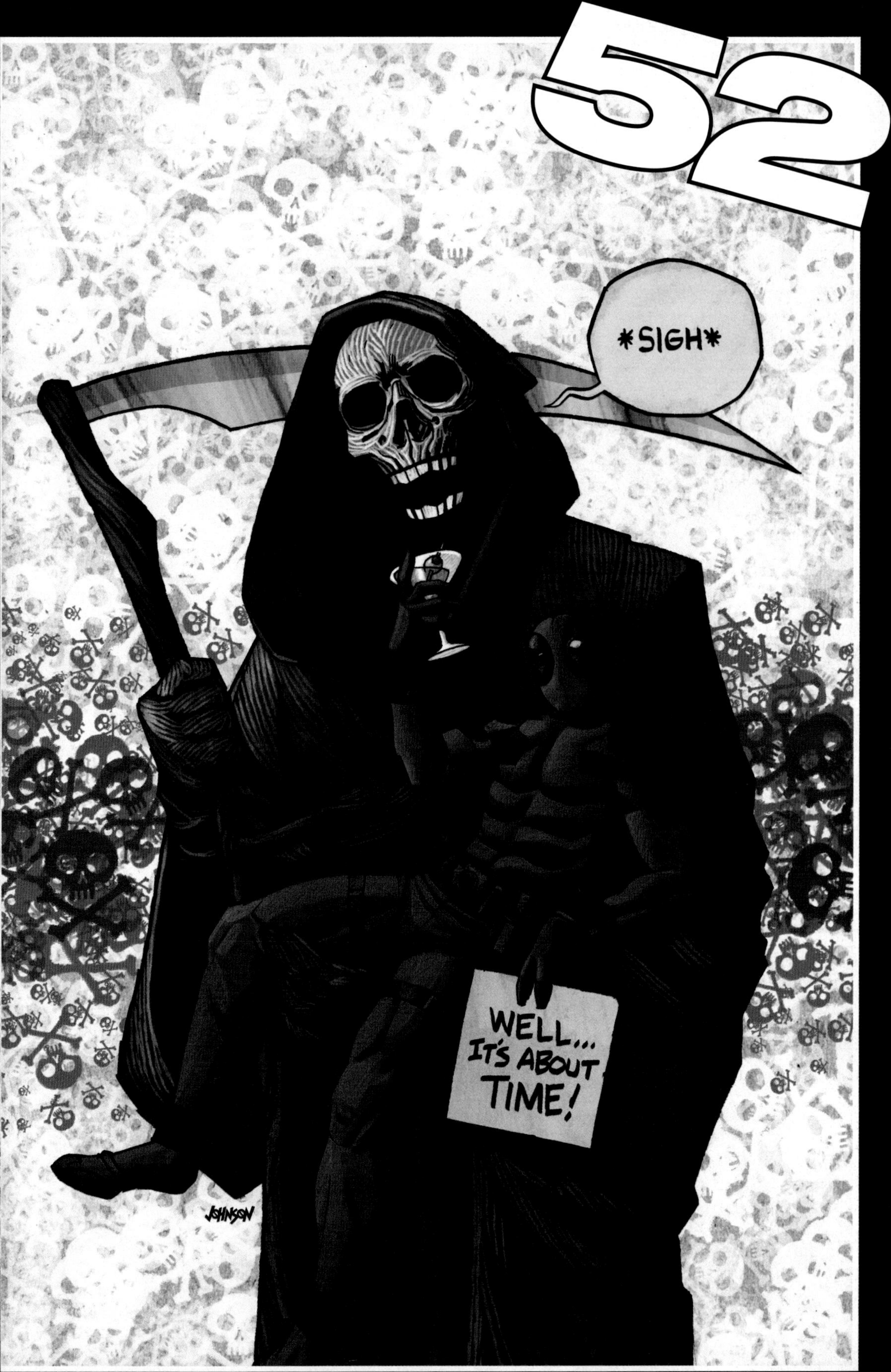
52
SIGH
WELL... IT'S ABOUT TIME!
JOHNSON

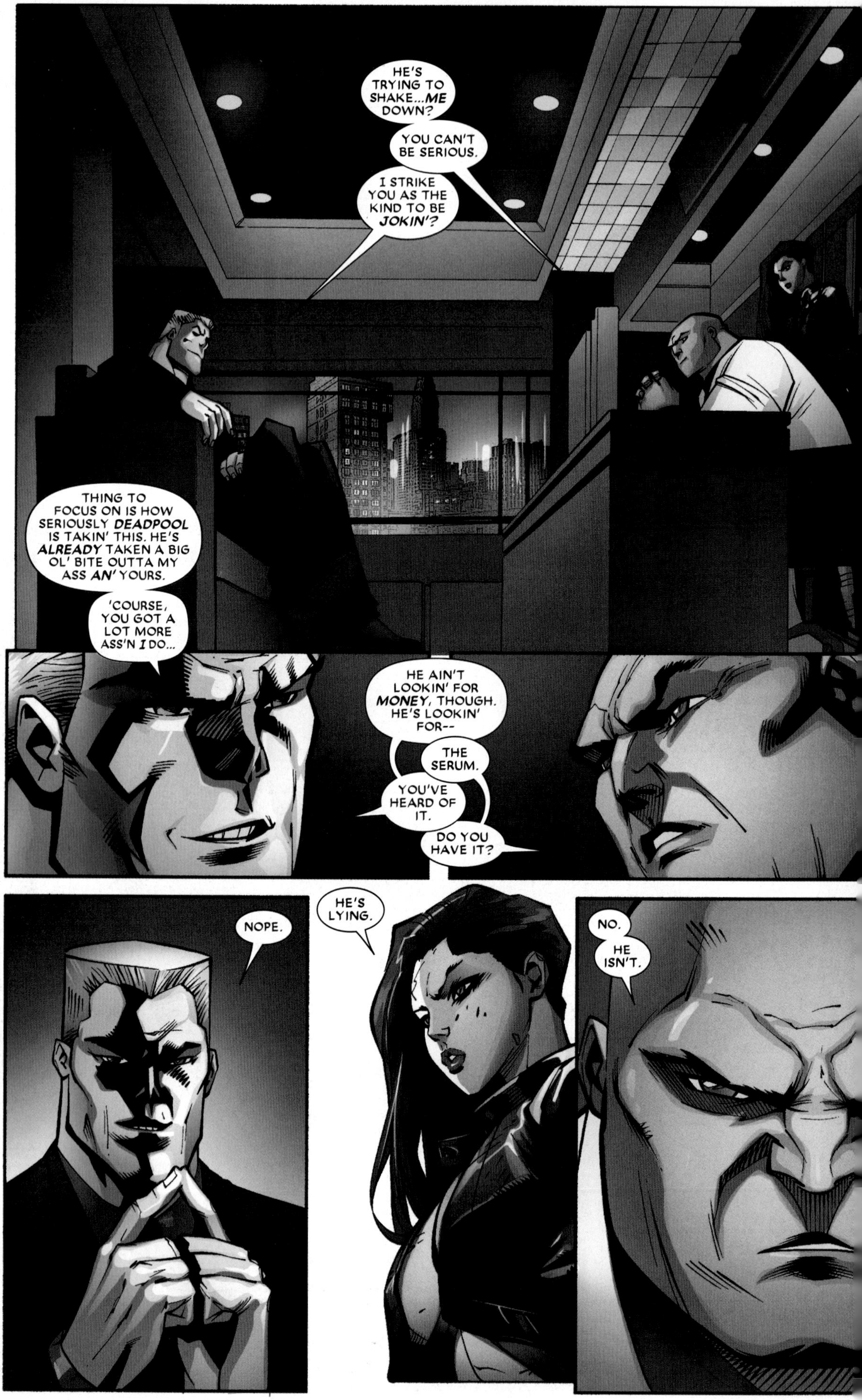
HE'S TRYING TO SHAKE...ME DOWN?
YOU CAN'T BE SERIOUS.
I STRIKE YOU AS THE KIND TO BE JOKIN'?
THING TO FOCUS ON IS HOW SERIOUSLY DEADPOOL IS TAKIN' THIS. HE'S ALREADY TAKEN A BIG OL' BITE OUTTA MY ASS AN' YOURS.
'COURSE, YOU GOT A LOT MORE ASS'N I DO...
HE AIN'T LOOKIN' FOR MONEY, THOUGH. HE'S LOOKIN' FOR--
THE SERUM.
YOU'VE HEARD OF IT.
DO YOU HAVE IT?
NOPE.
HE'S LYING.
NO. HE ISN'T.

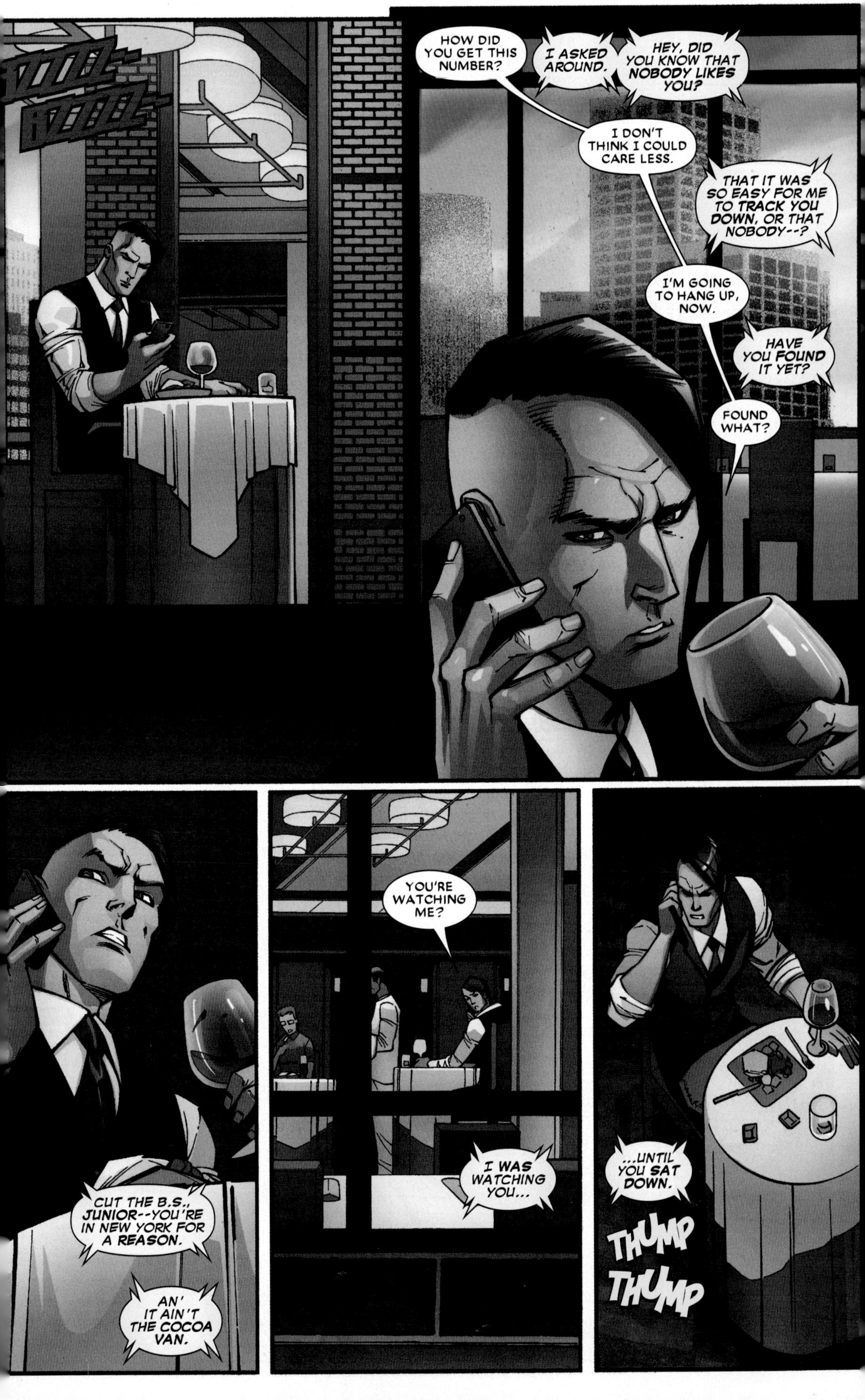
HOW DID YOU GET THIS NUMBER?
I ASKED AROUND.
HEY, DID YOU KNOW THAT NOBODY LIKES YOU?
I DON'T THINK I COULD CARE LESS.
THAT IT WAS SO EASY FOR ME TO TRACK YOU DOWN, OR THAT NOBODY--?
I'M GOING TO HANG UP, NOW.
HAVE YOU FOUND IT YET?
FOUND WHAT?
CUT THE B.S., JUNIOR--YOU'RE IN NEW YORK FOR A REASON.
AN' IT AIN'T THE COCOA VAN.
YOU'RE WATCHING ME?
I WAS WATCHING YOU...
...UNTIL YOU SAT DOWN.
THUMP
THUMP

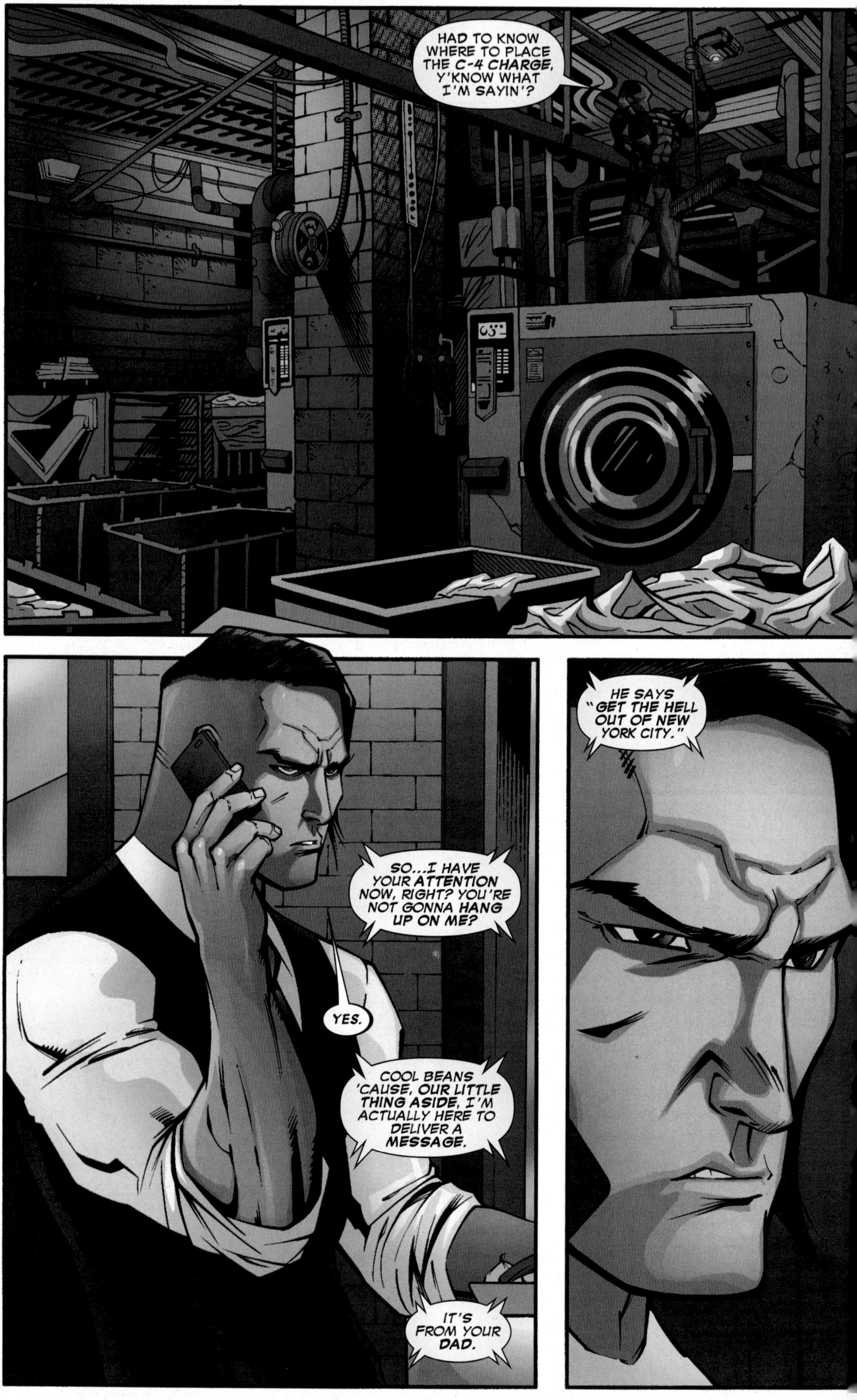
HAD TO KNOW WHERE TO PLACE THE C-4 CHARGE, Y'KNOW WHAT I'M SAYIN'?
SO...I HAVE YOUR ATTENTION NOW, RIGHT? YOU'RE NOT GONNA HANG UP ON ME?
YES.
COOL BEANS 'CAUSE, OUR LITTLE THING ASIDE, I'M ACTUALLY HERE TO DELIVER A MESSAGE.
IT'S FROM YOUR DAD.
HE SAYS "GET THE HELL OUT OF NEW YORK CITY."

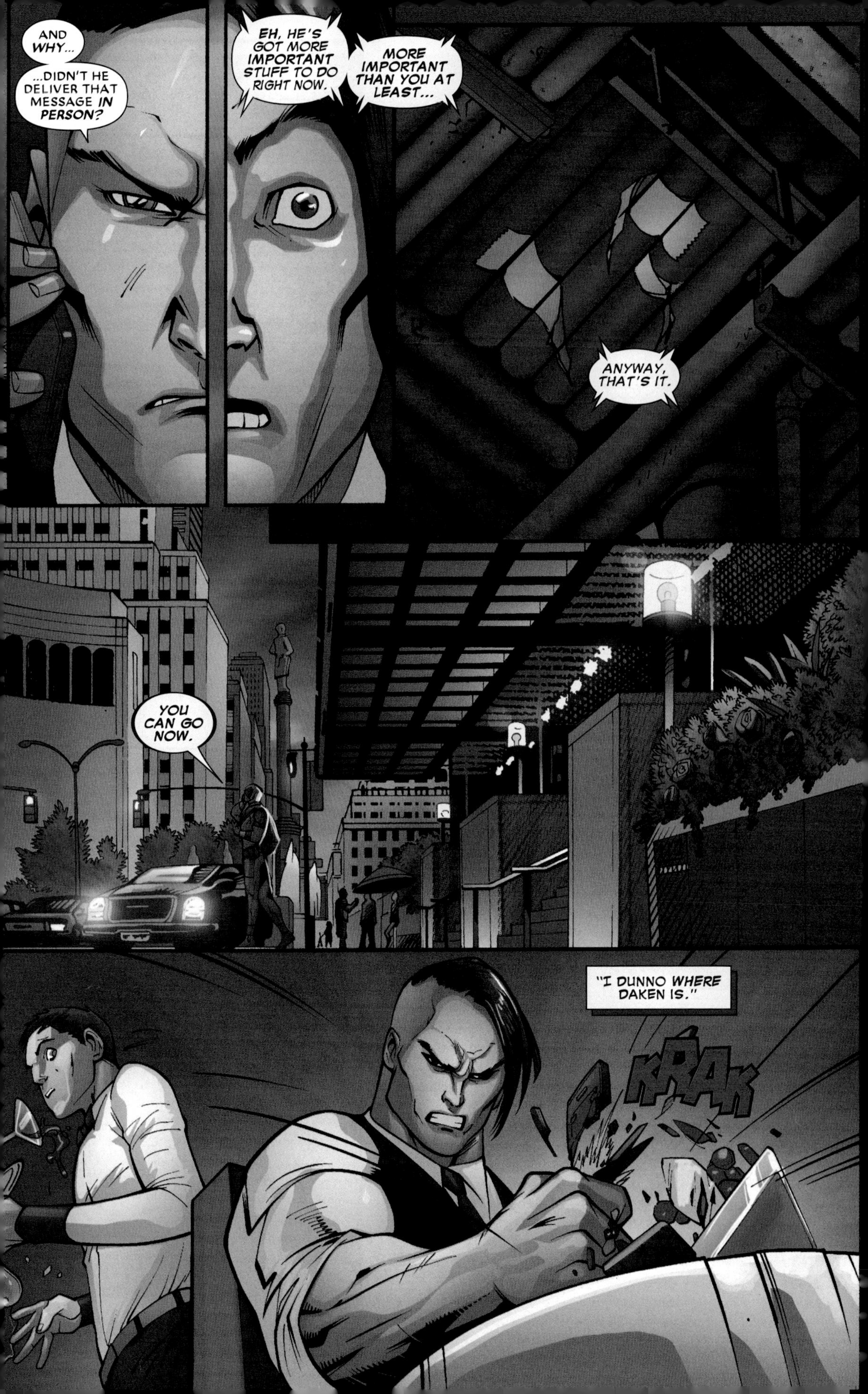

AND WHY...
...DIDN'T HE DELIVER THAT MESSAGE IN PERSON?
EH, HE'S GOT MORE IMPORTANT STUFF TO DO RIGHT NOW.
MORE IMPORTANT THAN YOU AT LEAST...
ANYWAY, THAT'S IT.
YOU CAN GO NOW.
"I DUNNO WHERE DAKEN IS."
KRAK

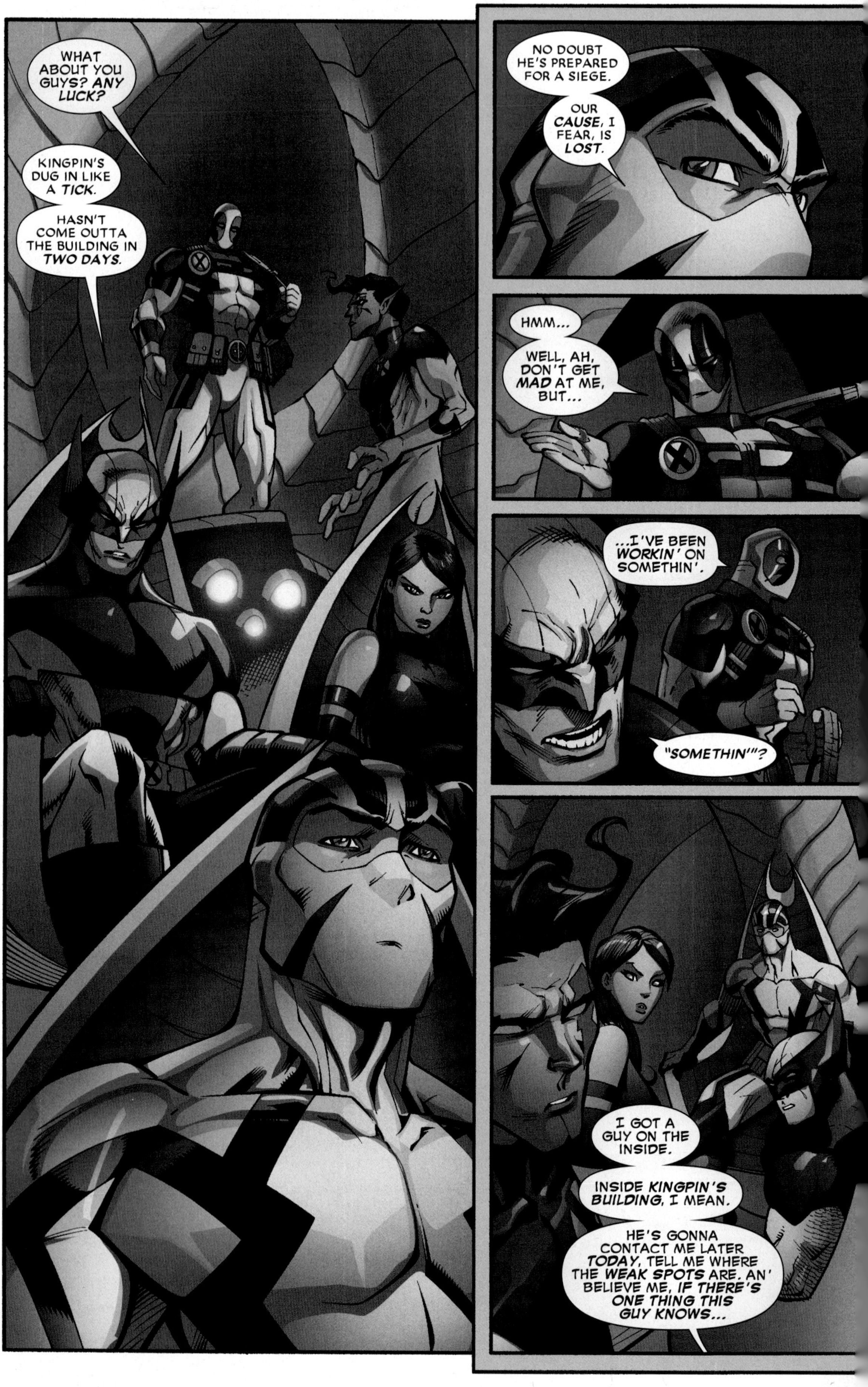
WHAT ABOUT YOU GUYS? ANY LUCK?
KINGPIN'S DUG IN LIKE A TICK.
HASN'T COME OUTTA THE BUILDING IN TWO DAYS.
NO DOUBT HE'S PREPARED FOR A SIEGE.
OUR CAUSE, I FEAR, IS LOST.
HMM...
WELL, AH, DON'T GET MAD AT ME, BUT...
...I'VE BEEN WORKIN' ON SOMETHIN'.
"SOMETHIN'"?
I GOT A GUY ON THE INSIDE.
INSIDE KINGPIN'S BUILDING, I MEAN.
HE'S GONNA CONTACT ME LATER TODAY, TELL ME WHERE THE WEAK SPOTS ARE. AN' BELIEVE ME, IF THERE'S ONE THING THIS GUY KNOWS...

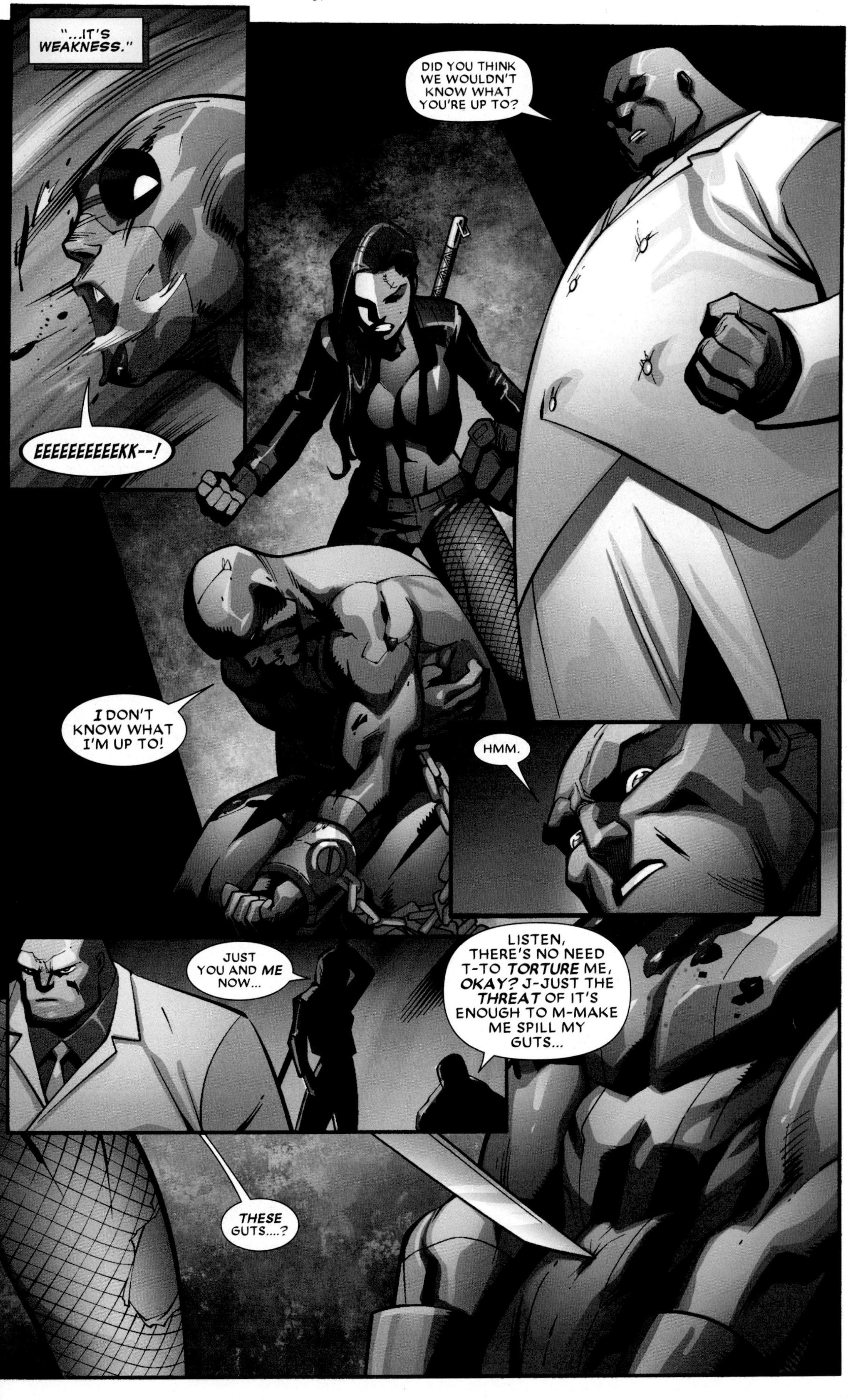
"...IT'S WEAKNESS."
EEEEEEEEEEKK--!
DID YOU THINK WE WOULDN'T KNOW WHAT YOU'RE UP TO?
I DON'T KNOW WHAT I'M UP TO!
HMM.
JUST YOU AND ME NOW...
LISTEN, THERE'S NO NEED T-TO TORTURE ME, OKAY? J-JUST THE THREAT OF IT'S ENOUGH TO M-MAKE ME SPILL MY GUTS...
THESE GUTS....?

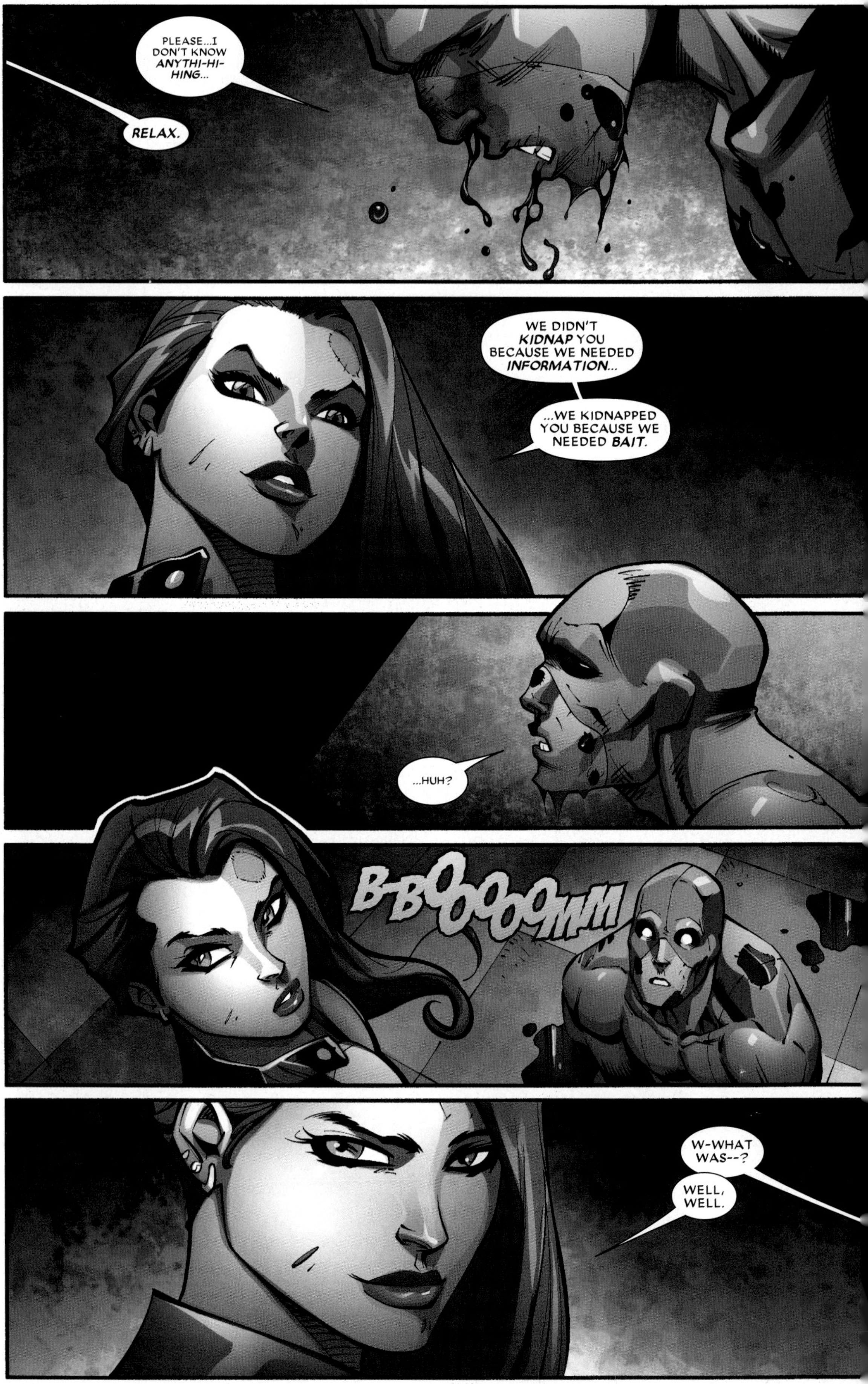
PLEASE...I DON'T KNOW ANYTHI-HI-HING...
RELAX.
WE DIDN'T KIDNAP YOU BECAUSE WE NEEDED INFORMATION...
...WE KIDNAPPED YOU BECAUSE WE NEEDED BAIT.
...HUH?
B-BOOOOOOMM
W-WHAT WAS--?
WELL, WELL.

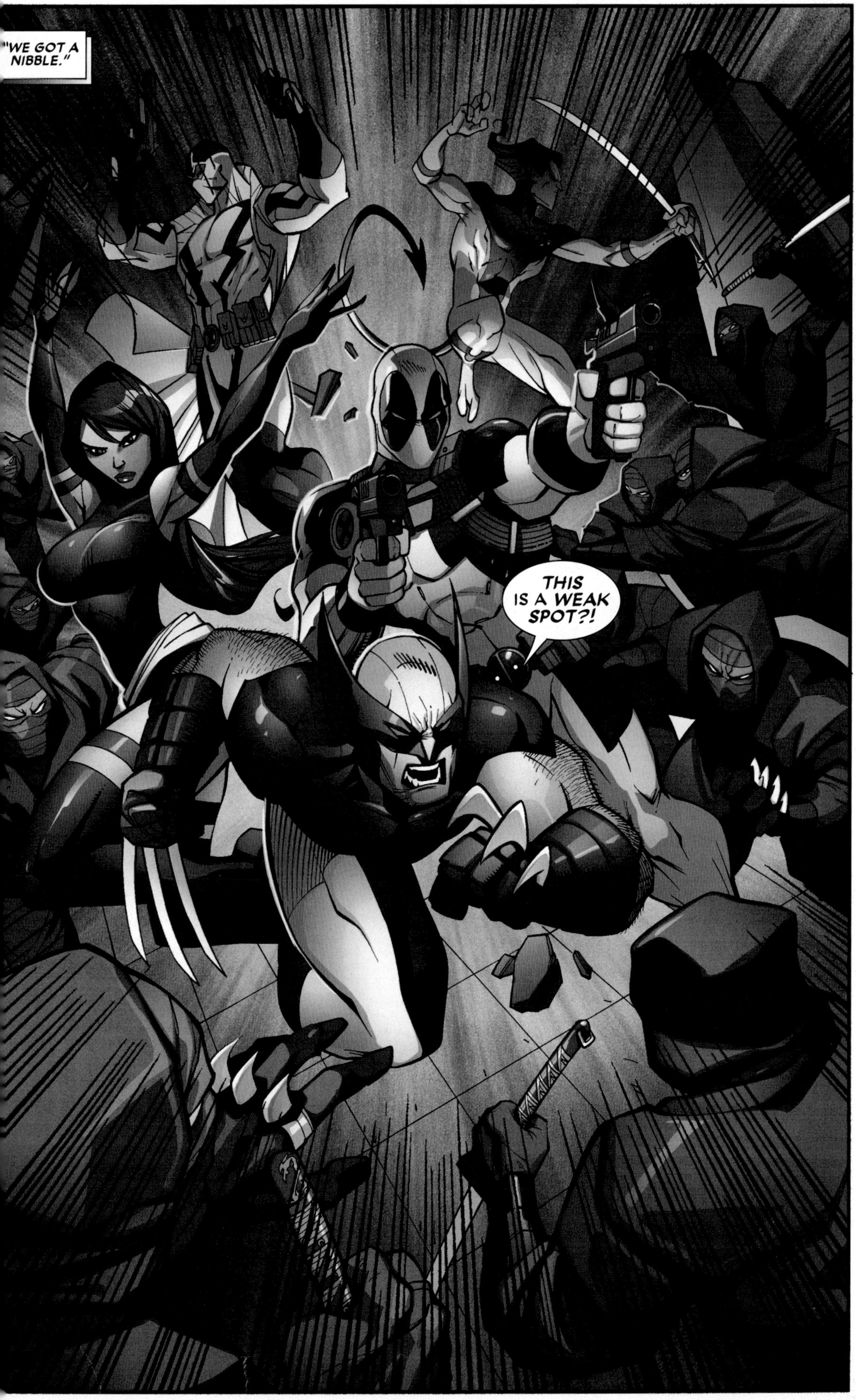
"WE GOT A NIBBLE."
THIS IS A WEAK SPOT?!

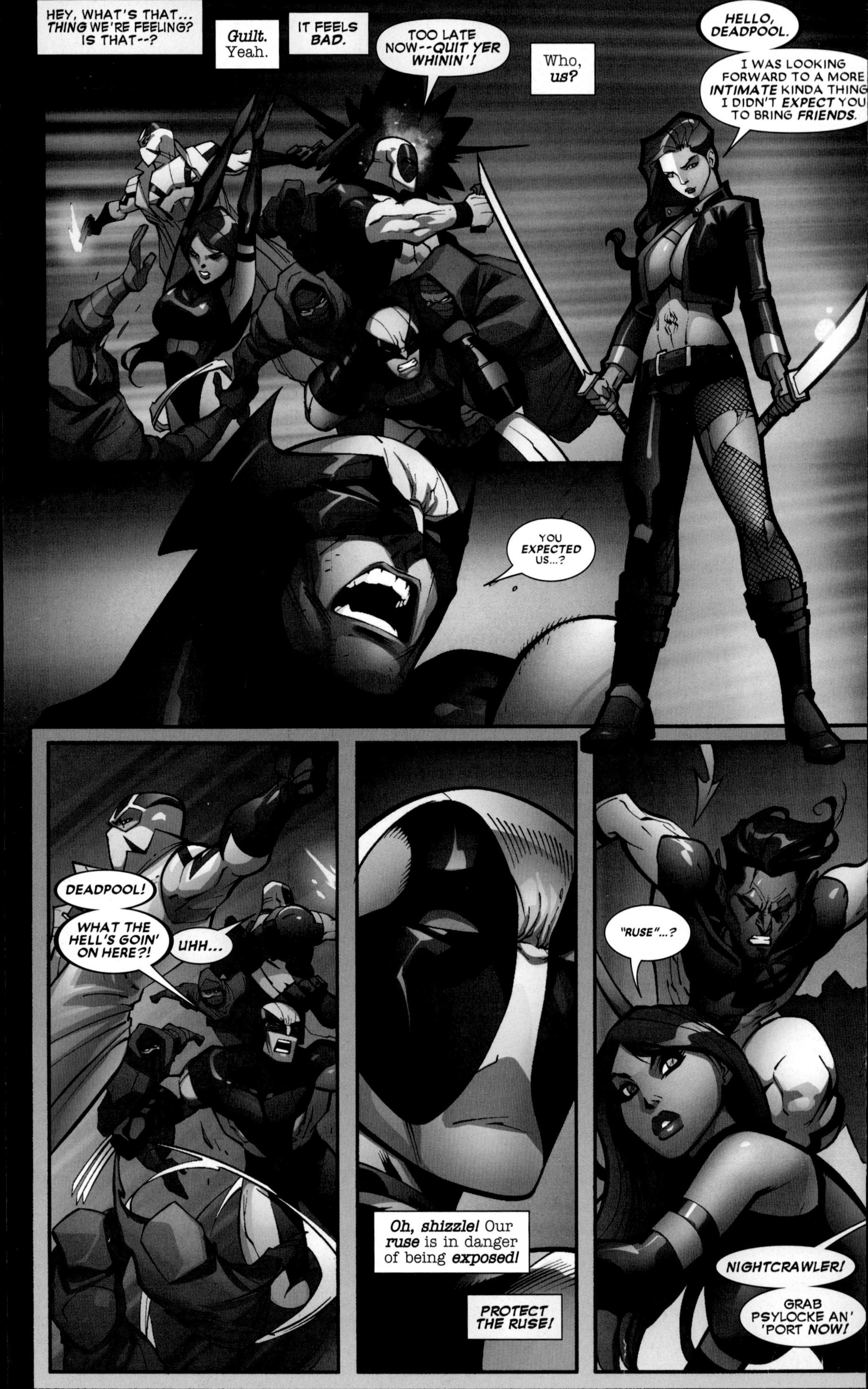
HEY, WHAT'S THAT... THING WE'RE FEELING? IS THAT--?
Guilt. Yeah.
IT FEELS BAD.
TOO LATE NOW--QUIT YER WHININ'!
Who, us?
HELLO, DEADPOOL.
I WAS LOOKING FORWARD TO A MORE INTIMATE KINDA THING. I DIDN'T EXPECT YOU TO BRING FRIENDS.
YOU EXPECTED US...?
DEADPOOL!
WHAT THE HELL'S GOIN' ON HERE?!
UHH...
Oh, shizzle! Our ruse is in danger of being exposed!
PROTECT THE RUSE!
"RUSE"...?
NIGHTCRAWLER!
GRAB PSYLOCKE AN' 'PORT NOW!

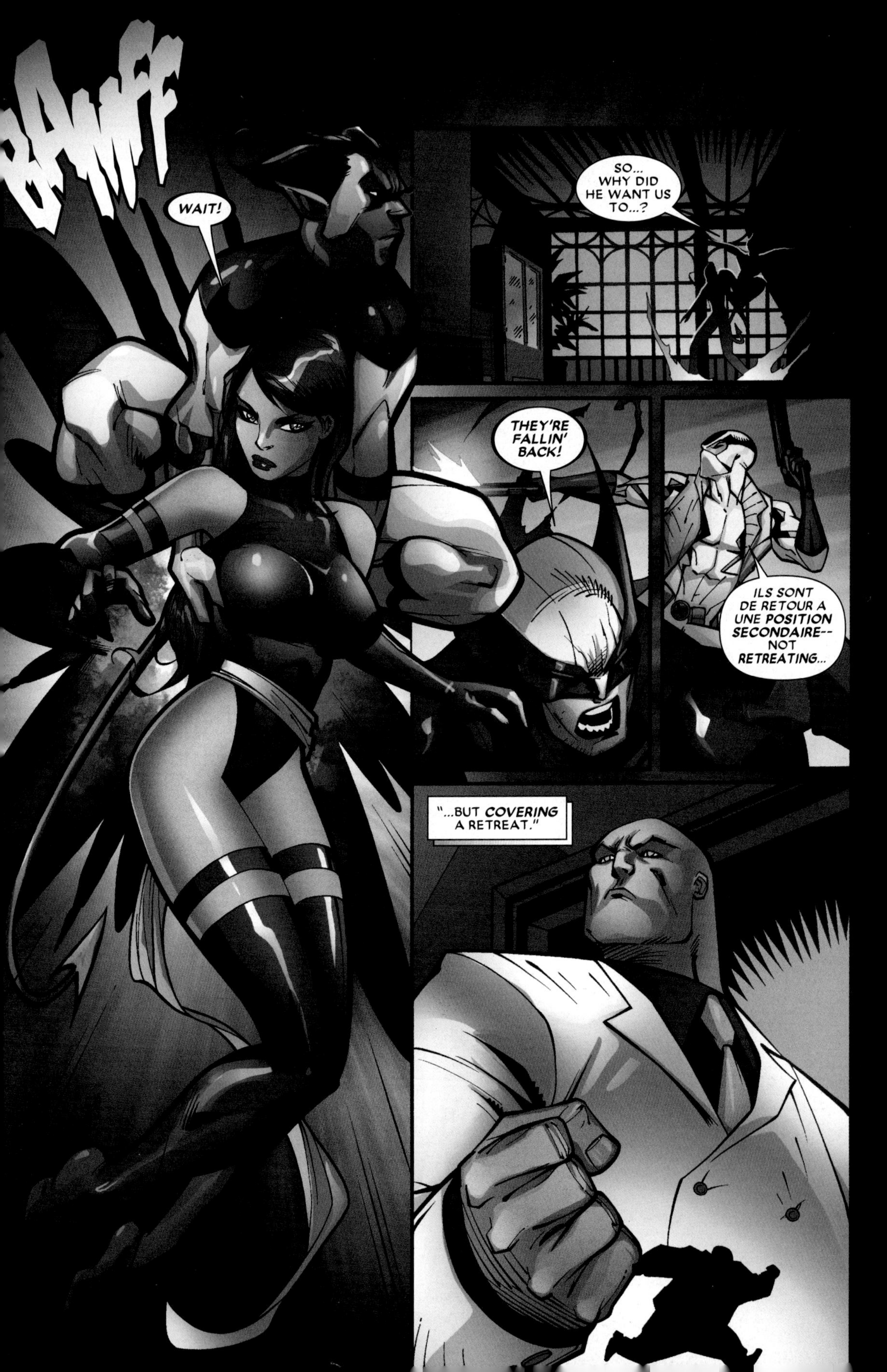
BAMFF
WAIT!
SO... WHY DID HE WANT US TO...?
THEY'RE FALLIN' BACK!
ILS SONT DE RETOUR A UNE POSITION SECONDAIRE-- NOT RETREATING...
"...BUT COVERING A RETREAT."

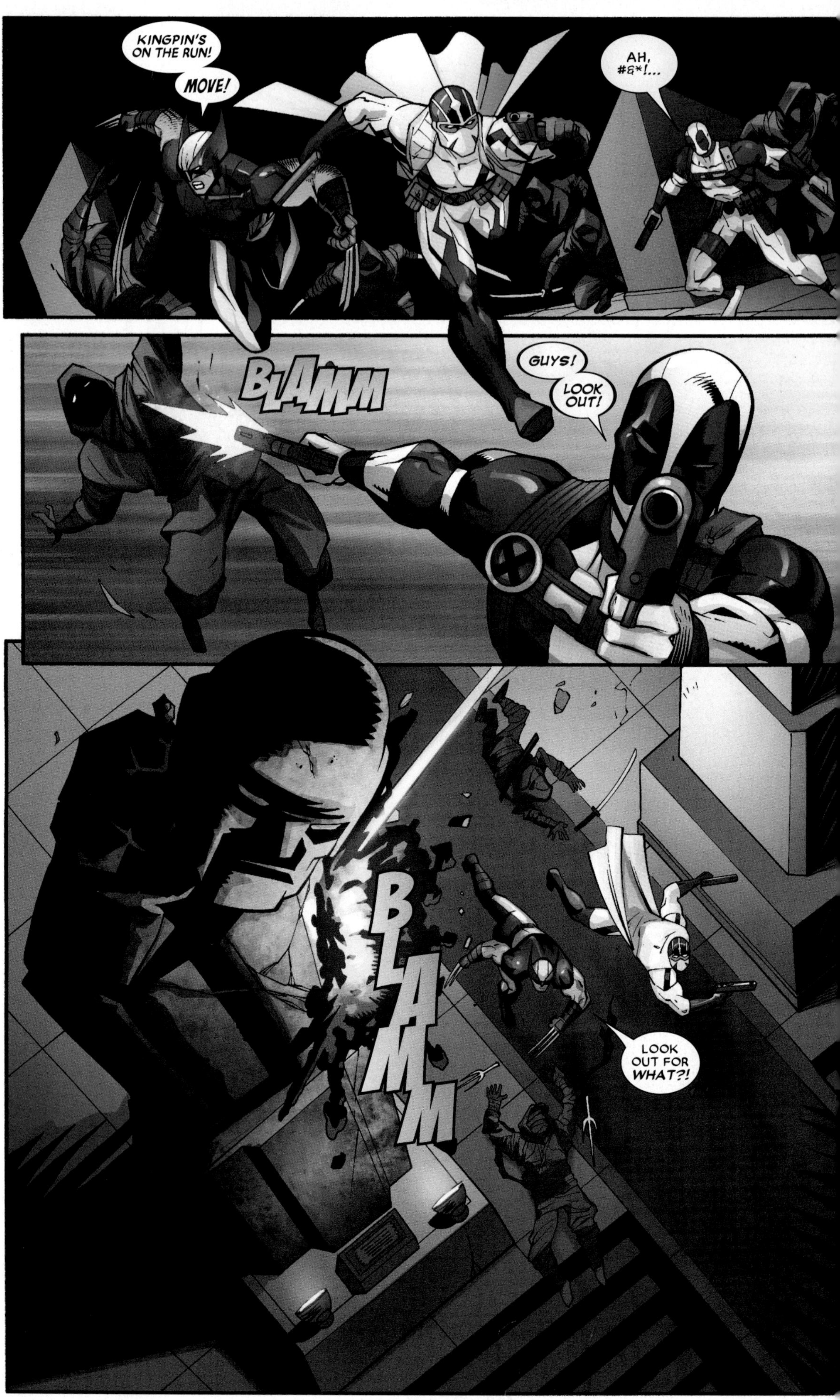
KINGPIN'S ON THE RUN!
MOVE!
AH, #&*!...
BLAMM
GUYS!
LOOK OUT!
BLAMM
LOOK OUT FOR WHAT?!

WHAT THE HELL'S HE SHOOTIN' AT?

APPAREMMENT, THE *STATUE.*

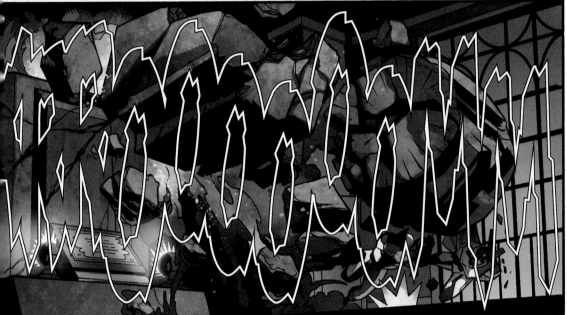

OW'RE WE 'NA EXPLAIN THAT?

mm...we missed?

THEY'RE NOT *IDIOTS*-- THEY'RE GONNA KNOW I'M UP TO SOMETHIN'.

BUT THAT DOESN'T MATTER, NOW.

AT?! BUT T WAS A ET SHOT!

NO *POINT* IN EXPLAININ' IT.

"IT'S *DO OR DIE* TIME."

DO AND DIE, Y'MEAN.

"YEAH.

"ONE WAY OR ANOTHER..."

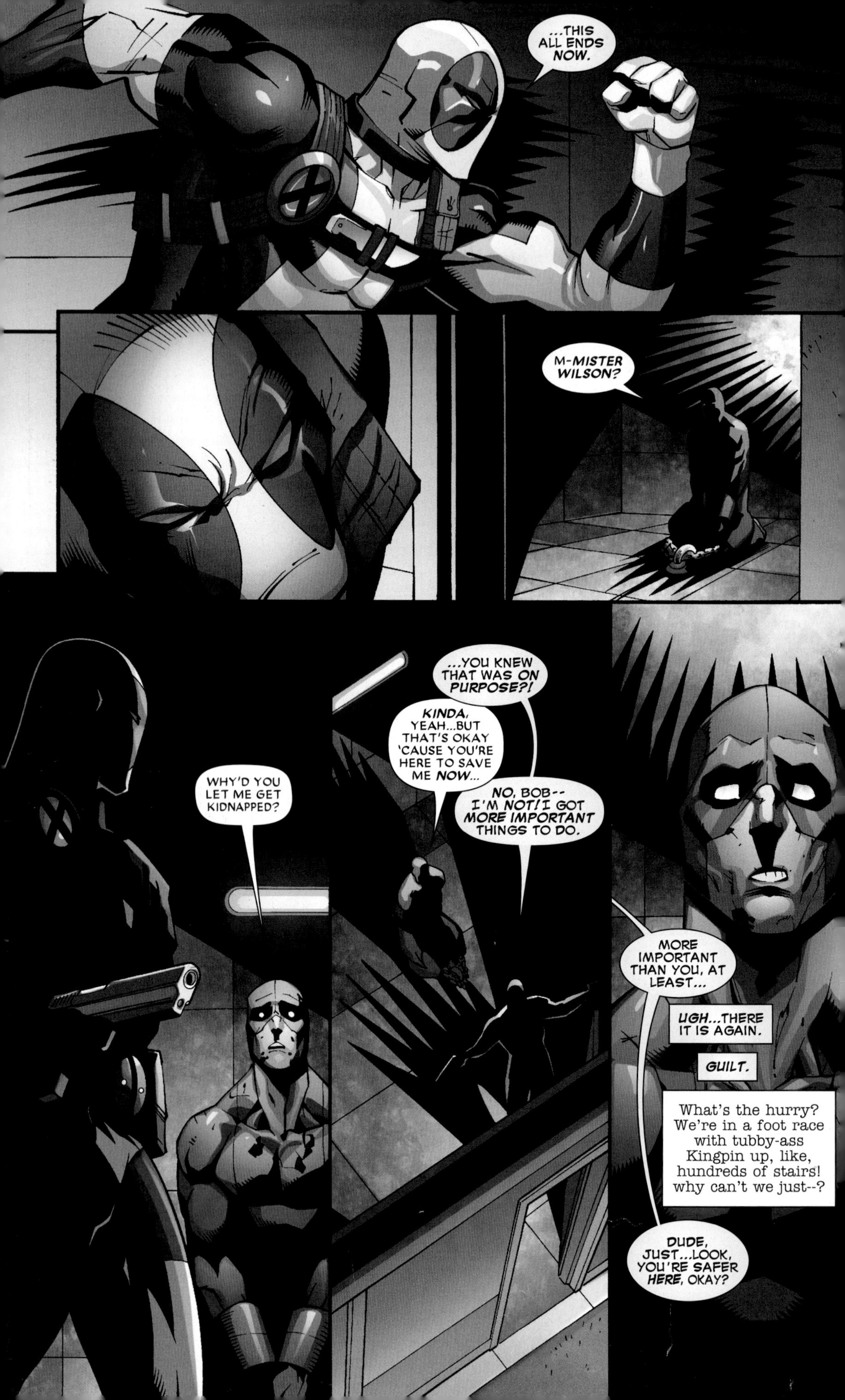
...THIS ALL ENDS NOW.
M-MISTER WILSON?
WHY'D YOU LET ME GET KIDNAPPED?
...YOU KNEW THAT WAS ON PURPOSE?!
KINDA, YEAH...BUT THAT'S OKAY 'CAUSE YOU'RE HERE TO SAVE ME NOW...
NO, BOB-- I'M NOT! I GOT MORE IMPORTANT THINGS TO DO.
MORE IMPORTANT THAN YOU, AT LEAST...
UGH...THERE IT IS AGAIN.
GUILT.
What's the hurry? We're in a foot race with tubby-ass Kingpin up, like, hundreds of stairs! why can't we just--?
DUDE, JUST...LOOK, YOU'RE SAFER HERE, OKAY?

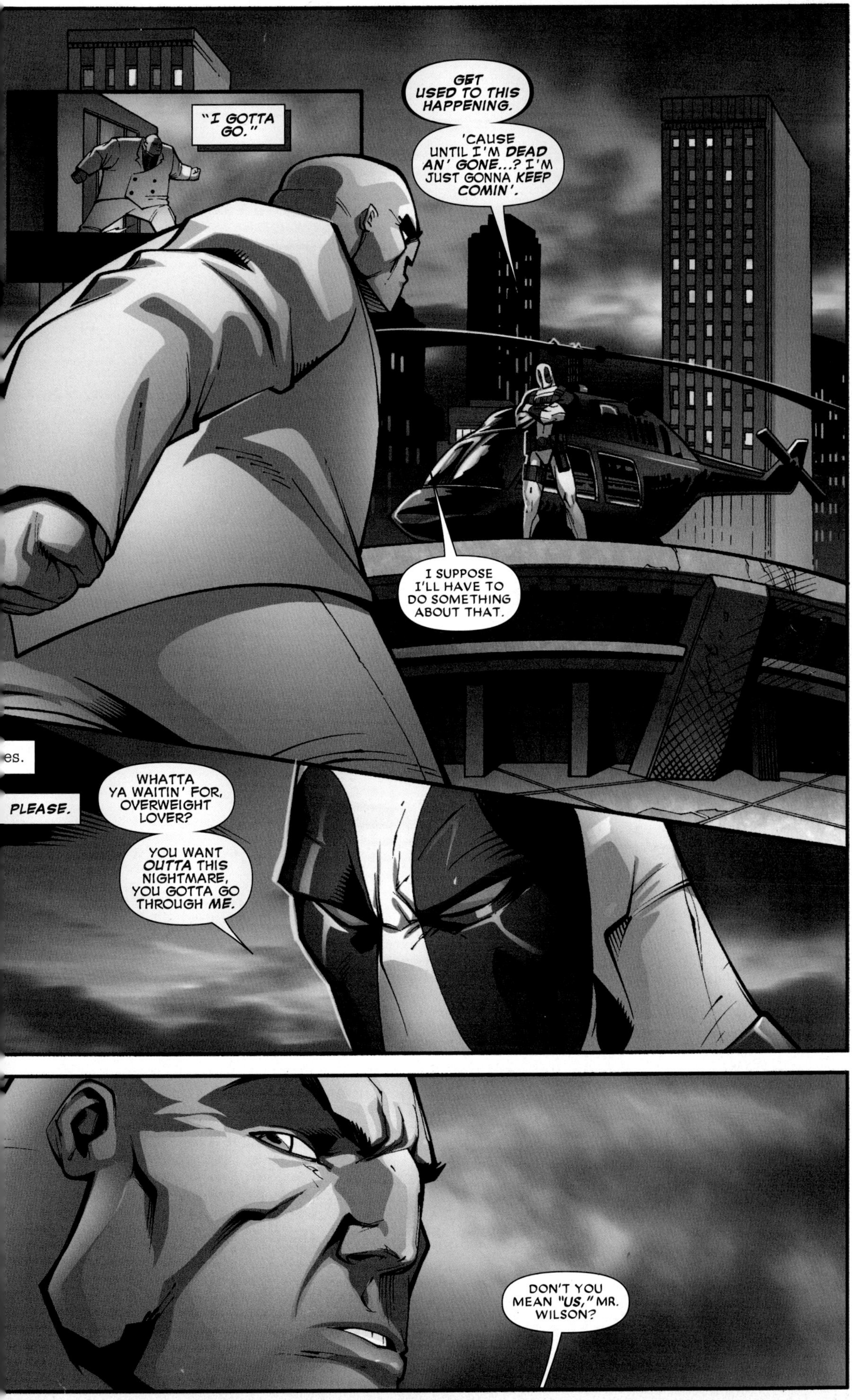

"I GOTTA GO."
GET USED TO THIS HAPPENING.
'CAUSE UNTIL I'M DEAD AN' GONE...? I'M JUST GONNA KEEP COMIN'.
I SUPPOSE I'LL HAVE TO DO SOMETHING ABOUT THAT.
es.
PLEASE.
WHATTA YA WAITIN' FOR, OVERWEIGHT LOVER?
YOU WANT OUTTA THIS NIGHTMARE, YOU GOTTA GO THROUGH ME.
DON'T YOU MEAN "US," MR. WILSON?

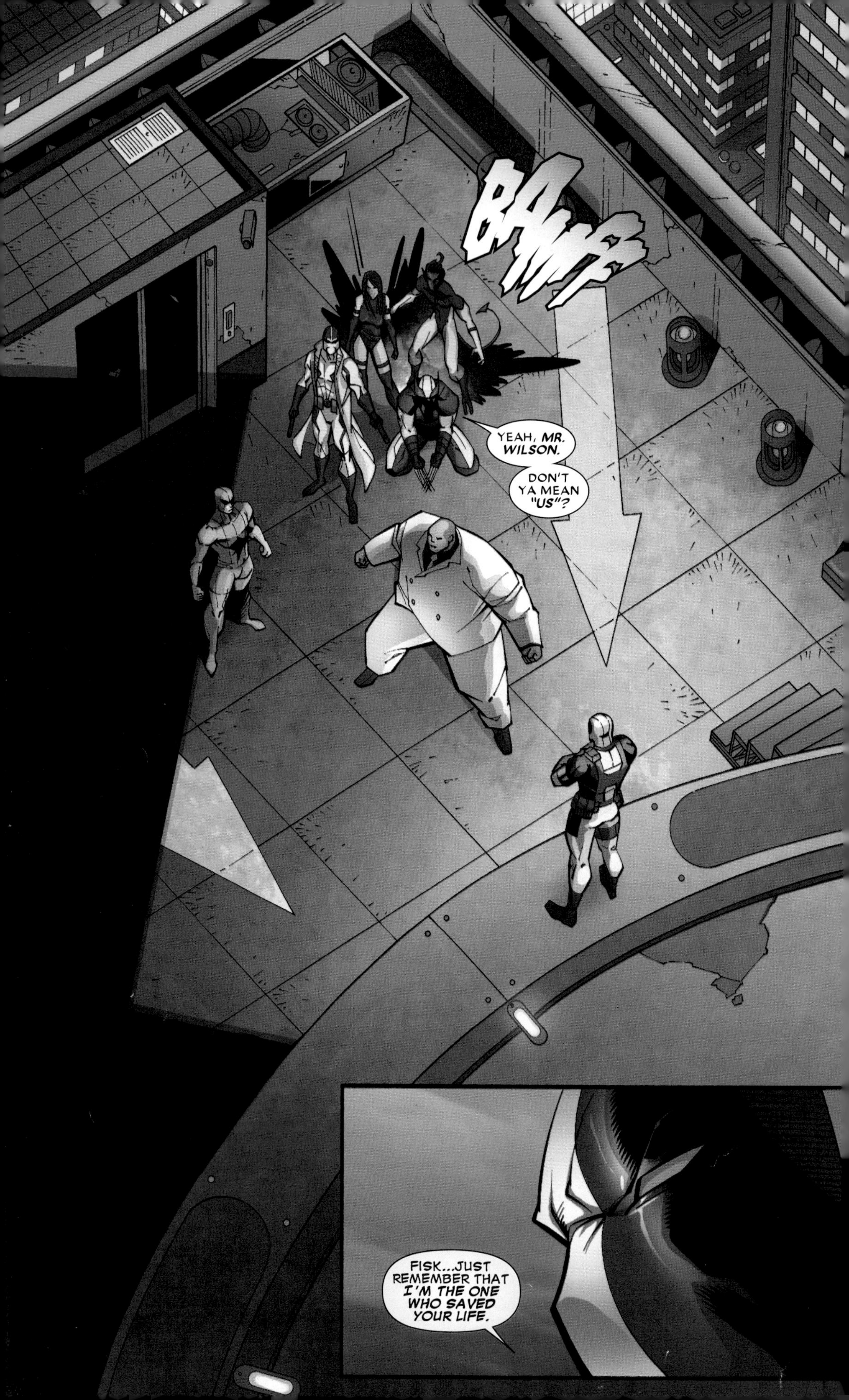
BAMF
YEAH, MR. WILSON.
DON'T YA MEAN "US"?
FISK...JUST REMEMBER THAT I'M THE ONE WHO SAVED YOUR LIFE.

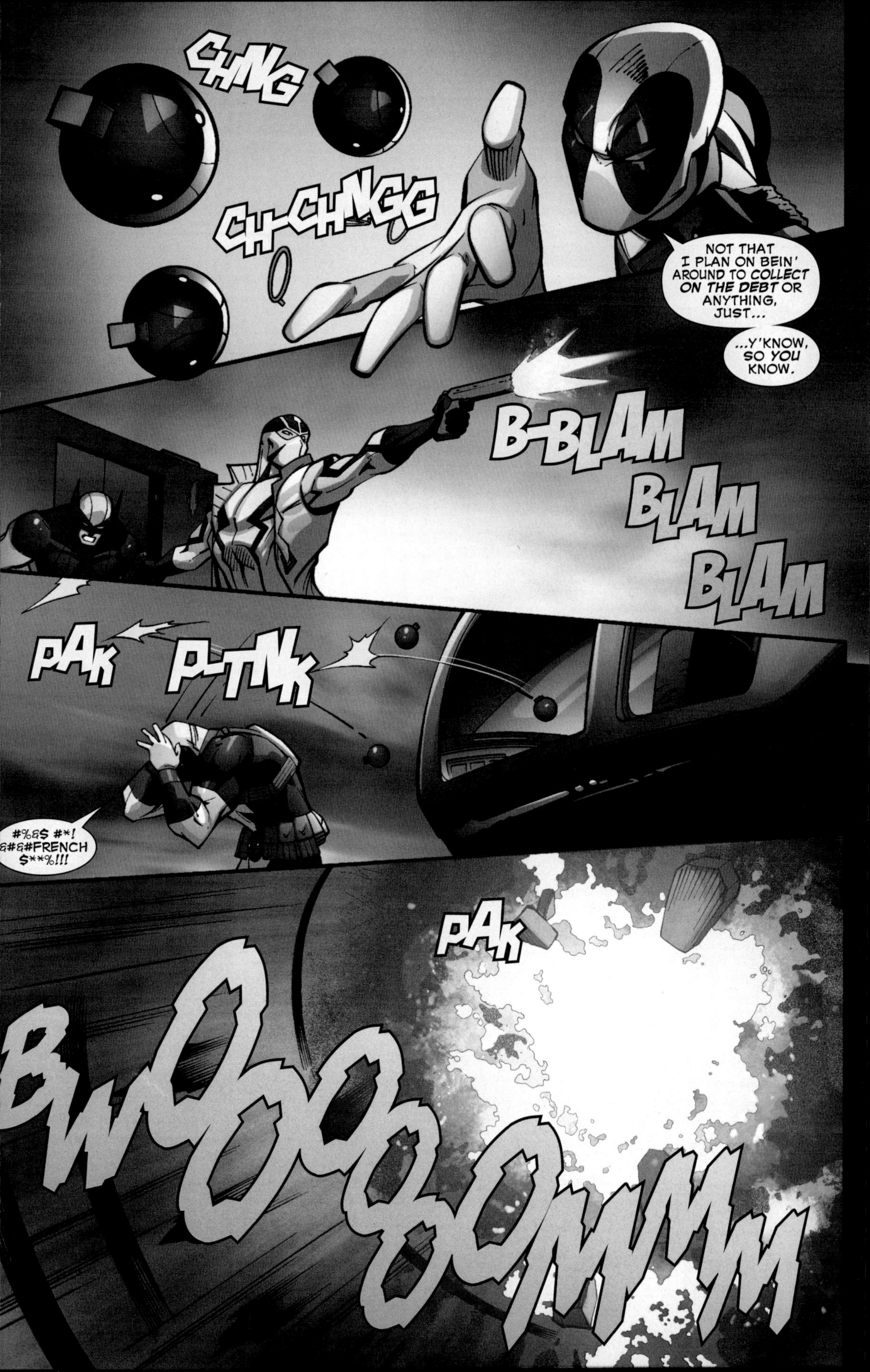
CHNG
CH-CHNGG
NOT THAT I PLAN ON BEIN' AROUND TO COLLECT ON THE DEBT OR ANYTHING, JUST...
...Y'KNOW, SO YOU KNOW.
B-BLAM
BLAM
BLAM
PAK
P-TINK
#%&$ #*! &#&#FRENCH $**%!!!
PAK
BWOOOOOMMMM

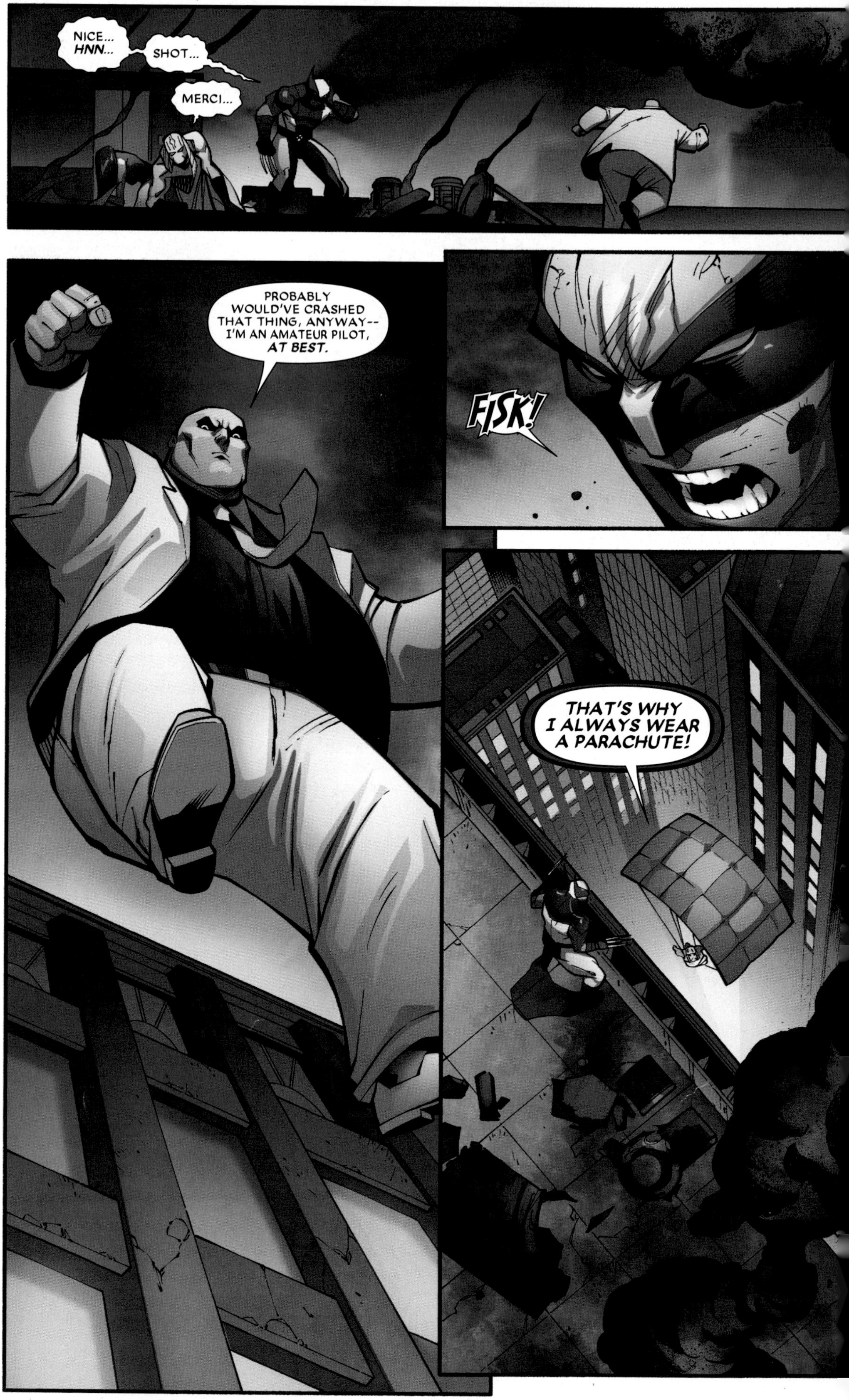

NICE... HNN...
SHOT...
MERCI...
PROBABLY WOULD'VE CRASHED THAT THING, ANYWAY-- I'M AN AMATEUR PILOT, AT BEST.
FISK!
THAT'S WHY I ALWAYS WEAR A PARACHUTE!

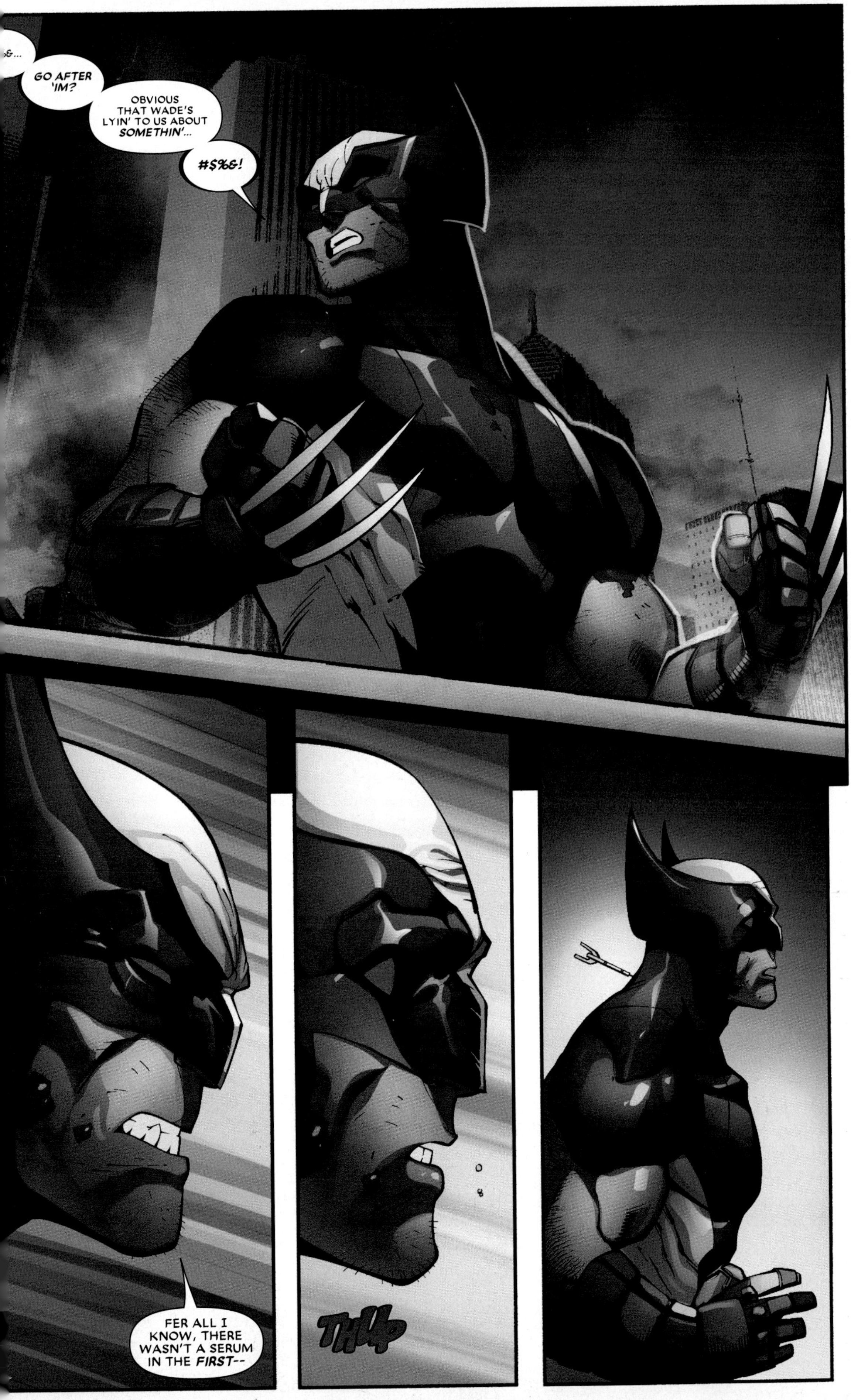
GO AFTER 'IM?
OBVIOUS THAT WADE'S LYIN' TO US ABOUT *SOMETHIN'*...
#$%&!
FER ALL I KNOW, THERE WASN'T A SERUM IN THE *FIRST*--
THUP

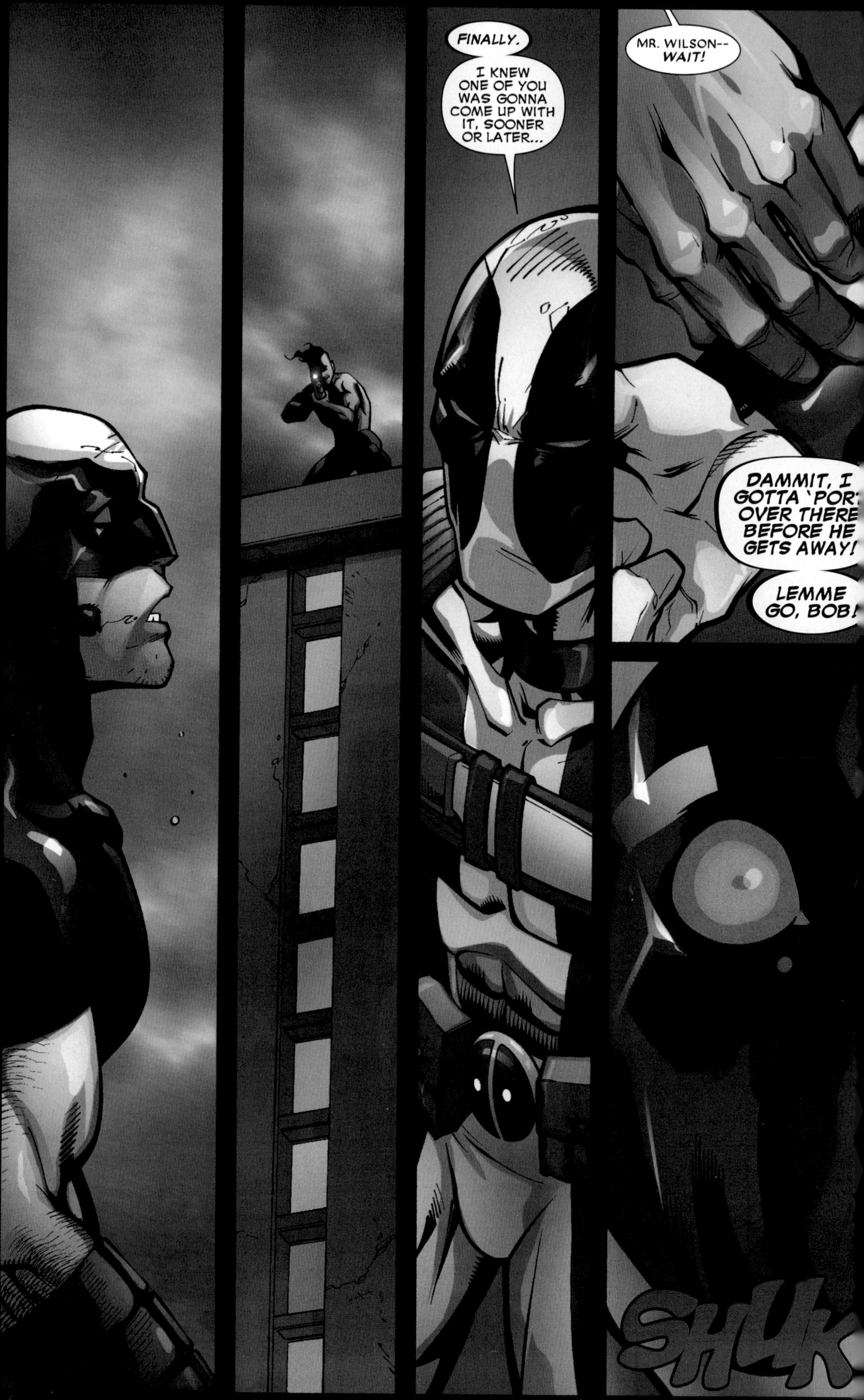
FINALLY.
I KNEW ONE OF YOU WAS GONNA COME UP WITH IT, SOONER OR LATER...
MR. WILSON-- WAIT!
DAMMIT, I GOTTA 'PORT OVER THERE BEFORE HE GETS AWAY!
LEMME GO, BOB!
SHUK

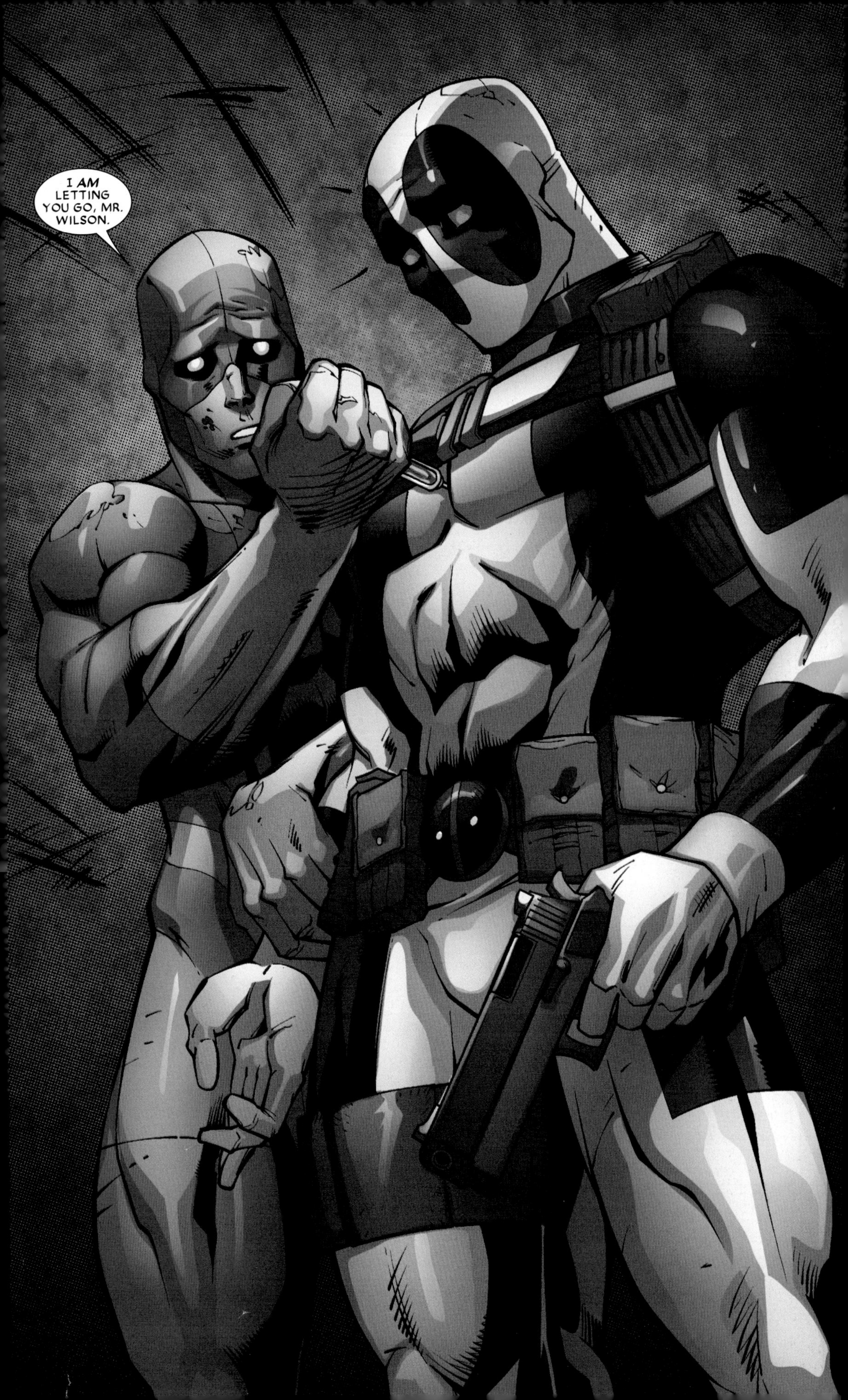
I *AM* LETTING YOU GO, MR. WILSON.

53

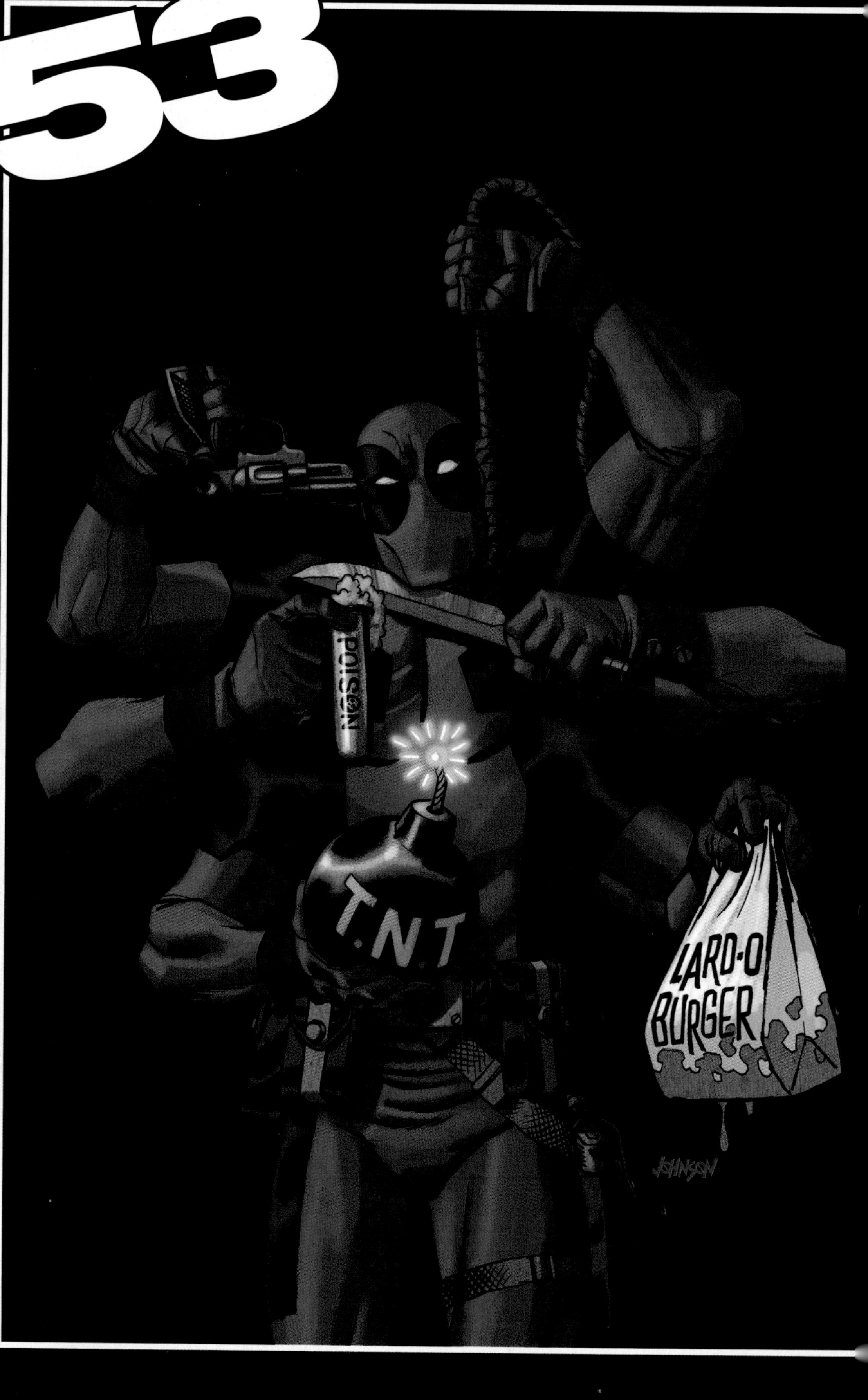
POISON
T.N.T
LARD-O BURGER
JOHNSON

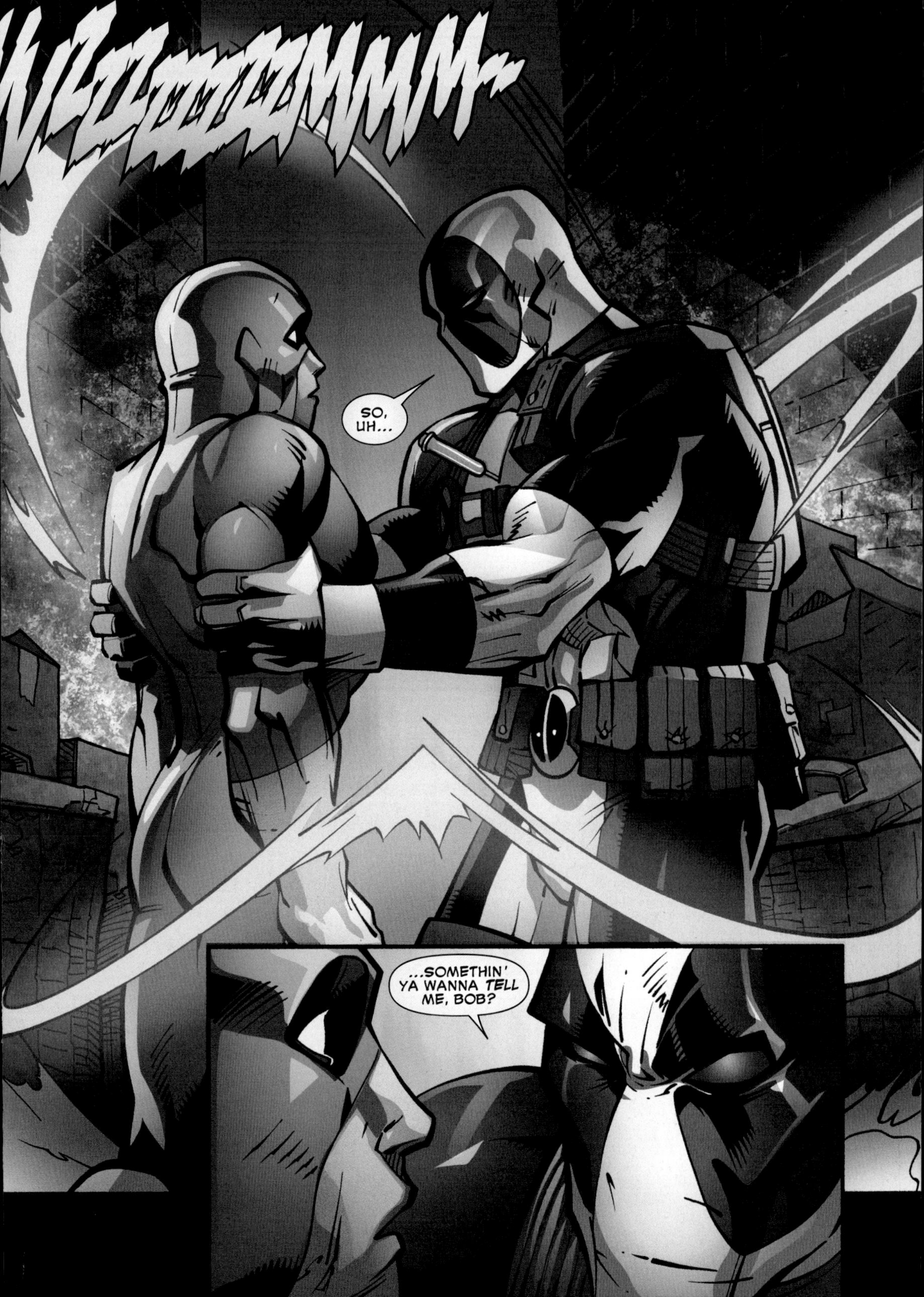
VVZZZZZMMMM--
SO, UH...
...SOMETHIN' YA WANNA TELL ME, BOB?

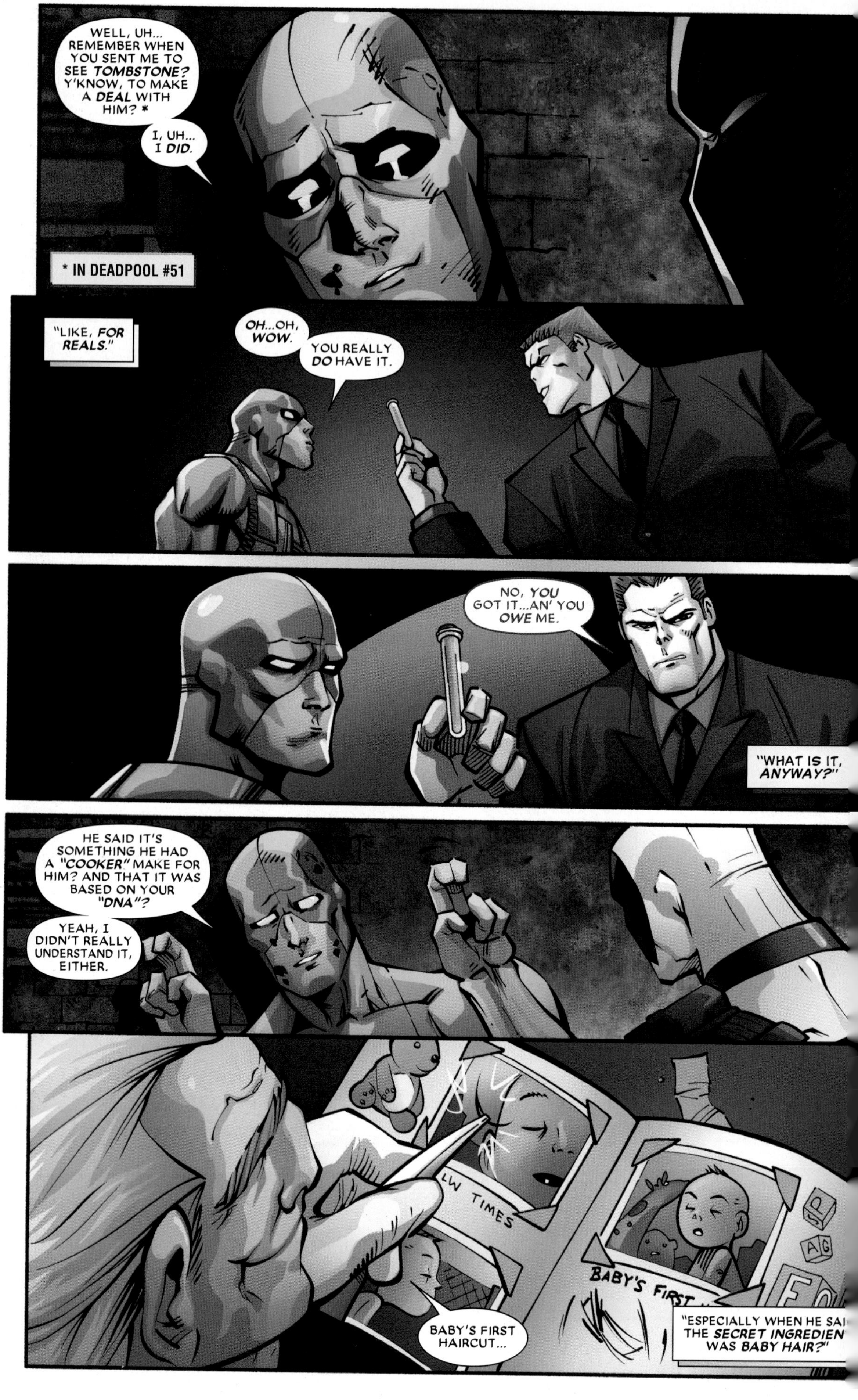
WELL, UH... REMEMBER WHEN YOU SENT ME TO SEE TOMBSTONE? Y'KNOW, TO MAKE A DEAL WITH HIM? *
I, UH... I DID.
* IN DEADPOOL #51
"LIKE, FOR REALS."
OH...OH, WOW.
YOU REALLY DO HAVE IT.
NO, YOU GOT IT...AN' YOU OWE ME.
"WHAT IS IT, ANYWAY?"
HE SAID IT'S SOMETHING HE HAD A "COOKER" MAKE FOR HIM? AND THAT IT WAS BASED ON YOUR "DNA"?
YEAH, I DIDN'T REALLY UNDERSTAND IT, EITHER.
LW TIMES
BABY'S FIRST
BABY'S FIRST HAIRCUT...
"ESPECIALLY WHEN HE SAI THE SECRET INGREDIEN WAS BABY HAIR?"

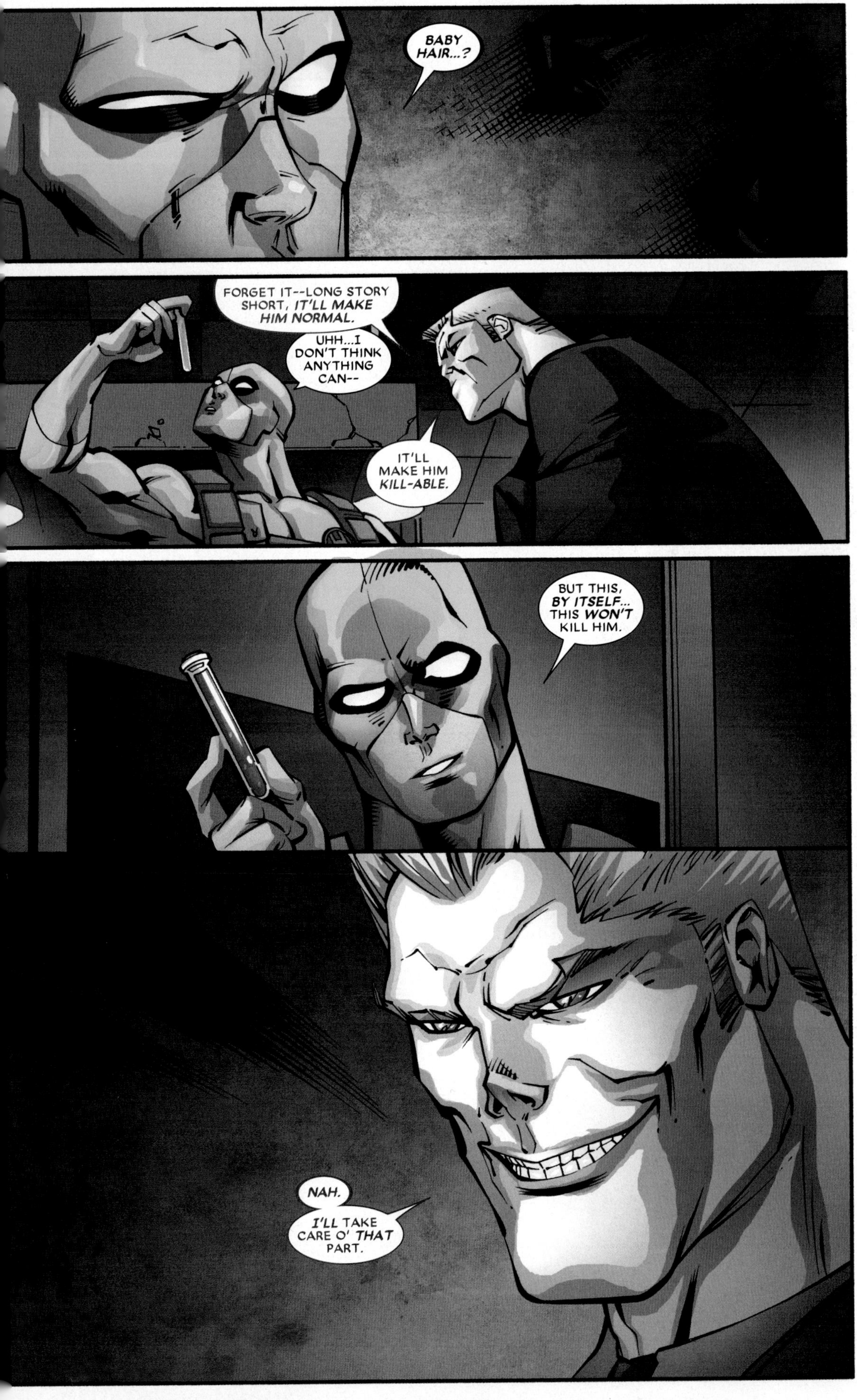
BABY HAIR...?
FORGET IT--LONG STORY SHORT, IT'LL MAKE HIM NORMAL.
UHH...I DON'T THINK ANYTHING CAN--
IT'LL MAKE HIM KILL-ABLE.
BUT THIS, BY ITSELF... THIS WON'T KILL HIM.
NAH.
I'LL TAKE CARE O' THAT PART.

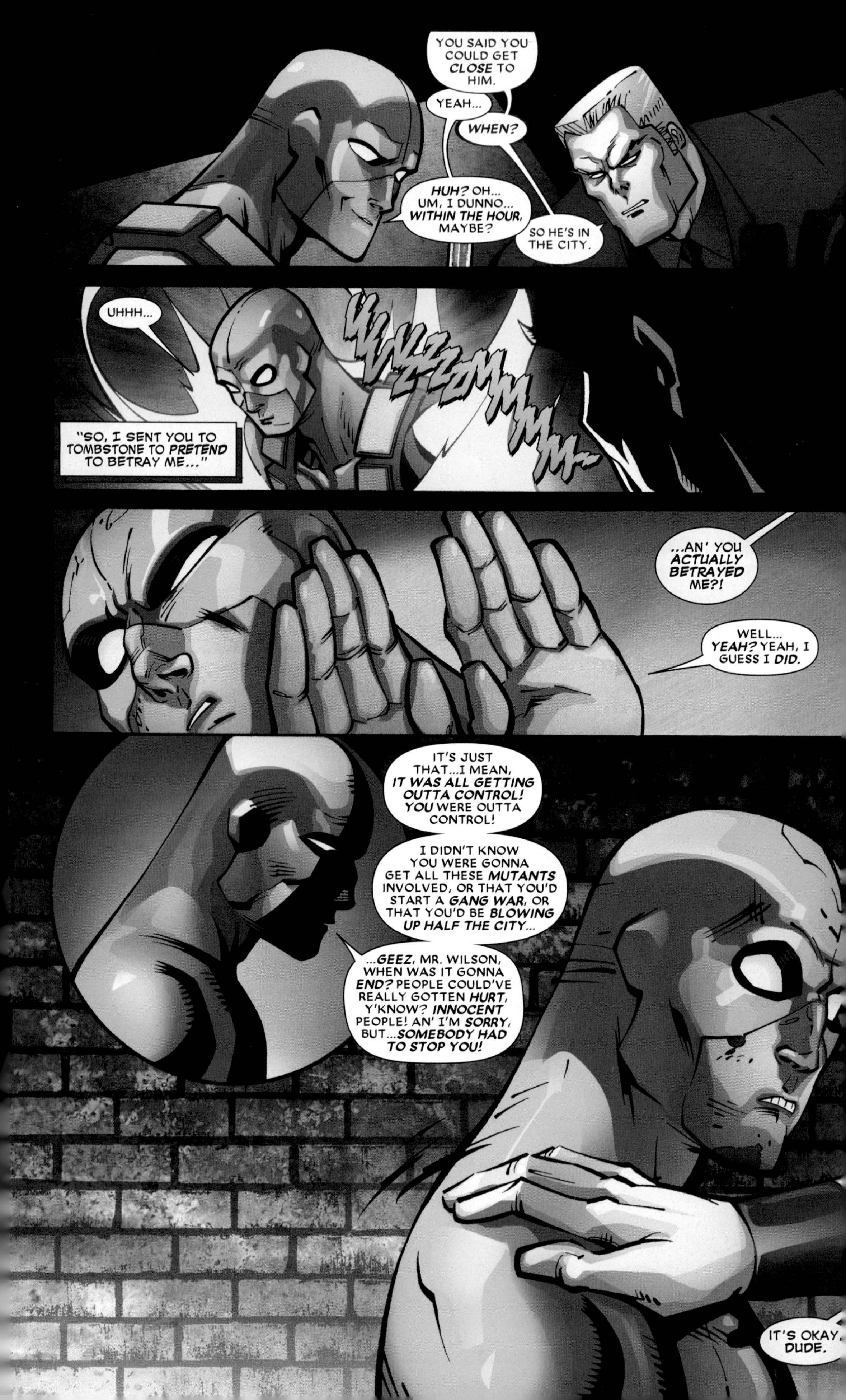
YOU SAID YOU COULD GET CLOSE TO HIM.
YEAH...
WHEN?
HUH? OH... UM, I DUNNO... WITHIN THE HOUR, MAYBE?
SO HE'S IN THE CITY.
UHHH...
"SO, I SENT YOU TO TOMBSTONE TO PRETEND TO BETRAY ME..."
WWZZOMMMM
...AN' YOU ACTUALLY BETRAYED ME?!
WELL... YEAH? YEAH, I GUESS I DID.
IT'S JUST THAT...I MEAN, IT WAS ALL GETTING OUTTA CONTROL! YOU WERE OUTTA CONTROL!
I DIDN'T KNOW YOU WERE GONNA GET ALL THESE MUTANTS INVOLVED, OR THAT YOU'D START A GANG WAR, OR THAT YOU'D BE BLOWING UP HALF THE CITY...
...GEEZ, MR. WILSON, WHEN WAS IT GONNA END? PEOPLE COULD'VE REALLY GOTTEN HURT, Y'KNOW? INNOCENT PEOPLE! AN' I'M SORRY, BUT...SOMEBODY HAD TO STOP YOU!
IT'S OKAY, DUDE.

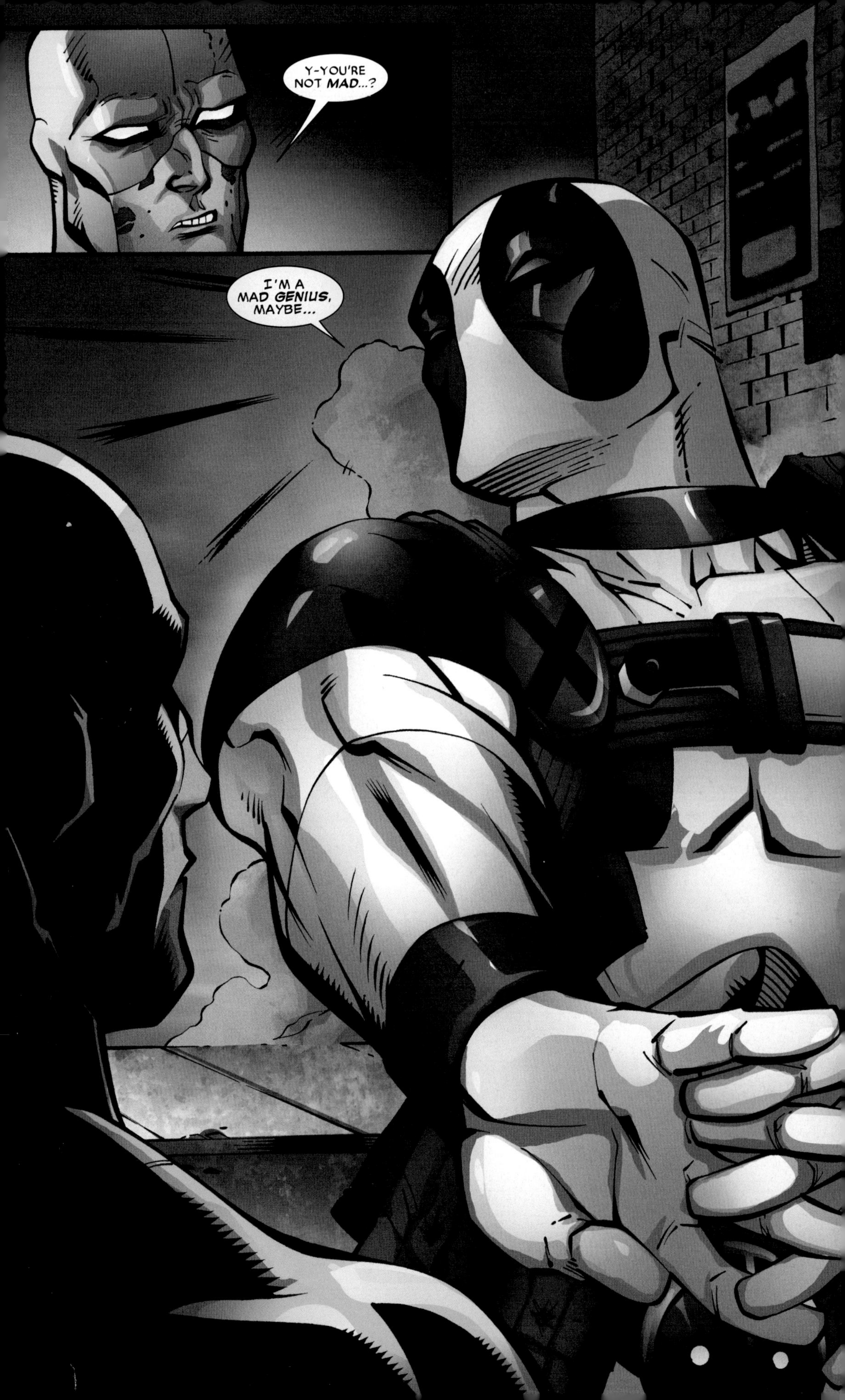
Y-YOU'RE NOT MAD...?
I'M A MAD GENIUS, MAYBE...

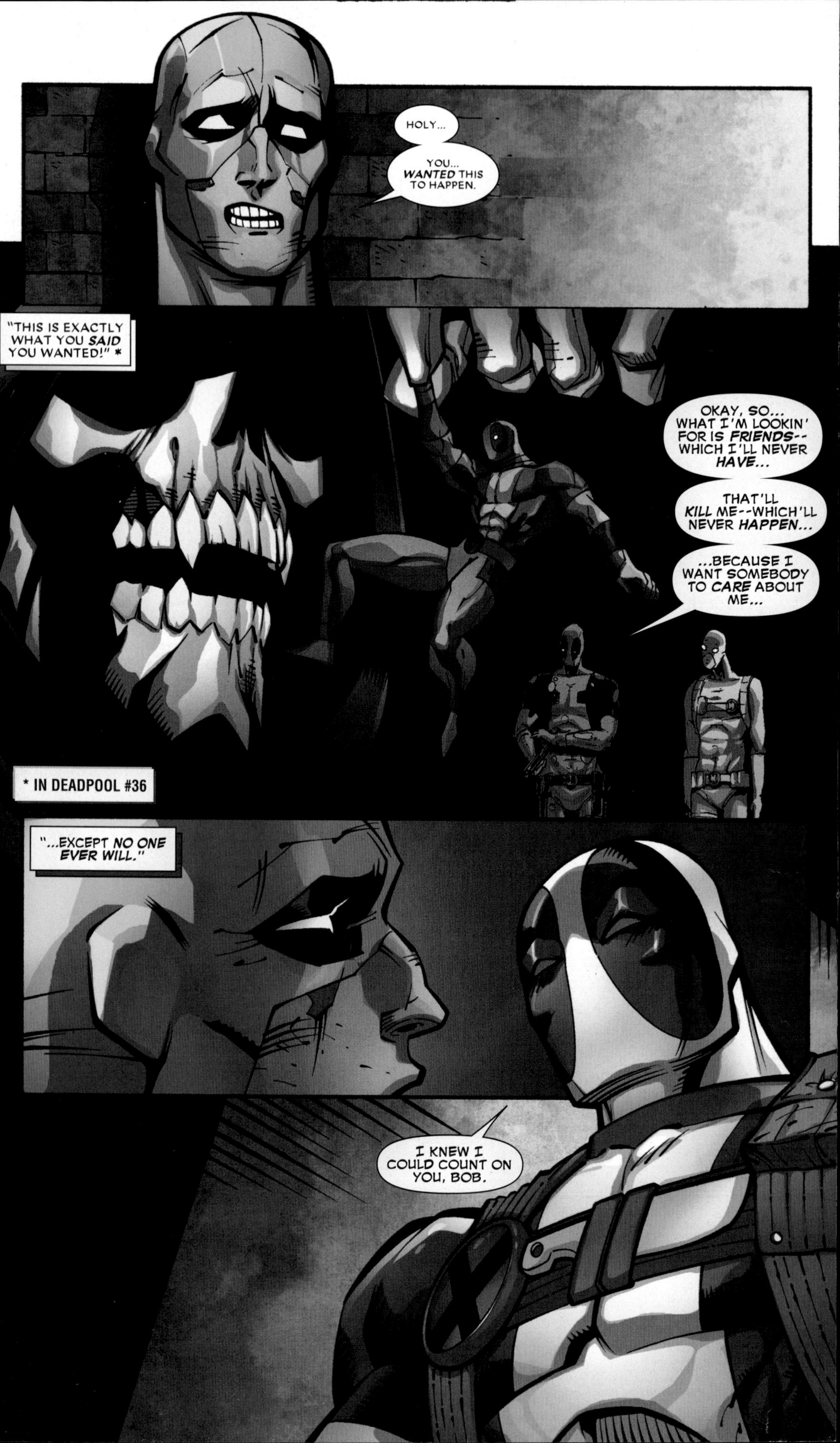
HOLY...
YOU... WANTED THIS TO HAPPEN.
"THIS IS EXACTLY WHAT YOU SAID YOU WANTED!" *
OKAY, SO... WHAT I'M LOOKIN' FOR IS FRIENDS-- WHICH I'LL NEVER HAVE...
THAT'LL KILL ME--WHICH'LL NEVER HAPPEN...
...BECAUSE I WANT SOMEBODY TO CARE ABOUT ME...
* IN DEADPOOL #36
"...EXCEPT NO ONE EVER WILL."
I KNEW I COULD COUNT ON YOU, BOB.

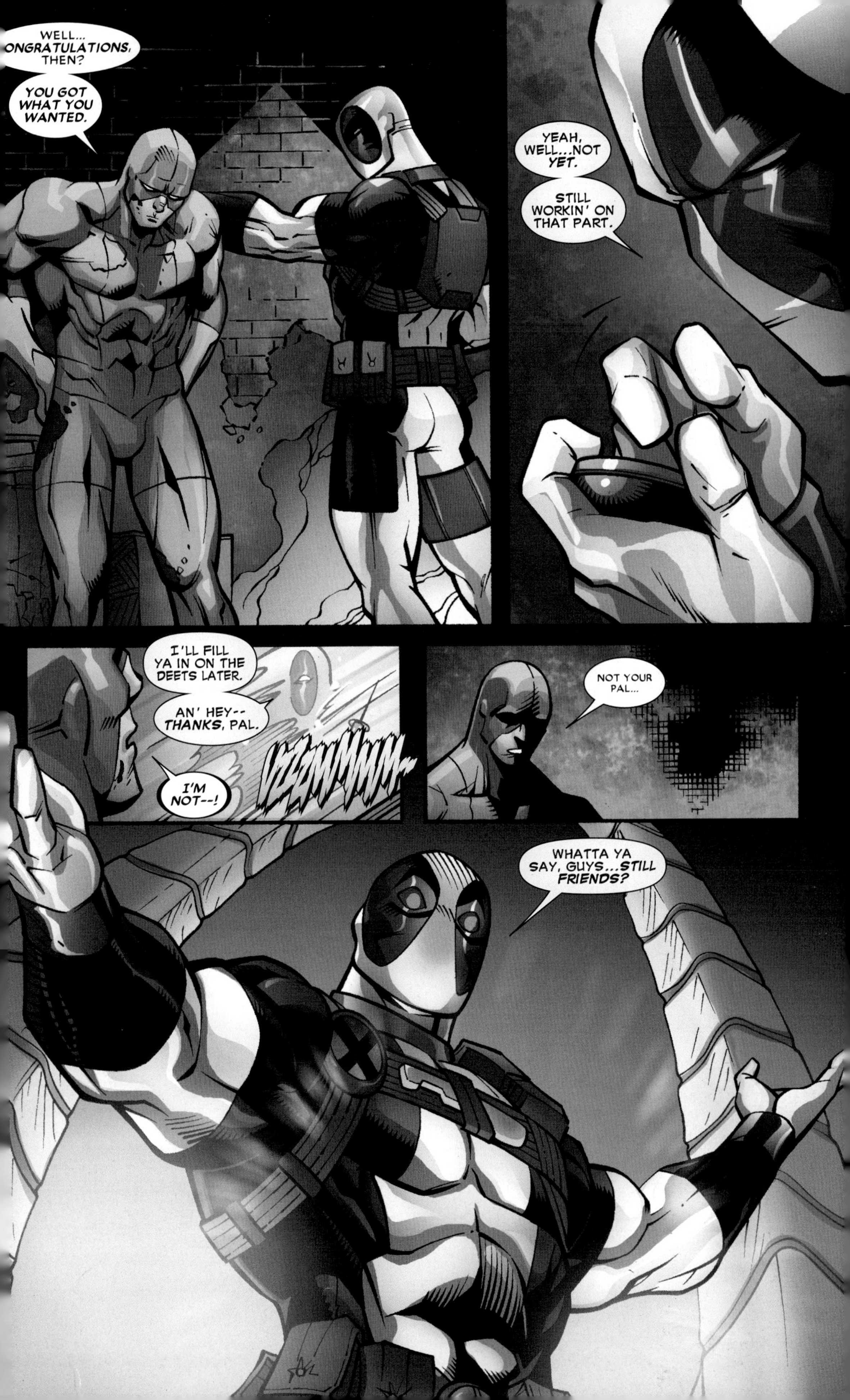

WELL... ONGRATULATIONS, THEN?
YOU GOT WHAT YOU WANTED.
YEAH, WELL...NOT YET.
STILL WORKIN' ON THAT PART.
I'LL FILL YA IN ON THE DEETS LATER.
AN' HEY-- THANKS, PAL.
I'M NOT--!
VZZMMMM
NOT YOUR PAL...
WHATTA YA SAY, GUYS...STILL FRIENDS?

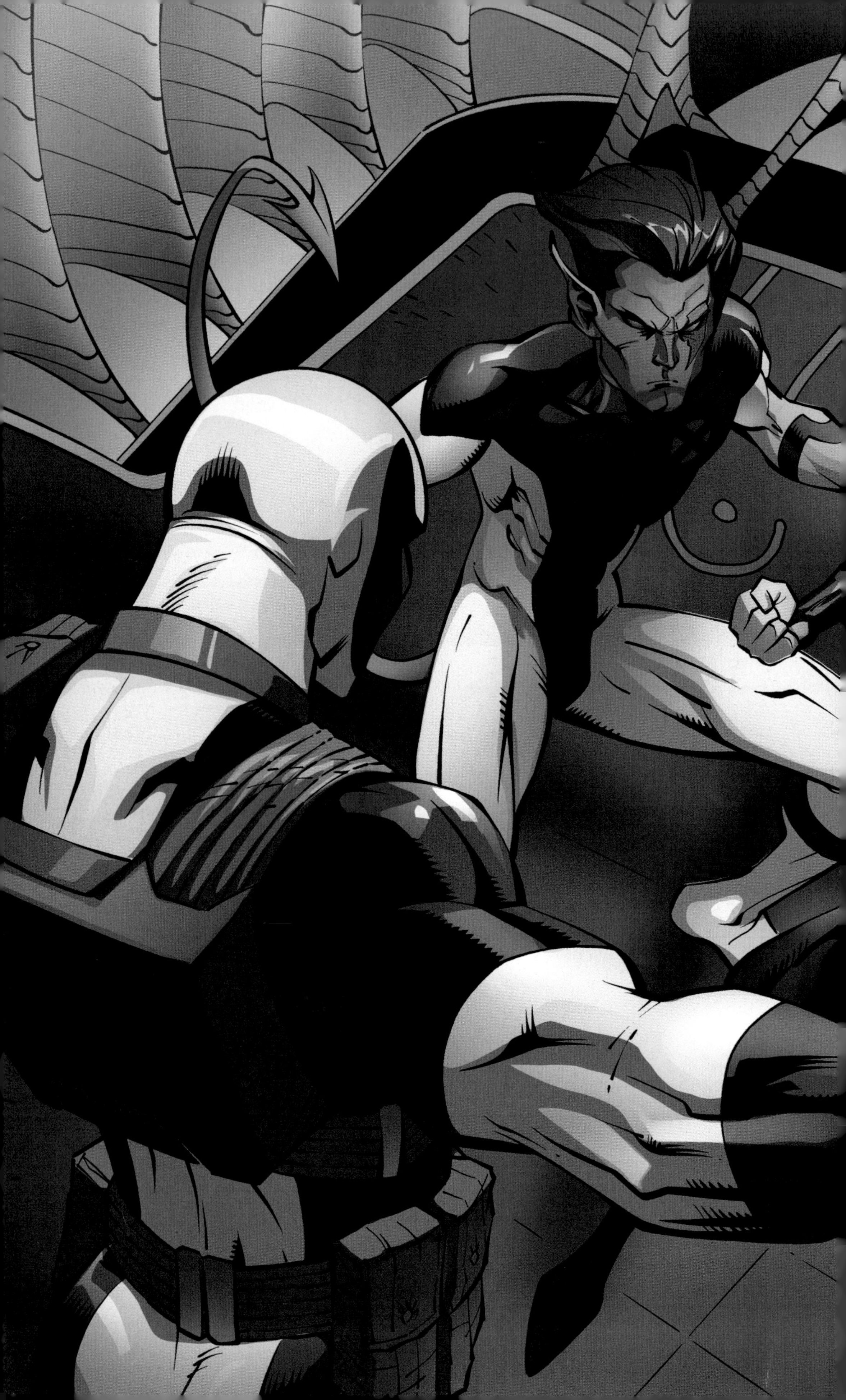

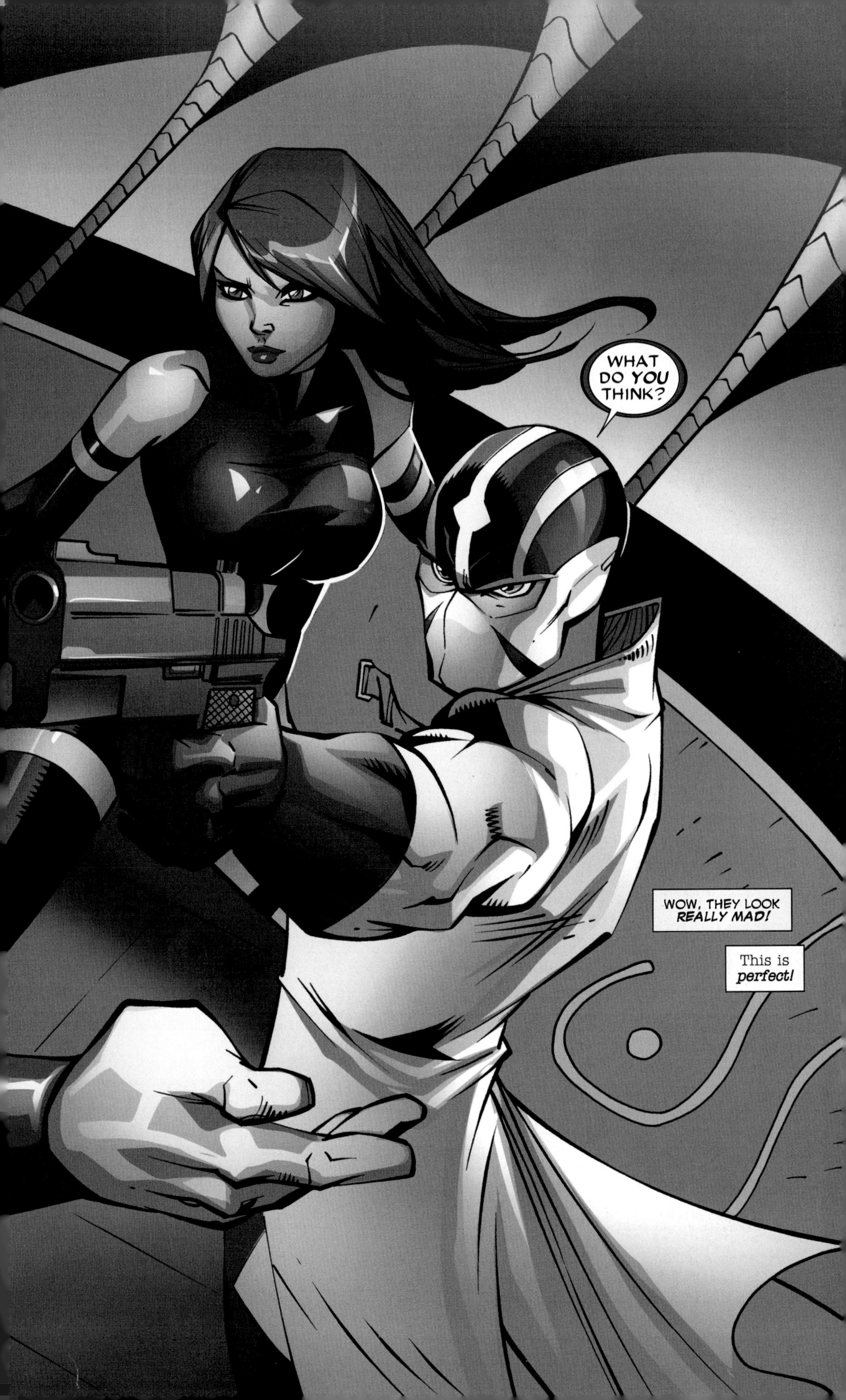
WHAT DO YOU THINK?
WOW, THEY LOOK REALLY MAD!
This is perfect!

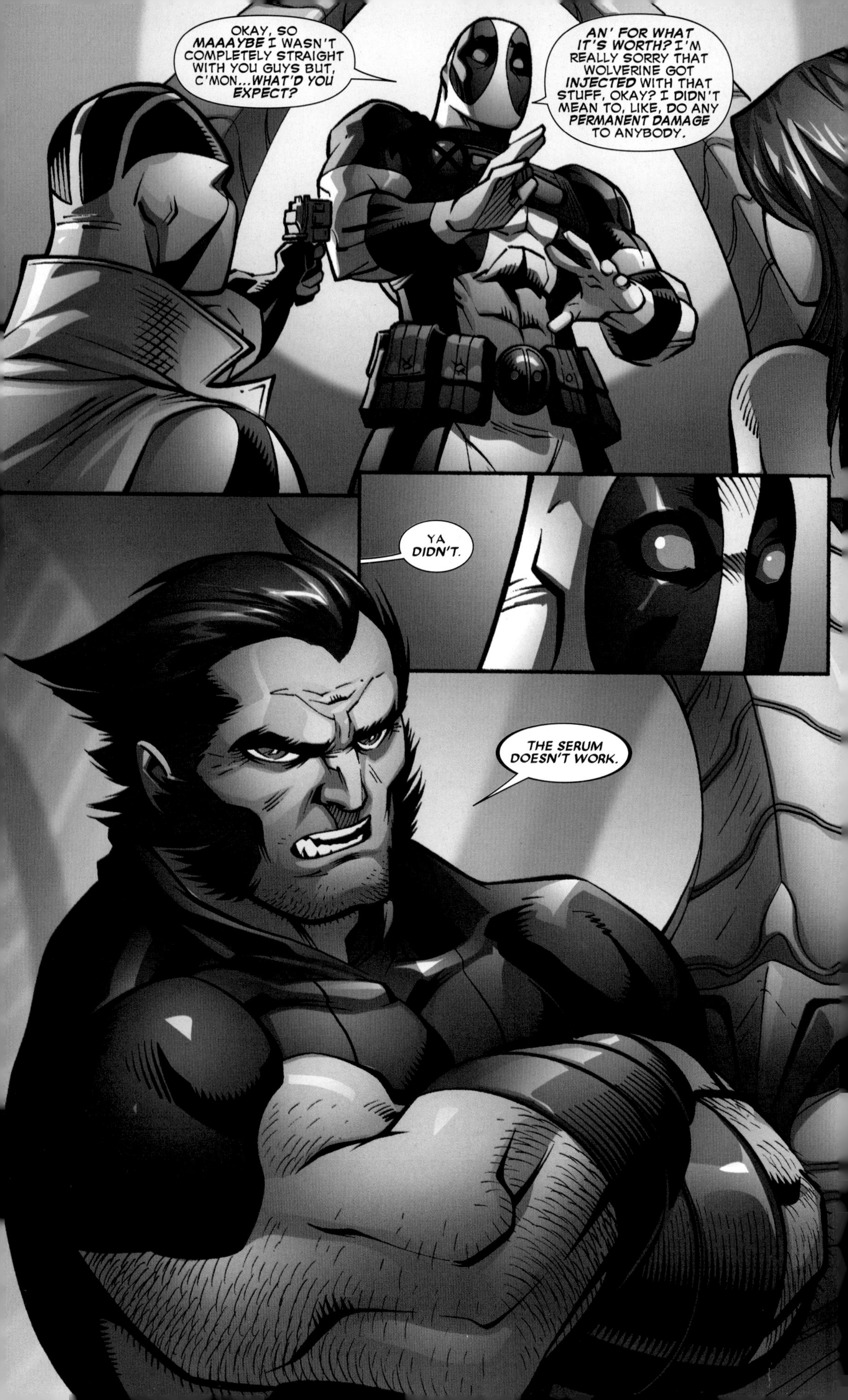
OKAY, SO MAAAYBE I WASN'T COMPLETELY STRAIGHT WITH YOU GUYS BUT, C'MON...WHAT'D YOU EXPECT?
AN' FOR WHAT IT'S WORTH? I'M REALLY SORRY THAT WOLVERINE GOT INJECTED WITH THAT STUFF, OKAY? I DIDN'T MEAN TO, LIKE, DO ANY PERMANENT DAMAGE TO ANYBODY.
YA DIDN'T.
THE SERUM DOESN'T WORK.

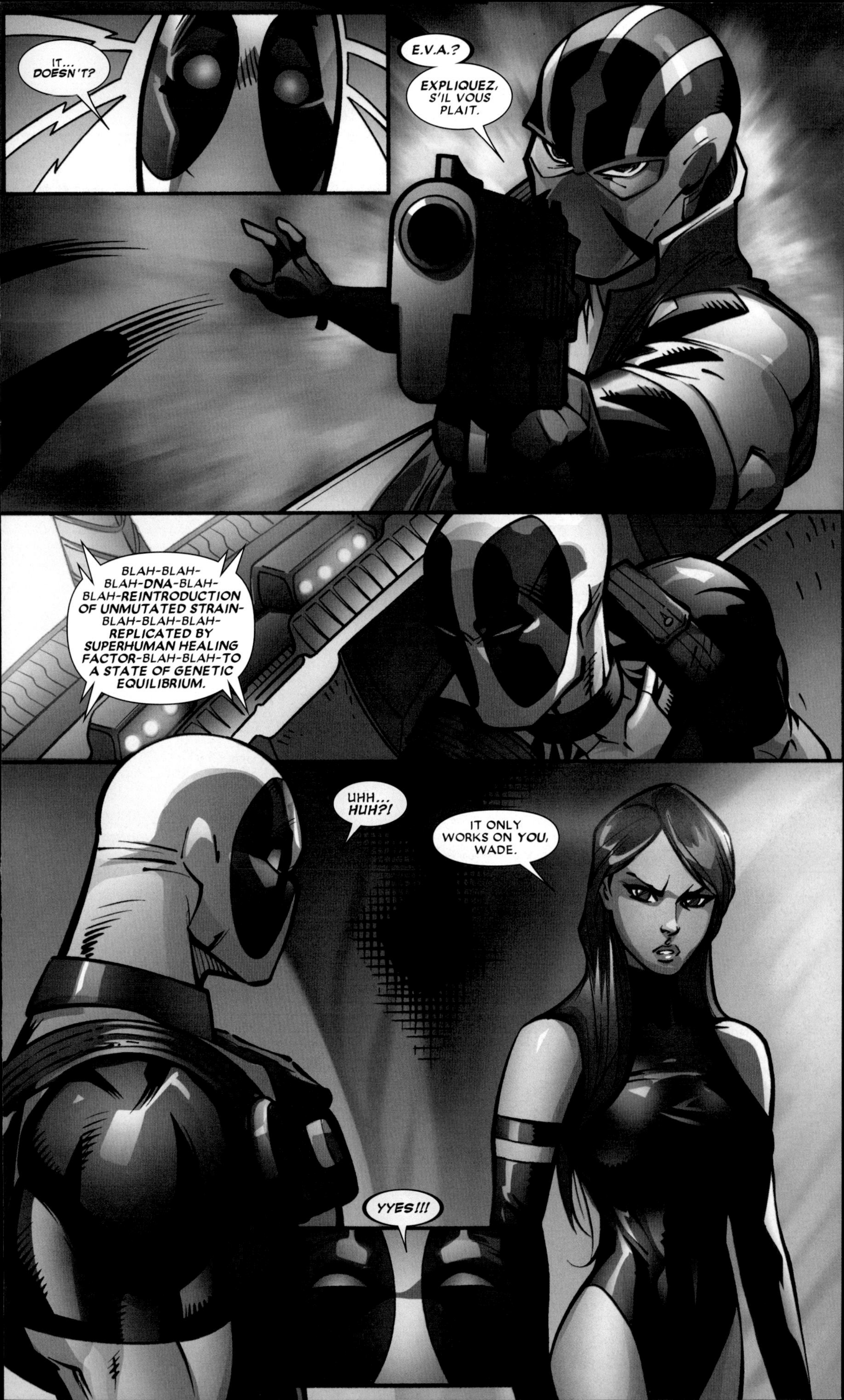

IT... DOESN'T?
E.V.A.?
EXPLIQUEZ, S'IL VOUS PLAIT.
BLAH-BLAH-BLAH-DNA-BLAH-BLAH-REINTRODUCTION OF UNMUTATED STRAIN-BLAH-BLAH-BLAH-REPLICATED BY SUPERHUMAN HEALING FACTOR-BLAH-BLAH-TO A STATE OF GENETIC EQUILIBRIUM.
UHH... HUH?!
IT ONLY WORKS ON YOU, WADE.
YYES!!!

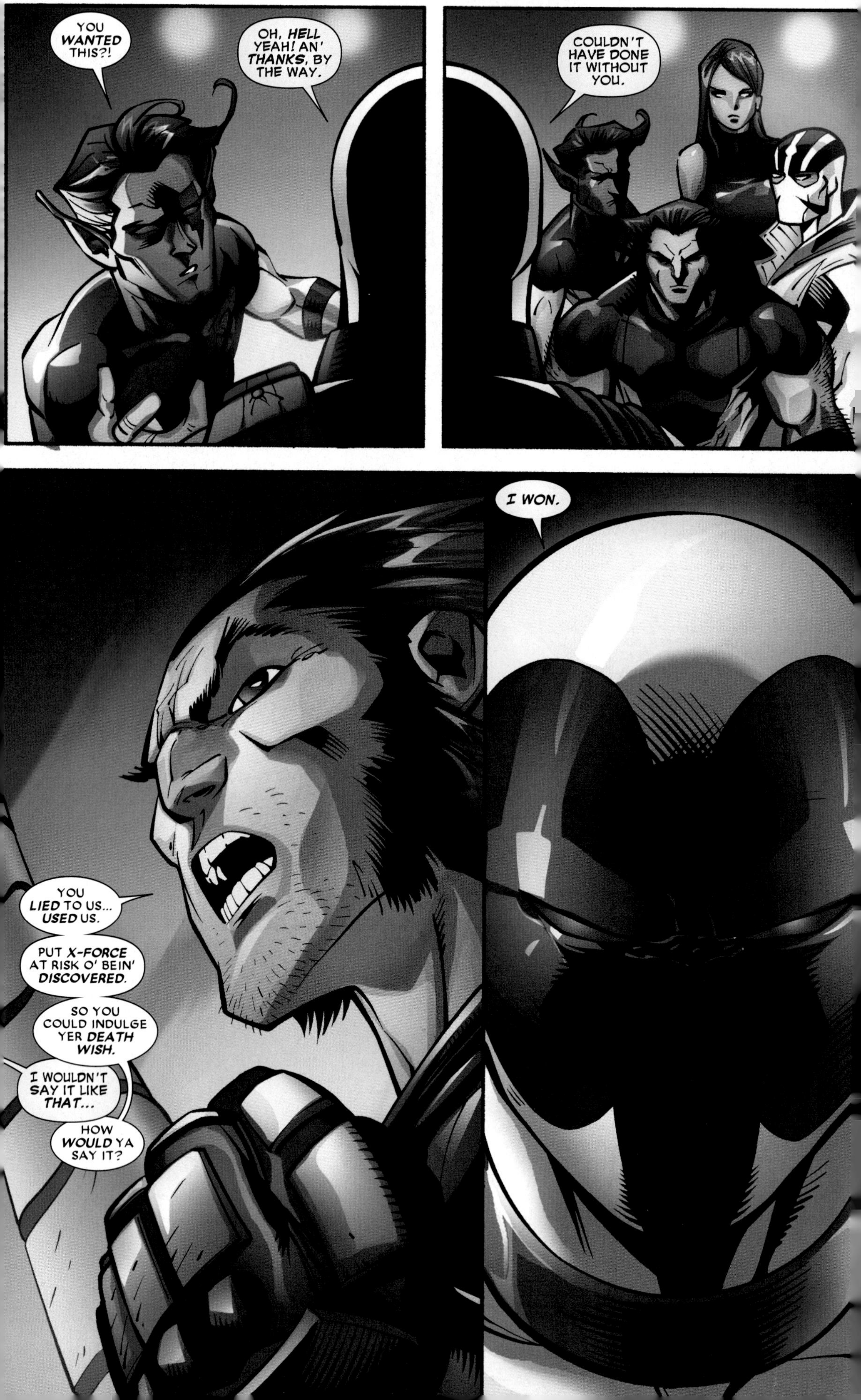
YOU WANTED THIS?!
OH, HELL YEAH! AN' THANKS, BY THE WAY.
COULDN'T HAVE DONE IT WITHOUT YOU.
I WON.
YOU LIED TO US... USED US.
PUT X-FORCE AT RISK O' BEIN' DISCOVERED.
SO YOU COULD INDULGE YER DEATH WISH.
I WOULDN'T SAY IT LIKE THAT...
HOW WOULD YA SAY IT?

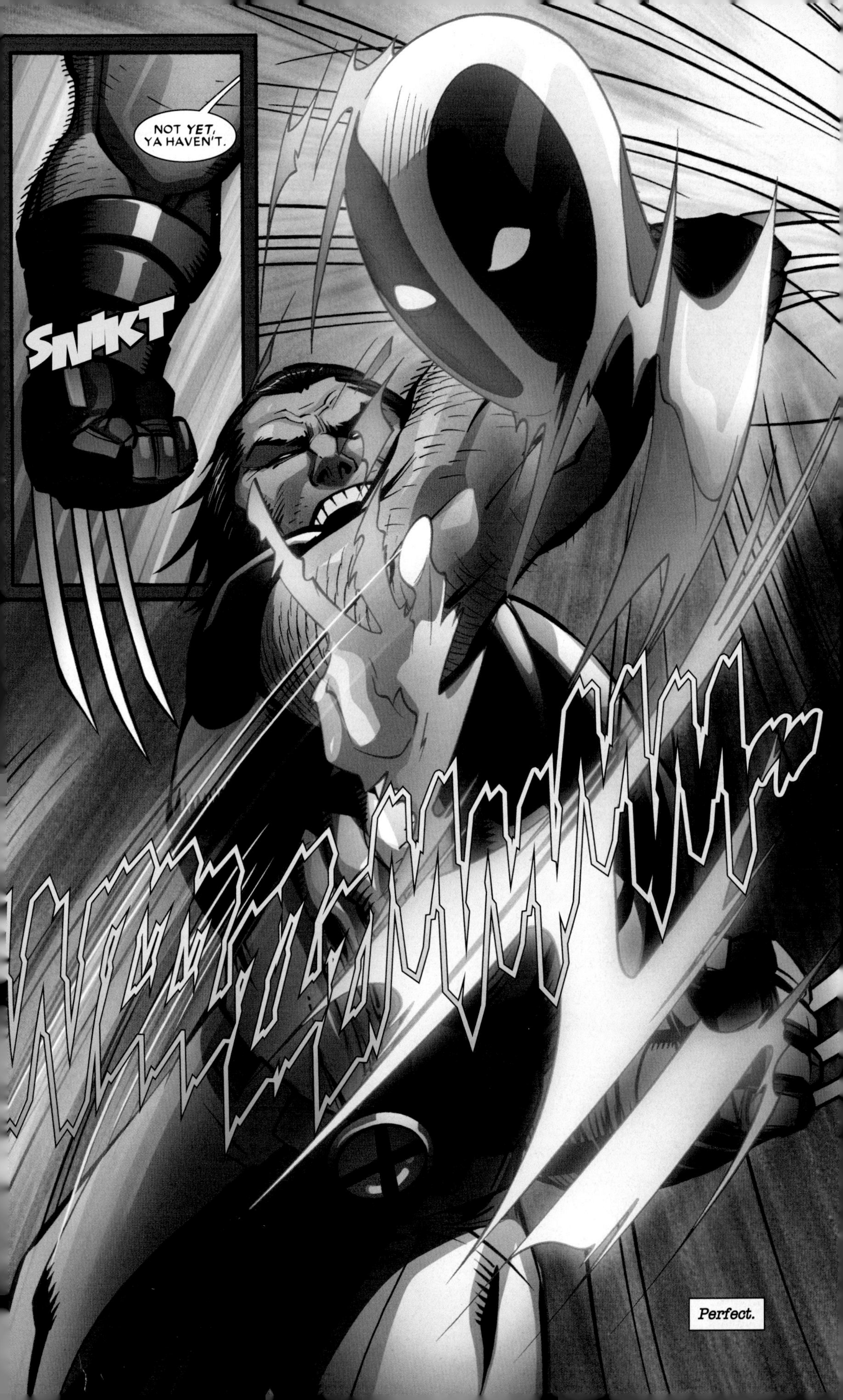
NOT YET, YA HAVEN'T.
SNIKT
Perfect.

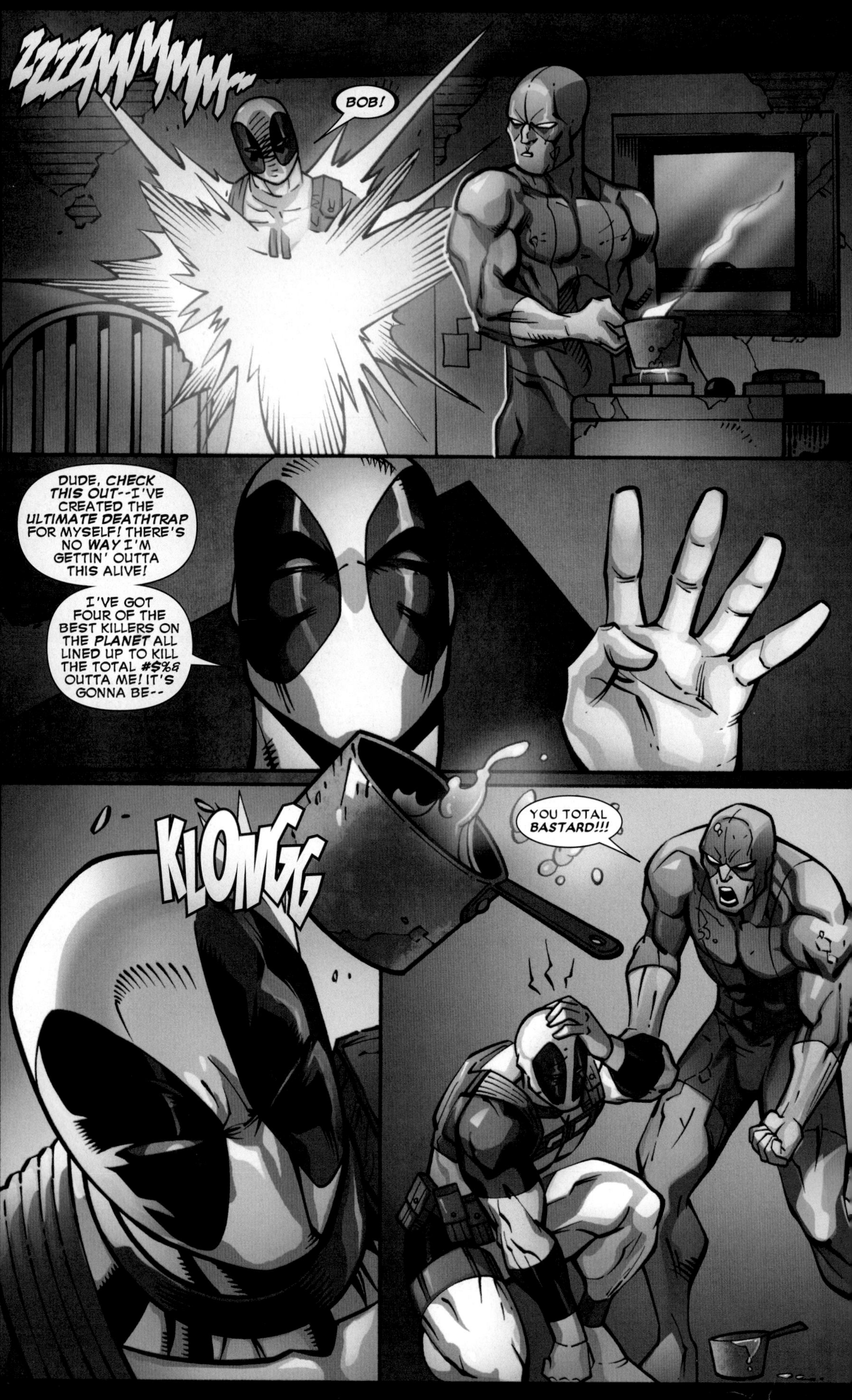
ZZZZMMMMM--
BOB!
DUDE, CHECK THIS OUT--I'VE CREATED THE ULTIMATE DEATHTRAP FOR MYSELF! THERE'S NO WAY I'M GETTIN' OUTTA THIS ALIVE!
I'VE GOT FOUR OF THE BEST KILLERS ON THE PLANET ALL LINED UP TO KILL THE TOTAL #$%& OUTTA ME! IT'S GONNA BE--
KLONGG
YOU TOTAL BASTARD!!!

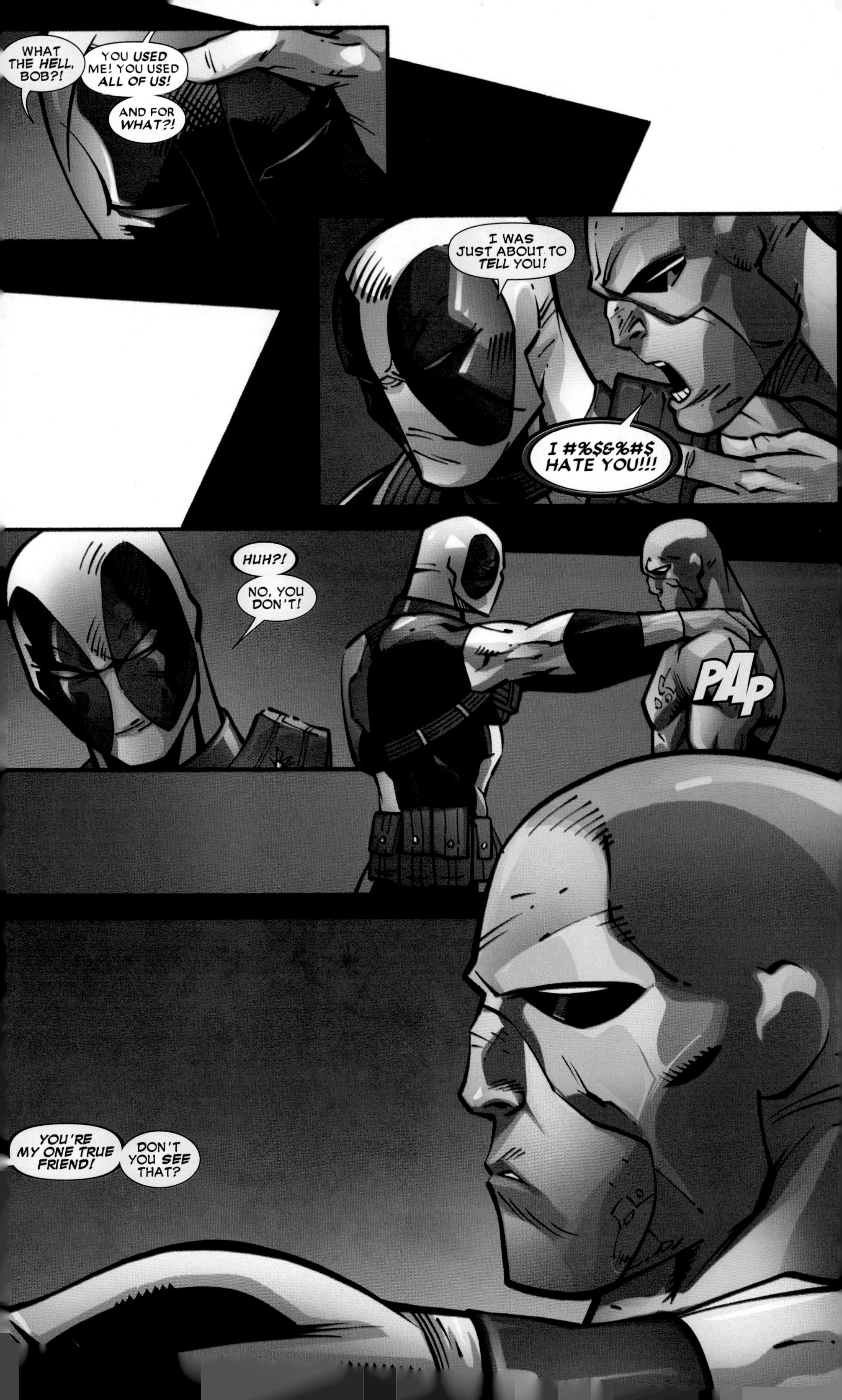
WHAT THE HELL, BOB?!
YOU USED ME! YOU USED ALL OF US!
AND FOR WHAT?!
I WAS JUST ABOUT TO TELL YOU!
I #%$&%#$ HATE YOU!!!
HUH?!
NO, YOU DON'T!
PAP
YOU'RE MY ONE TRUE FRIEND!
DON'T YOU SEE THAT?

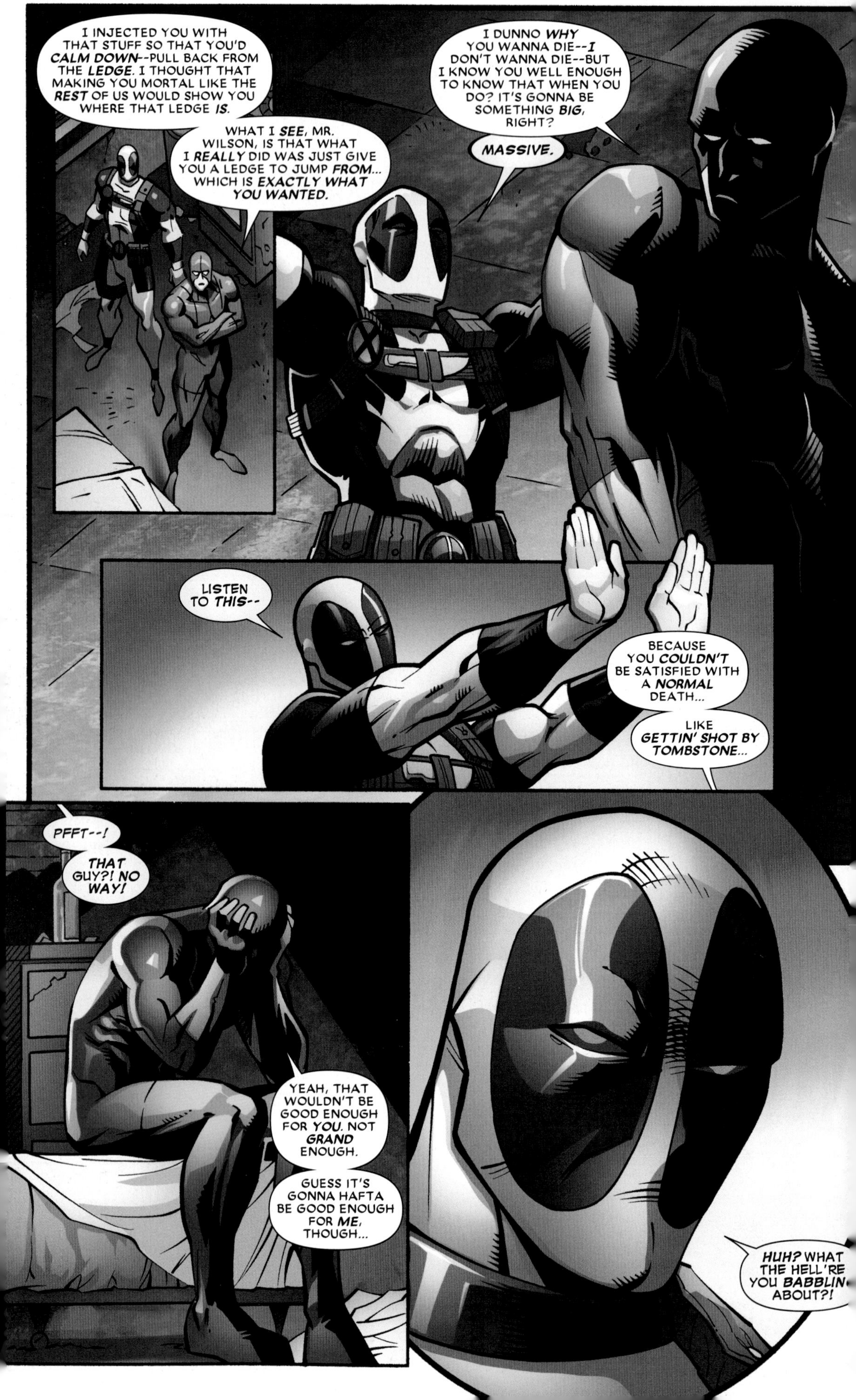
I INJECTED YOU WITH THAT STUFF SO THAT YOU'D CALM DOWN--PULL BACK FROM THE LEDGE. I THOUGHT THAT MAKING YOU MORTAL LIKE THE REST OF US WOULD SHOW YOU WHERE THAT LEDGE IS.
WHAT I SEE, MR. WILSON, IS THAT WHAT I REALLY DID WAS JUST GIVE YOU A LEDGE TO JUMP FROM... WHICH IS EXACTLY WHAT YOU WANTED.
I DUNNO WHY YOU WANNA DIE--I DON'T WANNA DIE--BUT I KNOW YOU WELL ENOUGH TO KNOW THAT WHEN YOU DO? IT'S GONNA BE SOMETHING BIG, RIGHT?
MASSIVE.
LISTEN TO THIS--
BECAUSE YOU COULDN'T BE SATISFIED WITH A NORMAL DEATH...
LIKE GETTIN' SHOT BY TOMBSTONE...
PFFT--!
THAT GUY?! NO WAY!
YEAH, THAT WOULDN'T BE GOOD ENOUGH FOR YOU. NOT GRAND ENOUGH.
GUESS IT'S GONNA HAFTA BE GOOD ENOUGH FOR ME, THOUGH...
HUH? WHAT THE HELL'RE YOU BABBLIN' ABOUT?!

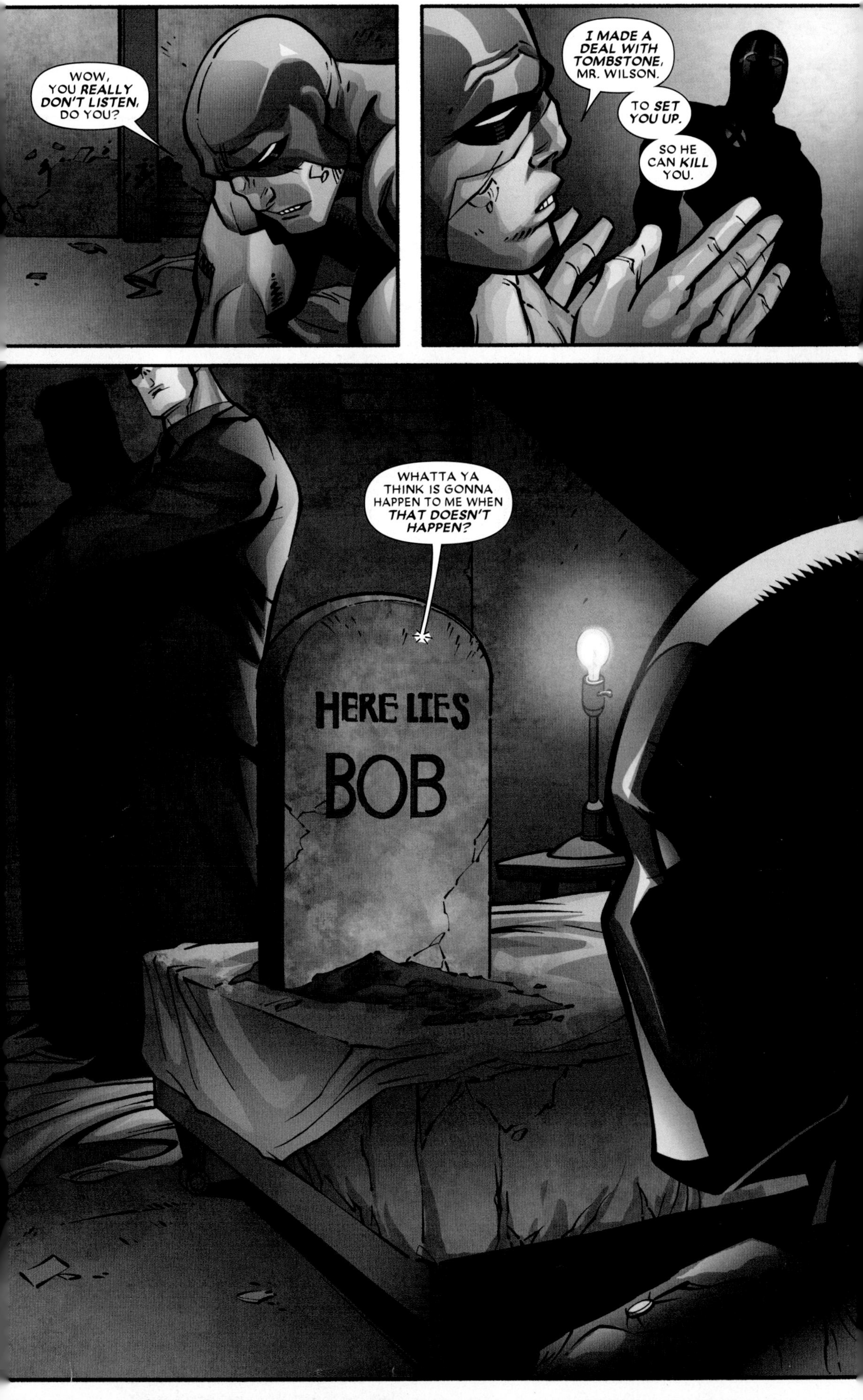
HERE LIES
WOW, YOU REALLY DON'T LISTEN, DO YOU?
I MADE A DEAL WITH TOMBSTONE, MR. WILSON.
TO SET YOU UP.
SO HE CAN KILL YOU.
WHATTA YA THINK IS GONNA HAPPEN TO ME WHEN THAT DOESN'T HAPPEN?
HERE LIES
BOB

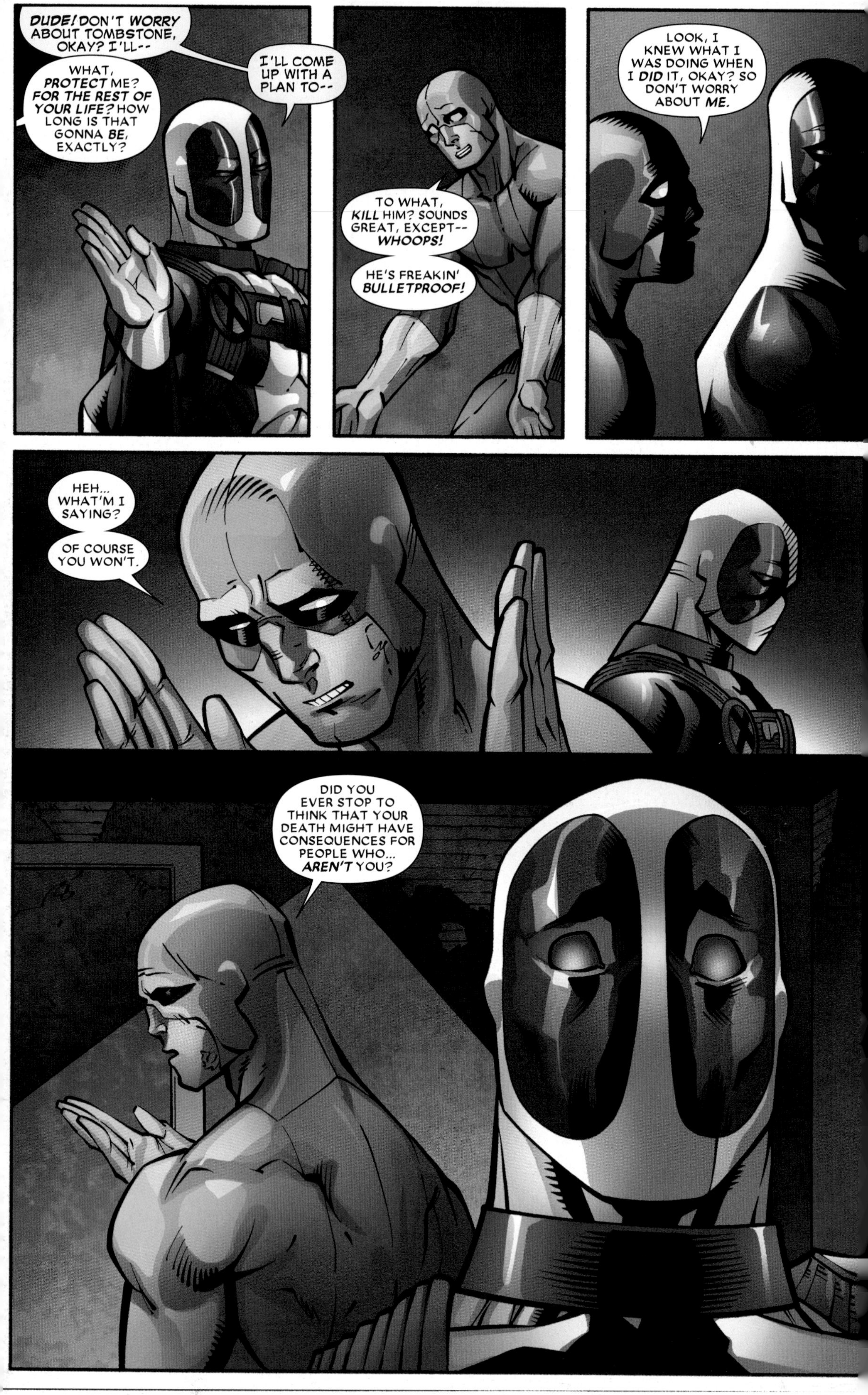
DUDE! DON'T WORRY ABOUT TOMBSTONE, OKAY? I'LL--
WHAT, PROTECT ME? FOR THE REST OF YOUR LIFE? HOW LONG IS THAT GONNA BE, EXACTLY?
I'LL COME UP WITH A PLAN TO--
TO WHAT, KILL HIM? SOUNDS GREAT, EXCEPT-- WHOOPS!
HE'S FREAKIN' BULLETPROOF!
LOOK, I KNEW WHAT I WAS DOING WHEN I DID IT, OKAY? SO DON'T WORRY ABOUT ME.
HEH... WHAT'M I SAYING?
OF COURSE YOU WON'T.
DID YOU EVER STOP TO THINK THAT YOUR DEATH MIGHT HAVE CONSEQUENCES FOR PEOPLE WHO... AREN'T YOU?

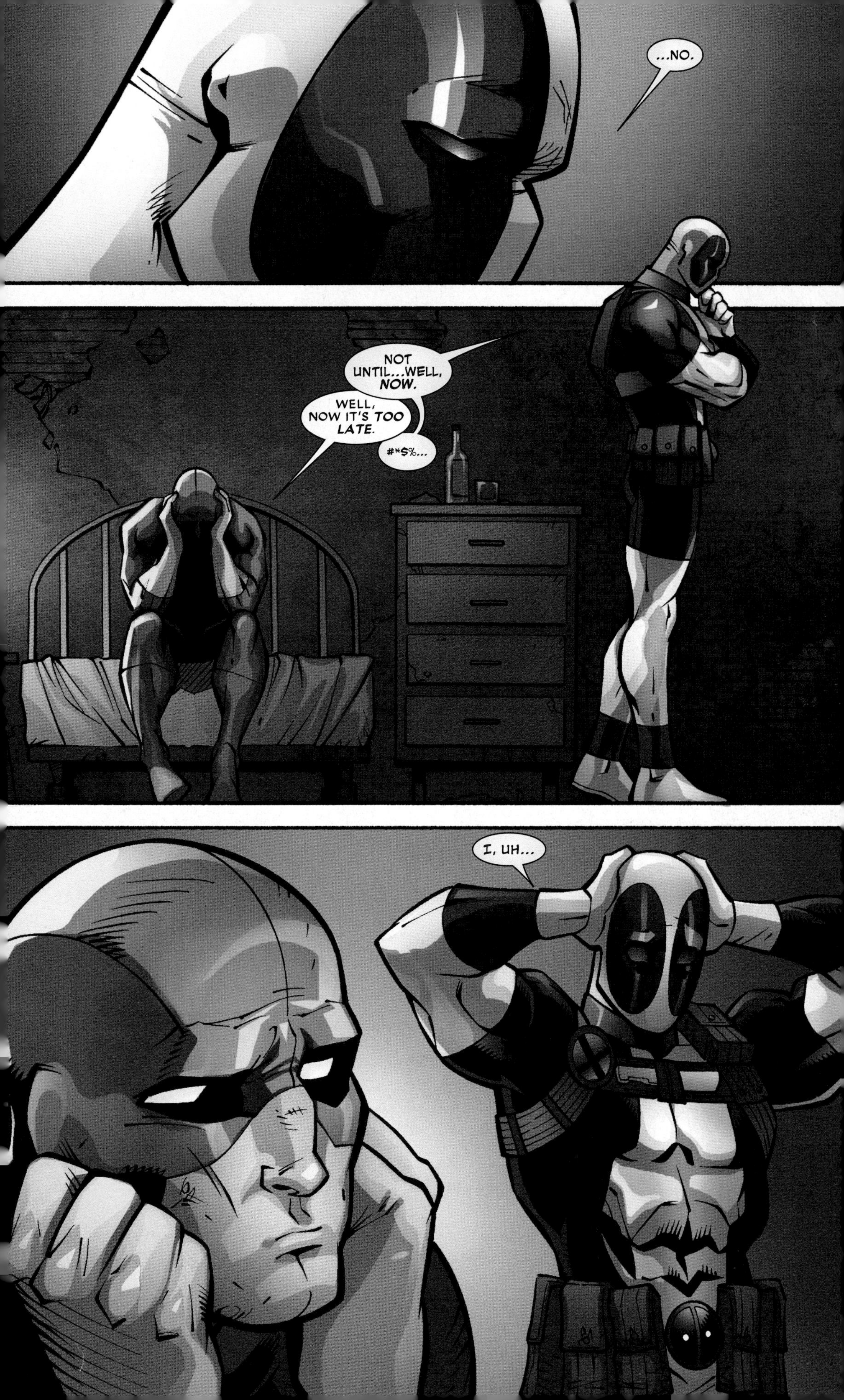

...NO.
NOT UNTIL...WELL, NOW.
#*$%...
WELL, NOW IT'S TOO LATE.
I, UH...

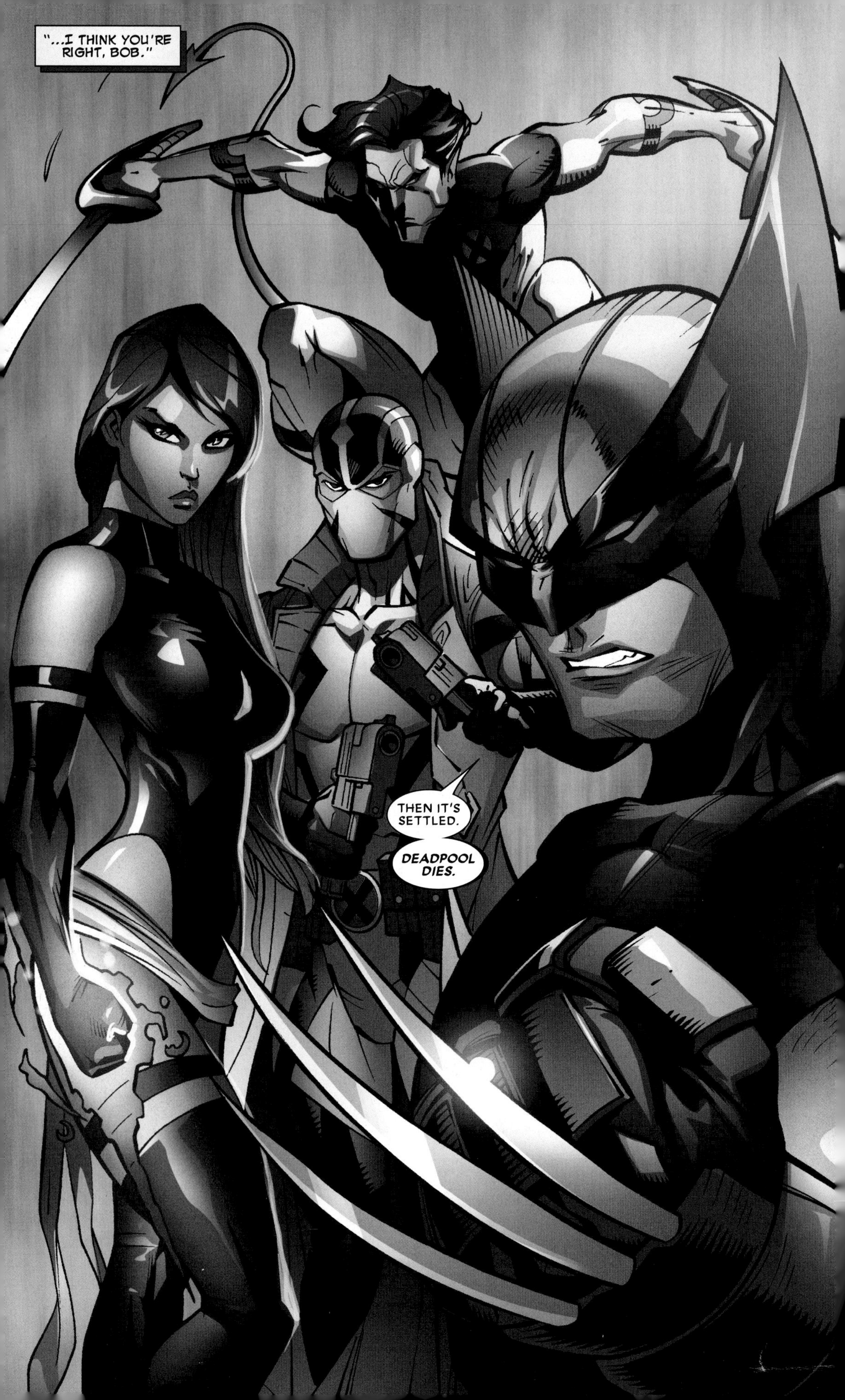
"...I THINK YOU'RE RIGHT, BOB."
THEN IT'S SETTLED.
DEADPOOL DIES.

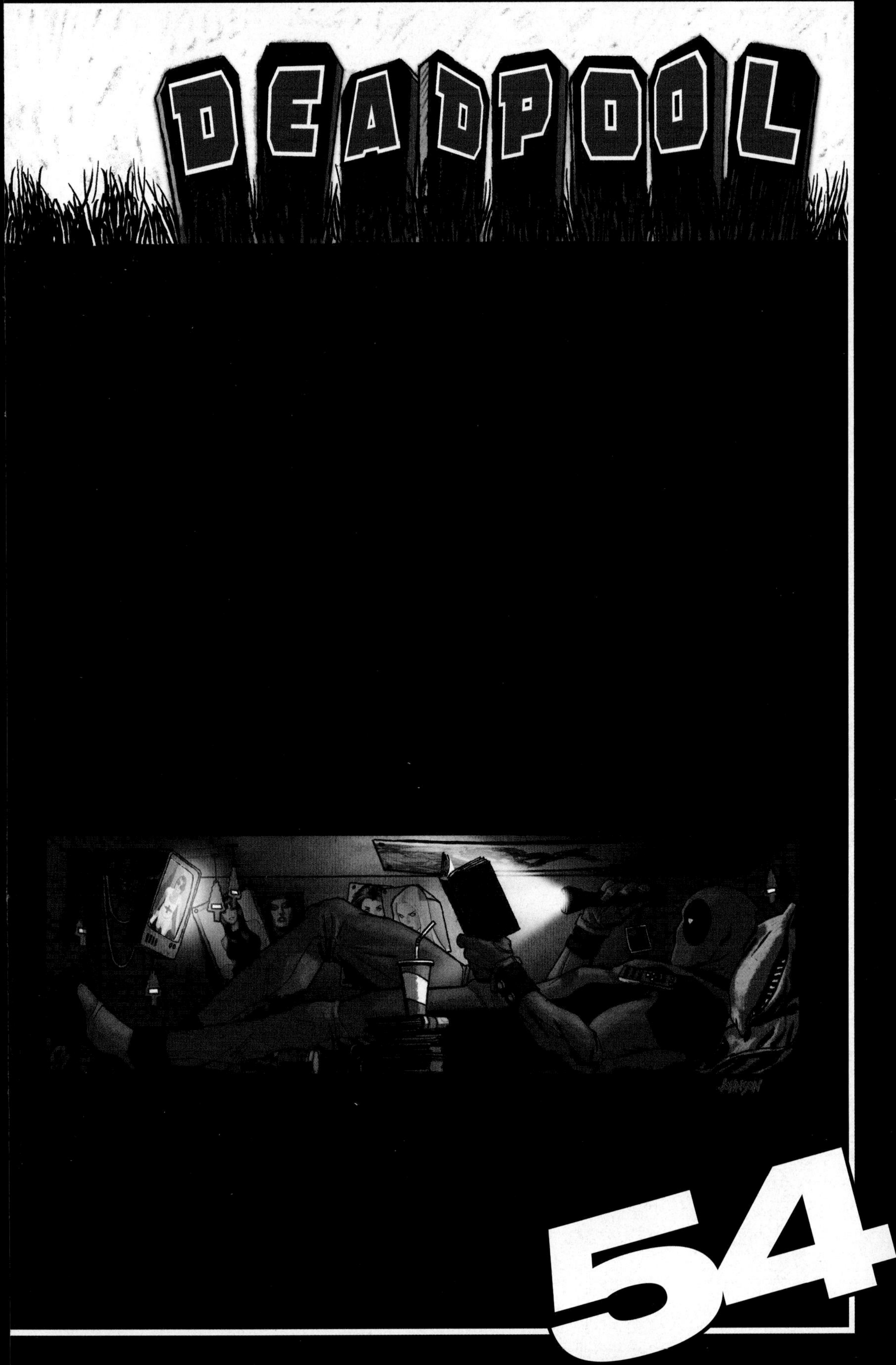
DEADPOOL
54

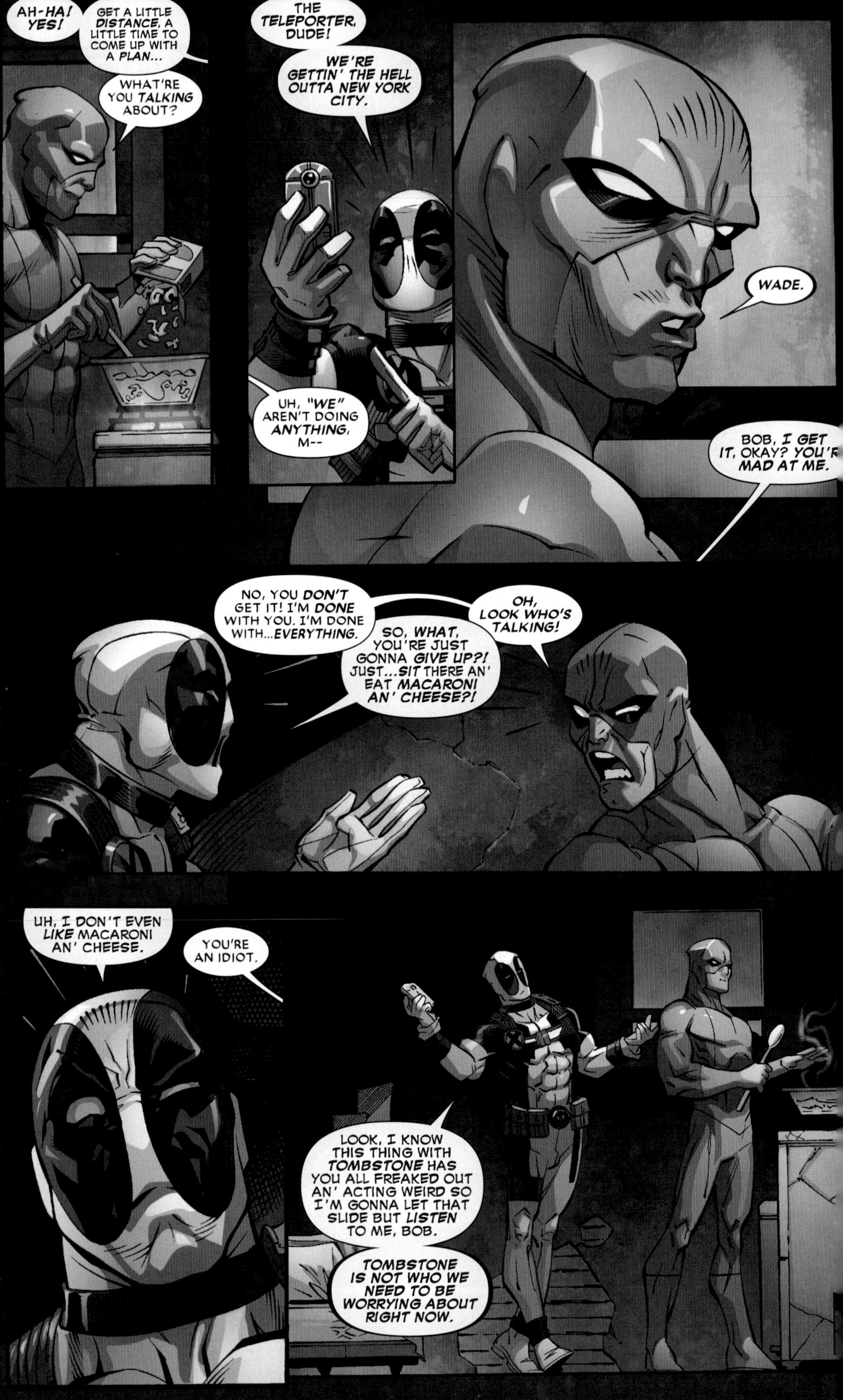
AH-HA! YES!
GET A LITTLE DISTANCE, A LITTLE TIME TO COME UP WITH A PLAN...
WHAT'RE YOU TALKING ABOUT?
THE TELEPORTER, DUDE!
WE'RE GETTIN' THE HELL OUTTA NEW YORK CITY.
UH, "WE" AREN'T DOING ANYTHING, M--
WADE.
BOB, I GET IT, OKAY? YOU'R MAD AT ME.
NO, YOU DON'T GET IT! I'M DONE WITH YOU. I'M DONE WITH...EVERYTHING.
OH, LOOK WHO'S TALKING!
SO, WHAT, YOU'RE JUST GONNA GIVE UP?! JUST...SIT THERE AN' EAT MACARONI AN' CHEESE?!
UH, I DON'T EVEN LIKE MACARONI AN' CHEESE.
YOU'RE AN IDIOT.
LOOK, I KNOW THIS THING WITH TOMBSTONE HAS YOU ALL FREAKED OUT AN' ACTING WEIRD SO I'M GONNA LET THAT SLIDE BUT LISTEN TO ME, BOB.
TOMBSTONE IS NOT WHO WE NEED TO BE WORRYING ABOUT RIGHT NOW.

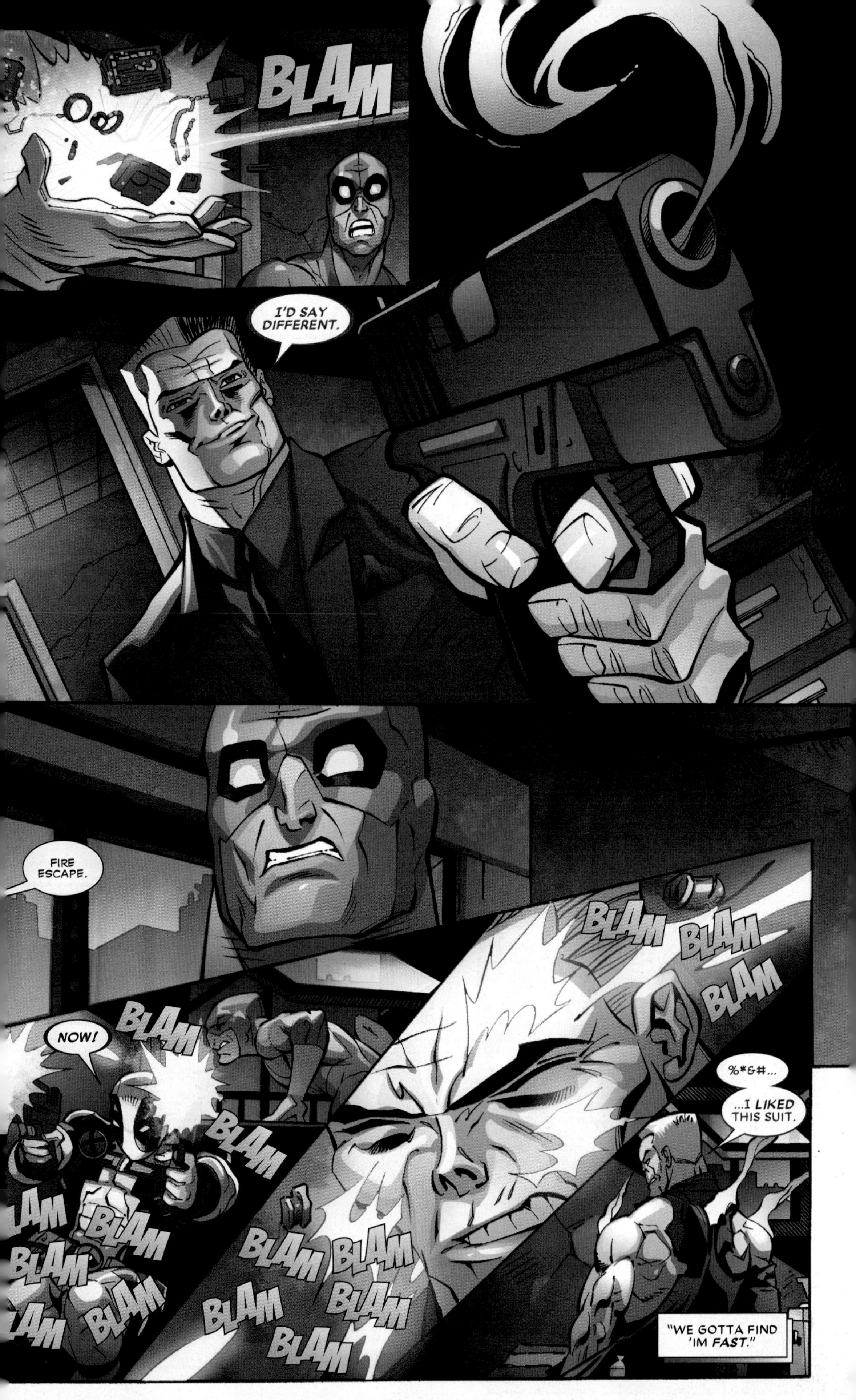
BLAM
I'D SAY DIFFERENT.
FIRE ESCAPE.
NOW!
BLAM
BLAM
BLAM
BLAM
BLAM
BLAM
BLAM
BLAM
BLAM
BLAM
BLAM
BLAM
BLAM
%*&#...
...I LIKED THIS SUIT.
"WE GOTTA FIND 'IM FAST."

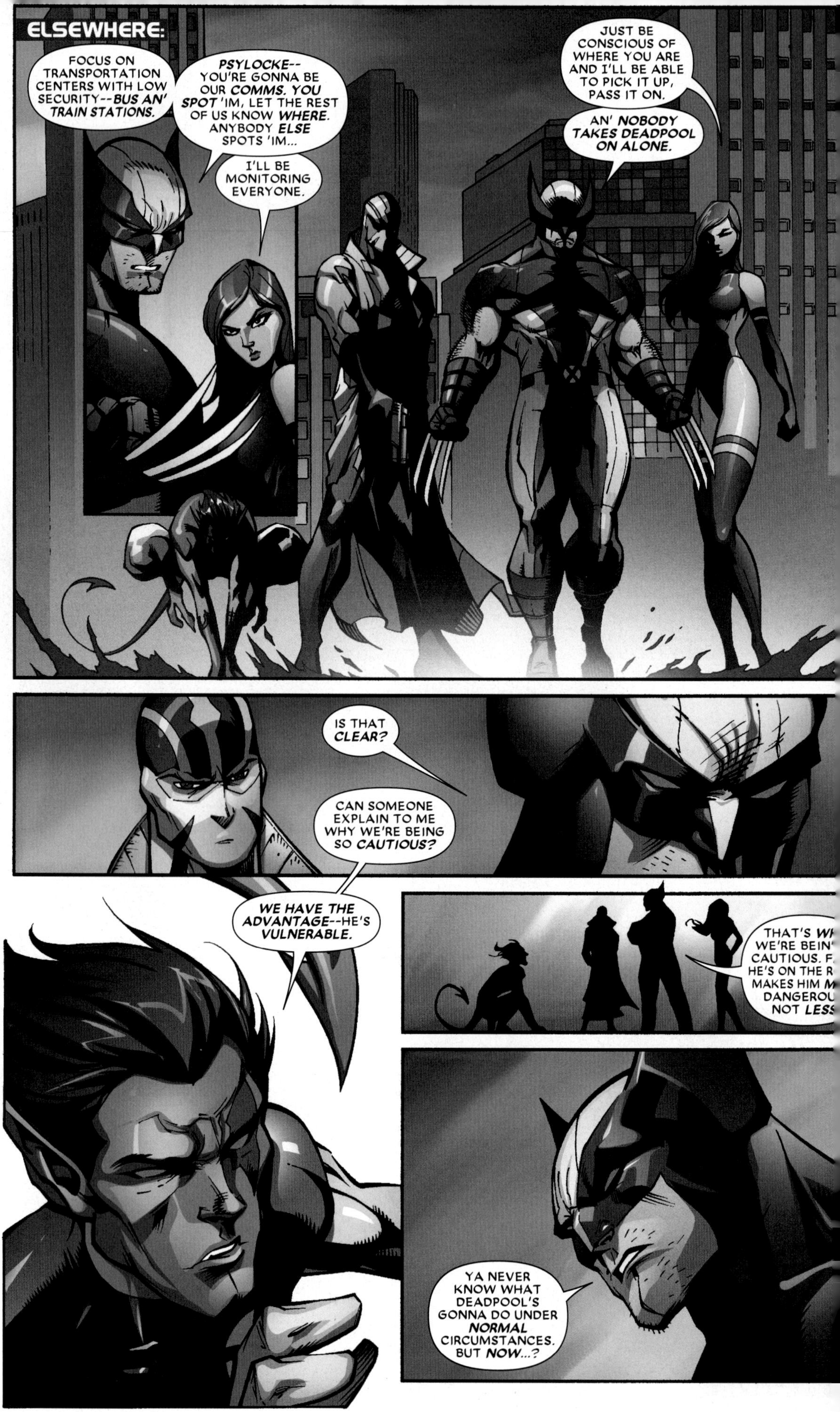
ELSEWHERE:
FOCUS ON TRANSPORTATION CENTERS WITH LOW SECURITY--BUS AN' TRAIN STATIONS.
PSYLOCKE--YOU'RE GONNA BE OUR COMMS. YOU SPOT 'IM, LET THE REST OF US KNOW WHERE. ANYBODY ELSE SPOTS 'IM...
I'LL BE MONITORING EVERYONE.
JUST BE CONSCIOUS OF WHERE YOU ARE AND I'LL BE ABLE TO PICK IT UP, PASS IT ON.
AN' NOBODY TAKES DEADPOOL ON ALONE.
IS THAT CLEAR?
CAN SOMEONE EXPLAIN TO ME WHY WE'RE BEING SO CAUTIOUS?
WE HAVE THE ADVANTAGE--HE'S VULNERABLE.
YA NEVER KNOW WHAT DEADPOOL'S GONNA DO UNDER NORMAL CIRCUMSTANCES. BUT NOW...?

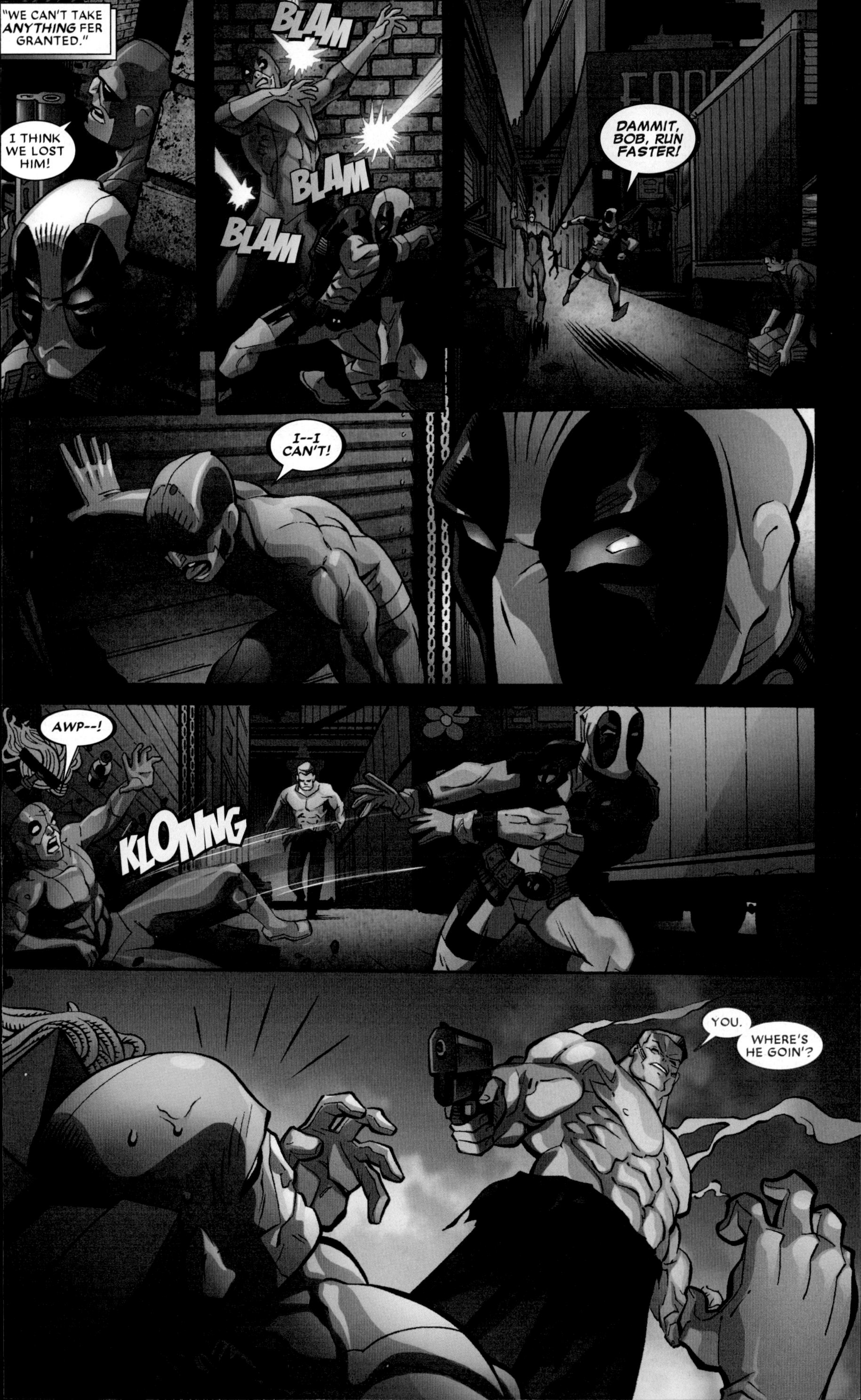
"WE CAN'T TAKE ANYTHING FER GRANTED."
I THINK WE LOST HIM!
BLAM
BLAM
BLAM
DAMMIT, BOB, RUN FASTER!
I--I CAN'T!
AWP--!
KLONNG
YOU.
WHERE'S HE GOIN'?

NOT GONNA...*HHH*... TELL YOU...

DID WHAT YOU WANTED... *HHH*

NOT GONNA DO ANYTHING... *HHH*...ELSE...

GOT A *POINT*, THERE-- YA *DID* DO WHAT I WANTED.

MAKES YA PRETTY DAMN *USELESS* T'ME NOW, DON'T IT?

VRRRRRMM

HON HON

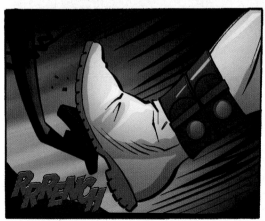

RRRENCH

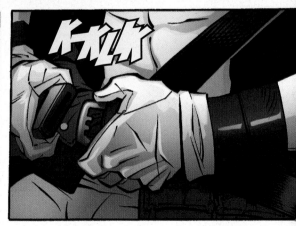

K-KLK

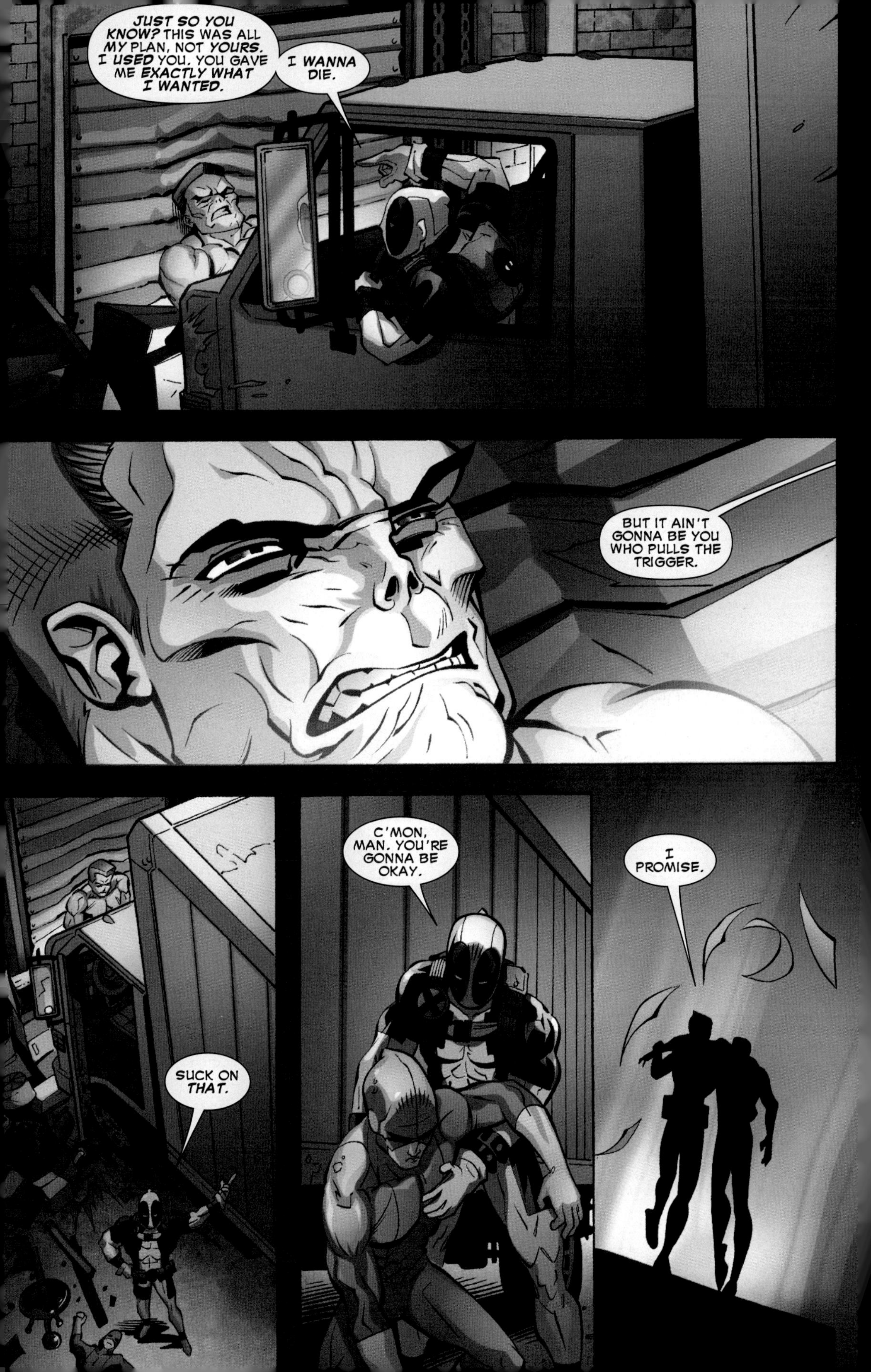
JUST SO YOU KNOW? THIS WAS ALL MY PLAN, NOT YOURS. I USED YOU. YOU GAVE ME EXACTLY WHAT I WANTED.
I WANNA DIE.
BUT IT AIN'T GONNA BE YOU WHO PULLS THE TRIGGER.
SUCK ON THAT.
C'MON, MAN. YOU'RE GONNA BE OKAY.
I PROMISE.

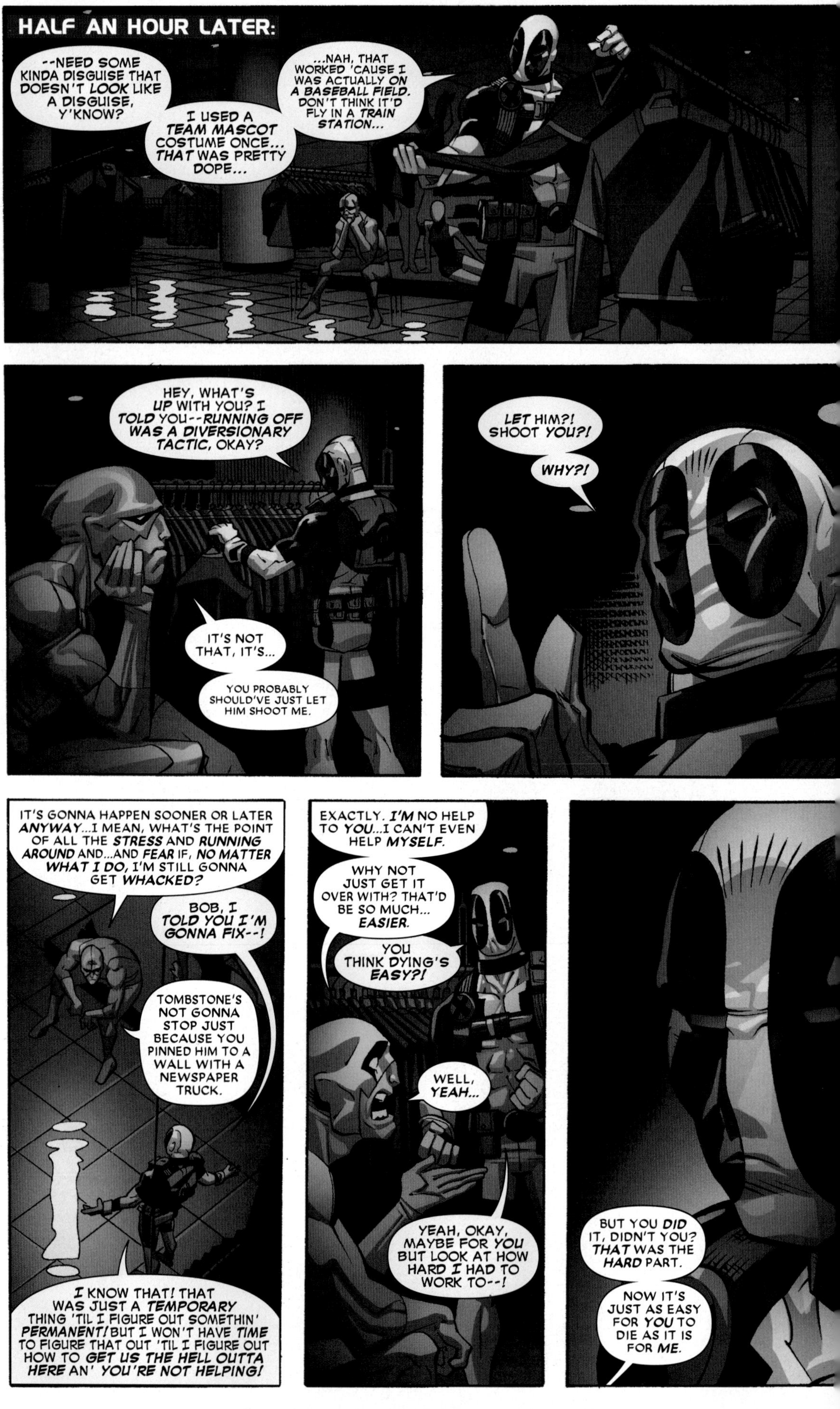
HALF AN HOUR LATER:
--NEED SOME KINDA DISGUISE THAT DOESN'T LOOK LIKE A DISGUISE, Y'KNOW?
I USED A TEAM MASCOT COSTUME ONCE... THAT WAS PRETTY DOPE...
...NAH, THAT WORKED 'CAUSE I WAS ACTUALLY ON A BASEBALL FIELD. DON'T THINK IT'D FLY IN A TRAIN STATION...
HEY, WHAT'S UP WITH YOU? I TOLD YOU--RUNNING OFF WAS A DIVERSIONARY TACTIC, OKAY?
IT'S NOT THAT, IT'S...
YOU PROBABLY SHOULD'VE JUST LET HIM SHOOT ME.
LET HIM?! SHOOT YOU?!
WHY?!
IT'S GONNA HAPPEN SOONER OR LATER ANYWAY...I MEAN, WHAT'S THE POINT OF ALL THE STRESS AND RUNNING AROUND AND...AND FEAR IF, NO MATTER WHAT I DO, I'M STILL GONNA GET WHACKED?
BOB, I TOLD YOU I'M GONNA FIX--!
TOMBSTONE'S NOT GONNA STOP JUST BECAUSE YOU PINNED HIM TO A WALL WITH A NEWSPAPER TRUCK.
I KNOW THAT! THAT WAS JUST A TEMPORARY THING 'TIL I FIGURE OUT SOMETHIN' PERMANENT! BUT I WON'T HAVE TIME TO FIGURE THAT OUT 'TIL I FIGURE OUT HOW TO GET US THE HELL OUTTA HERE AN' YOU'RE NOT HELPING!
EXACTLY. I'M NO HELP TO YOU...I CAN'T EVEN HELP MYSELF.
WHY NOT JUST GET IT OVER WITH? THAT'D BE SO MUCH... EASIER.
YOU THINK DYING'S EASY?!
WELL, YEAH...
YEAH, OKAY, MAYBE FOR YOU BUT LOOK AT HOW HARD I HAD TO WORK TO--!
BUT YOU DID IT, DIDN'T YOU? THAT WAS THE HARD PART.
NOW IT'S JUST AS EASY FOR YOU TO DIE AS IT IS FOR ME.

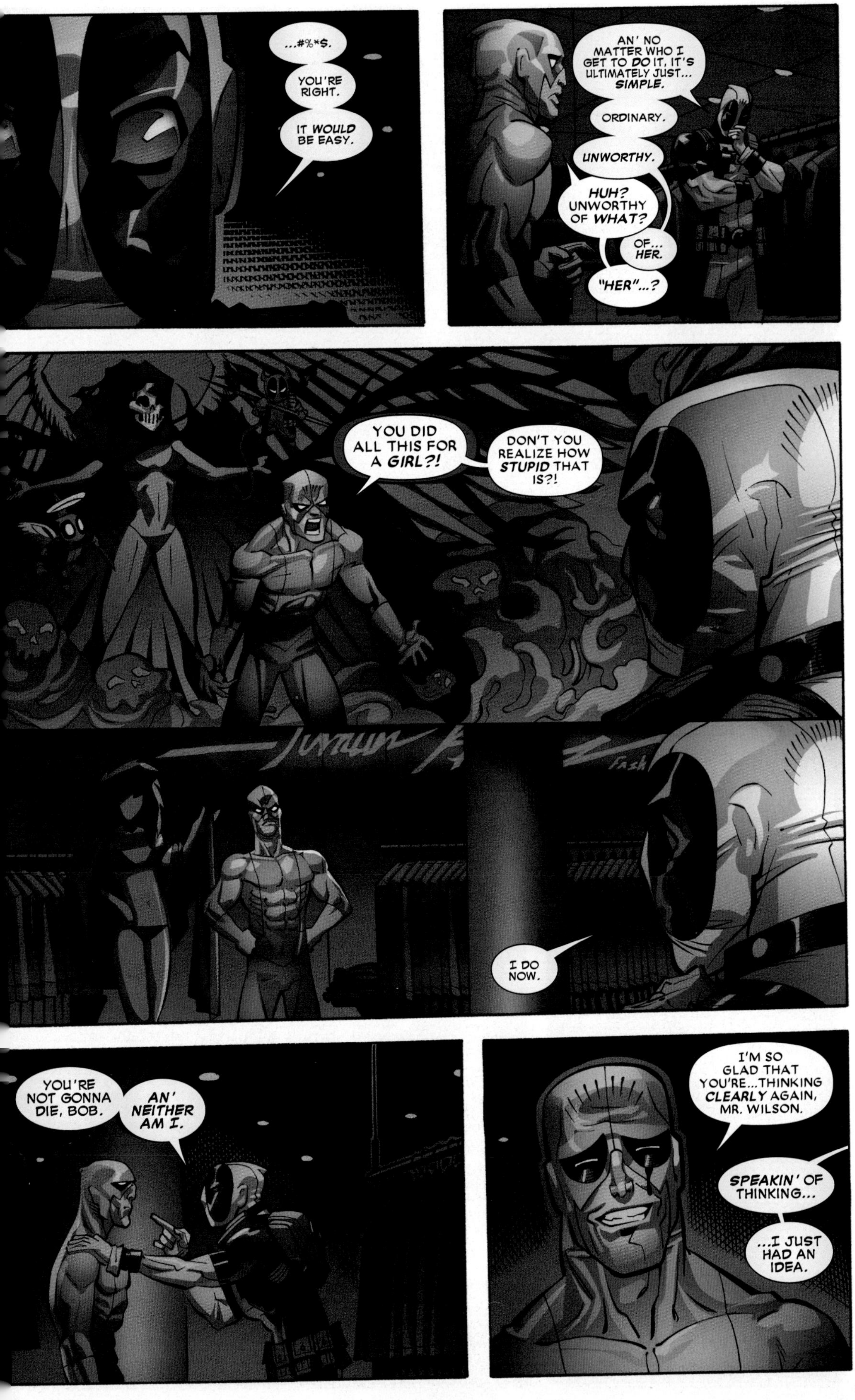
...#%*$.
YOU'RE RIGHT.
IT WOULD BE EASY.
AN' NO MATTER WHO I GET TO DO IT, IT'S ULTIMATELY JUST... SIMPLE.
ORDINARY.
UNWORTHY.
HUH? UNWORTHY OF WHAT?
OF... HER.
"HER"...?
YOU DID ALL THIS FOR A GIRL?!
DON'T YOU REALIZE HOW STUPID THAT IS?!
I DO NOW.
YOU'RE NOT GONNA DIE, BOB.
AN' NEITHER AM I.
I'M SO GLAD THAT YOU'RE...THINKING CLEARLY AGAIN, MR. WILSON.
SPEAKIN' OF THINKING...
...I JUST HAD AN IDEA.

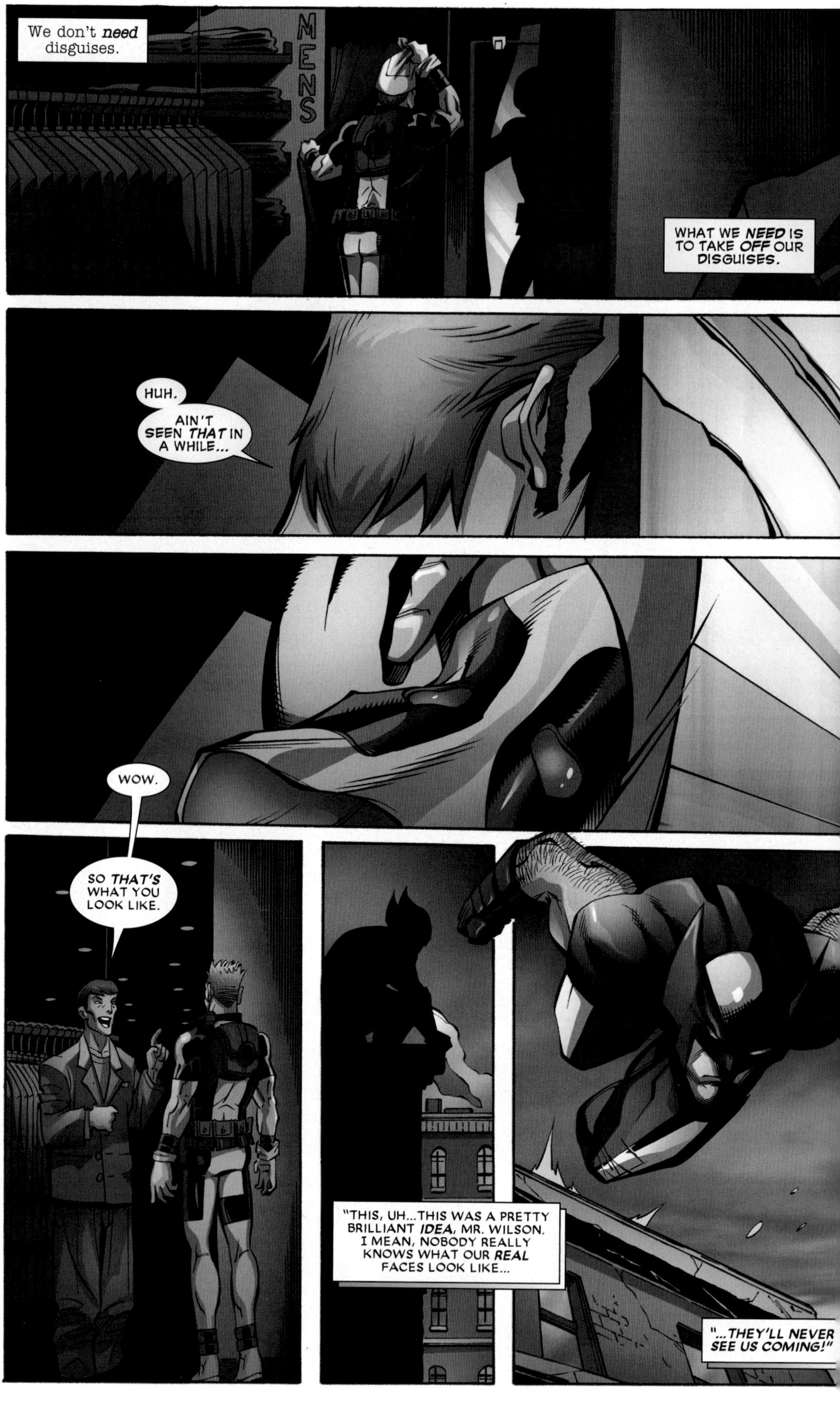
We don't **need** disguises.
WHAT WE **NEED** IS TO TAKE **OFF** OUR DISGUISES.
HUH.
AIN'T SEEN **THAT** IN A WHILE...
WOW.
SO **THAT'S** WHAT YOU LOOK LIKE.
"THIS, UH...THIS WAS A PRETTY BRILLIANT **IDEA**, MR. WILSON. I MEAN, NOBODY REALLY KNOWS WHAT OUR **REAL** FACES LOOK LIKE...
"...THEY'LL NEVER SEE US COMING!"

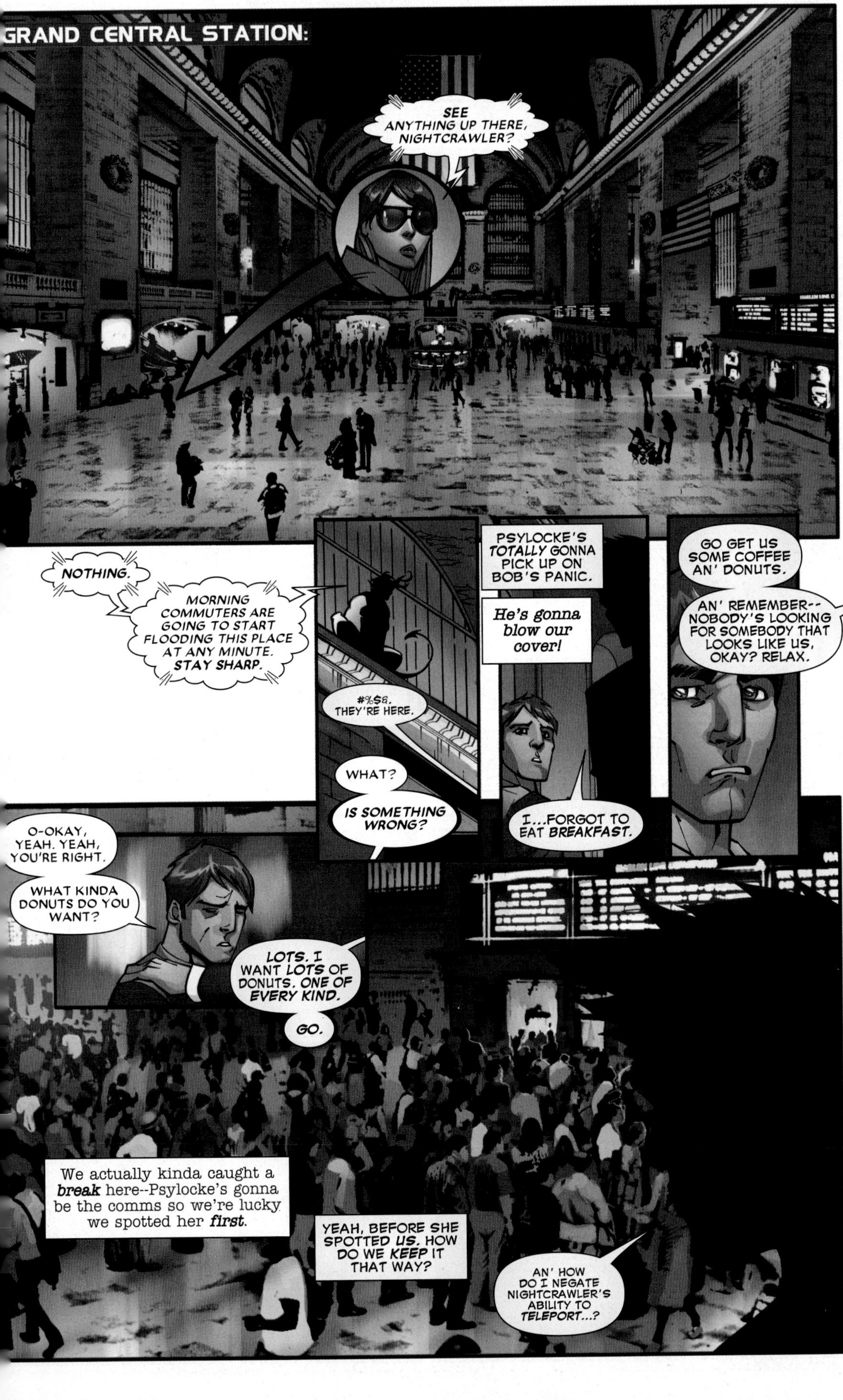
GRAND CENTRAL STATION:
SEE ANYTHING UP THERE, NIGHTCRAWLER?
NOTHING.
MORNING COMMUTERS ARE GOING TO START FLOODING THIS PLACE AT ANY MINUTE. STAY SHARP.
#%$&. THEY'RE HERE.
WHAT?
IS SOMETHING WRONG?
PSYLOCKE'S TOTALLY GONNA PICK UP ON BOB'S PANIC.
He's gonna blow our cover!
I...FORGOT TO EAT BREAKFAST.
GO GET US SOME COFFEE AN' DONUTS.
AN' REMEMBER--NOBODY'S LOOKING FOR SOMEBODY THAT LOOKS LIKE US, OKAY? RELAX.
O-OKAY, YEAH. YEAH, YOU'RE RIGHT.
WHAT KINDA DONUTS DO YOU WANT?
LOTS. I WANT LOTS OF DONUTS. ONE OF EVERY KIND.
GO.
We actually kinda caught a break here--Psylocke's gonna be the comms so we're lucky we spotted her first.
YEAH, BEFORE SHE SPOTTED US. HOW DO WE KEEP IT THAT WAY?
AN' HOW DO I NEGATE NIGHTCRAWLER'S ABILITY TO TELEPORT...?

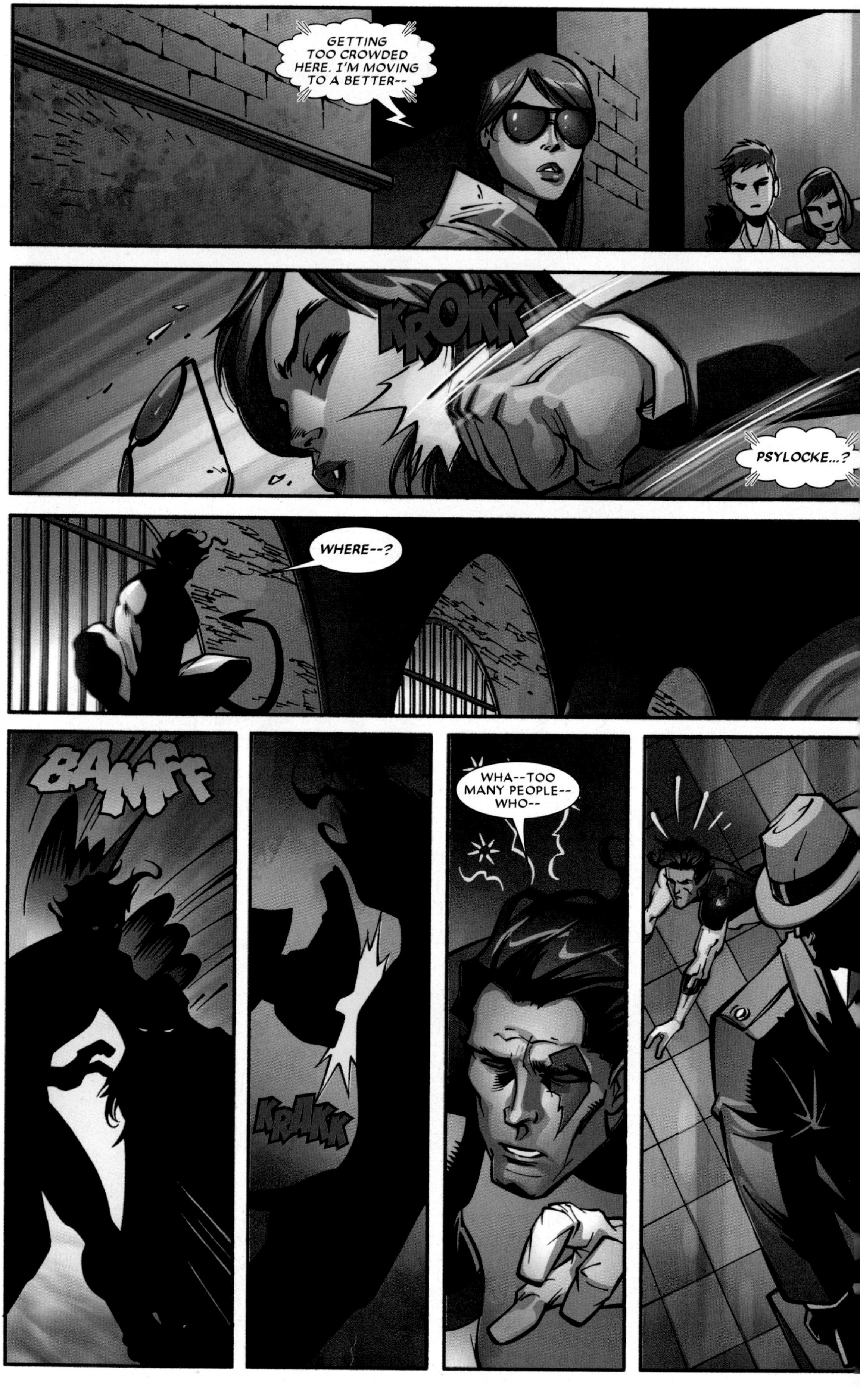
GETTING TOO CROWDED HERE. I'M MOVING TO A BETTER--
KROKK
PSYLOCKE...?
WHERE--?
BAMFF
KRAKK
WHA--TOO MANY PEOPLE-- WHO--

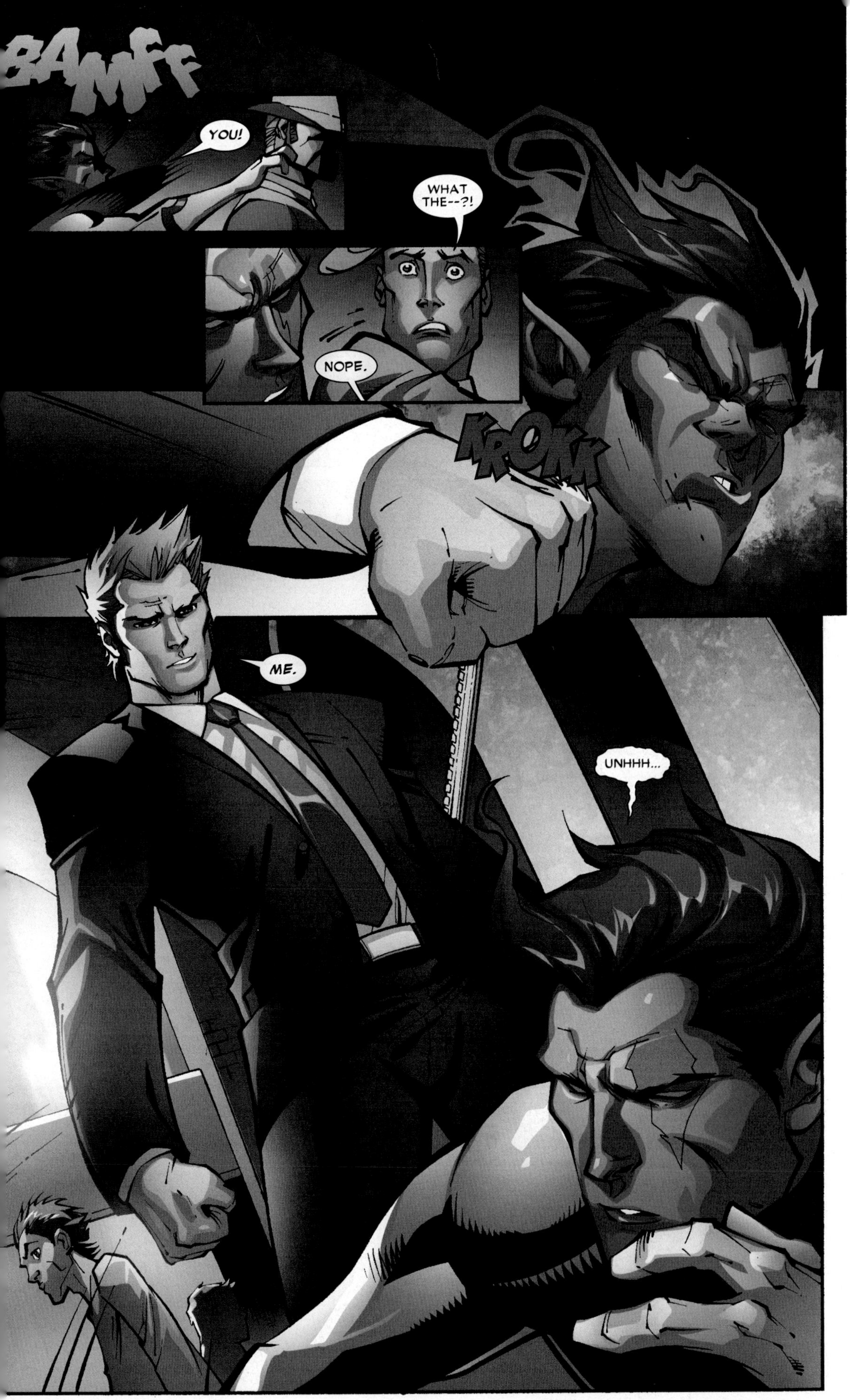
BAMFF
YOU!
WHAT THE--?!
NOPE.
KROKK
ME.
UNHHH...

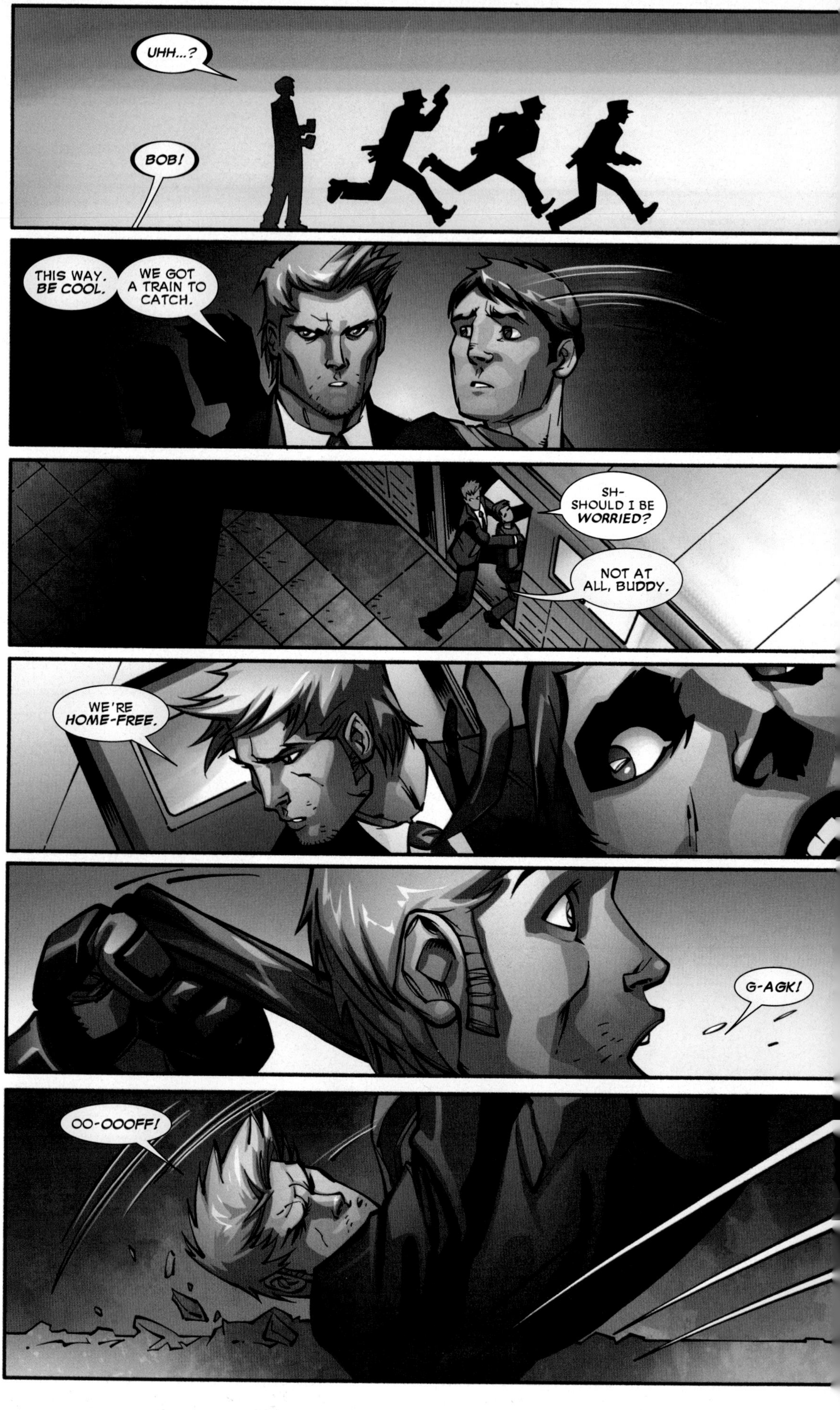
UHH...?
BOB!
THIS WAY. BE COOL.
WE GOT A TRAIN TO CATCH.
SH-SHOULD I BE WORRIED?
NOT AT ALL, BUDDY.
WE'RE HOME-FREE.
G-AGK!
OO-OOOFF!

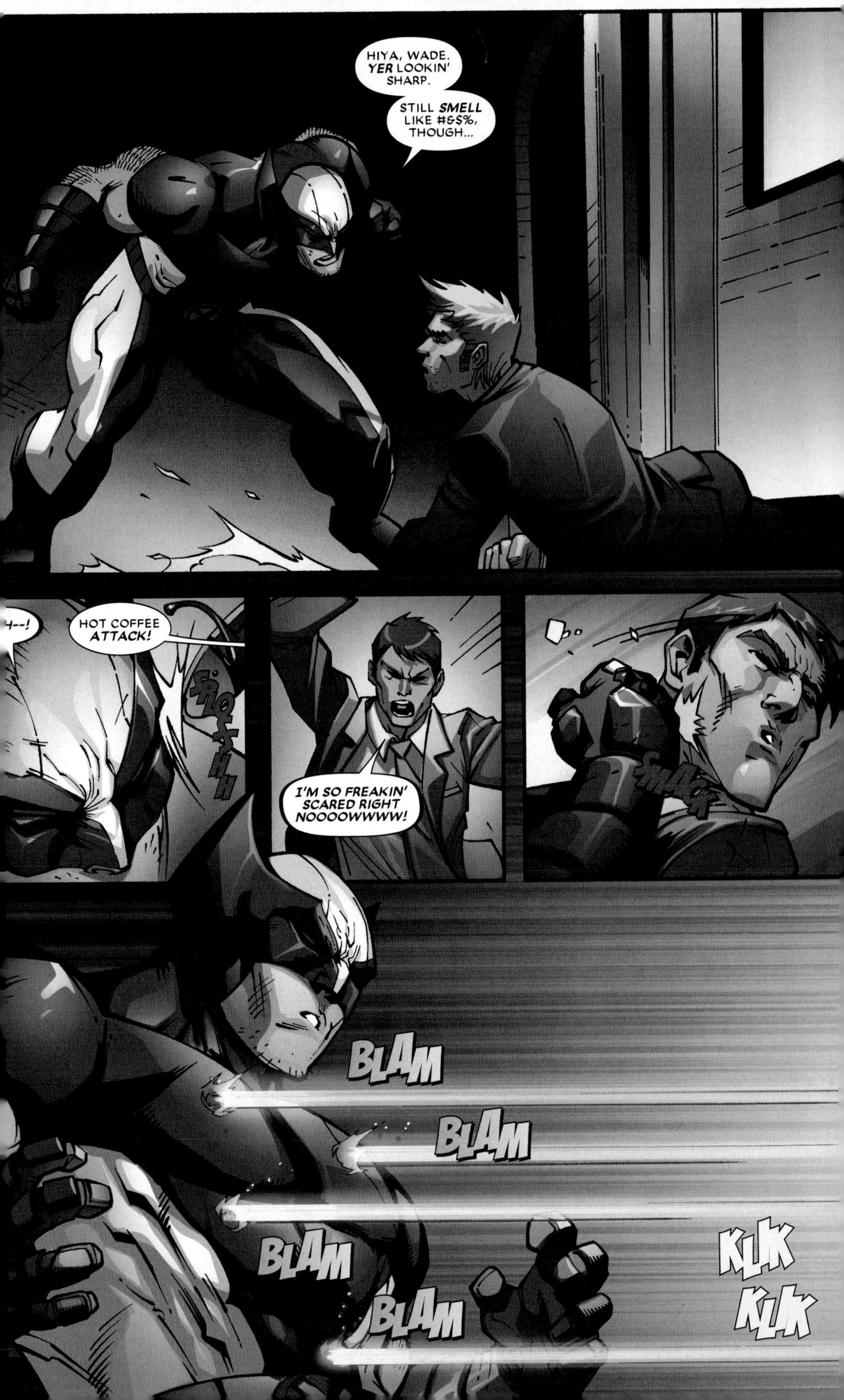

HIYA, WADE. YER LOOKIN' SHARP.
STILL SMELL LIKE #&$%, THOUGH...
HOT COFFEE ATTACK!
SPLOOSHHH
I'M SO FREAKIN' SCARED RIGHT NOOOOWWWW!
SMACK
BLAM
BLAM
BLAM
BLAM
KLIK
KLIK

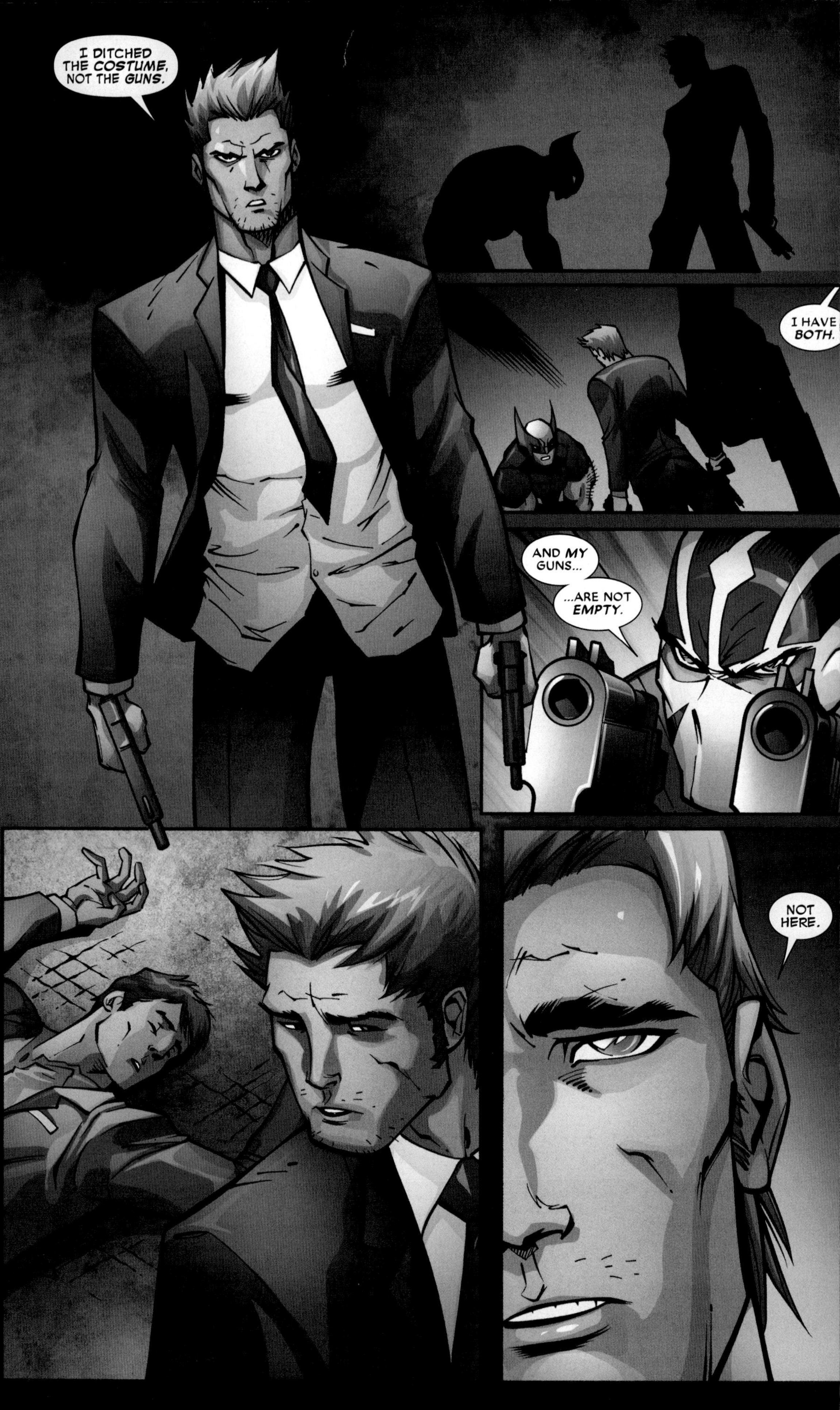
I DITCHED THE COSTUME, NOT THE GUNS.
I HAVE BOTH.
AND MY GUNS...
...ARE NOT EMPTY.
NOT HERE.

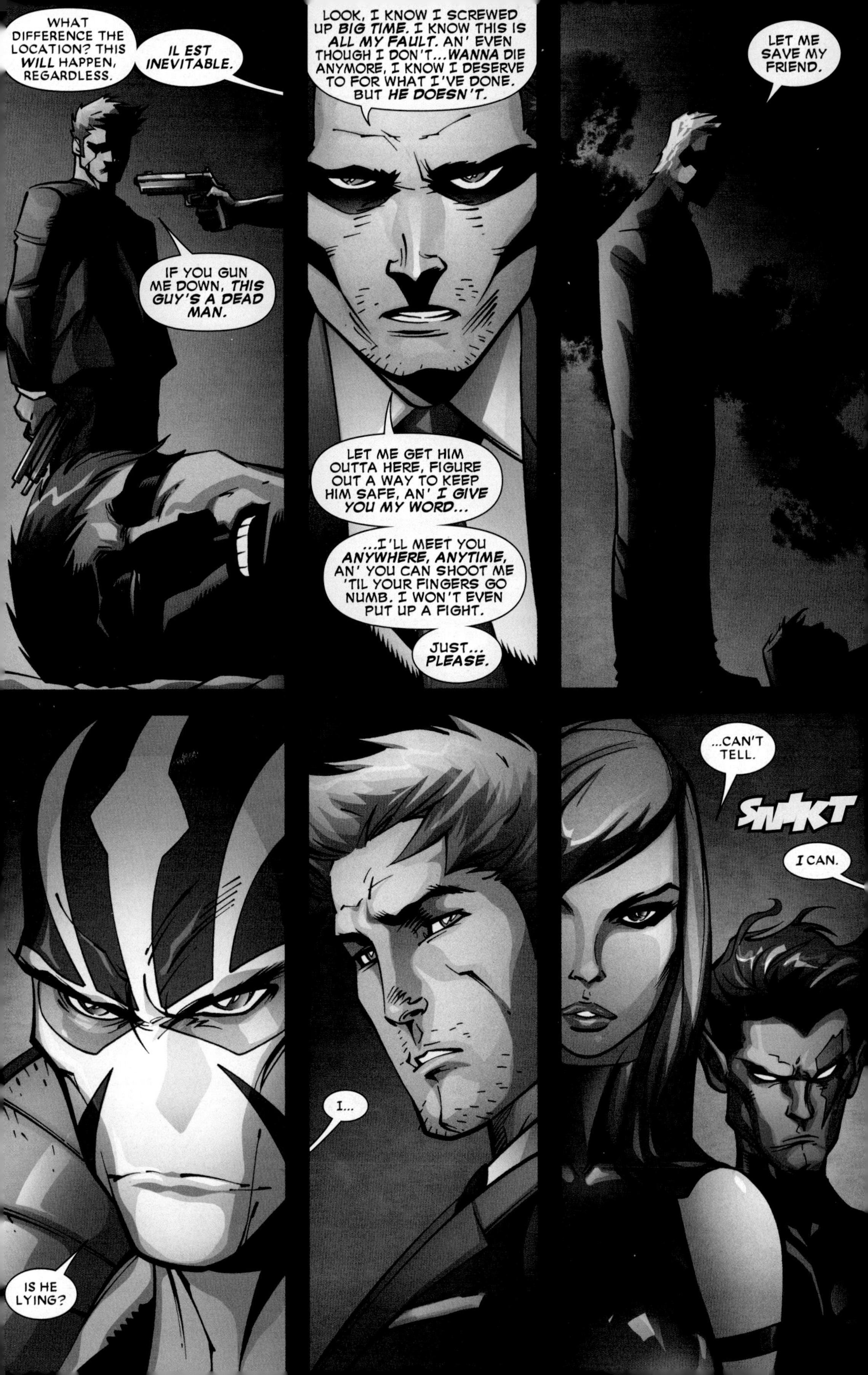
WHAT DIFFERENCE THE LOCATION? THIS WILL HAPPEN, REGARDLESS.
IL EST INEVITABLE.
IF YOU GUN ME DOWN, THIS GUY'S A DEAD MAN.
LOOK, I KNOW I SCREWED UP BIG TIME. I KNOW THIS IS ALL MY FAULT. AN' EVEN THOUGH I DON'T... WANNA DIE ANYMORE, I KNOW I DESERVE TO FOR WHAT I'VE DONE. BUT HE DOESN'T.
LET ME GET HIM OUTTA HERE, FIGURE OUT A WAY TO KEEP HIM SAFE, AN' I GIVE YOU MY WORD...
...I'LL MEET YOU ANYWHERE, ANYTIME, AN' YOU CAN SHOOT ME 'TIL YOUR FINGERS GO NUMB. I WON'T EVEN PUT UP A FIGHT.
JUST... PLEASE.
LET ME SAVE MY FRIEND.
IS HE LYING?
I...
...CAN'T TELL.
SNIKT
I CAN.

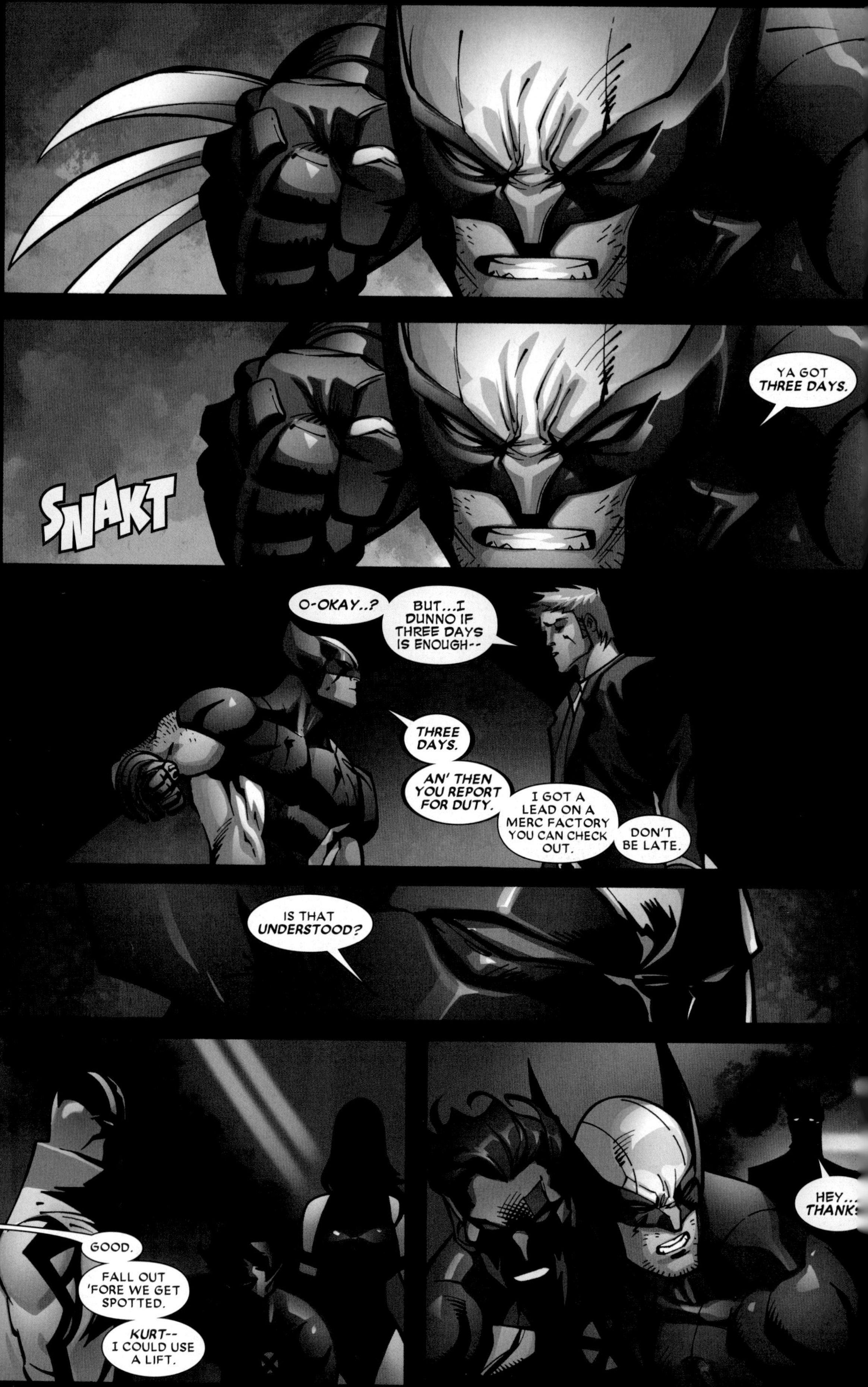
SNAKT
YA GOT THREE DAYS.
O-OKAY..?
BUT...I DUNNO IF THREE DAYS IS ENOUGH--
THREE DAYS.
AN' THEN YOU REPORT FOR DUTY.
I GOT A LEAD ON A MERC FACTORY YOU CAN CHECK OUT.
DON'T BE LATE.
IS THAT UNDERSTOOD?
GOOD.
FALL OUT 'FORE WE GET SPOTTED.
KURT-- I COULD USE A LIFT.
HEY...

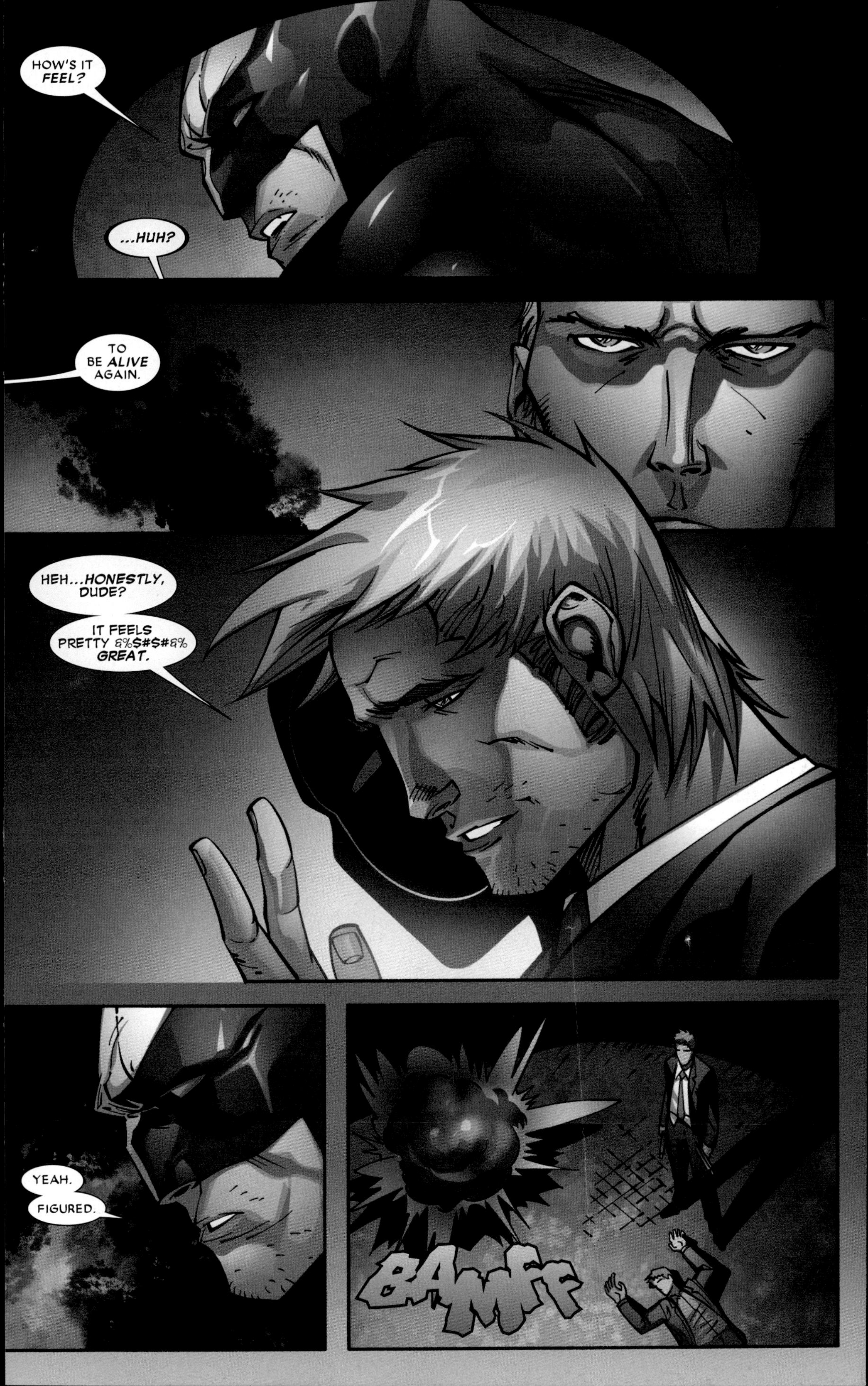
HOW'S IT FEEL?
...HUH?
TO BE ALIVE AGAIN.
HEH...HONESTLY, DUDE?
IT FEELS PRETTY &%$#$#&% GREAT.
YEAH.
FIGURED.
BAMFF

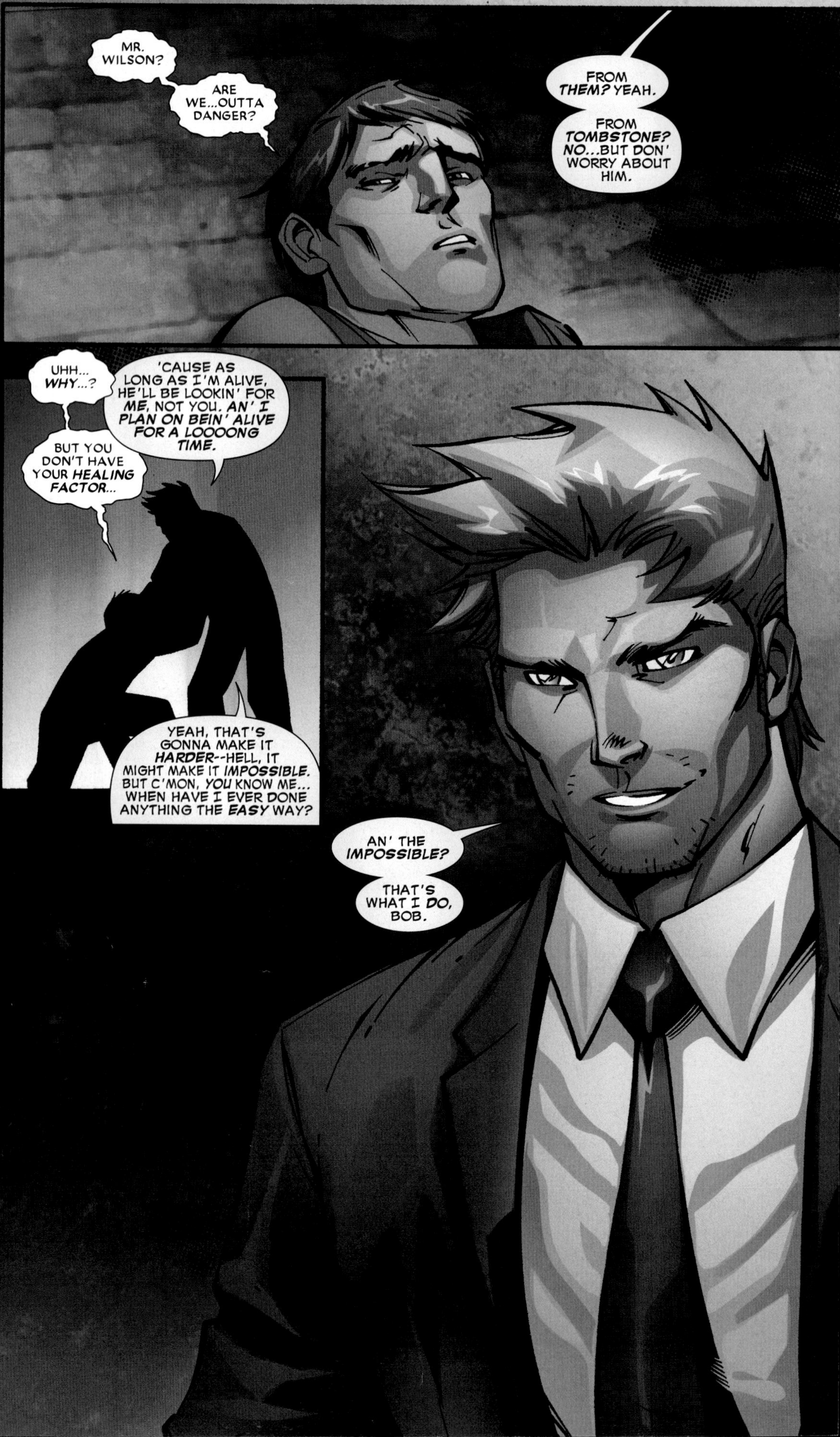
MR. WILSON?
ARE WE...OUTTA DANGER?
FROM THEM? YEAH.
FROM TOMBSTONE? NO...BUT DON' WORRY ABOUT HIM.
UHH... WHY...?
'CAUSE AS LONG AS I'M ALIVE, HE'LL BE LOOKIN' FOR ME, NOT YOU. AN' I PLAN ON BEIN' ALIVE FOR A LOOOONG TIME.
BUT YOU DON'T HAVE YOUR HEALING FACTOR...
YEAH, THAT'S GONNA MAKE IT HARDER--HELL, IT MIGHT MAKE IT IMPOSSIBLE. BUT C'MON, YOU KNOW ME... WHEN HAVE I EVER DONE ANYTHING THE EASY WAY?
AN' THE IMPOSSIBLE?
THAT'S WHAT I DO, BOB.

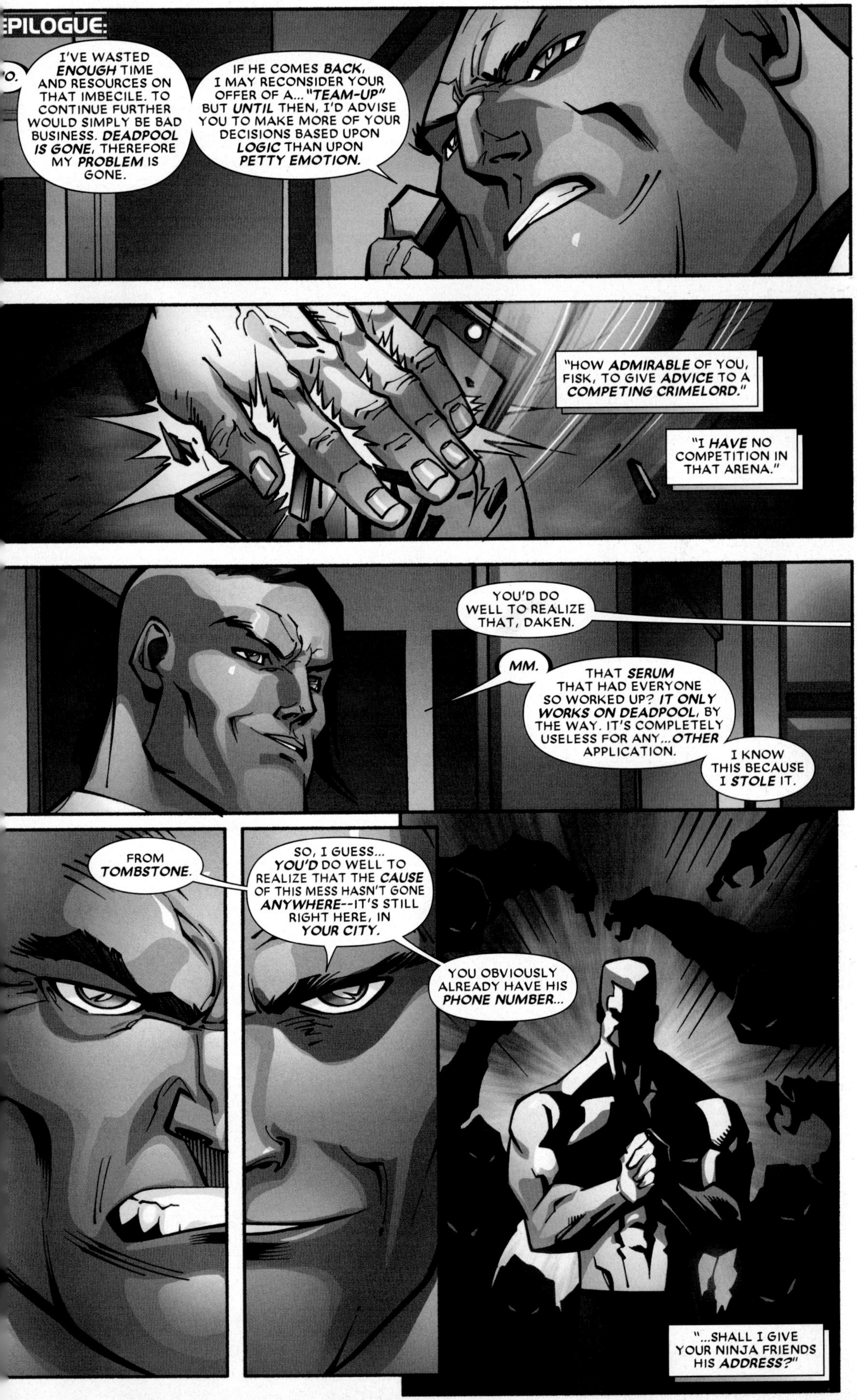
EPILOGUE:
I'VE WASTED ENOUGH TIME AND RESOURCES ON THAT IMBECILE. TO CONTINUE FURTHER WOULD SIMPLY BE BAD BUSINESS. DEADPOOL IS GONE, THEREFORE MY PROBLEM IS GONE.
IF HE COMES BACK, I MAY RECONSIDER YOUR OFFER OF A..."TEAM-UP" BUT UNTIL THEN, I'D ADVISE YOU TO MAKE MORE OF YOUR DECISIONS BASED UPON LOGIC THAN UPON PETTY EMOTION.
"HOW ADMIRABLE OF YOU, FISK, TO GIVE ADVICE TO A COMPETING CRIMELORD."
"I HAVE NO COMPETITION IN THAT ARENA."
YOU'D DO WELL TO REALIZE THAT, DAKEN.
MM.
THAT SERUM THAT HAD EVERYONE SO WORKED UP? IT ONLY WORKS ON DEADPOOL, BY THE WAY. IT'S COMPLETELY USELESS FOR ANY...OTHER APPLICATION.
I KNOW THIS BECAUSE I STOLE IT.
FROM TOMBSTONE.
SO, I GUESS... YOU'D DO WELL TO REALIZE THAT THE CAUSE OF THIS MESS HASN'T GONE ANYWHERE--IT'S STILL RIGHT HERE, IN YOUR CITY.
YOU OBVIOUSLY ALREADY HAVE HIS PHONE NUMBER...
"...SHALL I GIVE YOUR NINJA FRIENDS HIS ADDRESS?"

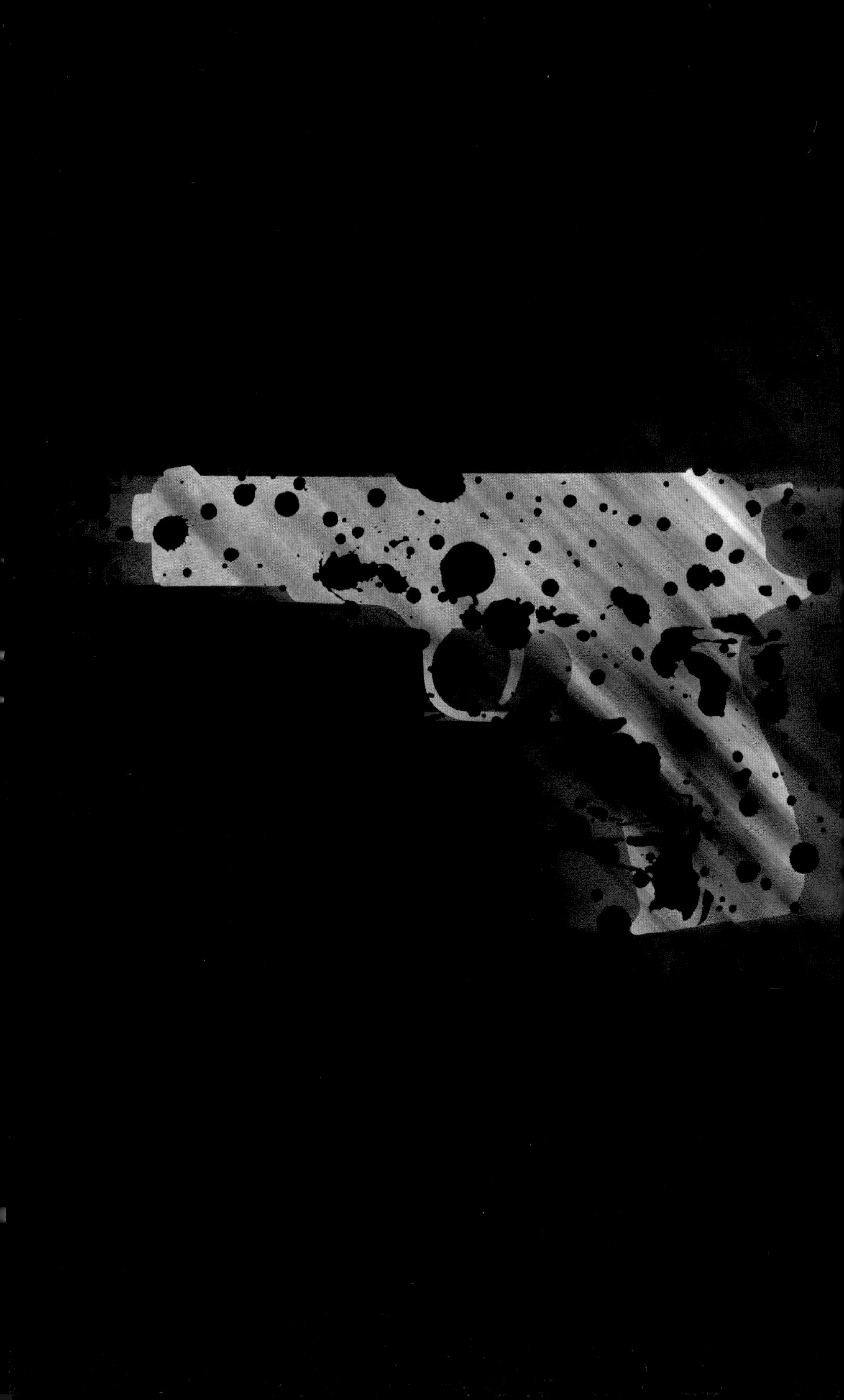

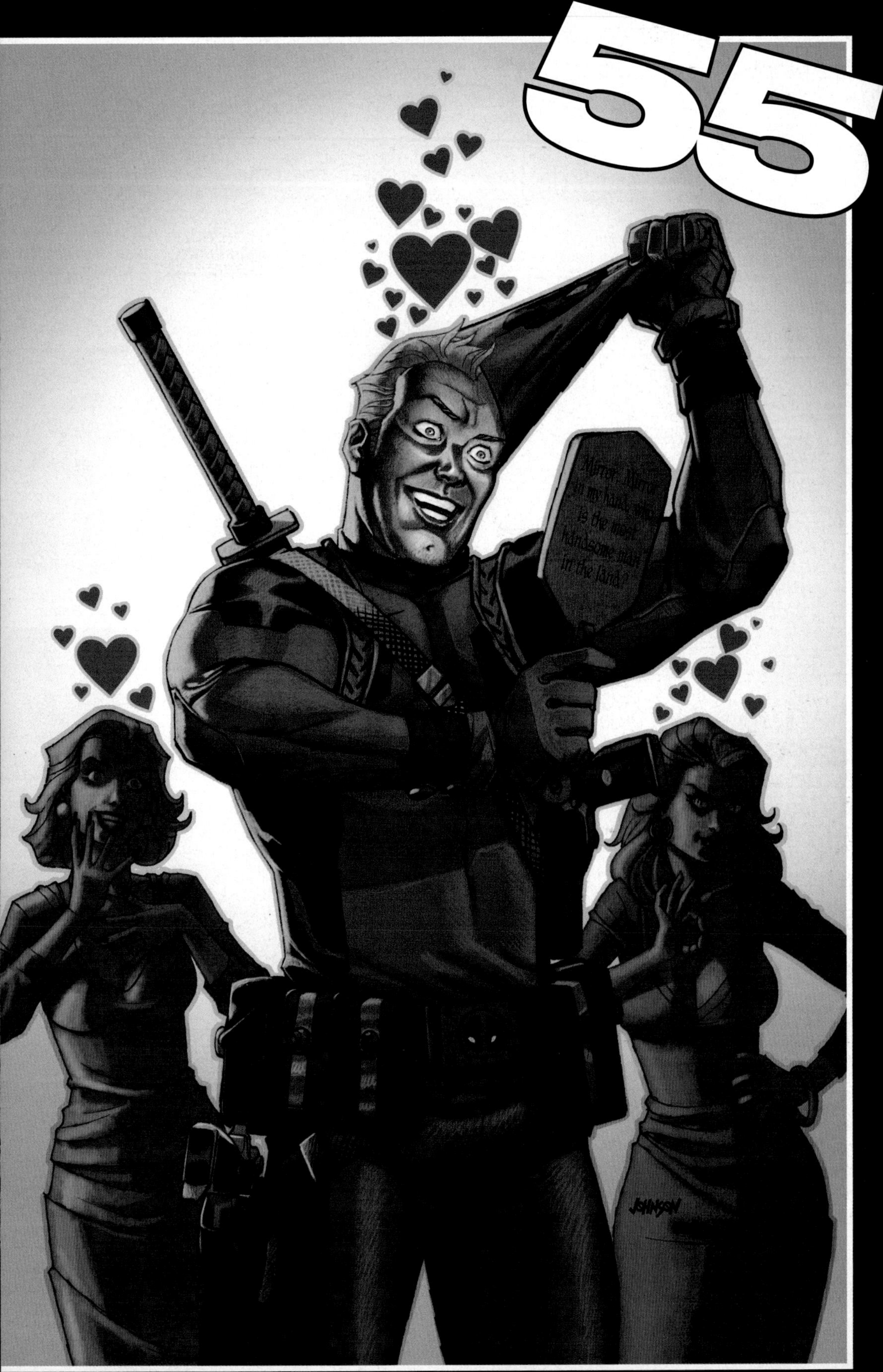
55
Mirror, Mirror in my hand, who is the most handsome man in the land?
JOHNSON

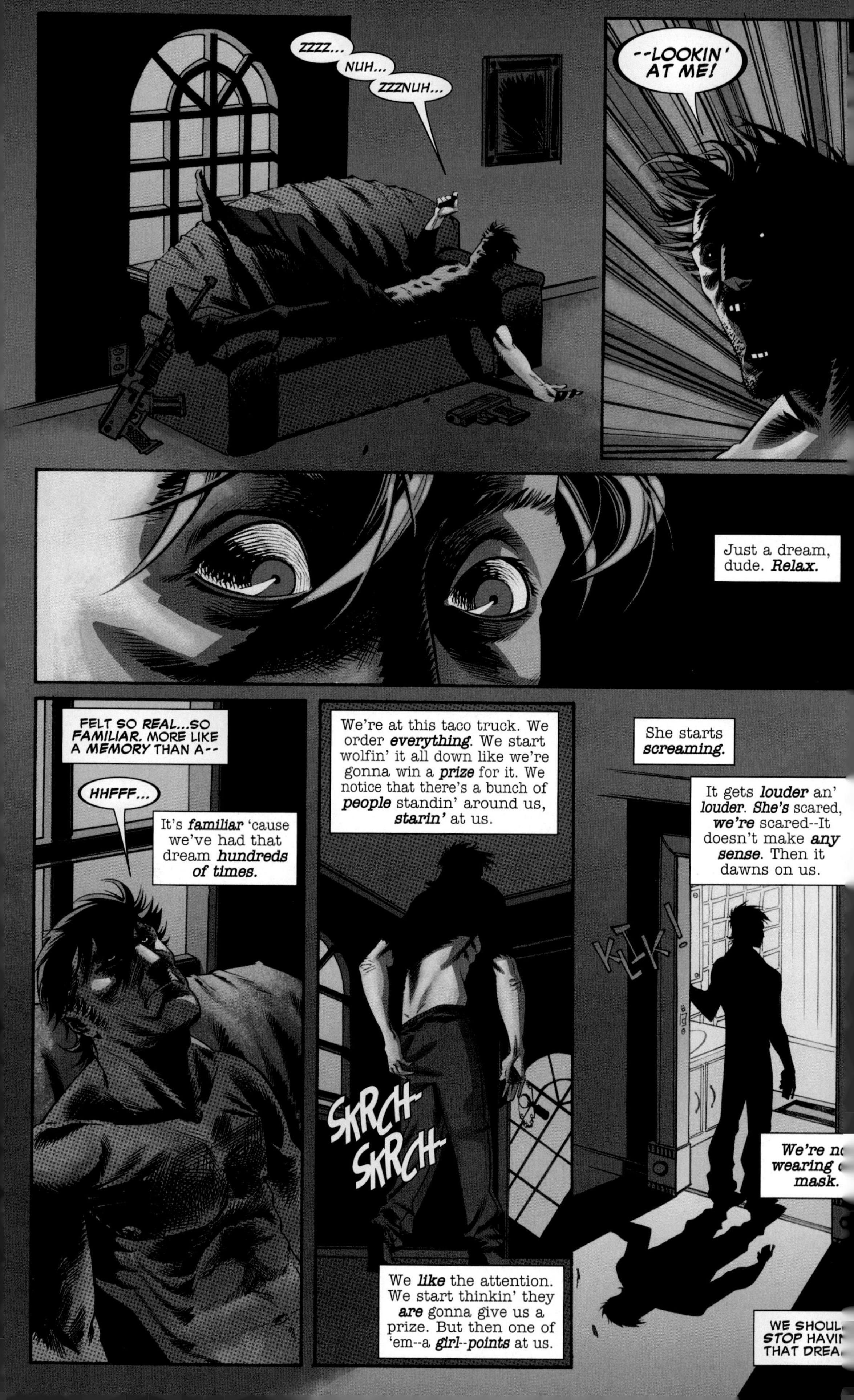
ZZZZ... NUH... ZZZNUH...
--LOOKIN' AT ME!
Just a dream, dude. Relax.
FELT SO REAL...SO FAMILIAR. MORE LIKE A MEMORY THAN A--
HHFFF...
It's familiar 'cause we've had that dream hundreds of times.
We're at this taco truck. We order everything. We start wolfin' it all down like we're gonna win a prize for it. We notice that there's a bunch of people standin' around us, starin' at us.
SKRCH SKRCH
We like the attention. We start thinkin' they are gonna give us a prize. But then one of 'em--a girl--points at us.
She starts screaming.
It gets louder an' louder. She's scared, we're scared--It doesn't make any sense. Then it dawns on us.
KLIK!
We're n wearing mask.
WE SHOUL STOP HAVIN THAT DREA

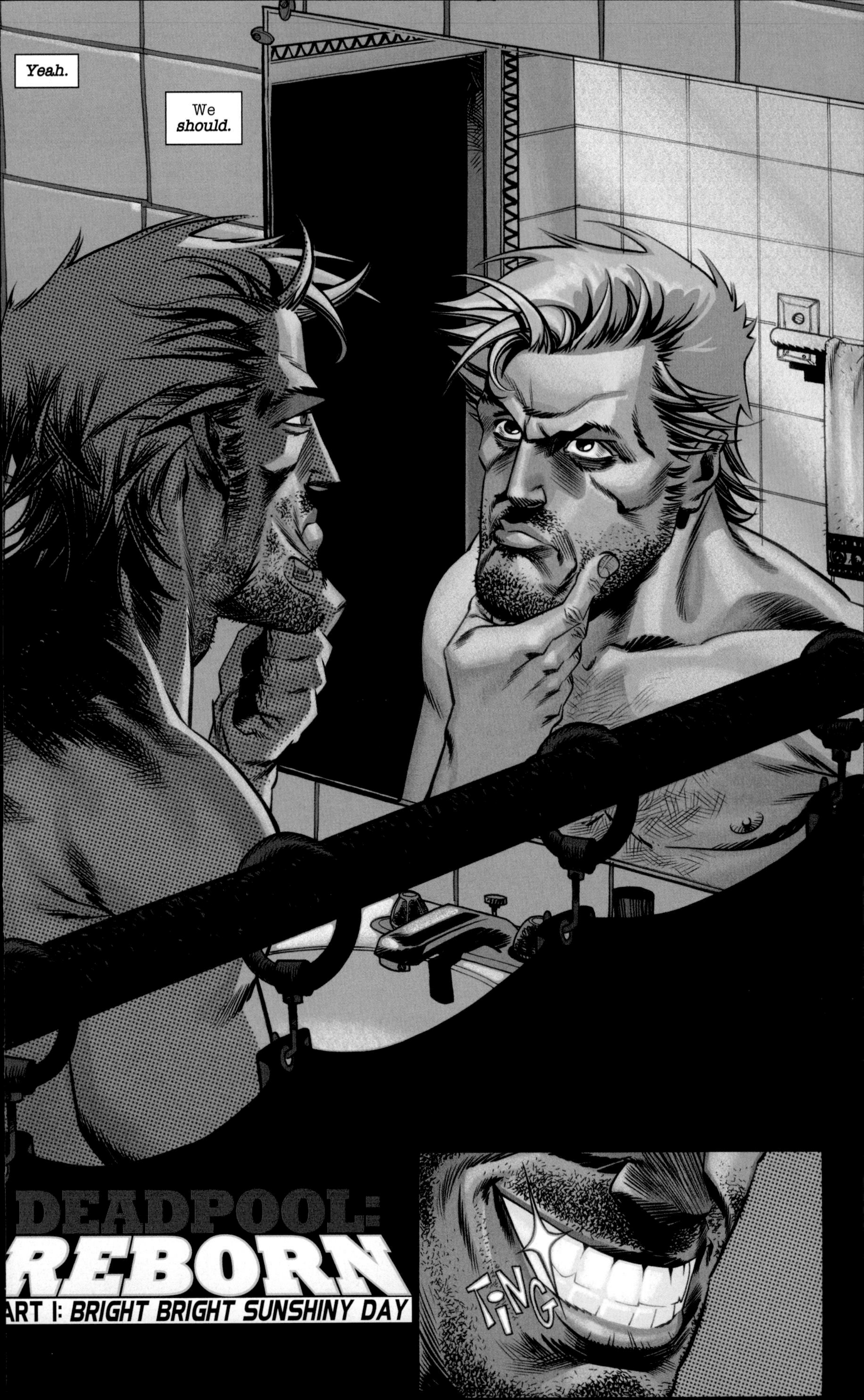
Yeah.
We should.
DEADPOOL: REBORN
ART I: BRIGHT BRIGHT SUNSHINY DAY
TING

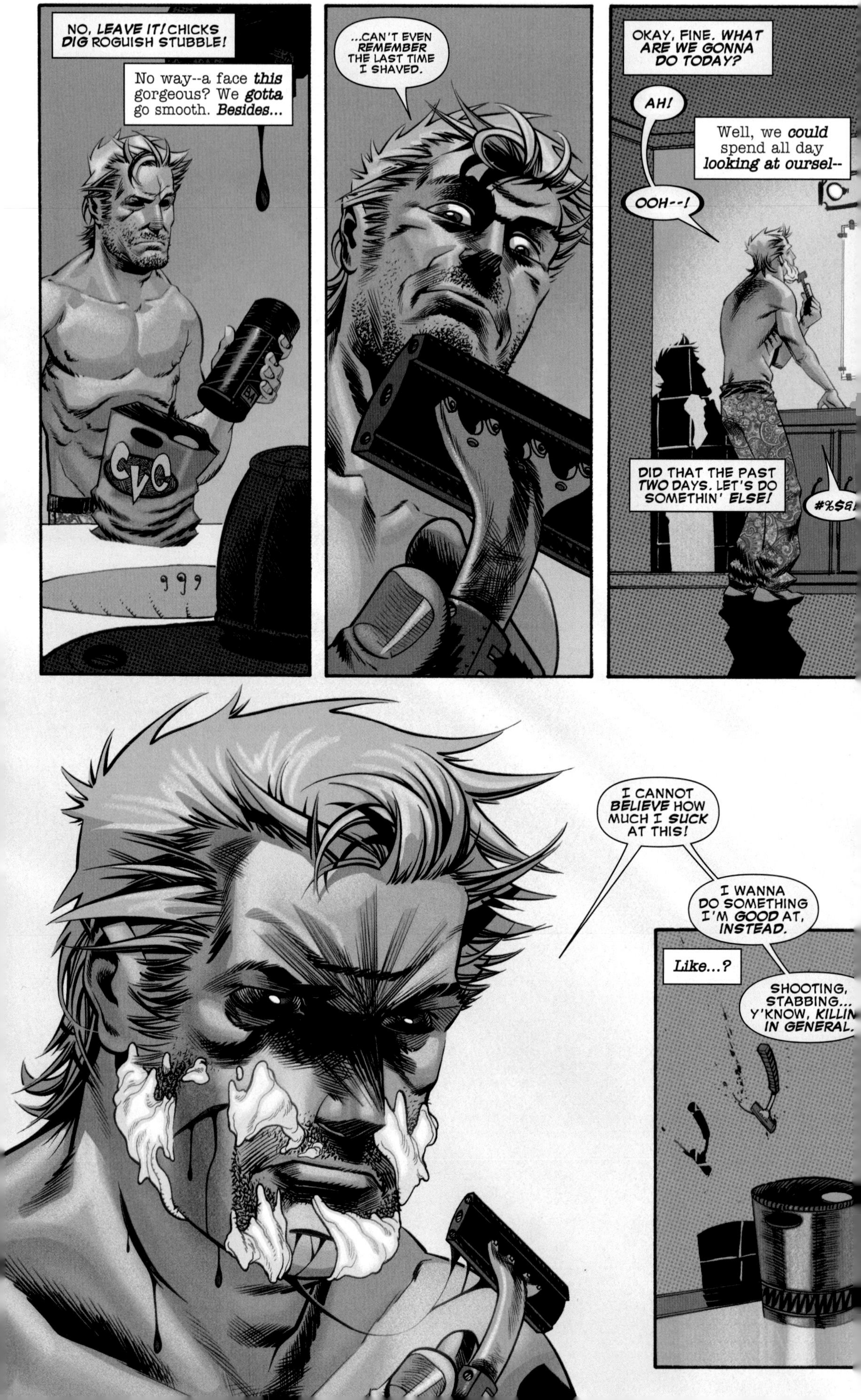
NO, LEAVE IT! CHICKS DIG ROGUISH STUBBLE!
No way--a face this gorgeous? We gotta go smooth. Besides...
...CAN'T EVEN REMEMBER THE LAST TIME I SHAVED.
OKAY, FINE. WHAT ARE WE GONNA DO TODAY?
AH!
Well, we could spend all day looking at oursel--
OOH--!
DID THAT THE PAST TWO DAYS. LET'S DO SOMETHIN' ELSE!
I CANNOT BELIEVE HOW MUCH I SUCK AT THIS!
I WANNA DO SOMETHING I'M GOOD AT, INSTEAD.
Like...?
SHOOTING, STABBING... Y'KNOW, KILLIN IN GENERAL.

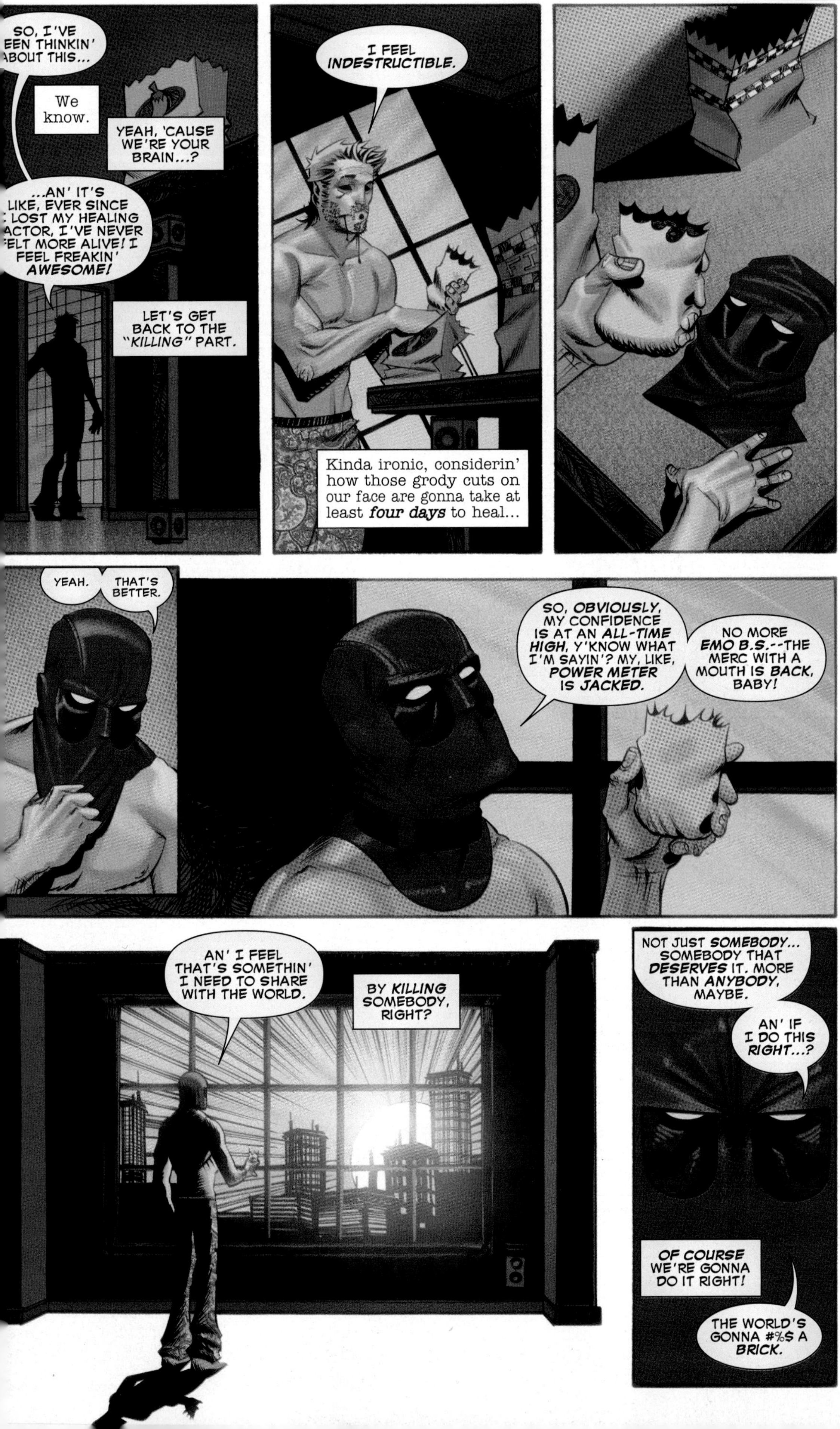
SO, I'VE BEEN THINKIN' ABOUT THIS...
We know.
YEAH, 'CAUSE WE'RE YOUR BRAIN...?
...AN' IT'S LIKE, EVER SINCE I LOST MY HEALING FACTOR, I'VE NEVER FELT MORE ALIVE! I FEEL FREAKIN' AWESOME!
LET'S GET BACK TO THE "KILLING" PART.
I FEEL INDESTRUCTIBLE.
Kinda ironic, considerin' how those grody cuts on our face are gonna take at least four days to heal...
YEAH.
THAT'S BETTER.
SO, OBVIOUSLY, MY CONFIDENCE IS AT AN ALL-TIME HIGH, Y'KNOW WHAT I'M SAYIN'? MY, LIKE, POWER METER IS JACKED.
NO MORE EMO B.S.--THE MERC WITH A MOUTH IS BACK, BABY!
AN' I FEEL THAT'S SOMETHIN' I NEED TO SHARE WITH THE WORLD.
BY KILLING SOMEBODY, RIGHT?
NOT JUST SOMEBODY... SOMEBODY THAT DESERVES IT. MORE THAN ANYBODY, MAYBE.
AN' IF I DO THIS RIGHT...?
OF COURSE WE'RE GONNA DO IT RIGHT!
THE WORLD'S GONNA #%$ A BRICK.

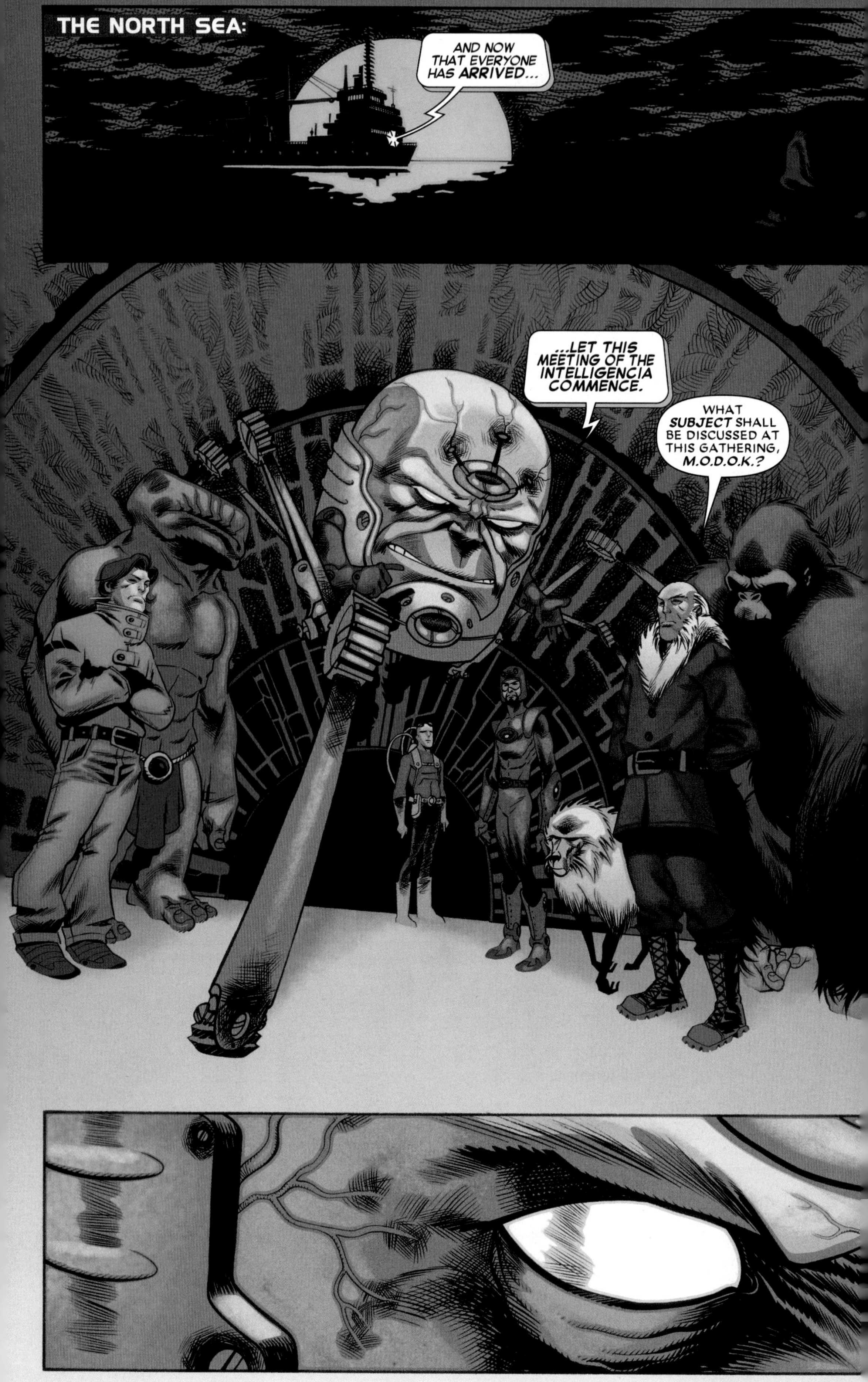
THE NORTH SEA:
AND NOW THAT EVERYONE HAS ARRIVED...
...LET THIS MEETING OF THE INTELLIGENCIA COMMENCE.
WHAT SUBJECT SHALL BE DISCUSSED AT THIS GATHERING, M.O.D.O.K.?

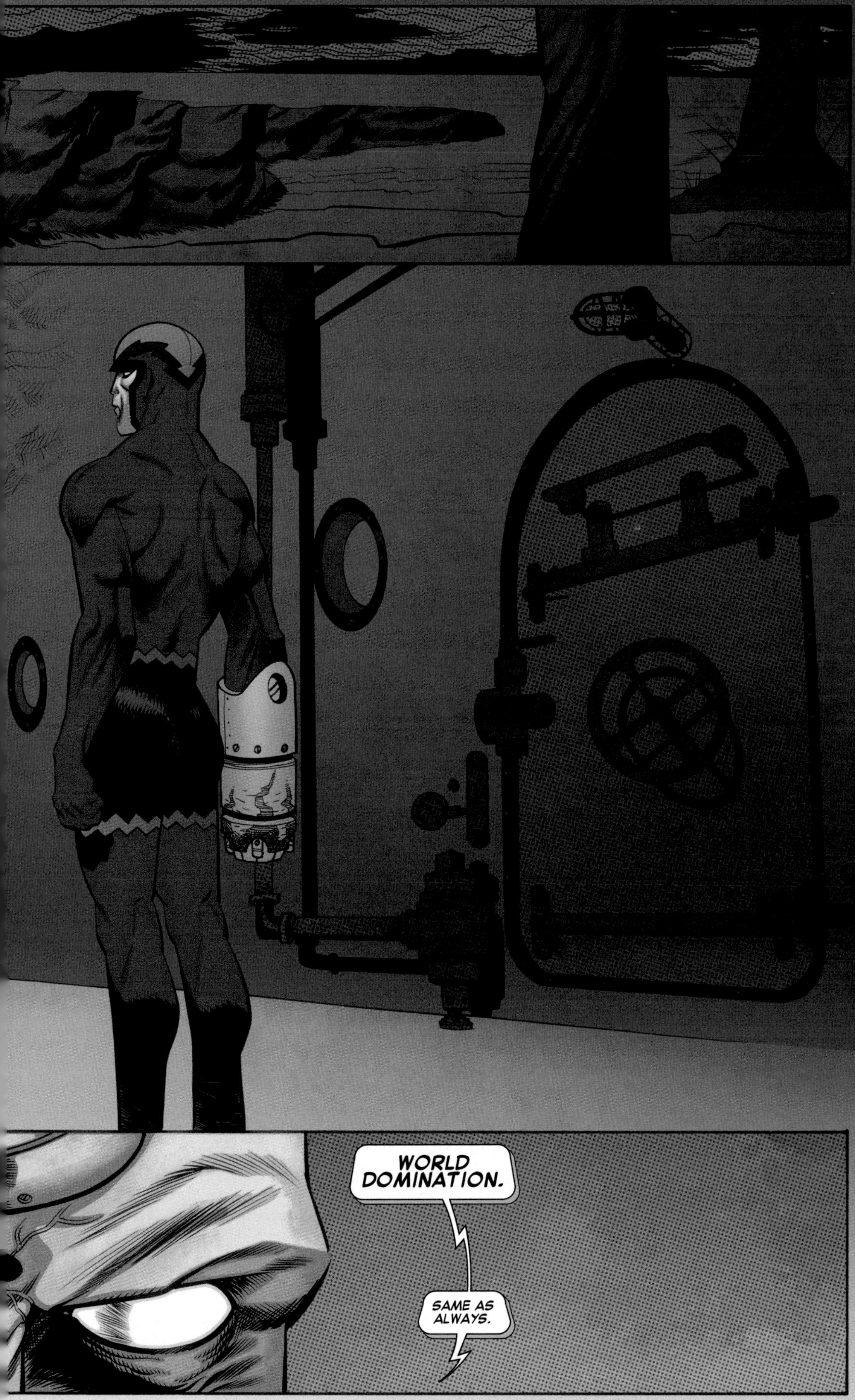
WORLD DOMINATION.
SAME AS ALWAYS.

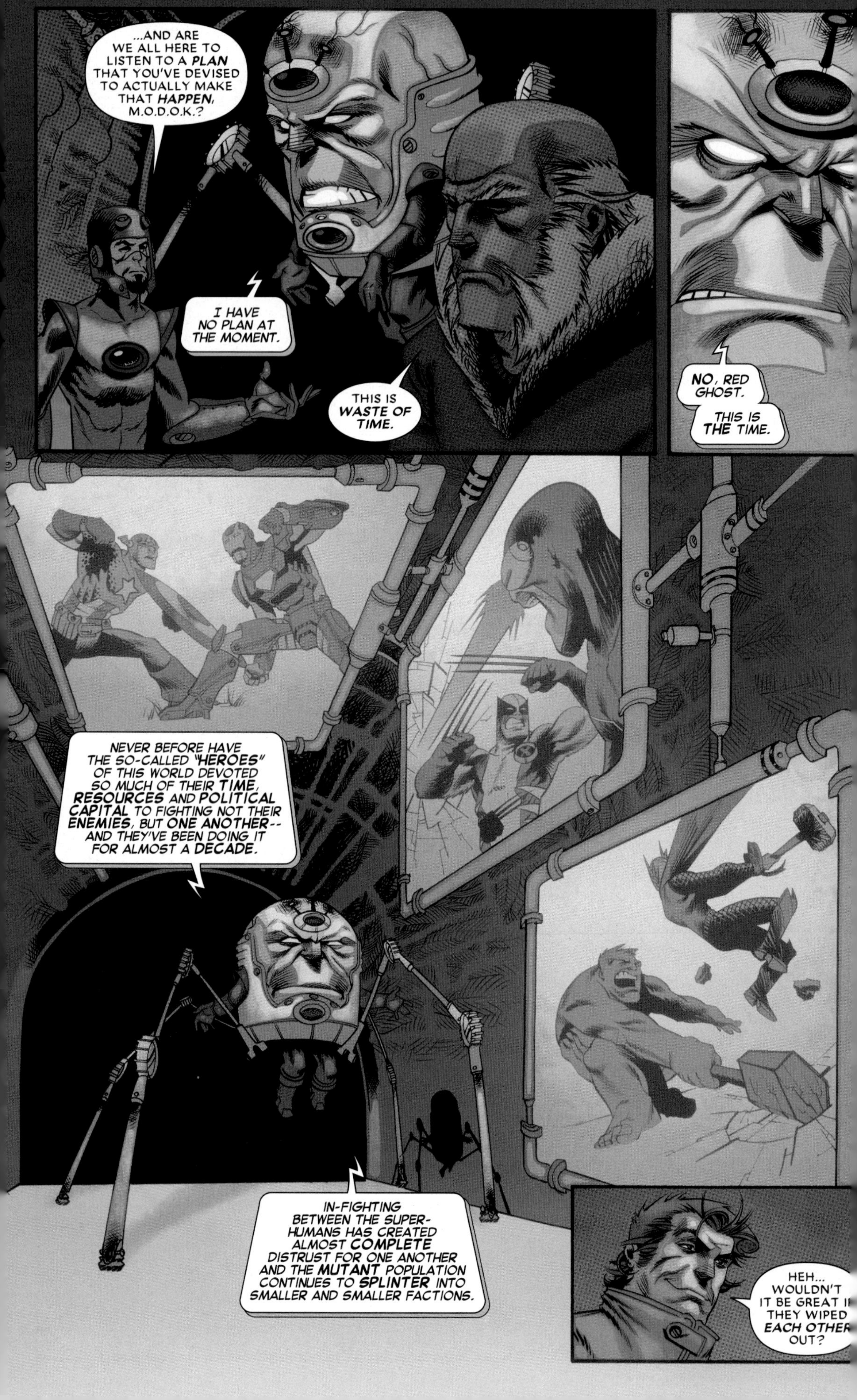
...AND ARE WE ALL HERE TO LISTEN TO A PLAN THAT YOU'VE DEVISED TO ACTUALLY MAKE THAT HAPPEN, M.O.D.O.K.?
I HAVE NO PLAN AT THE MOMENT.
THIS IS WASTE OF TIME.
NO, RED GHOST.
THIS IS THE TIME.
NEVER BEFORE HAVE THE SO-CALLED "HEROES" OF THIS WORLD DEVOTED SO MUCH OF THEIR TIME, RESOURCES AND POLITICAL CAPITAL TO FIGHTING NOT THEIR ENEMIES, BUT ONE ANOTHER-- AND THEY'VE BEEN DOING IT FOR ALMOST A DECADE.
IN-FIGHTING BETWEEN THE SUPER-HUMANS HAS CREATED ALMOST COMPLETE DISTRUST FOR ONE ANOTHER AND THE MUTANT POPULATION CONTINUES TO SPLINTER INTO SMALLER AND SMALLER FACTIONS.
HEH... WOULDN'T IT BE GREAT IF THEY WIPED EACH OTHER OUT?

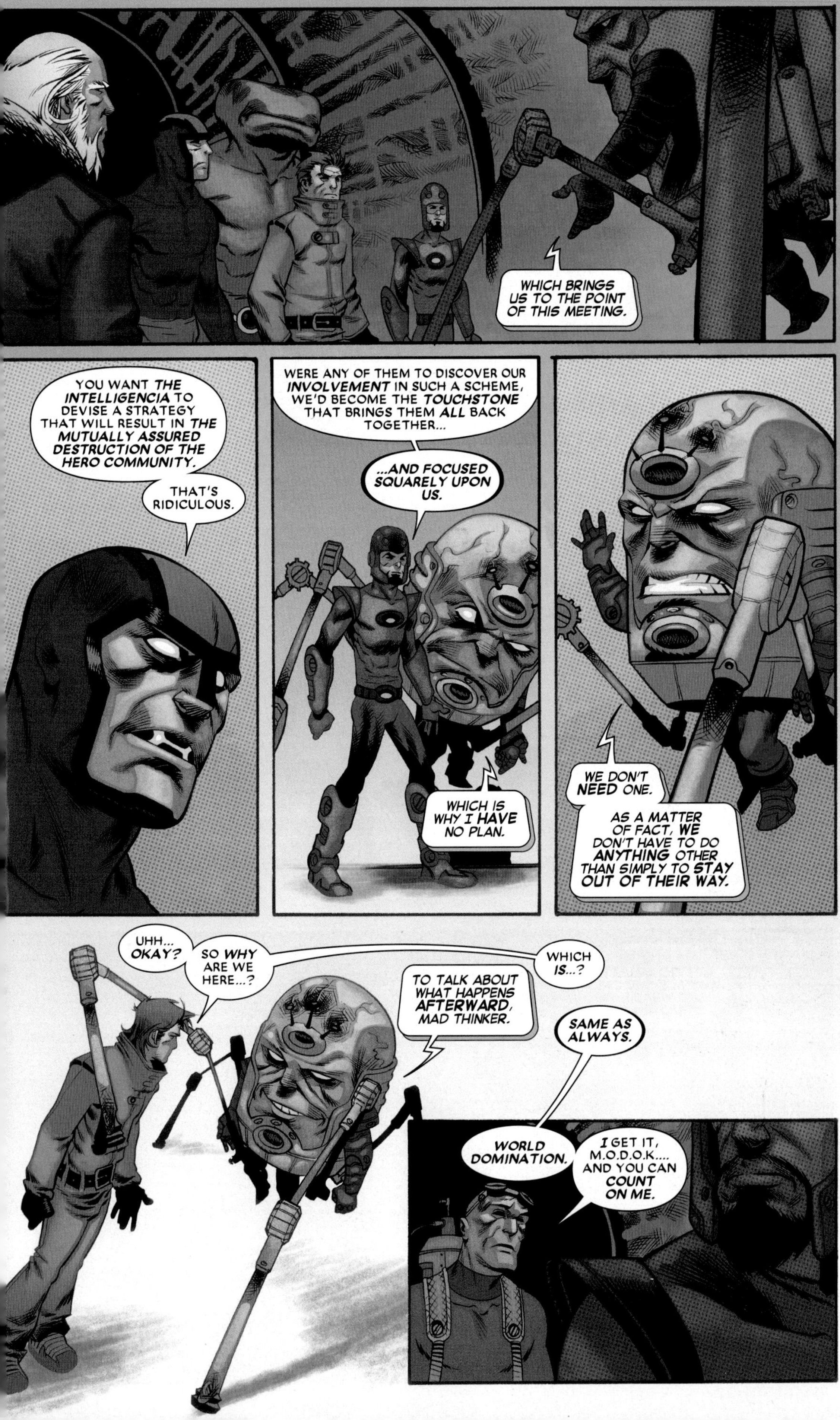
WHICH BRINGS US TO THE POINT OF THIS MEETING.
YOU WANT THE INTELLIGENCIA TO DEVISE A STRATEGY THAT WILL RESULT IN THE MUTUALLY ASSURED DESTRUCTION OF THE HERO COMMUNITY.
THAT'S RIDICULOUS.
WERE ANY OF THEM TO DISCOVER OUR INVOLVEMENT IN SUCH A SCHEME, WE'D BECOME THE TOUCHSTONE THAT BRINGS THEM ALL BACK TOGETHER...
...AND FOCUSED SQUARELY UPON US.
WHICH IS WHY I HAVE NO PLAN.
WE DON'T NEED ONE.
AS A MATTER OF FACT, WE DON'T HAVE TO DO ANYTHING OTHER THAN SIMPLY TO STAY OUT OF THEIR WAY.
UHH... OKAY?
SO WHY ARE WE HERE...?
TO TALK ABOUT WHAT HAPPENS AFTERWARD, MAD THINKER.
WHICH IS...?
SAME AS ALWAYS.
WORLD DOMINATION.
I GET IT, M.O.D.O.K.... AND YOU CAN COUNT ON ME.

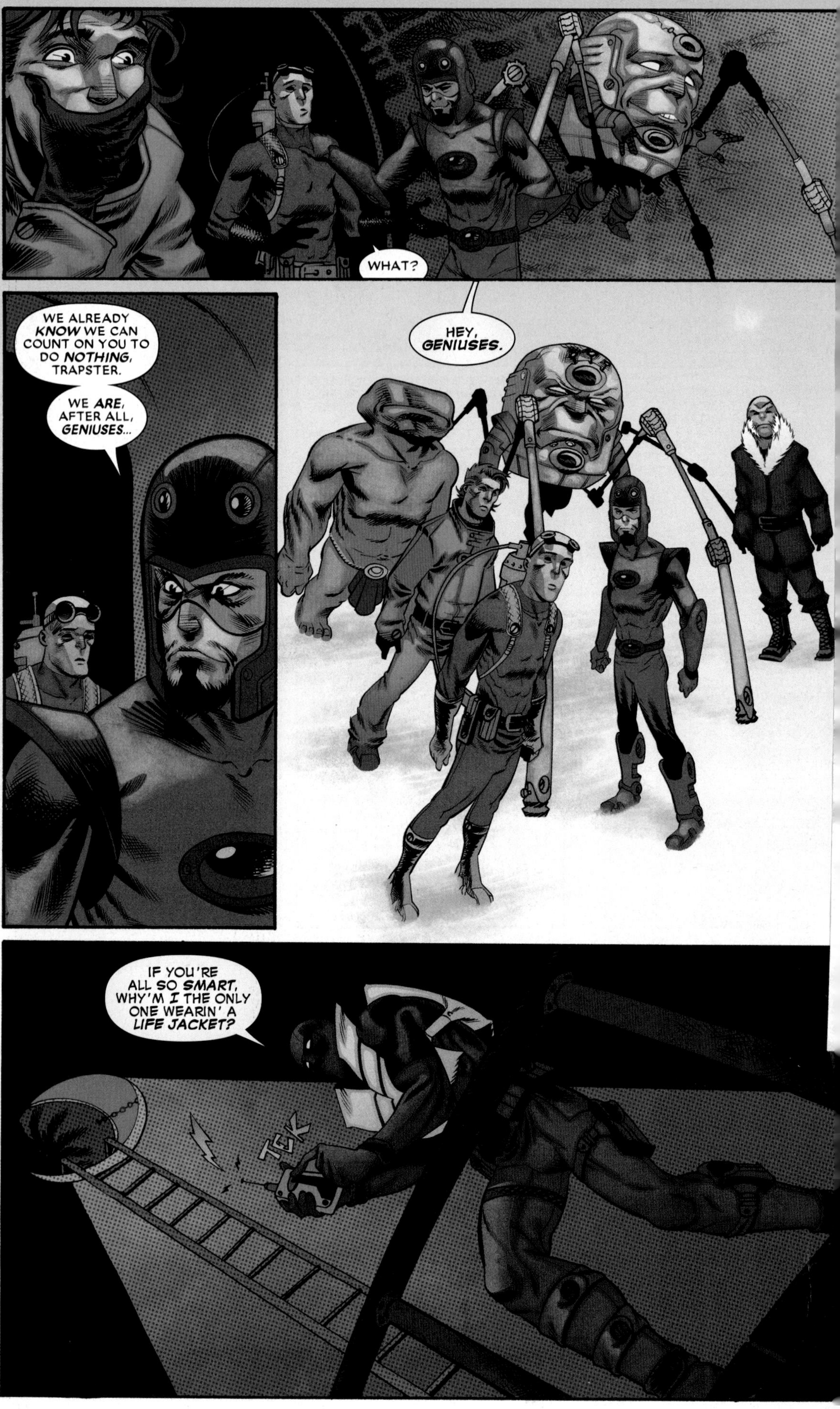

WHAT?
HEY, GENIUSES.
WE ALREADY KNOW WE CAN COUNT ON YOU TO DO NOTHING, TRAPSTER.
WE ARE, AFTER ALL, GENIUSES...
IF YOU'RE ALL SO SMART, WHY'M I THE ONLY ONE WEARIN' A LIFE JACKET?
TCK

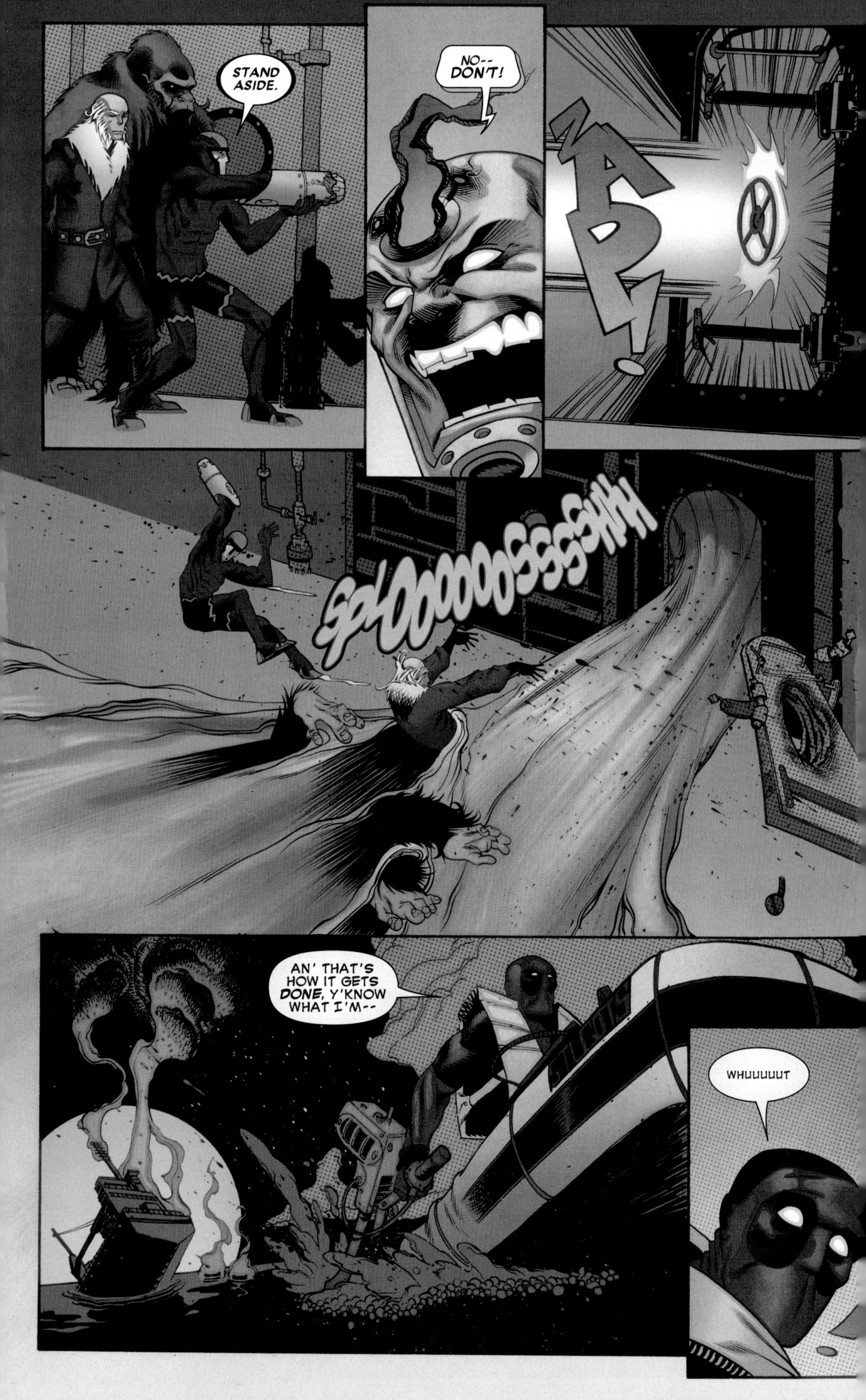
STAND ASIDE.
NO-- DON'T!
ZAP!
SPLOOOOOOSSSSHHH
AN' THAT'S HOW IT GETS DONE, Y'KNOW WHAT I'M--
WHUUUUUT

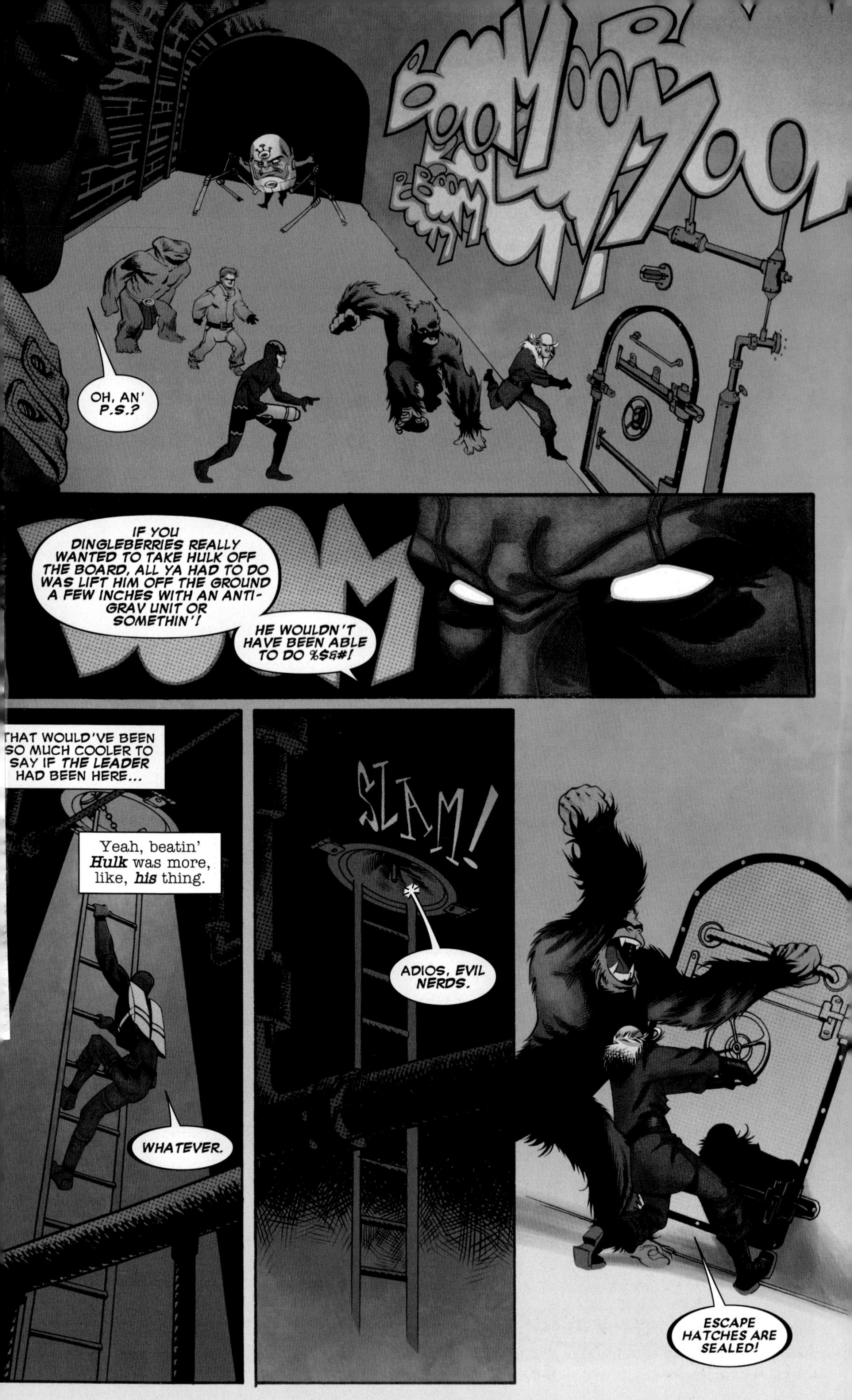

OH, AN' P.S.?
IF YOU DINGLEBERRIES REALLY WANTED TO TAKE HULK OFF THE BOARD, ALL YA HAD TO DO WAS LIFT HIM OFF THE GROUND A FEW INCHES WITH AN ANTI-GRAV UNIT OR SOMETHIN'!
HE WOULDN'T HAVE BEEN ABLE TO DO %$&#!
THAT WOULD'VE BEEN SO MUCH COOLER TO SAY IF THE LEADER HAD BEEN HERE...
Yeah, beatin' Hulk was more, like, his thing.
WHATEVER.
SLAM!
ADIOS, EVIL NERDS.
ESCAPE HATCHES ARE SEALED!

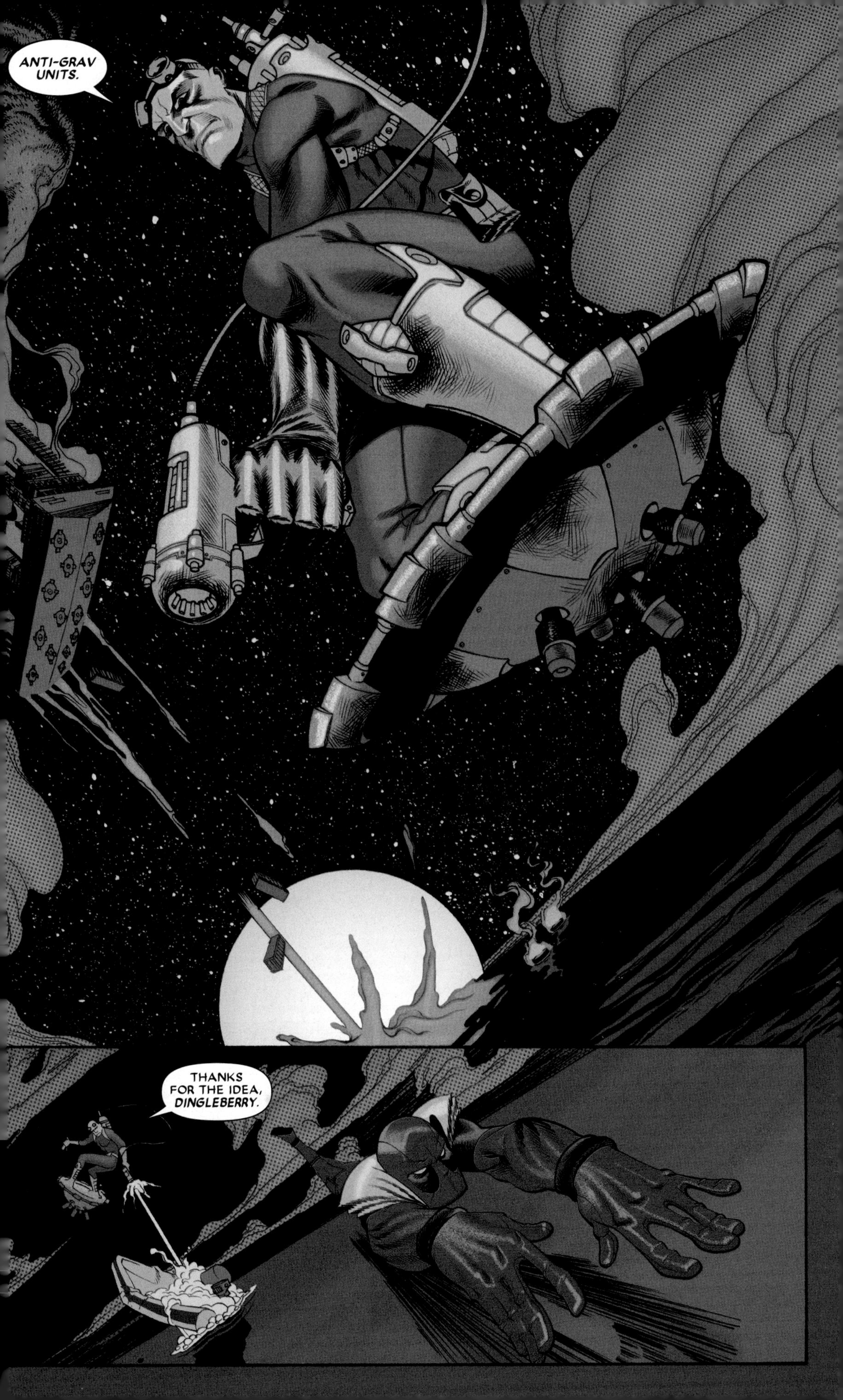
ANTI-GRAV UNITS.
THANKS FOR THE IDEA, DINGLEBERRY.

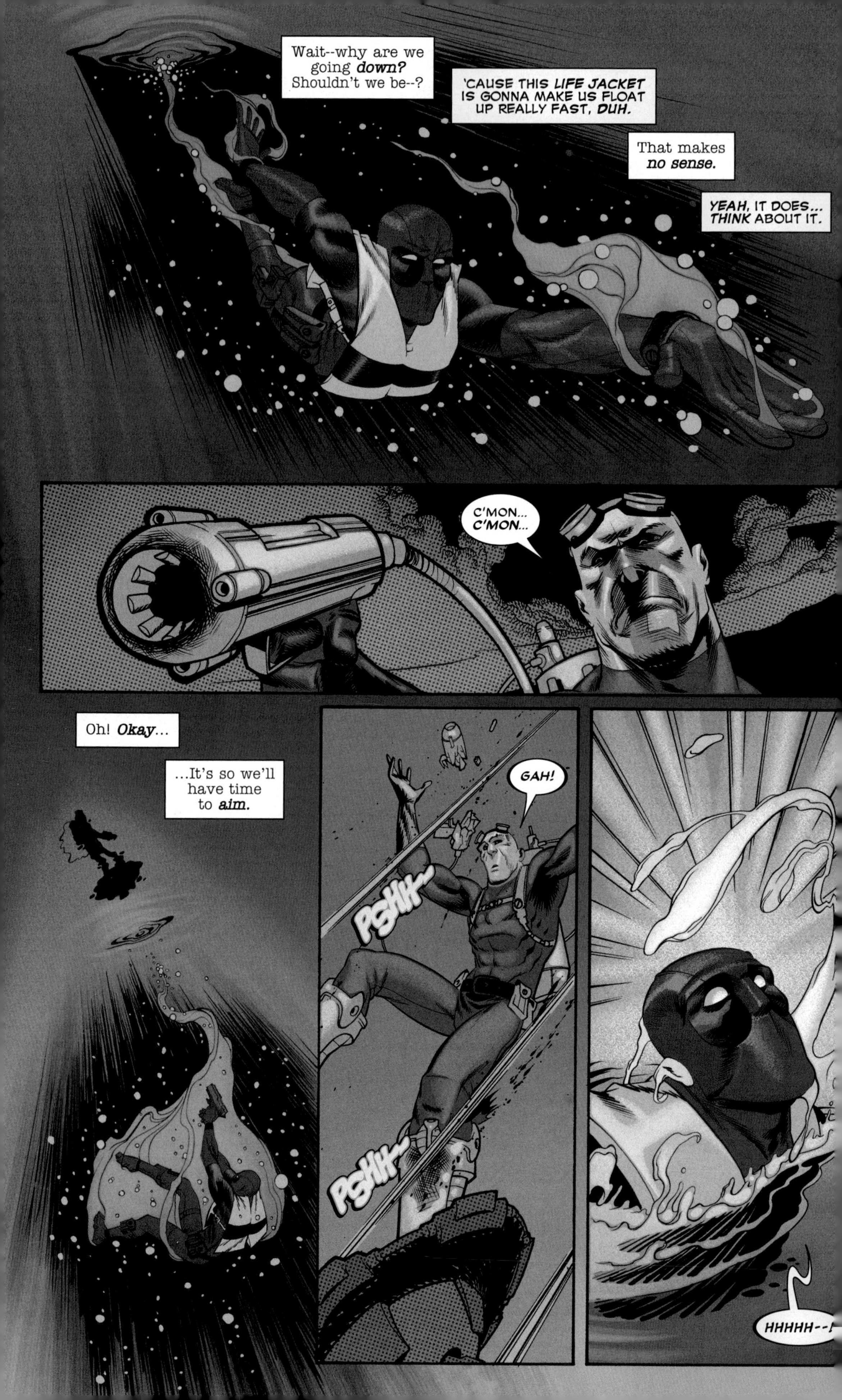

Wait--why are we going **down?** Shouldn't we be--?
'CAUSE THIS ***LIFE JACKET*** IS GONNA MAKE US FLOAT UP REALLY FAST, ***DUH.***
That makes ***no sense.***
YEAH, IT DOES... ***THINK*** ABOUT IT.
C'MON... ***C'MON...***
Oh! ***Okay...***
...It's so we'll have time to ***aim.***
GAH!
PSHH--
PSHH--
HHHHH--

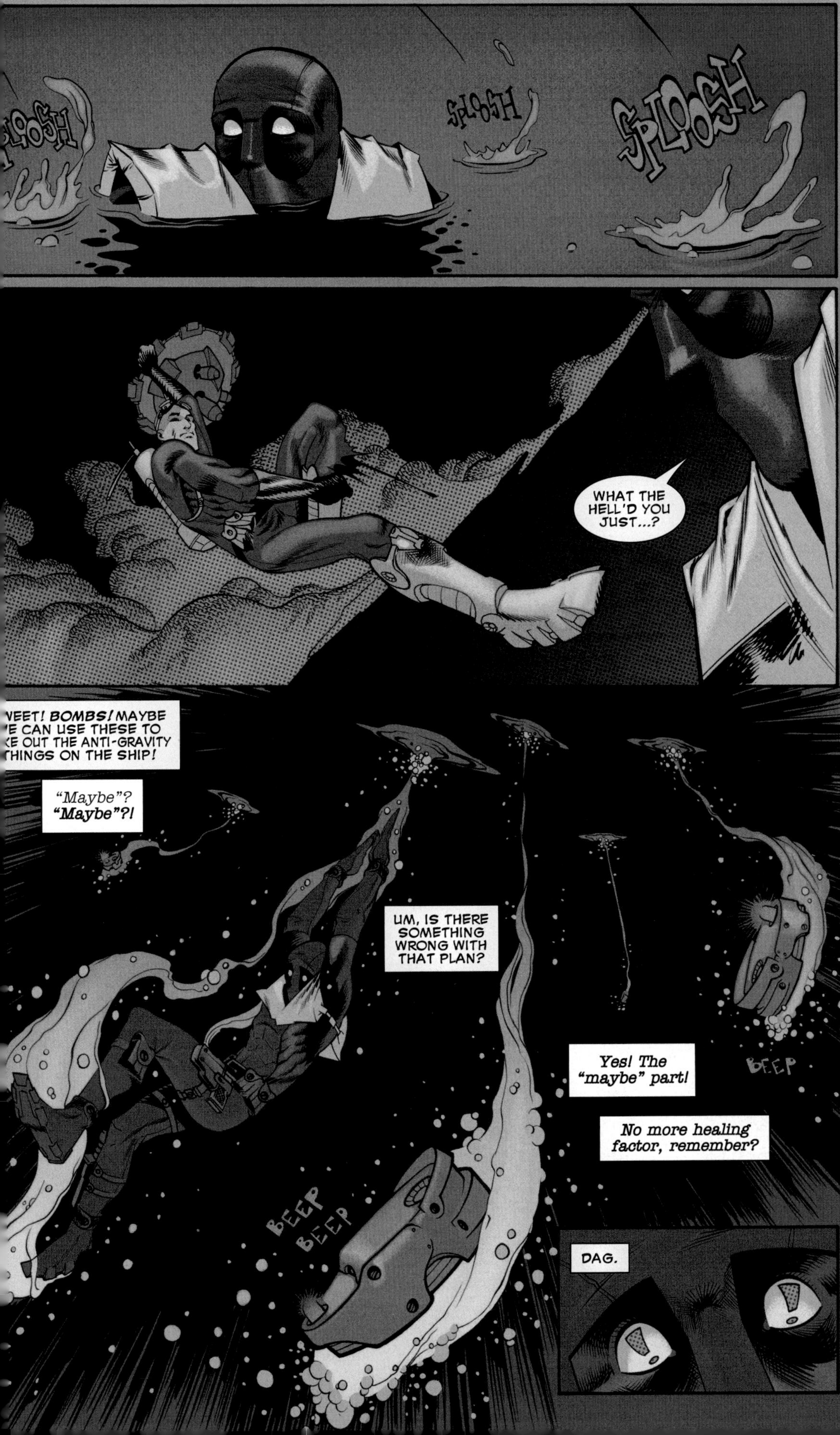

SPLOOSH
SPLOOSH
SPLOOSH
WHAT THE HELL'D YOU JUST...?
WEET! BOMBS! MAYBE E CAN USE THESE TO E OUT THE ANTI-GRAVITY THINGS ON THE SHIP!
"Maybe"? "Maybe"?!
UM, IS THERE SOMETHING WRONG WITH THAT PLAN?
Yes! The "maybe" part!
No more healing factor, remember?
BEEP
BEEP BEEP
DAG.

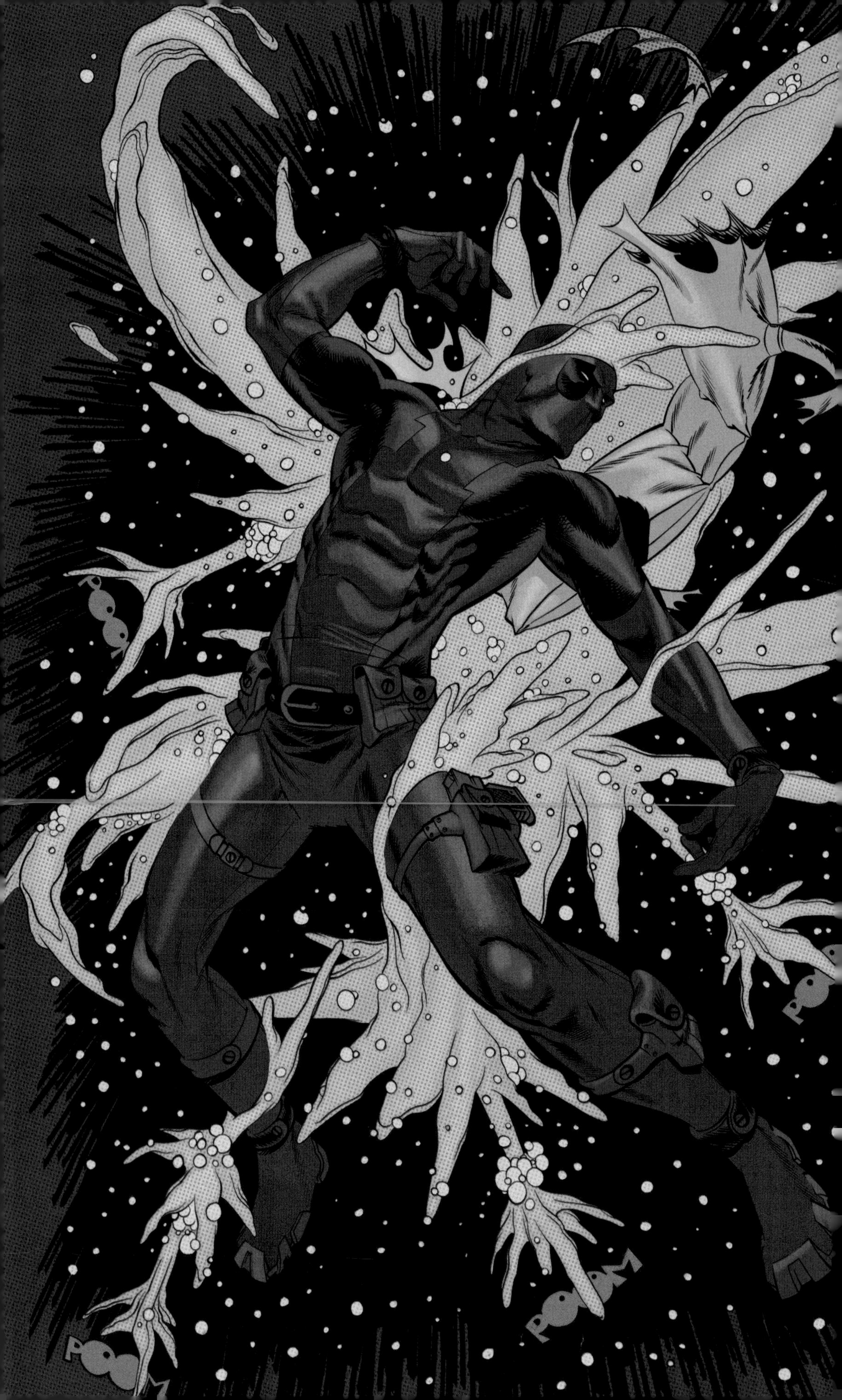
POOM
POOM
POOM

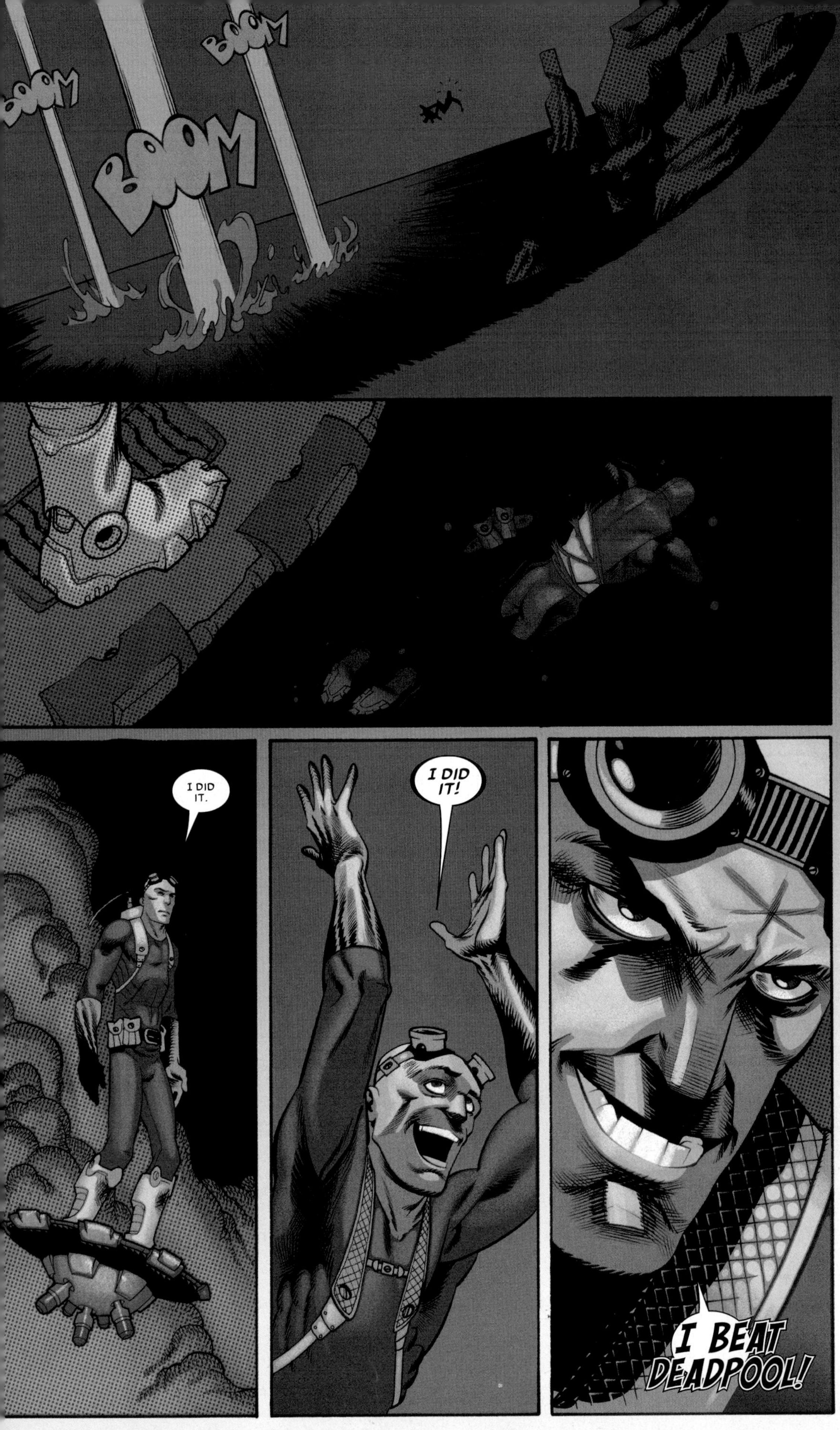

BOOM
BOOM
BOOM
I DID IT.
I DID IT!
I BEAT DEADPOOL!

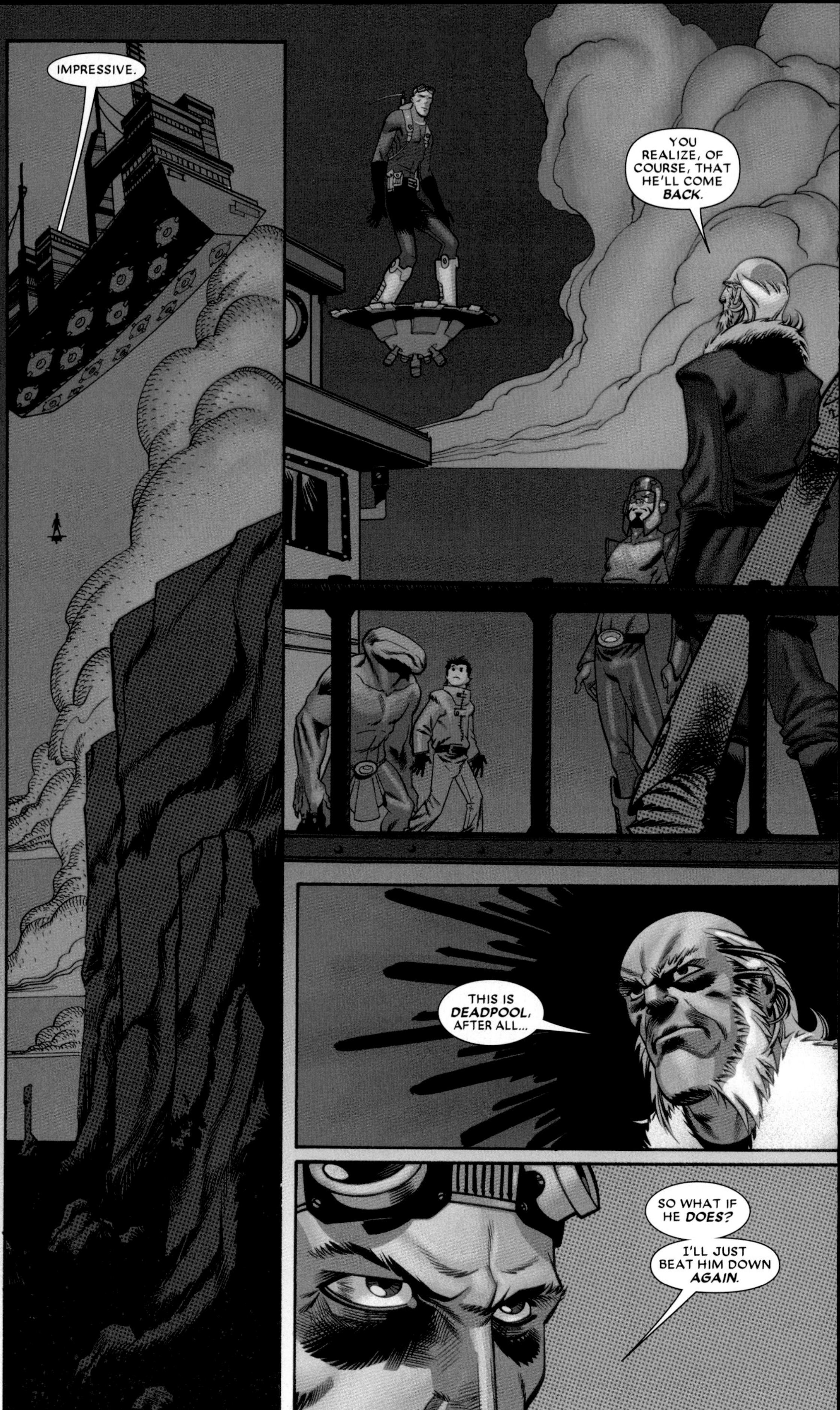
IMPRESSIVE.
YOU REALIZE, OF COURSE, THAT HE'LL COME BACK.
THIS IS DEADPOOL, AFTER ALL...
SO WHAT IF HE DOES?
I'LL JUST BEAT HIM DOWN AGAIN.

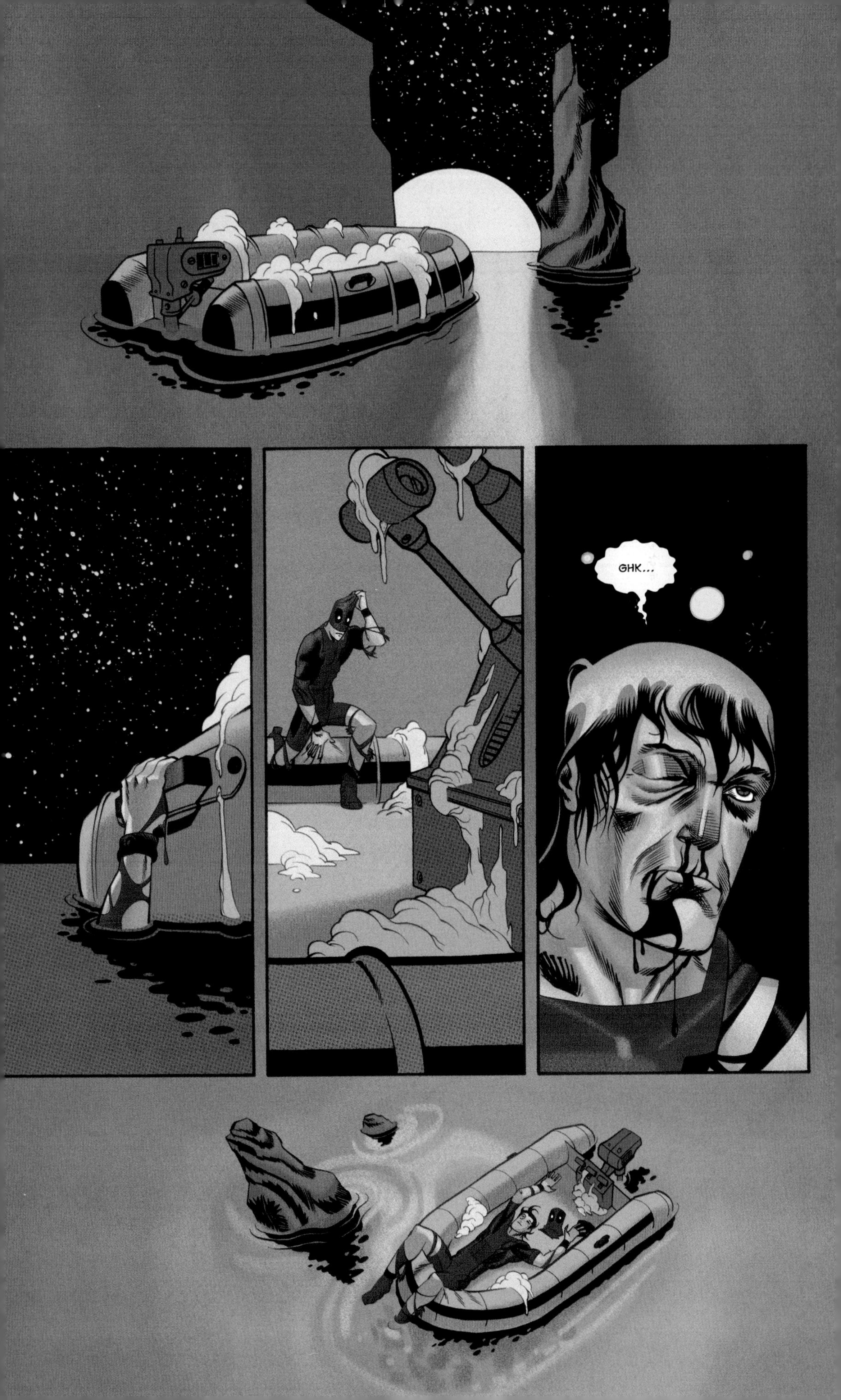
GHK...

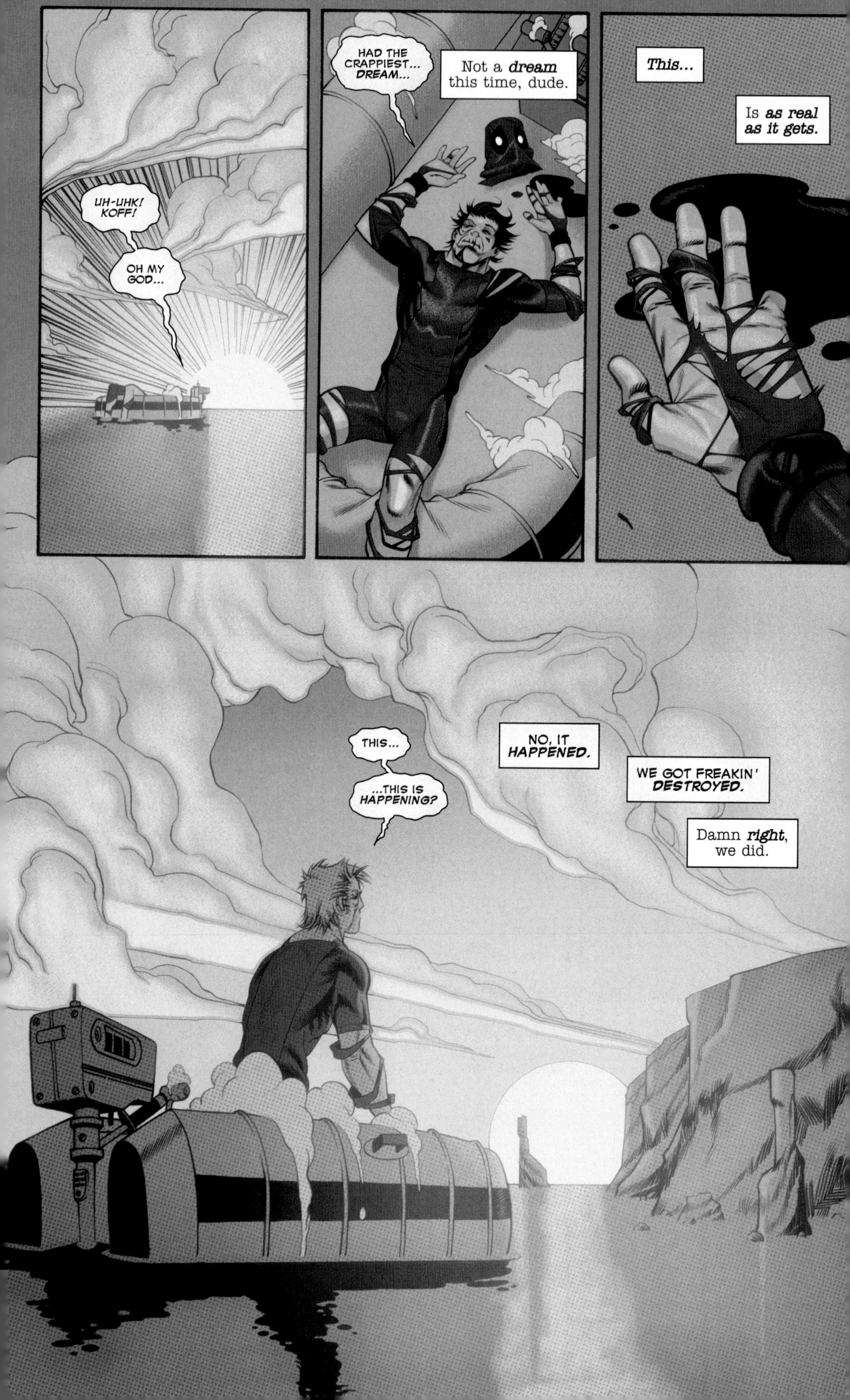
UH-UHK! KOFF!
OH MY GOD...
HAD THE CRAPPIEST... DREAM...
Not a dream this time, dude.
This...
Is as real as it gets.
THIS...
...THIS IS HAPPENING?
NO, IT HAPPENED.
WE GOT FREAKIN' DESTROYED.
Damn right, we did.

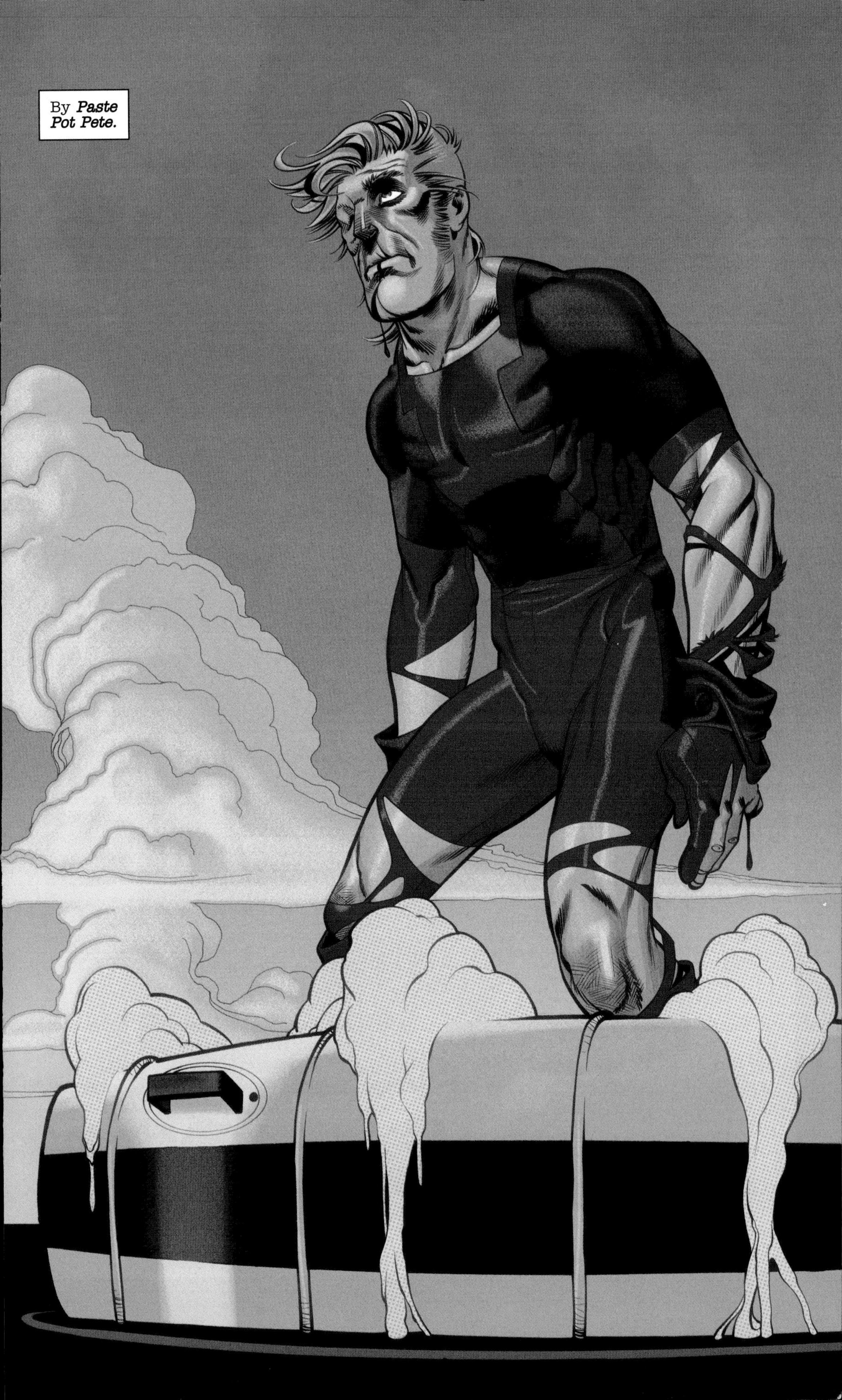
By Paste Pot Pete.

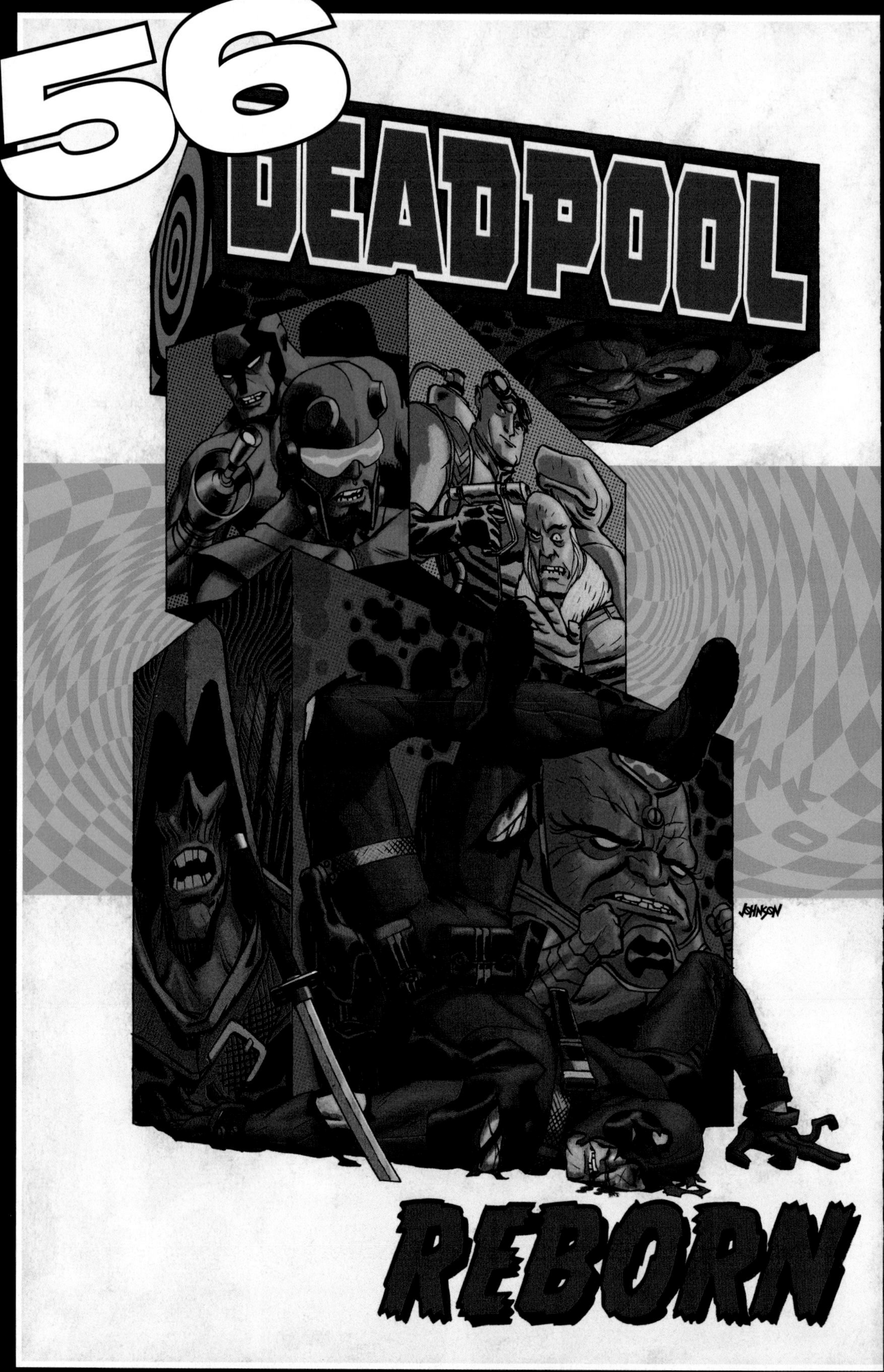
56
DEADPOOL
JOHNSON
REBORN

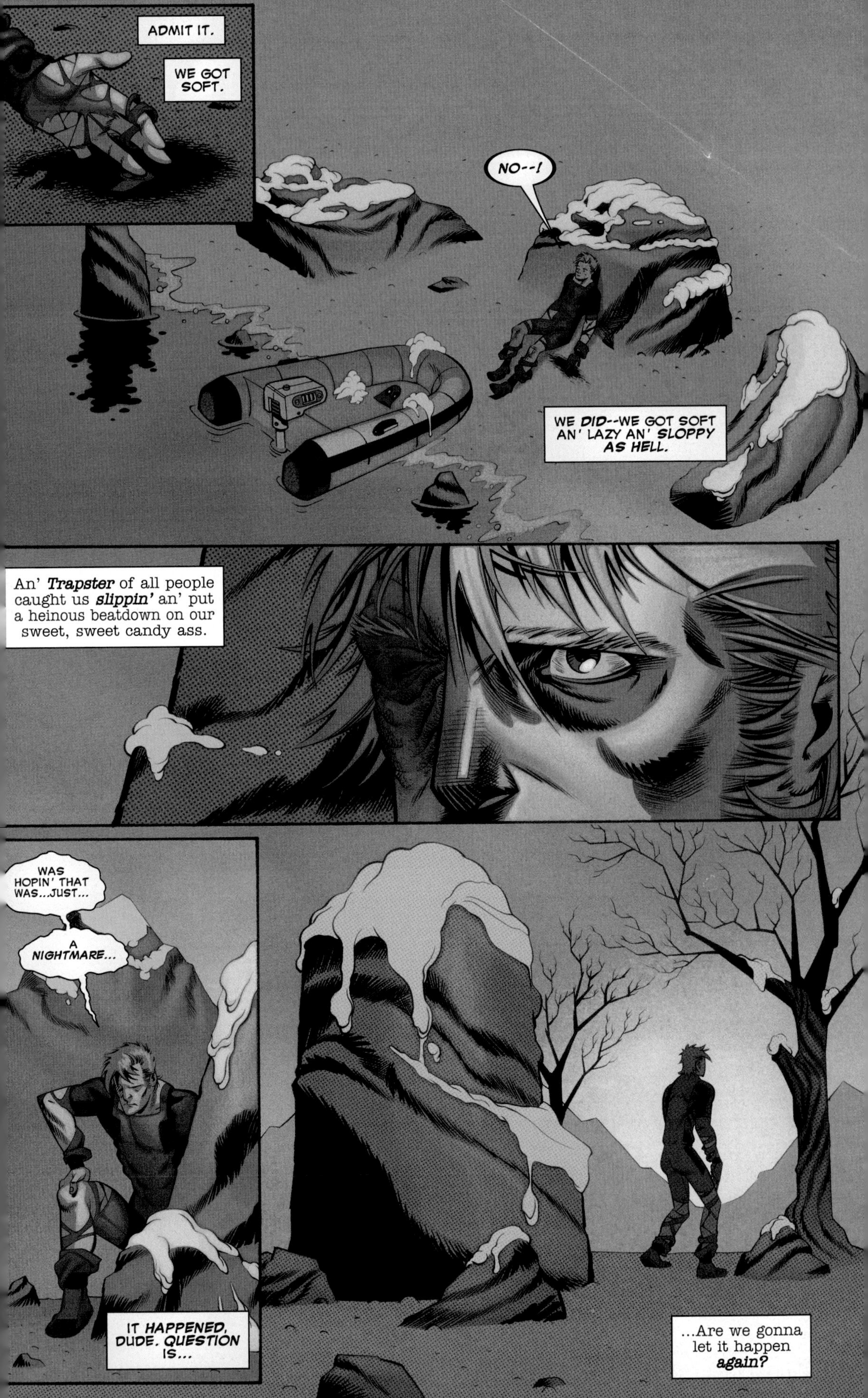
ADMIT IT.
WE GOT SOFT.
NO--!
WE DID--WE GOT SOFT AN' LAZY AN' SLOPPY AS HELL.
An' Trapster of all people caught us slippin' an' put a heinous beatdown on our sweet, sweet candy ass.
WAS HOPIN' THAT WAS...JUST...
A NIGHTMARE...
IT HAPPENED, DUDE. QUESTION IS...
...Are we gonna let it happen again?

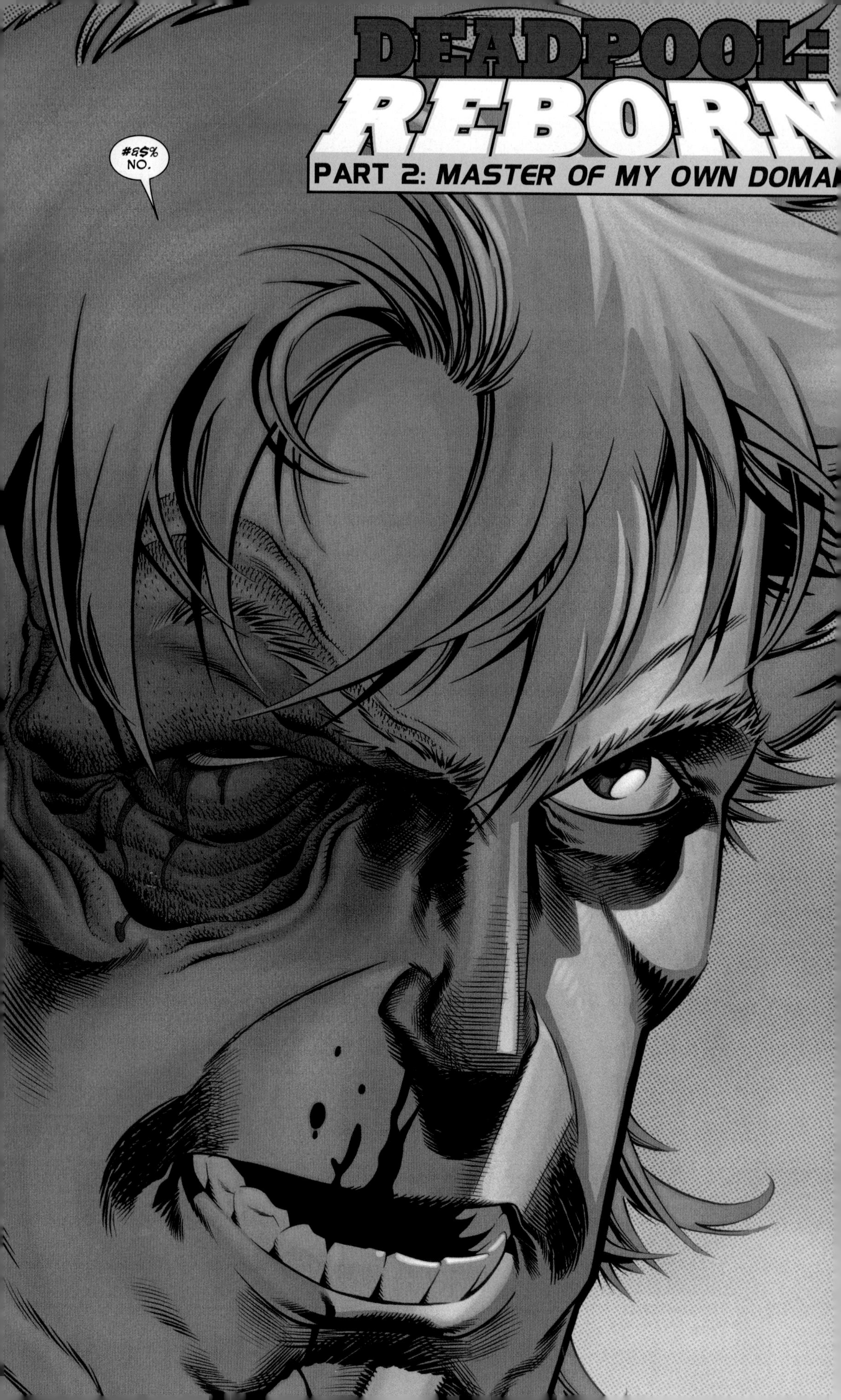
DEADPOOL:
REBORN
PART 2: MASTER OF MY OWN DOMAI
#&$%
NO.

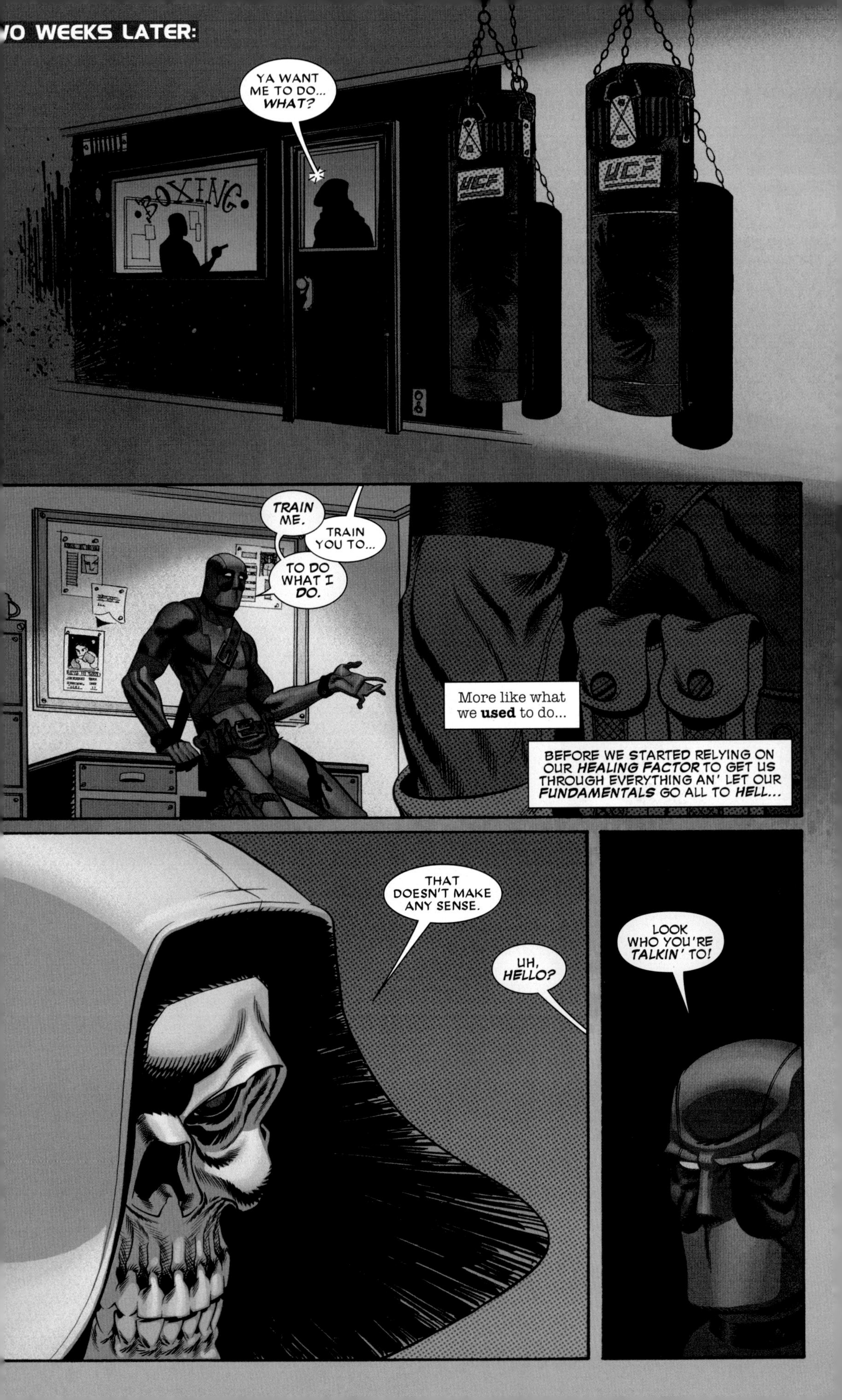

O WEEKS LATER:
YA WANT ME TO DO... WHAT?
BOXING
UCF
UCF
TRAIN ME.
TRAIN YOU TO...
TO DO WHAT I DO.
More like what we used to do...
BEFORE WE STARTED RELYING ON OUR HEALING FACTOR TO GET US THROUGH EVERYTHING AN' LET OUR FUNDAMENTALS GO ALL TO HELL...
THAT DOESN'T MAKE ANY SENSE.
UH, HELLO?
LOOK WHO YOU'RE TALKIN' TO!

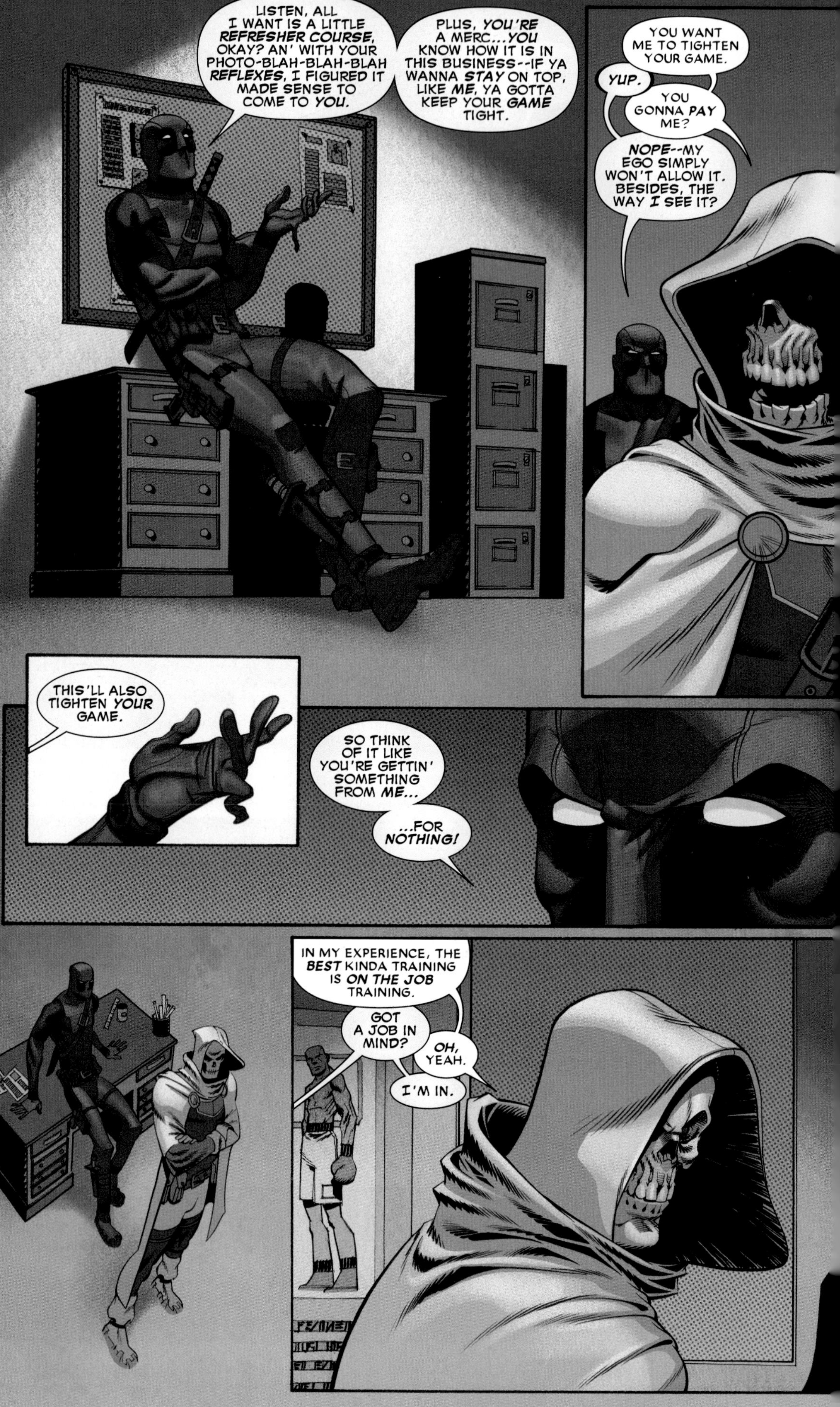
LISTEN, ALL I WANT IS A LITTLE REFRESHER COURSE, OKAY? AN' WITH YOUR PHOTO-BLAH-BLAH-BLAH REFLEXES, I FIGURED IT MADE SENSE TO COME TO YOU.
PLUS, YOU'RE A MERC...YOU KNOW HOW IT IS IN THIS BUSINESS--IF YA WANNA STAY ON TOP, LIKE ME, YA GOTTA KEEP YOUR GAME TIGHT.
YOU WANT ME TO TIGHTEN YOUR GAME.
YUP.
YOU GONNA PAY ME?
NOPE--MY EGO SIMPLY WON'T ALLOW IT. BESIDES, THE WAY I SEE IT?
THIS'LL ALSO TIGHTEN YOUR GAME.
SO THINK OF IT LIKE YOU'RE GETTIN' SOMETHING FROM ME...
...FOR NOTHING!
IN MY EXPERIENCE, THE BEST KINDA TRAINING IS ON THE JOB TRAINING.
GOT A JOB IN MIND?
OH, YEAH.
I'M IN.

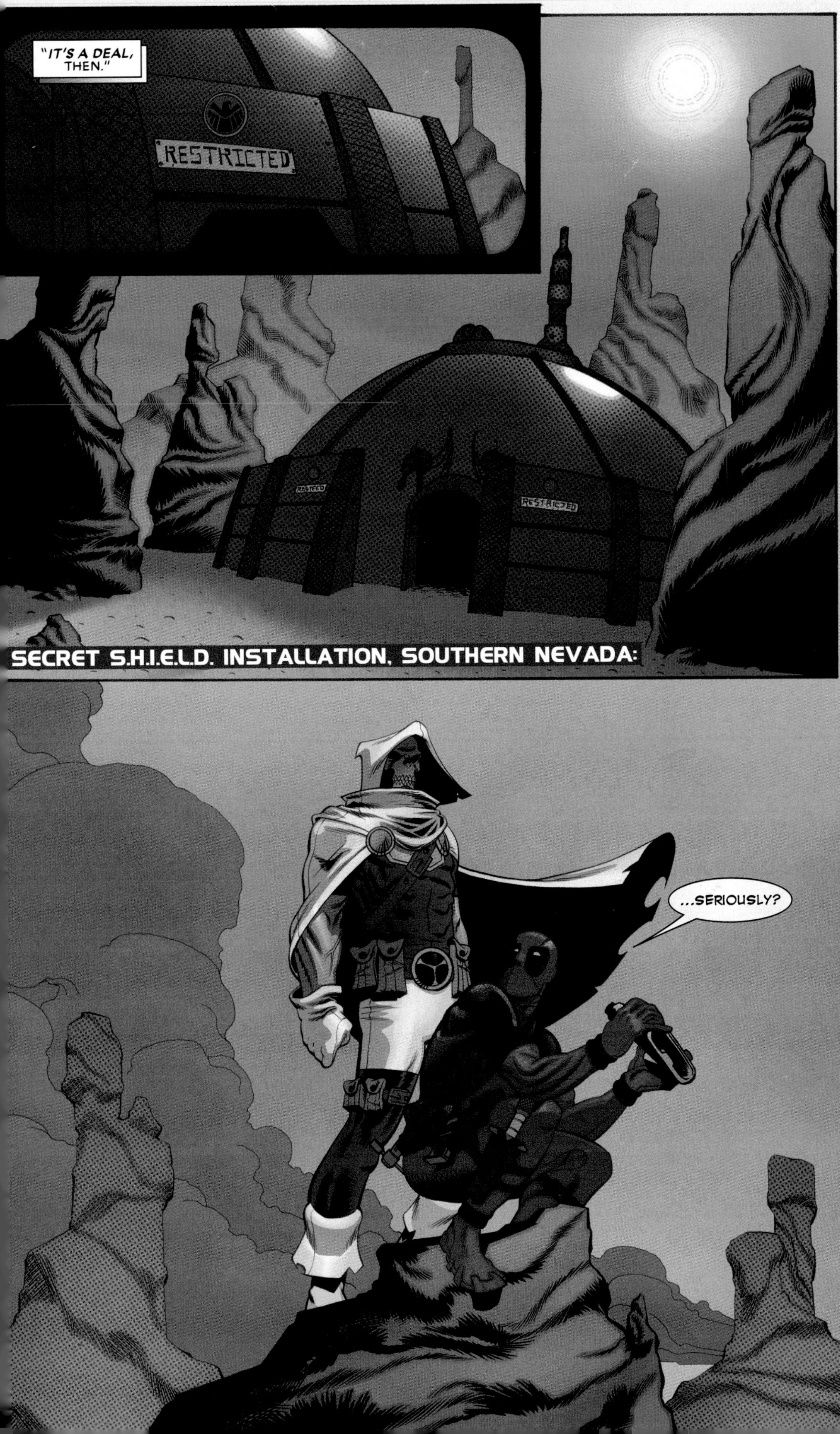
"IT'S A DEAL, THEN."
RESTRICTED
SECRET S.H.I.E.L.D. INSTALLATION, SOUTHERN NEVADA:
RESTRICTED
...SERIOUSLY?

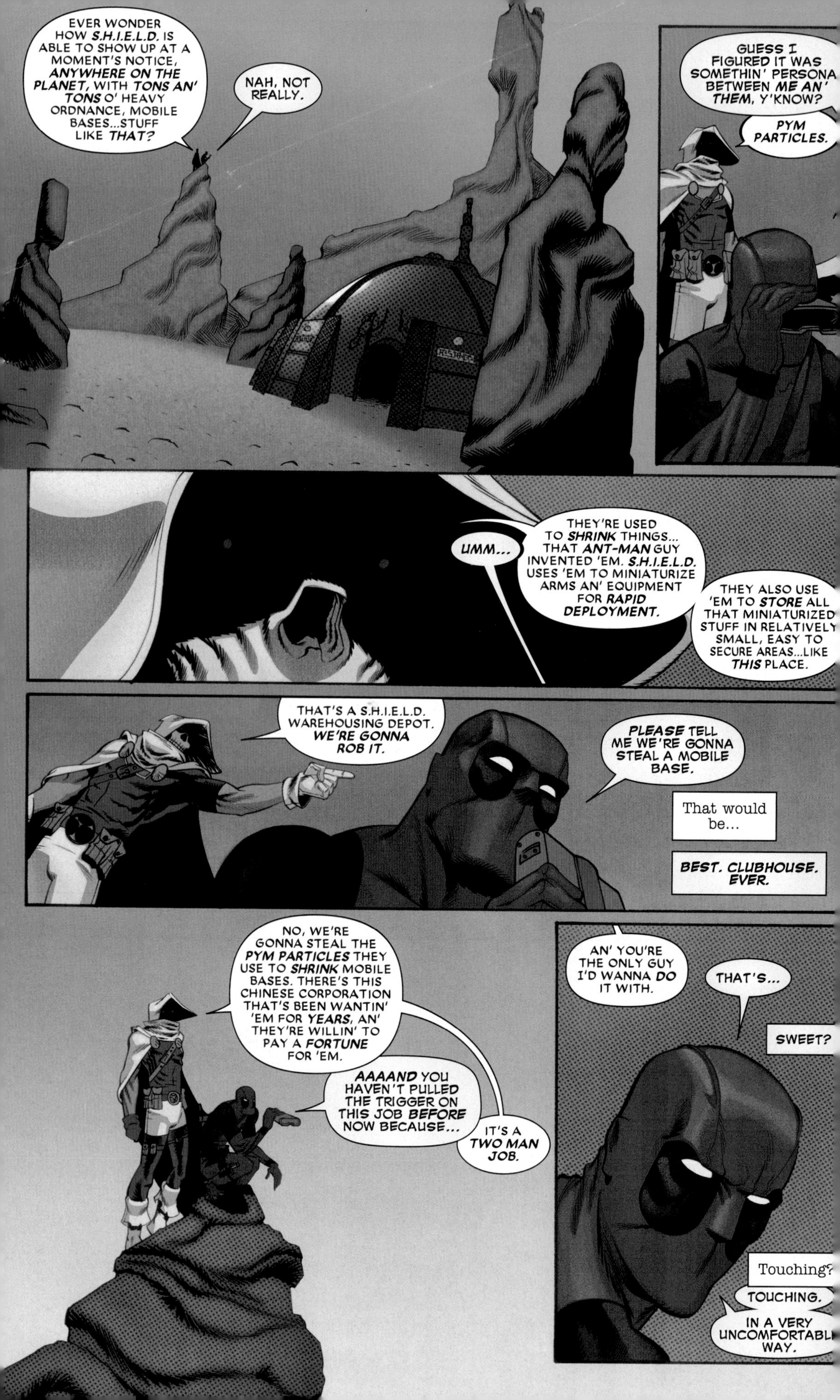
EVER WONDER HOW S.H.I.E.L.D. IS ABLE TO SHOW UP AT A MOMENT'S NOTICE, ANYWHERE ON THE PLANET, WITH TONS AN' TONS O' HEAVY ORDNANCE, MOBILE BASES...STUFF LIKE THAT?
NAH, NOT REALLY.
GUESS I FIGURED IT WAS SOMETHIN' PERSONA BETWEEN ME AN' THEM, Y'KNOW?
PYM PARTICLES.
UMM...
THEY'RE USED TO SHRINK THINGS... THAT ANT-MAN GUY INVENTED 'EM. S.H.I.E.L.D. USES 'EM TO MINIATURIZE ARMS AN' EQUIPMENT FOR RAPID DEPLOYMENT.
THEY ALSO USE 'EM TO STORE ALL THAT MINIATURIZED STUFF IN RELATIVELY SMALL, EASY TO SECURE AREAS...LIKE THIS PLACE.
THAT'S A S.H.I.E.L.D. WAREHOUSING DEPOT. WE'RE GONNA ROB IT.
PLEASE TELL ME WE'RE GONNA STEAL A MOBILE BASE.
That would be...
BEST. CLUBHOUSE. EVER.
NO, WE'RE GONNA STEAL THE PYM PARTICLES THEY USE TO SHRINK MOBILE BASES. THERE'S THIS CHINESE CORPORATION THAT'S BEEN WANTIN' 'EM FOR YEARS, AN' THEY'RE WILLIN' TO PAY A FORTUNE FOR 'EM.
AAAAND YOU HAVEN'T PULLED THE TRIGGER ON THIS JOB BEFORE NOW BECAUSE...
IT'S A TWO MAN JOB.
AN' YOU'RE THE ONLY GUY I'D WANNA DO IT WITH.
THAT'S...
SWEET?
Touching?
TOUCHING.
IN A VERY UNCOMFORTABL WAY.

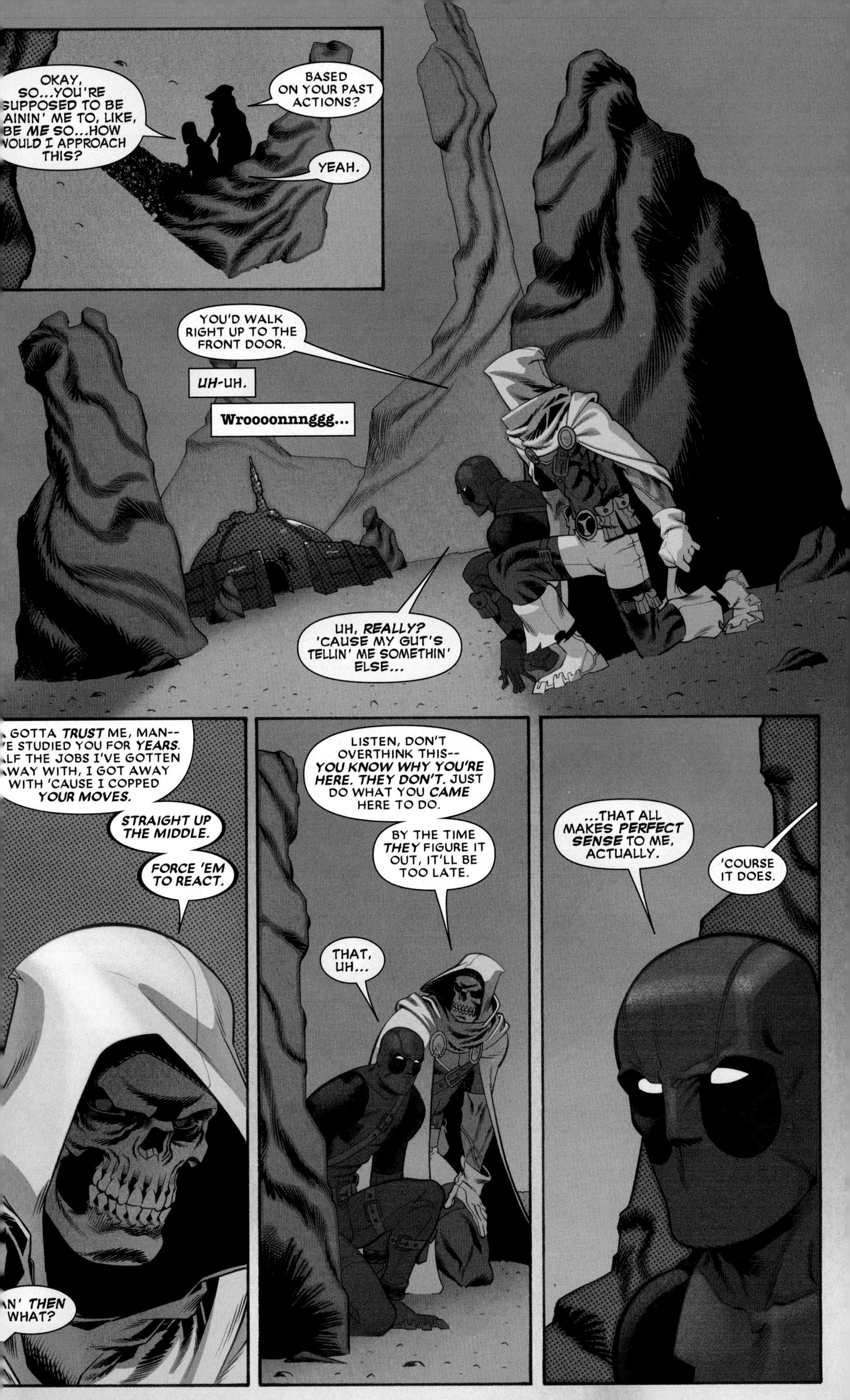
OKAY, SO...YOU'RE SUPPOSED TO BE AININ' ME TO, LIKE, BE ME SO...HOW WOULD I APPROACH THIS?
BASED ON YOUR PAST ACTIONS?
YEAH.
YOU'D WALK RIGHT UP TO THE FRONT DOOR.
UH-UH.
Wroooonnnggg...
UH, REALLY? 'CAUSE MY GUT'S TELLIN' ME SOMETHIN' ELSE...
GOTTA TRUST ME, MAN-- 'E STUDIED YOU FOR YEARS. LF THE JOBS I'VE GOTTEN AWAY WITH, I GOT AWAY WITH 'CAUSE I COPPED YOUR MOVES.
STRAIGHT UP THE MIDDLE.
FORCE 'EM TO REACT.
N' THEN WHAT?
LISTEN, DON'T OVERTHINK THIS-- YOU KNOW WHY YOU'RE HERE. THEY DON'T. JUST DO WHAT YOU CAME HERE TO DO.
BY THE TIME THEY FIGURE IT OUT, IT'LL BE TOO LATE.
THAT, UH...
...THAT ALL MAKES PERFECT SENSE TO ME, ACTUALLY.
'COURSE IT DOES.

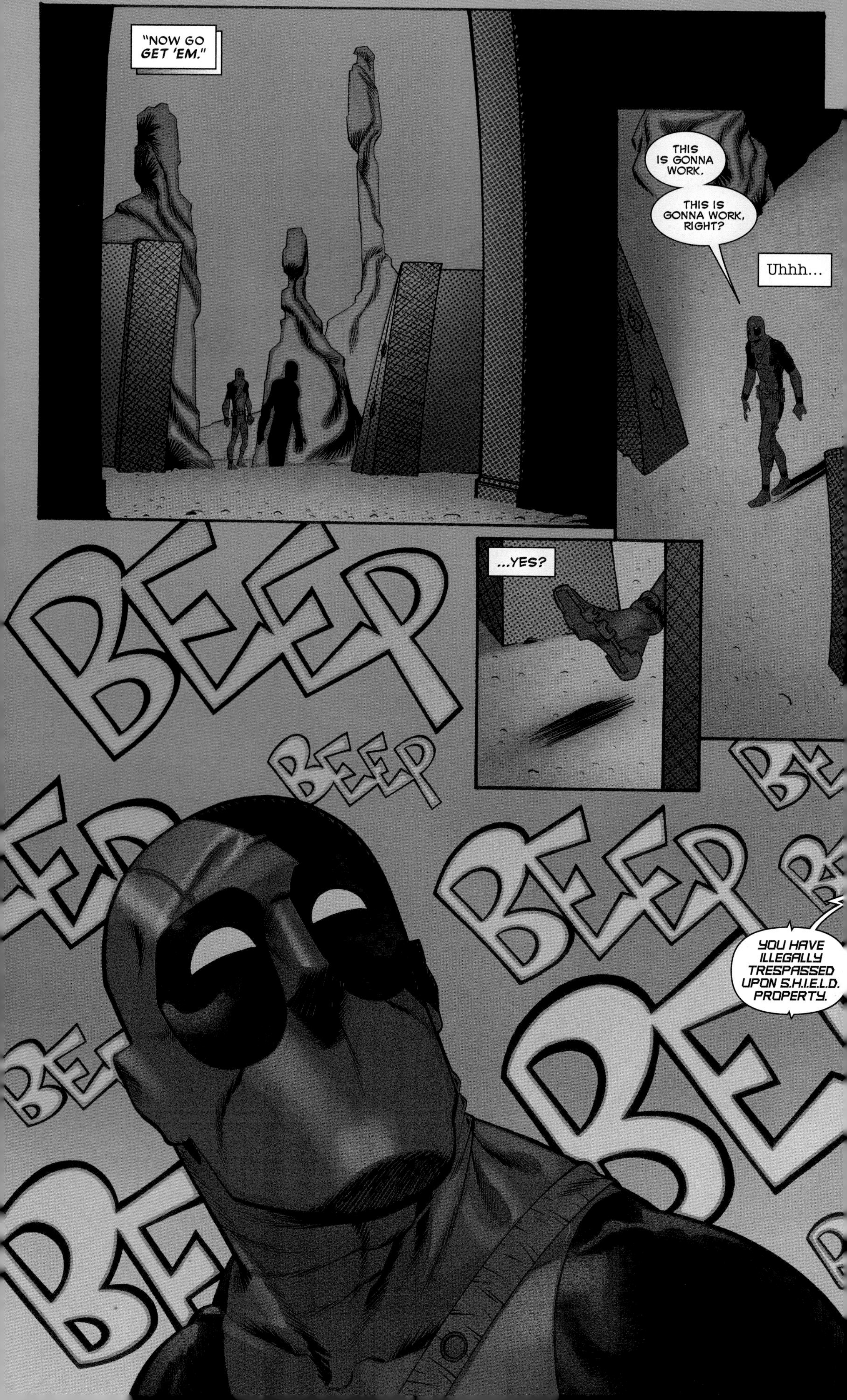
"NOW GO GET 'EM."
THIS IS GONNA WORK.
THIS IS GONNA WORK, RIGHT?
Uhhh...
...YES?
BEEP
BEEP
BEEP
YOU HAVE ILLEGALLY TRESPASSED UPON S.H.I.E.L.D. PROPERTY.

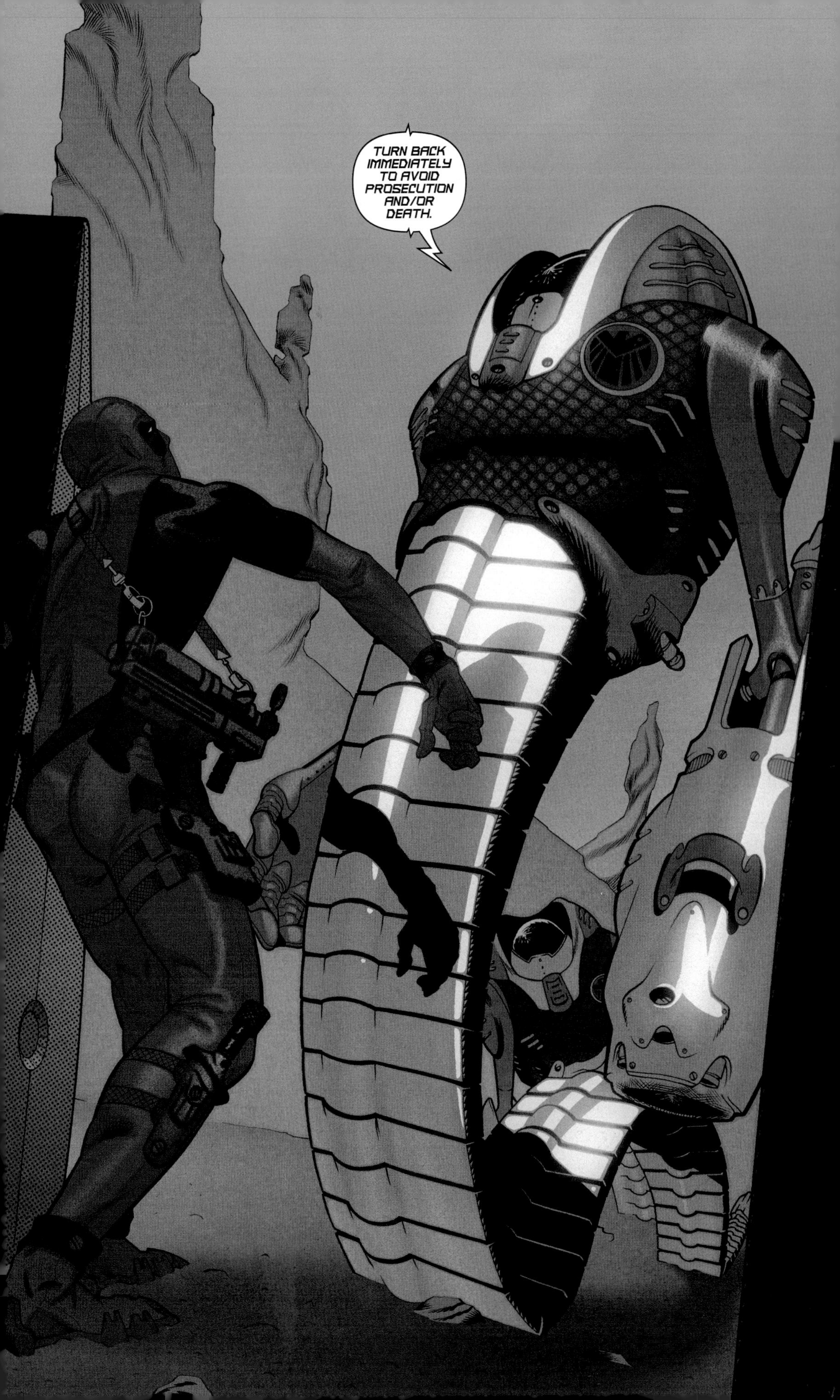
TURN BACK IMMEDIATELY TO AVOID PROSECUTION AND/OR DEATH.

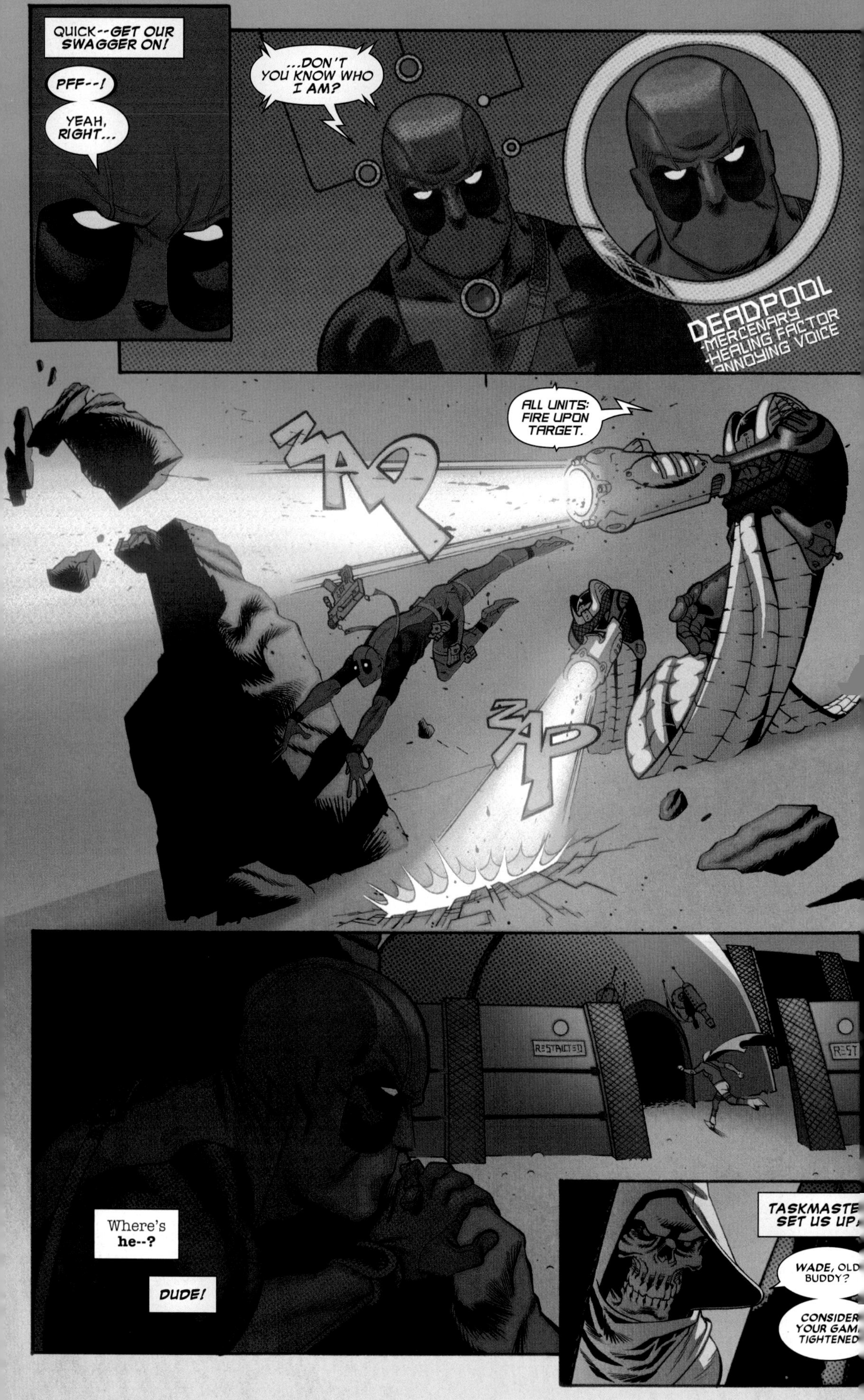
QUICK--GET OUR SWAGGER ON!
PFF--!
YEAH, RIGHT...
...DON'T YOU KNOW WHO I AM?
DEADPOOL
-MERCENARY
-HEALING FACTOR
-ANNOYING VOICE
ALL UNITS: FIRE UPON TARGET.
ZAP
ZAP
RESTRICTED
Where's he--?
DUDE!
TASKMASTE SET US UP,
WADE, OLD BUDDY?
CONSIDER YOUR GAM TIGHTENED

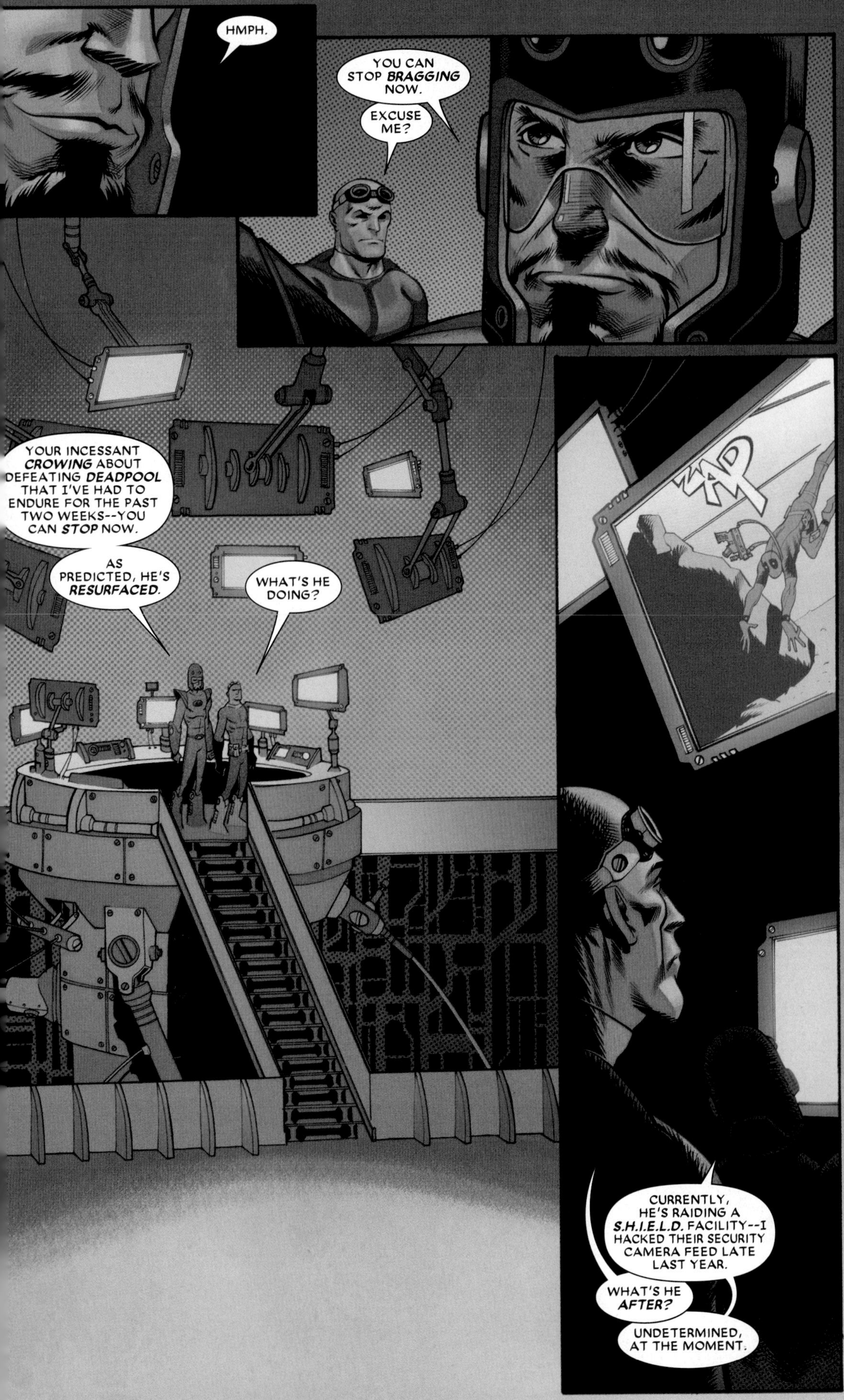
HMPH.
YOU CAN STOP BRAGGING NOW.
EXCUSE ME?
YOUR INCESSANT CROWING ABOUT DEFEATING DEADPOOL THAT I'VE HAD TO ENDURE FOR THE PAST TWO WEEKS--YOU CAN STOP NOW.
AS PREDICTED, HE'S RESURFACED.
WHAT'S HE DOING?
ZAP
CURRENTLY, HE'S RAIDING A S.H.I.E.L.D. FACILITY--I HACKED THEIR SECURITY CAMERA FEED LATE LAST YEAR.
WHAT'S HE AFTER?
UNDETERMINED, AT THE MOMENT.

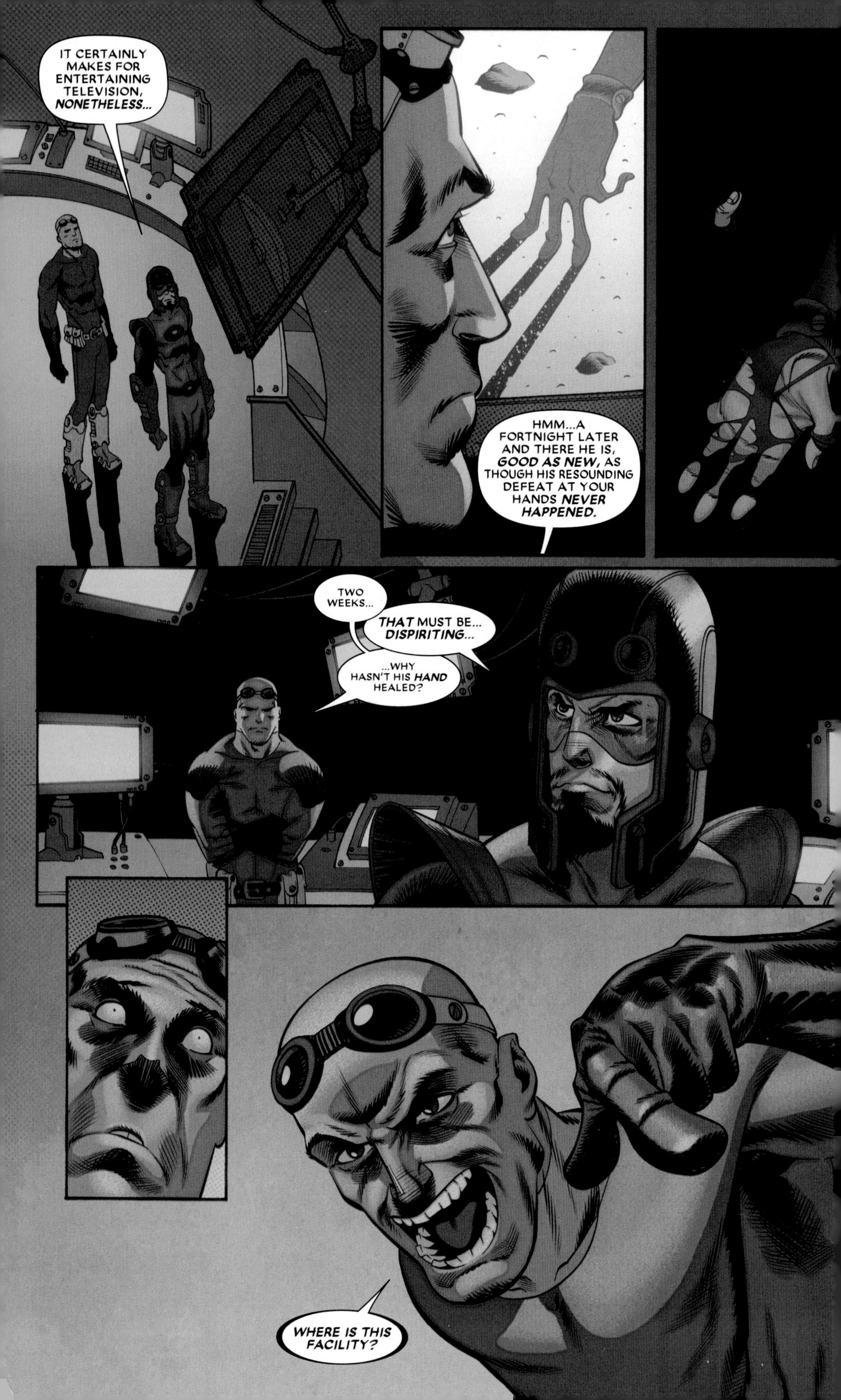

IT CERTAINLY MAKES FOR ENTERTAINING TELEVISION, NONETHELESS...
HMM...A FORTNIGHT LATER AND THERE HE IS, GOOD AS NEW, AS THOUGH HIS RESOUNDING DEFEAT AT YOUR HANDS NEVER HAPPENED.
TWO WEEKS...
THAT MUST BE... DISPIRITING...
...WHY HASN'T HIS HAND HEALED?
WHERE IS THIS FACILITY?

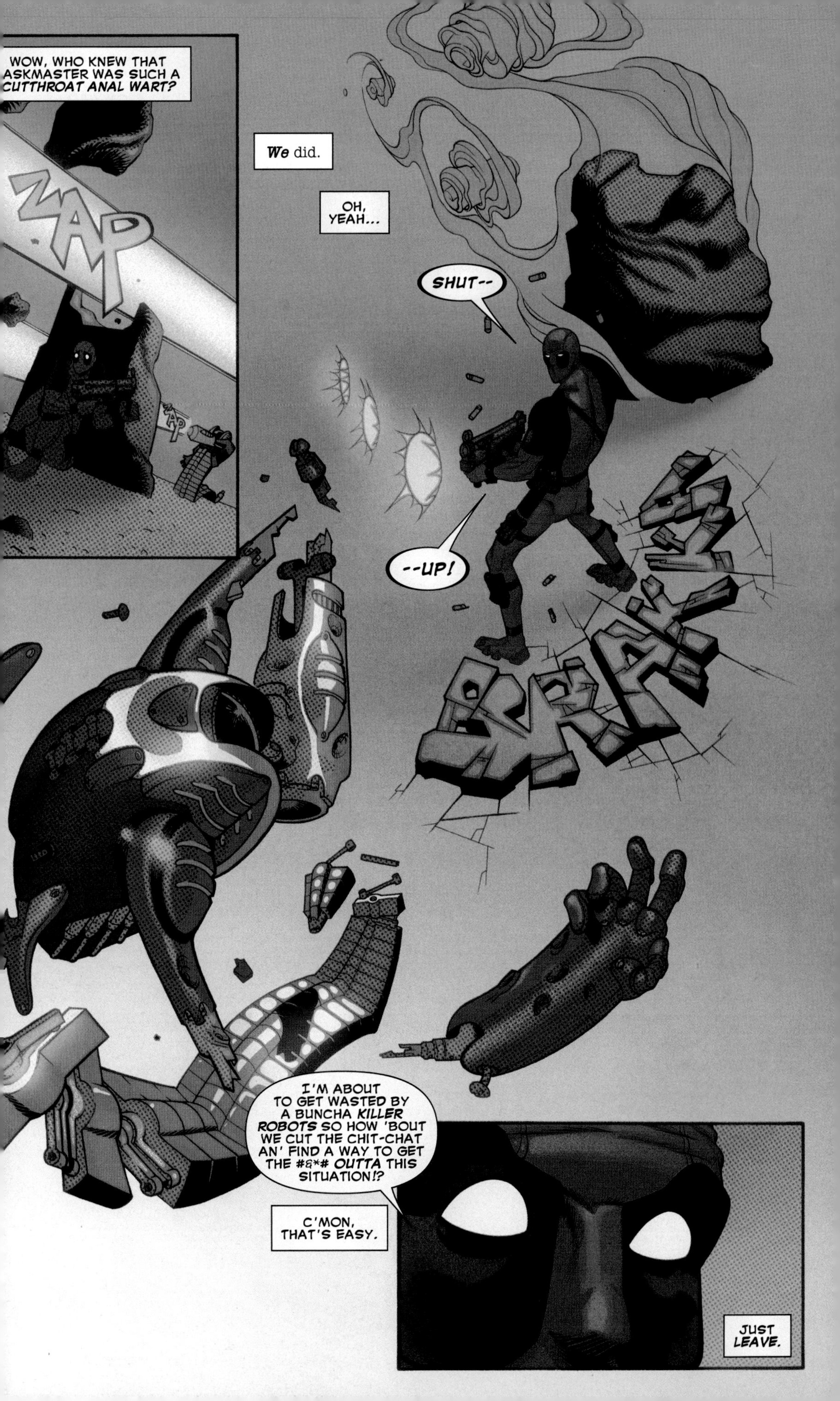
WOW, WHO KNEW THAT ASKMASTER WAS SUCH A CUTTHROAT ANAL WART?
ZAP
ZAP
We did.
OH, YEAH...
SHUT--
--UP!
BRAK
I'M ABOUT TO GET WASTED BY A BUNCHA KILLER ROBOTS SO HOW 'BOUT WE CUT THE CHIT-CHAT AN' FIND A WAY TO GET THE #&*# OUTTA THIS SITUATION!?
C'MON, THAT'S EASY.
JUST LEAVE.

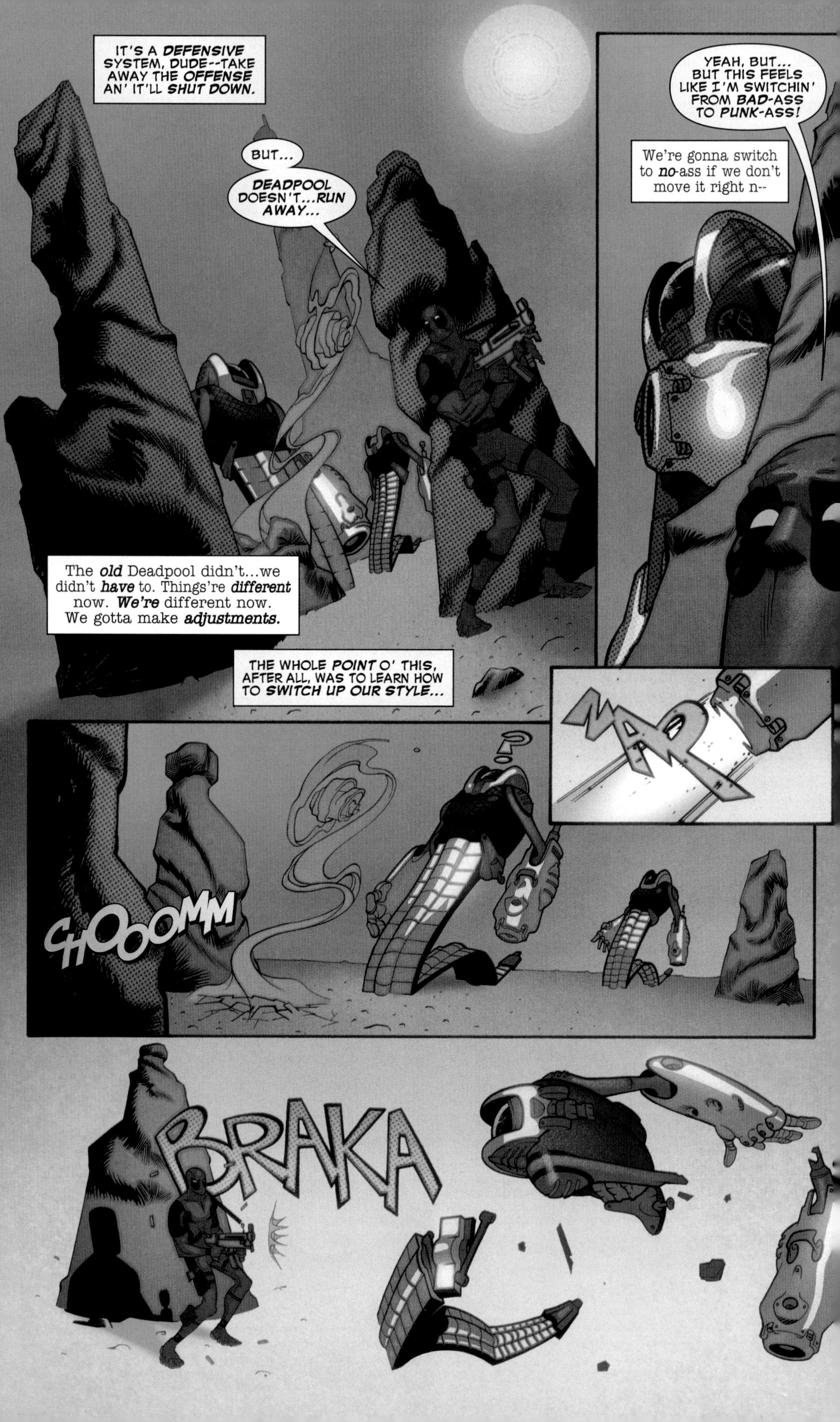

IT'S A DEFENSIVE SYSTEM, DUDE--TAKE AWAY THE OFFENSE AN' IT'LL SHUT DOWN.
BUT...
DEADPOOL DOESN'T...RUN AWAY...
The old Deadpool didn't...we didn't have to. Things're different now. We're different now. We gotta make adjustments.
THE WHOLE POINT O' THIS, AFTER ALL, WAS TO LEARN HOW TO SWITCH UP OUR STYLE...
YEAH, BUT... BUT THIS FEELS LIKE I'M SWITCHIN' FROM BAD-ASS TO PUNK-ASS!
We're gonna switch to no-ass if we don't move it right n--
WAP
CHOOOMM
?
BRAKA

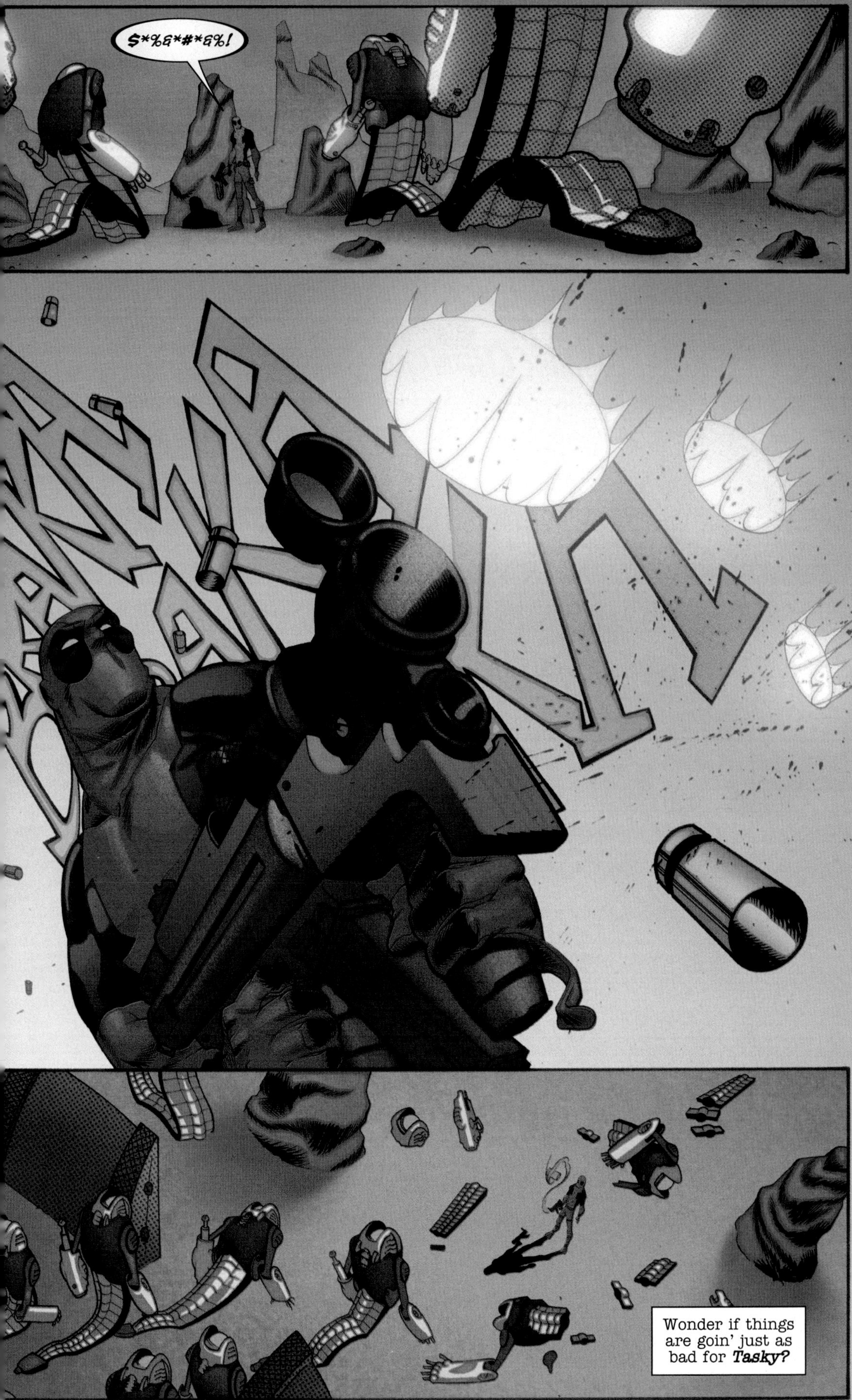
$*%&*#*&%!
Wonder if things are goin' just as bad for *Tasky?*

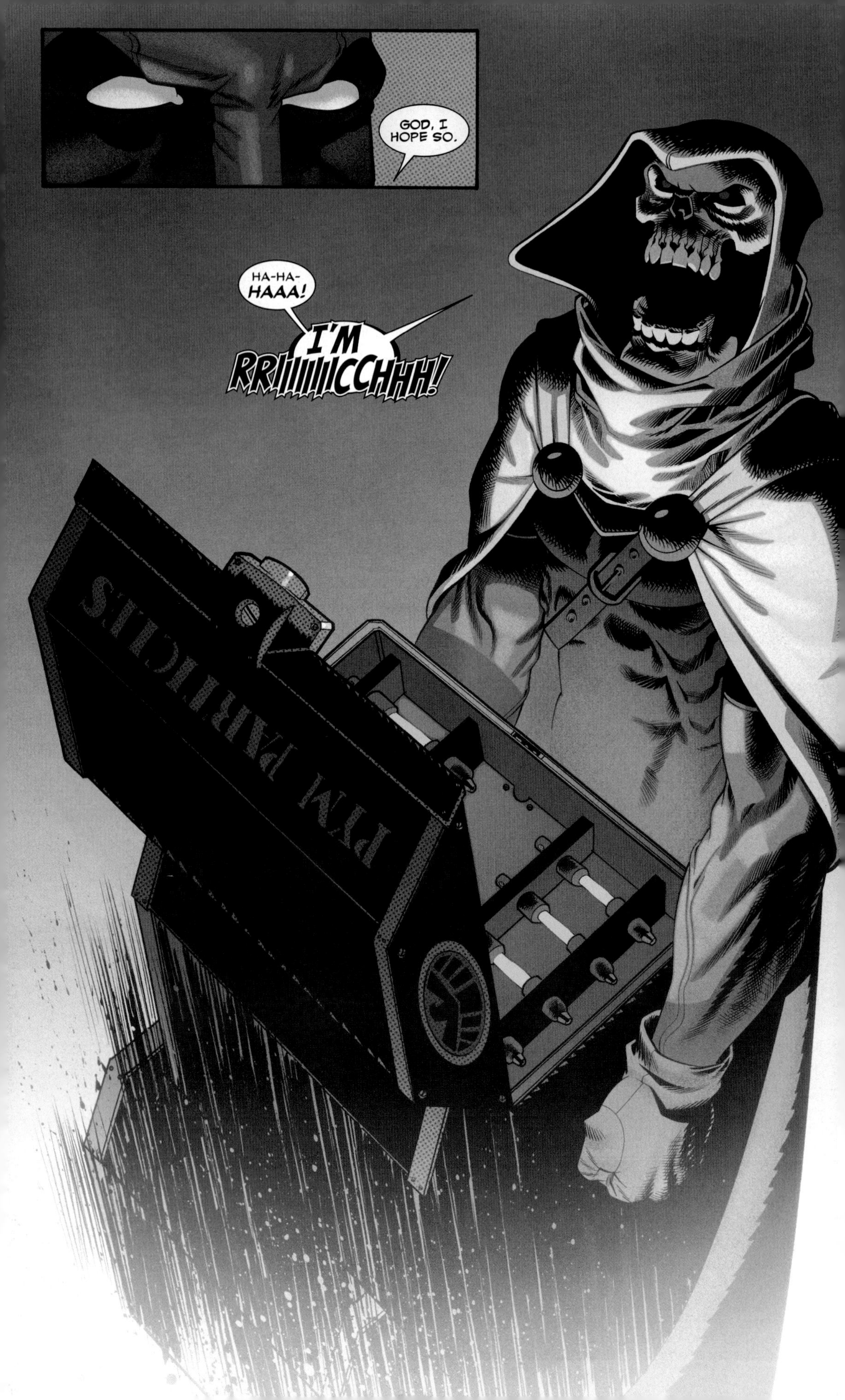

GOD, I HOPE SO.
HA-HA-HAAA!
I'M RRIIIIIIIICCHHH!

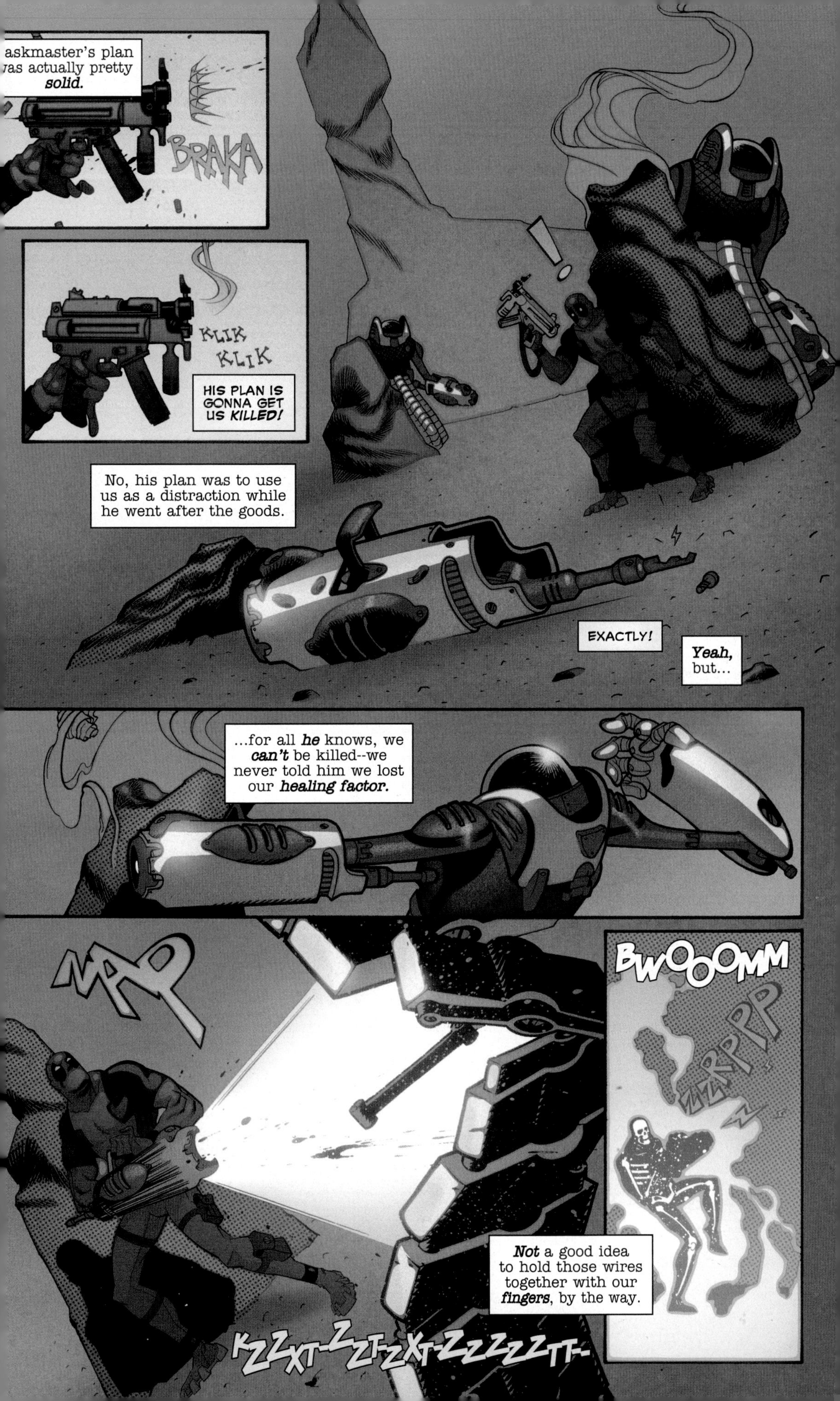
askmaster's plan
vas actually pretty
solid.
BRAKA
KLIK KLIK
HIS PLAN IS GONNA GET US *KILLED!*
No, his plan was to use us as a distraction while he went after the goods.
EXACTLY!
Yeah, but...
...for all *he* knows, we *can't* be killed--we never told him we lost our *healing factor.*
NAP
BWOOOMM
ZZRPPP
Not a good idea to hold those wires together with our *fingers*, by the way.
KZZXT-ZZTZXT-ZZZZZZTT-

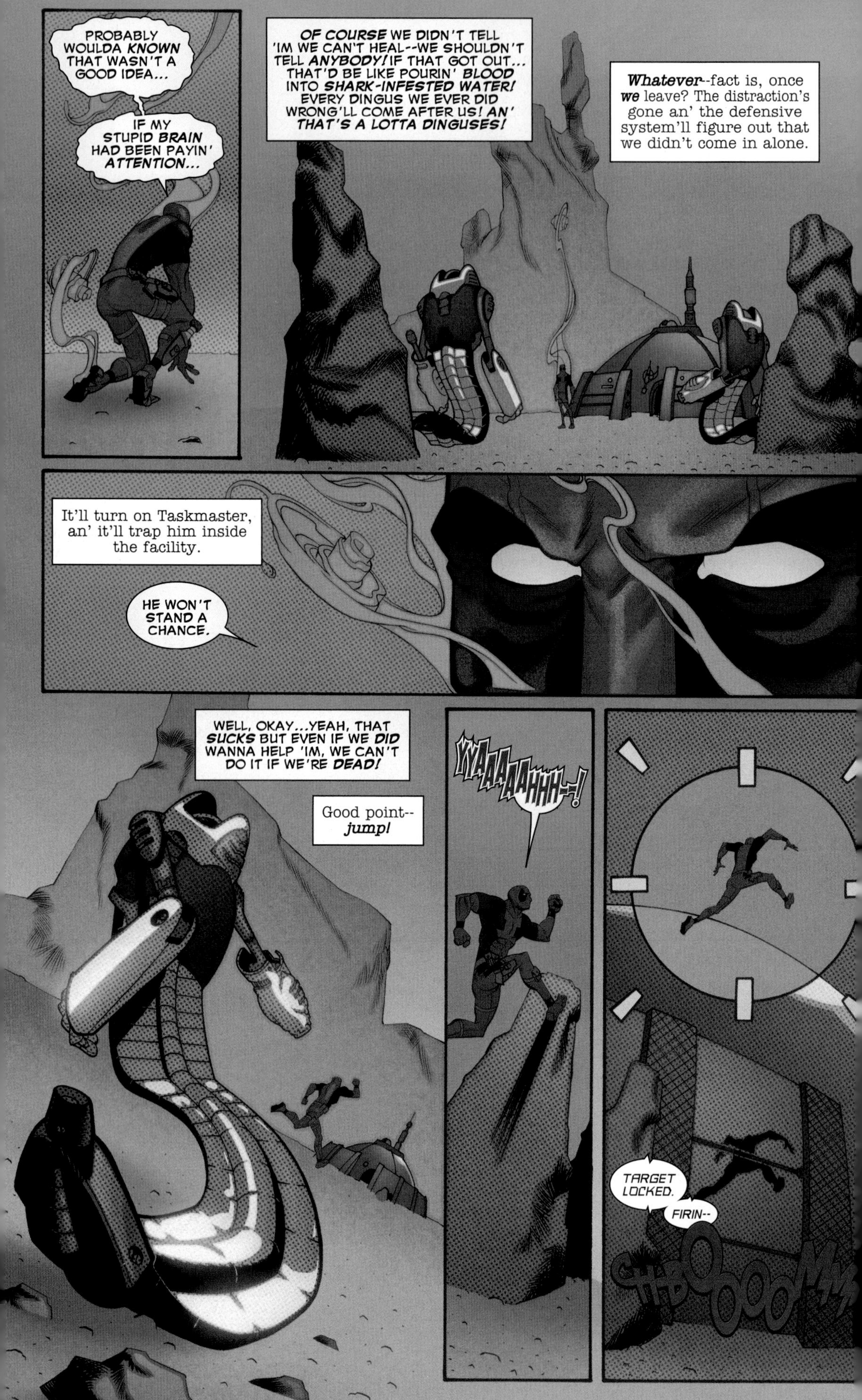
PROBABLY WOULDA KNOWN THAT WASN'T A GOOD IDEA...
IF MY STUPID BRAIN HAD BEEN PAYIN' ATTENTION...
OF COURSE WE DIDN'T TELL 'IM WE CAN'T HEAL--WE SHOULDN'T TELL ANYBODY! IF THAT GOT OUT... THAT'D BE LIKE POURIN' BLOOD INTO SHARK-INFESTED WATER! EVERY DINGUS WE EVER DID WRONG'LL COME AFTER US! AN' THAT'S A LOTTA DINGUSES!
Whatever--fact is, once we leave? The distraction's gone an' the defensive system'll figure out that we didn't come in alone.
It'll turn on Taskmaster, an' it'll trap him inside the facility.
HE WON'T STAND A CHANCE.
WELL, OKAY...YEAH, THAT SUCKS BUT EVEN IF WE DID WANNA HELP 'IM, WE CAN'T DO IT IF WE'RE DEAD!
Good point-- jump!
YYAAAAAHHH--!
TARGET LOCKED.
FIRIN--

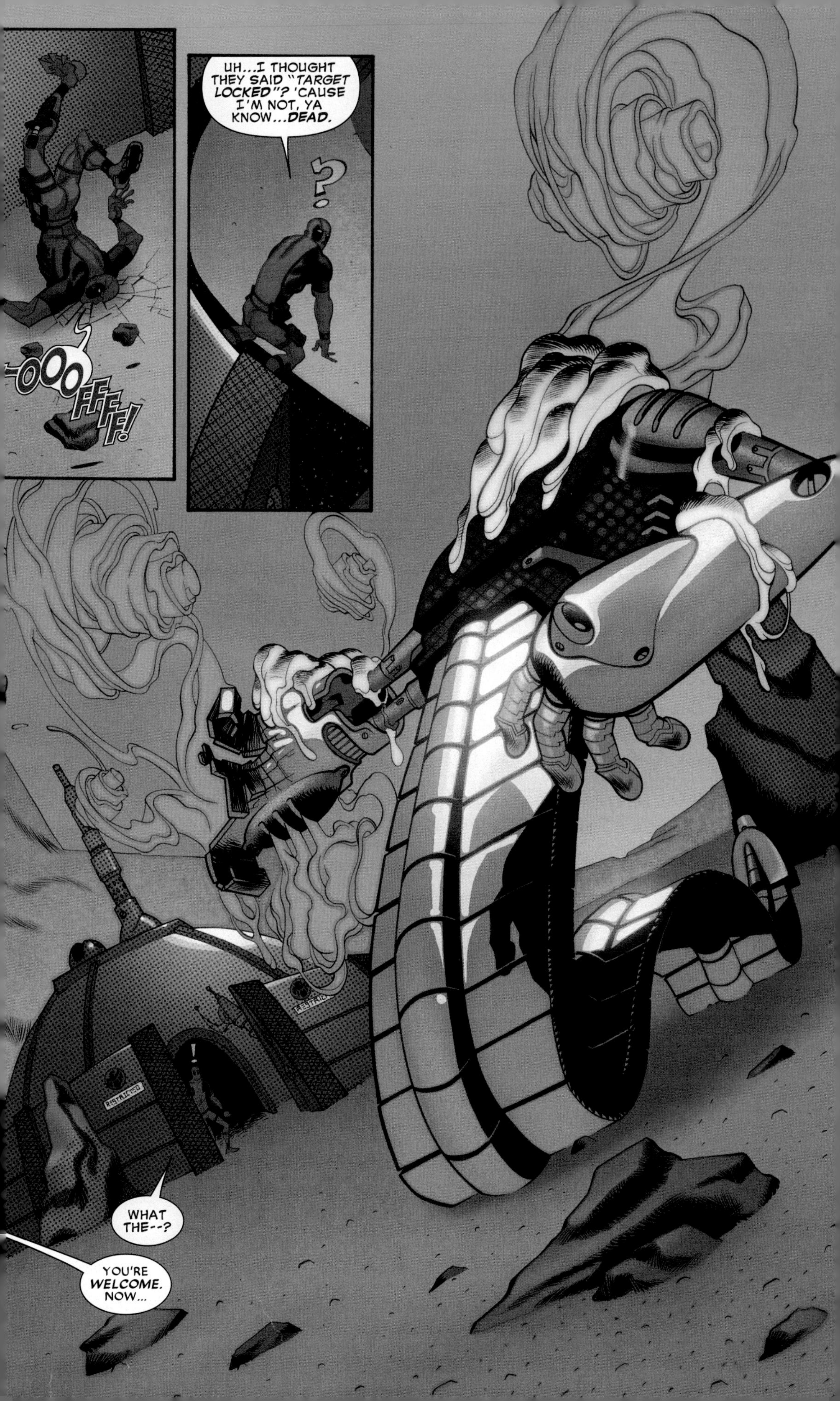
OOOFFFF!
UH...I THOUGHT THEY SAID "TARGET LOCKED"? 'CAUSE I'M NOT, YA KNOW...DEAD.
?
WHAT THE--?
YOU'RE WELCOME. NOW...

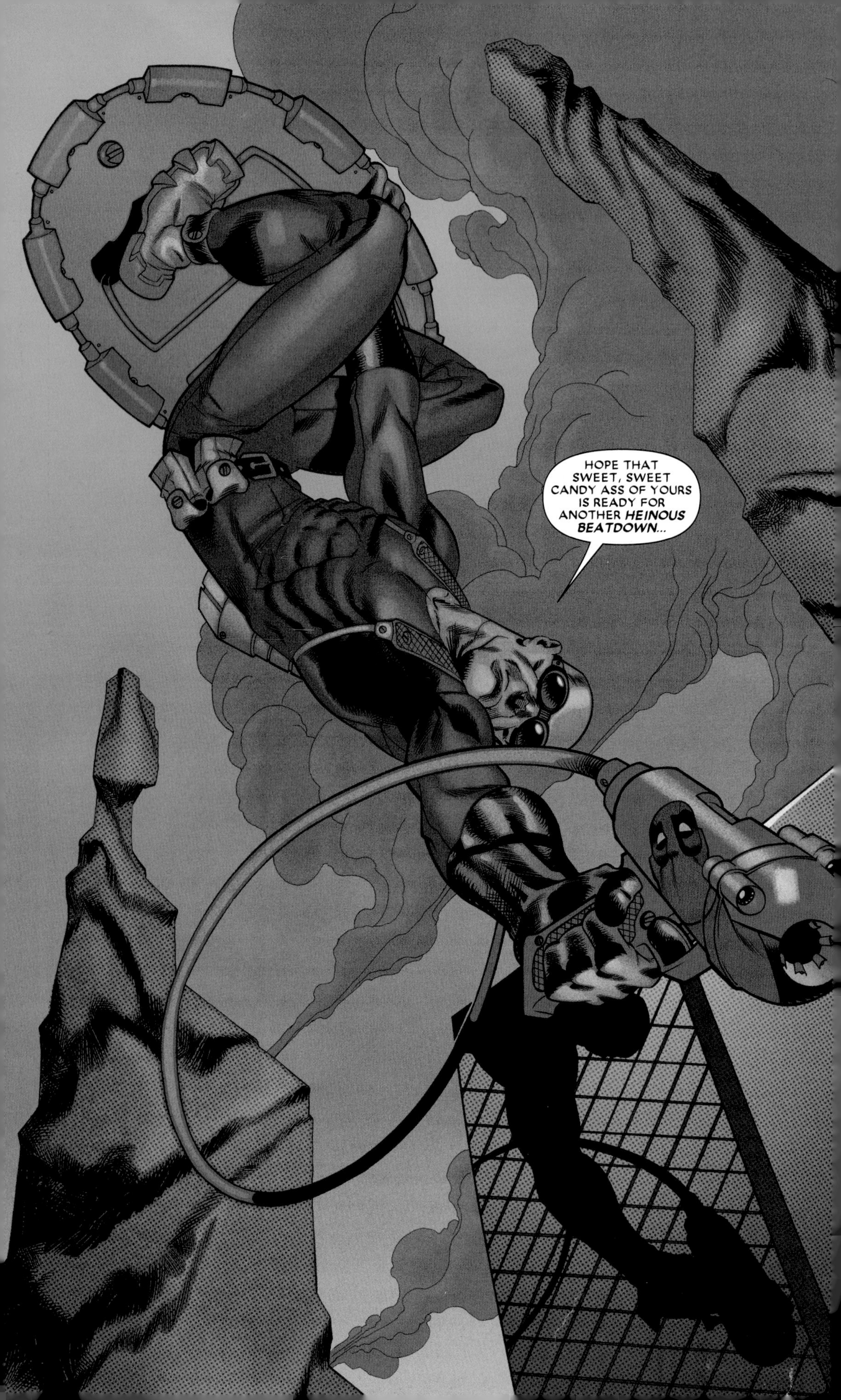
HOPE THAT SWEET, SWEET CANDY ASS OF YOURS IS READY FOR ANOTHER *HEINOUS BEATDOWN*...

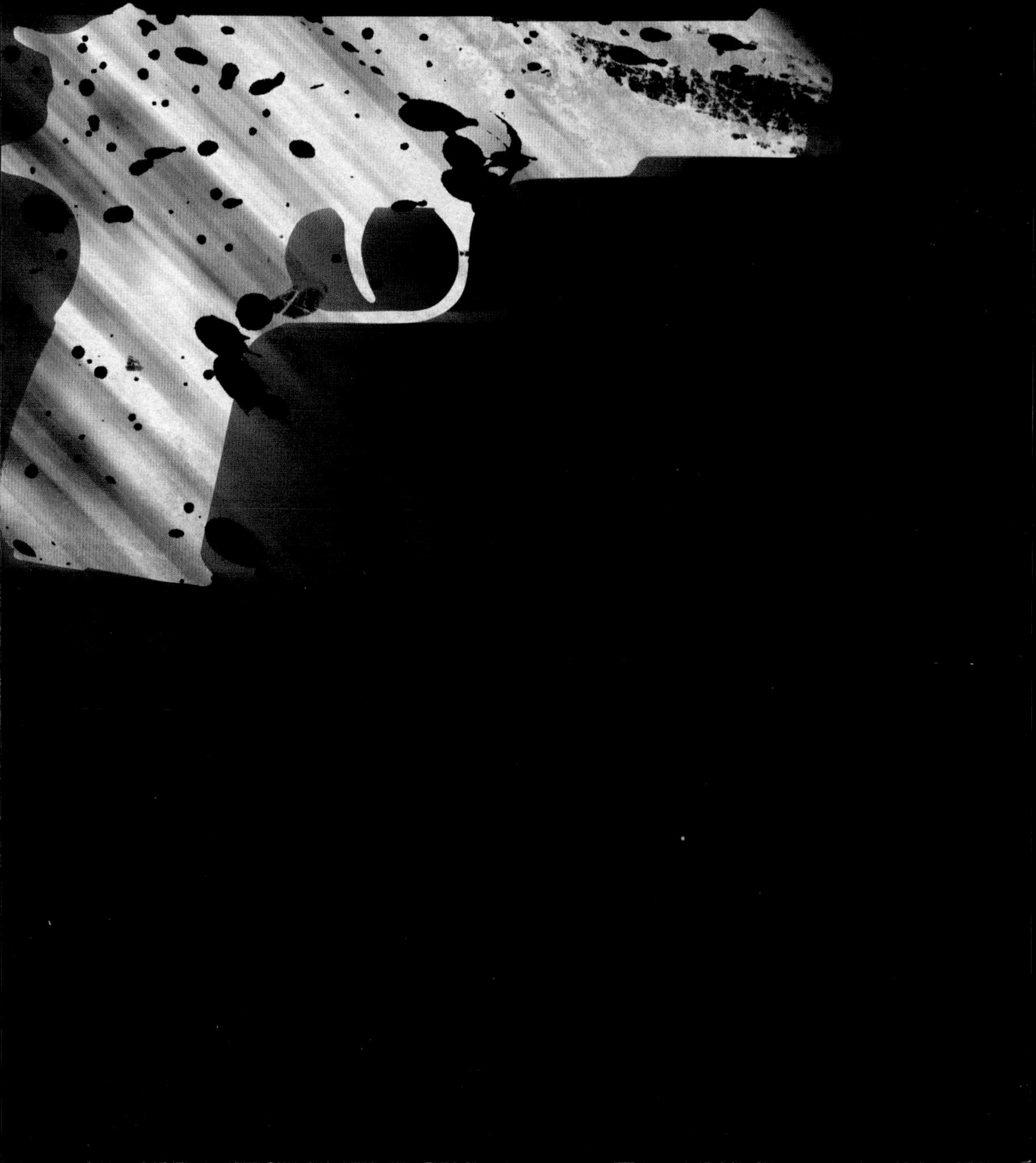

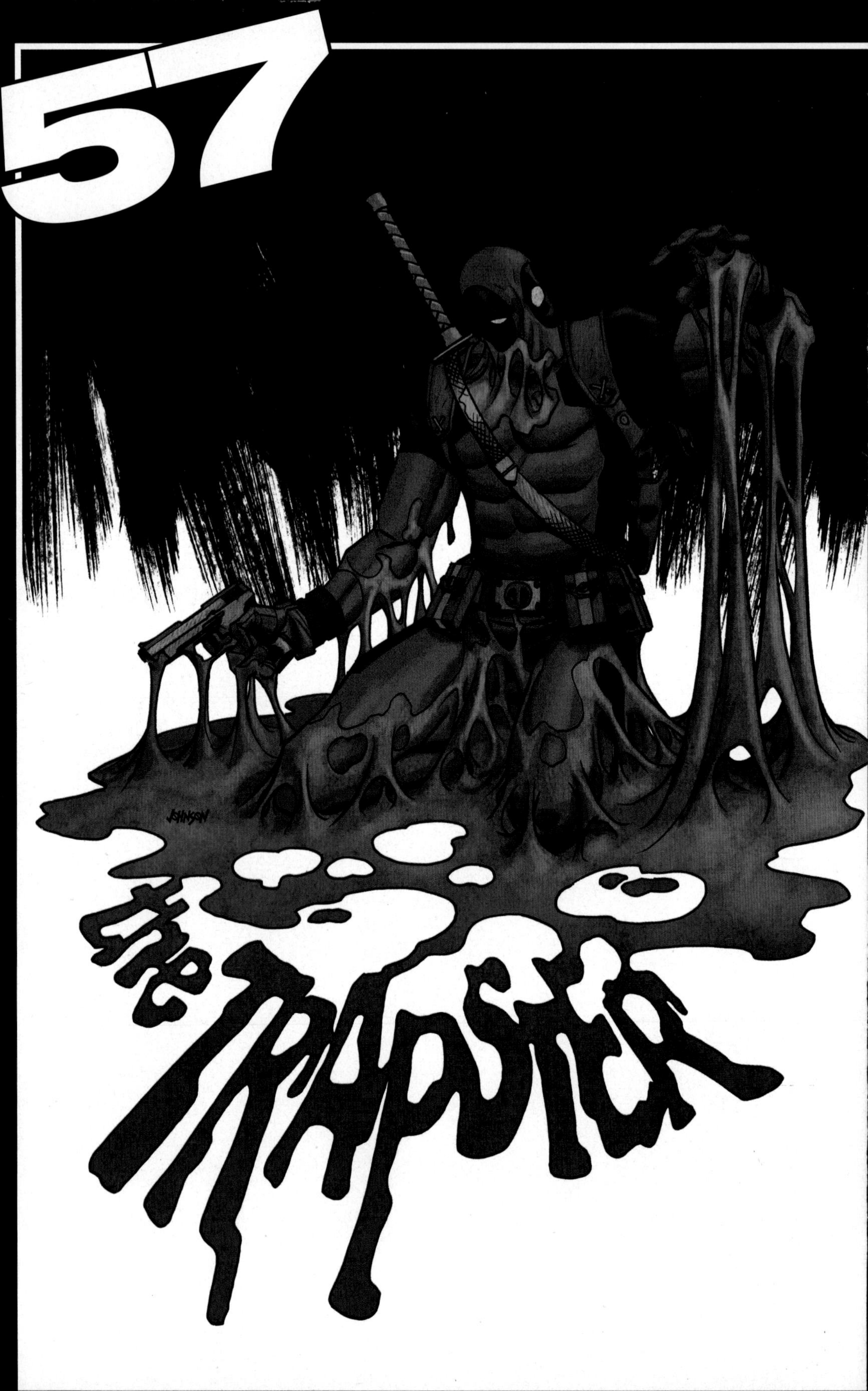
57
JOHNSON
the TRAPSTER

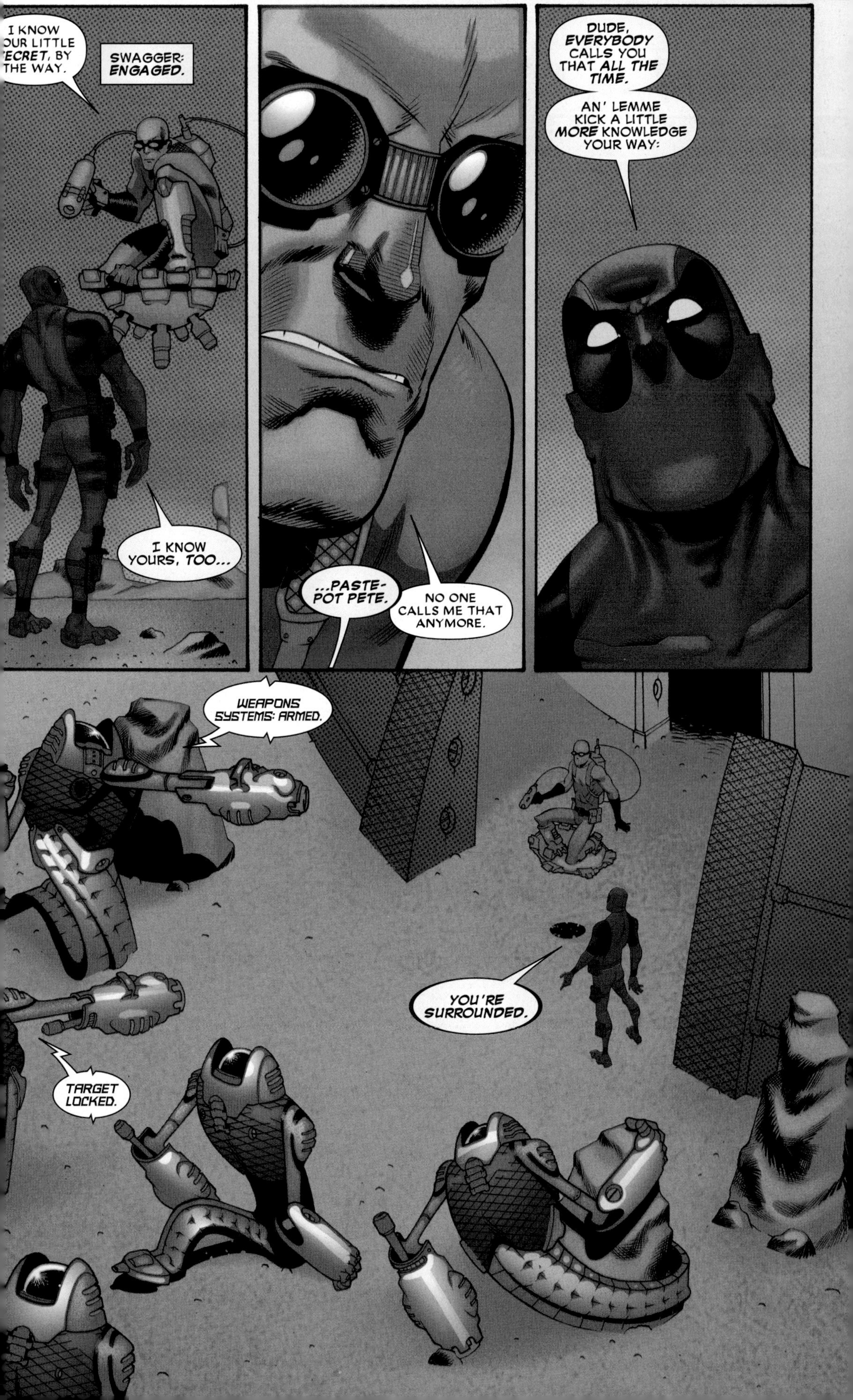
I KNOW
OUR LITTLE
ECRET, BY
THE WAY.
SWAGGER: ENGAGED.
I KNOW YOURS, TOO...
...PASTE-POT PETE.
NO ONE CALLS ME THAT ANYMORE.
DUDE, EVERYBODY CALLS YOU THAT ALL THE TIME.
AN' LEMME KICK A LITTLE MORE KNOWLEDGE YOUR WAY:
WEAPONS SYSTEMS: ARMED.
YOU'RE SURROUNDED.
TARGET LOCKED.

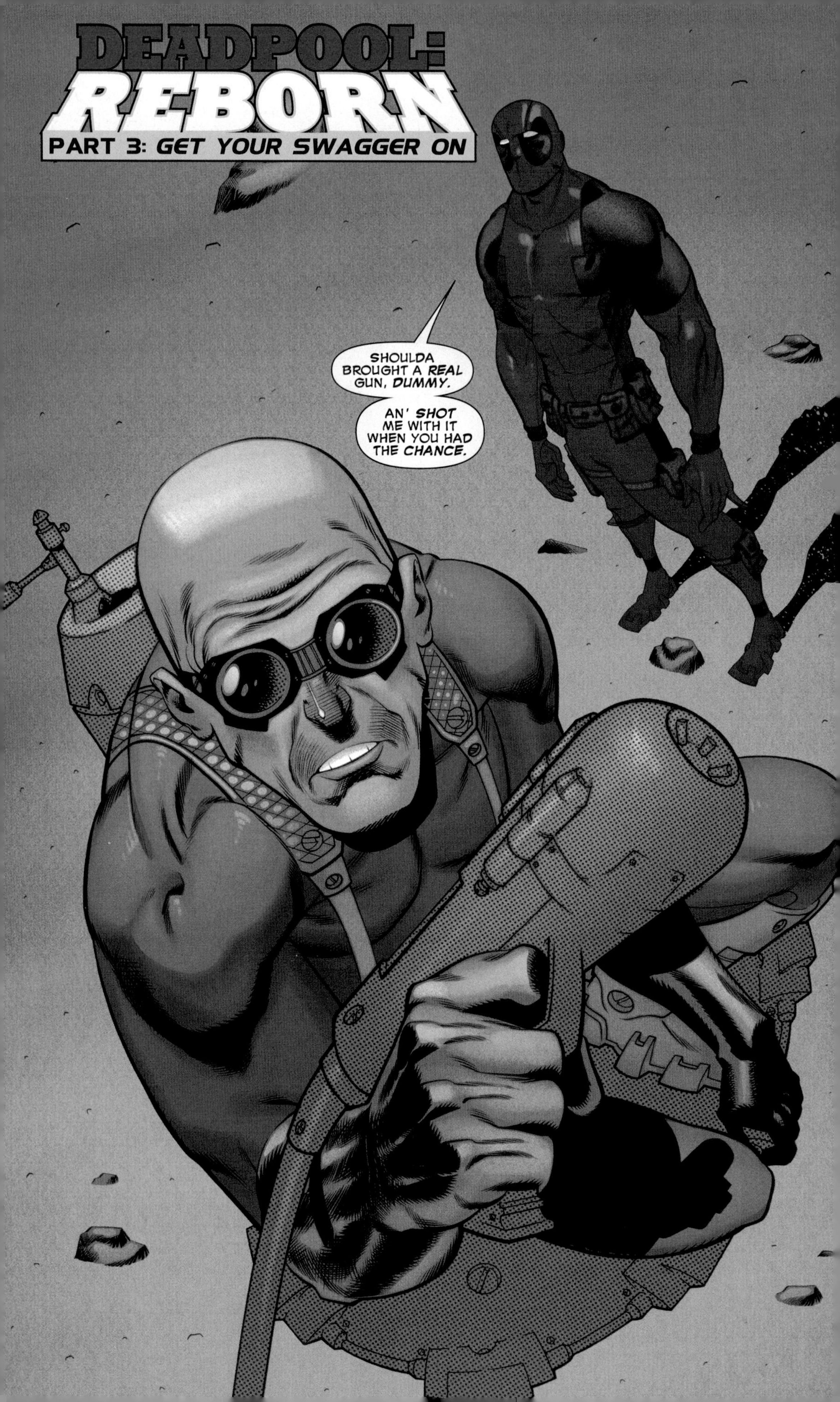
DEADPOOL: REBORN
PART 3: GET YOUR SWAGGER ON
SHOULDA BROUGHT A REAL GUN, DUMMY.
AN' SHOT ME WITH IT WHEN YOU HAD THE CHANCE.

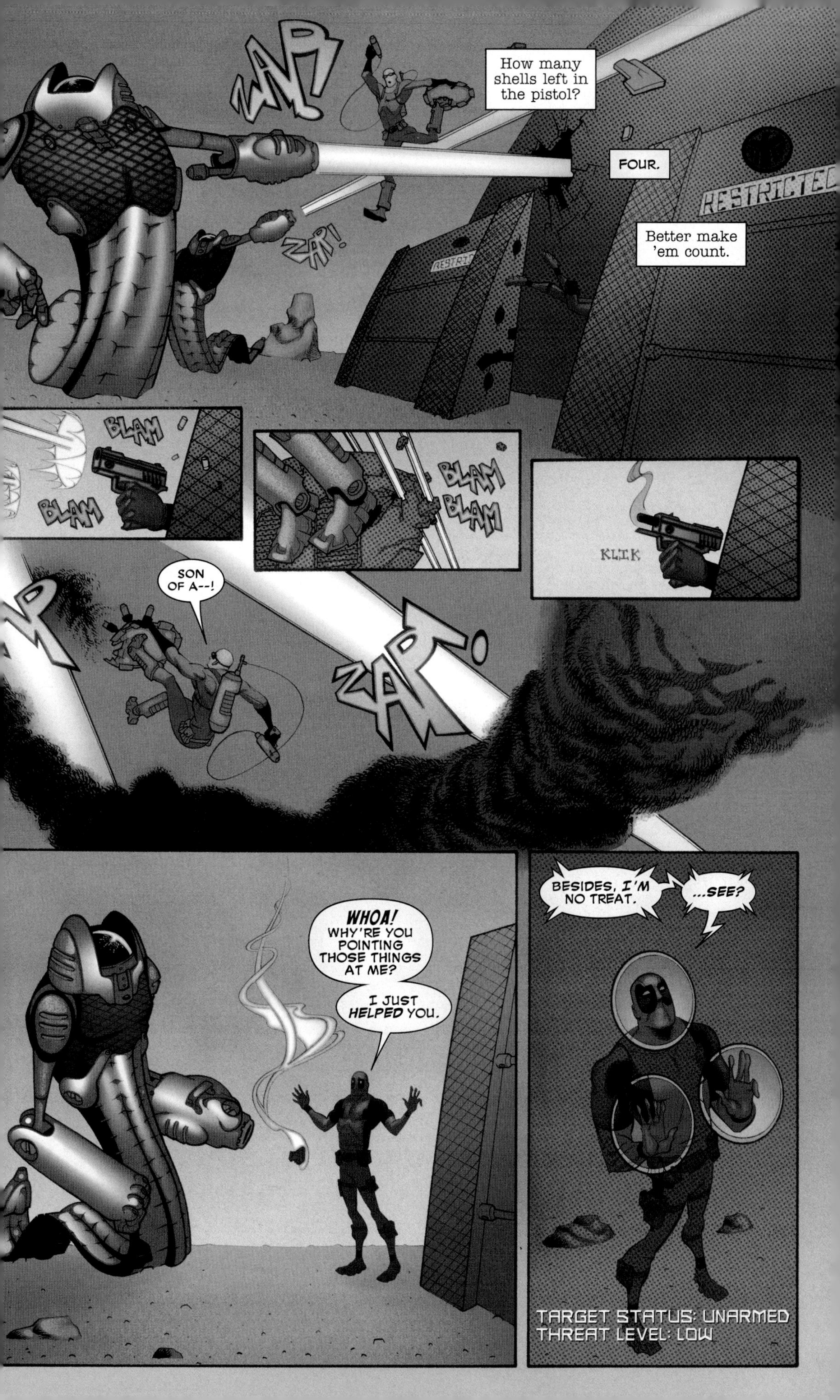
ZAP!
How many shells left in the pistol?
FOUR.
RESTRICTED
ZAP!
RESTRIC
Better make 'em count.
BLAM
BLAM
BLAM
BLAM
KLIK
SON OF A--!
ZAP!
WHOA! WHY'RE YOU POINTING THOSE THINGS AT ME?
I JUST HELPED YOU.
BESIDES, I'M NO TREAT.
...SEE?
TARGET STATUS: UNARMED
THREAT LEVEL: LOW

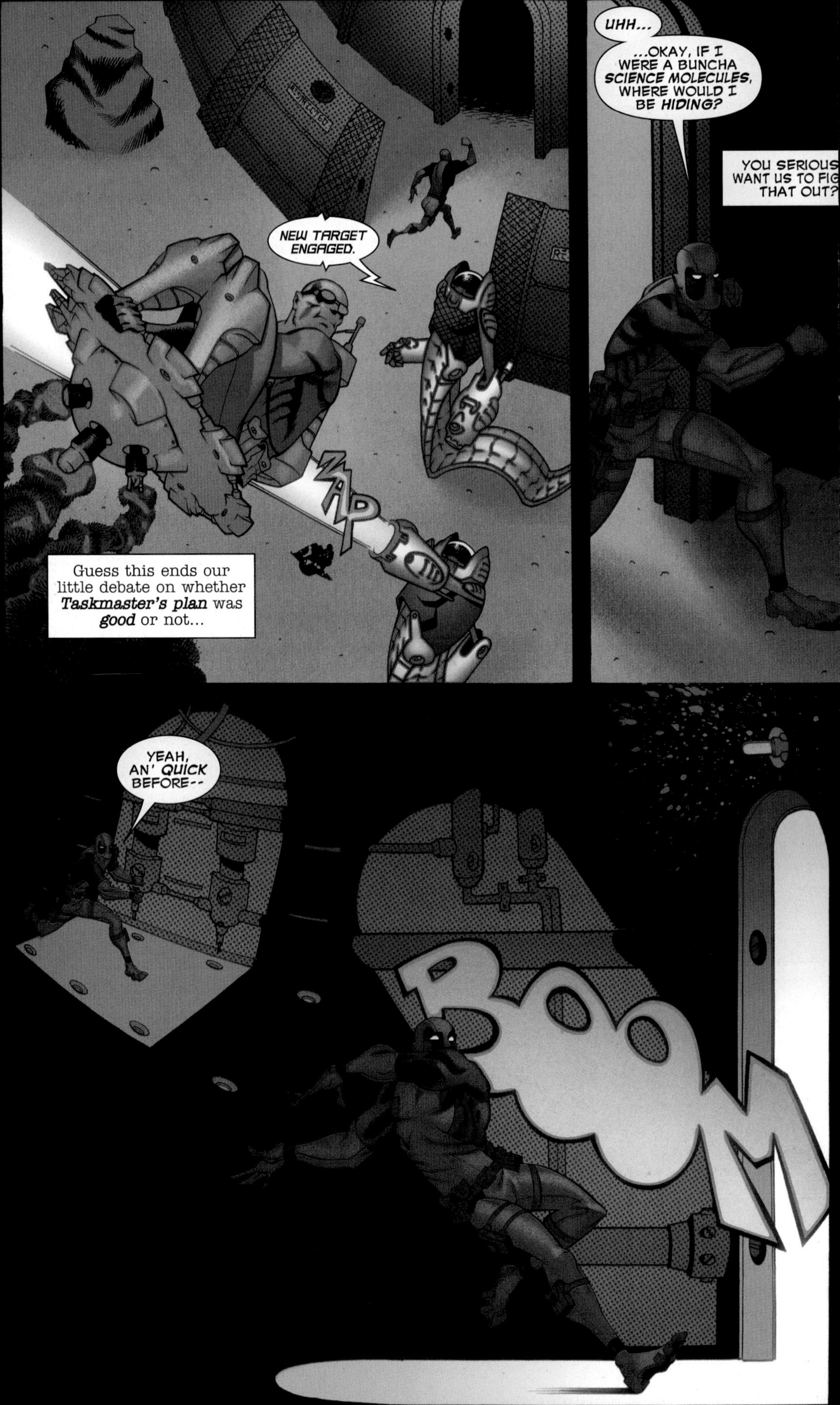
NEW TARGET ENGAGED.
ZAP
Guess this ends our little debate on whether *Taskmaster's plan* was *good* or not...
UHH...
...OKAY, IF I WERE A BUNCHA SCIENCE MOLECULES, WHERE WOULD I BE HIDING?
YOU SERIOUS WANT US TO FIG THAT OUT?
YEAH, AN' QUICK BEFORE--
BOOM

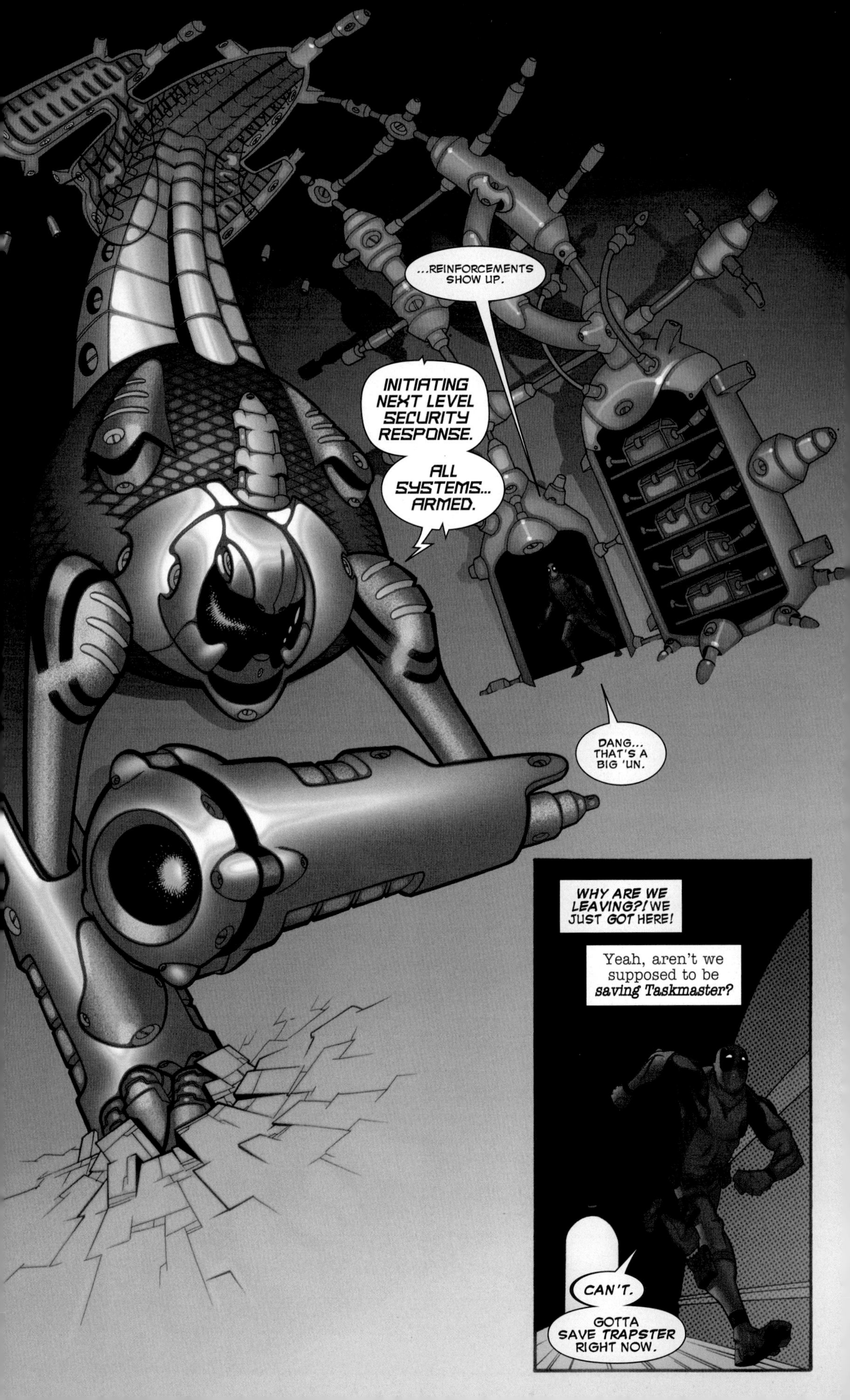

...REINFORCEMENTS SHOW UP.
INITIATING NEXT LEVEL SECURITY RESPONSE.
ALL SYSTEMS... ARMED.
DANG... THAT'S A BIG 'UN.
WHY ARE WE LEAVING?! WE JUST GOT HERE!
Yeah, aren't we supposed to be saving Taskmaster?
CAN'T.
GOTTA SAVE TRAPSTER RIGHT NOW.

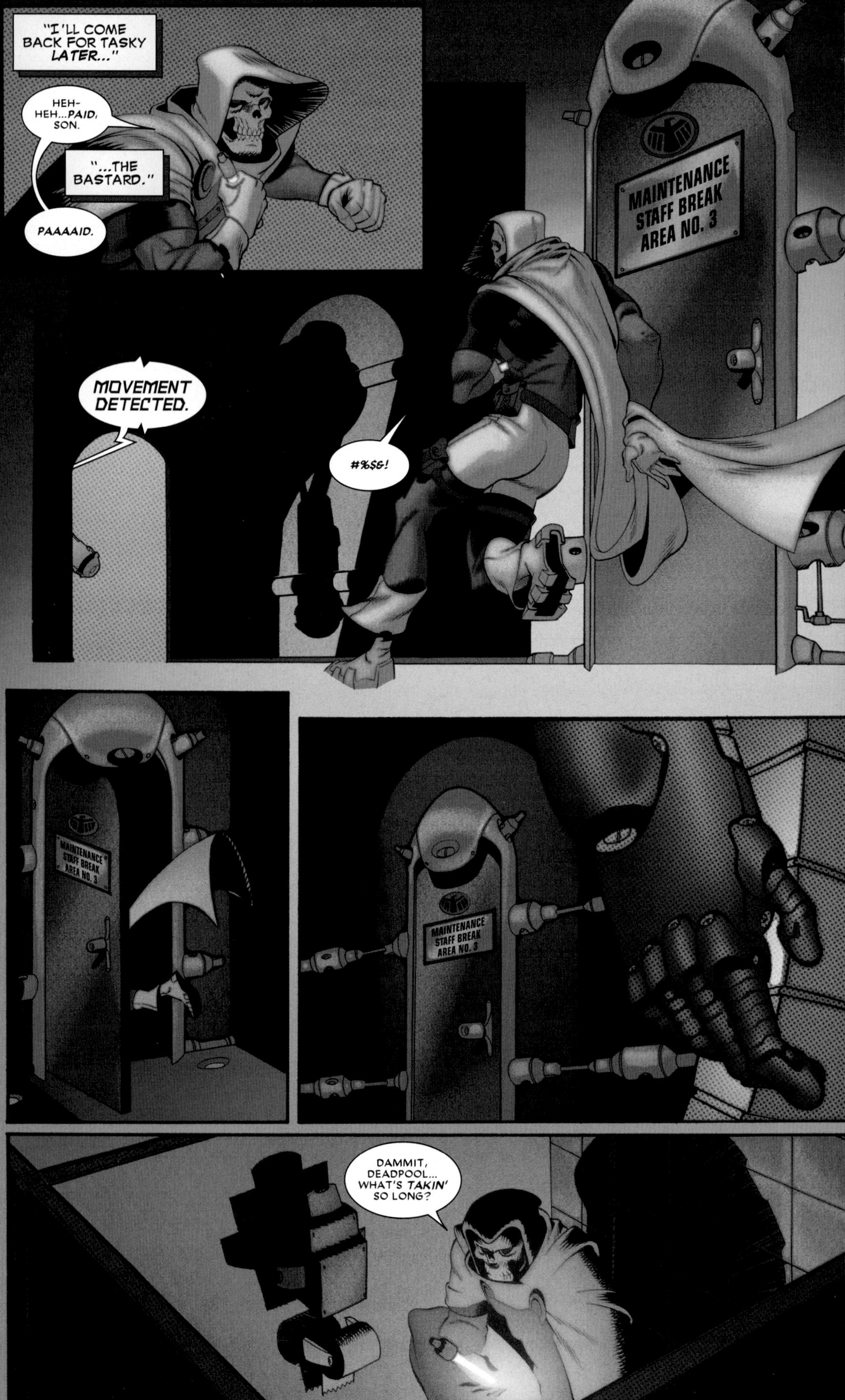
"I'LL COME BACK FOR TASKY LATER..."
HEH-HEH...PAID, SON.
"...THE BASTARD."
PAAAAID.
MAINTENANCE STAFF BREAK AREA NO. 3
MOVEMENT DETECTED.
#%$&!
MAINTENANCE STAFF BREAK AREA NO. 3
MAINTENANCE STAFF BREAK AREA NO. 3
DAMMIT, DEADPOOL... WHAT'S TAKIN' SO LONG?

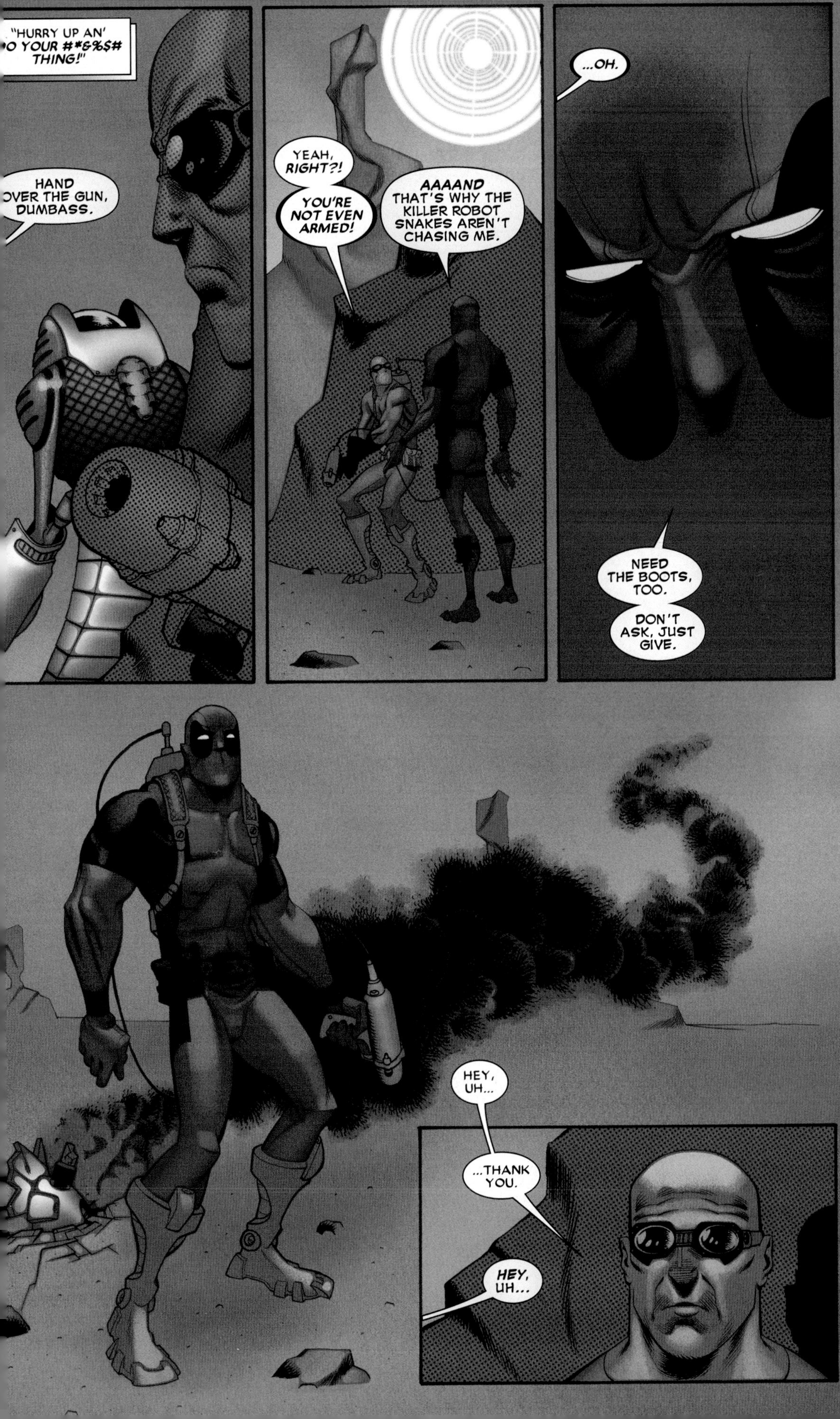
"HURRY UP AN' DO YOUR #*&%$# THING!"
HAND OVER THE GUN, DUMBASS.
YEAH, RIGHT?!
YOU'RE NOT EVEN ARMED!
AAAAND THAT'S WHY THE KILLER ROBOT SNAKES AREN'T CHASING ME.
...OH.
NEED THE BOOTS, TOO.
DON'T ASK, JUST GIVE.
HEY, UH...
...THANK YOU.
HEY, UH...

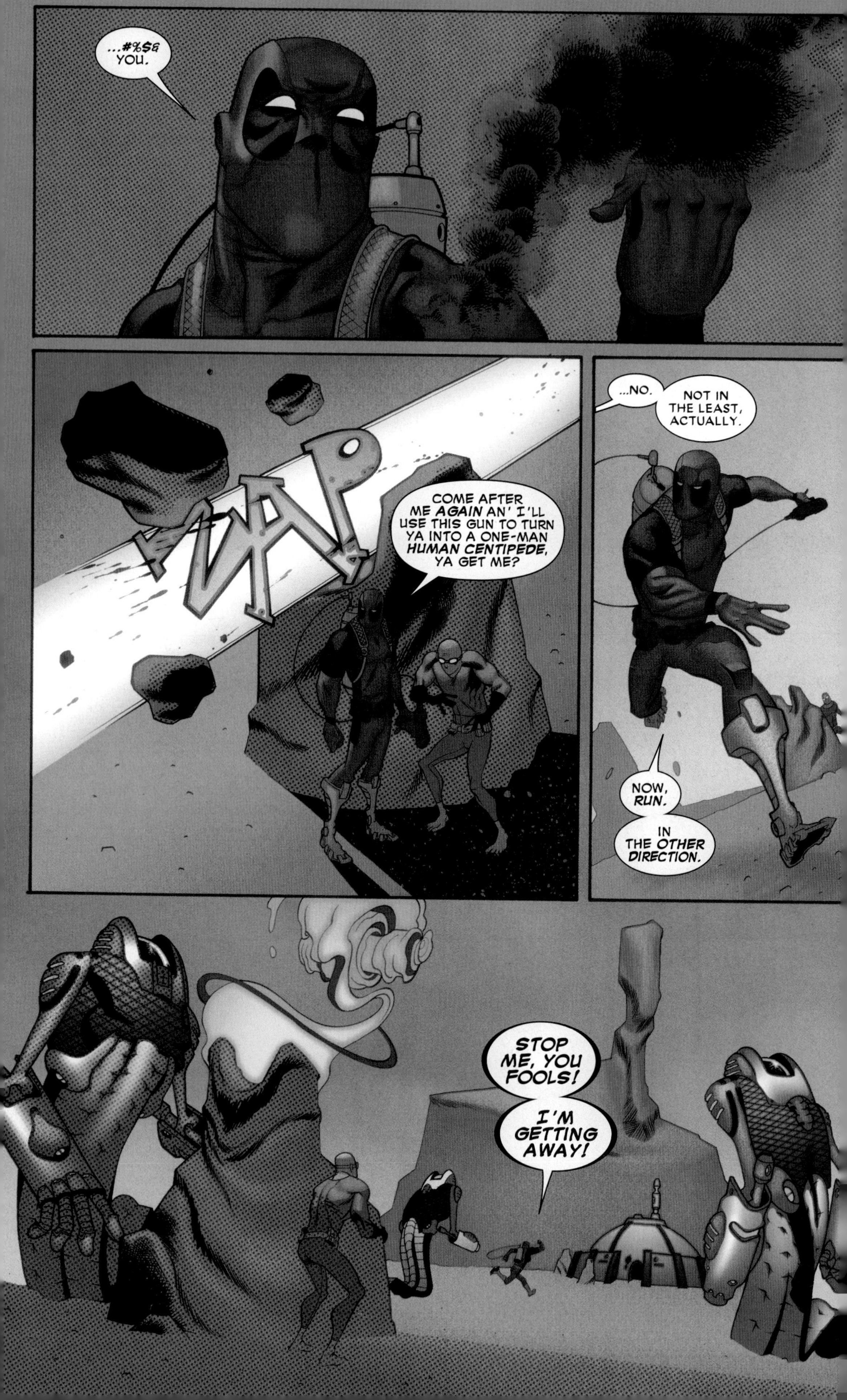
...#%$& YOU.
COME AFTER ME AGAIN AN' I'LL USE THIS GUN TO TURN YA INTO A ONE-MAN HUMAN CENTIPEDE, YA GET ME?
...NO.
NOT IN THE LEAST, ACTUALLY.
NOW, RUN.
IN THE OTHER DIRECTION.
STOP ME, YOU FOOLS!
I'M GETTING AWAY!

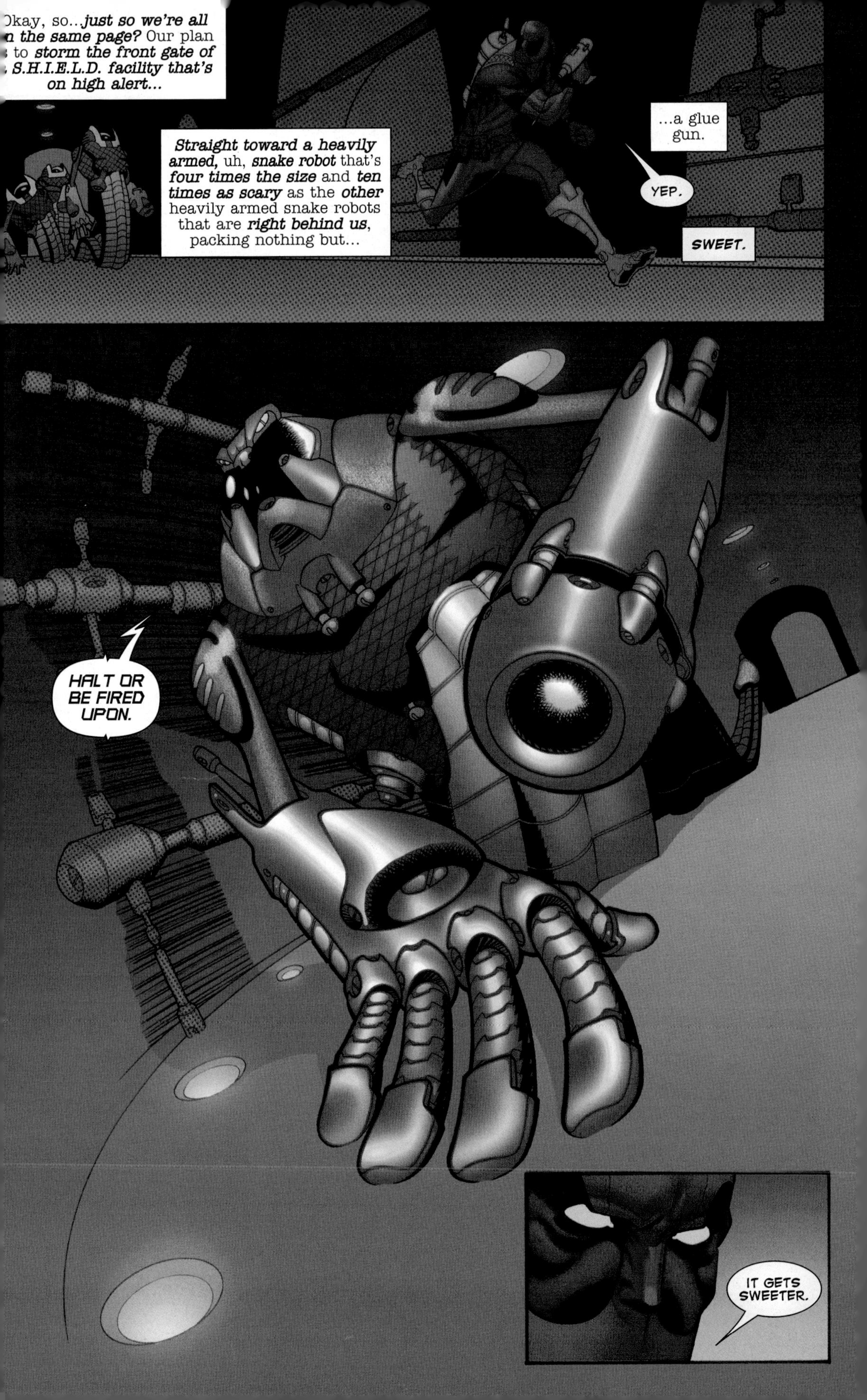

Okay, so…just so we're all on the same page? Our plan is to storm the front gate of a S.H.I.E.L.D. facility that's on high alert…
Straight toward a heavily armed, uh, snake robot that's four times the size and ten times as scary as the other heavily armed snake robots that are right behind us, packing nothing but…
…a glue gun.
YEP.
SWEET.
HALT OR BE FIRED UPON.
IT GETS SWEETER.

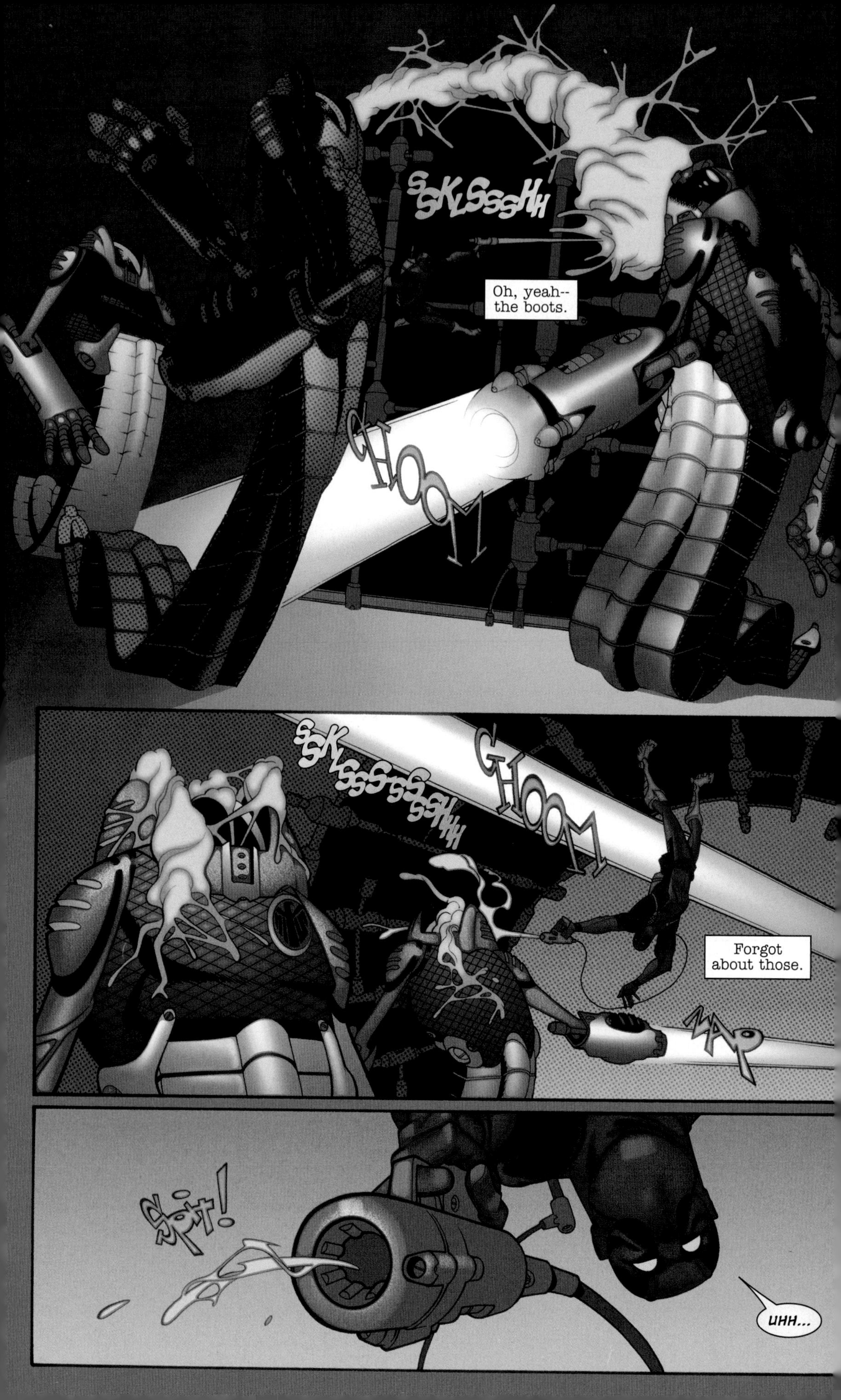

Oh, yeah--
the boots.
CHOOM
CHOOM
Forgot
about those.
UHH...

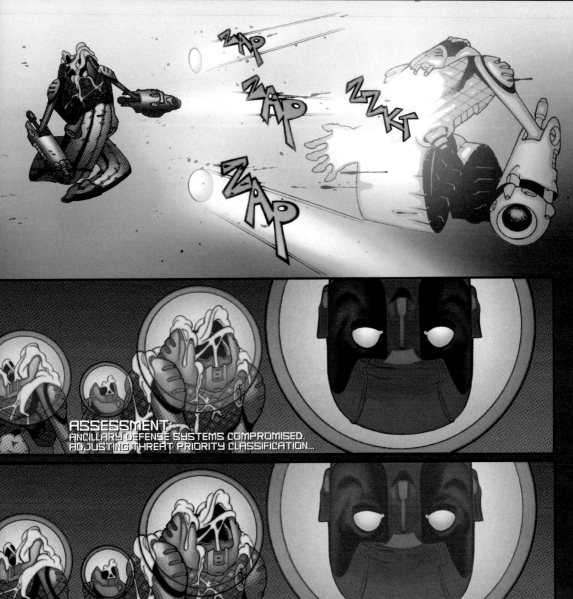

ASSESSMENT:
ANCILLARY DEFENSE SYSTEMS COMPROMISED.
ADJUSTING THREAT PRIORITY CLASSIFICATION...

...ADJUSTMENT
COMPLETE.

YOU GUYS
AREN'T GONNA
LET HIM *GET
AWAY WITH
THAT*, ARE
YOU?!

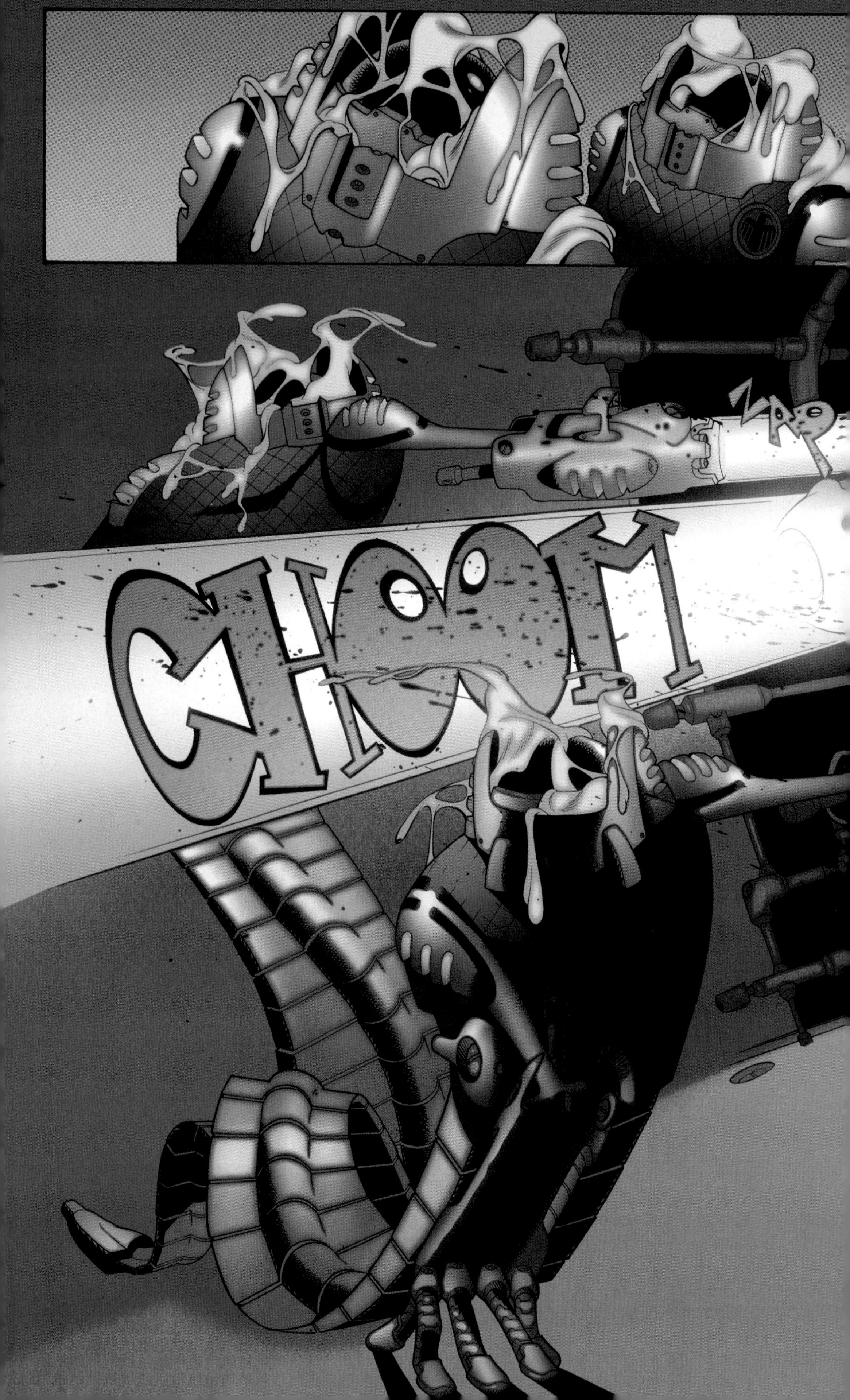
ZAP
CHOOM

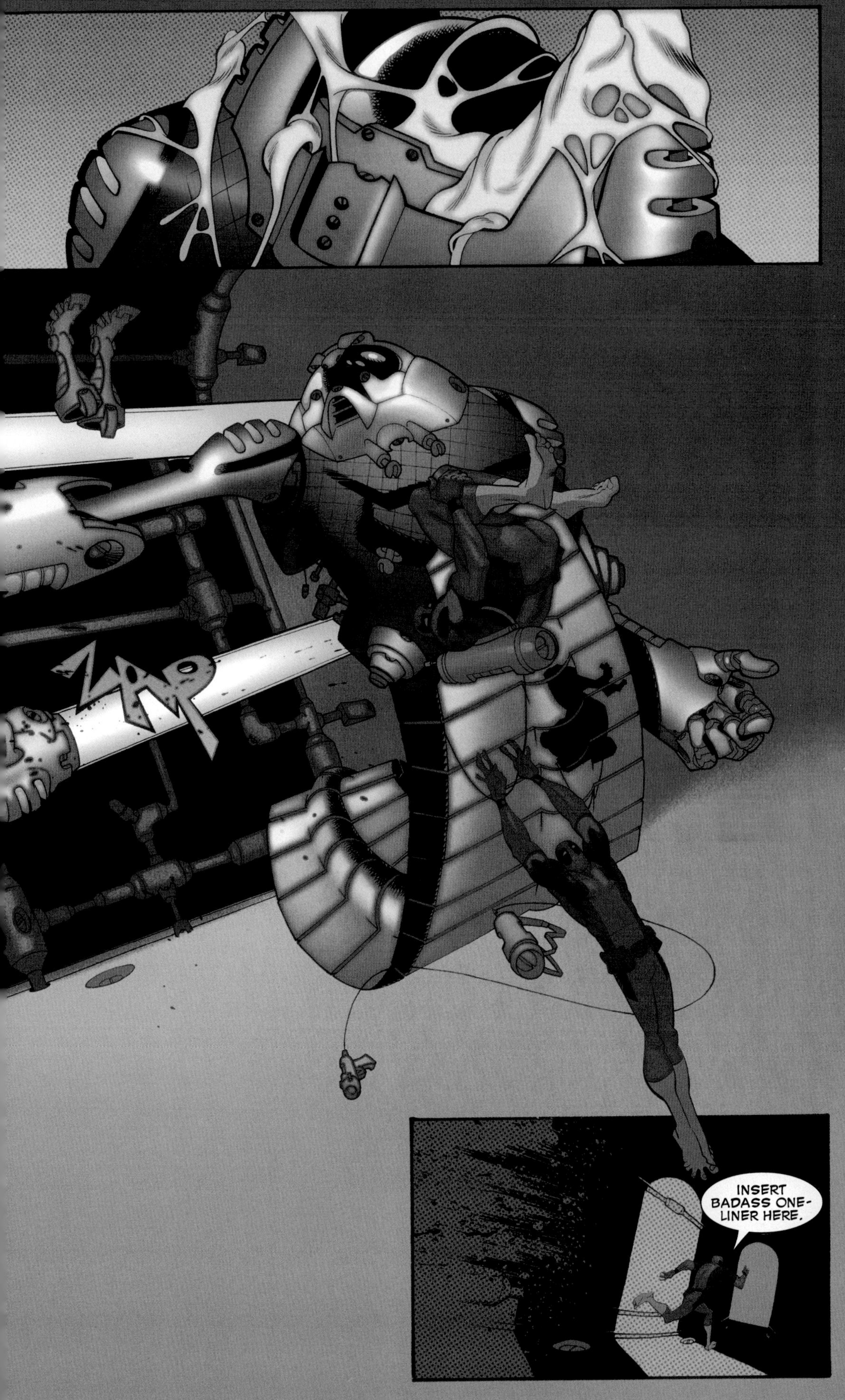
ZAP
INSERT BADASS ONE-LINER HERE.

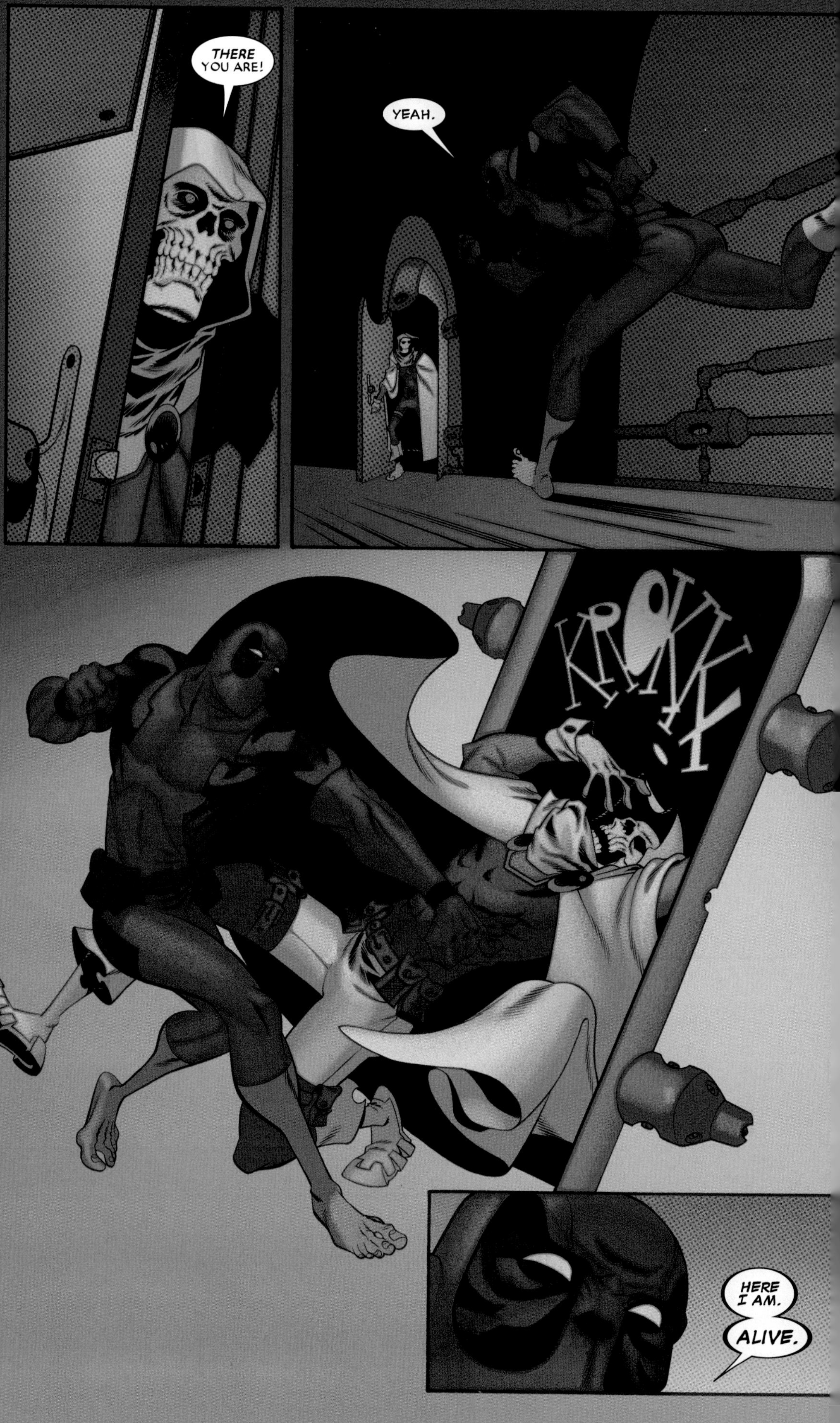
THERE YOU ARE!
YEAH.
KRACK
HERE I AM.
ALIVE.

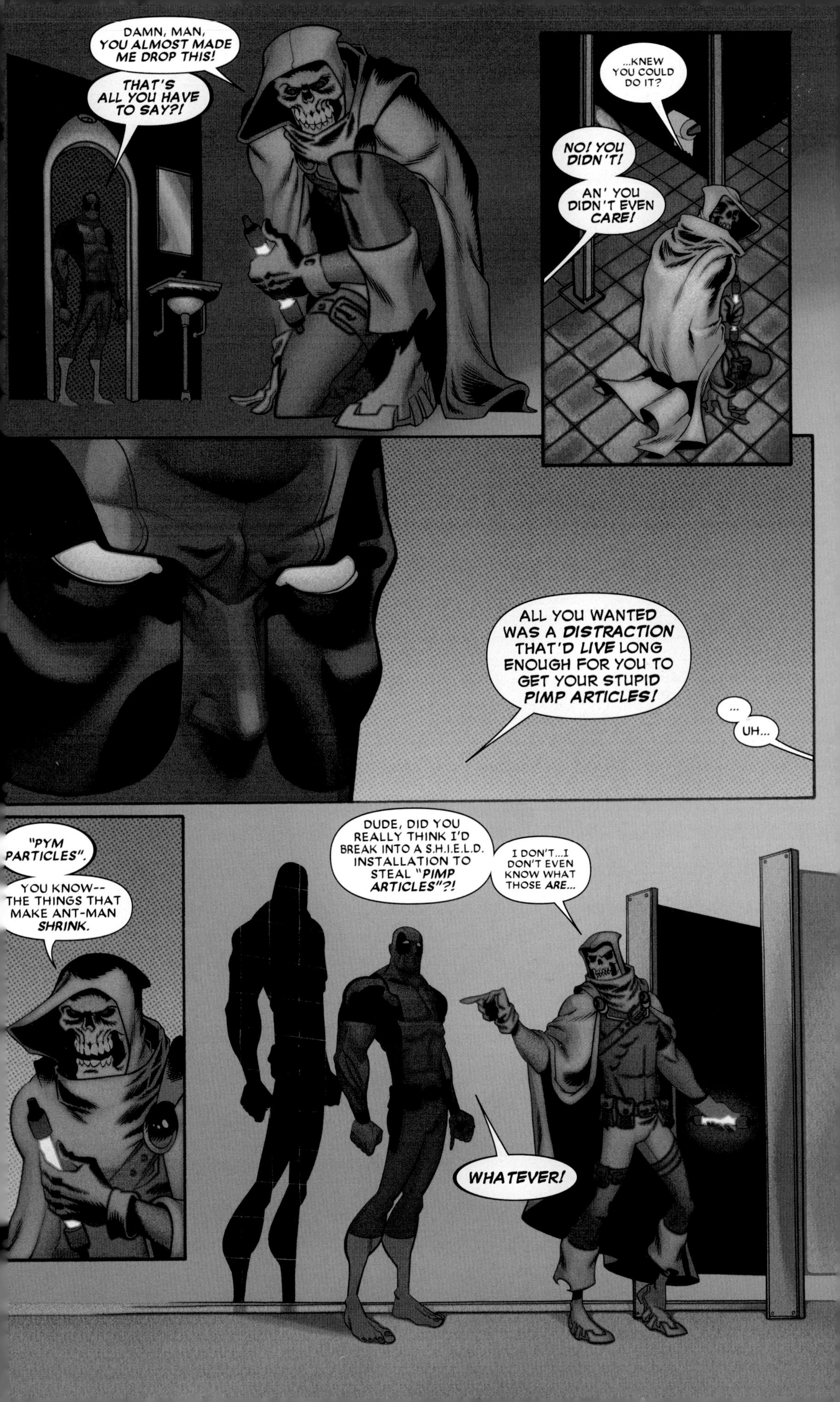

DAMN, MAN, YOU ALMOST MADE ME DROP THIS!
THAT'S ALL YOU HAVE TO SAY?!
...KNEW YOU COULD DO IT?
NO! YOU DIDN'T!
AN' YOU DIDN'T EVEN CARE!
ALL YOU WANTED WAS A DISTRACTION THAT'D LIVE LONG ENOUGH FOR YOU TO GET YOUR STUPID PIMP ARTICLES!
...
UH...
"PYM PARTICLES".
YOU KNOW-- THE THINGS THAT MAKE ANT-MAN SHRINK.
DUDE, DID YOU REALLY THINK I'D BREAK INTO A S.H.I.E.L.D. INSTALLATION TO STEAL "PIMP ARTICLES"?!
I DON'T...I DON'T EVEN KNOW WHAT THOSE ARE...
WHATEVER!

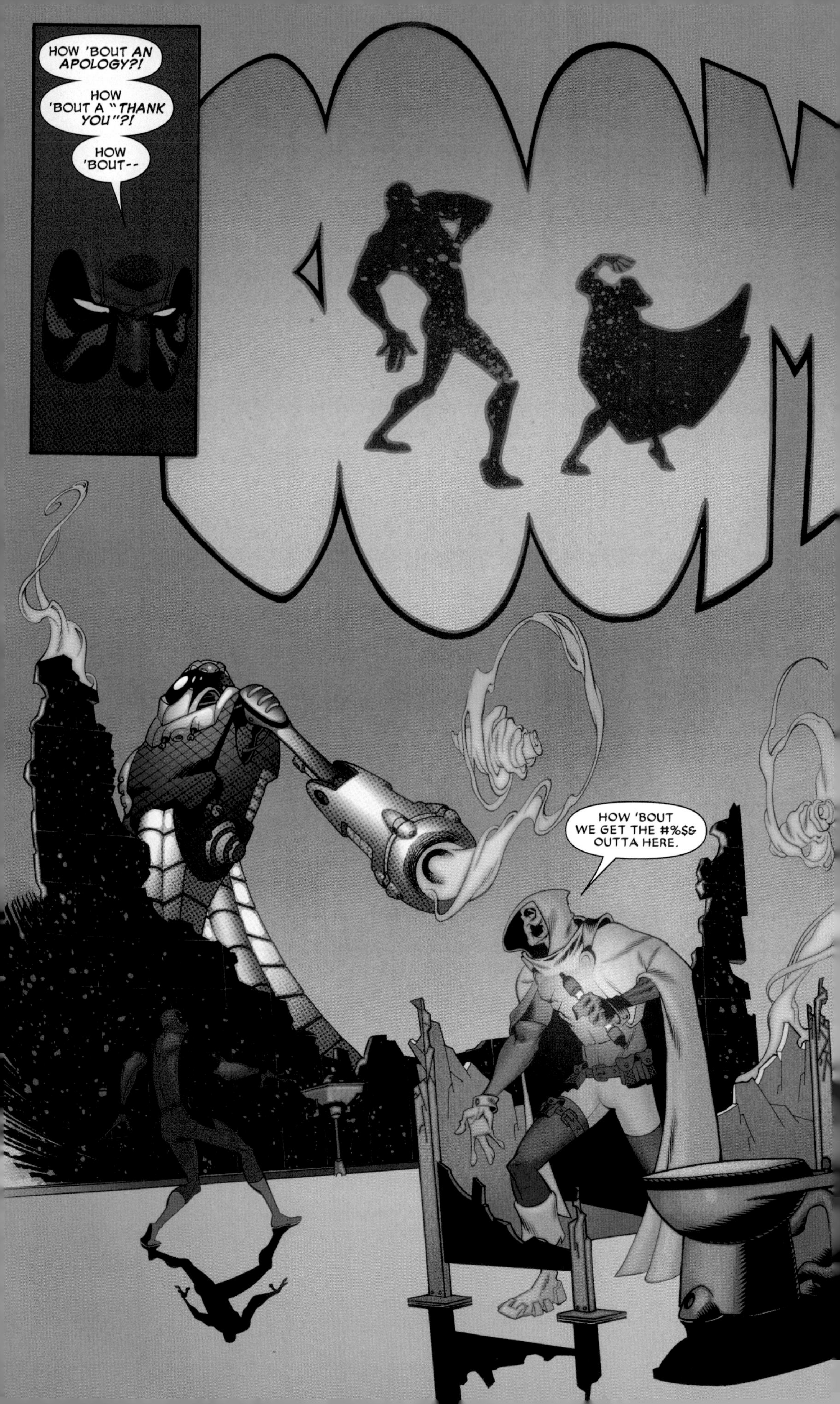

HOW 'BOUT AN APOLOGY?!
HOW 'BOUT A "THANK YOU"?!
HOW 'BOUT--
HOW 'BOUT WE GET THE #%$& OUTTA HERE.

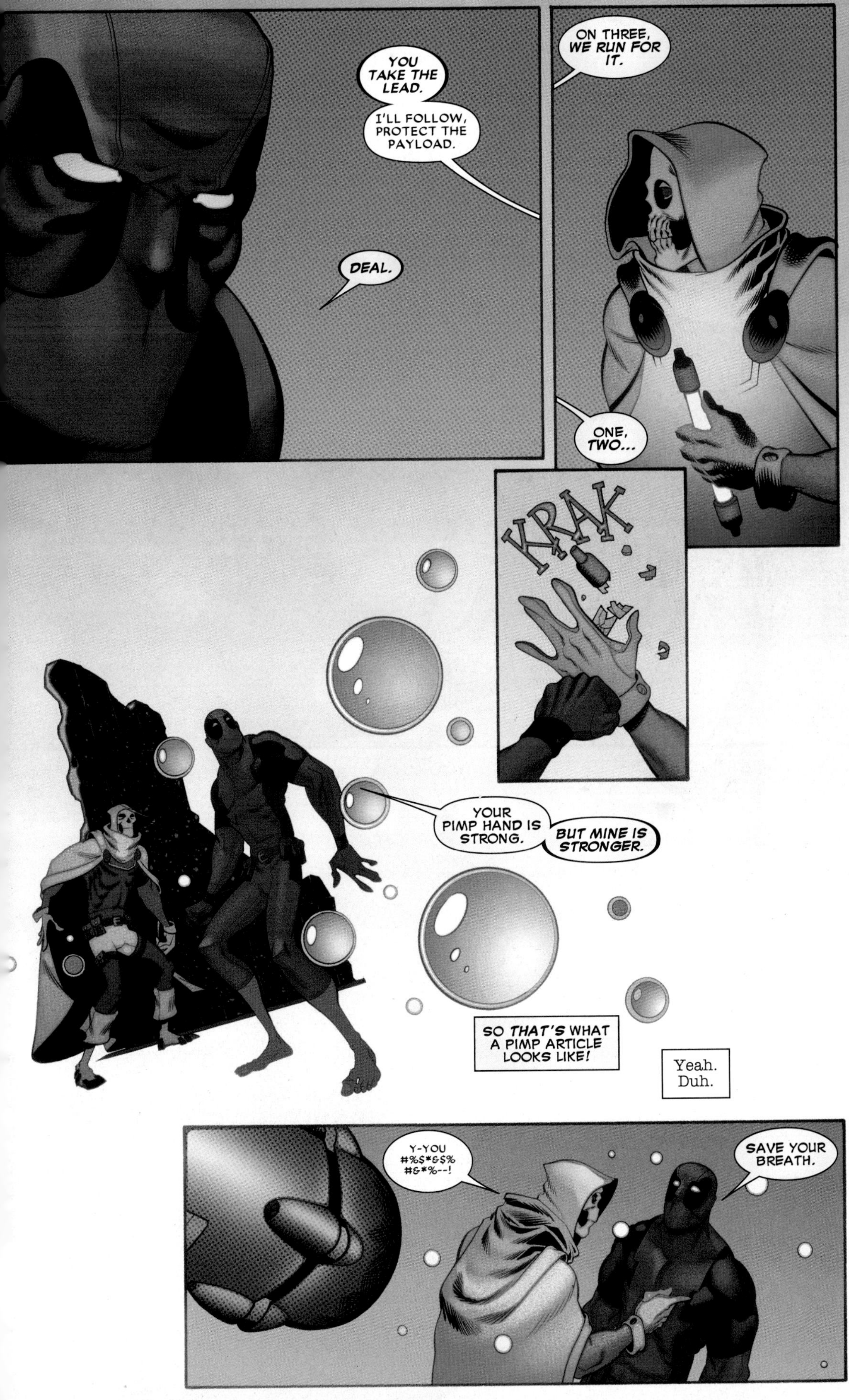
YOU TAKE THE LEAD.
I'LL FOLLOW, PROTECT THE PAYLOAD.
DEAL.
ON THREE, WE RUN FOR IT.
ONE, TWO...
KRAK
YOUR PIMP HAND IS STRONG.
BUT MINE IS STRONGER.
SO THAT'S WHAT A PIMP ARTICLE LOOKS LIKE!
Yeah. Duh.
Y-YOU #%$*&$% #&*%--!
SAVE YOUR BREATH.

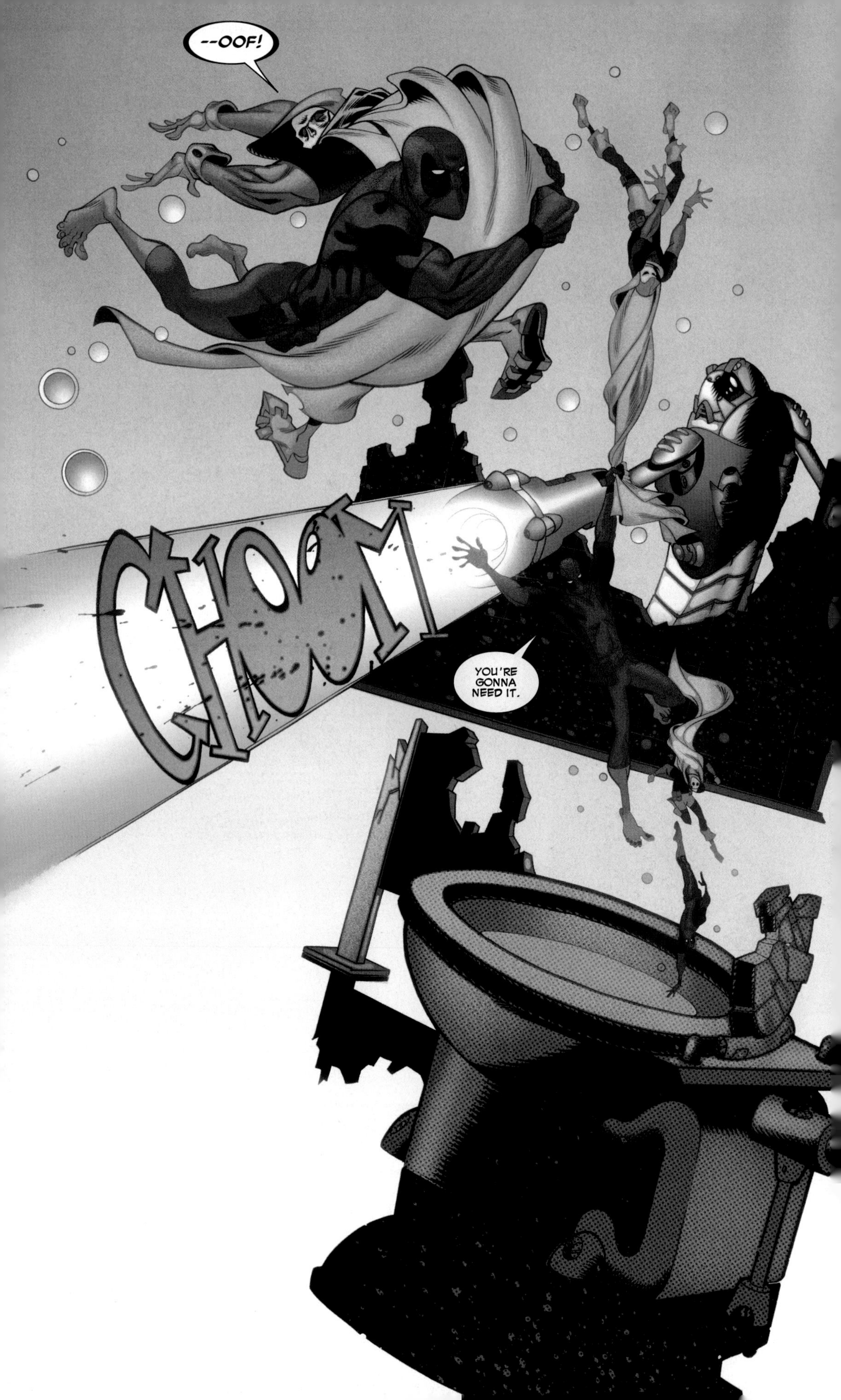
--OOF!
CHOOM
YOU'RE GONNA NEED IT.

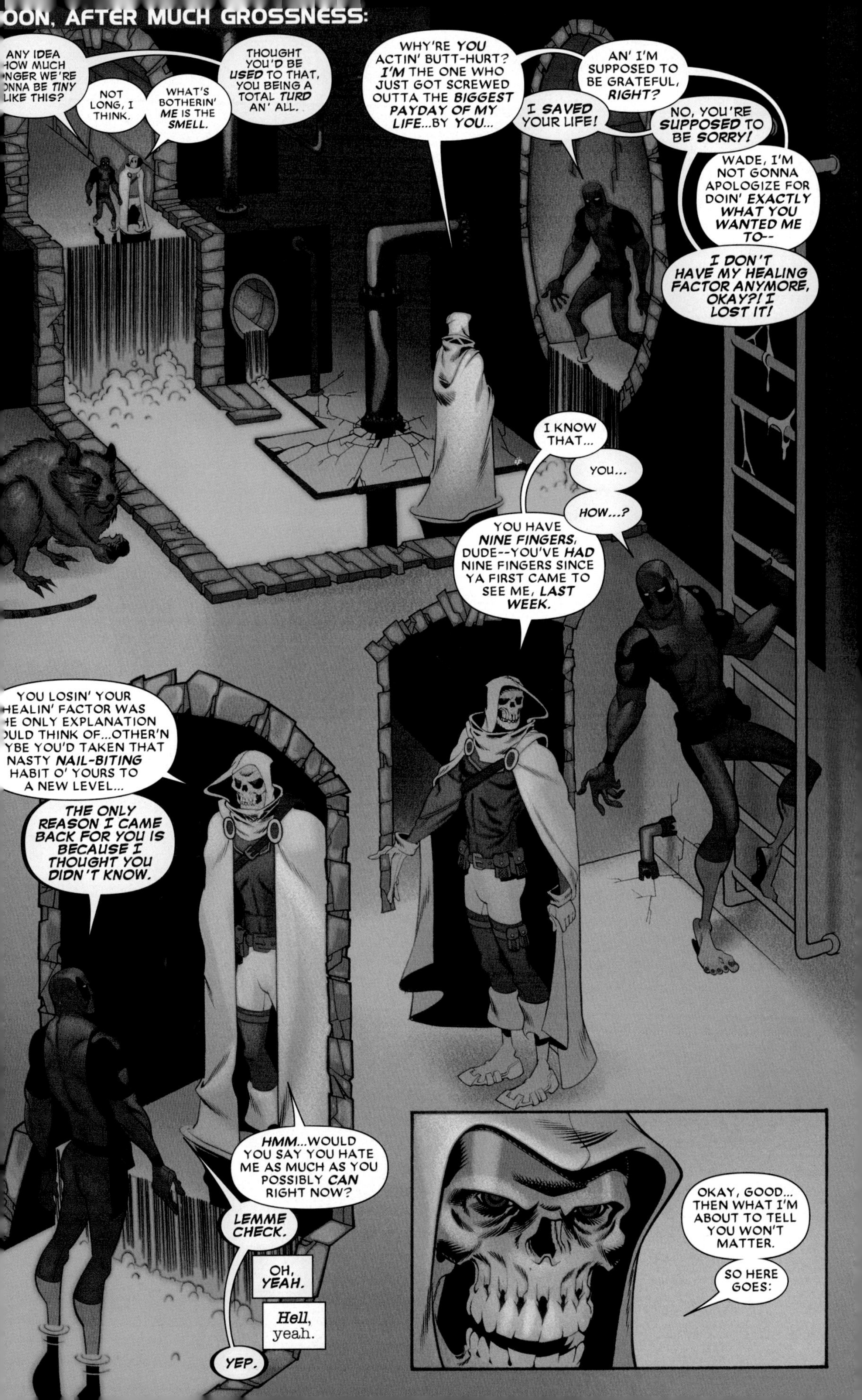

OON, AFTER MUCH GROSSNESS:
ANY IDEA HOW MUCH NGER WE'RE ONNA BE TINY LIKE THIS?
NOT LONG, I THINK.
WHAT'S BOTHERIN' ME IS THE SMELL.
THOUGHT YOU'D BE USED TO THAT, YOU BEING A TOTAL TURD AN' ALL.
WHY'RE YOU ACTIN' BUTT-HURT? I'M THE ONE WHO JUST GOT SCREWED OUTTA THE BIGGEST PAYDAY OF MY LIFE...BY YOU...
I SAVED YOUR LIFE!
AN' I'M SUPPOSED TO BE GRATEFUL, RIGHT?
NO, YOU'RE SUPPOSED TO BE SORRY!
WADE, I'M NOT GONNA APOLOGIZE FOR DOIN' EXACTLY WHAT YOU WANTED ME TO--
I DON'T HAVE MY HEALING FACTOR ANYMORE, OKAY?! I LOST IT!
I KNOW THAT...
YOU...
HOW...?
YOU HAVE NINE FINGERS, DUDE--YOU'VE HAD NINE FINGERS SINCE YA FIRST CAME TO SEE ME, LAST WEEK.
YOU LOSIN' YOUR HEALIN' FACTOR WAS HE ONLY EXPLANATION OULD THINK OF...OTHER'N YBE YOU'D TAKEN THAT NASTY NAIL-BITING HABIT O' YOURS TO A NEW LEVEL...
THE ONLY REASON I CAME BACK FOR YOU IS BECAUSE I THOUGHT YOU DIDN'T KNOW.
HMM...WOULD YOU SAY YOU HATE ME AS MUCH AS YOU POSSIBLY CAN RIGHT NOW?
LEMME CHECK.
OH, YEAH.
Hell, yeah.
YEP.
OKAY, GOOD... THEN WHAT I'M ABOUT TO TELL YOU WON'T MATTER.
SO HERE GOES:

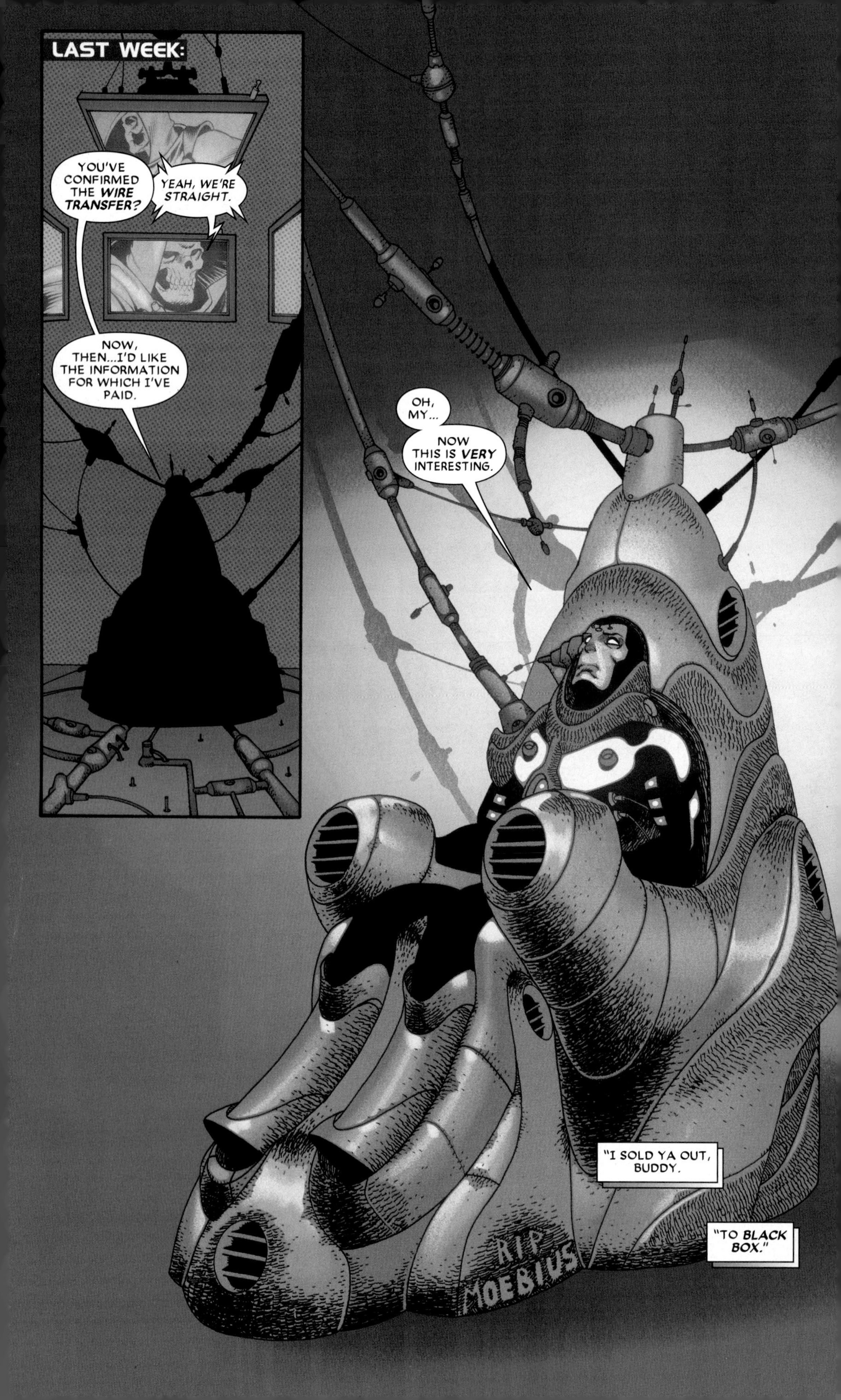
LAST WEEK:
YOU'VE CONFIRMED THE WIRE TRANSFER?
YEAH, WE'RE STRAIGHT.
NOW, THEN...I'D LIKE THE INFORMATION FOR WHICH I'VE PAID.
OH, MY...
NOW THIS IS VERY INTERESTING.
RIP MOEBIUS
"I SOLD YA OUT, BUDDY.
"TO BLACK BOX."

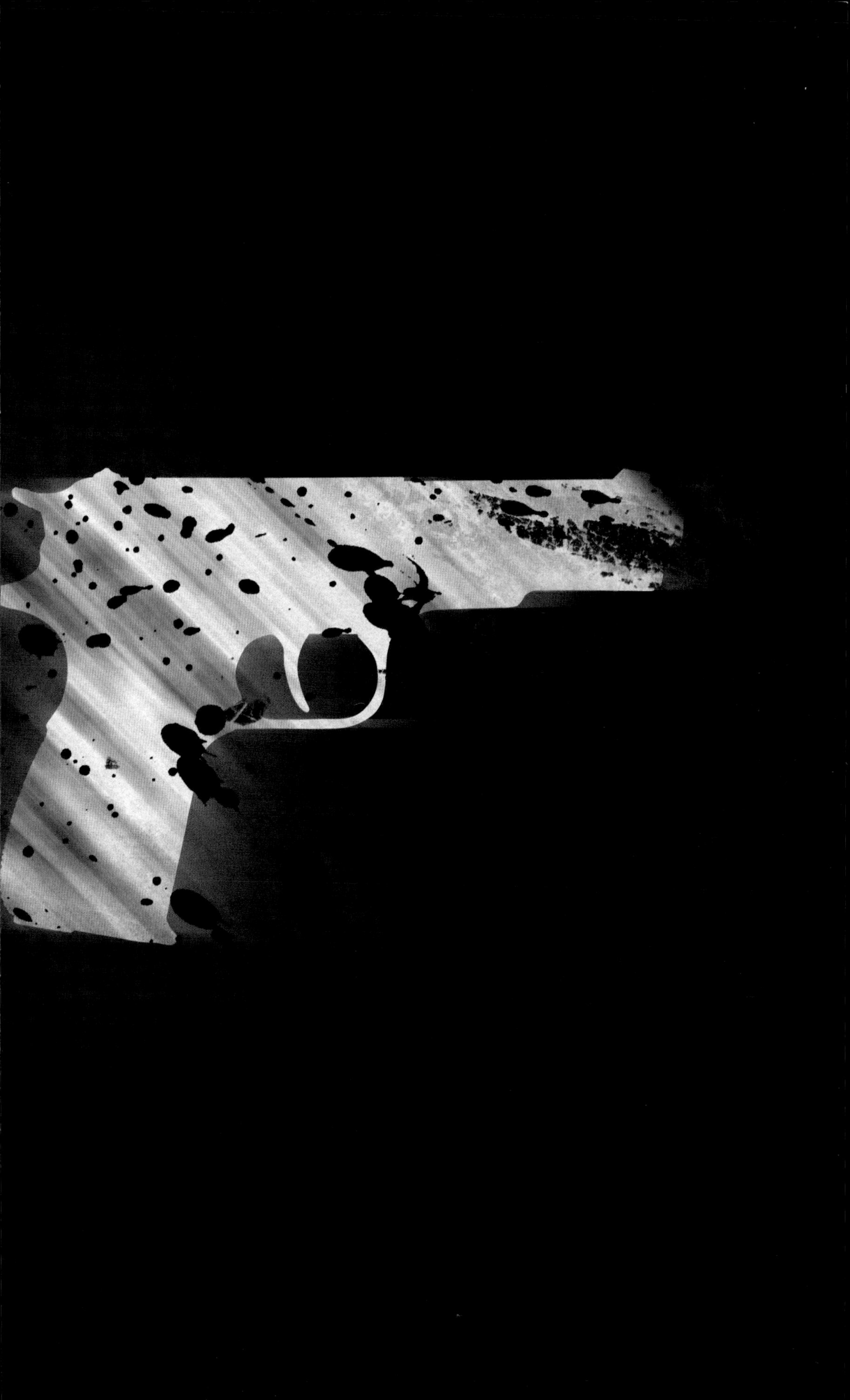

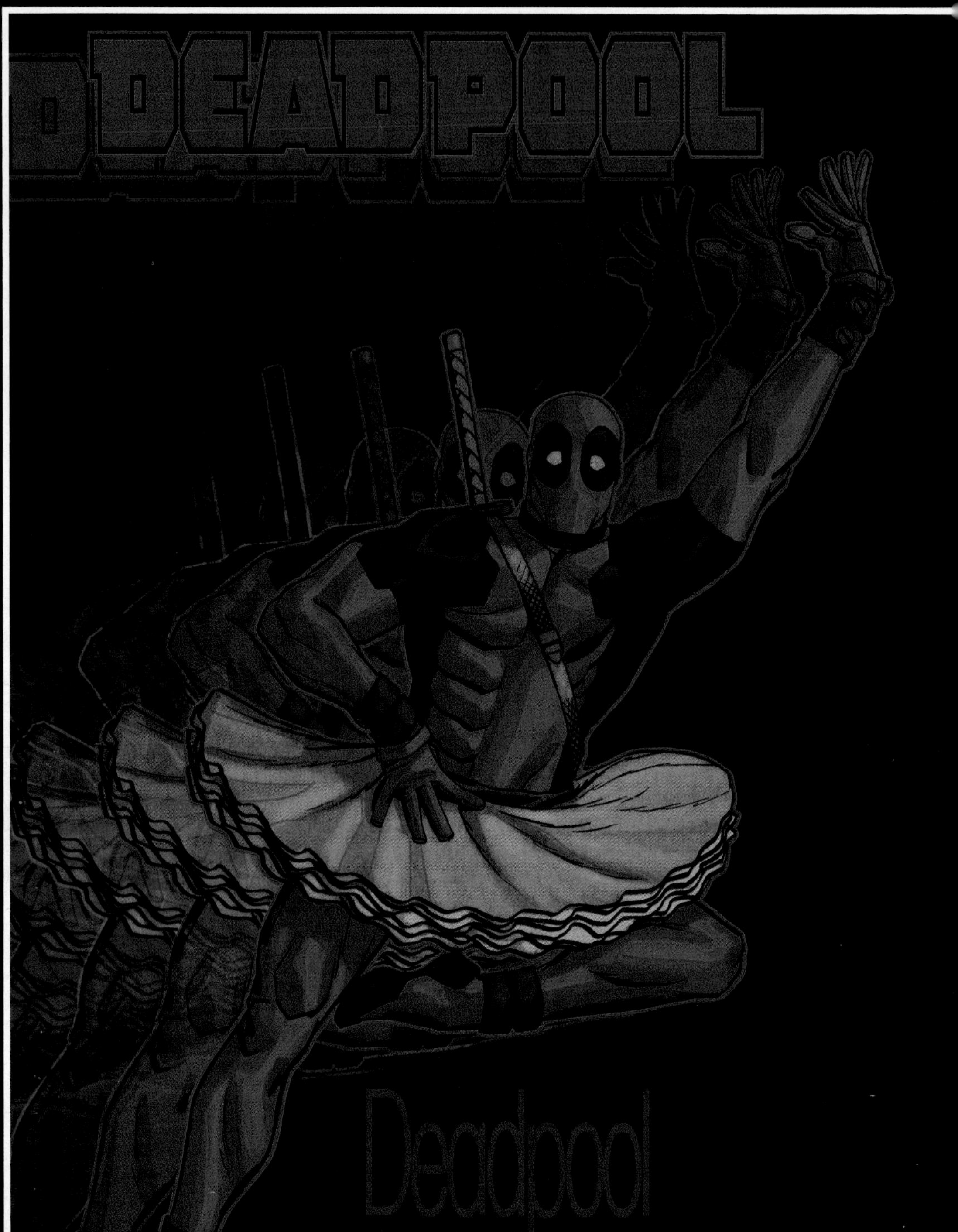
DEADPOOL
Deadpool
vs
BlackSwan
*Uh...no, the Super Villain

58

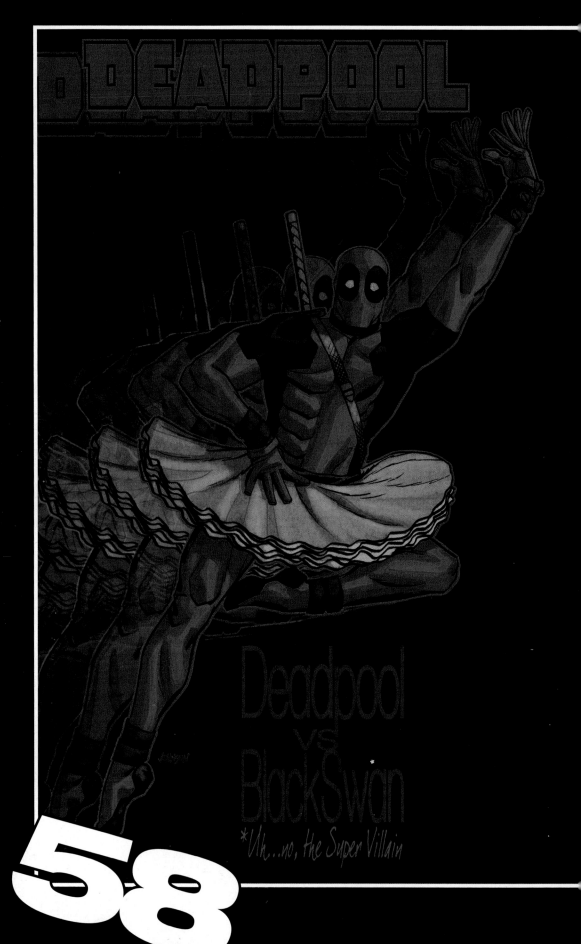

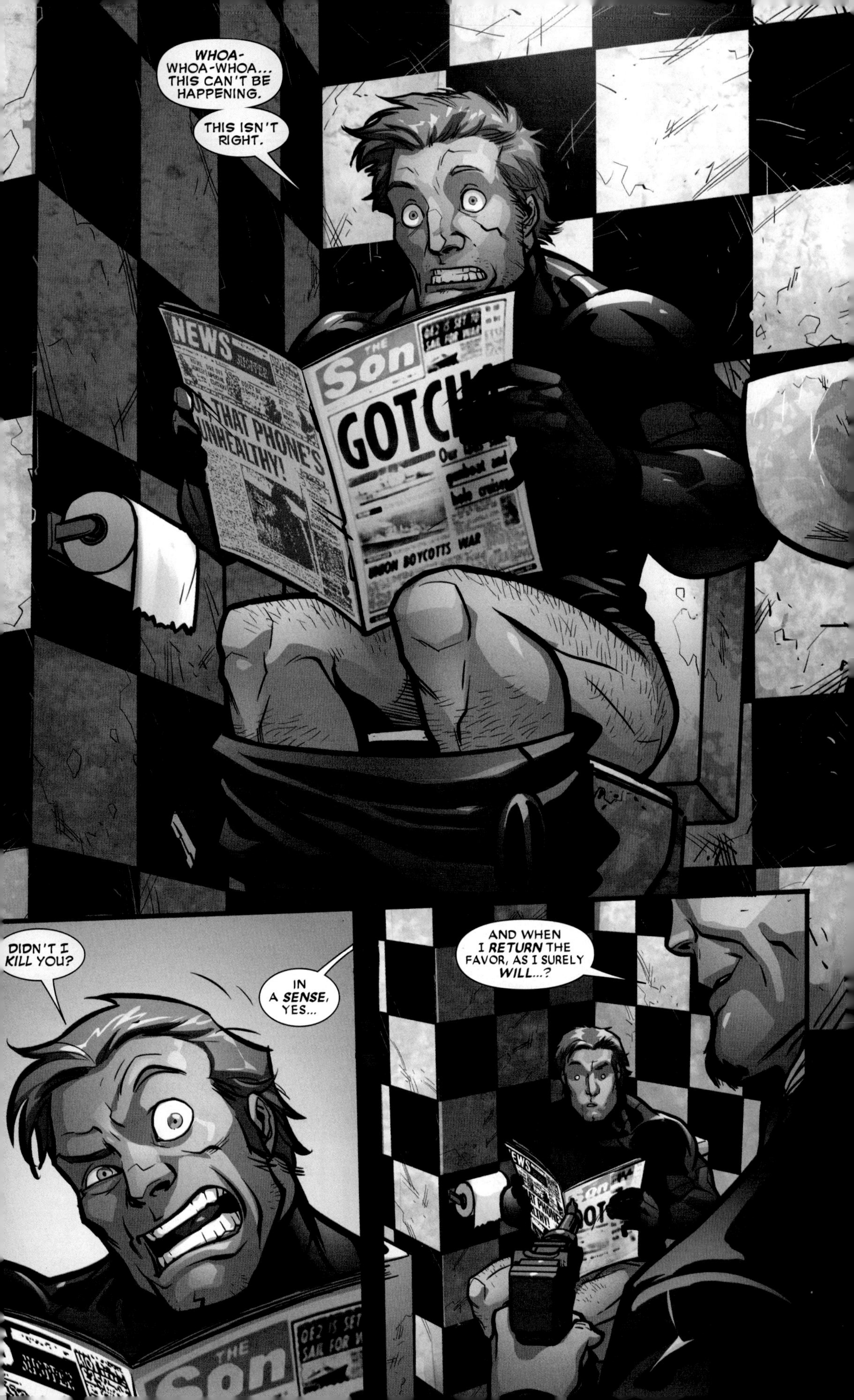
WHOA-WHOA-WHOA... THIS CAN'T BE HAPPENING.
THIS ISN'T RIGHT.
NEWS
THE Son
GOTCH
UNION BOYCOTTS WAR
DIDN'T I KILL YOU?
IN A SENSE, YES...
AND WHEN I RETURN THE FAVOR, AS I SURELY WILL...?

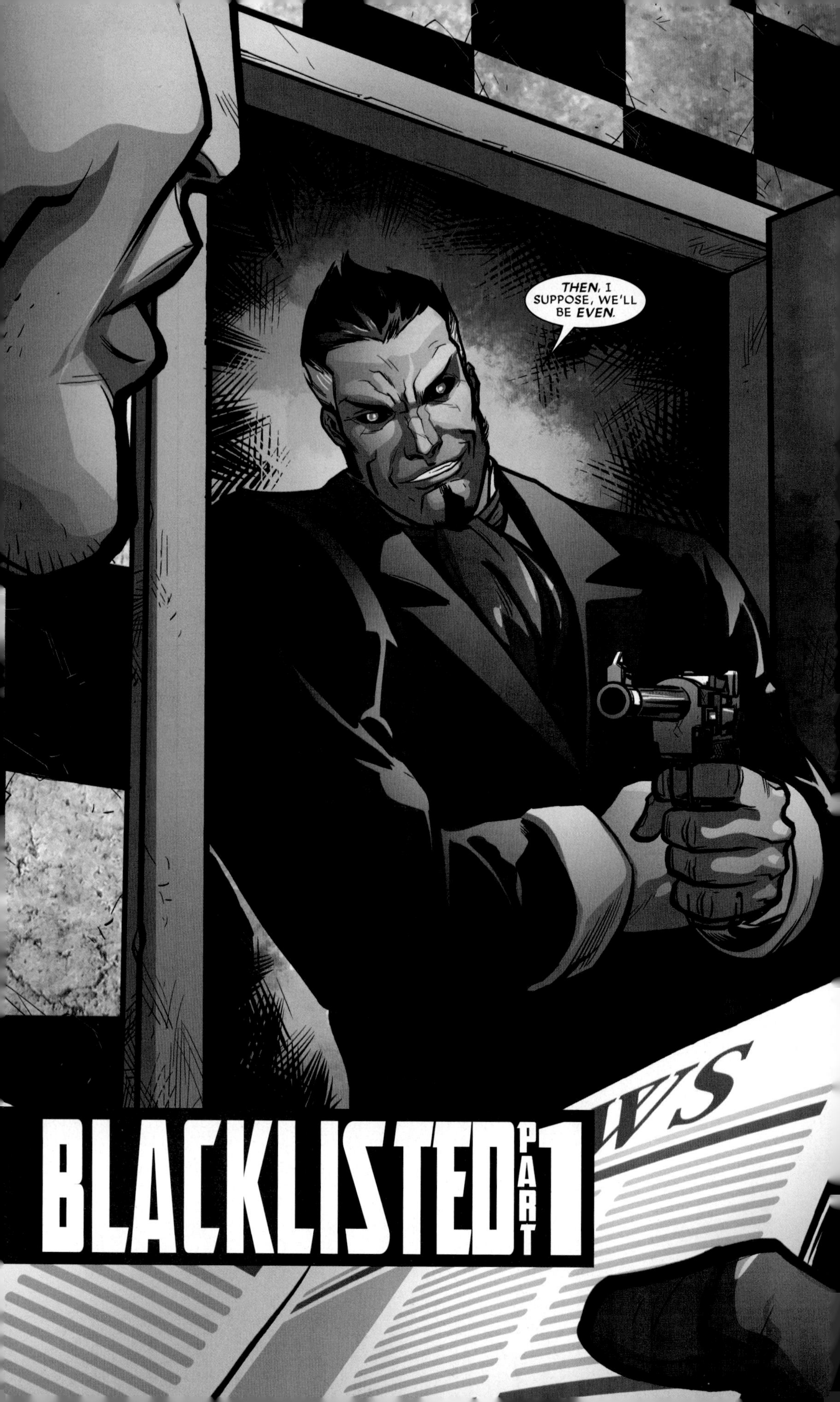
THEN, I SUPPOSE, WE'LL BE EVEN.
BLACKLISTED PART 1

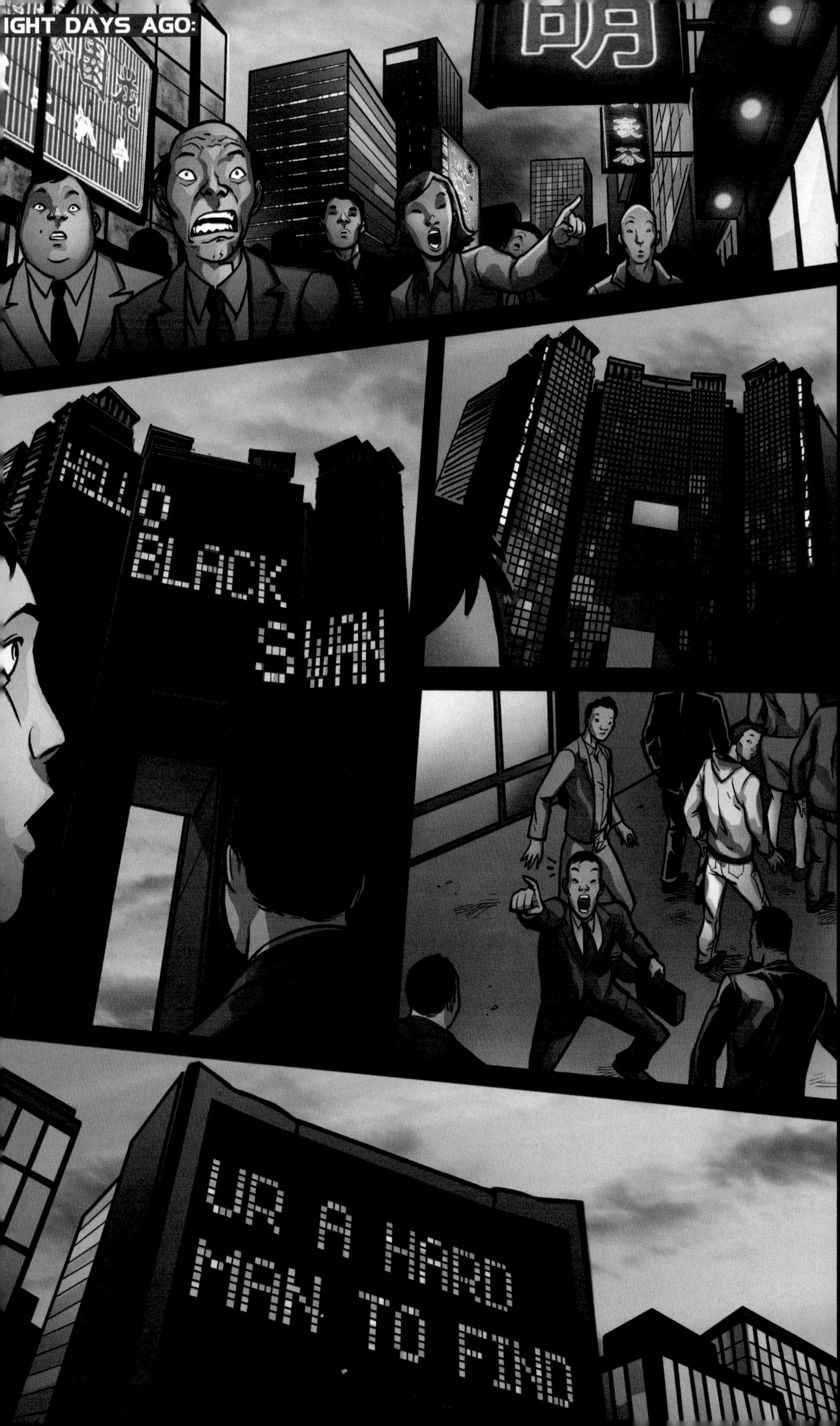
IGHT DAYS AGO:
HELLO BLACK SWAN
UR A HARD MAN TO FIND

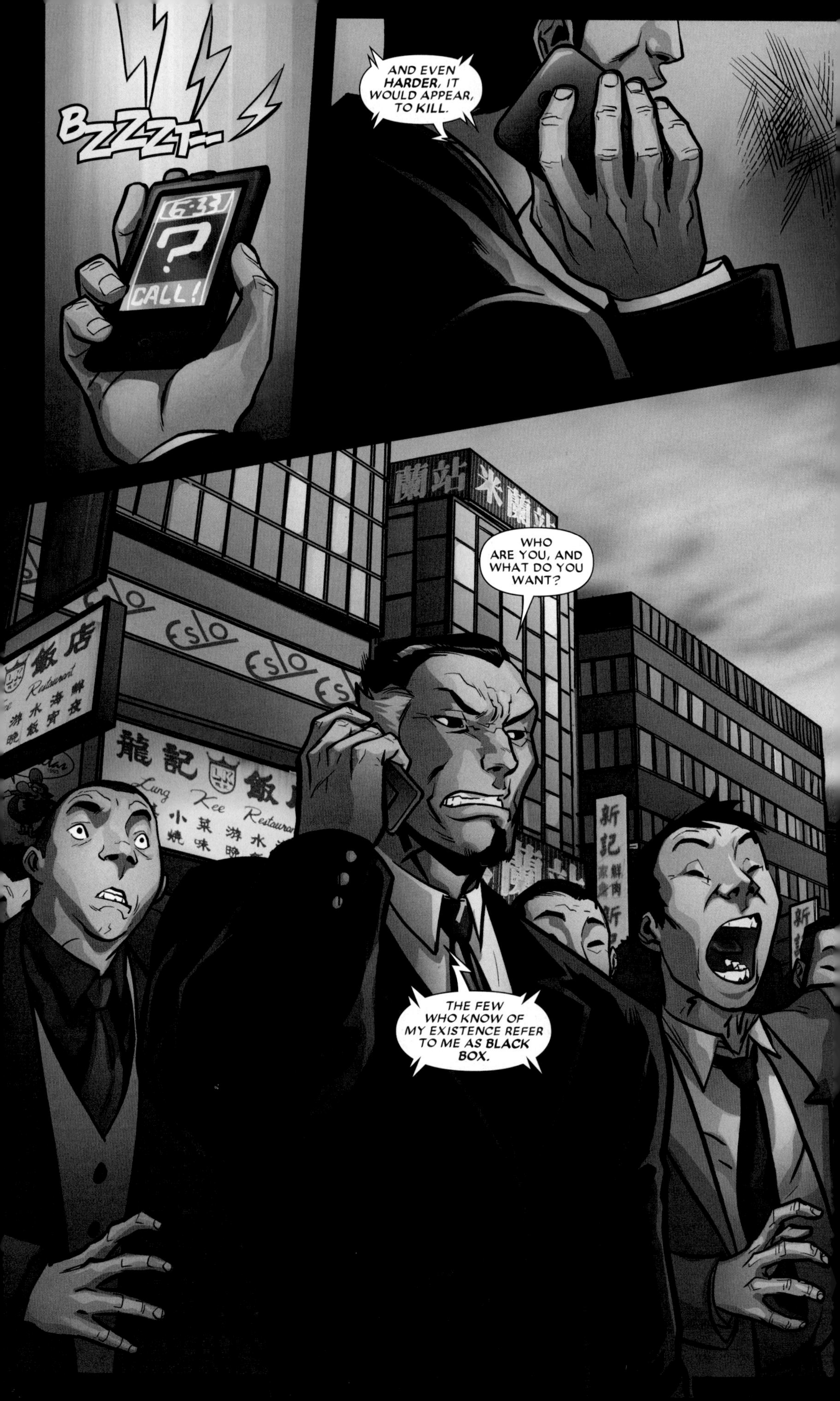
BZZZT—
CALL!
AND EVEN HARDER, IT WOULD APPEAR, TO KILL.
WHO ARE YOU, AND WHAT DO YOU WANT?
THE FEW WHO KNOW OF MY EXISTENCE REFER TO ME AS BLACK BOX.
龍記
Lung Kee Restaurant
Eslo

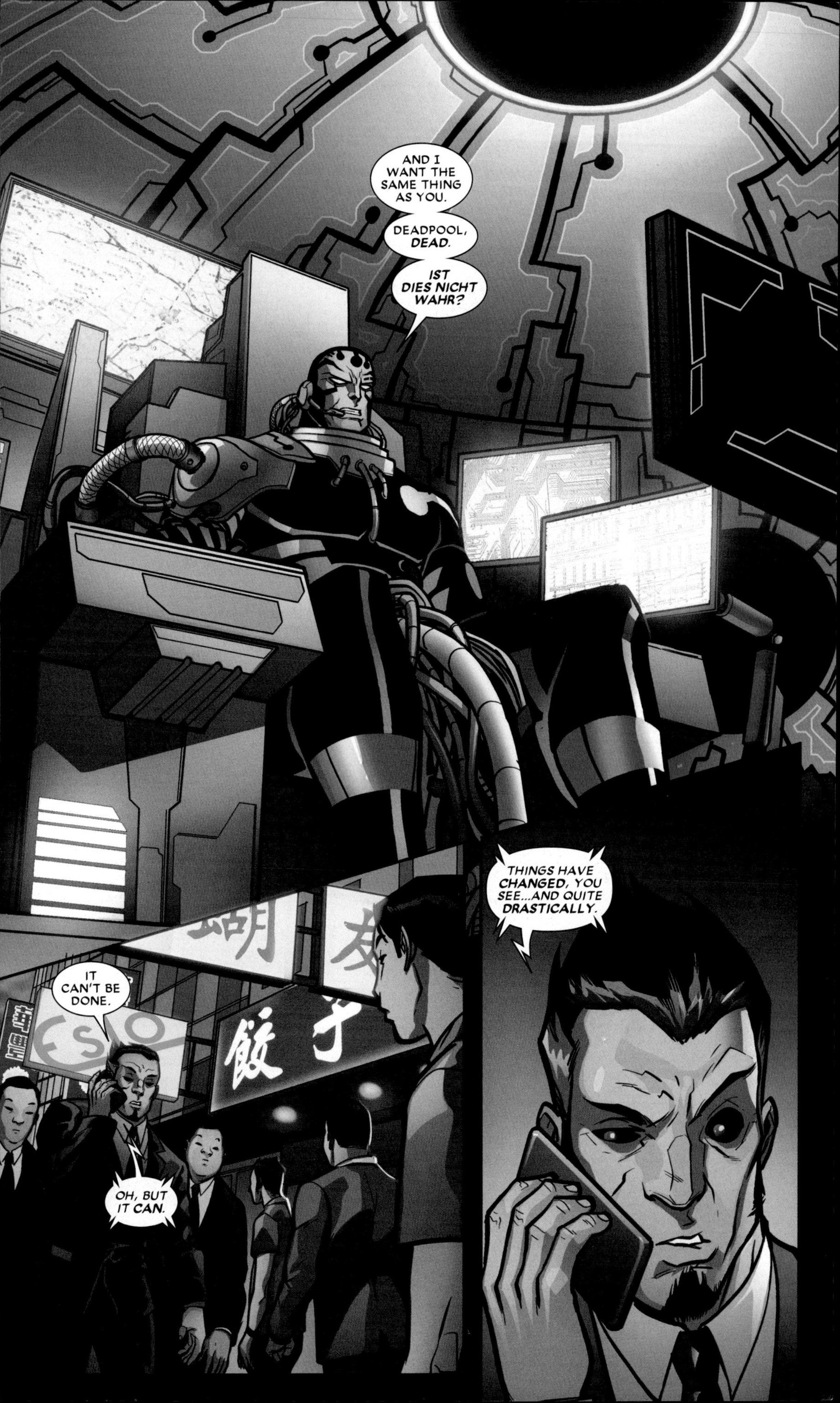
AND I WANT THE SAME THING AS YOU.
DEADPOOL, DEAD.
IST DIES NICHT WAHR?
IT CAN'T BE DONE.
OH, BUT IT CAN.
THINGS HAVE CHANGED, YOU SEE...AND QUITE DRASTICALLY.

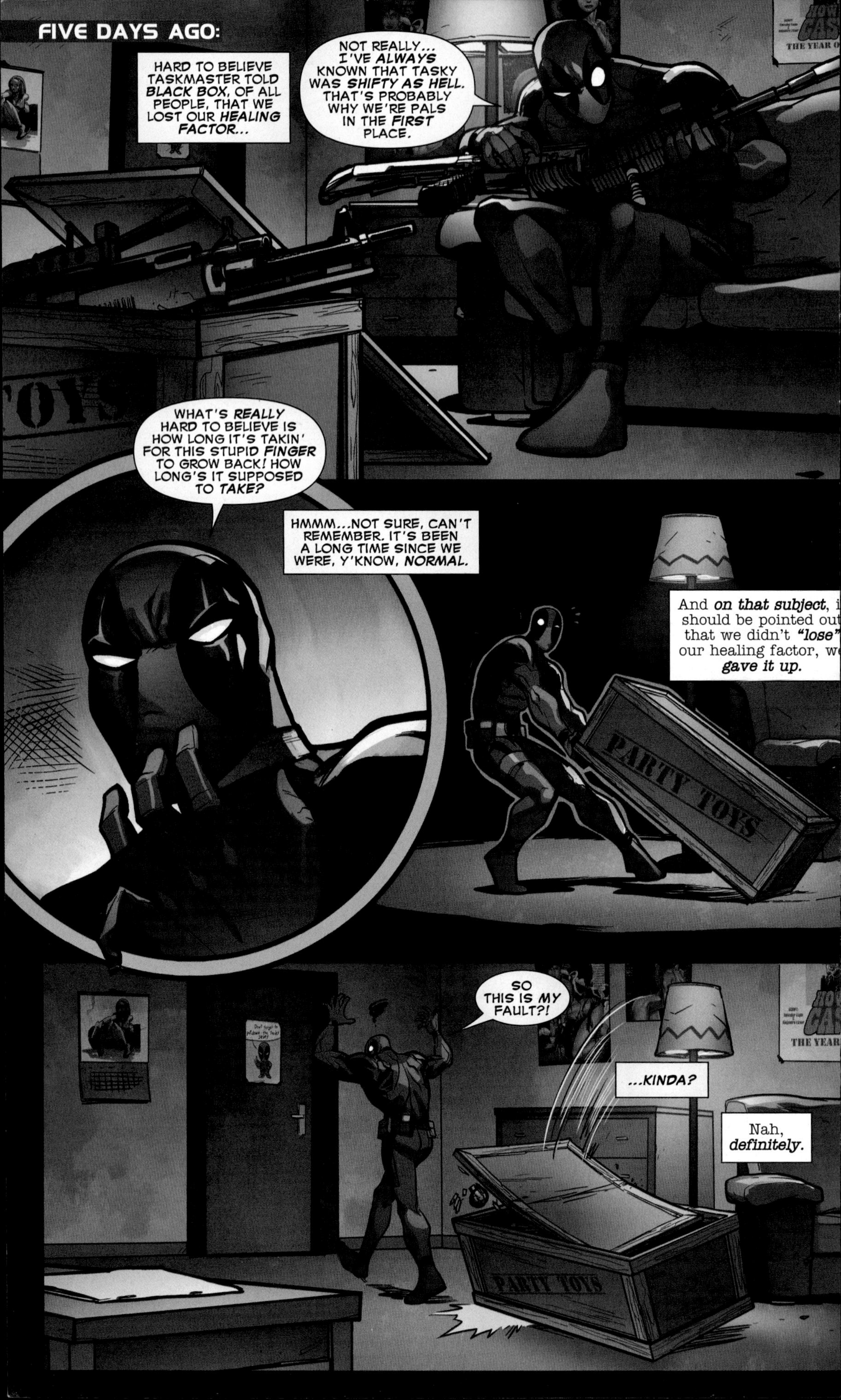
FIVE DAYS AGO:
HARD TO BELIEVE TASKMASTER TOLD BLACK BOX, OF ALL PEOPLE, THAT WE LOST OUR HEALING FACTOR...
NOT REALLY... I'VE ALWAYS KNOWN THAT TASKY WAS SHIFTY AS HELL. THAT'S PROBABLY WHY WE'RE PALS IN THE FIRST PLACE.
TOYS
WHAT'S REALLY HARD TO BELIEVE IS HOW LONG IT'S TAKIN' FOR THIS STUPID FINGER TO GROW BACK! HOW LONG'S IT SUPPOSED TO TAKE?
HMMM...NOT SURE, CAN'T REMEMBER. IT'S BEEN A LONG TIME SINCE WE WERE, Y'KNOW, NORMAL.
And on that subject, i should be pointed out that we didn't "lose" our healing factor, w gave it up.
PARTY TOYS
SO THIS IS MY FAULT?!
...KINDA?
Nah, definitely.
PARTY TOYS

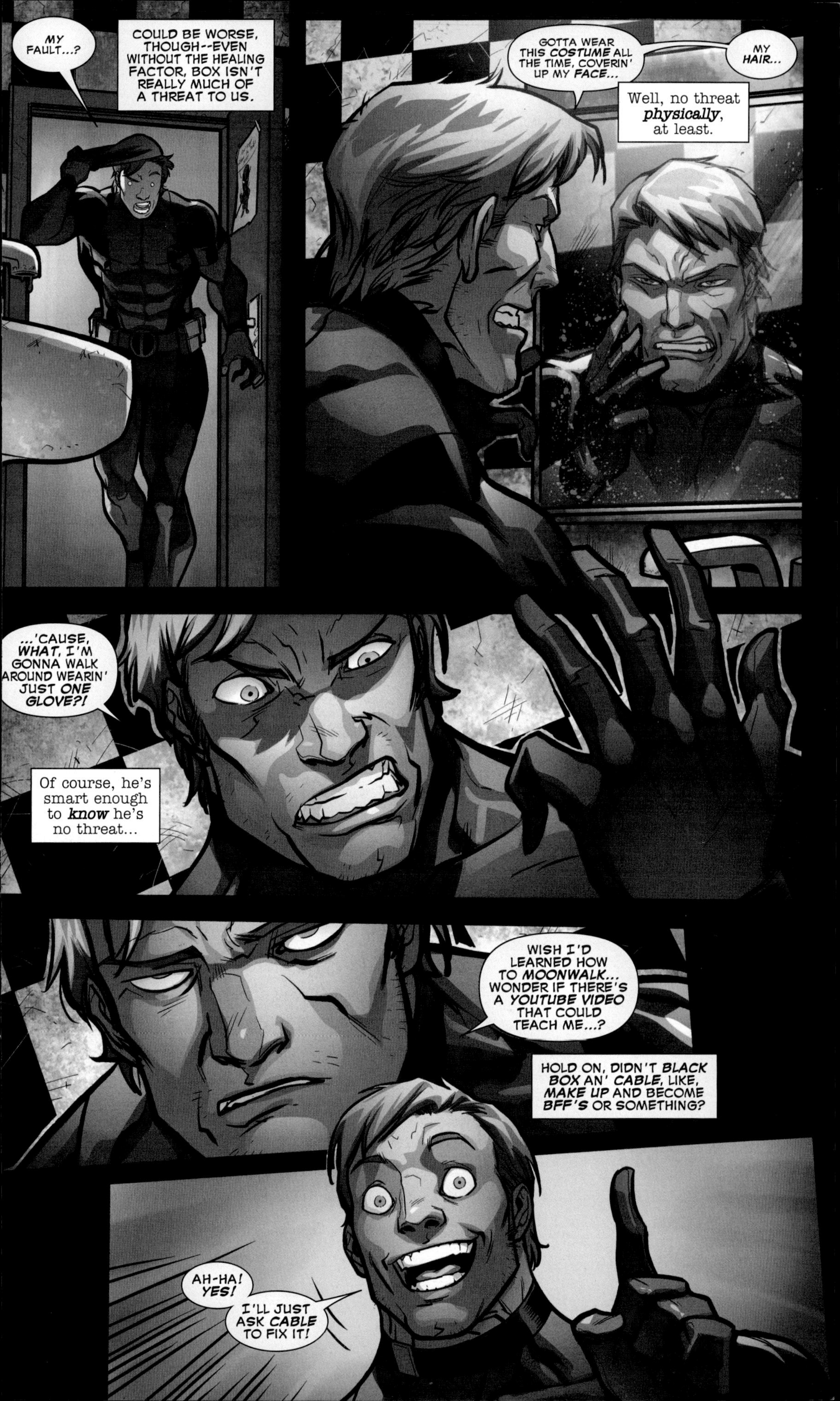
MY FAULT...?
COULD BE WORSE, THOUGH--EVEN WITHOUT THE HEALING FACTOR, BOX ISN'T REALLY MUCH OF A THREAT TO US.
GOTTA WEAR THIS COSTUME ALL THE TIME, COVERIN' UP MY FACE...
MY HAIR...
Well, no threat physically, at least.
...'CAUSE, WHAT, I'M GONNA WALK AROUND WEARIN' JUST ONE GLOVE?!
Of course, he's smart enough to know he's no threat...
WISH I'D LEARNED HOW TO MOONWALK... WONDER IF THERE'S A YOUTUBE VIDEO THAT COULD TEACH ME...?
HOLD ON, DIDN'T BLACK BOX AN' CABLE, LIKE, MAKE UP AND BECOME BFF'S OR SOMETHING?
AH-HA! YES!
I'LL JUST ASK CABLE TO FIX IT!

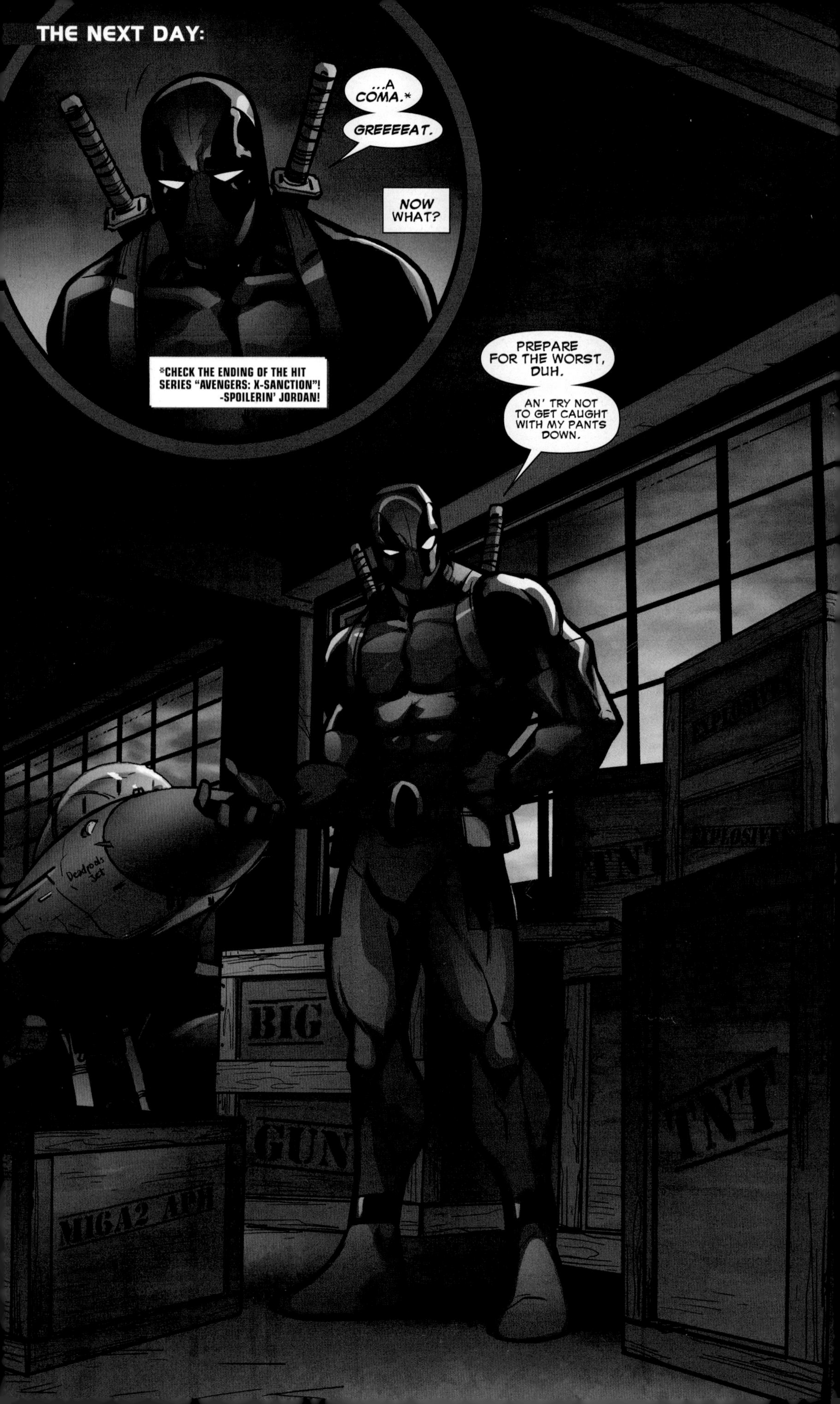

THE NEXT DAY:
...A COMA.*
GREEEEAT.
NOW WHAT?
*CHECK THE ENDING OF THE HIT SERIES "AVENGERS: X-SANCTION"! -SPOILERIN' JORDAN!
PREPARE FOR THE WORST, DUH.
AN' TRY NOT TO GET CAUGHT WITH MY PANTS DOWN.
BIG
GUN
TNT
M16A2 APH

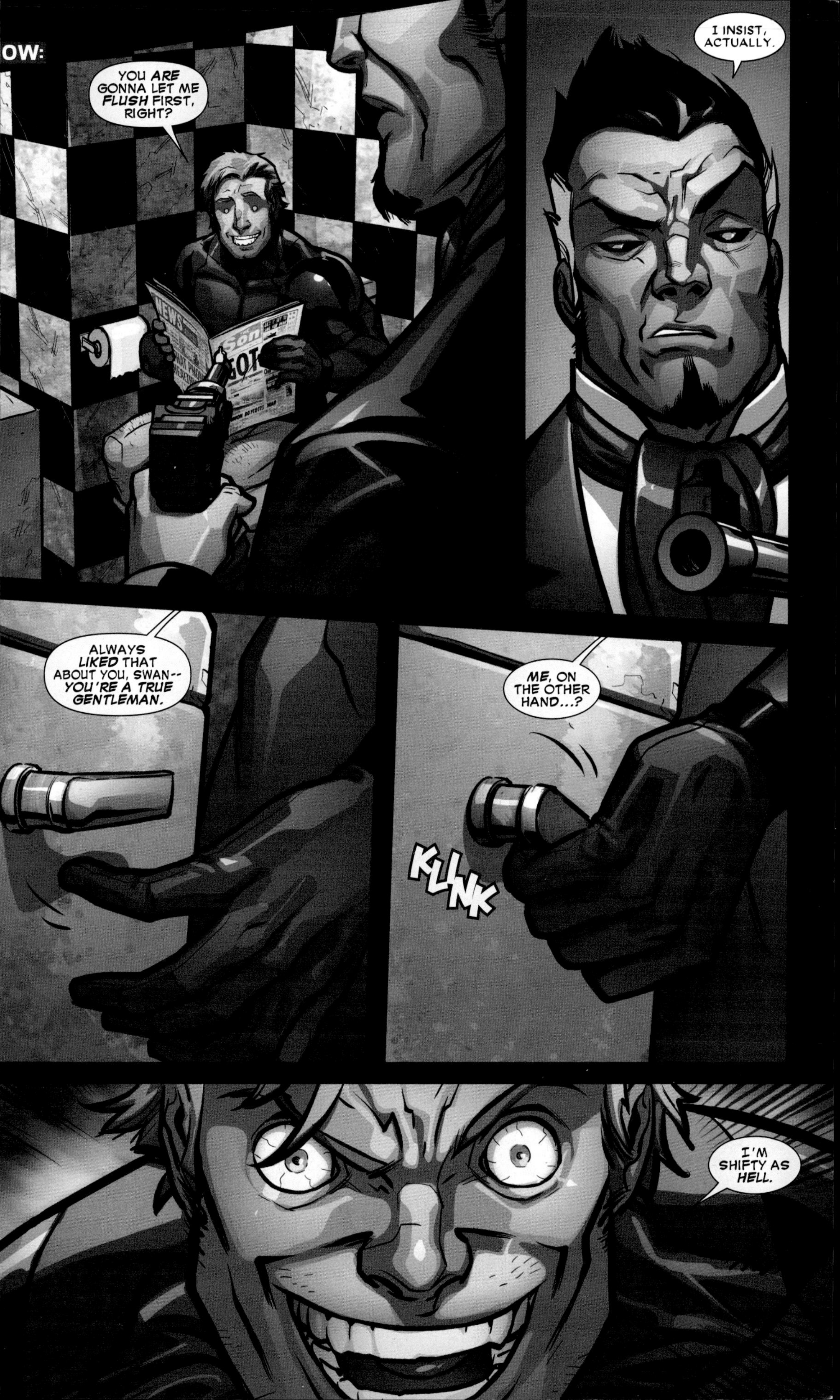
OW:
YOU ARE GONNA LET ME FLUSH FIRST, RIGHT?
I INSIST, ACTUALLY.
ALWAYS LIKED THAT ABOUT YOU, SWAN--YOU'RE A TRUE GENTLEMAN.
ME, ON THE OTHER HAND...?
KLINK
I'M SHIFTY AS HELL.

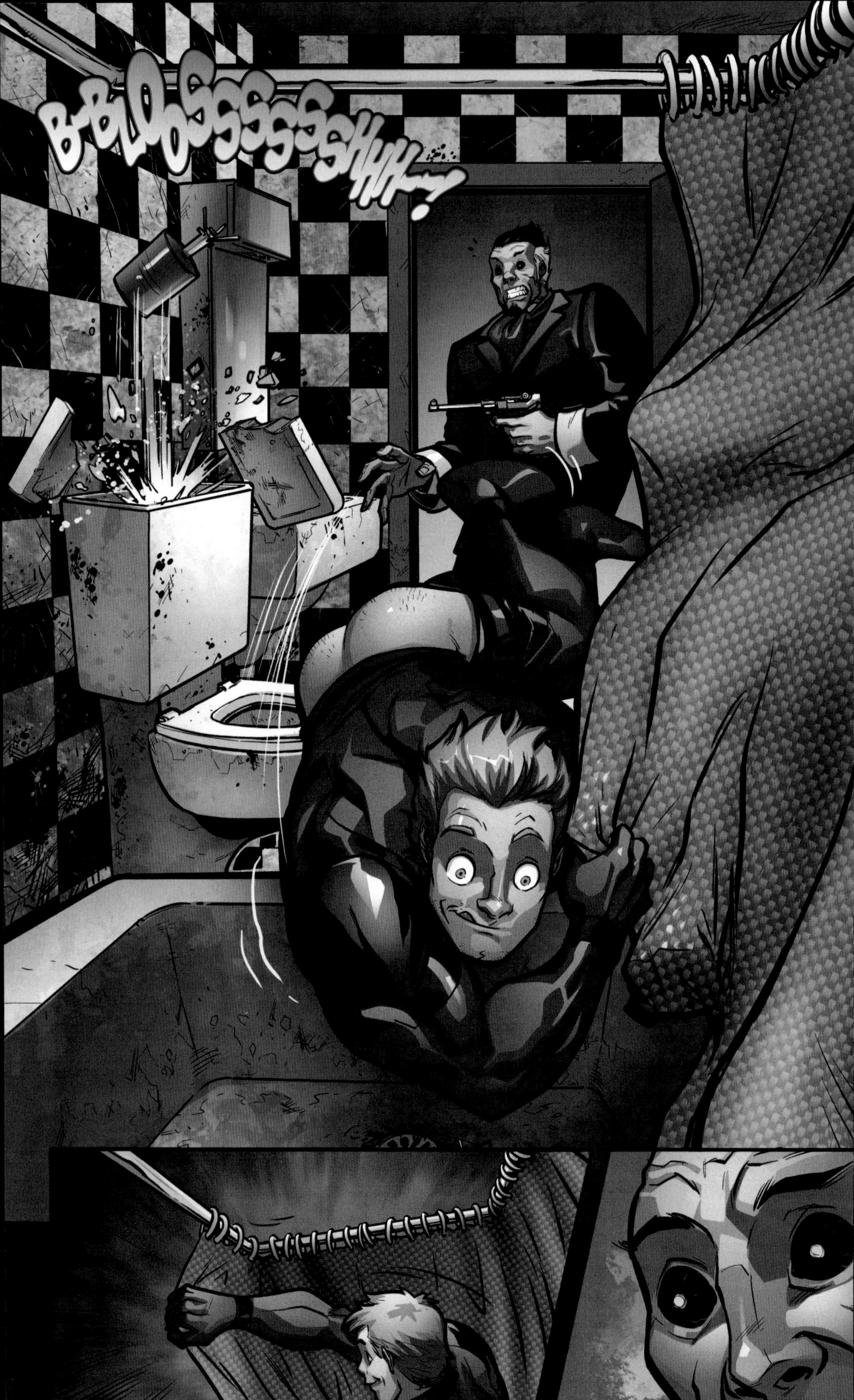
B-BLOOSSSSSSHHH~!

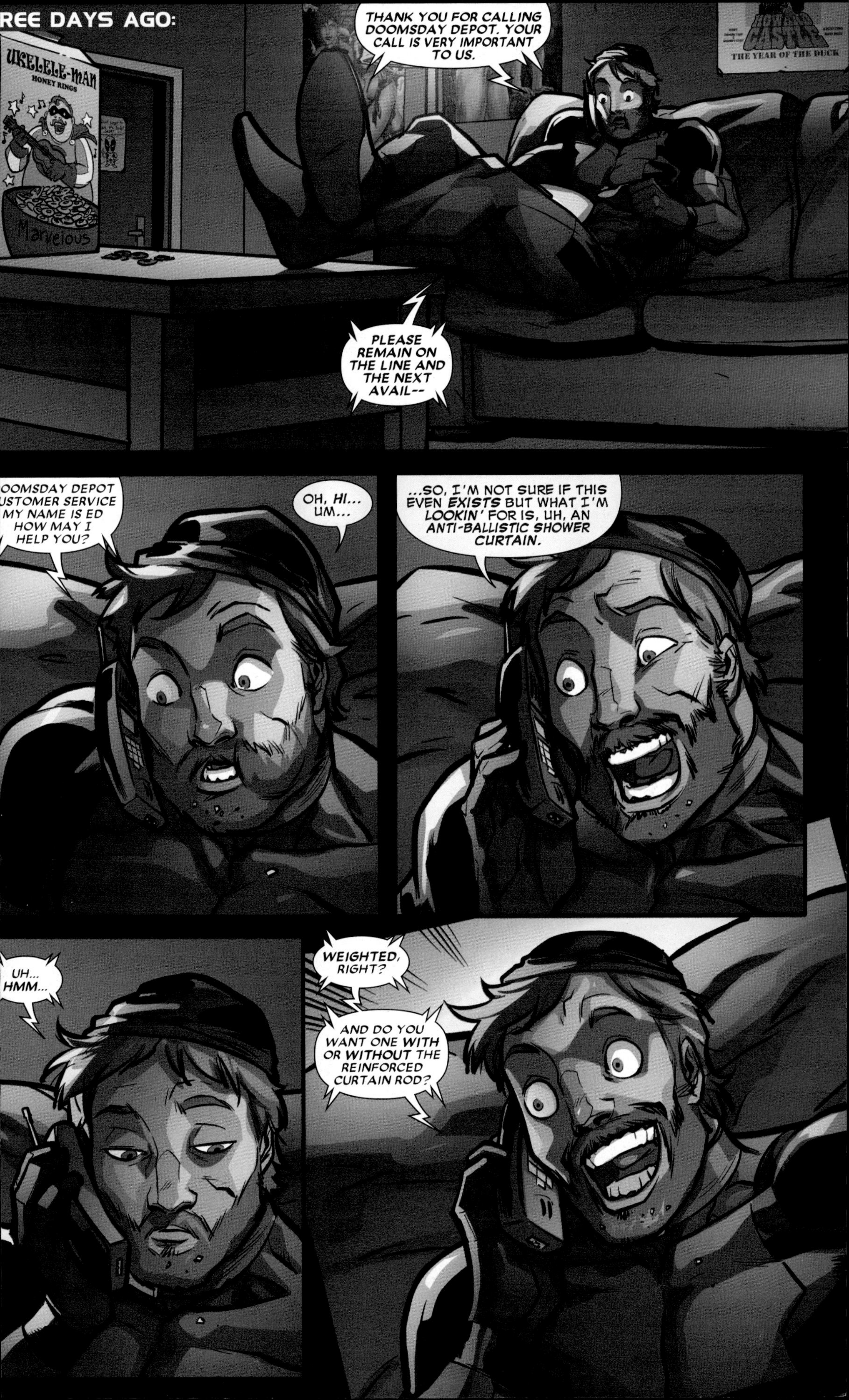

REE DAYS AGO:
UKELELE-MAN
HONEY RINGS
Marvelous
HOWARD CASTLE
THE YEAR OF THE DUCK
THANK YOU FOR CALLING DOOMSDAY DEPOT. YOUR CALL IS VERY IMPORTANT TO US.
PLEASE REMAIN ON THE LINE AND THE NEXT AVAIL--
OOMSDAY DEPOT USTOMER SERVICE MY NAME IS ED HOW MAY I HELP YOU?
OH, HI... UM...
...SO, I'M NOT SURE IF THIS EVEN EXISTS BUT WHAT I'M LOOKIN' FOR IS, UH, AN ANTI-BALLISTIC SHOWER CURTAIN.
UH... HMM...
WEIGHTED, RIGHT?
AND DO YOU WANT ONE WITH OR WITHOUT THE REINFORCED CURTAIN ROD?

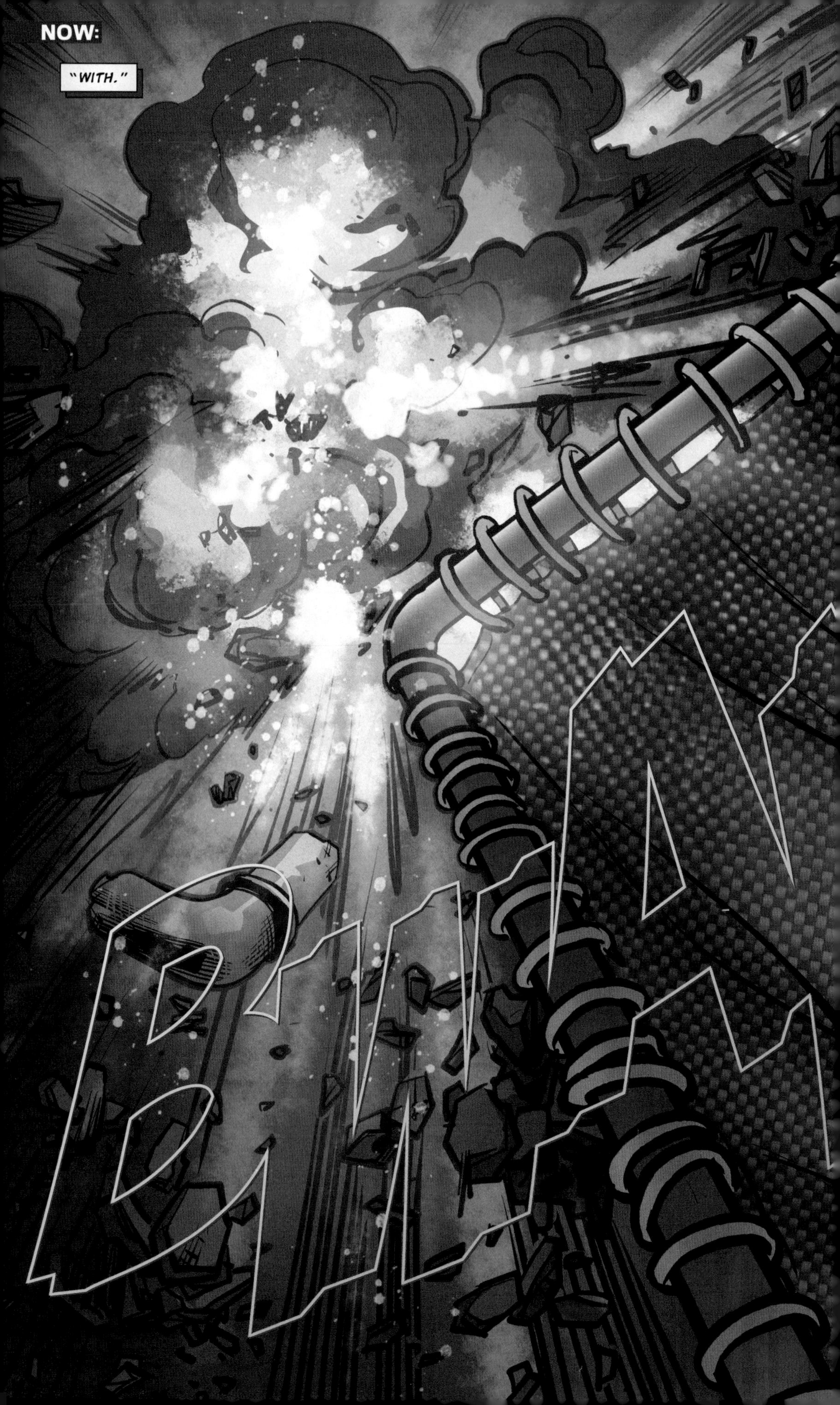
NOW:
"WITH."

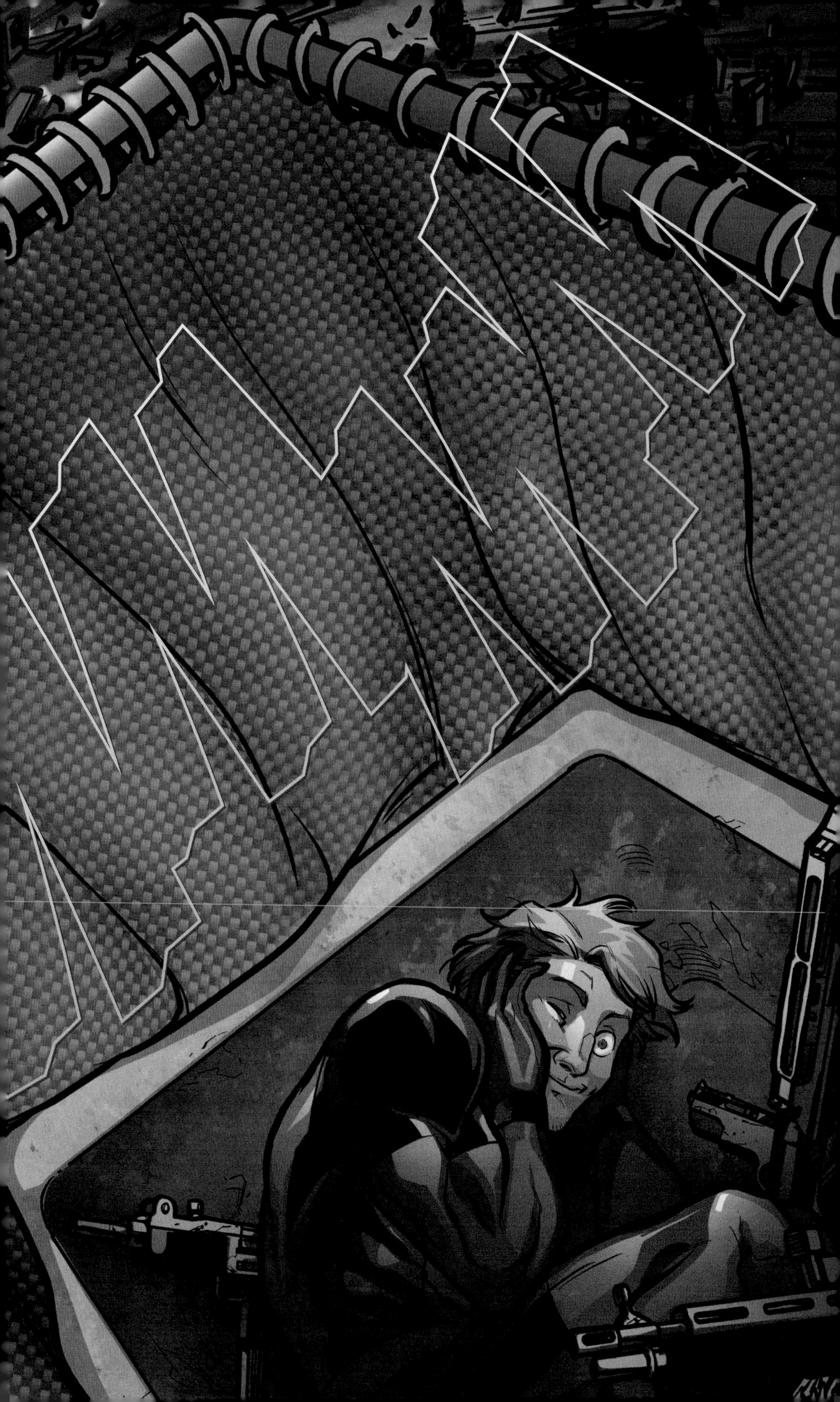

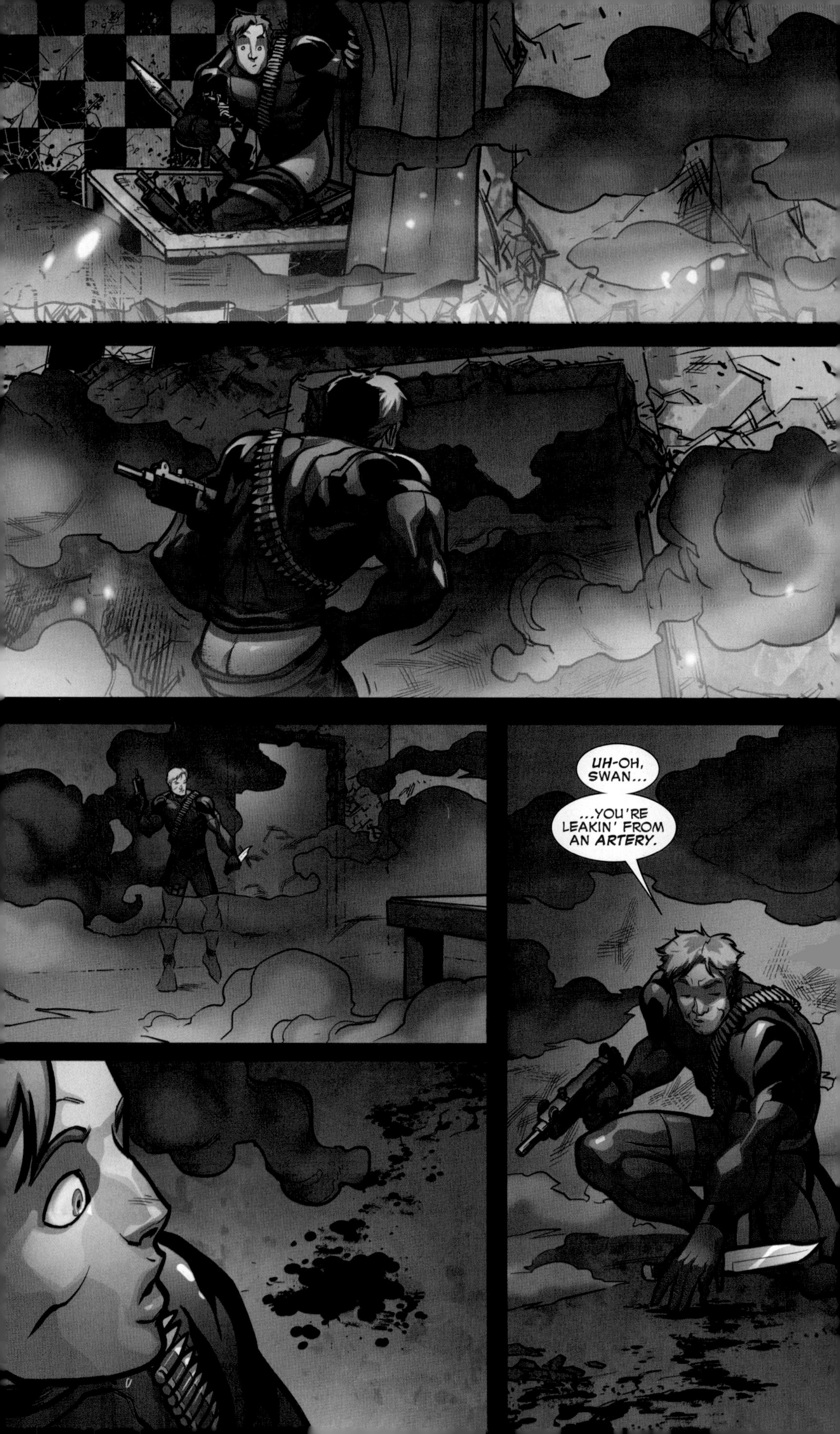
UH-OH, SWAN...
...YOU'RE LEAKIN' FROM AN ARTERY.

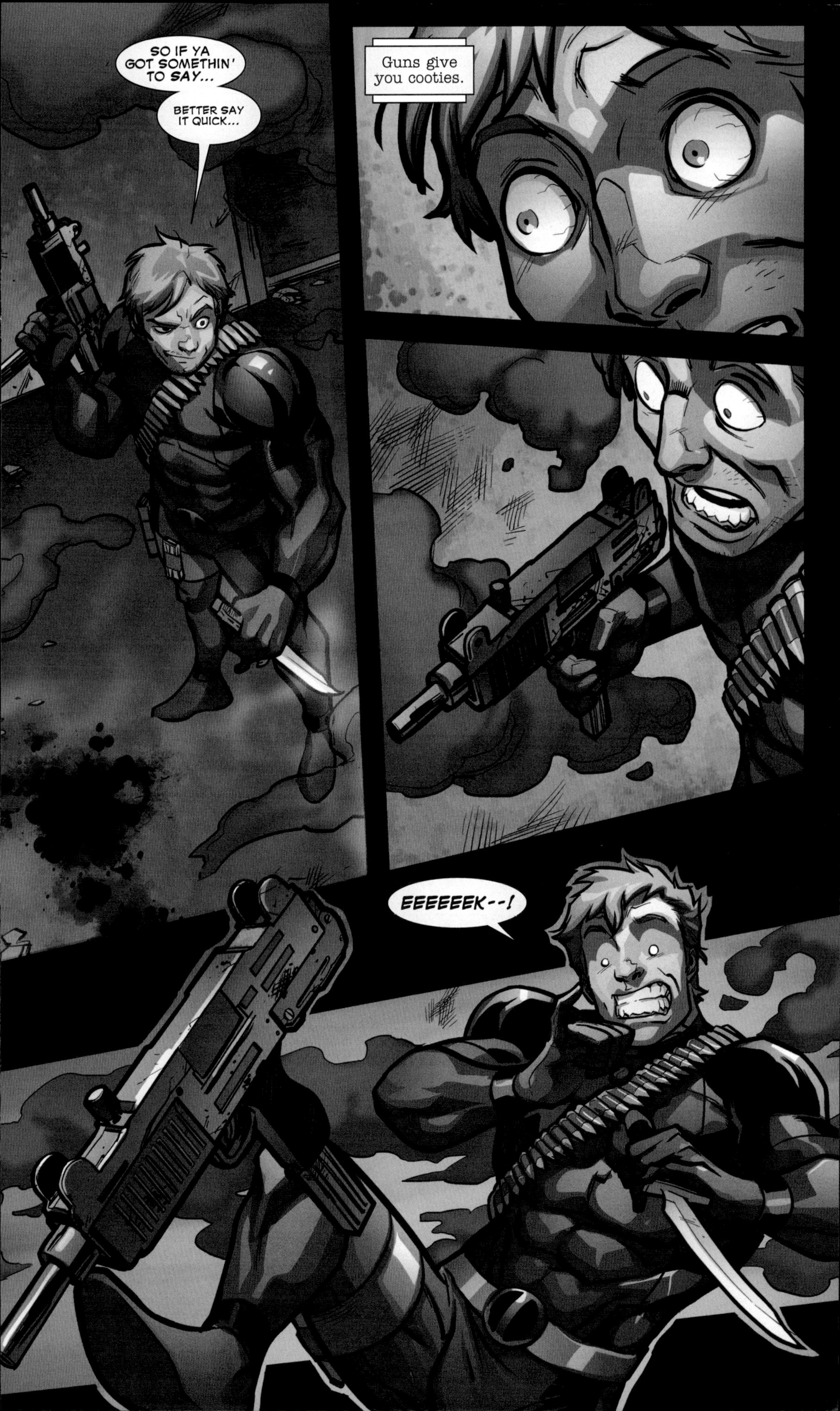
SO IF YA GOT SOMETHIN' TO SAY...
BETTER SAY IT QUICK...
Guns give you cooties.
EEEEEEK--!

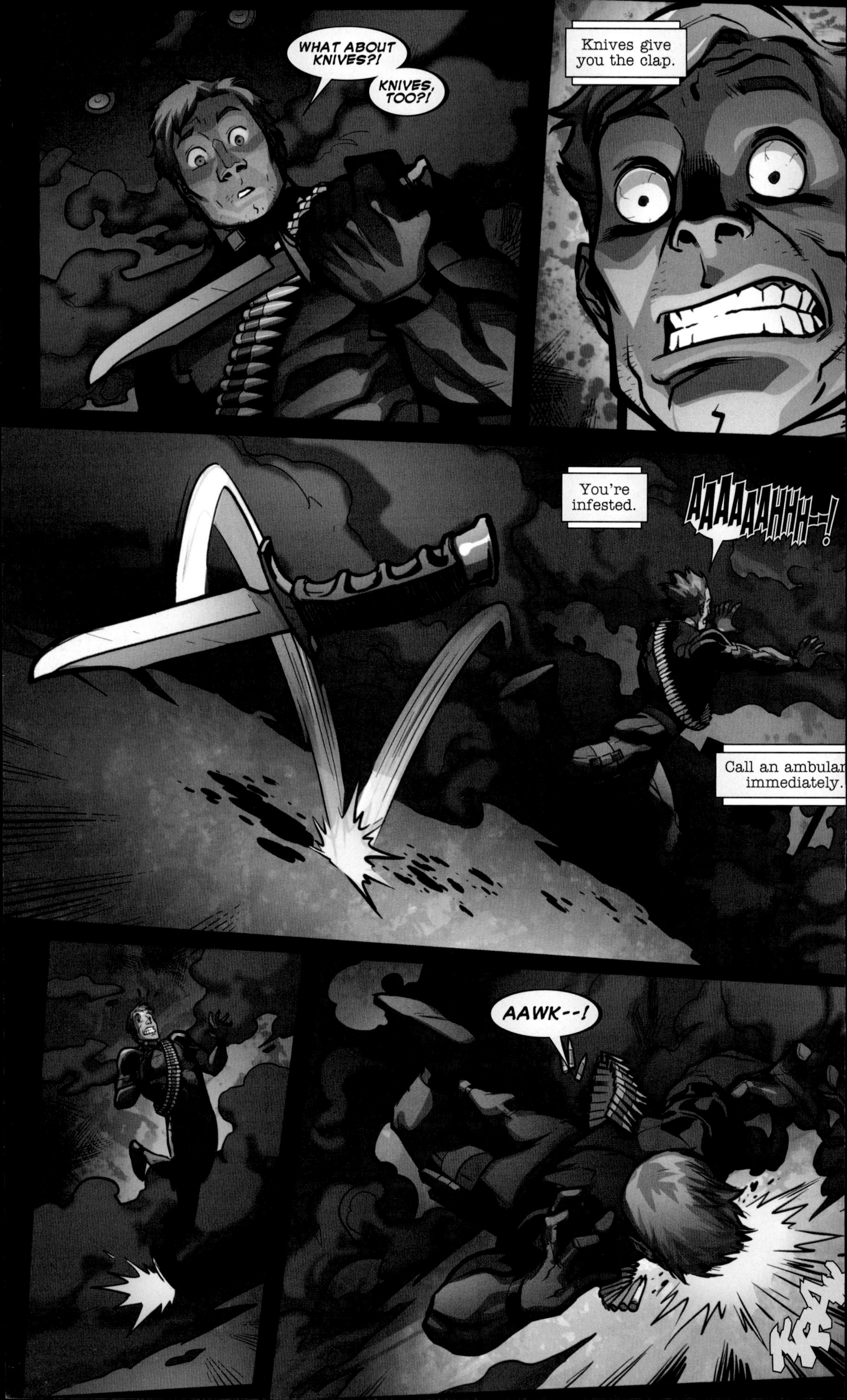
WHAT ABOUT KNIVES?!
KNIVES, TOO?!
Knives give you the clap.
You're infested.
AAAAAAHHH--!
Call an ambular
immediately.
AAWK--!

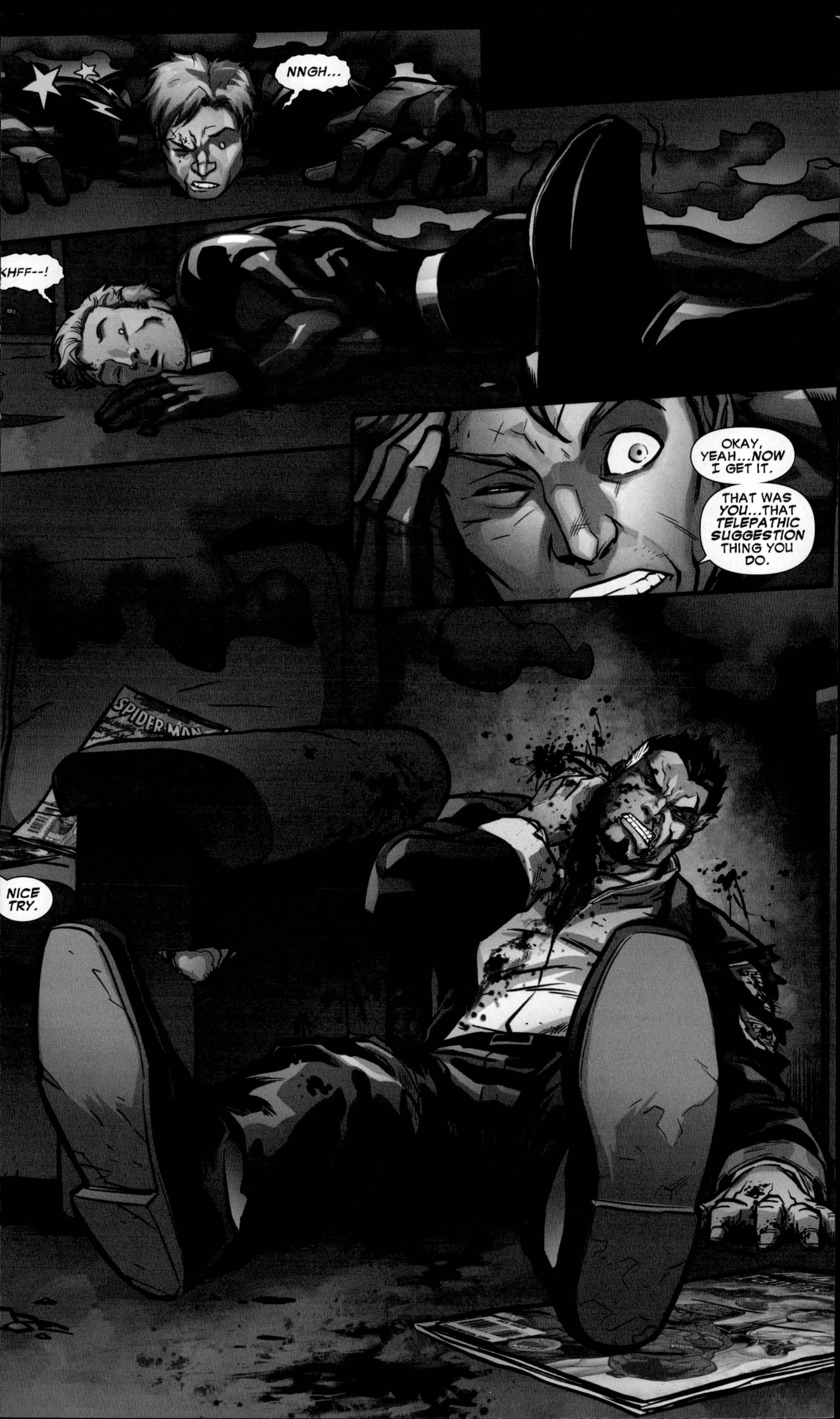
NNGH...
KHFF--!
OKAY, YEAH...NOW I GET IT.
THAT WAS YOU...THAT TELEPATHIC SUGGESTION THING YOU DO.
SPIDER-MAN
NICE TRY.

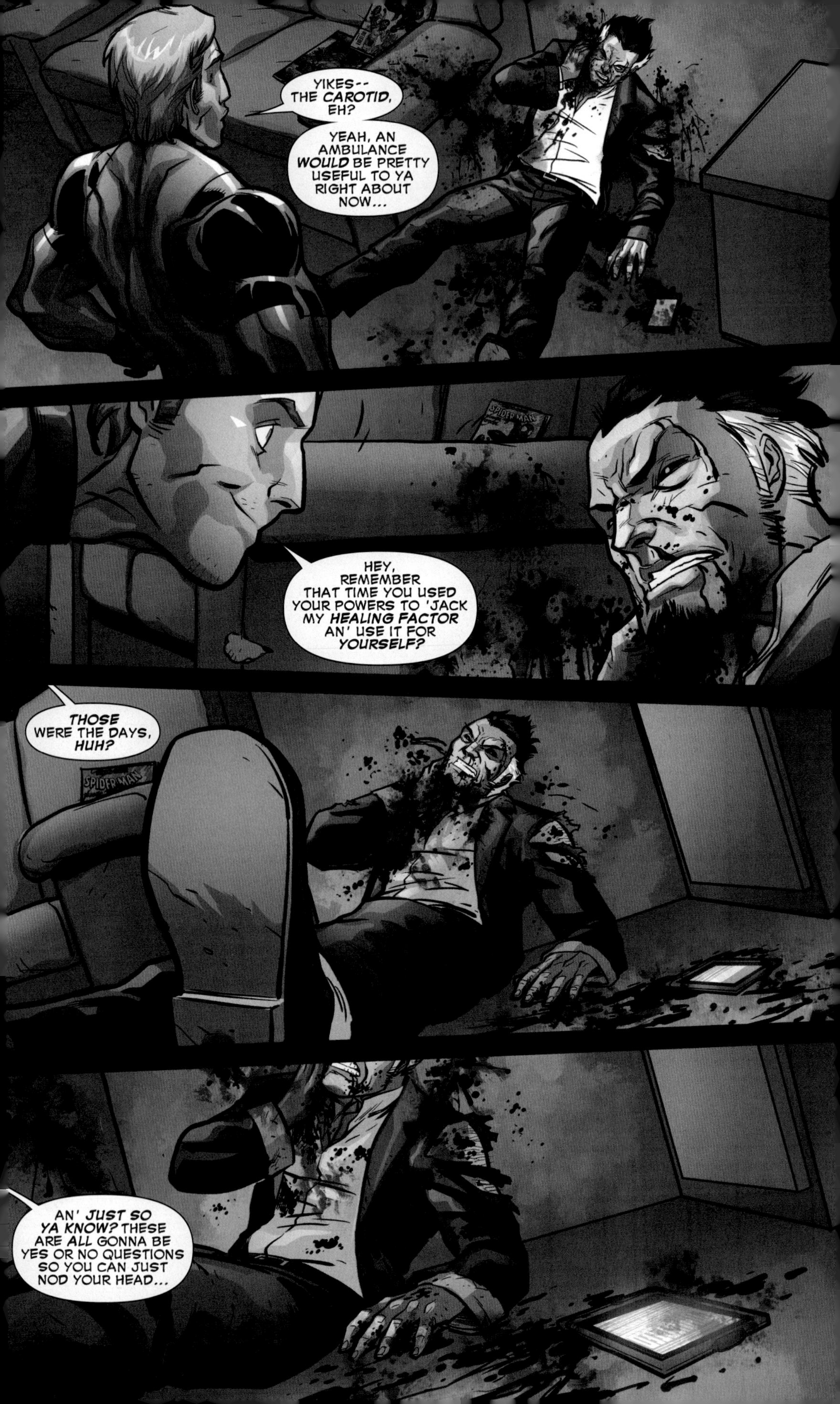
YIKES-- THE CAROTID, EH?
YEAH, AN AMBULANCE WOULD BE PRETTY USEFUL TO YA RIGHT ABOUT NOW...
HEY, REMEMBER THAT TIME YOU USED YOUR POWERS TO 'JACK MY HEALING FACTOR AN' USE IT FOR YOURSELF?
THOSE WERE THE DAYS, HUH?
AN' JUST SO YA KNOW? THESE ARE ALL GONNA BE YES OR NO QUESTIONS SO YOU CAN JUST NOD YOUR HEAD...

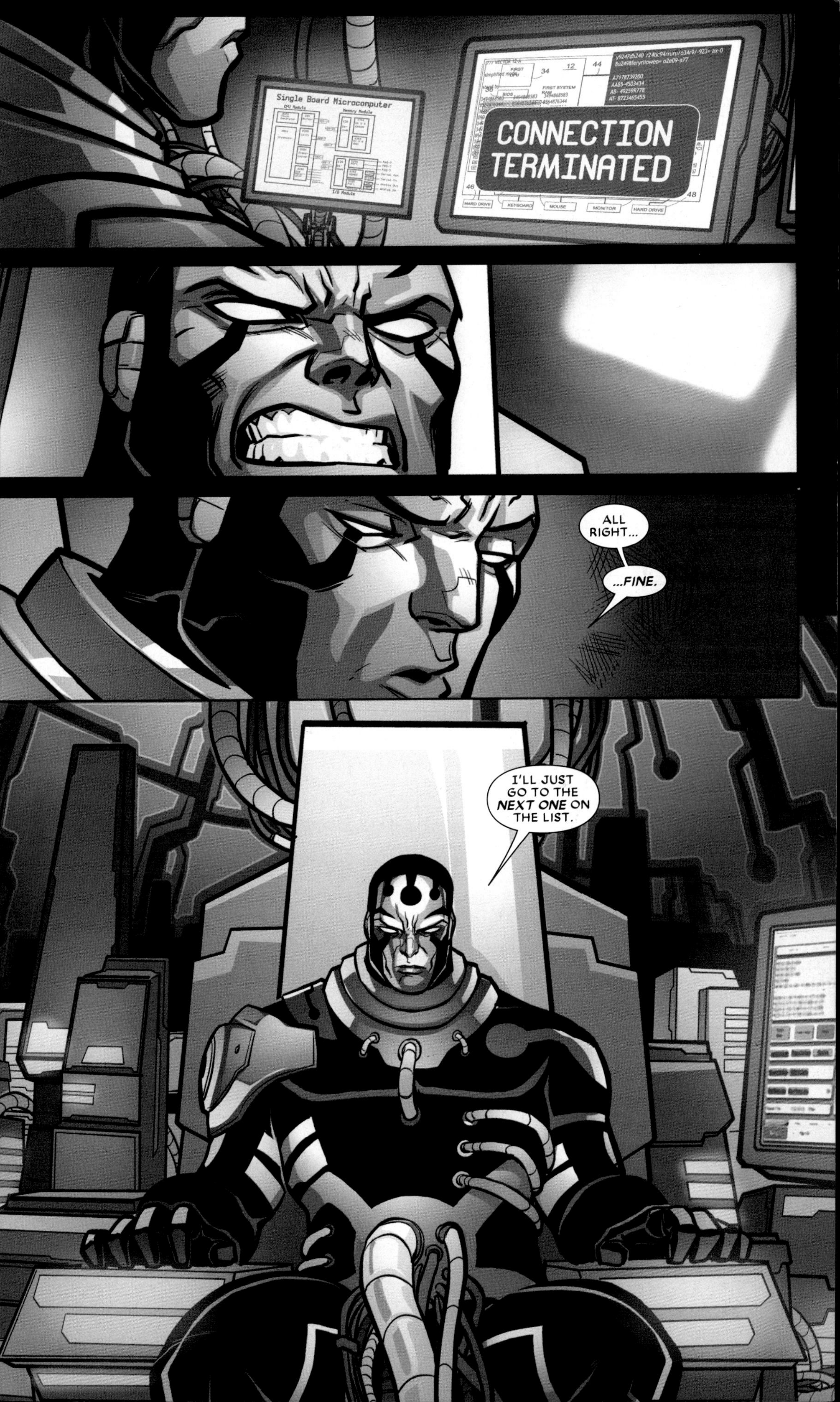
Single Board Microcomputer
CONNECTION TERMINATED
HARD DRIVE
KEYBOARD
MOUSE
MONITOR
HARD DRIVE
ALL RIGHT...
...FINE.
I'LL JUST GO TO THE NEXT ONE ON THE LIST.

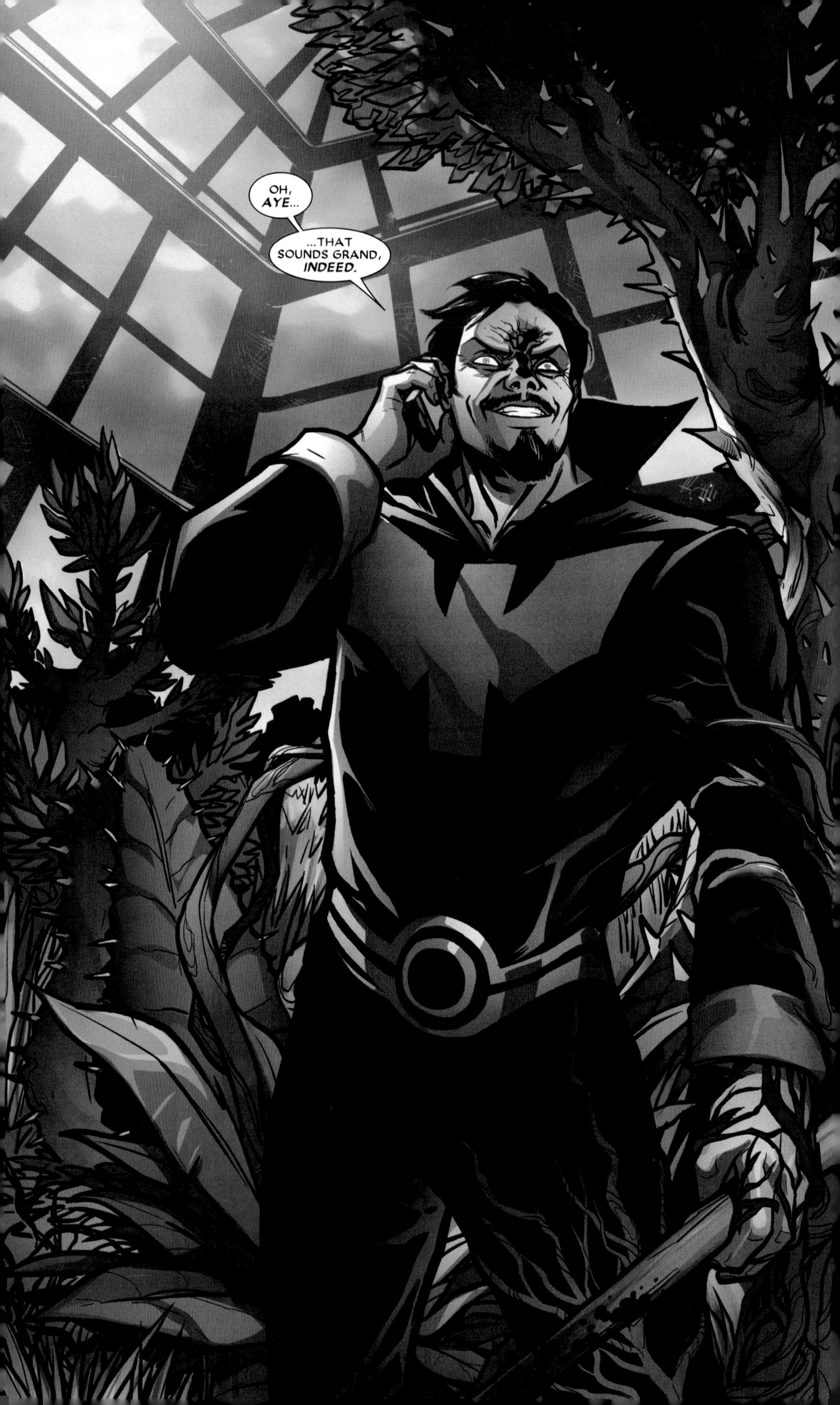
OH, AYE...
...THAT SOUNDS GRAND, INDEED.

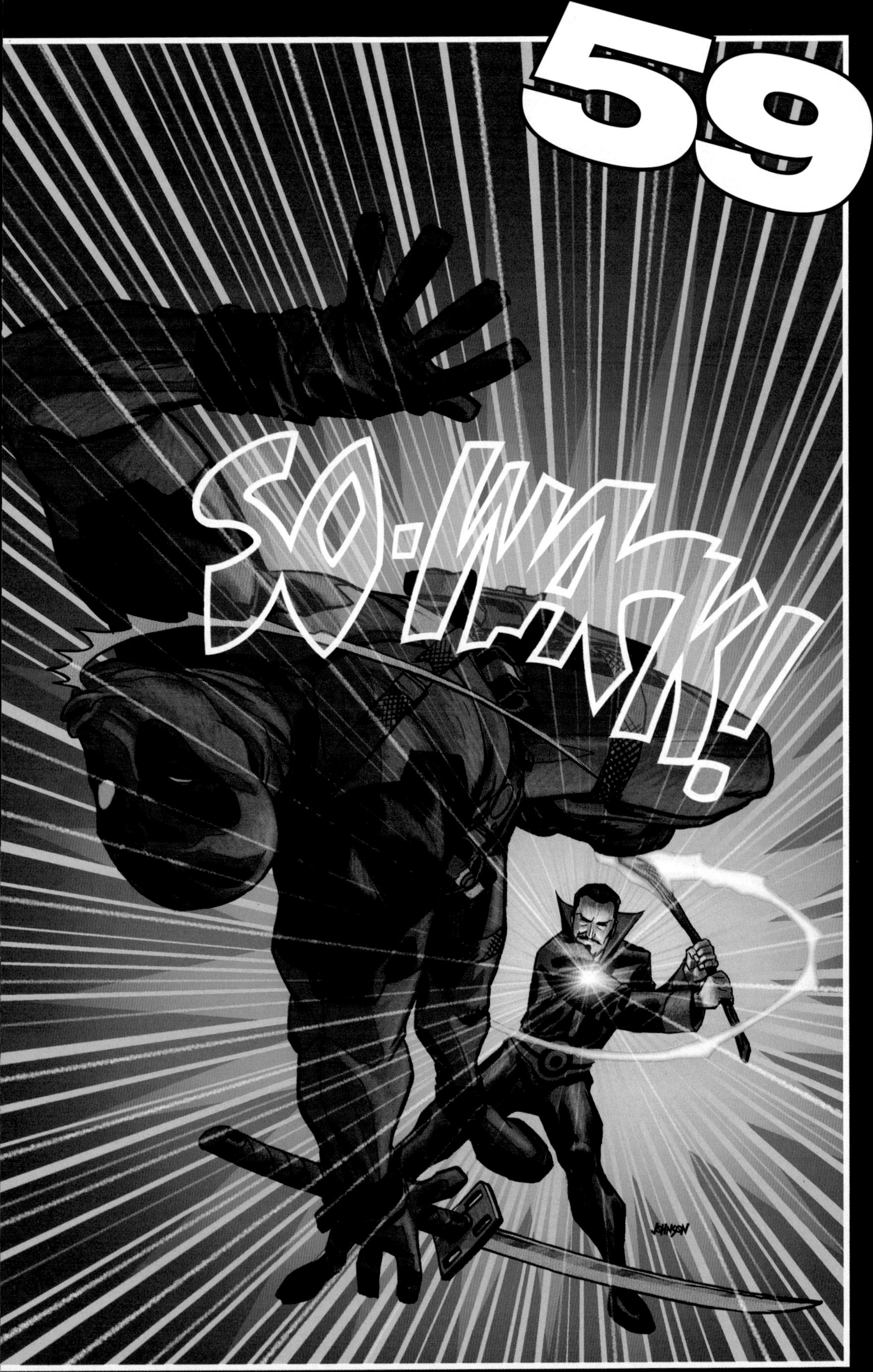
59
SQLUNK!
JOHNSON

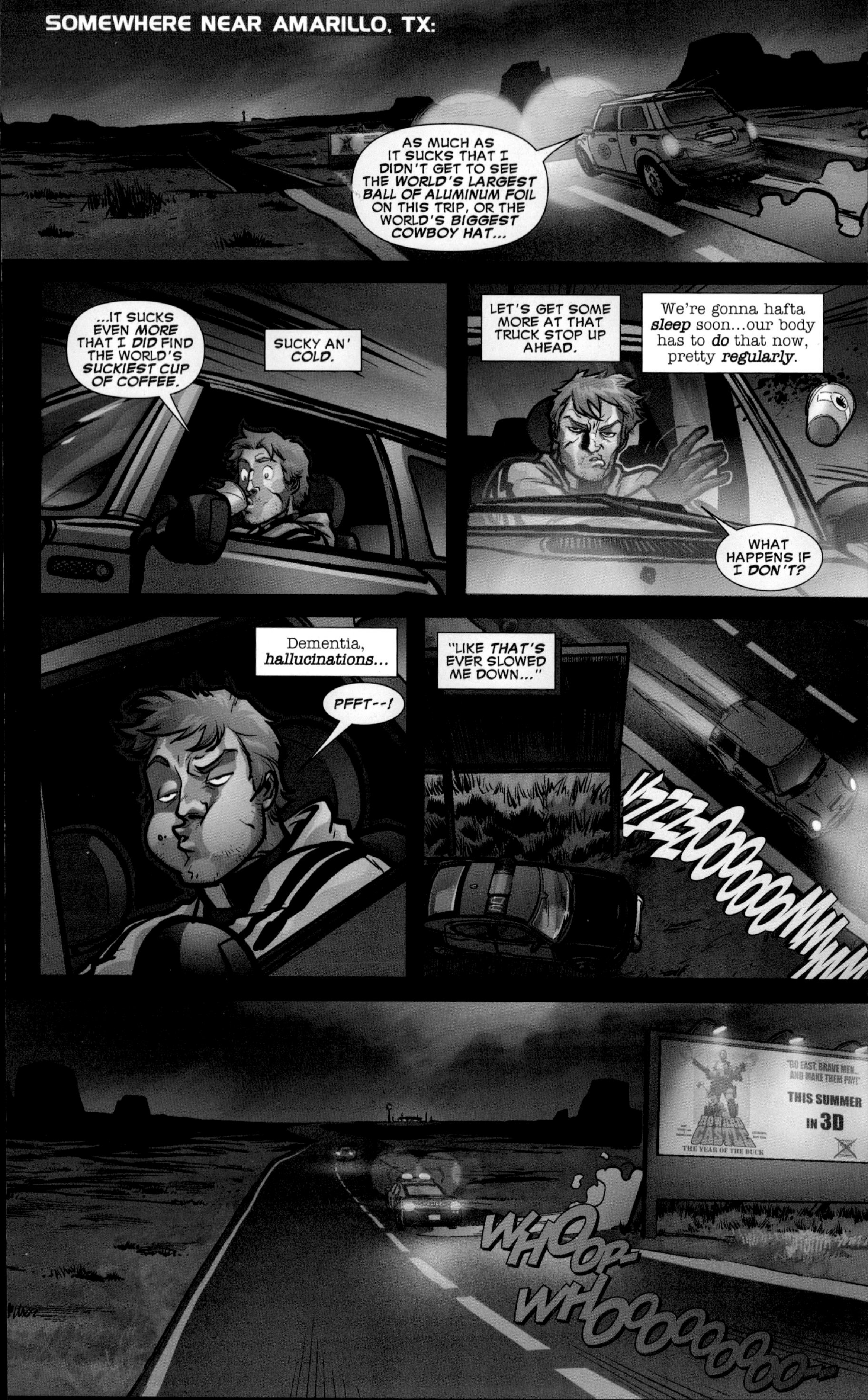
SOMEWHERE NEAR AMARILLO, TX:
AS MUCH AS IT SUCKS THAT I DIDN'T GET TO SEE THE WORLD'S LARGEST BALL OF ALUMINUM FOIL ON THIS TRIP, OR THE WORLD'S BIGGEST COWBOY HAT...
...IT SUCKS EVEN MORE THAT I DID FIND THE WORLD'S SUCKIEST CUP OF COFFEE.
SUCKY AN' COLD.
LET'S GET SOME MORE AT THAT TRUCK STOP UP AHEAD.
We're gonna hafta sleep soon...our body has to do that now, pretty regularly.
WHAT HAPPENS IF I DON'T?
Dementia, hallucinations...
PFFT--!
"LIKE THAT'S EVER SLOWED ME DOWN..."
"GO EAST, BRAVE MEN... AND MAKE THEM PAY!"
THIS SUMMER
IN 3D
HOWARD CASTLE
THE YEAR OF THE DUCK

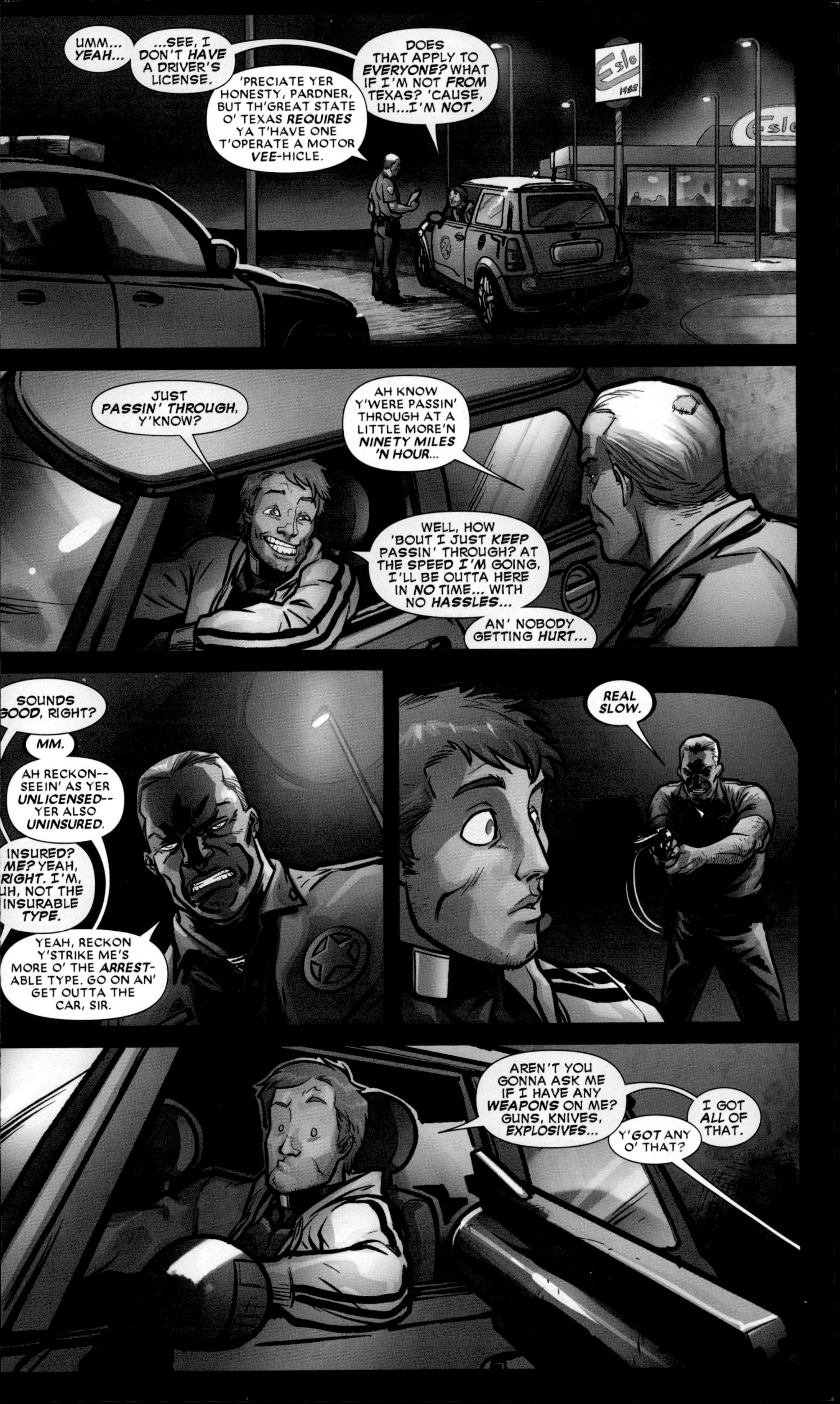
UMM... YEAH...
...SEE, I DON'T HAVE A DRIVER'S LICENSE.
'PRECIATE YER HONESTY, PARDNER, BUT TH'GREAT STATE O' TEXAS REQUIRES YA T'HAVE ONE T'OPERATE A MOTOR VEE-HICLE.
DOES THAT APPLY TO EVERYONE? WHAT IF I'M NOT FROM TEXAS? 'CAUSE, UH...I'M NOT.
Eslo
JUST PASSIN' THROUGH, Y'KNOW?
AH KNOW Y'WERE PASSIN' THROUGH AT A LITTLE MORE'N NINETY MILES 'N HOUR...
WELL, HOW 'BOUT I JUST KEEP PASSIN' THROUGH? AT THE SPEED I'M GOING, I'LL BE OUTTA HERE IN NO TIME... WITH NO HASSLES...
AN' NOBODY GETTING HURT...
SOUNDS GOOD, RIGHT?
MM.
AH RECKON--SEEIN' AS YER UNLICENSED--YER ALSO UNINSURED.
INSURED? ME? YEAH, RIGHT. I'M, UH, NOT THE INSURABLE TYPE.
YEAH, RECKON Y'STRIKE ME'S MORE O' THE ARREST-ABLE TYPE. GO ON AN' GET OUTTA THE CAR, SIR.
REAL SLOW.
AREN'T YOU GONNA ASK ME IF I HAVE ANY WEAPONS ON ME? GUNS, KNIVES, EXPLOSIVES...
Y'GOT ANY O' THAT?
I GOT ALL OF THAT.

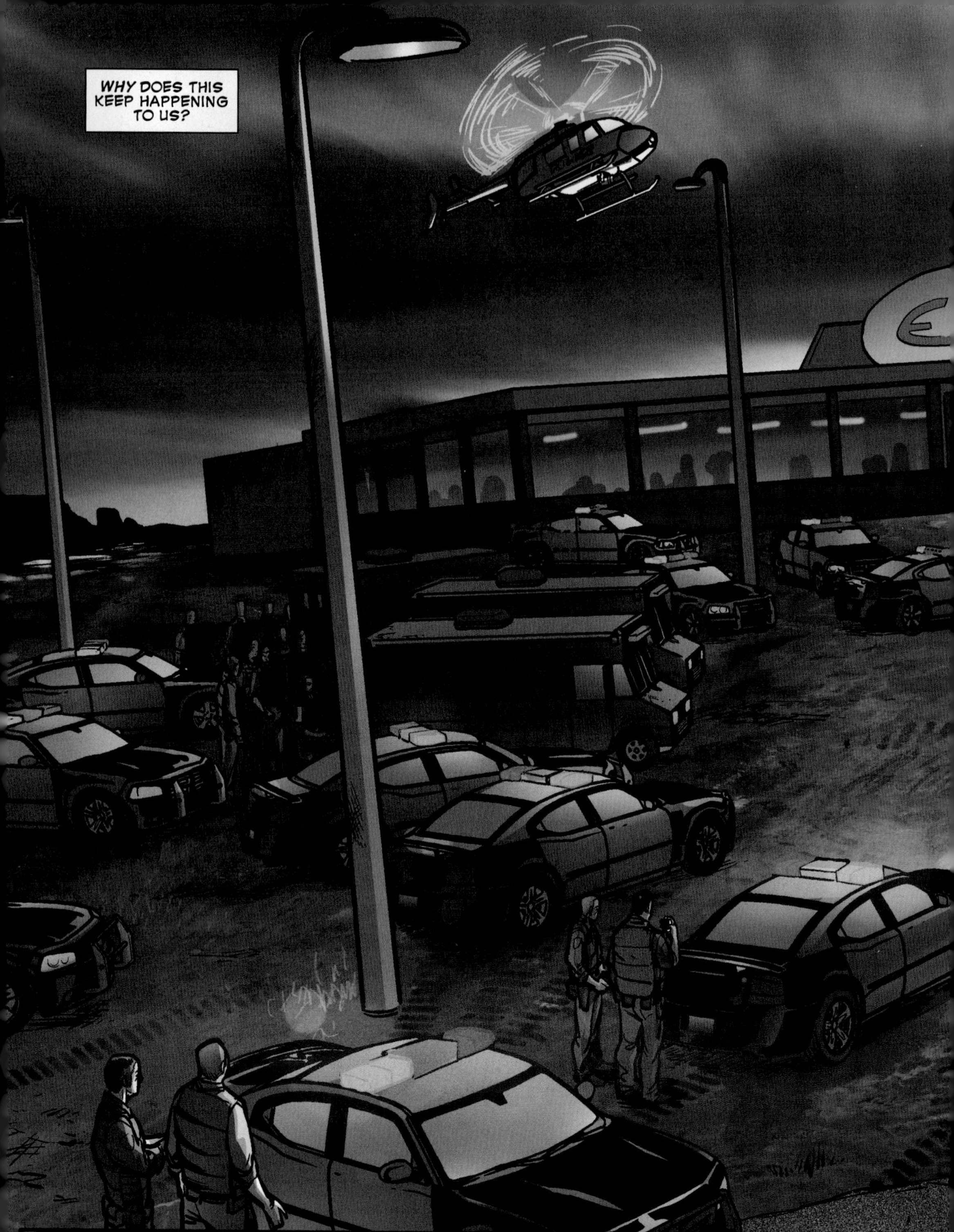
WHY DOES THIS KEEP HAPPENING TO US?
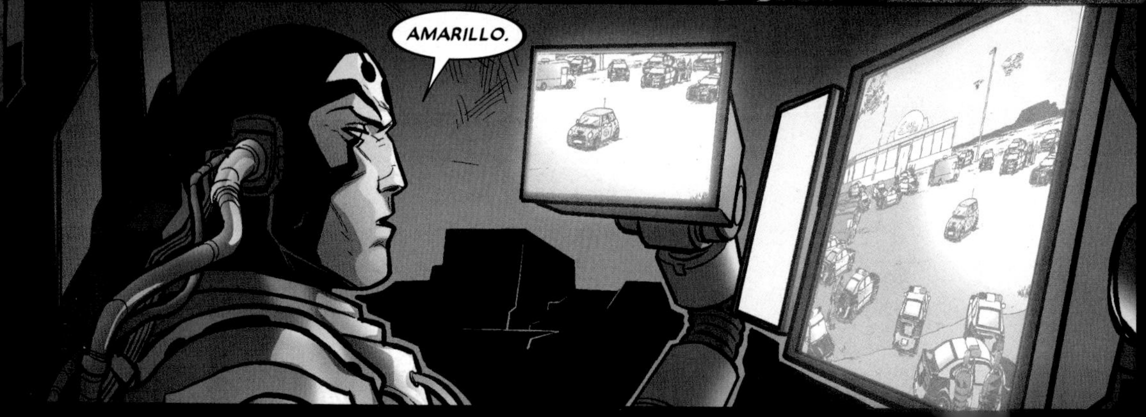
AMARILLO.

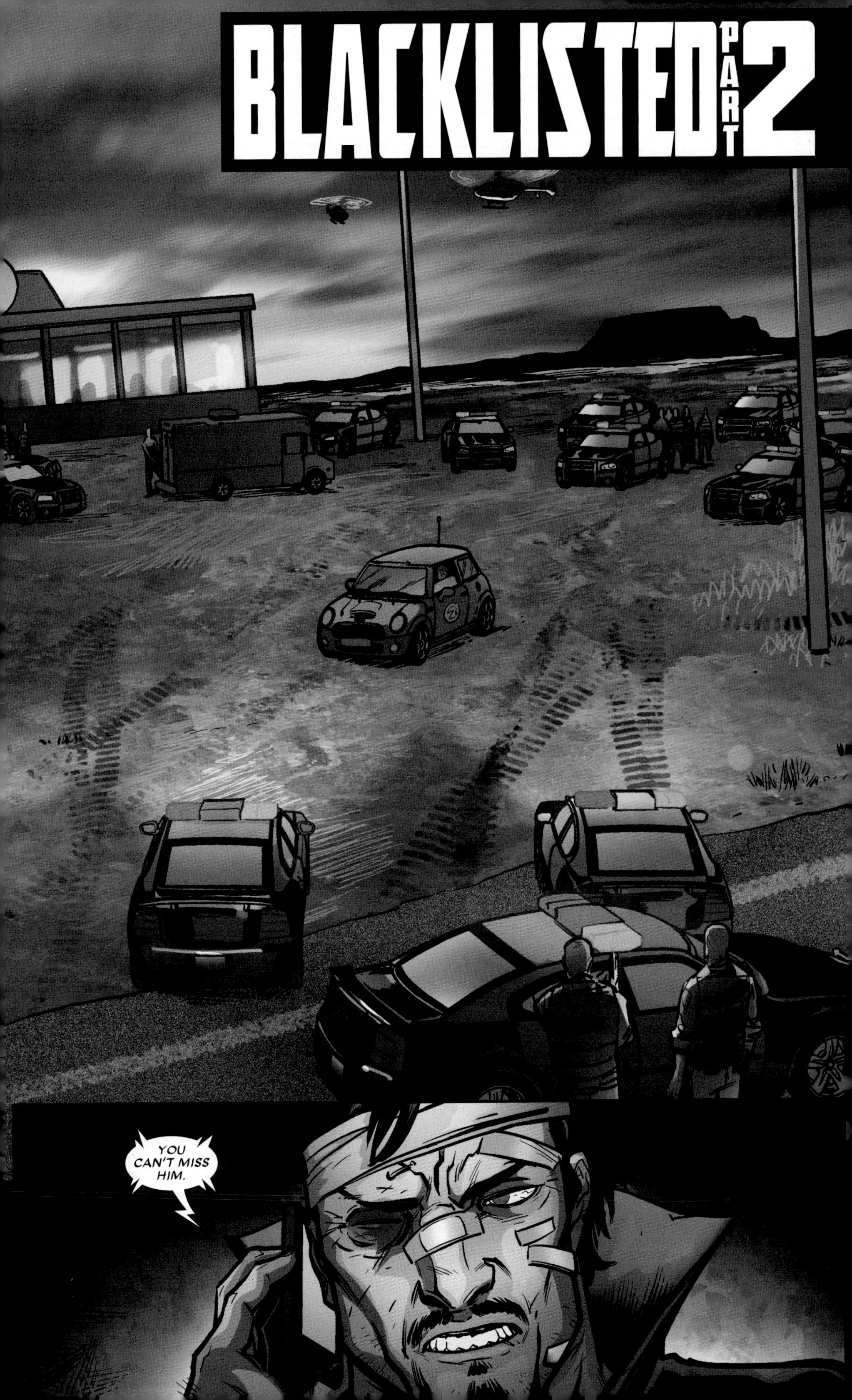
BLACKLISTED PART 2
YOU CAN'T MISS HIM.

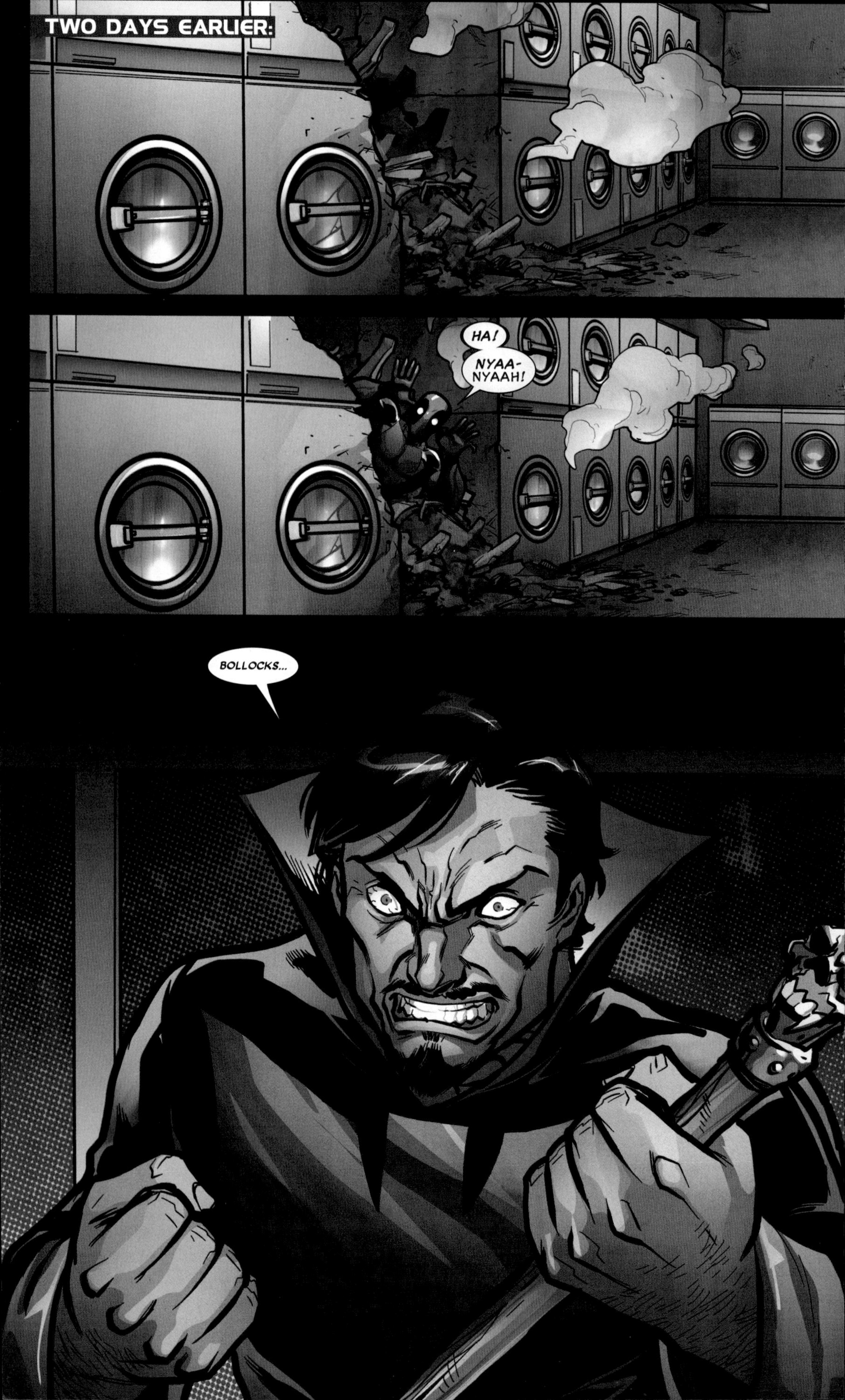
TWO DAYS EARLIER:
HA!
NYAA-NYAAH!
BOLLOCKS...

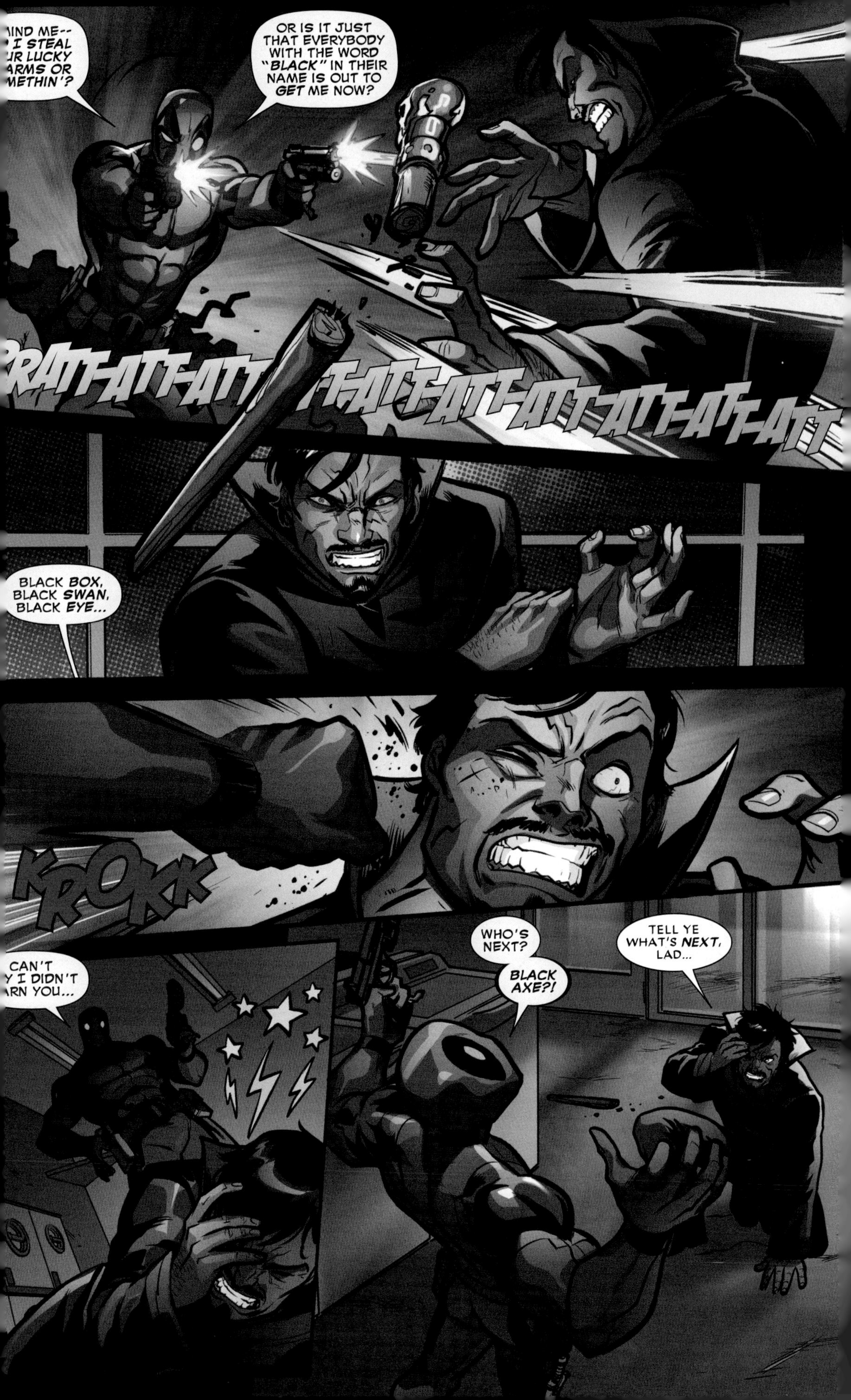

MIND ME-- I STEAL UR LUCKY ARMS OR METHIN'?
OR IS IT JUST THAT EVERYBODY WITH THE WORD "BLACK" IN THEIR NAME IS OUT TO GET ME NOW?
BRATT-ATT-ATT-ATT-ATT-ATT-ATT-ATT-ATT
BLACK BOX, BLACK SWAN, BLACK EYE...
KROKK
CAN'T Y I DIDN'T ARN YOU...
WHO'S NEXT?
BLACK AXE?!
TELL YE WHAT'S NEXT, LAD...

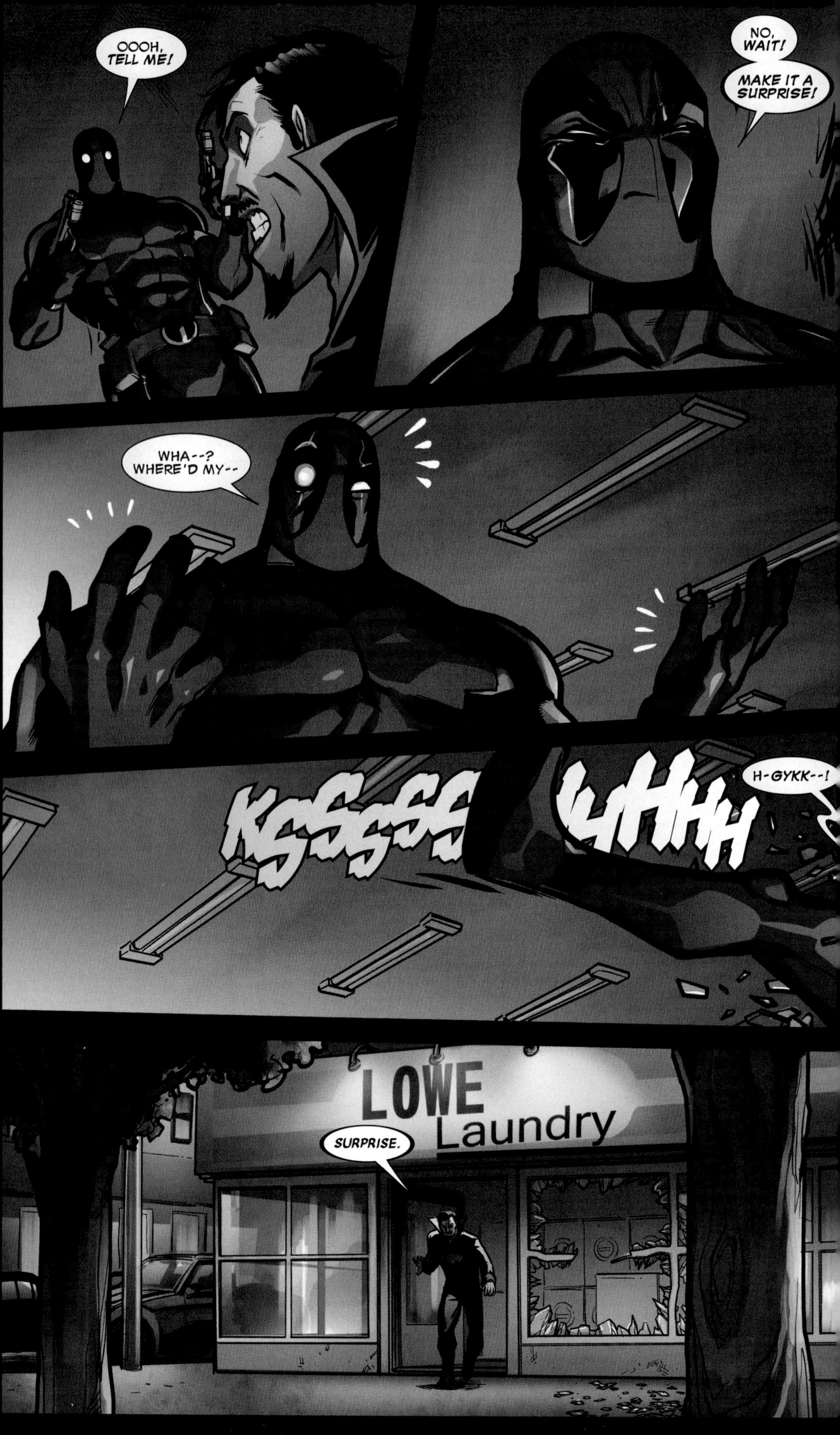
OOOH, TELL ME!
NO, WAIT!
MAKE IT A SURPRISE!
WHA--? WHERE'D MY--
KSSSSSHHHH
H-GYKK--!
LOWE Laundry
SURPRISE.

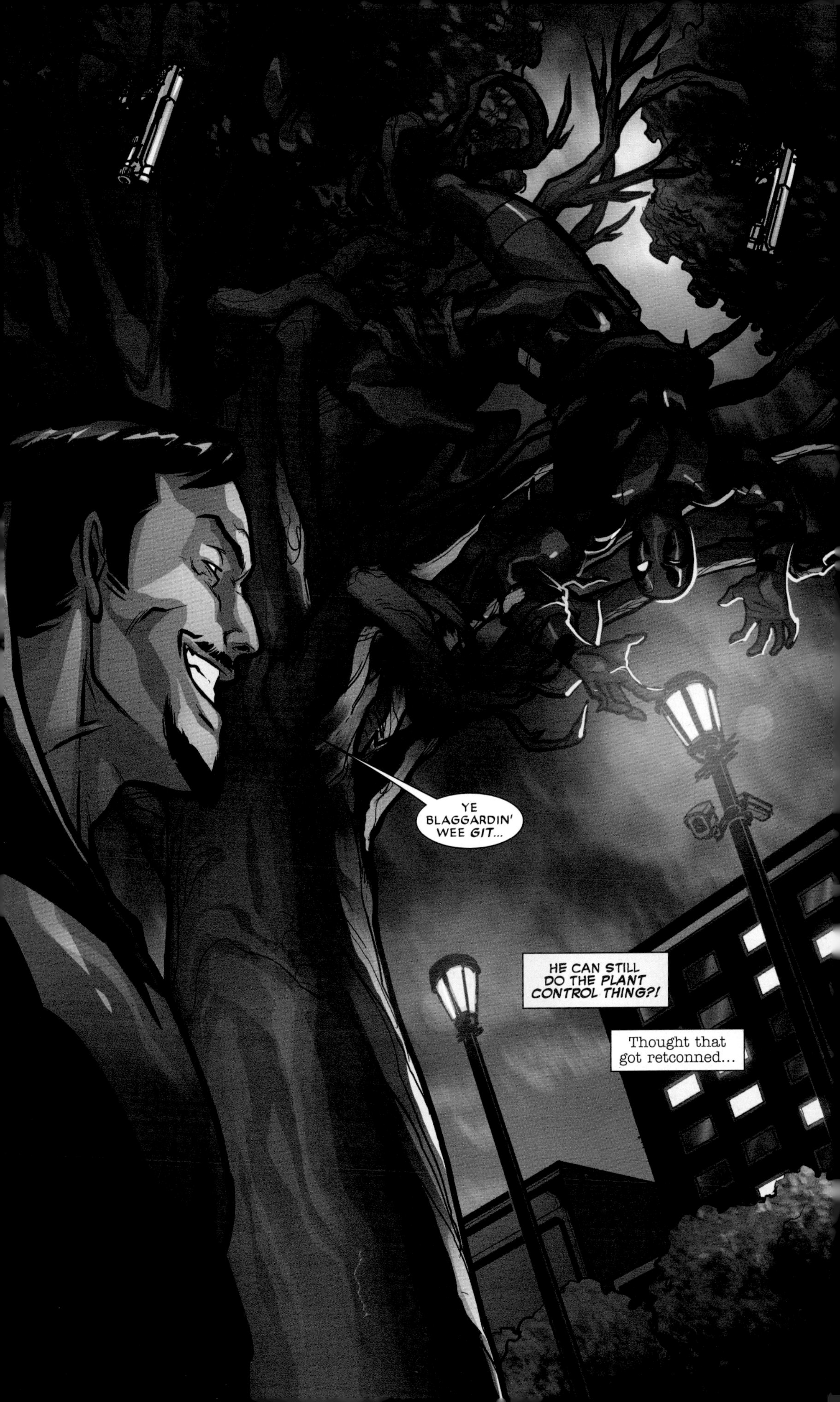
YE BLAGGARDIN' WEE GIT...
HE CAN STILL DO THE PLANT CONTROL THING?!
Thought that got retconned...

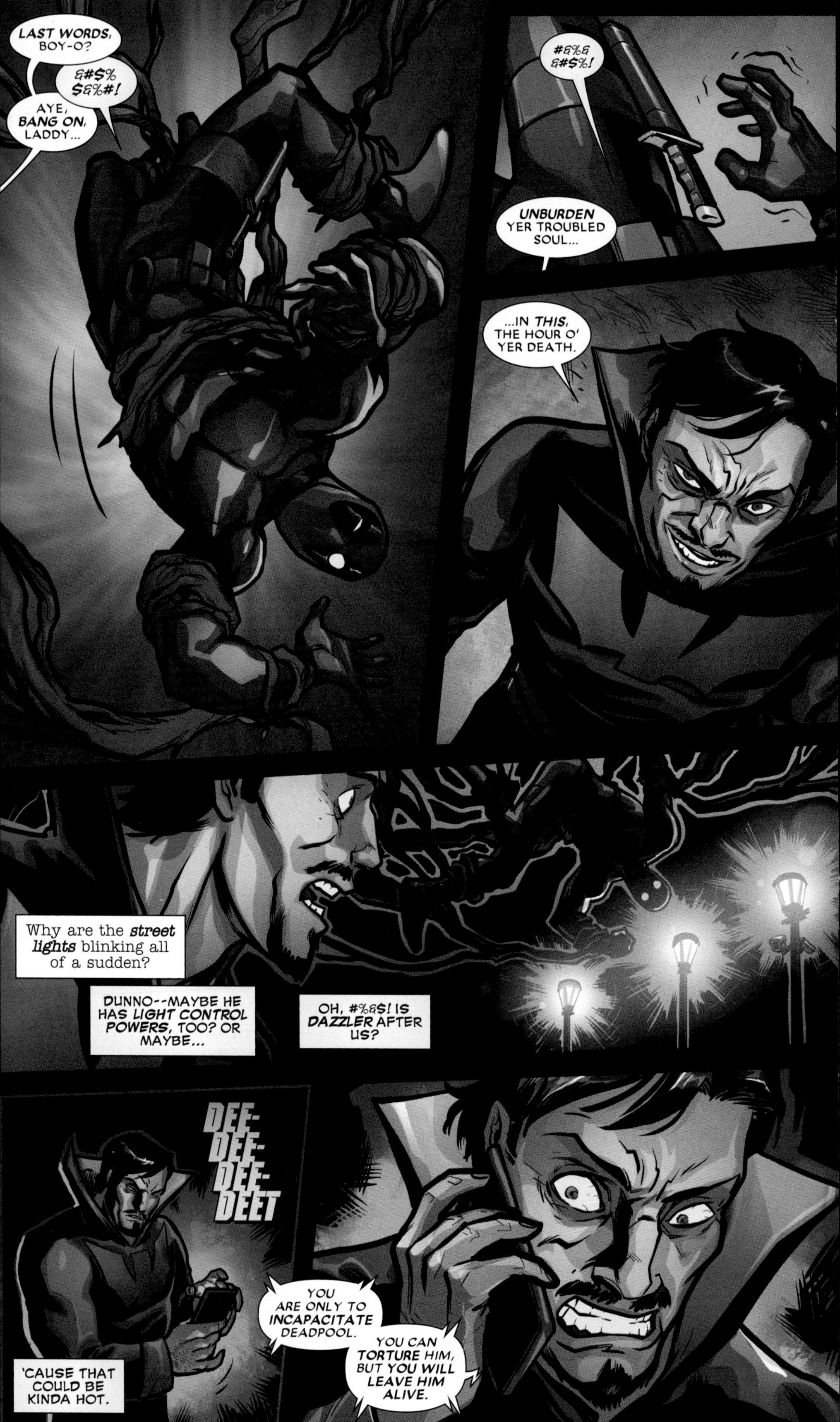
LAST WORDS, BOY-O?
&#$% $&%#!
AYE, BANG ON, LADDY...
#&%& &#$%!
UNBURDEN YER TROUBLED SOUL...
...IN THIS, THE HOUR O' YER DEATH.
Why are the street lights blinking all of a sudden?
DUNNO--MAYBE HE HAS LIGHT CONTROL POWERS, TOO? OR MAYBE...
OH, #%&$! IS DAZZLER AFTER US?
DEE-DEE-DEE-DEET
'CAUSE THAT COULD BE KINDA HOT.
YOU ARE ONLY TO INCAPACITATE DEADPOOL.
YOU CAN TORTURE HIM, BUT YOU WILL LEAVE HIM ALIVE.

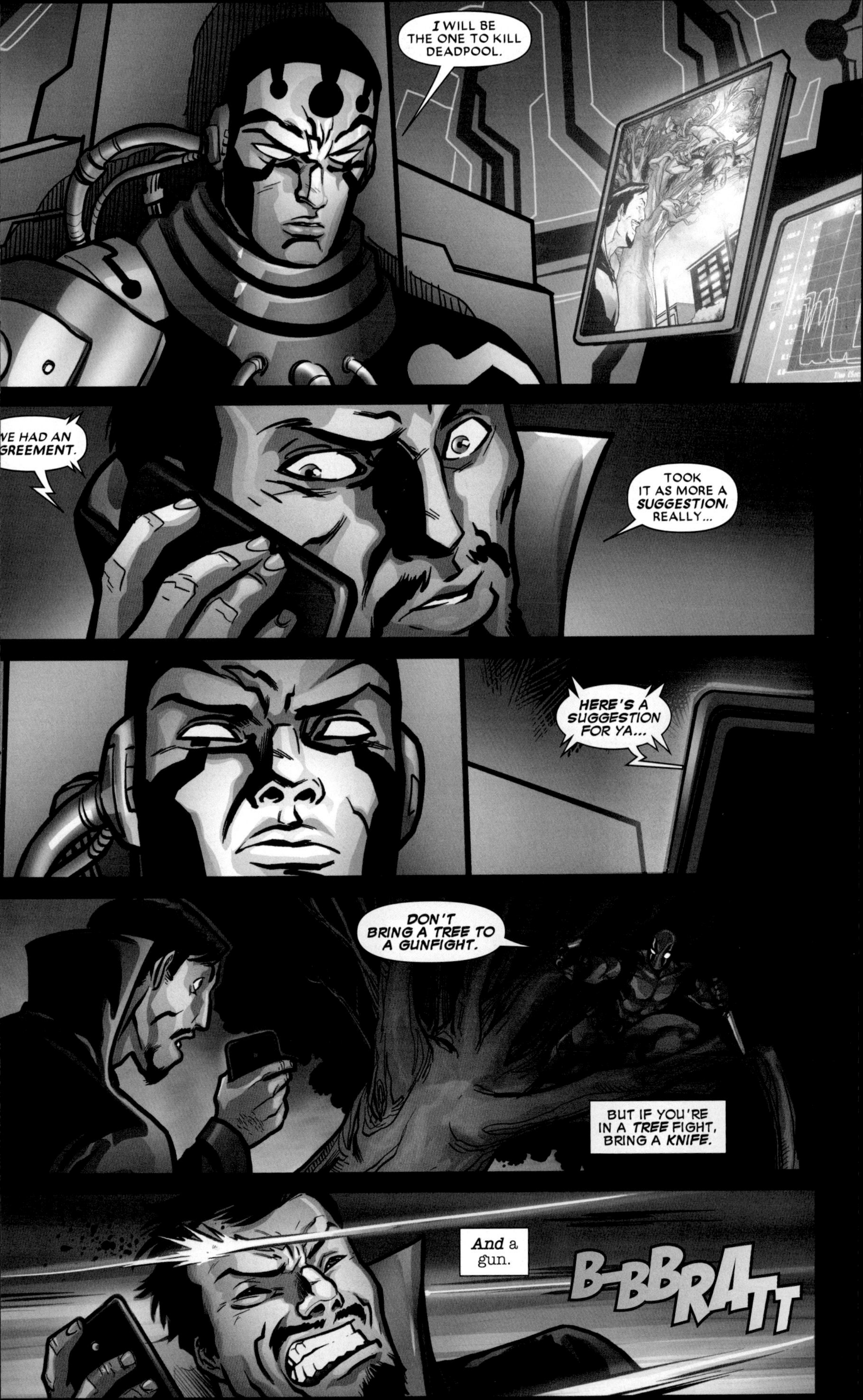
I WILL BE THE ONE TO KILL DEADPOOL.
WE HAD AN AGREEMENT.
TOOK IT AS MORE A SUGGESTION, REALLY...
HERE'S A SUGGESTION FOR YA...
DON'T BRING A TREE TO A GUNFIGHT.
BUT IF YOU'RE IN A TREE FIGHT, BRING A KNIFE.
And a gun.
B-BBRATT

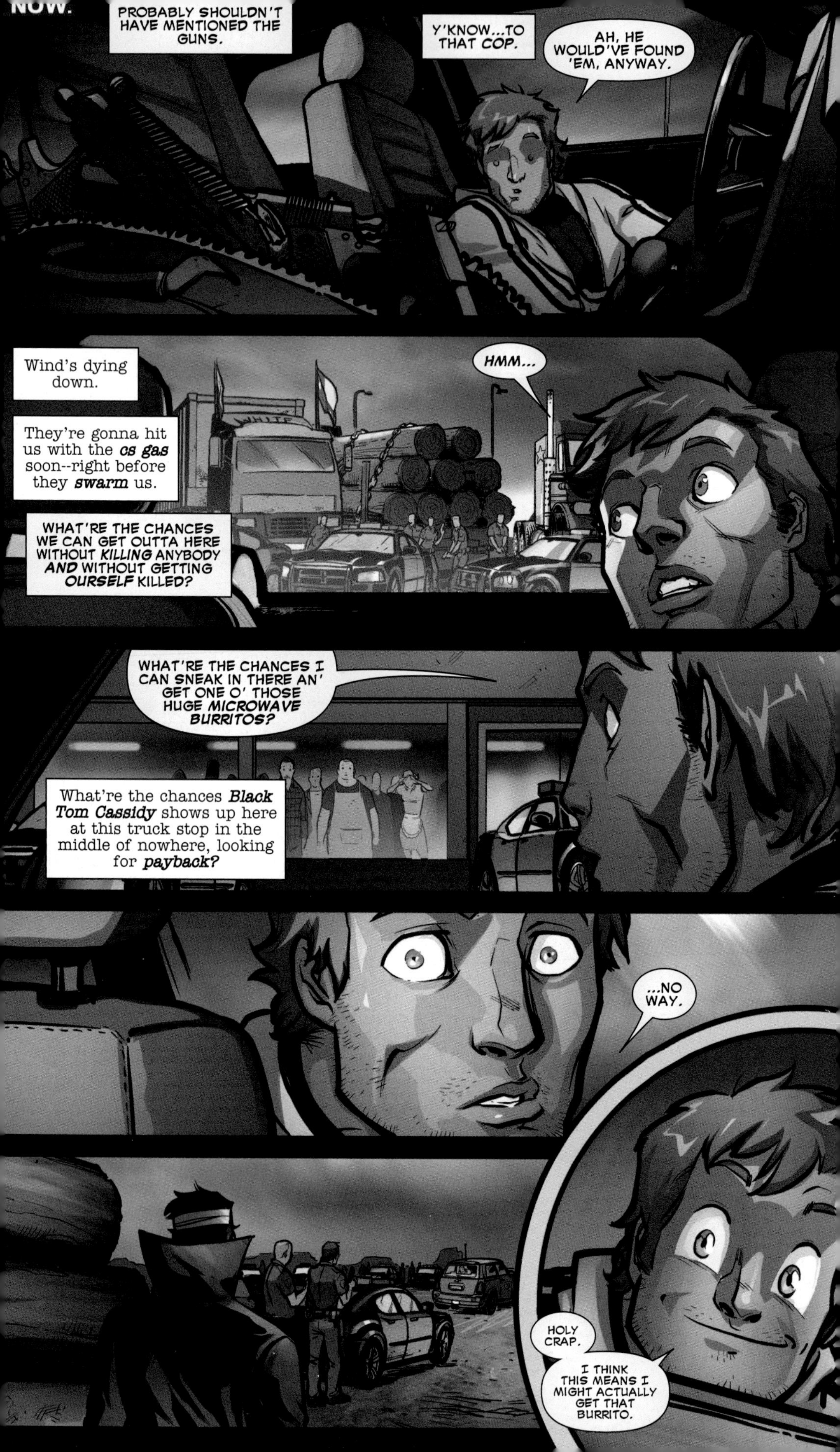
NOW.
PROBABLY SHOULDN'T HAVE MENTIONED THE GUNS.
Y'KNOW...TO THAT COP.
AH, HE WOULD'VE FOUND 'EM, ANYWAY.
Wind's dying down.
They're gonna hit us with the cs gas soon--right before they swarm us.
HMM...
WHAT'RE THE CHANCES WE CAN GET OUTTA HERE WITHOUT KILLING ANYBODY AND WITHOUT GETTING OURSELF KILLED?
WHAT'RE THE CHANCES I CAN SNEAK IN THERE AN' GET ONE O' THOSE HUGE MICROWAVE BURRITOS?
What're the chances Black Tom Cassidy shows up here at this truck stop in the middle of nowhere, looking for payback?
...NO WAY.
HOLY CRAP.
I THINK THIS MEANS I MIGHT ACTUALLY GET THAT BURRITO.

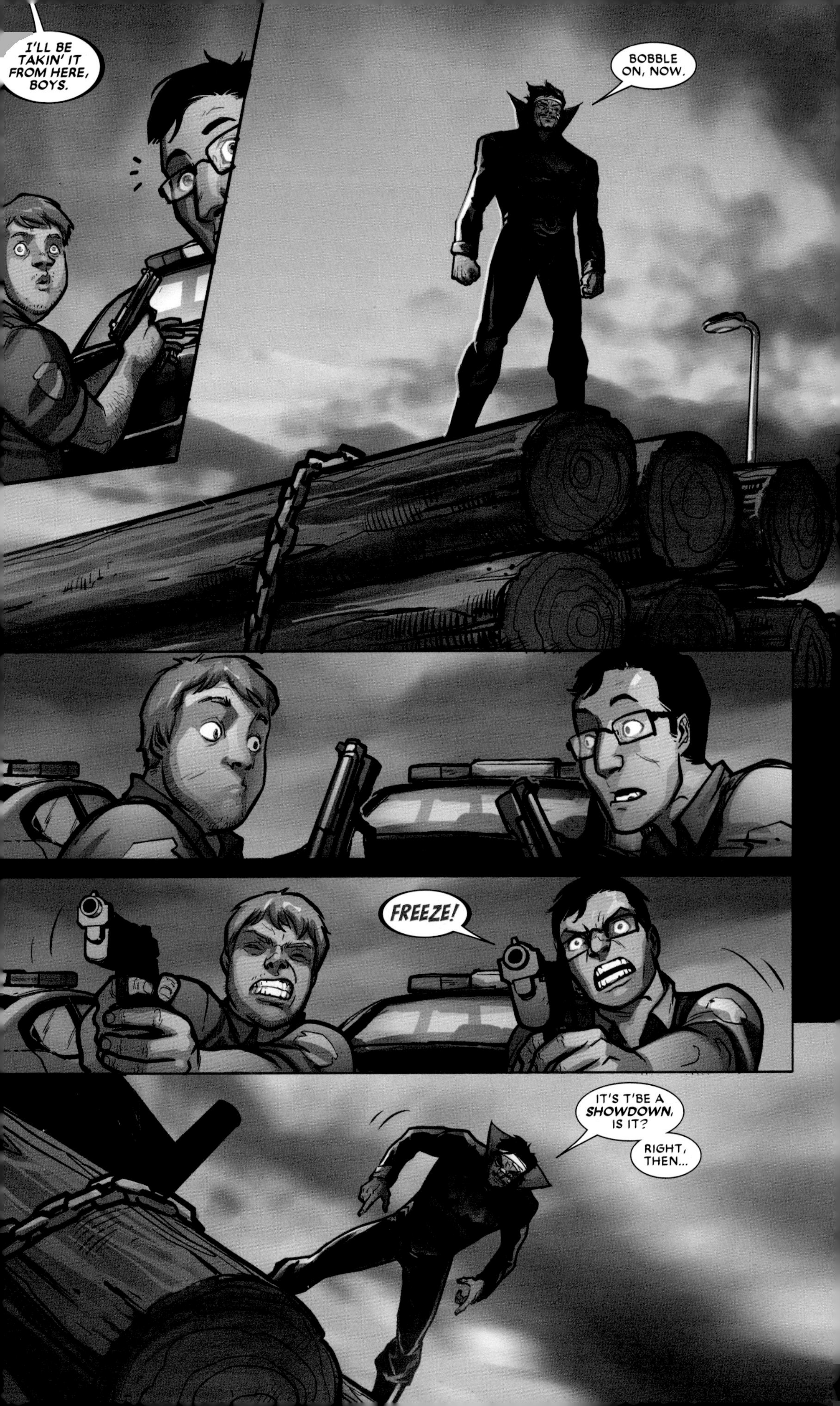
I'LL BE TAKIN' IT FROM HERE, BOYS.
BOBBLE ON, NOW.
FREEZE!
IT'S T'BE A SHOWDOWN, IS IT?
RIGHT, THEN...

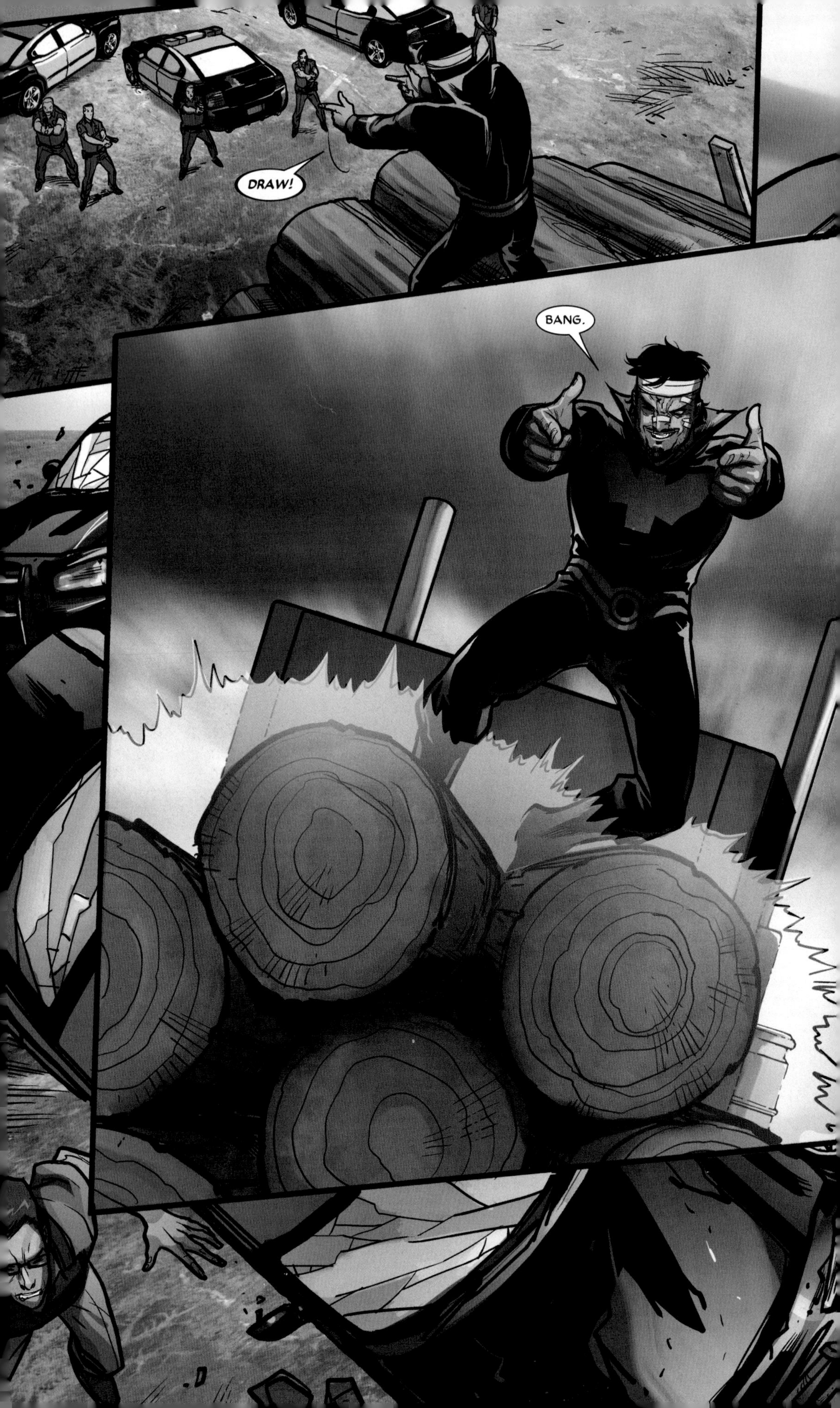
DRAW!
BANG.

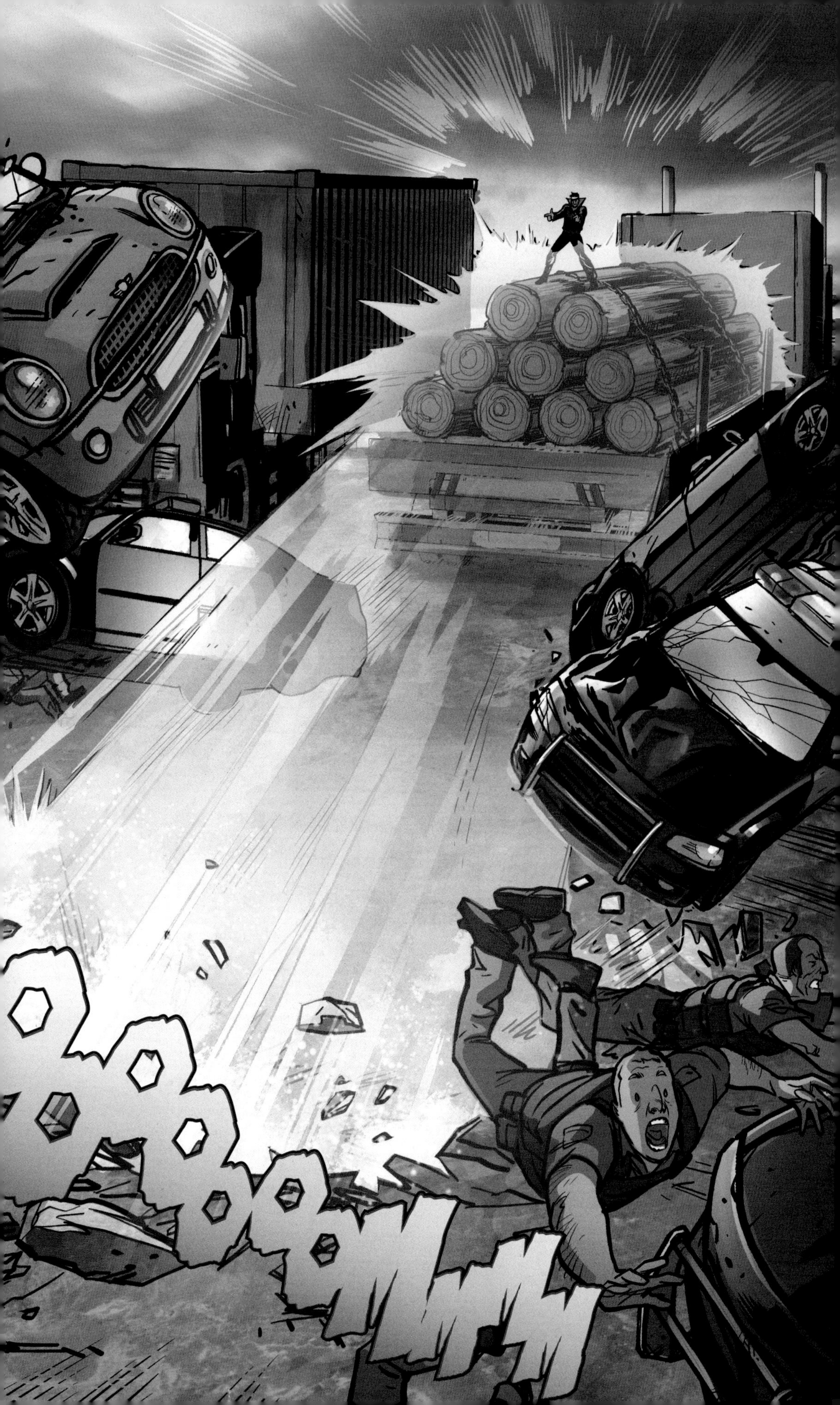

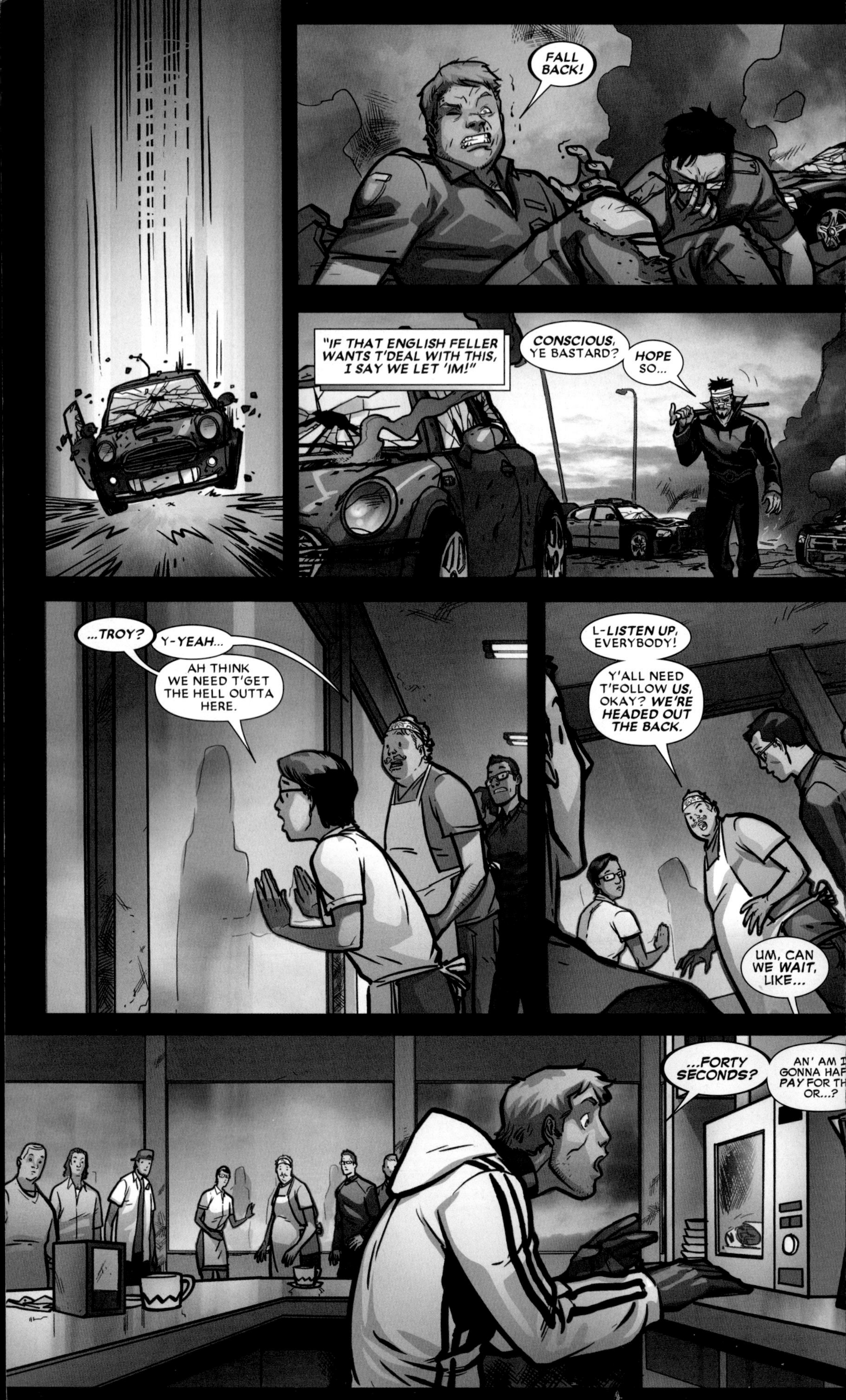
FALL BACK!
"IF THAT ENGLISH FELLER WANTS T'DEAL WITH THIS, I SAY WE LET 'IM!"
CONSCIOUS, YE BASTARD?
HOPE SO...
...TROY?
Y-YEAH...
AH THINK WE NEED T'GET THE HELL OUTTA HERE.
L-LISTEN UP, EVERYBODY!
Y'ALL NEED T'FOLLOW US, OKAY? WE'RE HEADED OUT THE BACK.
UM, CAN WE WAIT, LIKE...
...FORTY SECONDS?

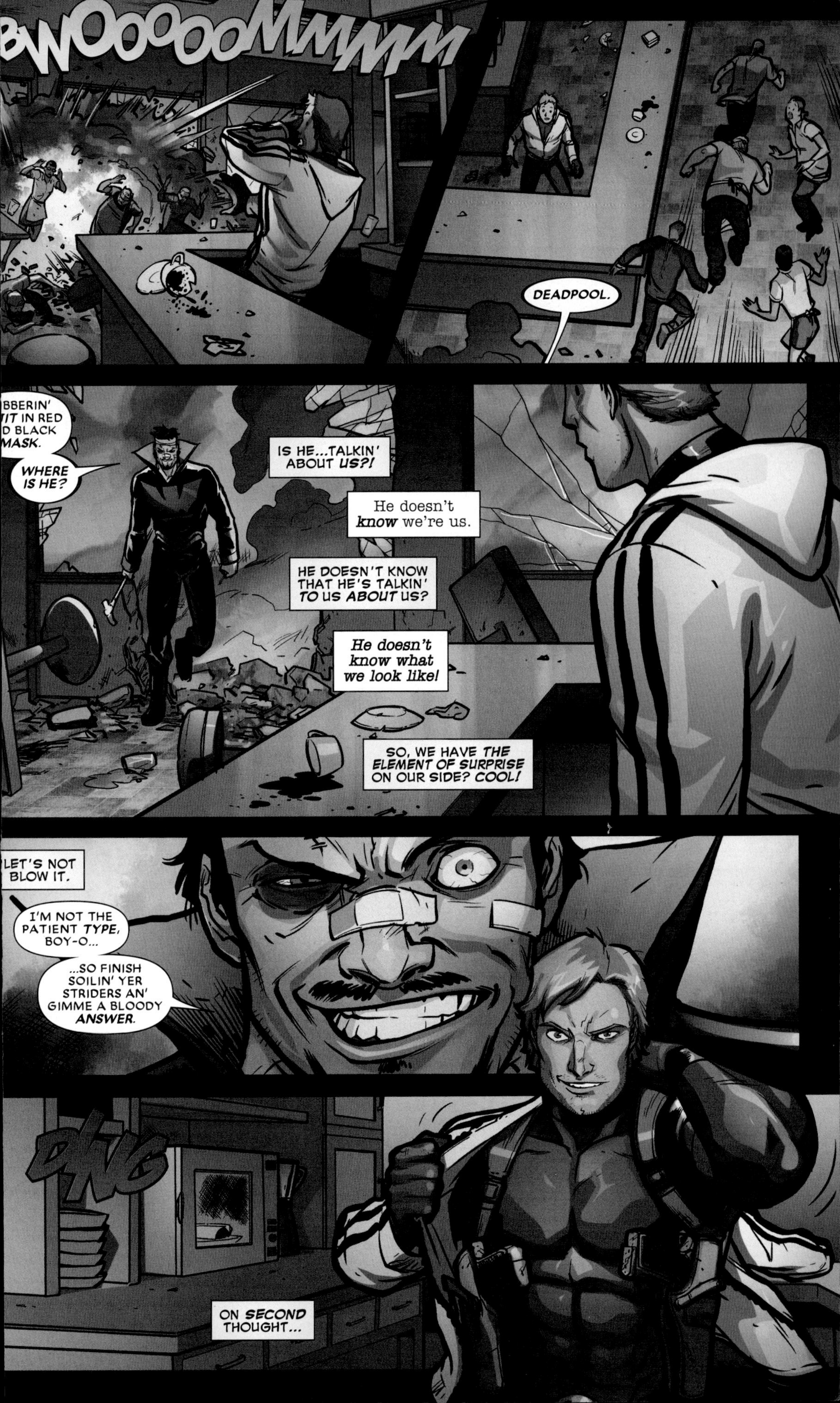
BWOOOOOMMMMM
DEADPOOL.
BBERIN'
IT IN RED
D BLACK
MASK.
WHERE IS HE?
IS HE...TALKIN' ABOUT US?!
He doesn't know we're us.
HE DOESN'T KNOW THAT HE'S TALKIN' TO US ABOUT US?
He doesn't know what we look like!
SO, WE HAVE THE ELEMENT OF SURPRISE ON OUR SIDE? COOL!
LET'S NOT BLOW IT.
I'M NOT THE PATIENT TYPE, BOY-O...
...SO FINISH SOILIN' YER STRIDERS AN' GIMME A BLOODY ANSWER.
ON SECOND THOUGHT...

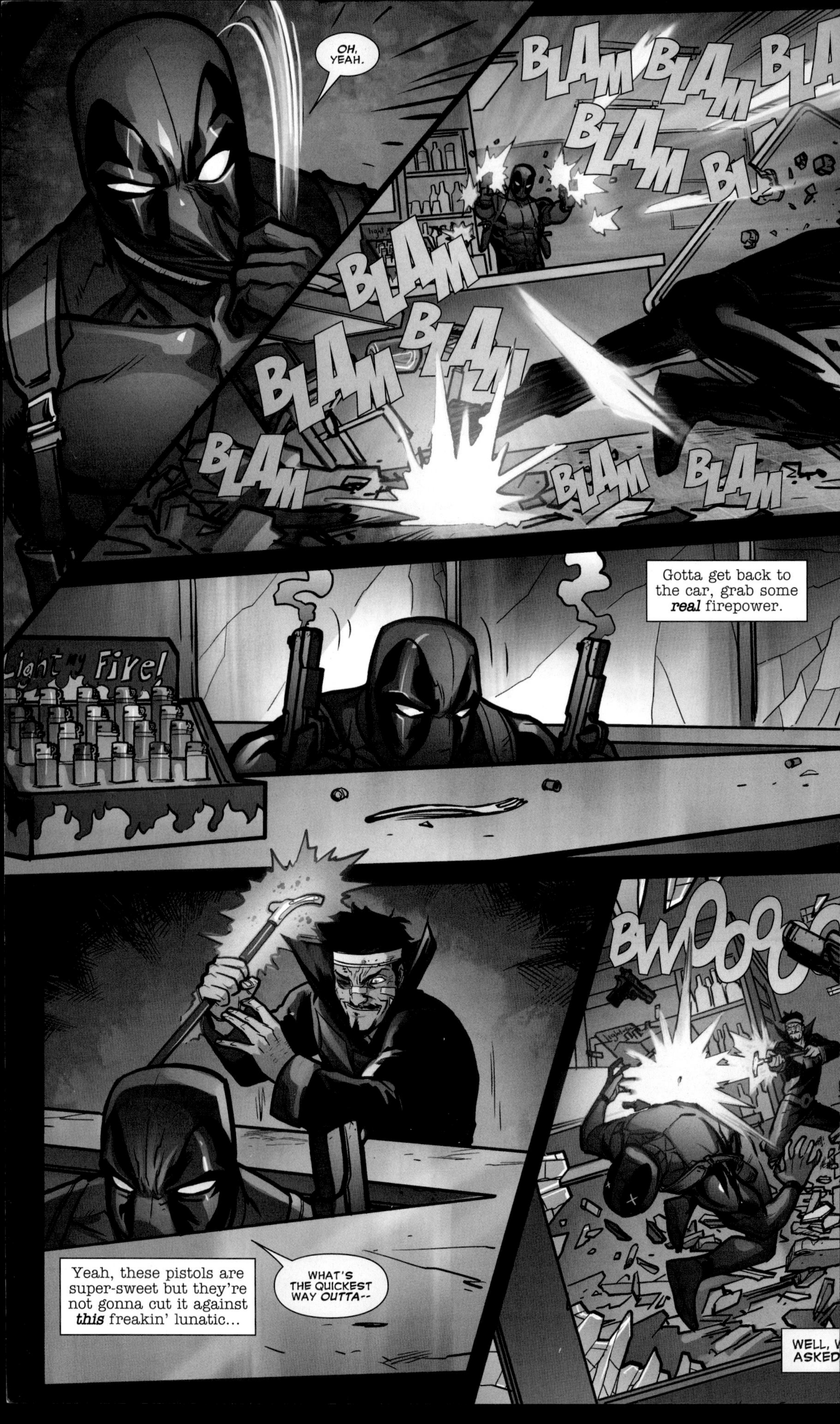
OH, YEAH.
BLAM BLAM BLA
BLAM
BL
BLAM
BLAM
BLAM
BLAM
BLAM BLAM
Gotta get back to the car, grab some *real* firepower.
Light my Fire!
Yeah, these pistols are super-sweet but they're not gonna cut it against *this* freakin' lunatic...
WHAT'S THE QUICKEST WAY *OUTTA*--
BWOOO
WELL, W
ASKED

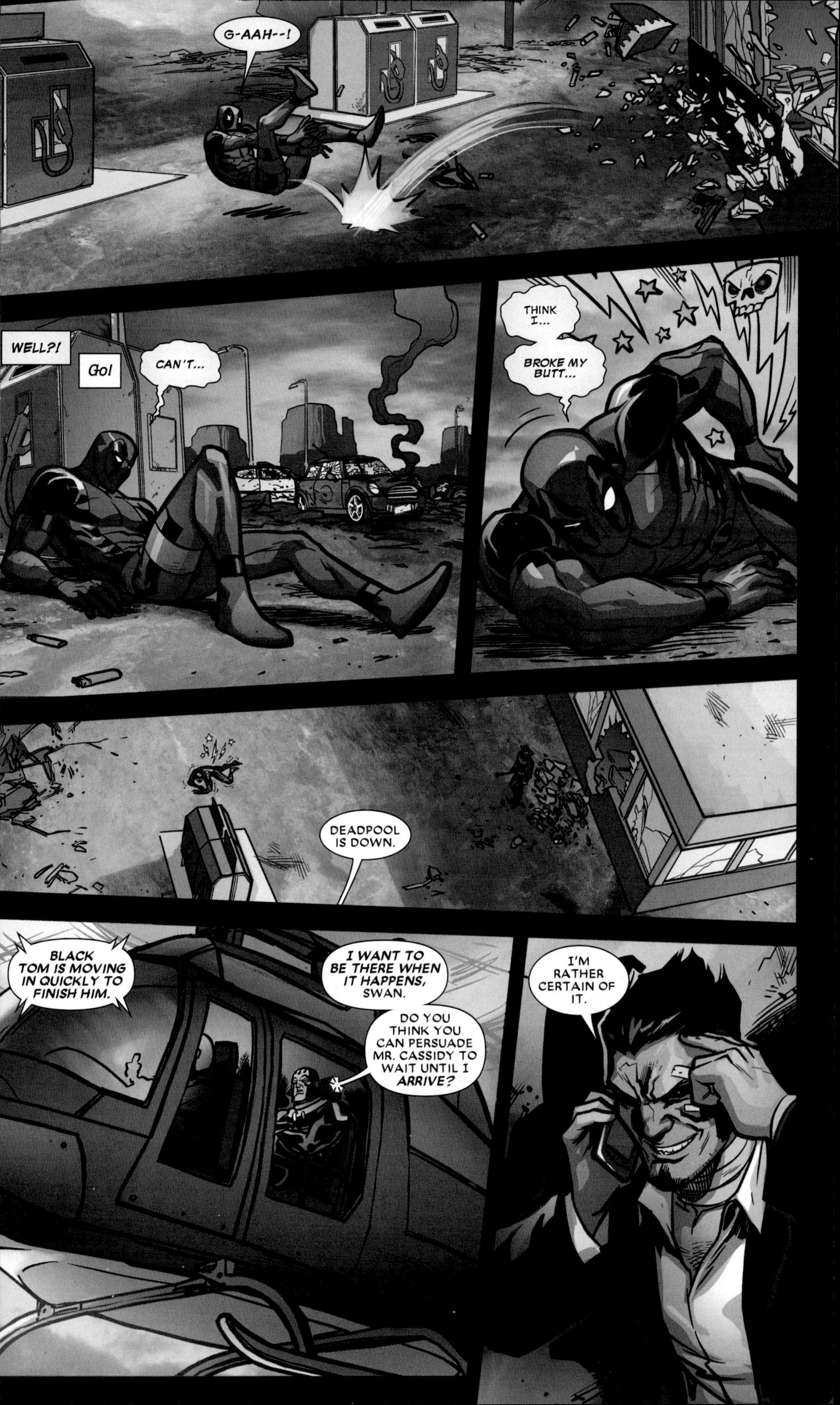
G-AAH--!
WELL?!
Go!
CAN'T...
THINK I...
BROKE MY BUTT...
DEADPOOL IS DOWN.
BLACK TOM IS MOVING IN QUICKLY TO FINISH HIM.
I WANT TO BE THERE WHEN IT HAPPENS, SWAN.
DO YOU THINK YOU CAN PERSUADE MR. CASSIDY TO WAIT UNTIL I ARRIVE?
I'M RATHER CERTAIN OF IT.

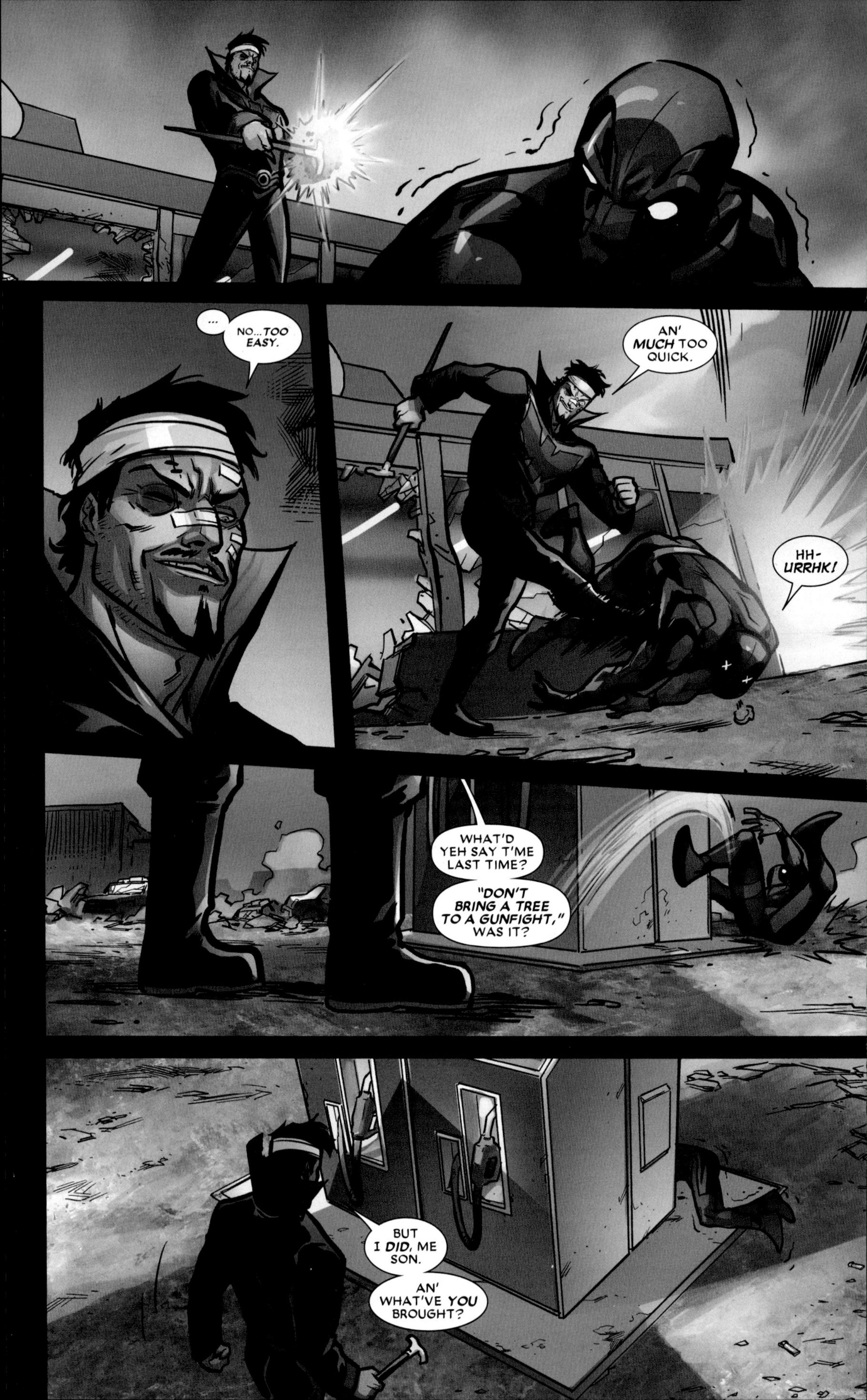
...
NO...TOO EASY.
AN' MUCH TOO QUICK.
HH-URRHK!
WHAT'D YEH SAY T'ME LAST TIME?
"DON'T BRING A TREE TO A GUNFIGHT," WAS IT?
BUT I DID, ME SON.
AN' WHAT'VE YOU BROUGHT?

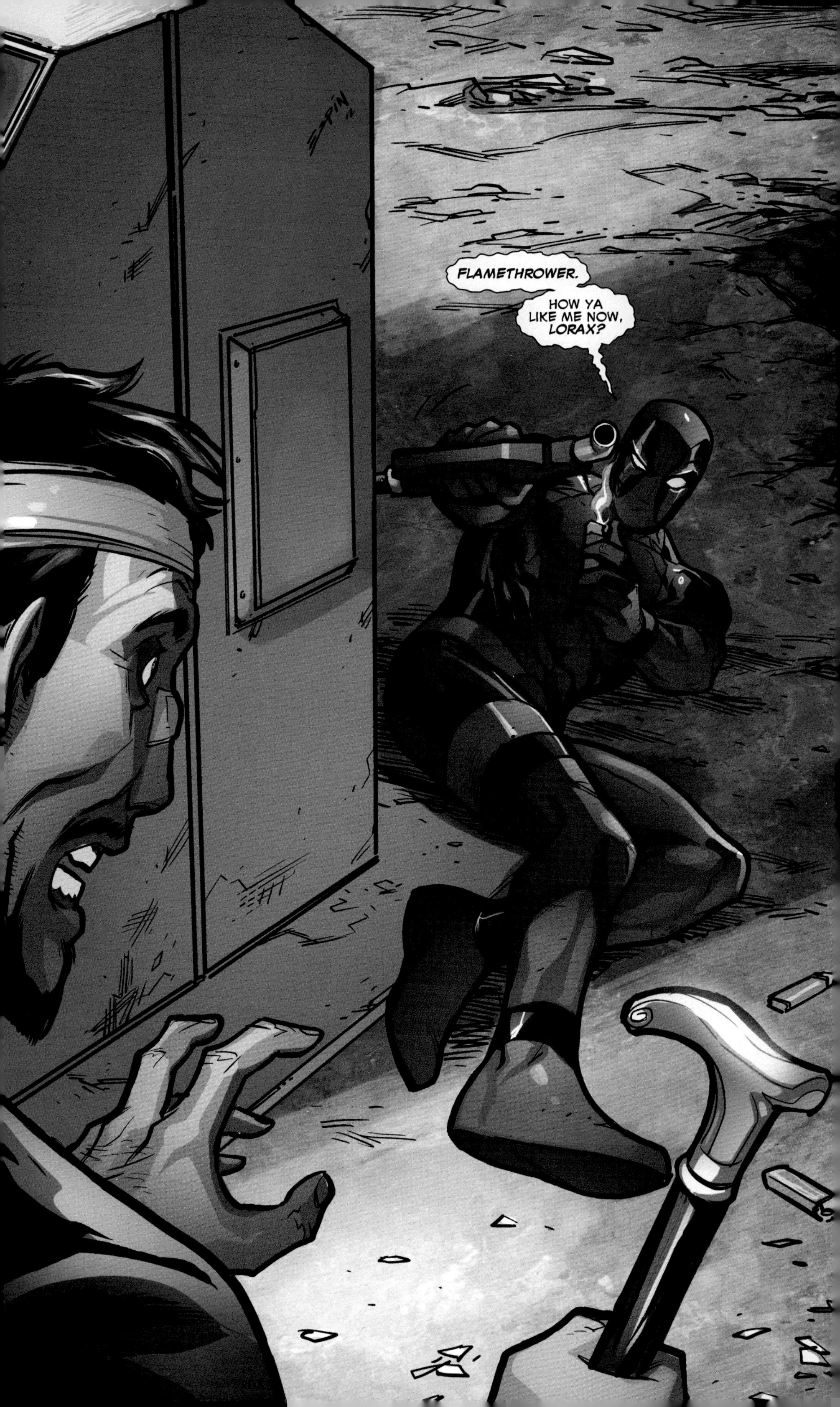
FLAMETHROWER.
HOW YA LIKE ME NOW, LORAX?

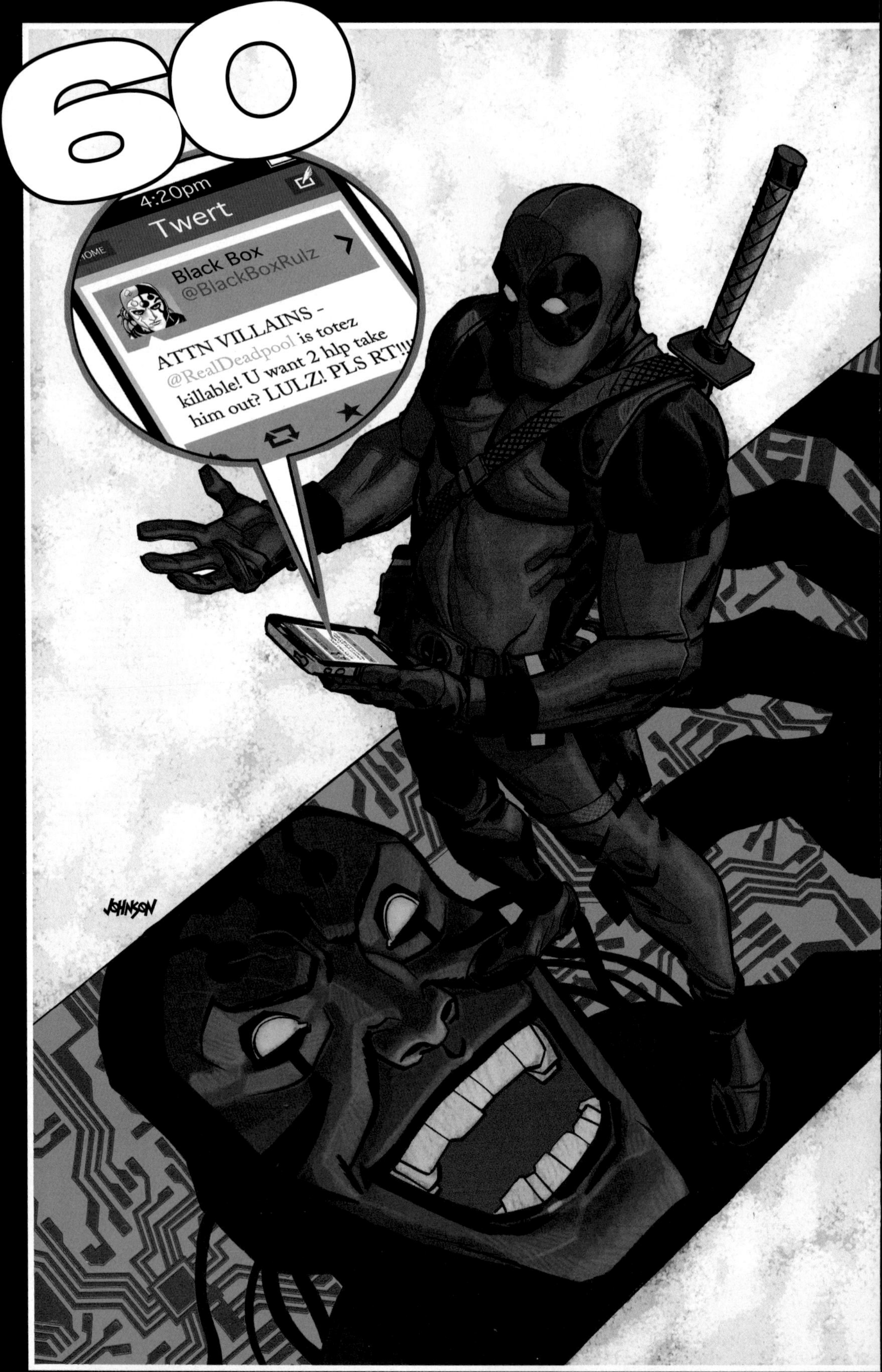
60
4:20pm
Twert
HOME
Black Box
@BlackBoxRulz
ATTN VILLAINS - @RealDeadpool is totez killable! U want 2 hlp take him out? LULZ! PLS RT!!!
JOHNSON

WHAT'D HE DO *THIS* TIME?

LEAST IT WASN'T THE *GIRLS'*...

HE WAS PLAYING WITH MATCHES IN THE BOYS' BATHROOM.

PRINCIPAL's OFFICE

THIS IS NOT SOMETHING THAT YOU SHOULD BE *JOKING* ABOUT, SERGEANT WILSON. IT APPEARS THAT YOUR SON WAS ATTEMPTING TO *LIGHT HIMSELF ON FIRE.*

SAY AGAIN, MA'AM?

THERE WERE OTHER BOYS IN THE BATHROOM AT THE TIME AND THEY SAY HE WAS HOLDING *LIT MATCHES* UP TO HIS...HIS *REAR END.*

DAMN IT, NOT AGAIN...

I *BEG* YOUR PARDON? ARE YOU SAYING THAT HE'S DONE THIS *BEFORE?*

COUPLE TIMES, YEAH. LOOK, HE WASN'T TRYIN' TO LIGHT HIMSELF ON FIRE, OKAY? HE WAS JUST... *PRETENDING.*

I *ASSURE* YOU, SERGEANT, THAT THE MATCHES WERE REAL.

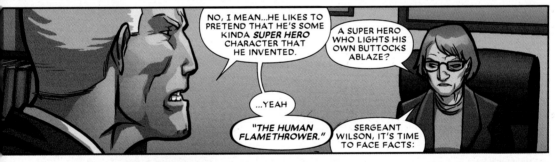

NO, I MEAN...HE LIKES TO PRETEND THAT HE'S SOME KINDA *SUPER HERO* CHARACTER THAT HE INVENTED.

A SUPER HERO WHO LIGHTS HIS OWN BUTTOCKS ABLAZE?

...YEAH

"THE HUMAN FLAMETHROWER."

SERGEANT WILSON, IT'S TIME TO FACE FACTS:

YOUR SON WADE HAS MENTAL ISSUES.

SILEN PLEAS

YEAH? AN' WHAT'M I SUPPOSED TO DO ABOUT IT?

I ALREADY TOOK HIM TO SEE THE *CHAPLAIN* AN' HE SAID THIS IS ALL JUST...*KID STUFF.* SAID THE BOY'LL *GROW* OUT OF IT.

IN MOST CASES, CHILDREN WHO DEVELOP MORBID FASCINATIONS DO LEAVE THEM BEHIND...*WHEN THEY MATURE.*

WHAT'S *THAT* SUPPOSED T'MEAN?

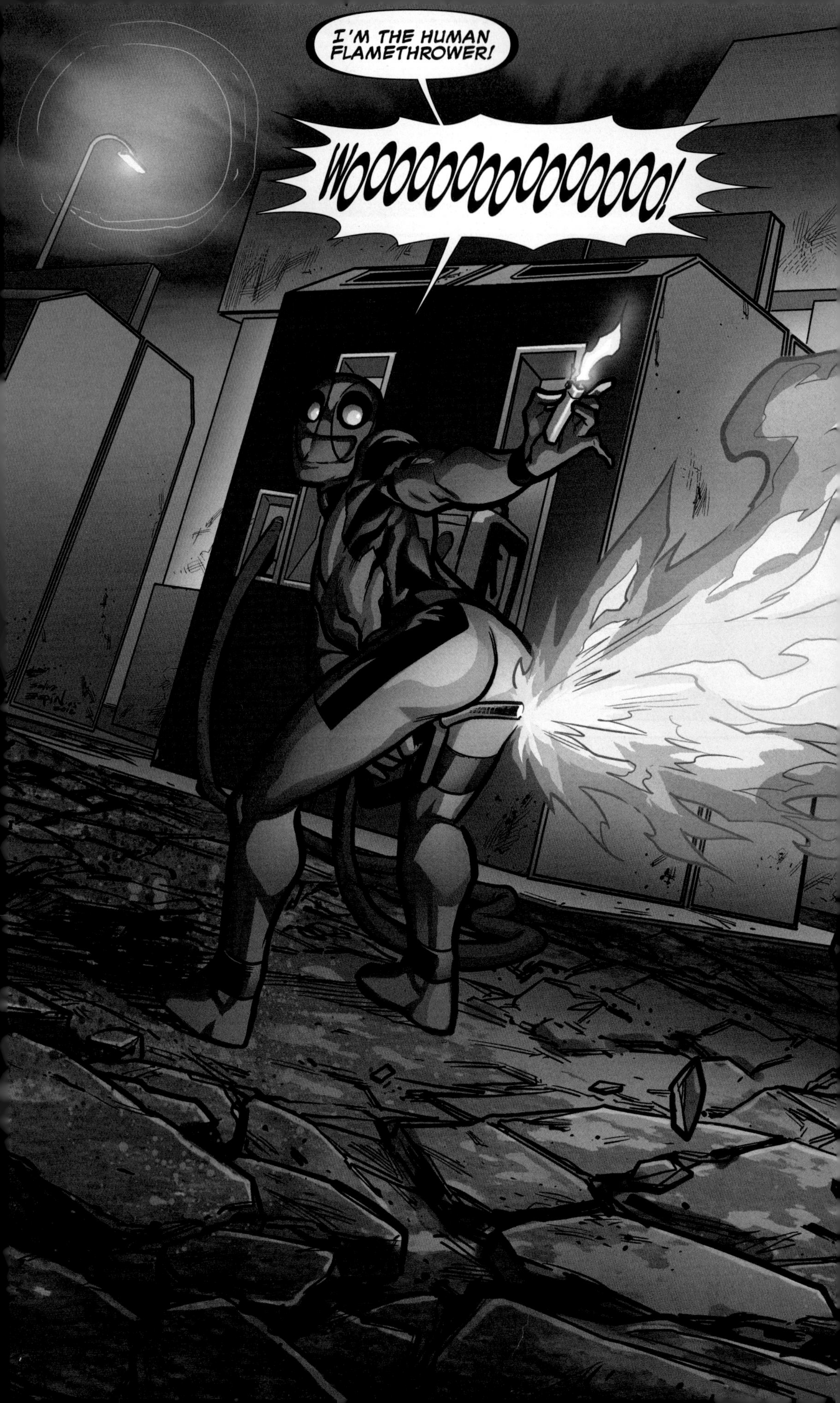
I'M THE HUMAN FLAMETHROWER!
WOOOOOOOOOOOOOOO!

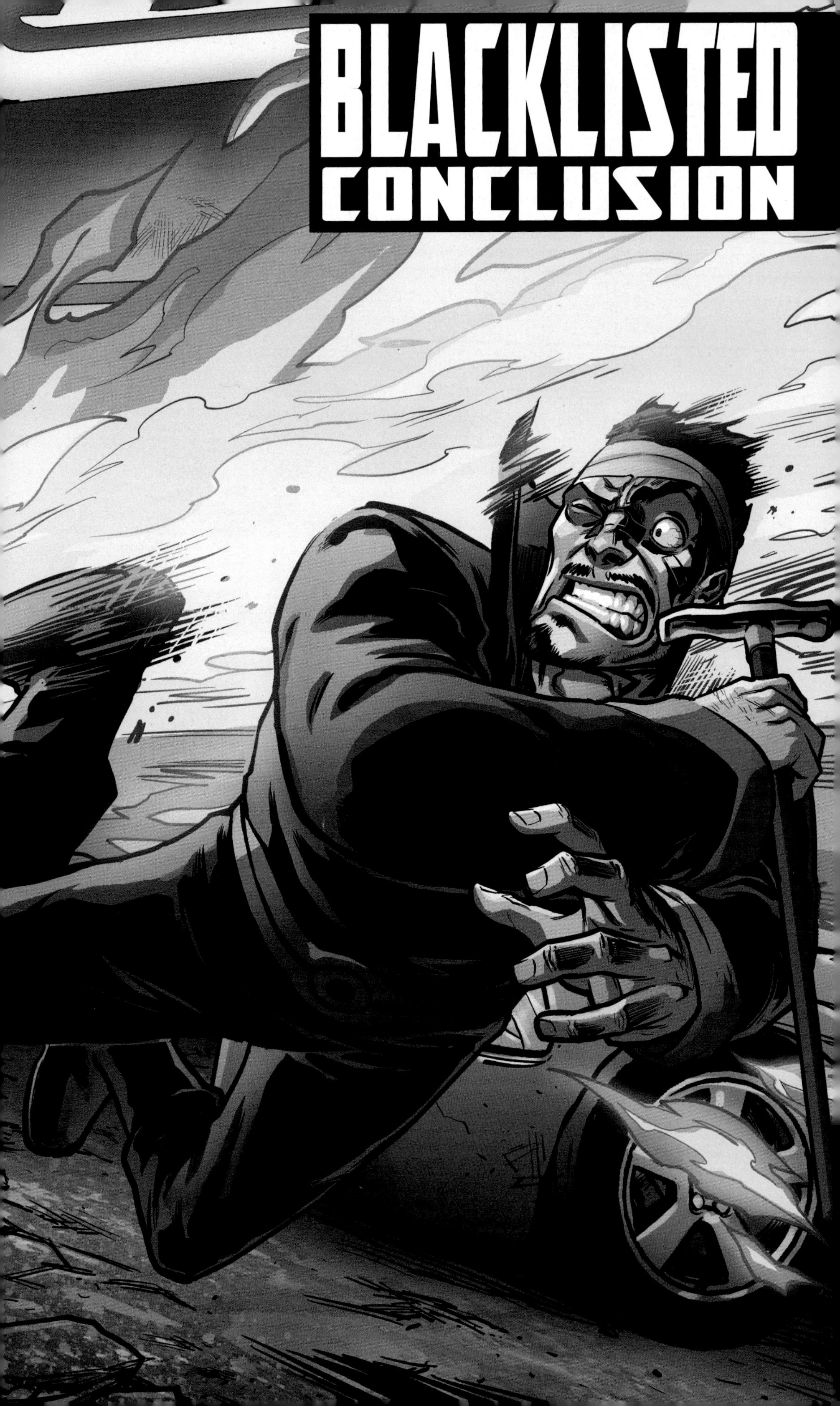
BLACKLISTED
CONCLUSION

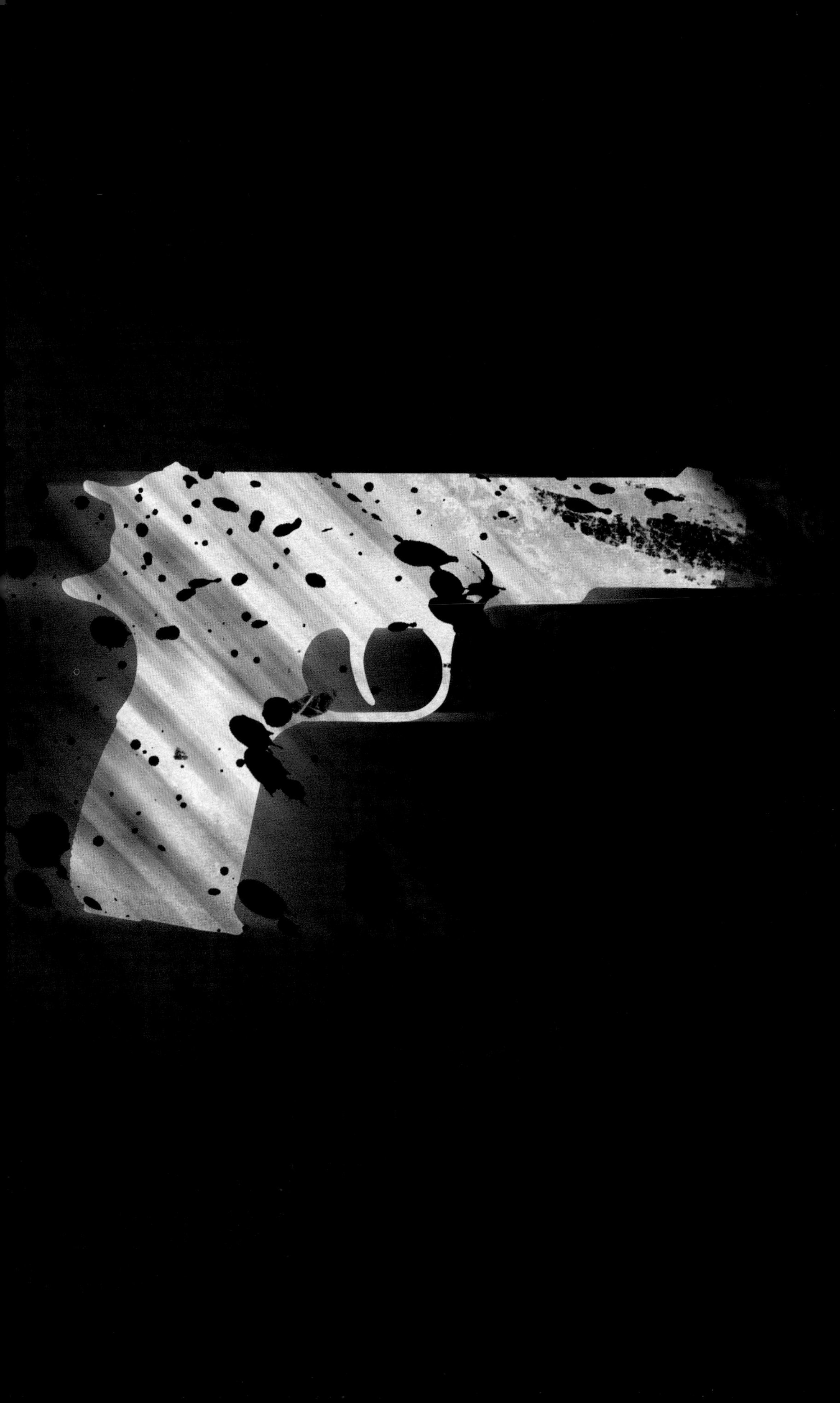

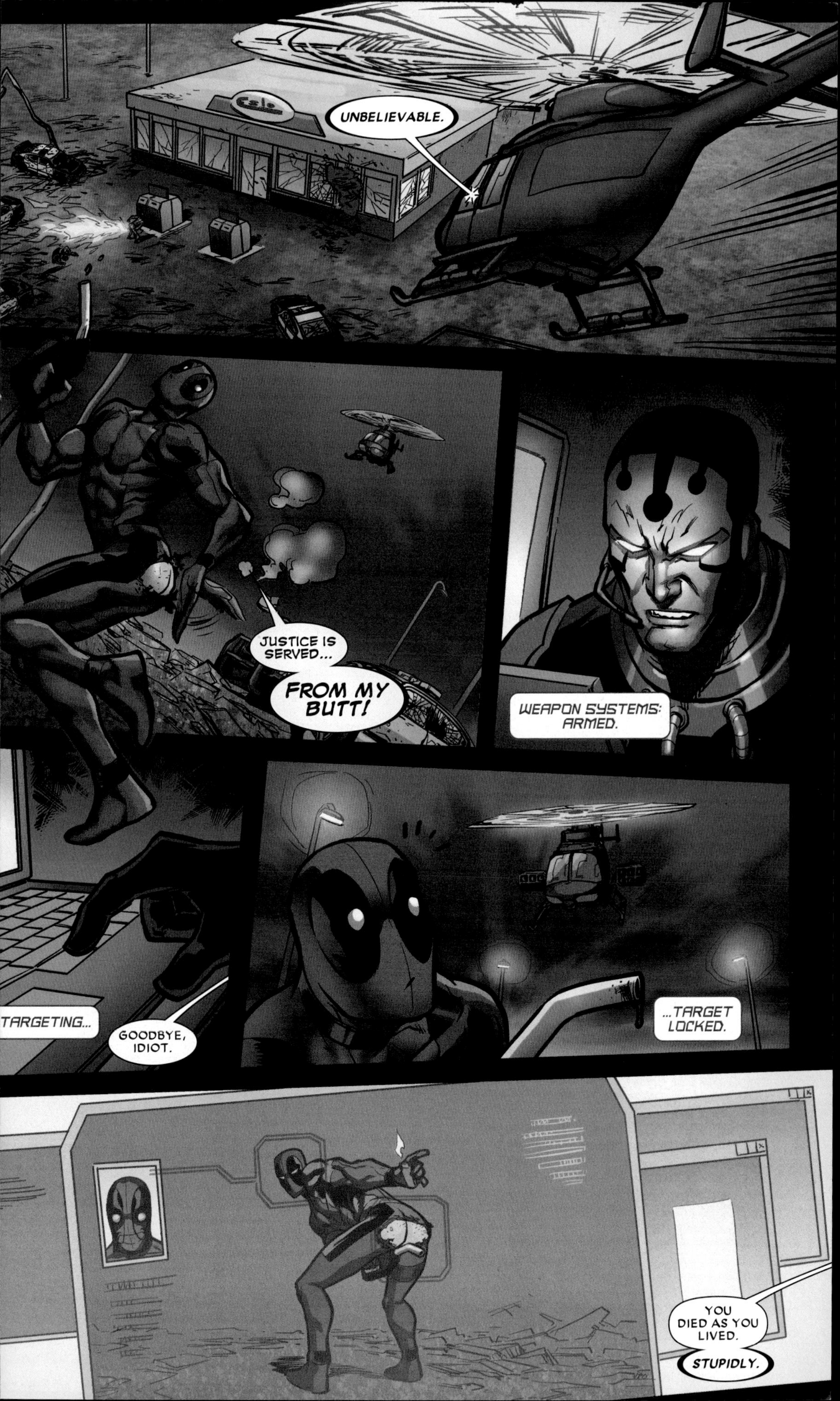
UNBELIEVABLE.
JUSTICE IS SERVED...
FROM MY BUTT!
WEAPON SYSTEMS: ARMED.
TARGETING...
GOODBYE, IDIOT.
...TARGET LOCKED.
YOU DIED AS YOU LIVED.
STUPIDLY.

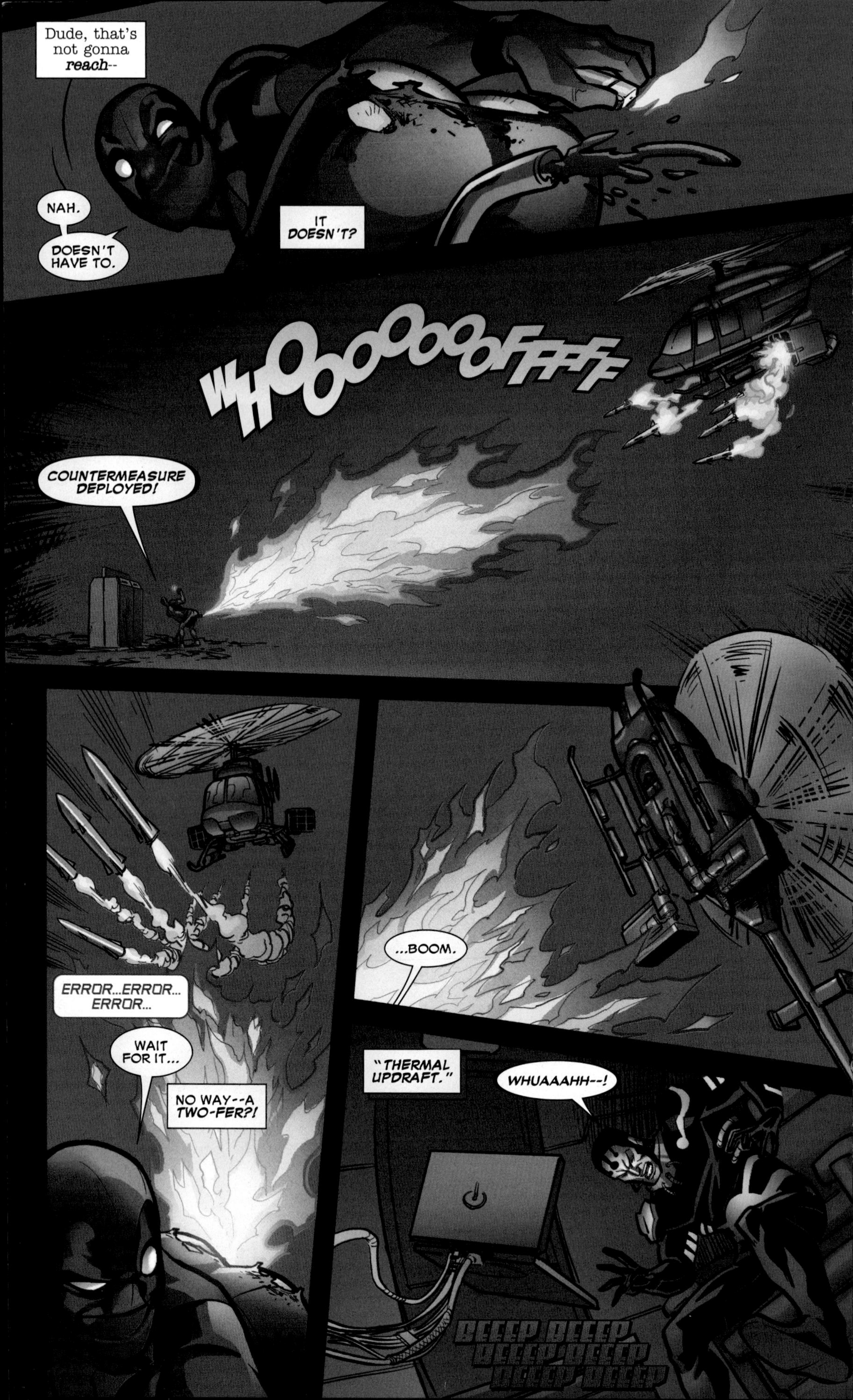
Dude, that's not gonna *reach*--
NAH.
DOESN'T HAVE TO.
IT DOESN'T?
WHOOOOOOOFFFF
COUNTERMEASURE DEPLOYED!
ERROR...ERROR... ERROR...
WAIT FOR IT...
NO WAY--A TWO-FER?!
...BOOM.
"THERMAL UPDRAFT."
WHUAAAHH--!

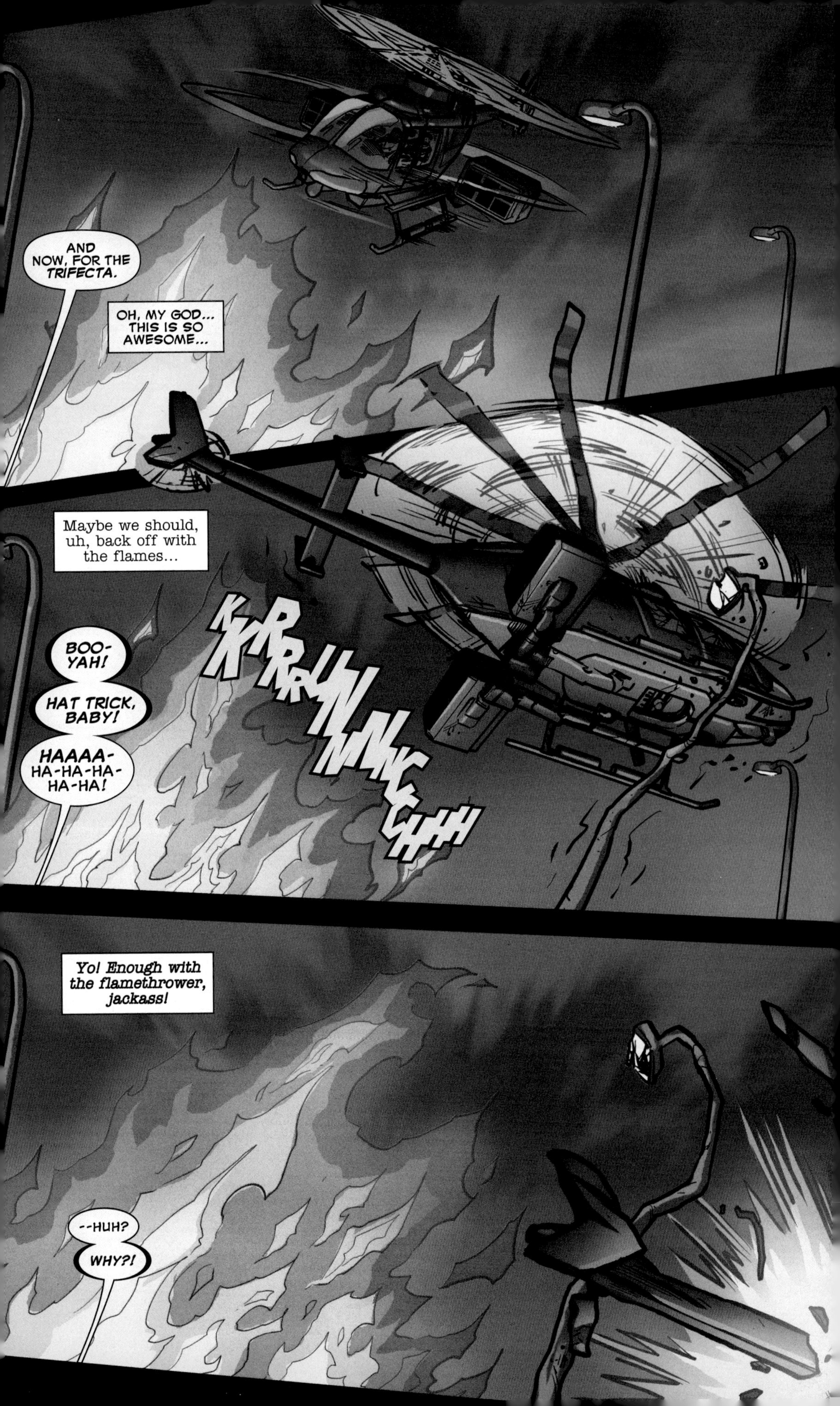
AND NOW, FOR THE TRIFECTA.
OH, MY GOD... THIS IS SO AWESOME...
Maybe we should, uh, back off with the flames...
KKRRRUNNNCHHH
BOO-YAH!
HAT TRICK, BABY!
HAAAA-HA-HA-HA-HA-HA!
Yo! Enough with the flamethrower, jackass!
--HUH?
WHY?!

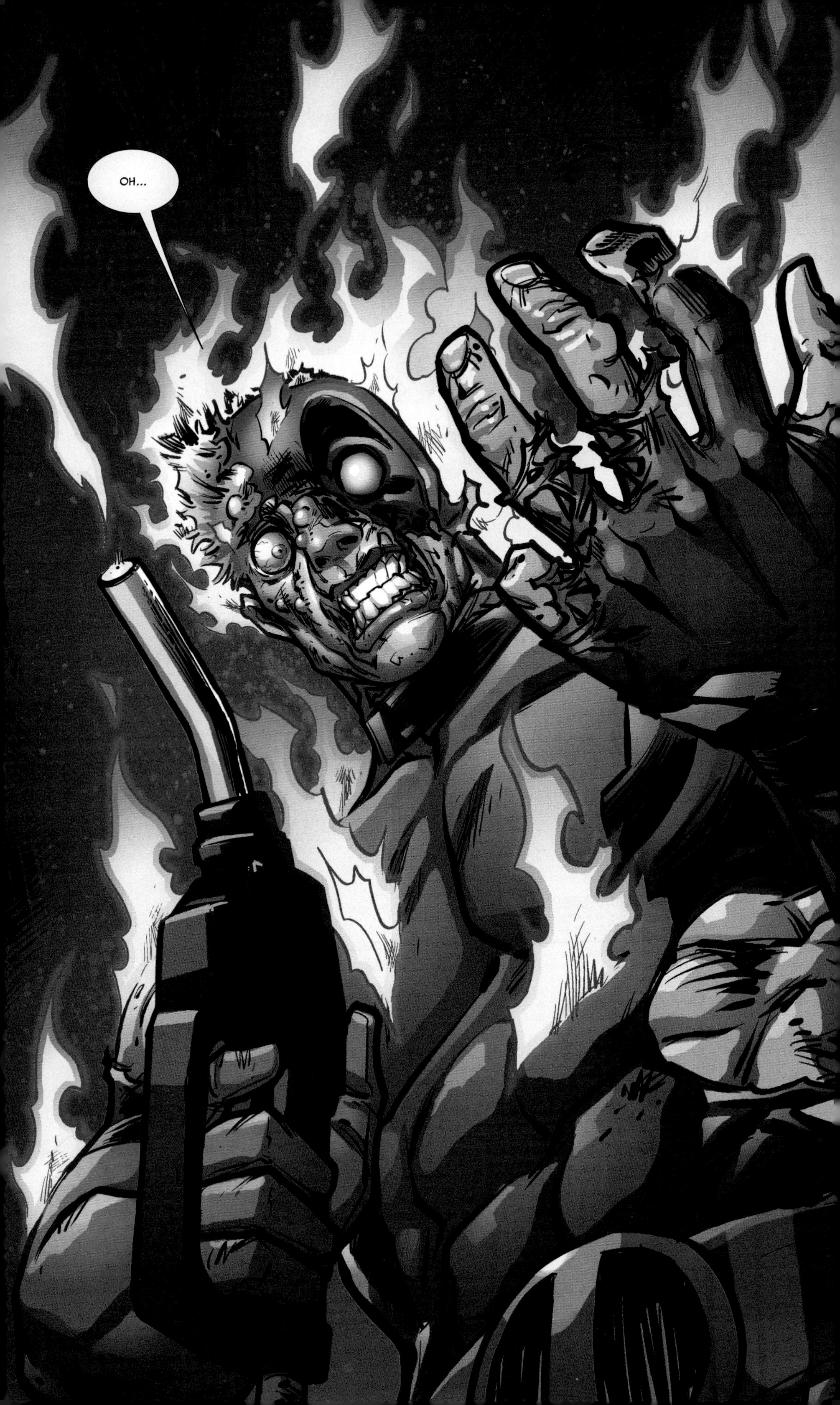
OH...

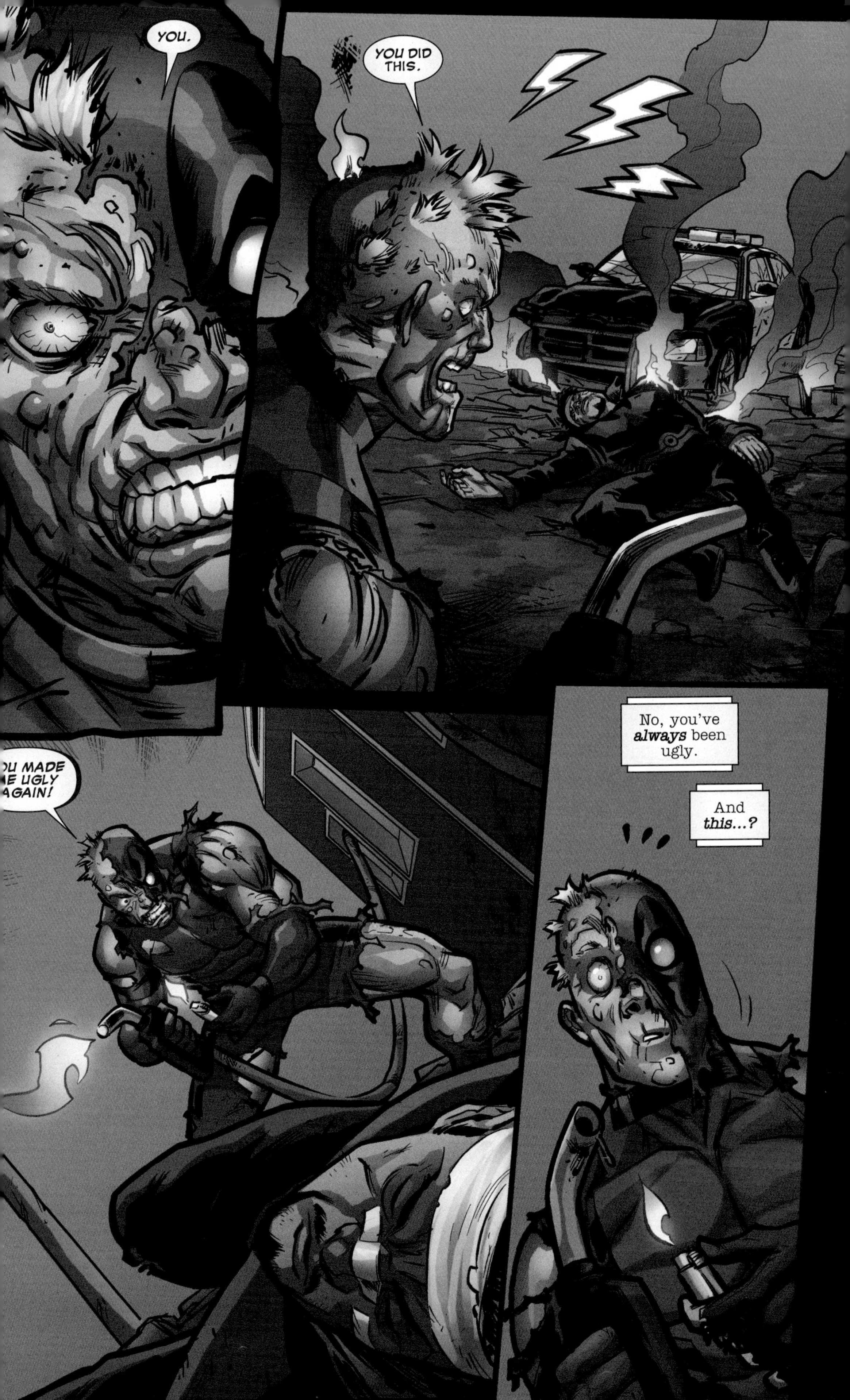
YOU.
YOU DID THIS.
OU MADE
E UGLY
AGAIN!
No, you've *always* been ugly.
And *this...?*

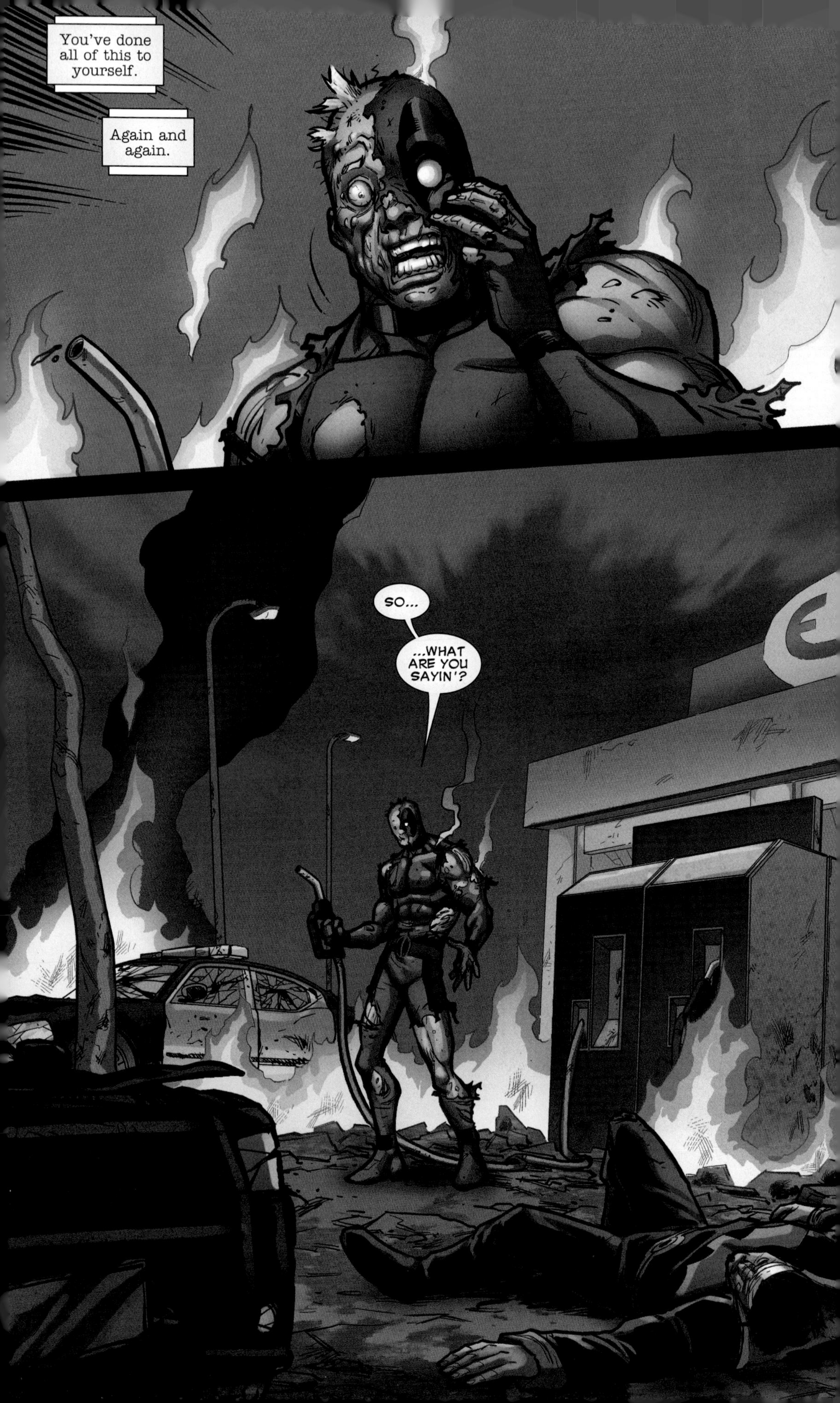
You've done all of this to yourself.
Again and again.
SO...
...WHAT ARE YOU SAYIN'?

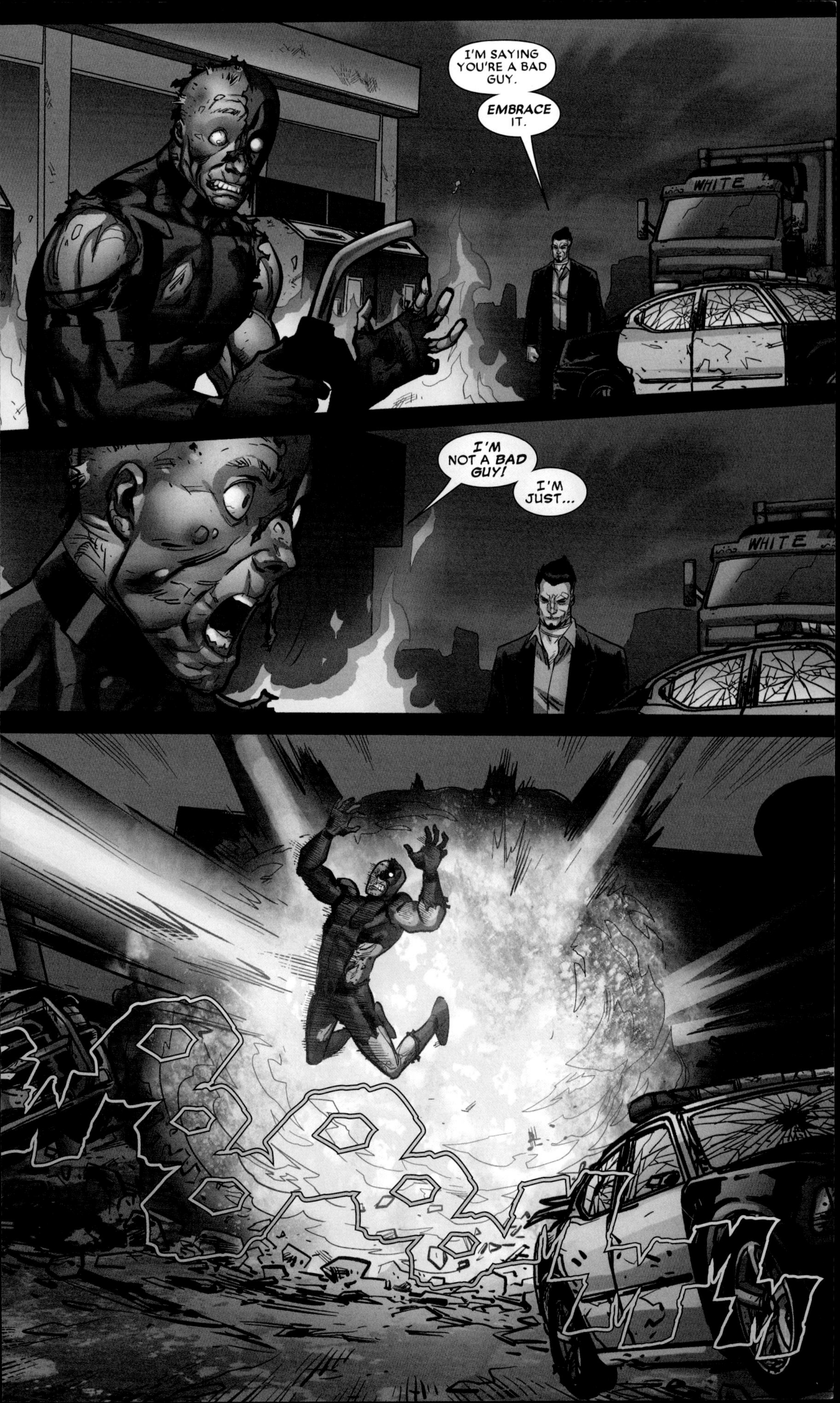
I'M SAYING YOU'RE A BAD GUY.
EMBRACE IT.
WHITE
I'M NOT A BAD GUY!
I'M JUST...
WHITE

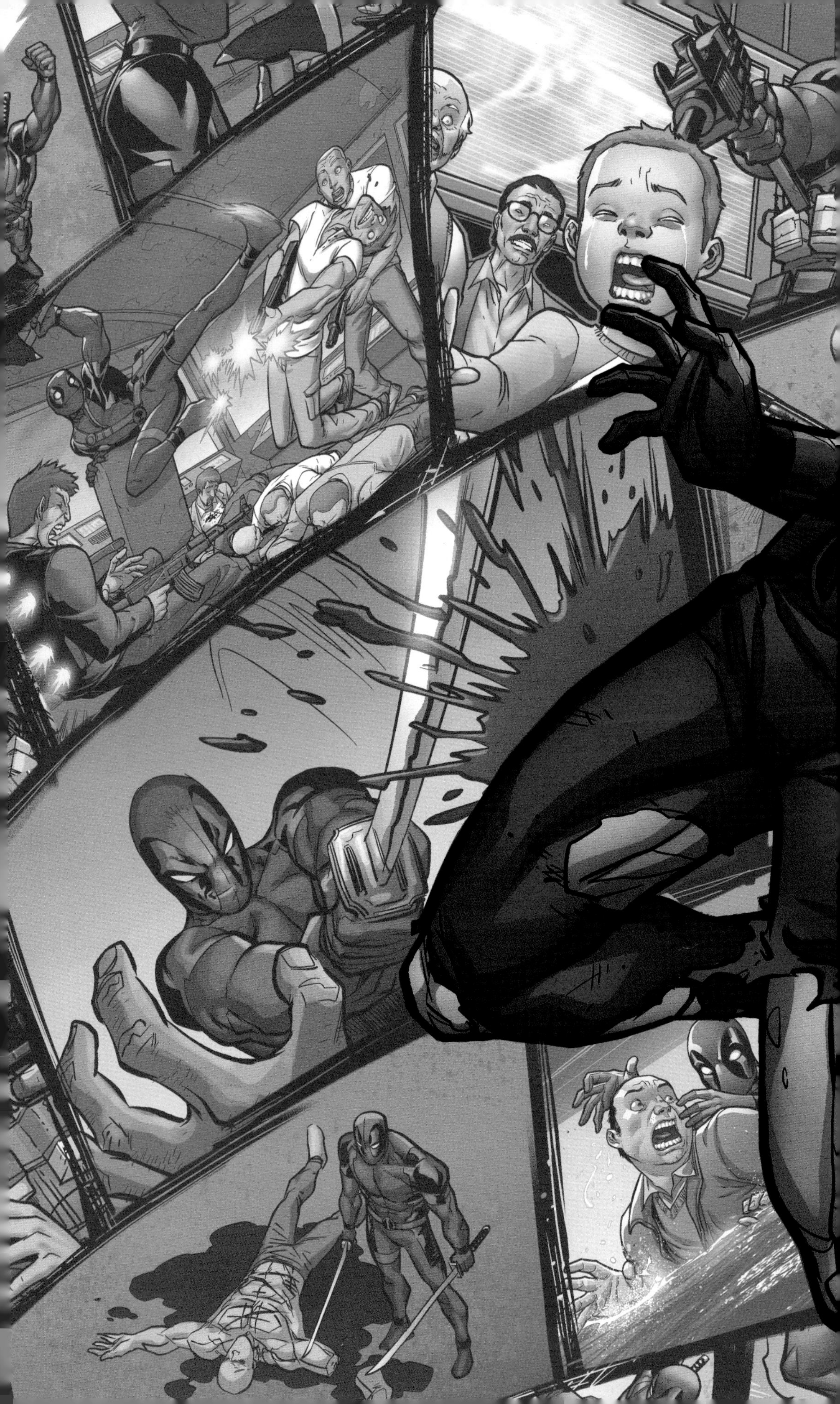

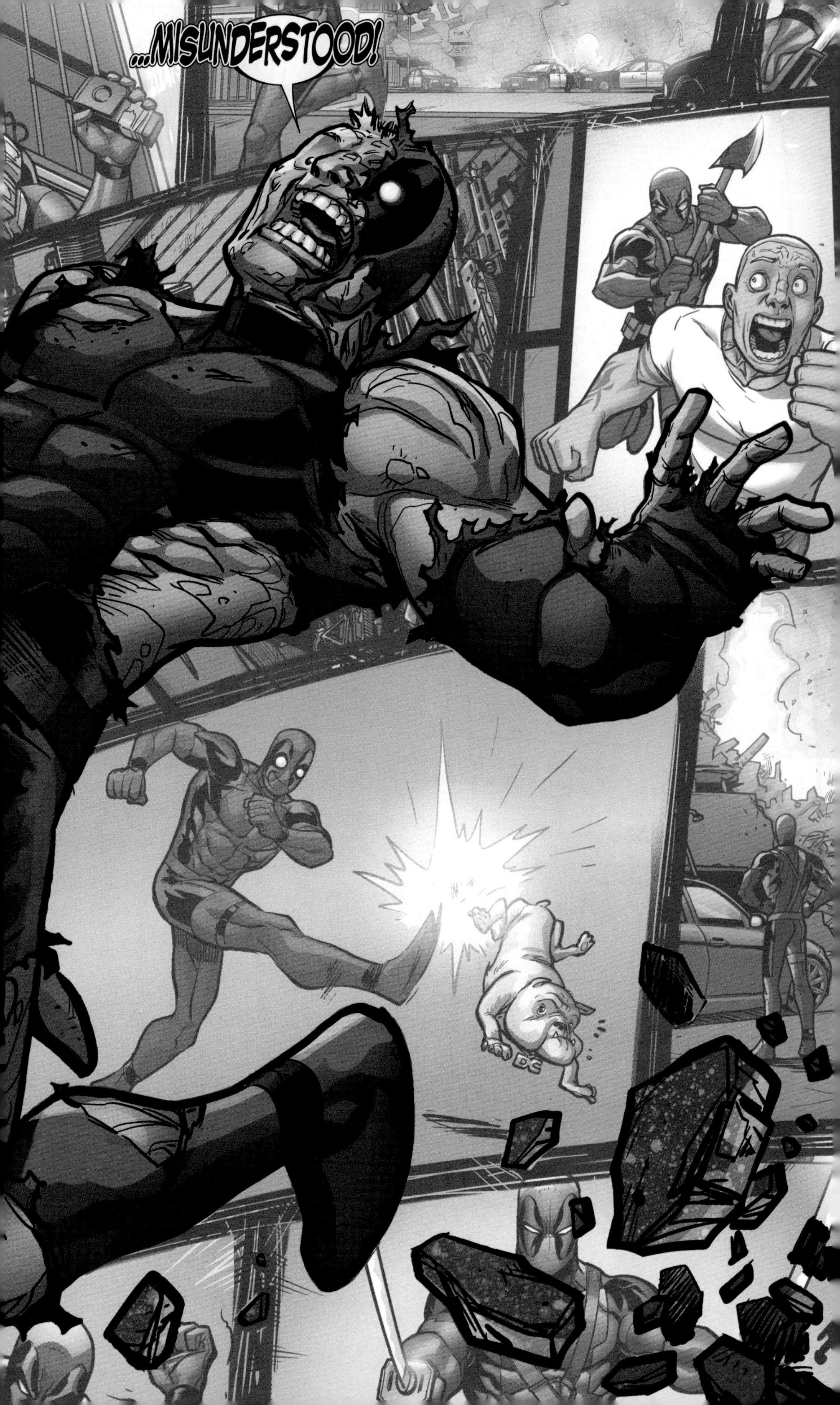
...MISUNDERSTOOD!

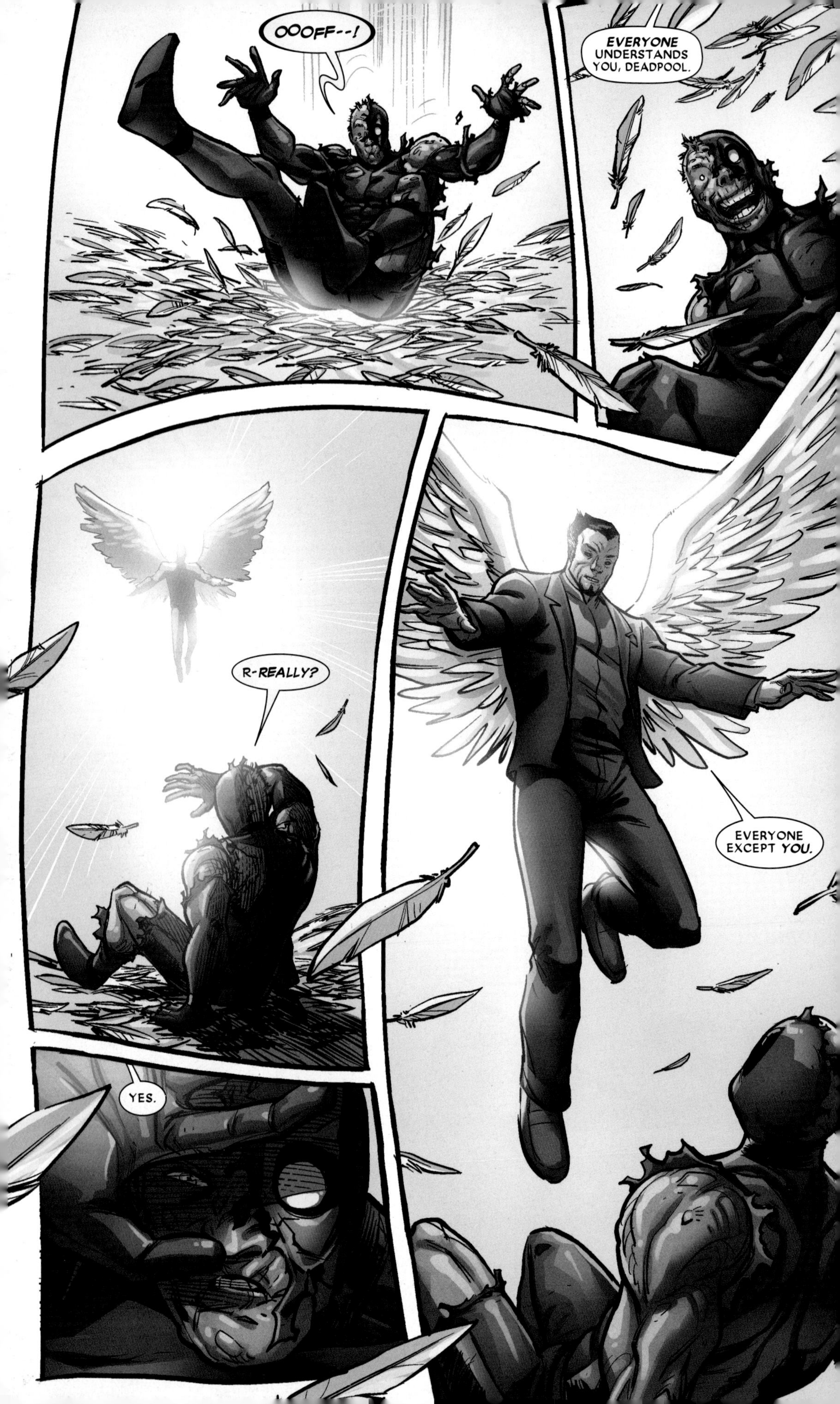
OOOFF--!
EVERYONE UNDERSTANDS YOU, DEADPOOL.
R-REALLY?
EVERYONE EXCEPT YOU.
YES.

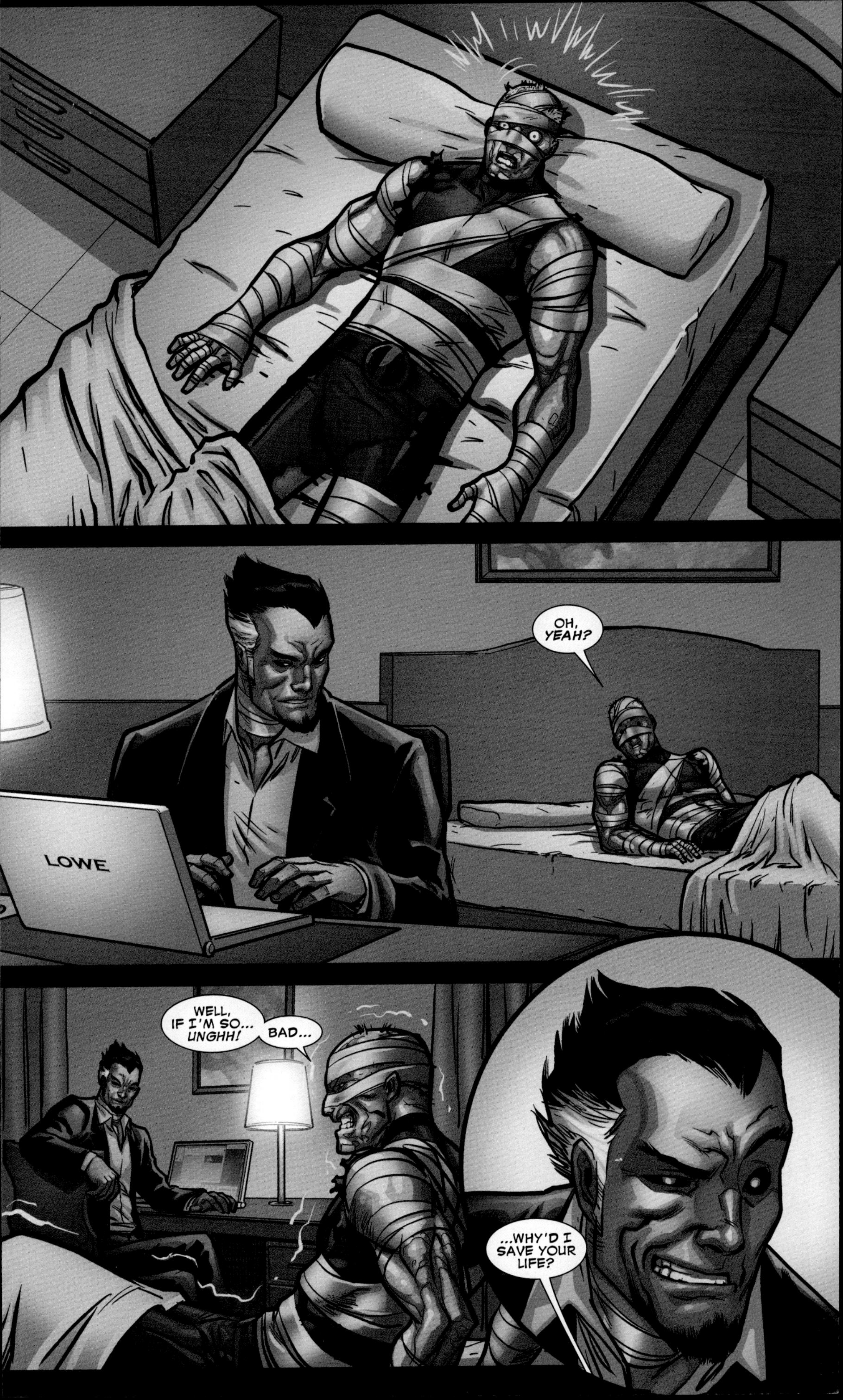
OH, YEAH?
LOWE
WELL, IF I'M SO... UNGHH!
BAD...
...WHY'D I SAVE YOUR LIFE?

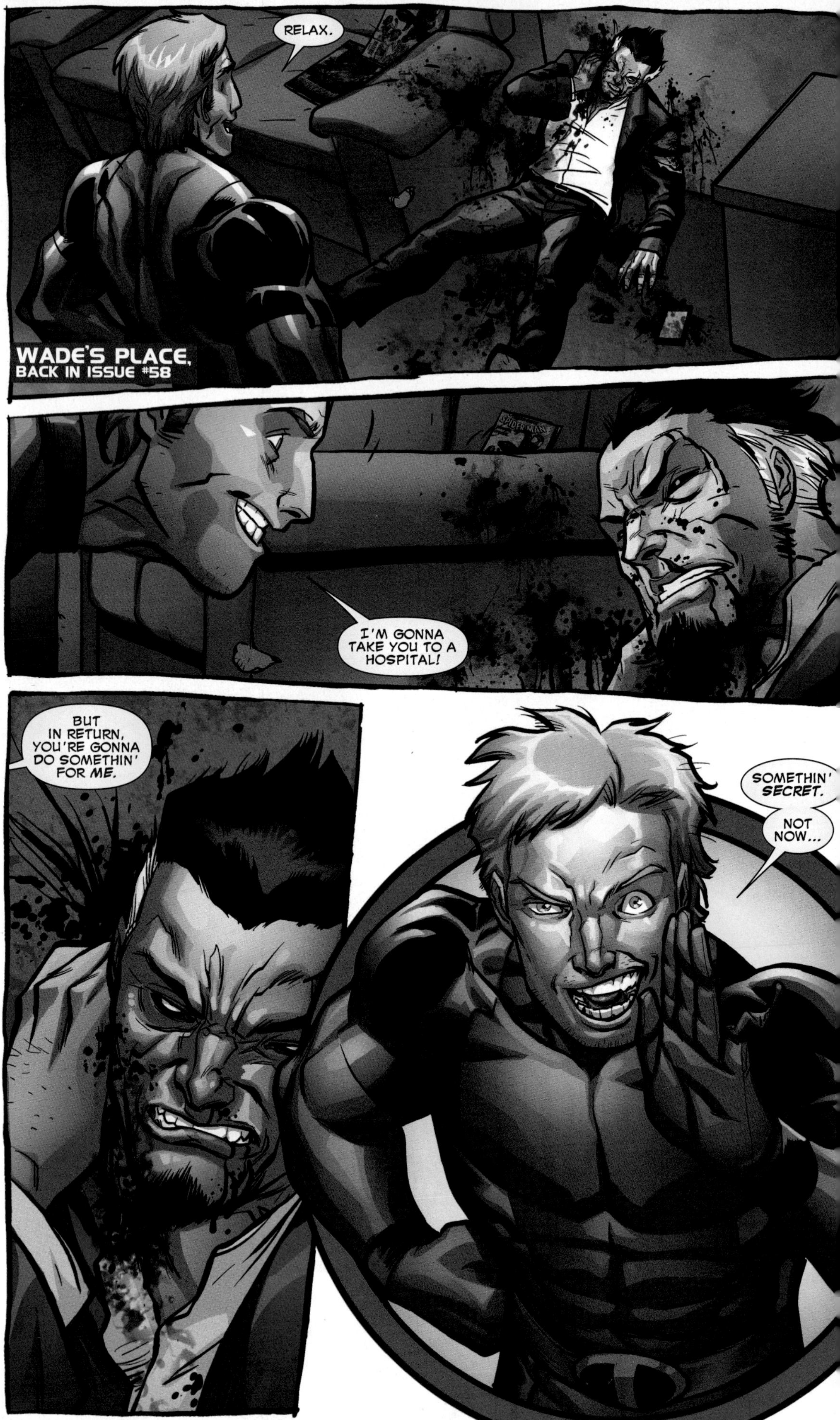
RELAX.
WADE'S PLACE, BACK IN ISSUE #58
I'M GONNA TAKE YOU TO A HOSPITAL!
BUT IN RETURN, YOU'RE GONNA DO SOMETHIN' FOR ME.
SOMETHIN' SECRET.
NOT NOW...

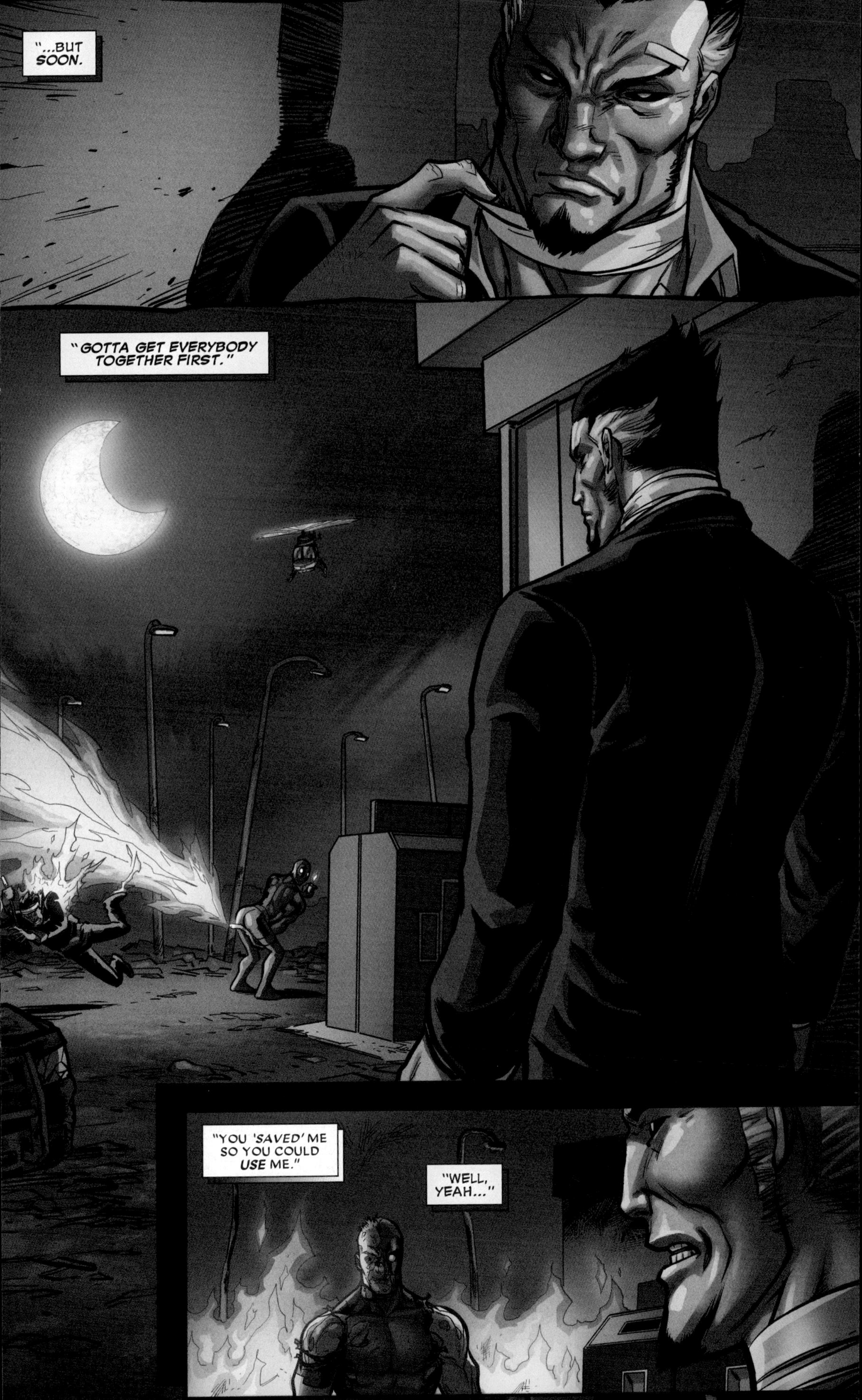
"...BUT SOON.
"GOTTA GET EVERYBODY TOGETHER FIRST."
"YOU 'SAVED' ME SO YOU COULD USE ME."
"WELL, YEAH..."

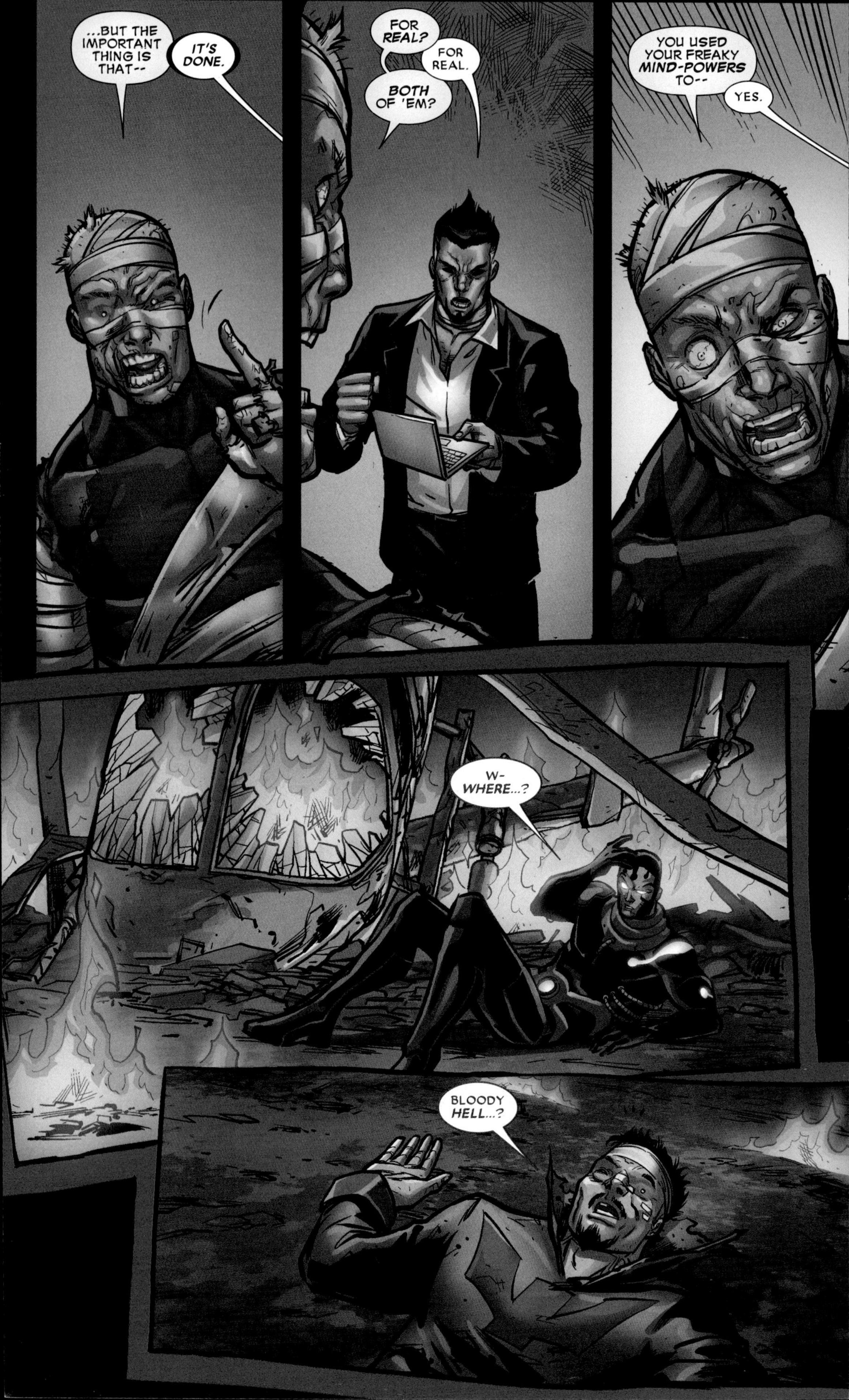
...BUT THE IMPORTANT THING IS THAT--
IT'S DONE.
FOR REAL?
FOR REAL.
BOTH OF 'EM?
YOU USED YOUR FREAKY MIND-POWERS TO--
YES.
W- WHERE...?
BLOODY HELL...?

OUR
~~RET~~ IS
~~AFE.~~

NEITHER
~~B~~LACK BOX NOR
~~C~~K TOM WILL EVER
~~R~~EMEMBER THAT YOU
~~L~~ST YOUR HEALING
FACTOR...

...FOR
AS LONG AS
I LIVE.

...WELL
PLAYED, SIR.

~~V~~E LEARNED FROM...BITTER
~~E~~XPERIENCE THAT, WHEN
~~DE~~ALING WITH YOU, INSURANCE
IS OF THE UTMOST
IMPORTANCE.

"DEALING"
WITH ME?

DUDE,
OUR DEAL IS
DONE.

PEACE IN THE
MIDDLE EAST--
I'M OUT.

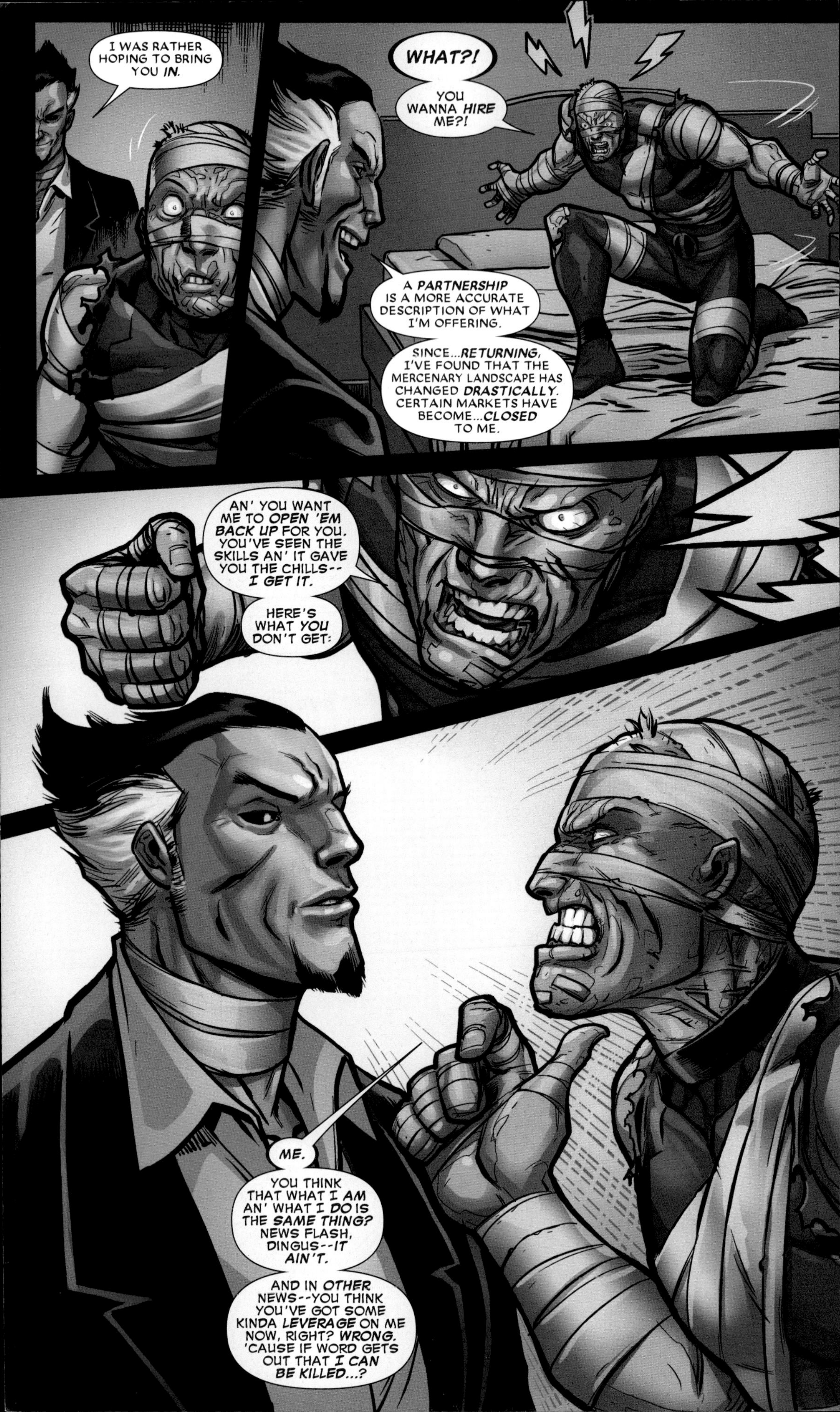
I WAS RATHER HOPING TO BRING YOU IN.
WHAT?!
YOU WANNA HIRE ME?!
A PARTNERSHIP IS A MORE ACCURATE DESCRIPTION OF WHAT I'M OFFERING.
SINCE...RETURNING, I'VE FOUND THAT THE MERCENARY LANDSCAPE HAS CHANGED DRASTICALLY. CERTAIN MARKETS HAVE BECOME...CLOSED TO ME.
AN' YOU WANT ME TO OPEN 'EM BACK UP FOR YOU. YOU'VE SEEN THE SKILLS AN' IT GAVE YOU THE CHILLS-- I GET IT.
HERE'S WHAT YOU DON'T GET:
ME.
YOU THINK THAT WHAT I AM AN' WHAT I DO IS THE SAME THING? NEWS FLASH, DINGUS--IT AIN'T.
AND IN OTHER NEWS--YOU THINK YOU'VE GOT SOME KINDA LEVERAGE ON ME NOW, RIGHT? WRONG. 'CAUSE IF WORD GETS OUT THAT I CAN BE KILLED...?

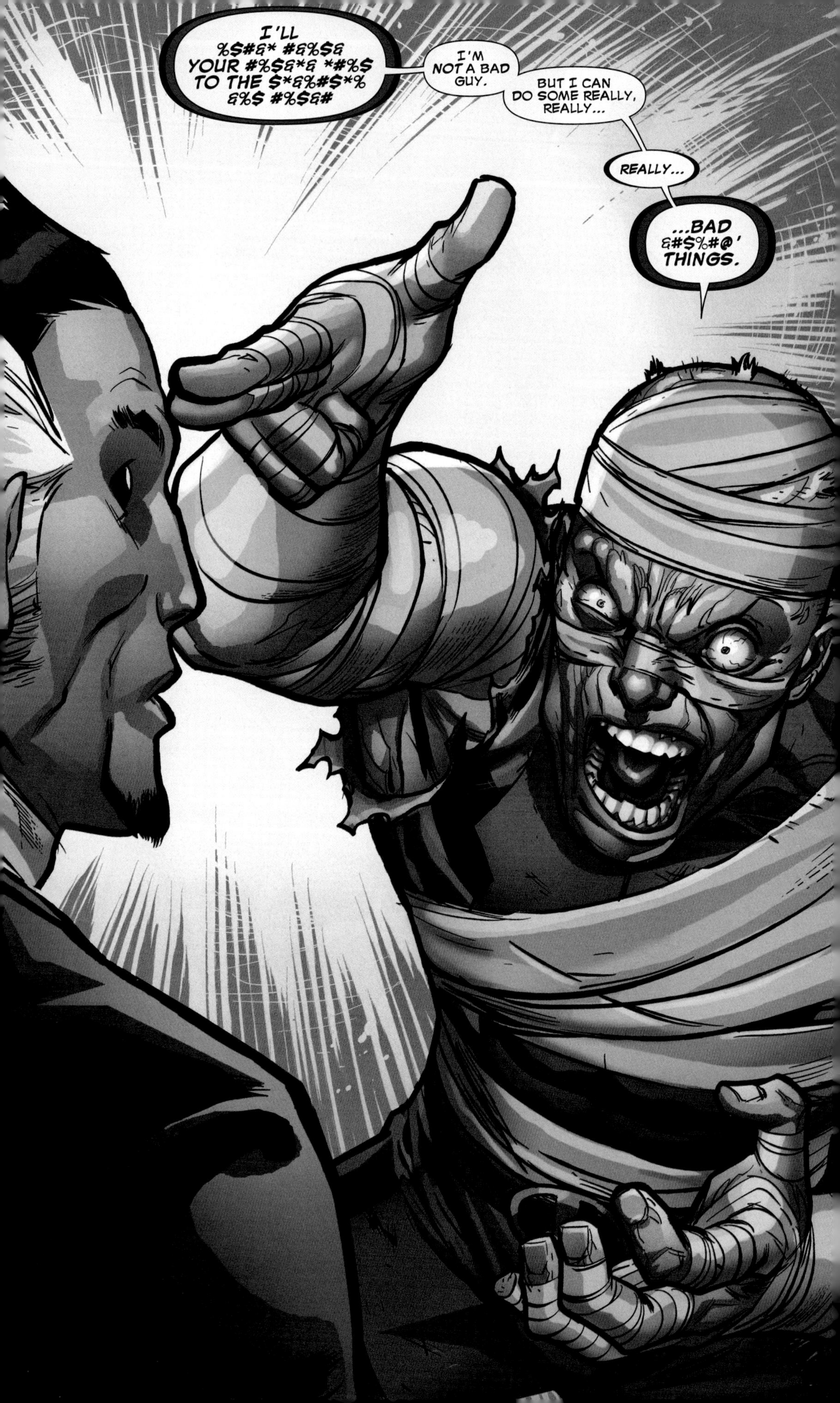
I'LL %$#&* #&%$& YOUR #%$&*& *#%$ TO THE $*&%#$*% &%$ #%$&#
I'M NOT A BAD GUY.
BUT I CAN DO SOME REALLY, REALLY...
REALLY...
...BAD &#$%#@' THINGS.

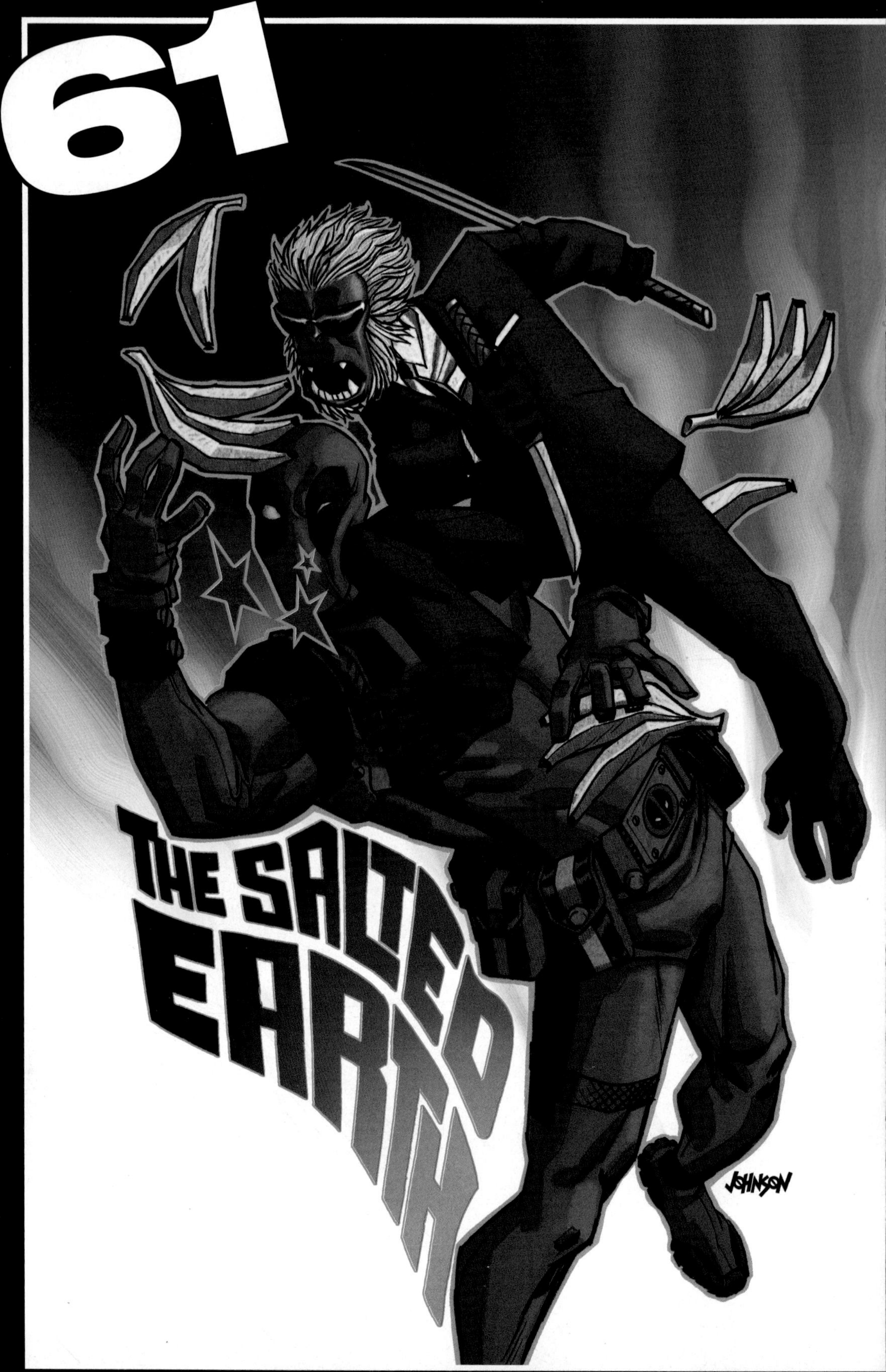
61
THE SALTED EARTH
JOHNSON

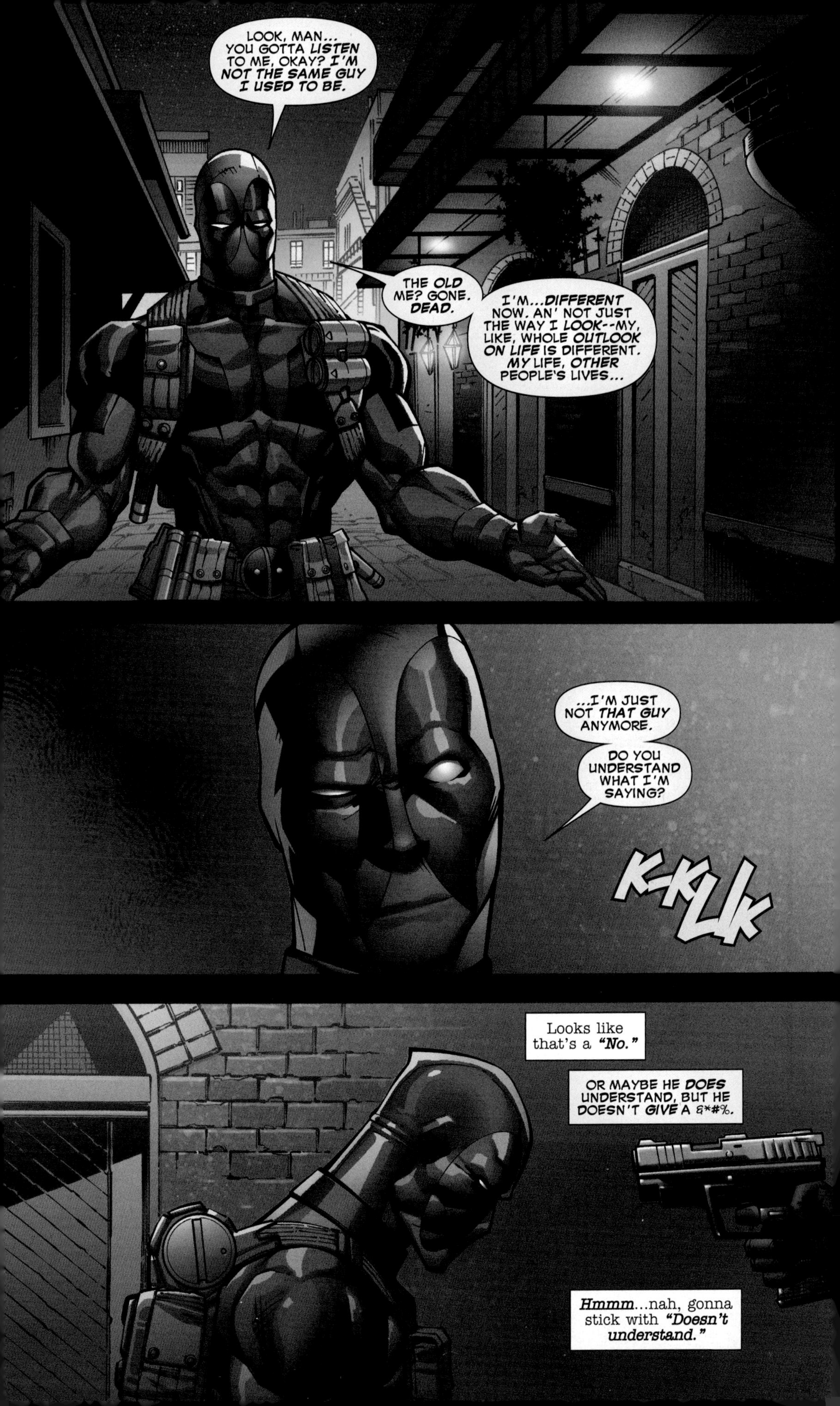
LOOK, MAN... YOU GOTTA LISTEN TO ME, OKAY? I'M NOT THE SAME GUY I USED TO BE.
THE OLD ME? GONE. DEAD.
I'M...DIFFERENT NOW. AN' NOT JUST THE WAY I LOOK--MY, LIKE, WHOLE OUTLOOK ON LIFE IS DIFFERENT. MY LIFE, OTHER PEOPLE'S LIVES...
...I'M JUST NOT THAT GUY ANYMORE.
DO YOU UNDERSTAND WHAT I'M SAYING?
K-KLIK
Looks like that's a "No."
OR MAYBE HE DOES UNDERSTAND, BUT HE DOESN'T GIVE A &*#%.
Hmmm...nah, gonna stick with "Doesn't understand."

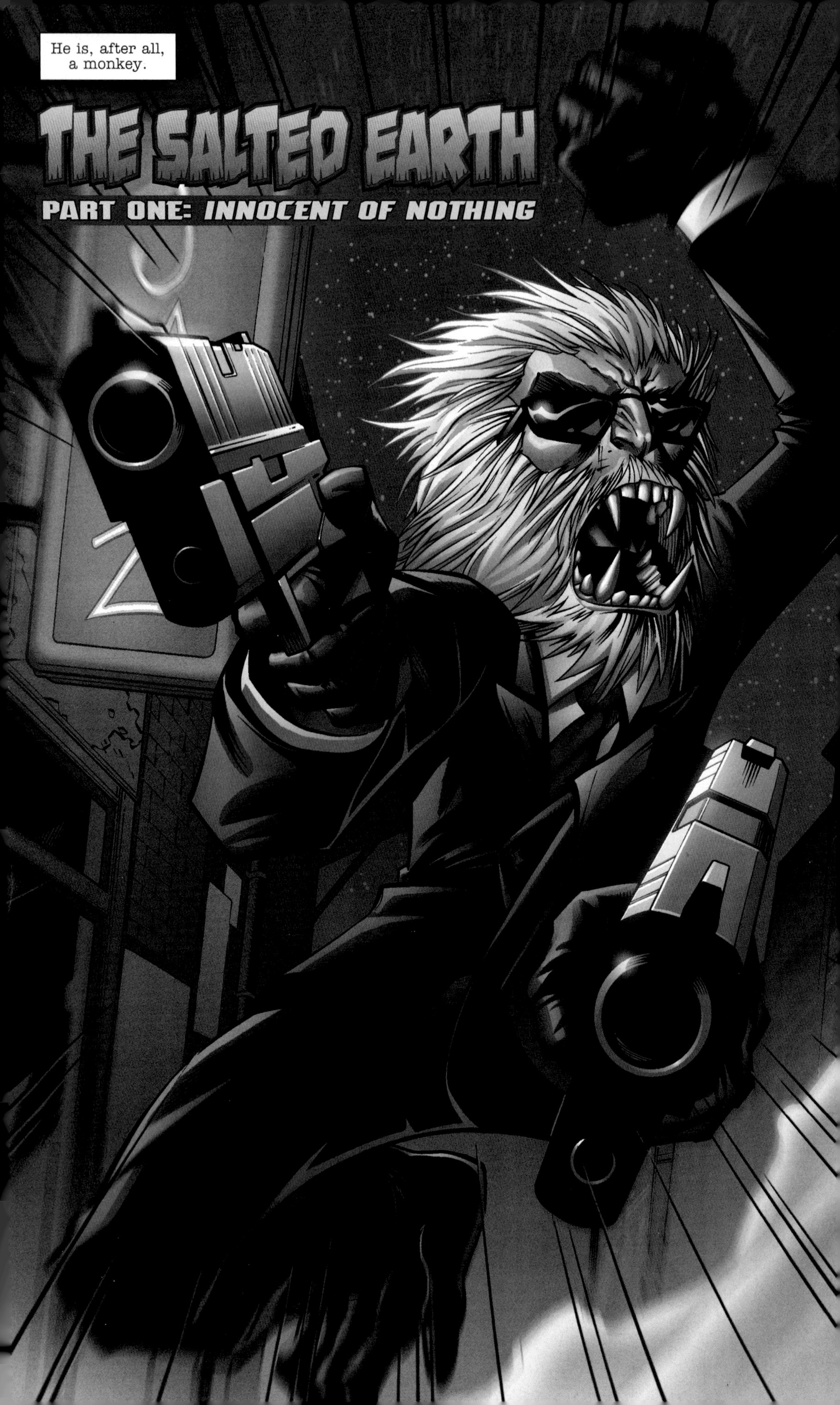
He is, after all, a monkey.
THE SALTED EARTH
PART ONE: INNOCENT OF NOTHING

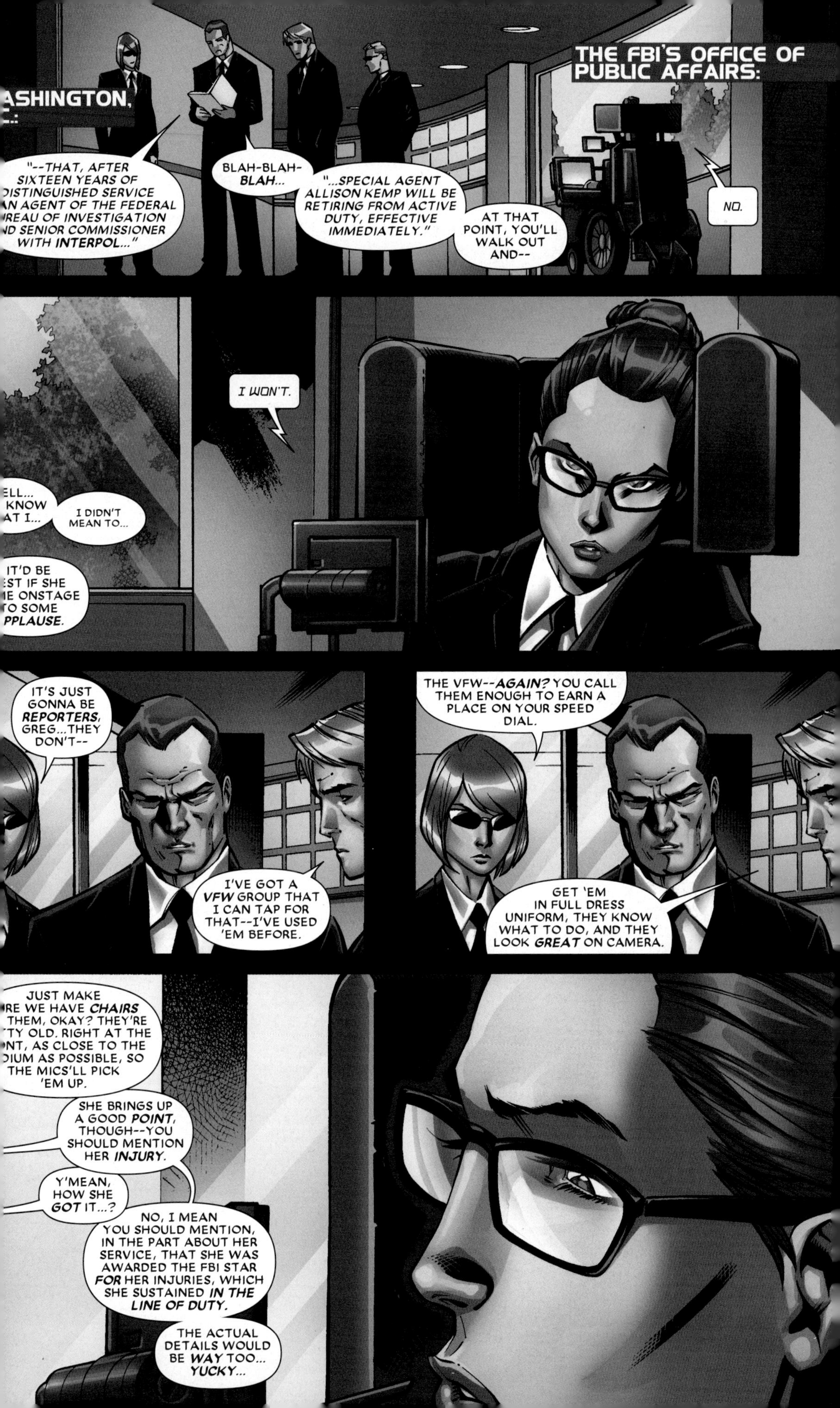
ASHINGTON,
THE FBI'S OFFICE OF PUBLIC AFFAIRS:
"--THAT, AFTER SIXTEEN YEARS OF DISTINGUISHED SERVICE AN AGENT OF THE FEDERAL REAU OF INVESTIGATION D SENIOR COMMISSIONER WITH INTERPOL..."
BLAH-BLAH-BLAH...
"...SPECIAL AGENT ALLISON KEMP WILL BE RETIRING FROM ACTIVE DUTY, EFFECTIVE IMMEDIATELY."
AT THAT POINT, YOU'LL WALK OUT AND--
NO.
I WON'T.
ELL... KNOW AT I...
I DIDN'T MEAN TO...
IT'D BE EST IF SHE E ONSTAGE TO SOME PPLAUSE.
IT'S JUST GONNA BE REPORTERS, GREG...THEY DON'T--
I'VE GOT A VFW GROUP THAT I CAN TAP FOR THAT--I'VE USED 'EM BEFORE.
THE VFW--AGAIN? YOU CALL THEM ENOUGH TO EARN A PLACE ON YOUR SPEED DIAL.
GET 'EM IN FULL DRESS UNIFORM, THEY KNOW WHAT TO DO, AND THEY LOOK GREAT ON CAMERA.
JUST MAKE RE WE HAVE CHAIRS THEM, OKAY? THEY'RE TY OLD. RIGHT AT THE NT, AS CLOSE TO THE DIUM AS POSSIBLE, SO THE MICS'LL PICK 'EM UP.
SHE BRINGS UP A GOOD POINT, THOUGH--YOU SHOULD MENTION HER INJURY.
Y'MEAN, HOW SHE GOT IT...?
NO, I MEAN YOU SHOULD MENTION, IN THE PART ABOUT HER SERVICE, THAT SHE WAS AWARDED THE FBI STAR FOR HER INJURIES, WHICH SHE SUSTAINED IN THE LINE OF DUTY.
THE ACTUAL DETAILS WOULD BE WAY TOO... YUCKY...

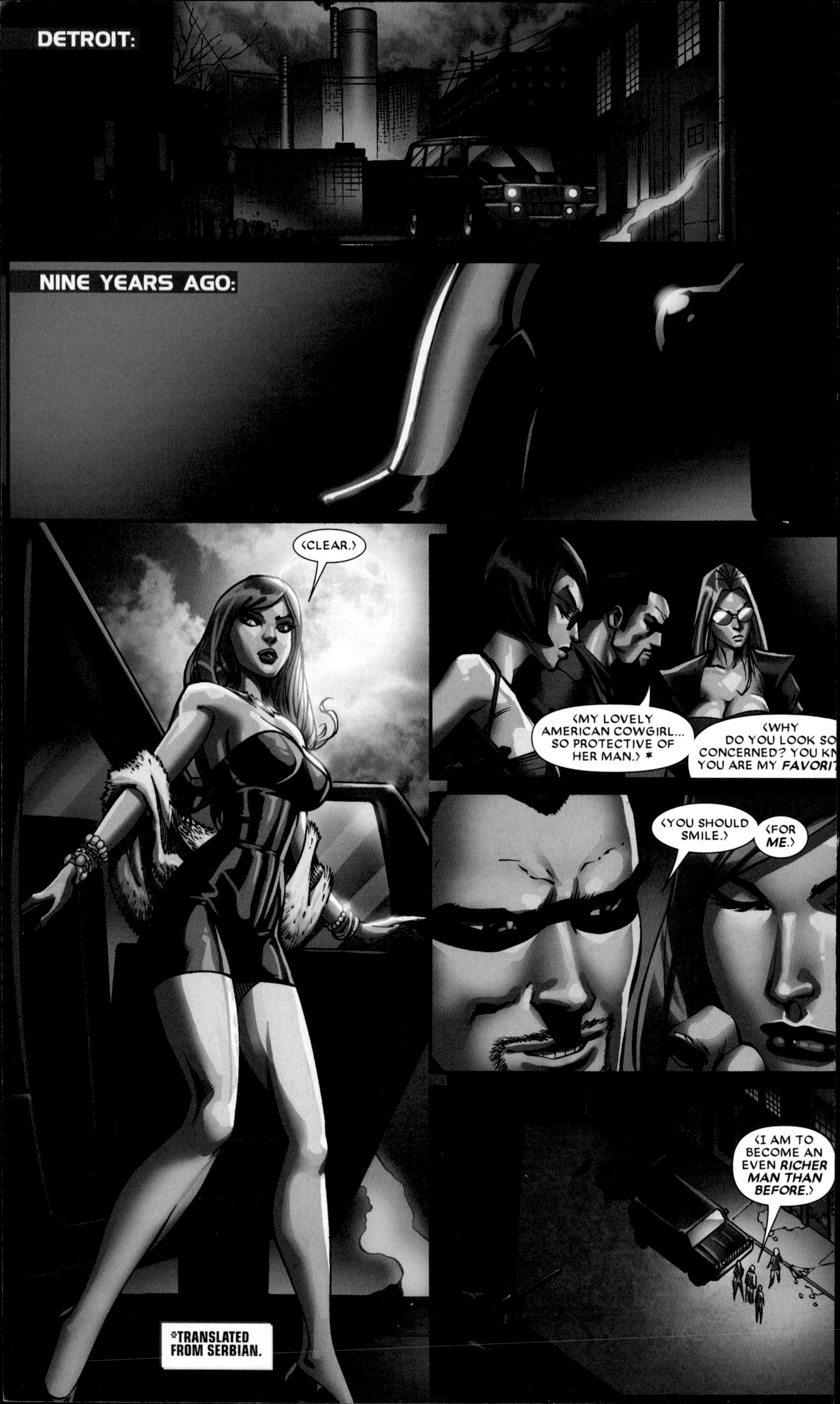

DETROIT:
NINE YEARS AGO:
‹CLEAR.›
‹MY LOVELY AMERICAN COWGIRL... SO PROTECTIVE OF HER MAN.› *
‹WHY DO YOU LOOK SO CONCERNED? YOU KN YOU ARE MY FAVORIT
‹YOU SHOULD SMILE.›
‹FOR ME.›
‹I AM TO BECOME AN EVEN RICHER MAN THAN BEFORE.›
*TRANSLATED FROM SERBIAN.

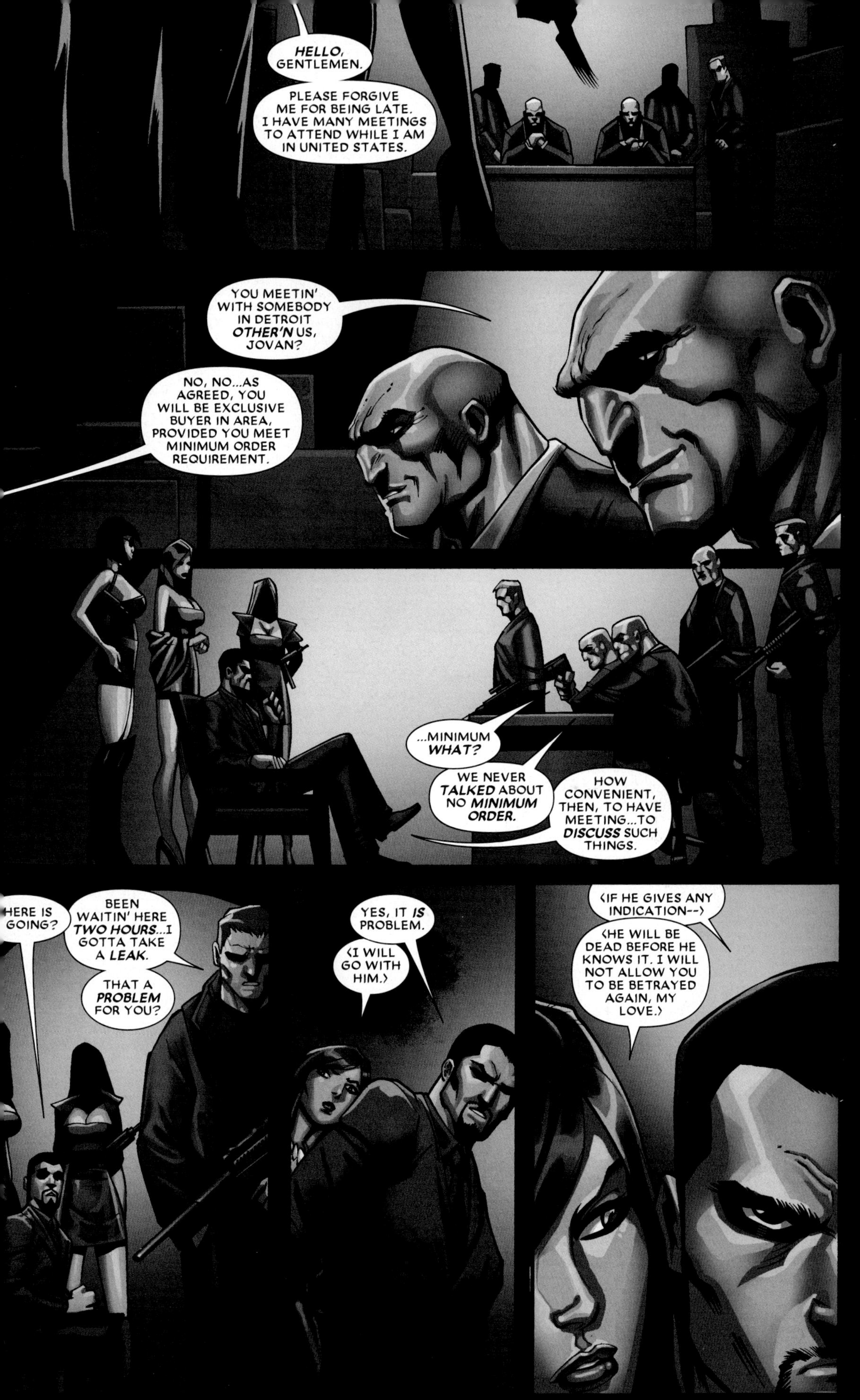
HELLO, GENTLEMEN.
PLEASE FORGIVE ME FOR BEING LATE. I HAVE MANY MEETINGS TO ATTEND WHILE I AM IN UNITED STATES.
YOU MEETIN' WITH SOMEBODY IN DETROIT OTHER'N US, JOVAN?
NO, NO...AS AGREED, YOU WILL BE EXCLUSIVE BUYER IN AREA, PROVIDED YOU MEET MINIMUM ORDER REQUIREMENT.
...MINIMUM WHAT?
WE NEVER TALKED ABOUT NO MINIMUM ORDER.
HOW CONVENIENT, THEN, TO HAVE MEETING...TO DISCUSS SUCH THINGS.
HERE IS GOING?
BEEN WAITIN' HERE TWO HOURS...I GOTTA TAKE A LEAK.
THAT A PROBLEM FOR YOU?
YES, IT IS PROBLEM.
‹I WILL GO WITH HIM.›
‹IF HE GIVES ANY INDICATION--›
‹HE WILL BE DEAD BEFORE HE KNOWS IT. I WILL NOT ALLOW YOU TO BE BETRAYED AGAIN, MY LOVE.›

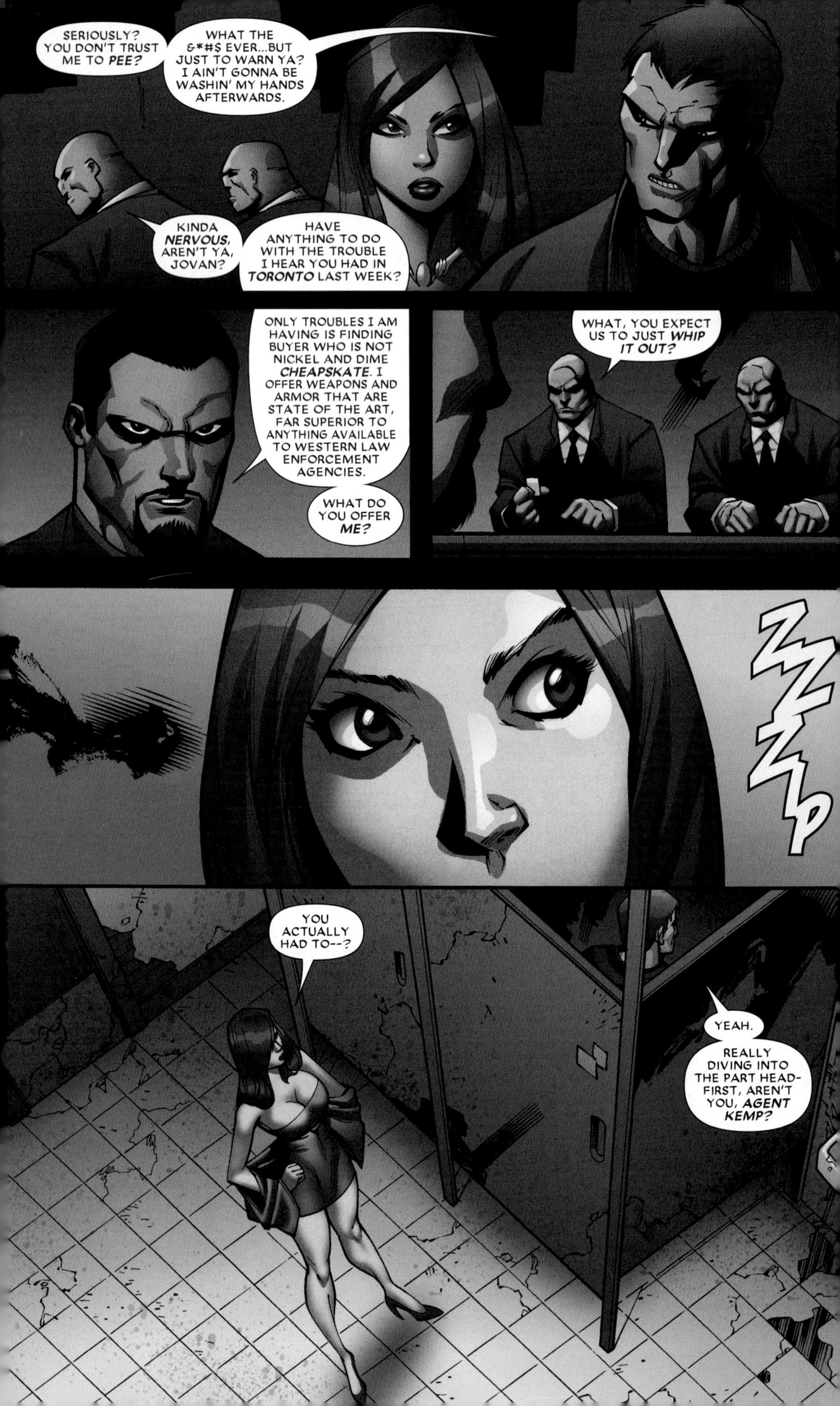
SERIOUSLY? YOU DON'T TRUST ME TO PEE?
WHAT THE &*#$ EVER...BUT JUST TO WARN YA? I AIN'T GONNA BE WASHIN' MY HANDS AFTERWARDS.
KINDA NERVOUS, AREN'T YA, JOVAN?
HAVE ANYTHING TO DO WITH THE TROUBLE I HEAR YOU HAD IN TORONTO LAST WEEK?
ONLY TROUBLES I AM HAVING IS FINDING BUYER WHO IS NOT NICKEL AND DIME CHEAPSKATE. I OFFER WEAPONS AND ARMOR THAT ARE STATE OF THE ART, FAR SUPERIOR TO ANYTHING AVAILABLE TO WESTERN LAW ENFORCEMENT AGENCIES.
WHAT DO YOU OFFER ME?
WHAT, YOU EXPECT US TO JUST WHIP IT OUT?
ZZZZIP
YOU ACTUALLY HAD TO--?
YEAH.
REALLY DIVING INTO THE PART HEAD-FIRST, AREN'T YOU, AGENT KEMP?

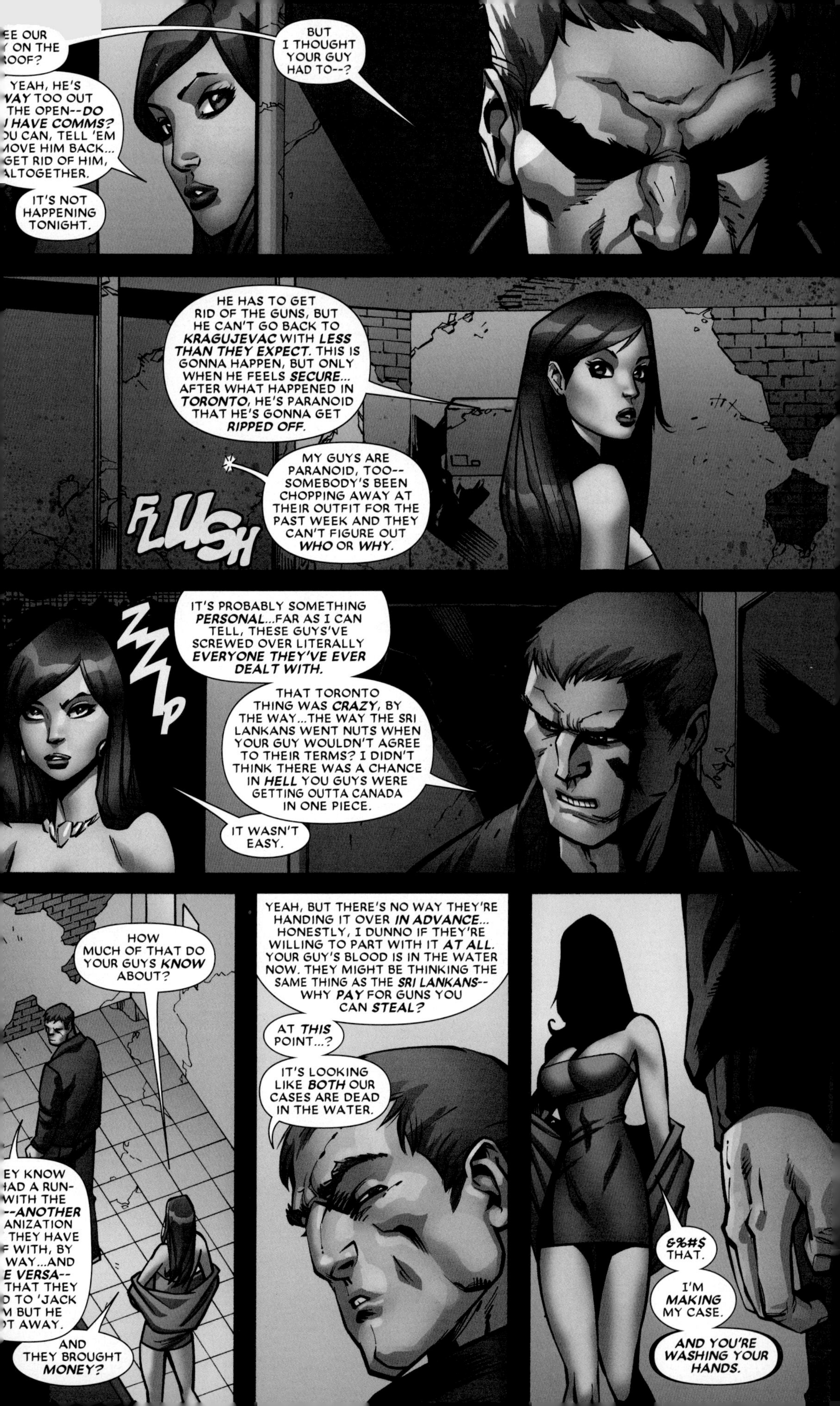

EE OUR
ON THE
ROOF?
BUT I THOUGHT YOUR GUY HAD TO--?
YEAH, HE'S WAY TOO OUT THE OPEN--DO I HAVE COMMS? OU CAN, TELL 'EM MOVE HIM BACK... GET RID OF HIM, ALTOGETHER.
IT'S NOT HAPPENING TONIGHT.
HE HAS TO GET RID OF THE GUNS, BUT HE CAN'T GO BACK TO KRAGUJEVAC WITH LESS THAN THEY EXPECT. THIS IS GONNA HAPPEN, BUT ONLY WHEN HE FEELS SECURE... AFTER WHAT HAPPENED IN TORONTO, HE'S PARANOID THAT HE'S GONNA GET RIPPED OFF.
FLUSH
MY GUYS ARE PARANOID, TOO-- SOMEBODY'S BEEN CHOPPING AWAY AT THEIR OUTFIT FOR THE PAST WEEK AND THEY CAN'T FIGURE OUT WHO OR WHY.
ZZZIP
IT'S PROBABLY SOMETHING PERSONAL...FAR AS I CAN TELL, THESE GUYS'VE SCREWED OVER LITERALLY EVERYONE THEY'VE EVER DEALT WITH.
THAT TORONTO THING WAS CRAZY, BY THE WAY...THE WAY THE SRI LANKANS WENT NUTS WHEN YOUR GUY WOULDN'T AGREE TO THEIR TERMS? I DIDN'T THINK THERE WAS A CHANCE IN HELL YOU GUYS WERE GETTING OUTTA CANADA IN ONE PIECE.
IT WASN'T EASY.
HOW MUCH OF THAT DO YOUR GUYS KNOW ABOUT?
EY KNOW HAD A RUN- WITH THE --ANOTHER ANIZATION THEY HAVE F WITH, BY WAY...AND E VERSA-- THAT THEY D TO 'JACK M BUT HE OT AWAY.
AND THEY BROUGHT MONEY?
YEAH, BUT THERE'S NO WAY THEY'RE HANDING IT OVER IN ADVANCE... HONESTLY, I DUNNO IF THEY'RE WILLING TO PART WITH IT AT ALL. YOUR GUY'S BLOOD IS IN THE WATER NOW. THEY MIGHT BE THINKING THE SAME THING AS THE SRI LANKANS-- WHY PAY FOR GUNS YOU CAN STEAL?
AT THIS POINT...?
IT'S LOOKING LIKE BOTH OUR CASES ARE DEAD IN THE WATER.
&%#$ THAT.
I'M MAKING MY CASE.
AND YOU'RE WASHING YOUR HANDS.

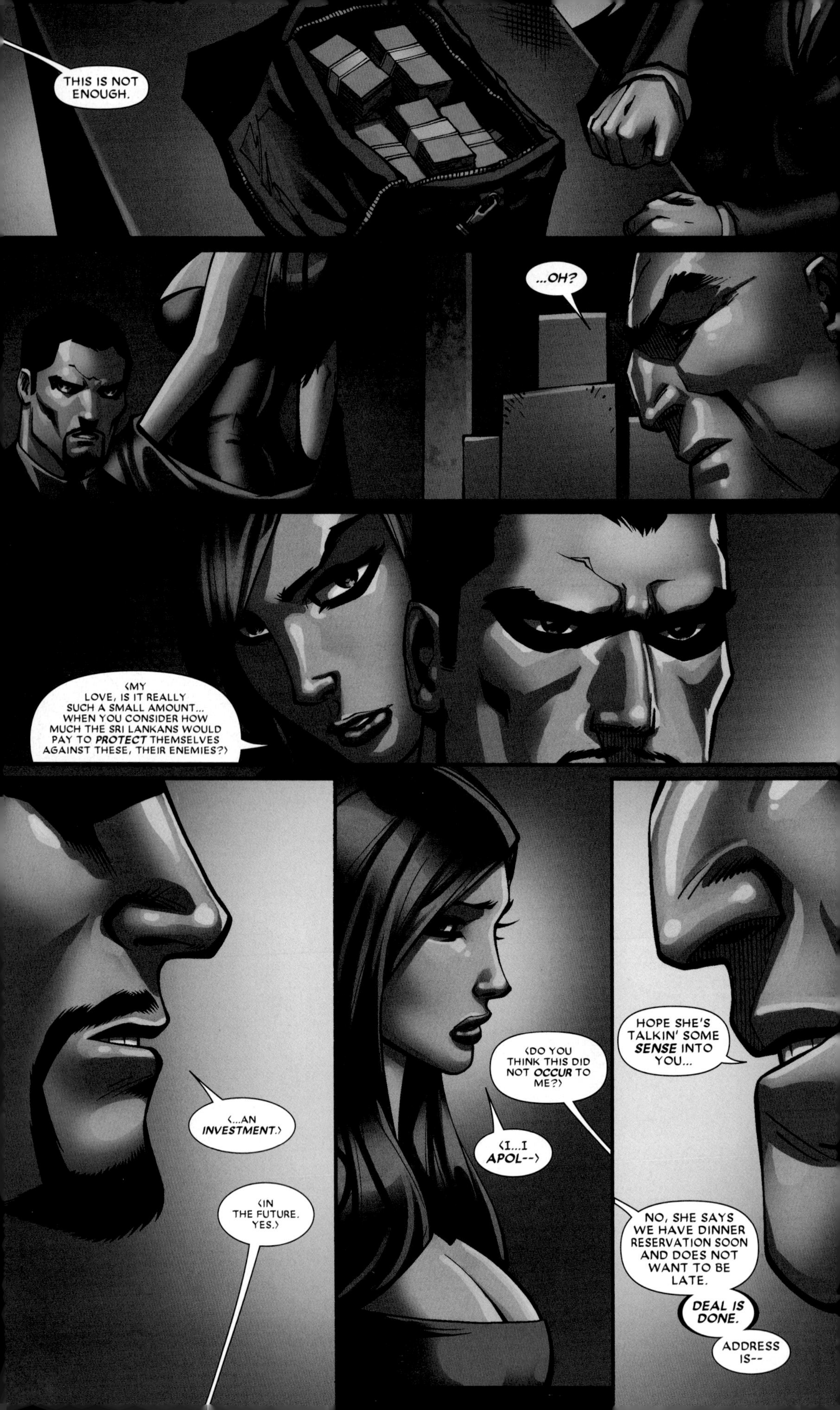
THIS IS NOT ENOUGH.
...OH?
‹MY LOVE, IS IT REALLY SUCH A SMALL AMOUNT... WHEN YOU CONSIDER HOW MUCH THE SRI LANKANS WOULD PAY TO *PROTECT* THEMSELVES AGAINST THESE, THEIR ENEMIES?›
‹...AN *INVESTMENT*.›
‹IN THE FUTURE. YES.›
‹DO YOU THINK THIS DID NOT *OCCUR* TO ME?›
‹I...I *APOL*--›
HOPE SHE'S TALKIN' SOME *SENSE* INTO YOU...
NO, SHE SAYS WE HAVE DINNER RESERVATION SOON AND DOES NOT WANT TO BE LATE.
DEAL IS DONE.
ADDRESS IS--

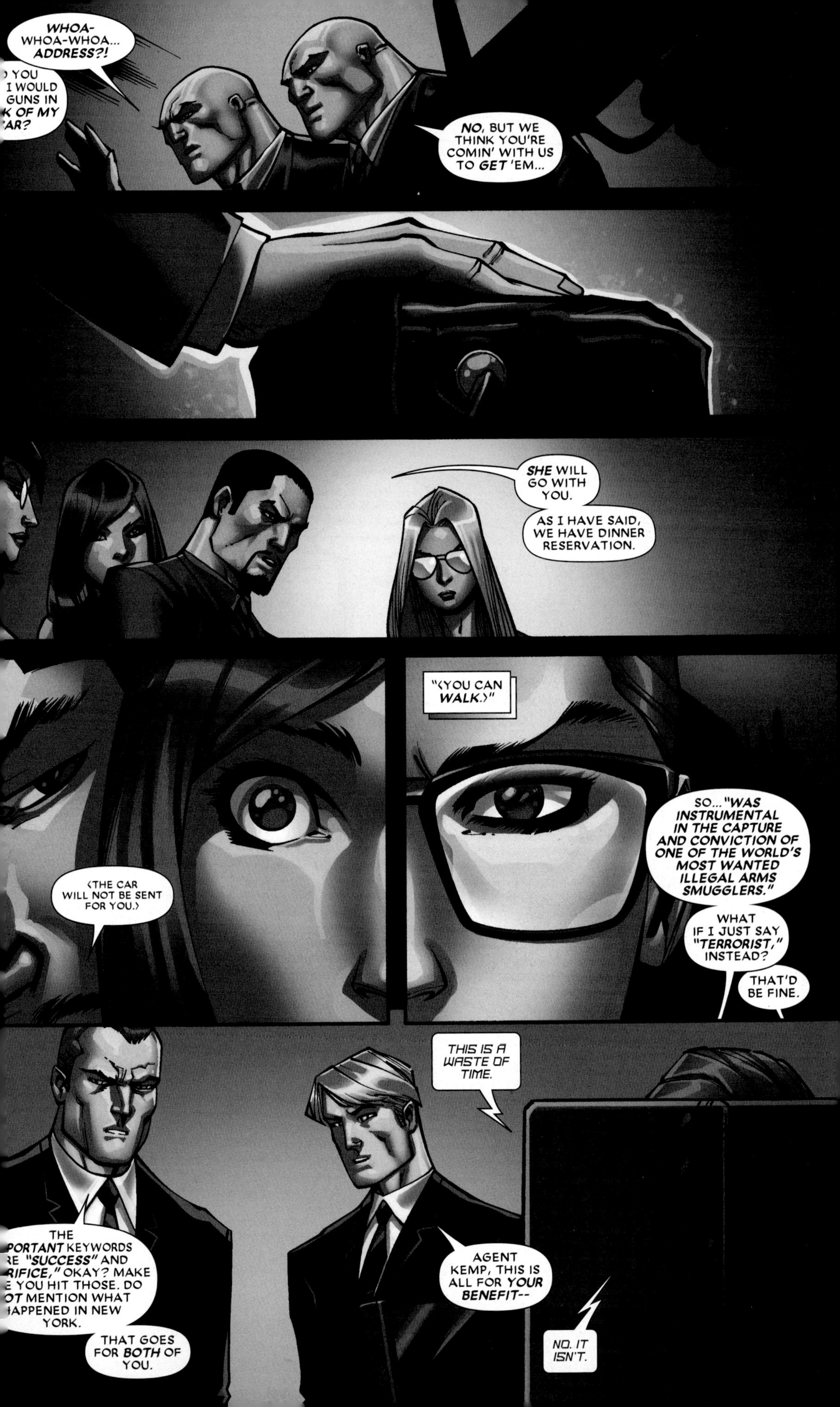

WHOA-WHOA-WHOA... ADDRESS?!
D YOU I WOULD GUNS IN K OF MY CAR?
NO, BUT WE THINK YOU'RE COMIN' WITH US TO GET 'EM...
SHE WILL GO WITH YOU.
AS I HAVE SAID, WE HAVE DINNER RESERVATION.
"‹YOU CAN WALK.›"
‹THE CAR WILL NOT BE SENT FOR YOU.›
SO... "WAS INSTRUMENTAL IN THE CAPTURE AND CONVICTION OF ONE OF THE WORLD'S MOST WANTED ILLEGAL ARMS SMUGGLERS."
WHAT IF I JUST SAY "TERRORIST," INSTEAD?
THAT'D BE FINE.
THIS IS A WASTE OF TIME.
THE PORTANT KEYWORDS RE "SUCCESS" AND RIFICE," OKAY? MAKE E YOU HIT THOSE. DO OT MENTION WHAT HAPPENED IN NEW YORK.
THAT GOES FOR BOTH OF YOU.
AGENT KEMP, THIS IS ALL FOR YOUR BENEFIT--
NO. IT ISN'T.

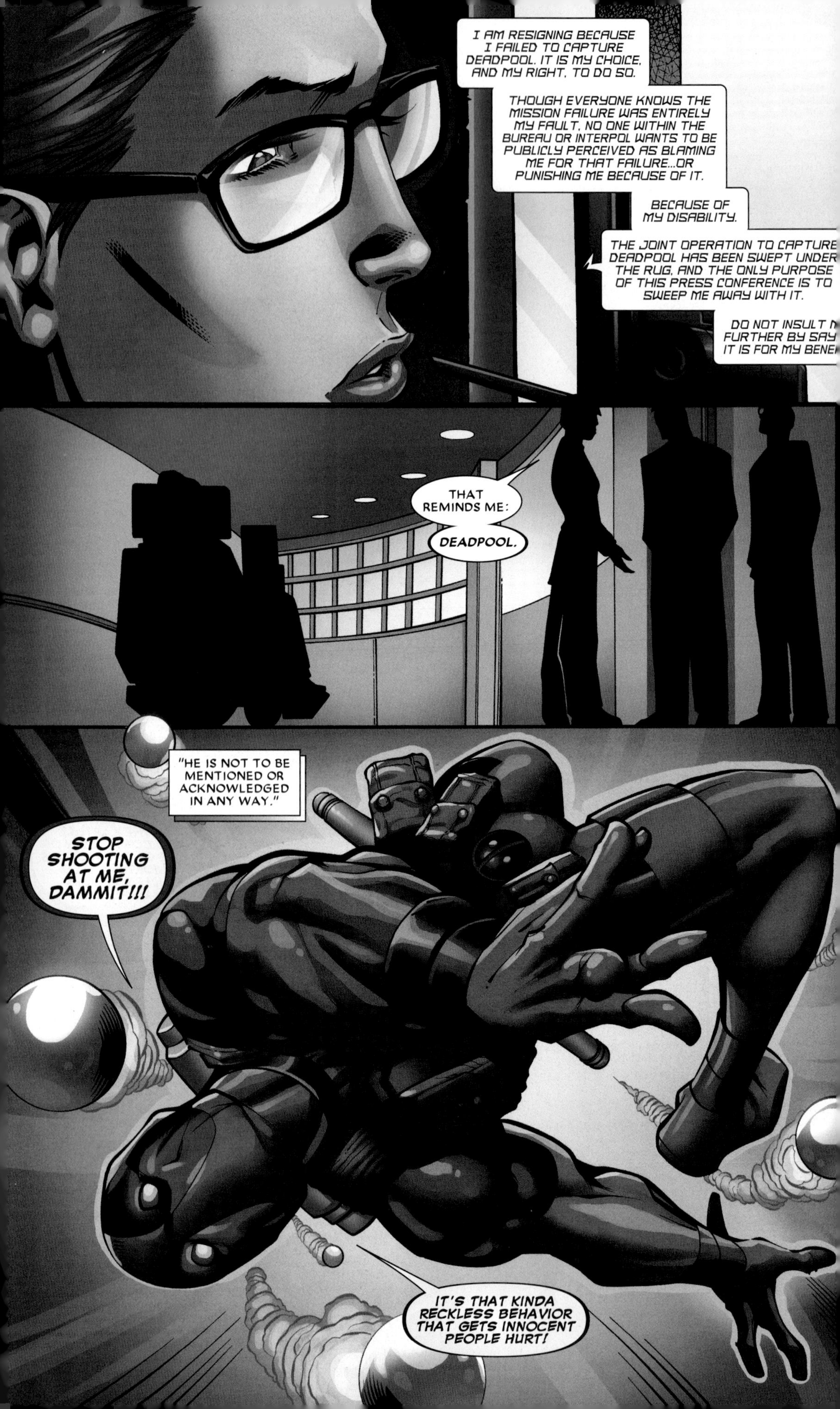

I AM RESIGNING BECAUSE I FAILED TO CAPTURE DEADPOOL. IT IS MY CHOICE, AND MY RIGHT, TO DO SO.
THOUGH EVERYONE KNOWS THE MISSION FAILURE WAS ENTIRELY MY FAULT, NO ONE WITHIN THE BUREAU OR INTERPOL WANTS TO BE PUBLICLY PERCEIVED AS BLAMING ME FOR THAT FAILURE...OR PUNISHING ME BECAUSE OF IT.
BECAUSE OF MY DISABILITY.
THE JOINT OPERATION TO CAPTURE DEADPOOL HAS BEEN SWEPT UNDER THE RUG, AND THE ONLY PURPOSE OF THIS PRESS CONFERENCE IS TO SWEEP ME AWAY WITH IT.
DO NOT INSULT M FURTHER BY SAY IT IS FOR MY BENE
THAT REMINDS ME:
DEADPOOL.
"HE IS NOT TO BE MENTIONED OR ACKNOWLEDGED IN ANY WAY."
STOP SHOOTING AT ME, DAMMIT!!!
IT'S THAT KINDA RECKLESS BEHAVIOR THAT GETS INNOCENT PEOPLE HURT!

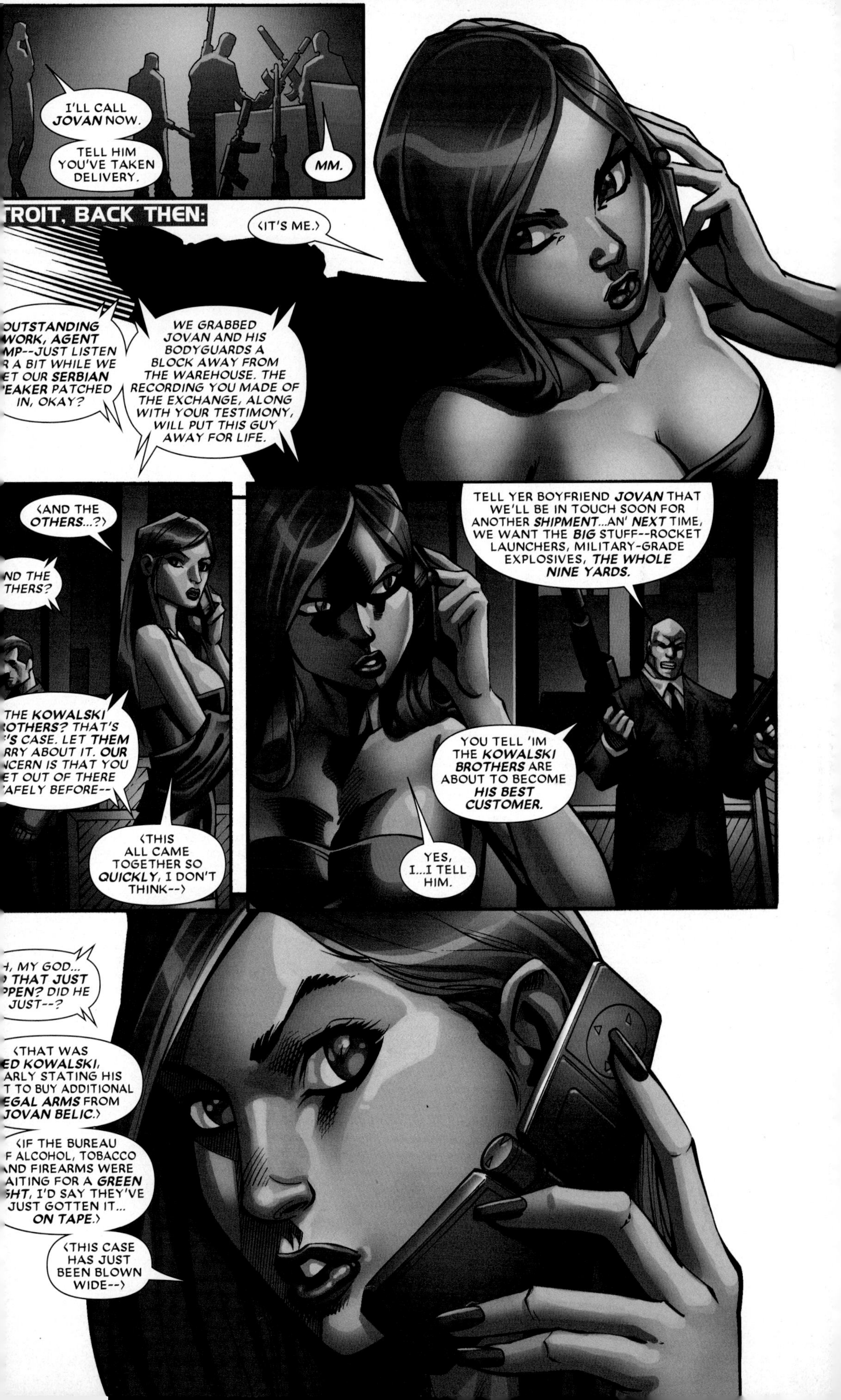
I'LL CALL JOVAN NOW.
TELL HIM YOU'VE TAKEN DELIVERY.
MM.
TROIT, BACK THEN:
‹IT'S ME.›
OUTSTANDING WORK, AGENT MP--JUST LISTEN R A BIT WHILE WE ET OUR SERBIAN PEAKER PATCHED IN, OKAY?
WE GRABBED JOVAN AND HIS BODYGUARDS A BLOCK AWAY FROM THE WAREHOUSE. THE RECORDING YOU MADE OF THE EXCHANGE, ALONG WITH YOUR TESTIMONY, WILL PUT THIS GUY AWAY FOR LIFE.
‹AND THE OTHERS...?›
ND THE THERS?
THE KOWALSKI ROTHERS? THAT'S 'S CASE. LET THEM RRY ABOUT IT. OUR NCERN IS THAT YOU ET OUT OF THERE AFELY BEFORE--
‹THIS ALL CAME TOGETHER SO QUICKLY, I DON'T THINK--›
TELL YER BOYFRIEND JOVAN THAT WE'LL BE IN TOUCH SOON FOR ANOTHER SHIPMENT...AN' NEXT TIME, WE WANT THE BIG STUFF--ROCKET LAUNCHERS, MILITARY-GRADE EXPLOSIVES, THE WHOLE NINE YARDS.
YOU TELL 'IM THE KOWALSKI BROTHERS ARE ABOUT TO BECOME HIS BEST CUSTOMER.
YES, I...I TELL HIM.
H, MY GOD... THAT JUST PPEN? DID HE JUST--?
‹THAT WAS ED KOWALSKI, ARLY STATING HIS T TO BUY ADDITIONAL EGAL ARMS FROM JOVAN BELIC.›
‹IF THE BUREAU F ALCOHOL, TOBACCO ND FIREARMS WERE AITING FOR A GREEN GHT, I'D SAY THEY'VE JUST GOTTEN IT... ON TAPE.›
‹THIS CASE HAS JUST BEEN BLOWN WIDE--›

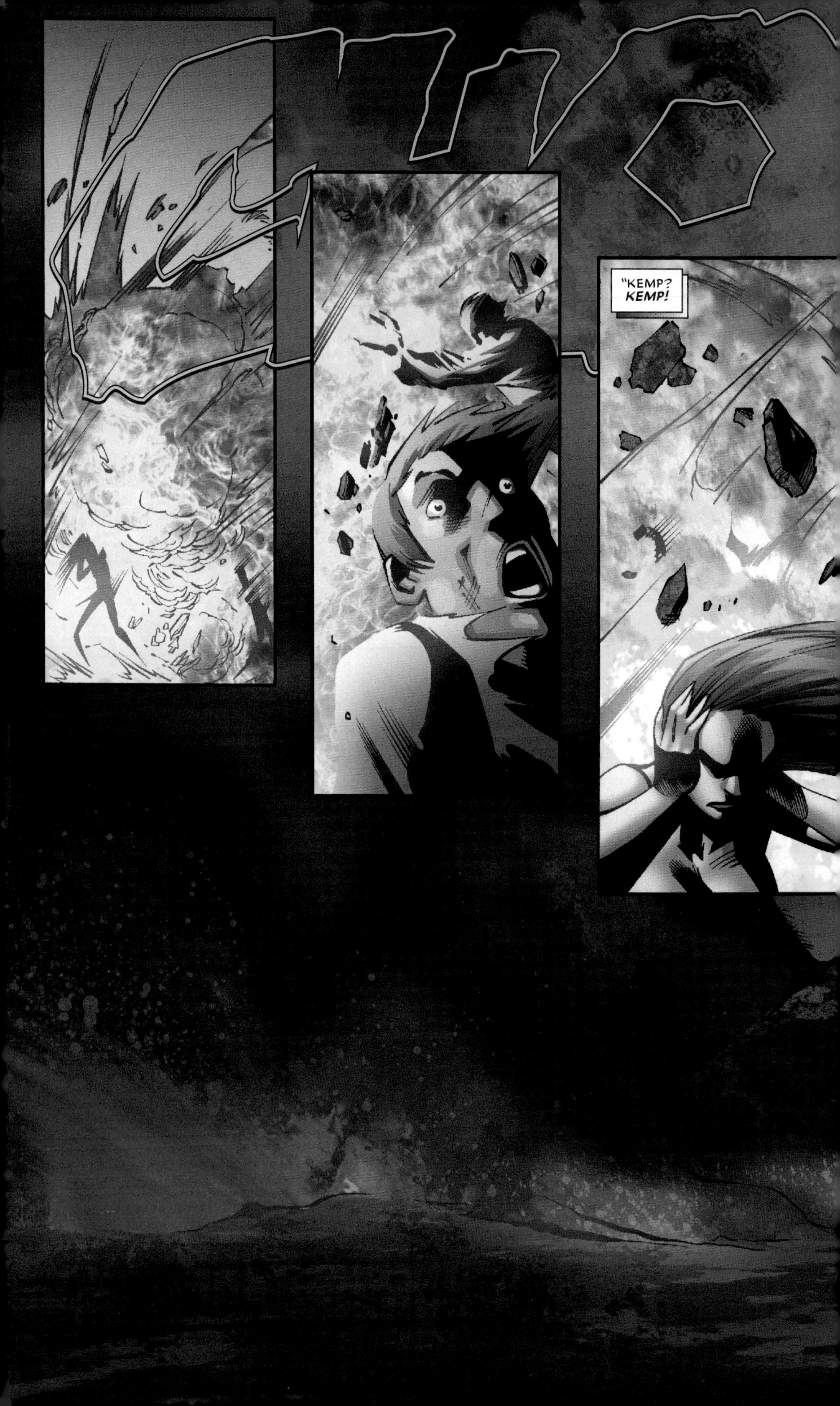
"KEMP? KEMP!

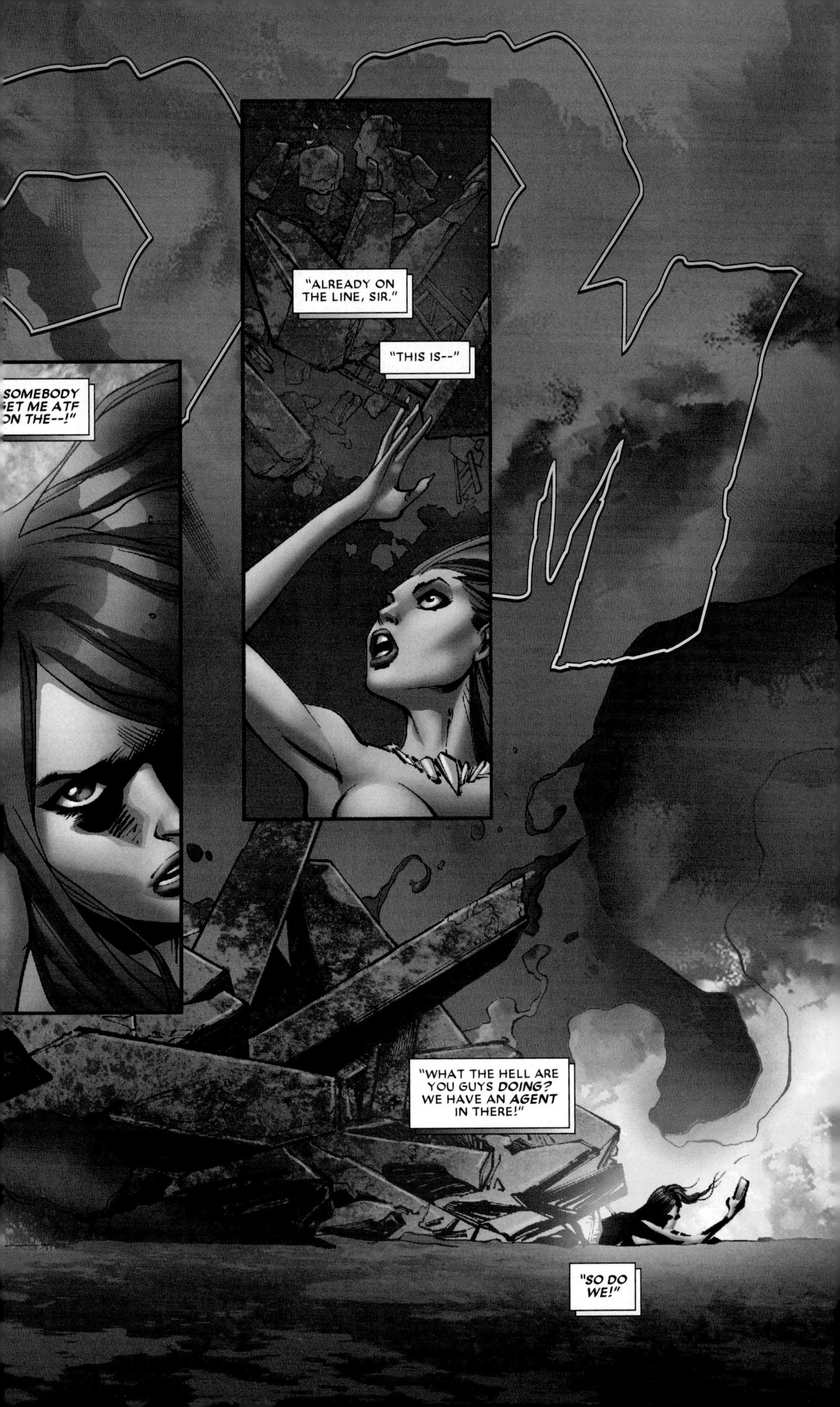

"SOMEBODY GET ME ATF ON THE--!"
"ALREADY ON THE LINE, SIR."
"THIS IS--"
"WHAT THE HELL ARE YOU GUYS DOING? WE HAVE AN AGENT IN THERE!"
"SO DO WE!"

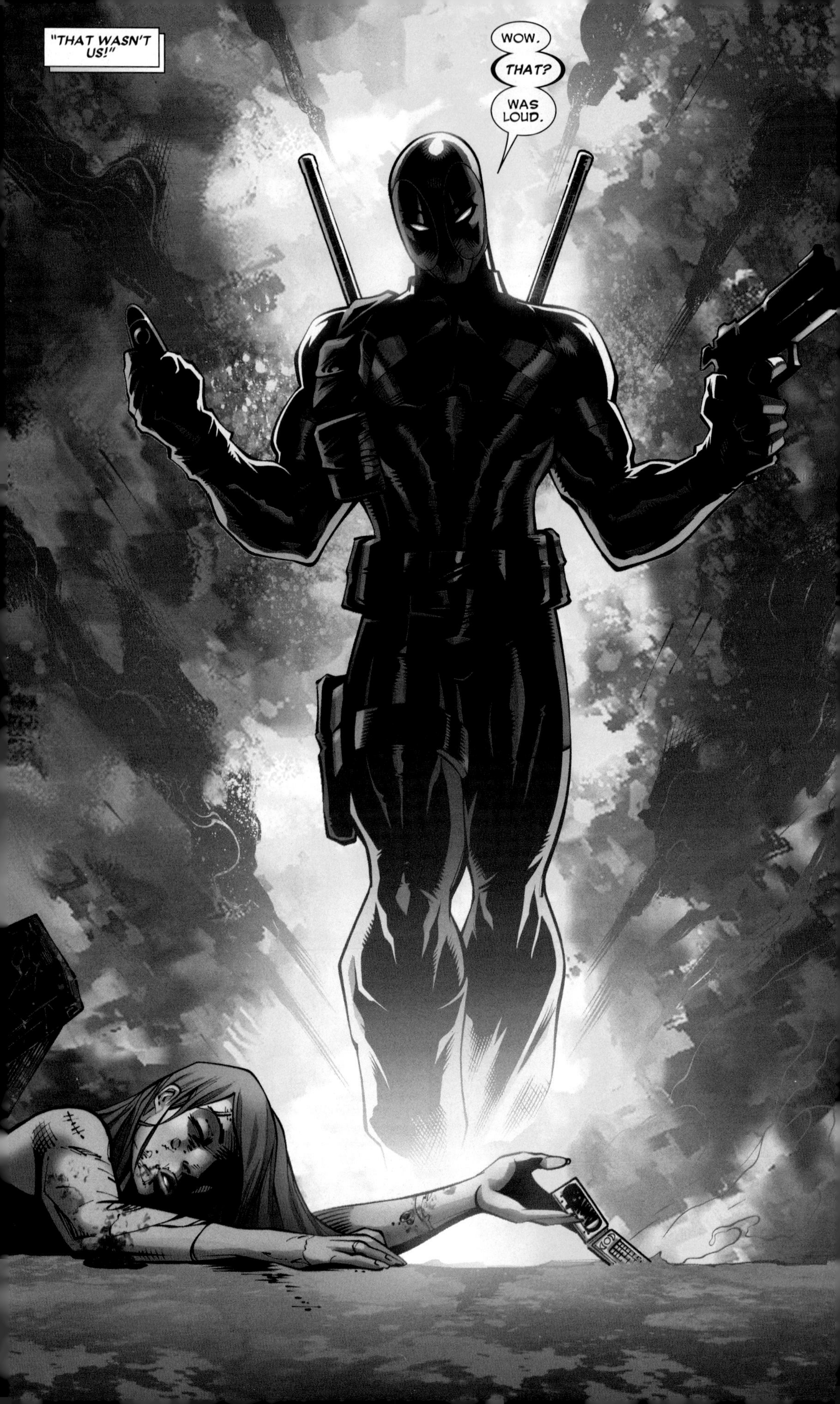
"THAT WASN'T US!"
WOW.
THAT?
WAS LOUD.

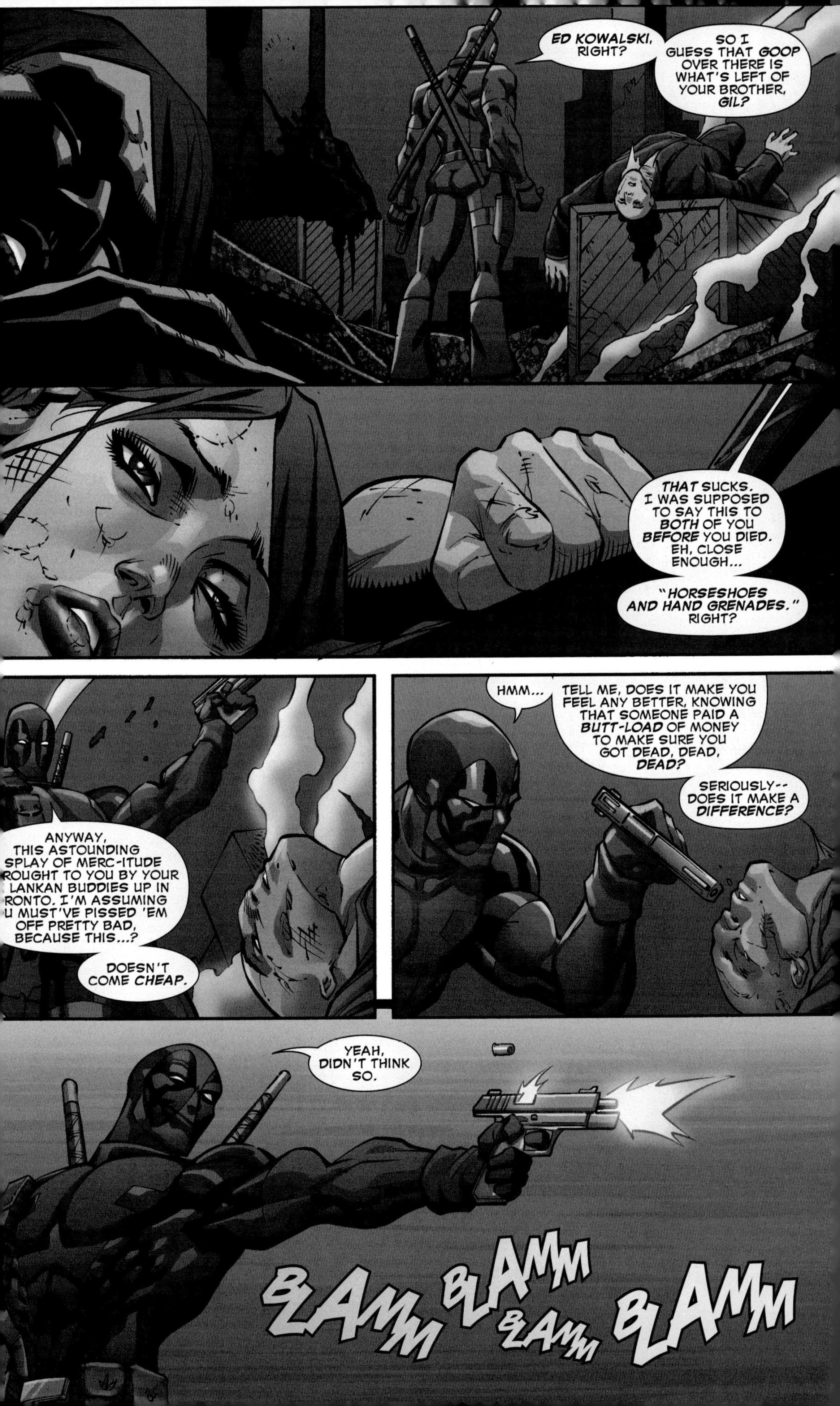

ED KOWALSKI, RIGHT?
SO I GUESS THAT GOOP OVER THERE IS WHAT'S LEFT OF YOUR BROTHER, GIL?
THAT SUCKS. I WAS SUPPOSED TO SAY THIS TO BOTH OF YOU BEFORE YOU DIED. EH, CLOSE ENOUGH...
"HORSESHOES AND HAND GRENADES." RIGHT?
ANYWAY, THIS ASTOUNDING SPLAY OF MERC-ITUDE ROUGHT TO YOU BY YOUR LANKAN BUDDIES UP IN RONTO. I'M ASSUMING U MUST'VE PISSED 'EM OFF PRETTY BAD, BECAUSE THIS...?
DOESN'T COME CHEAP.
HMM...
TELL ME, DOES IT MAKE YOU FEEL ANY BETTER, KNOWING THAT SOMEONE PAID A BUTT-LOAD OF MONEY TO MAKE SURE YOU GOT DEAD, DEAD, DEAD?
SERIOUSLY-- DOES IT MAKE A DIFFERENCE?
YEAH, DIDN'T THINK SO.
BLAMM BLAMM BLAMM BLAMM

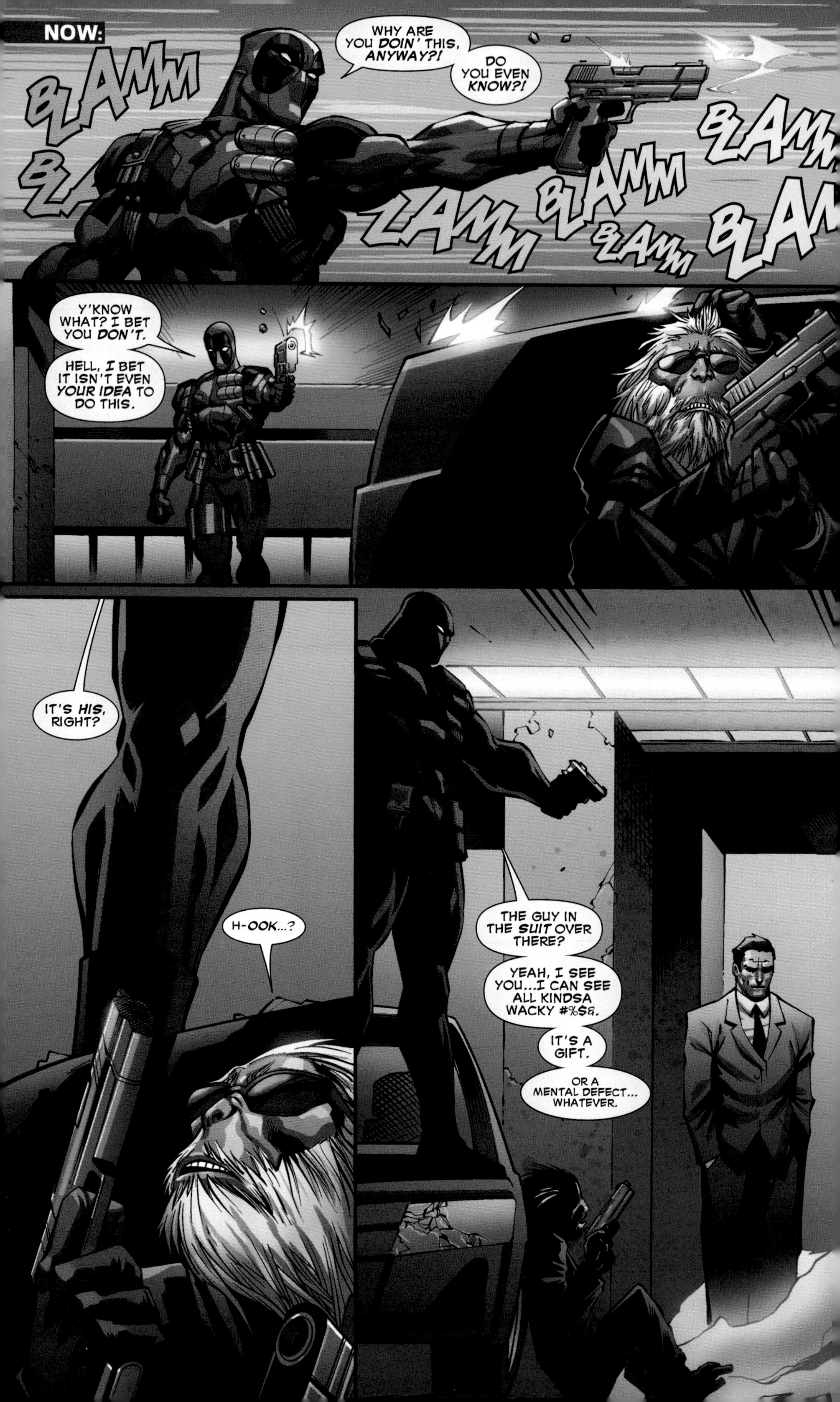
NOW:
WHY ARE YOU DOIN' THIS, ANYWAY?!
DO YOU EVEN KNOW?!
BLAMM
BLA
BLAMM
BLAMM
BLAMM
BLAMM
BLAMM
BLAM
Y'KNOW WHAT? I BET YOU DON'T.
HELL, I BET IT ISN'T EVEN YOUR IDEA TO DO THIS.
IT'S HIS, RIGHT?
H-OOK...?
THE GUY IN THE SUIT OVER THERE?
YEAH, I SEE YOU...I CAN SEE ALL KINDSA WACKY #%$&.
IT'S A GIFT.
OR A MENTAL DEFECT... WHATEVER.

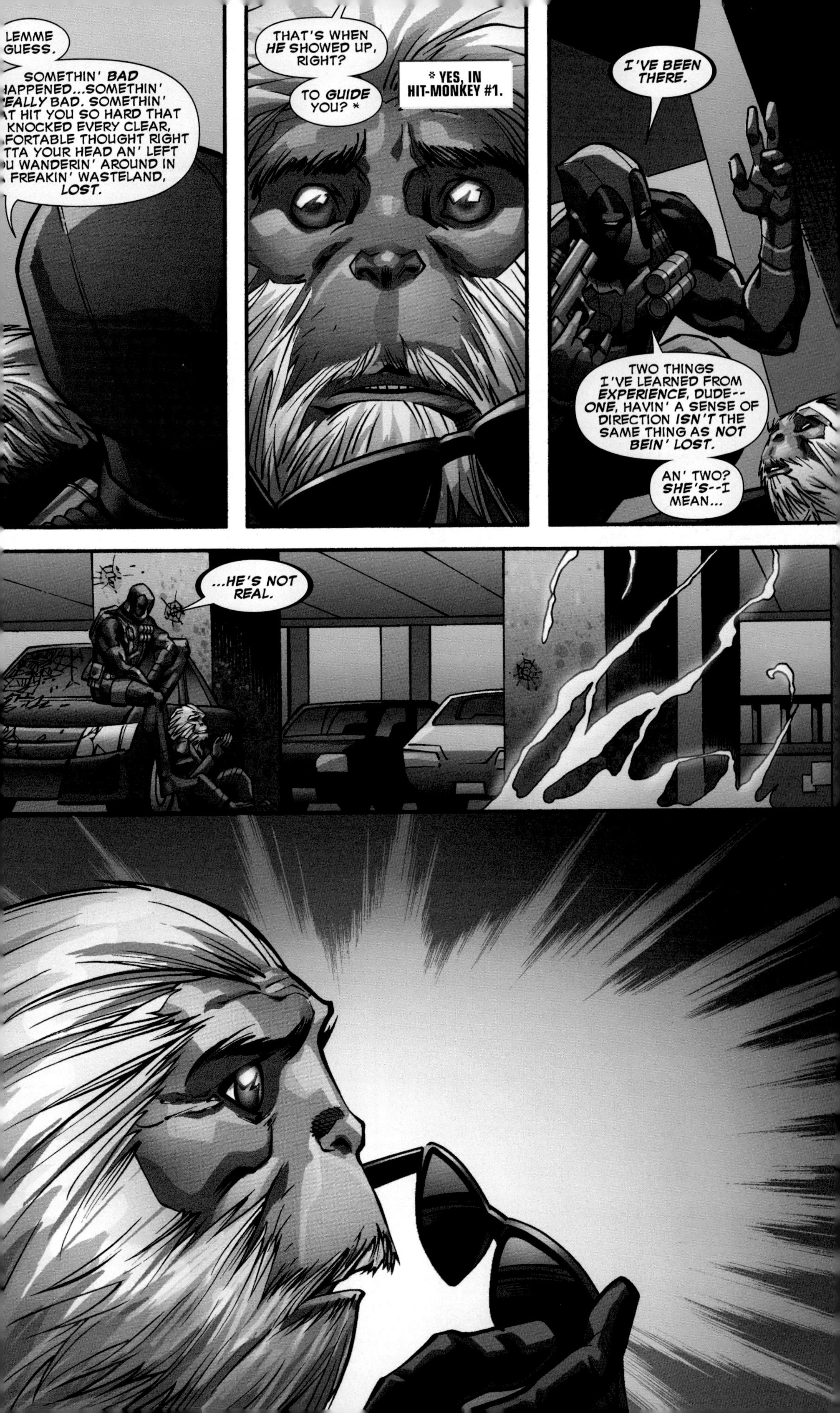
LEMME GUESS.
SOMETHIN' BAD HAPPENED...SOMETHIN' REALLY BAD. SOMETHIN' THAT HIT YOU SO HARD THAT KNOCKED EVERY CLEAR, FORTABLE THOUGHT RIGHT TTA YOUR HEAD AN' LEFT U WANDERIN' AROUND IN FREAKIN' WASTELAND, LOST.
THAT'S WHEN HE SHOWED UP, RIGHT?
TO GUIDE YOU? *
* YES, IN HIT-MONKEY #1.
I'VE BEEN THERE.
TWO THINGS I'VE LEARNED FROM EXPERIENCE, DUDE-- ONE, HAVIN' A SENSE OF DIRECTION ISN'T THE SAME THING AS NOT BEIN' LOST.
AN' TWO? SHE'S--I MEAN...
...HE'S NOT REAL.

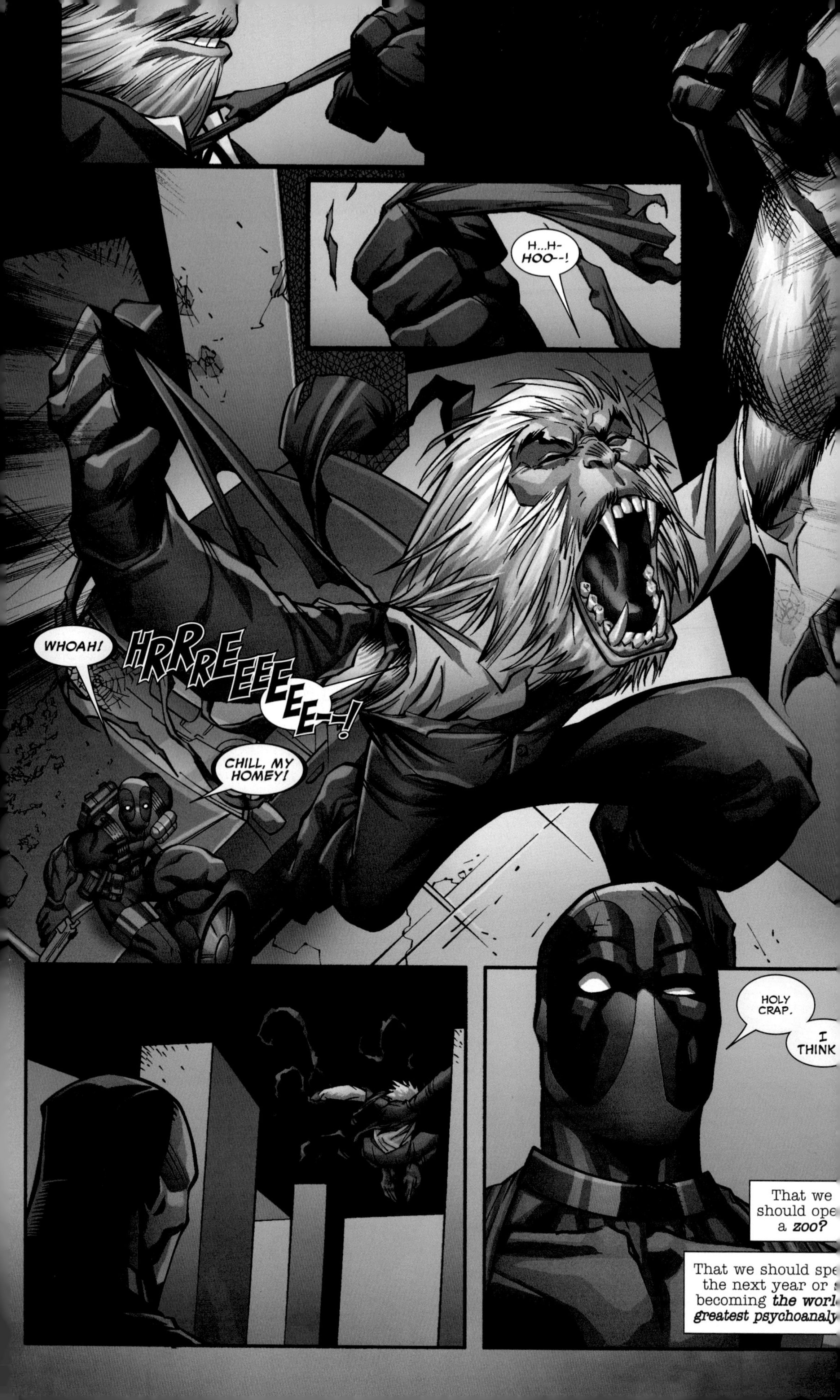

H...H-
HOO--!
WHOAH!
HRRREEEEEE--!
CHILL, MY HOMEY!
HOLY CRAP.
I THINK
That we should ope a zoo?
That we should spe the next year or becoming the worl greatest psychoanaly

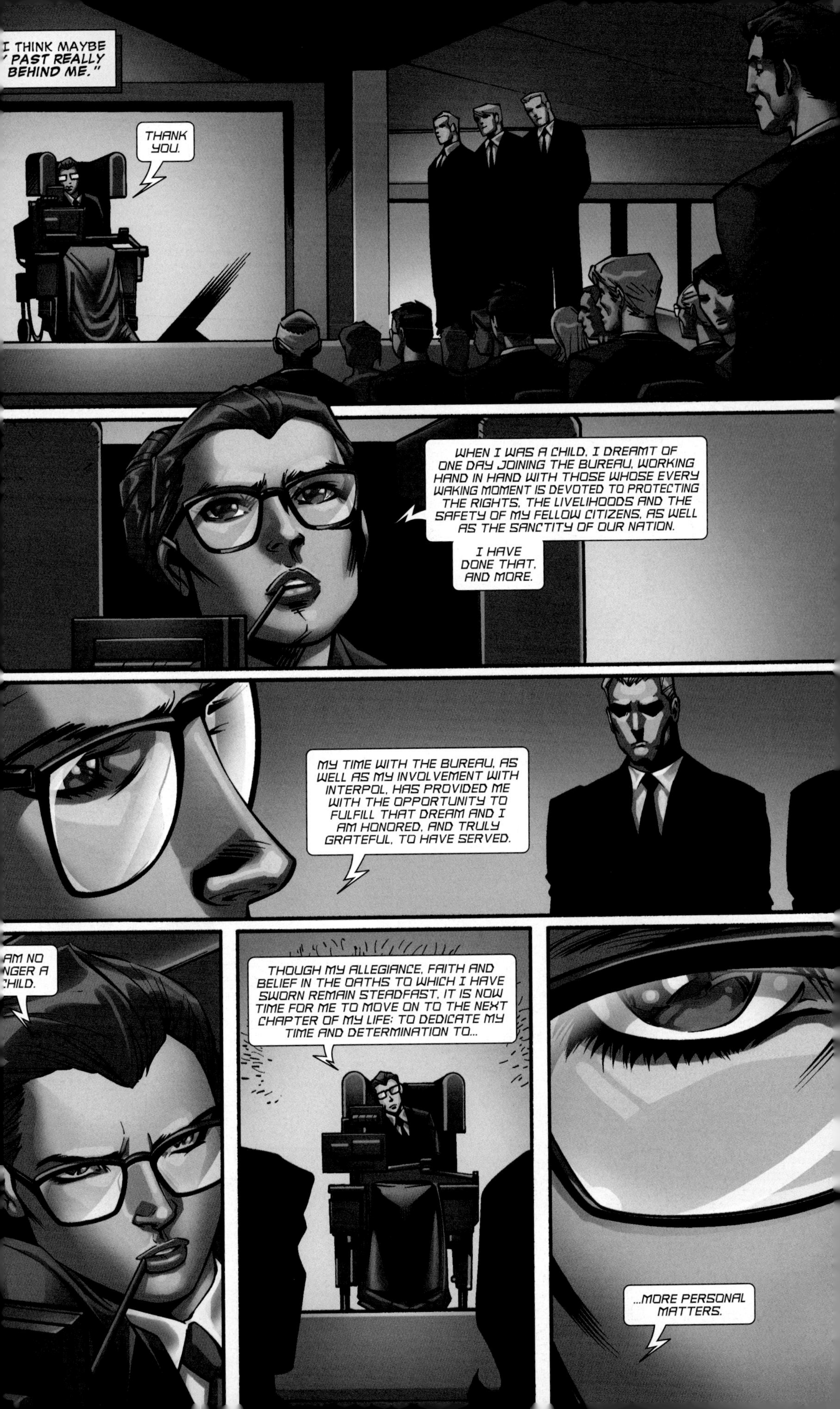

I THINK MAYBE
' PAST REALLY
BEHIND ME."
THANK YOU.
WHEN I WAS A CHILD, I DREAMT OF ONE DAY JOINING THE BUREAU, WORKING HAND IN HAND WITH THOSE WHOSE EVERY WAKING MOMENT IS DEVOTED TO PROTECTING THE RIGHTS, THE LIVELIHOODS AND THE SAFETY OF MY FELLOW CITIZENS, AS WELL AS THE SANCTITY OF OUR NATION.
I HAVE DONE THAT, AND MORE.
MY TIME WITH THE BUREAU, AS WELL AS MY INVOLVEMENT WITH INTERPOL, HAS PROVIDED ME WITH THE OPPORTUNITY TO FULFILL THAT DREAM AND I AM HONORED, AND TRULY GRATEFUL, TO HAVE SERVED.
AM NO
NGER A
CHILD.
THOUGH MY ALLEGIANCE, FAITH AND BELIEF IN THE OATHS TO WHICH I HAVE SWORN REMAIN STEADFAST, IT IS NOW TIME FOR ME TO MOVE ON TO THE NEXT CHAPTER OF MY LIFE: TO DEDICATE MY TIME AND DETERMINATION TO...
...MORE PERSONAL MATTERS.

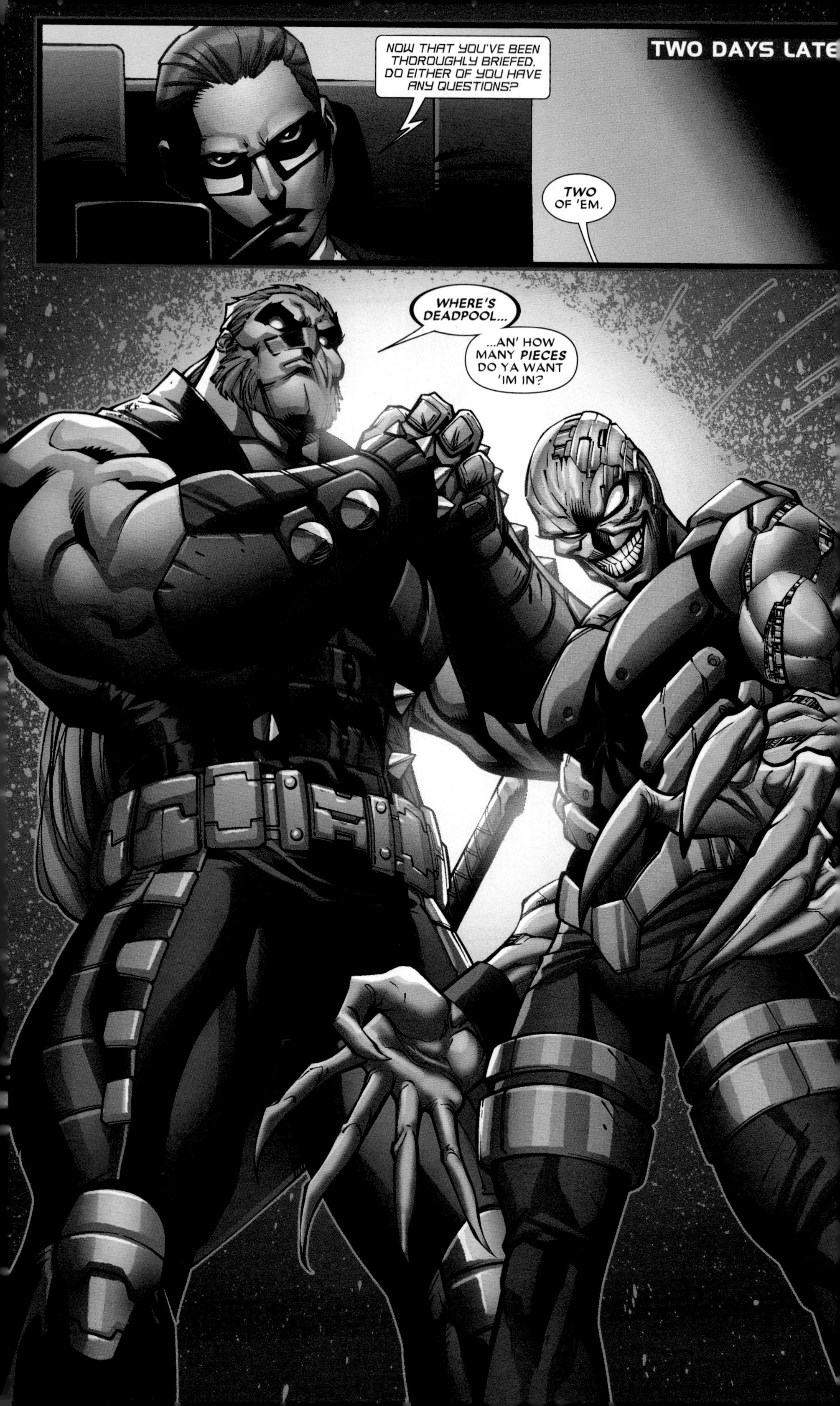
TWO DAYS LATE
NOW THAT YOU'VE BEEN THOROUGHLY BRIEFED, DO EITHER OF YOU HAVE ANY QUESTIONS?
TWO OF 'EM.
WHERE'S DEADPOOL...
...AN' HOW MANY PIECES DO YA WANT 'IM IN?

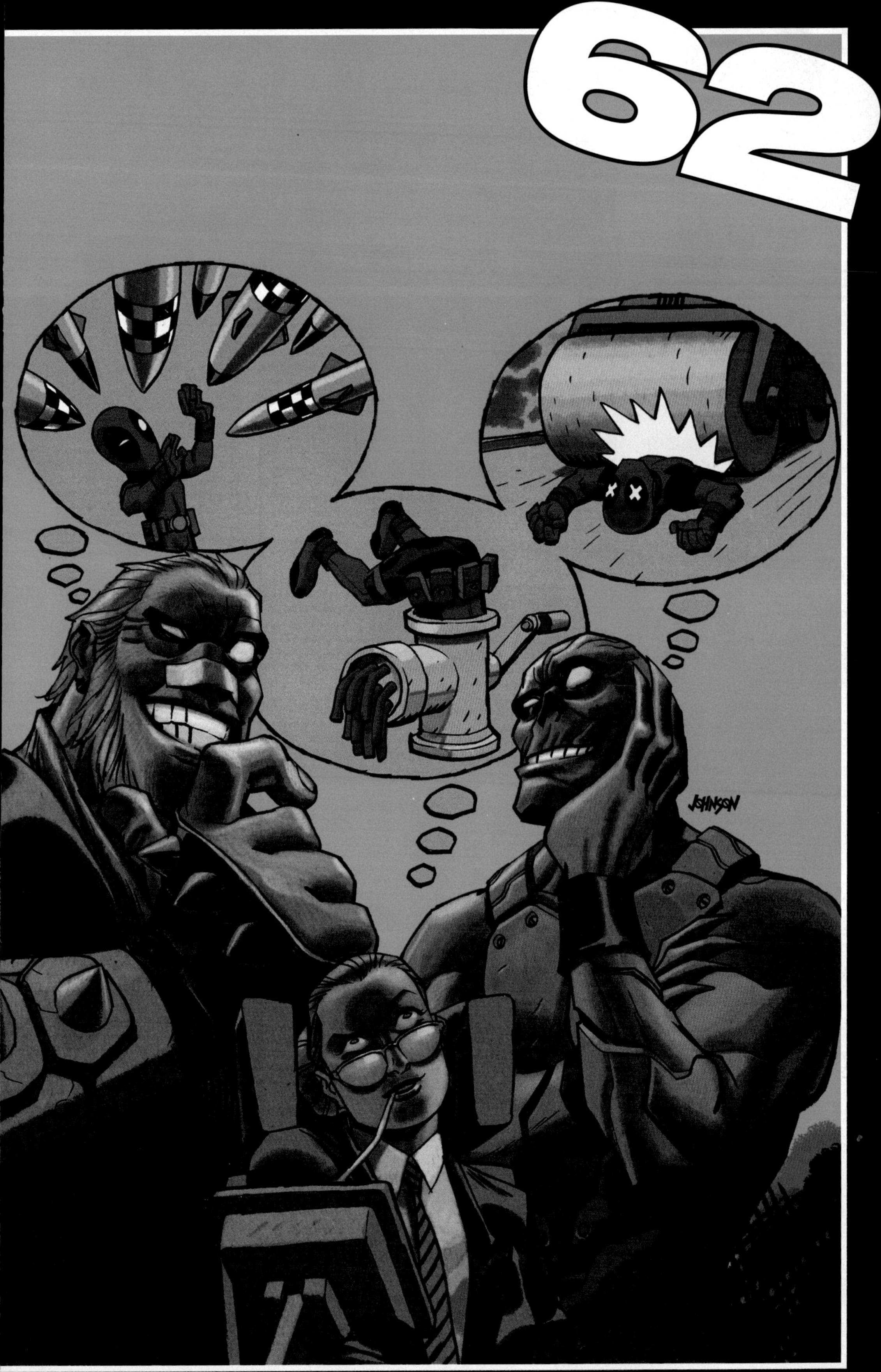
62
JOHNSON

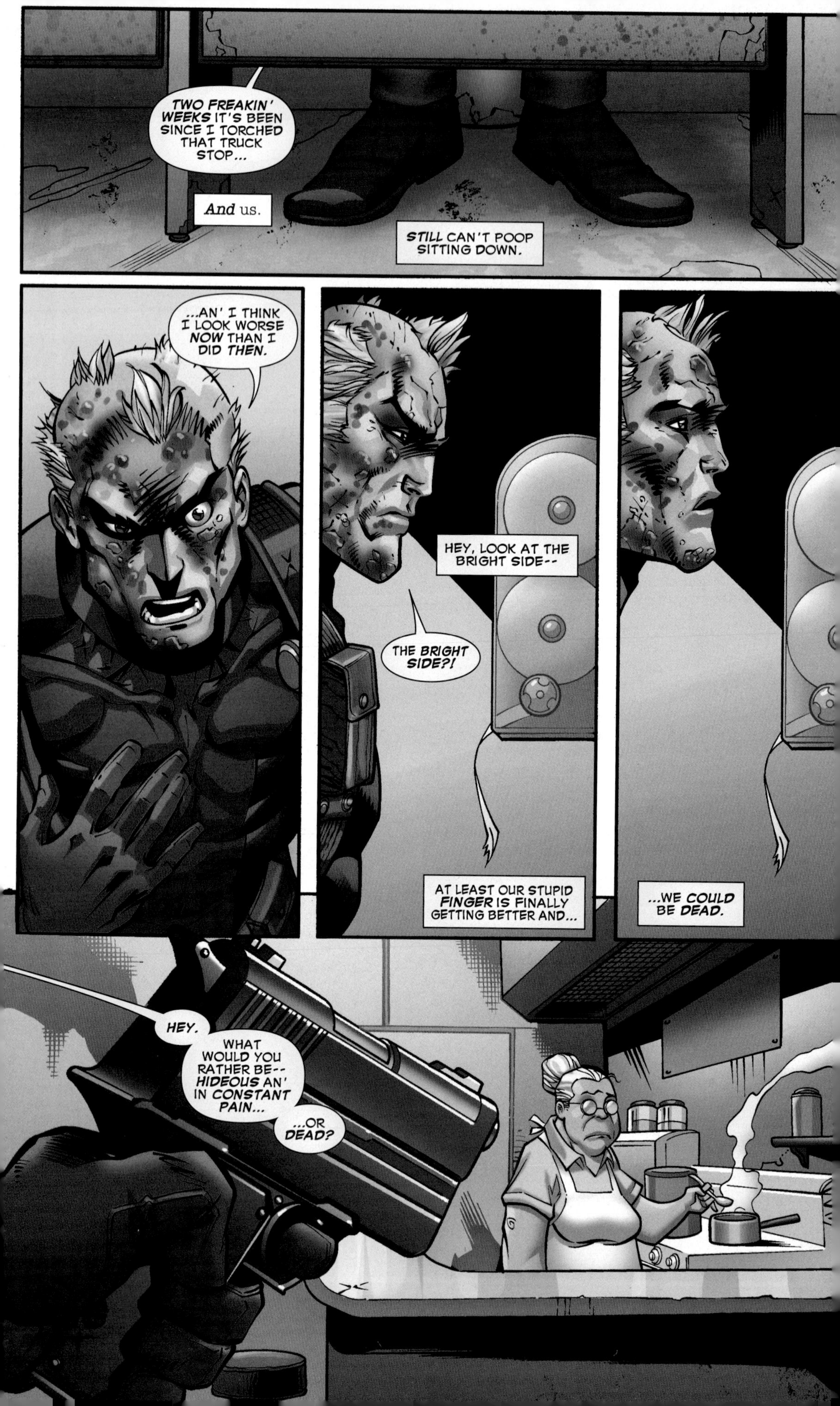
TWO FREAKIN' WEEKS IT'S BEEN SINCE I TORCHED THAT TRUCK STOP...
And us.
STILL CAN'T POOP SITTING DOWN.
...AN' I THINK I LOOK WORSE NOW THAN I DID THEN.
HEY, LOOK AT THE BRIGHT SIDE--
THE BRIGHT SIDE?!
AT LEAST OUR STUPID FINGER IS FINALLY GETTING BETTER AND...
...WE COULD BE DEAD.
HEY.
WHAT WOULD YOU RATHER BE--HIDEOUS AN' IN CONSTANT PAIN...
...OR DEAD?

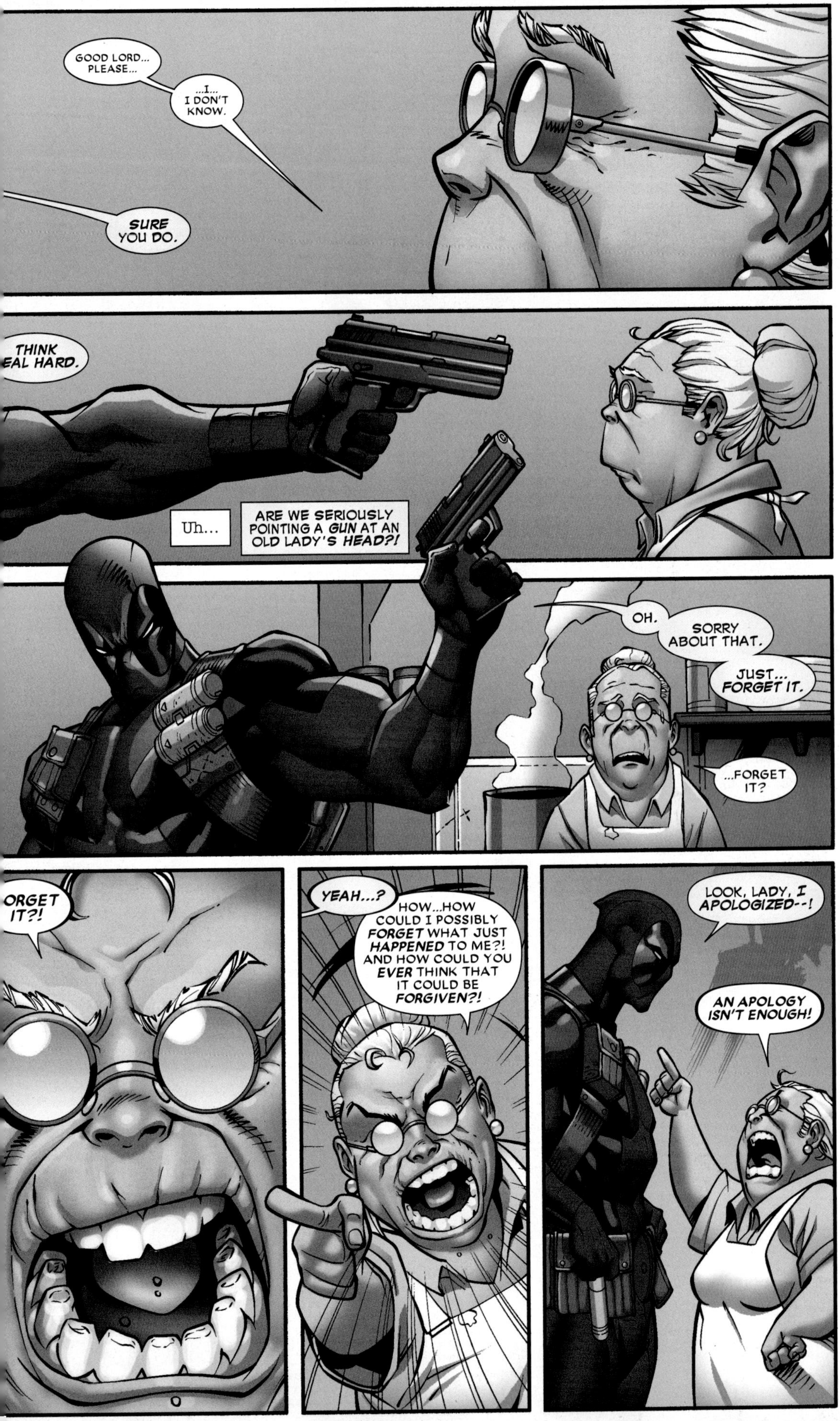

GOOD LORD... PLEASE...
...I... I DON'T KNOW.
SURE YOU DO.
THINK EAL HARD.
Uh...
ARE WE SERIOUSLY POINTING A GUN AT AN OLD LADY'S HEAD?!
OH.
SORRY ABOUT THAT.
JUST... FORGET IT.
...FORGET IT?
ORGET IT?!
YEAH...?
HOW...HOW COULD I POSSIBLY FORGET WHAT JUST HAPPENED TO ME?! AND HOW COULD YOU EVER THINK THAT IT COULD BE FORGIVEN?!
LOOK, LADY, I APOLOGIZED--!
AN APOLOGY ISN'T ENOUGH!

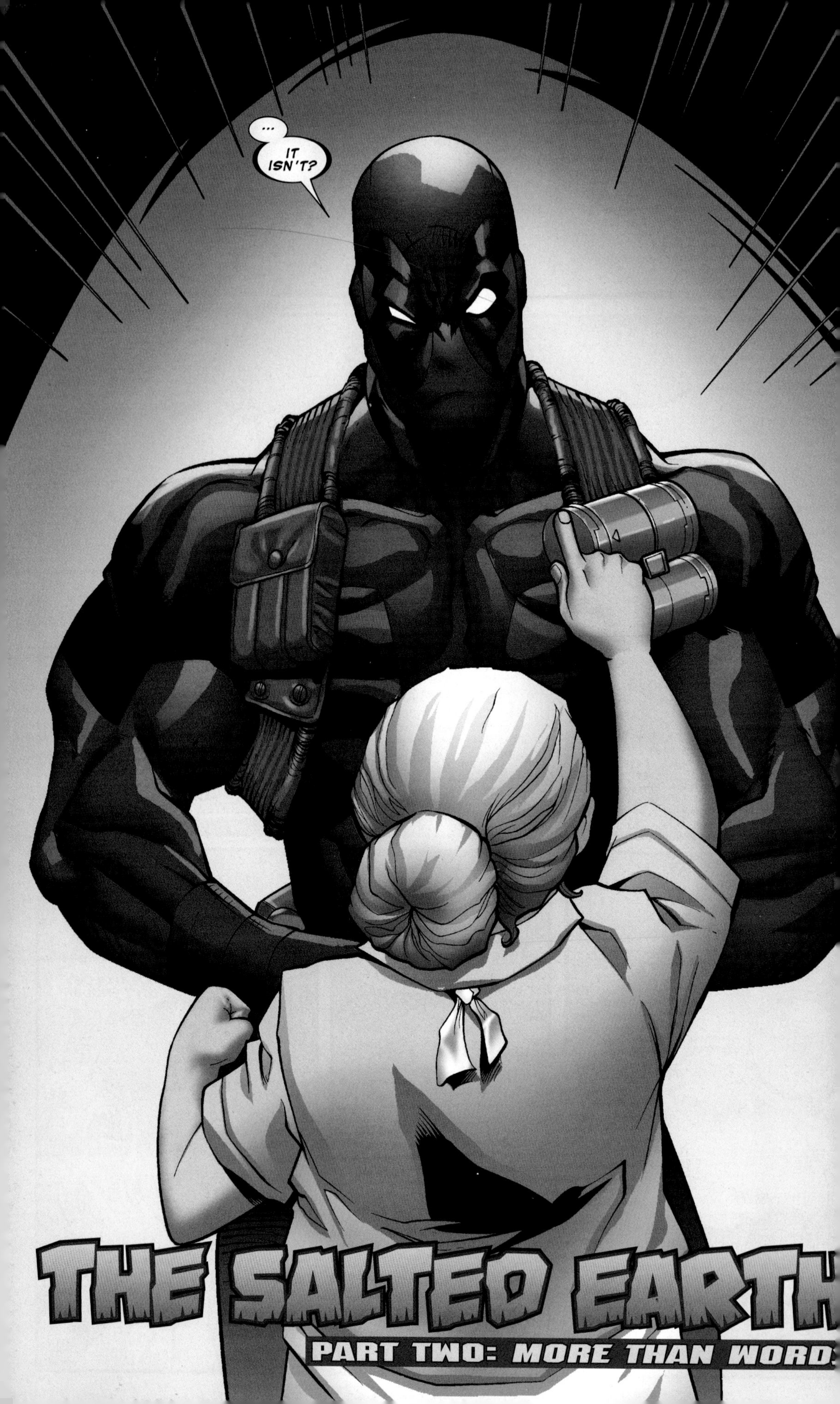
...
IT ISN'T?
THE SALTED EARTH
PART TWO: MORE THAN WORD

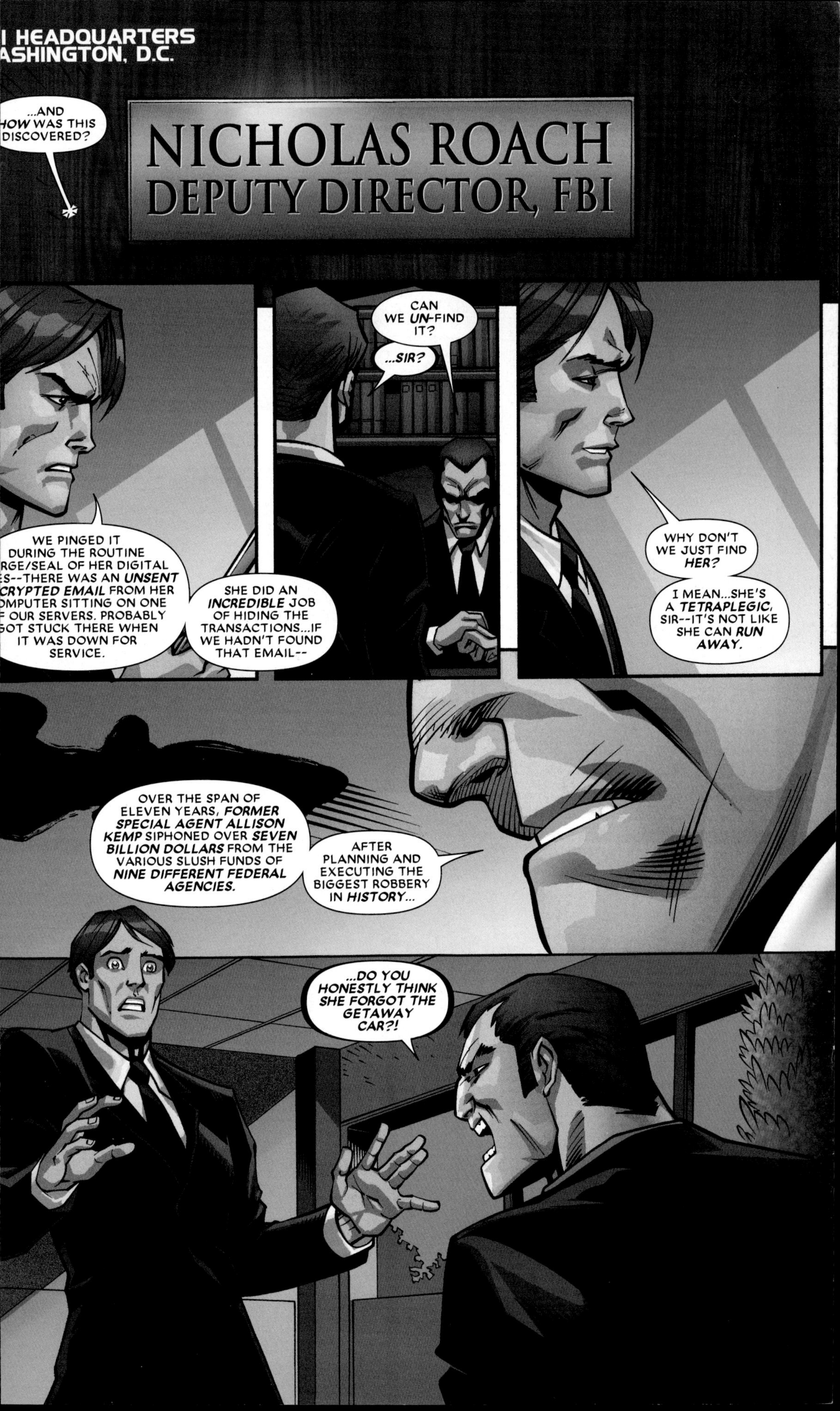

I HEADQUARTERS
ASHINGTON, D.C.
...AND HOW WAS THIS DISCOVERED?
NICHOLAS ROACH
DEPUTY DIRECTOR, FBI
WE PINGED IT DURING THE ROUTINE RGE/SEAL OF HER DIGITAL ES--THERE WAS AN UNSENT CRYPTED EMAIL FROM HER OMPUTER SITTING ON ONE F OUR SERVERS. PROBABLY GOT STUCK THERE WHEN IT WAS DOWN FOR SERVICE.
SHE DID AN INCREDIBLE JOB OF HIDING THE TRANSACTIONS...IF WE HADN'T FOUND THAT EMAIL--
CAN WE UN-FIND IT?
...SIR?
WHY DON'T WE JUST FIND HER?
I MEAN...SHE'S A TETRAPLEGIC, SIR--IT'S NOT LIKE SHE CAN RUN AWAY.
OVER THE SPAN OF ELEVEN YEARS, FORMER SPECIAL AGENT ALLISON KEMP SIPHONED OVER SEVEN BILLION DOLLARS FROM THE VARIOUS SLUSH FUNDS OF NINE DIFFERENT FEDERAL AGENCIES.
AFTER PLANNING AND EXECUTING THE BIGGEST ROBBERY IN HISTORY...
...DO YOU HONESTLY THINK SHE FORGOT THE GETAWAY CAR?!

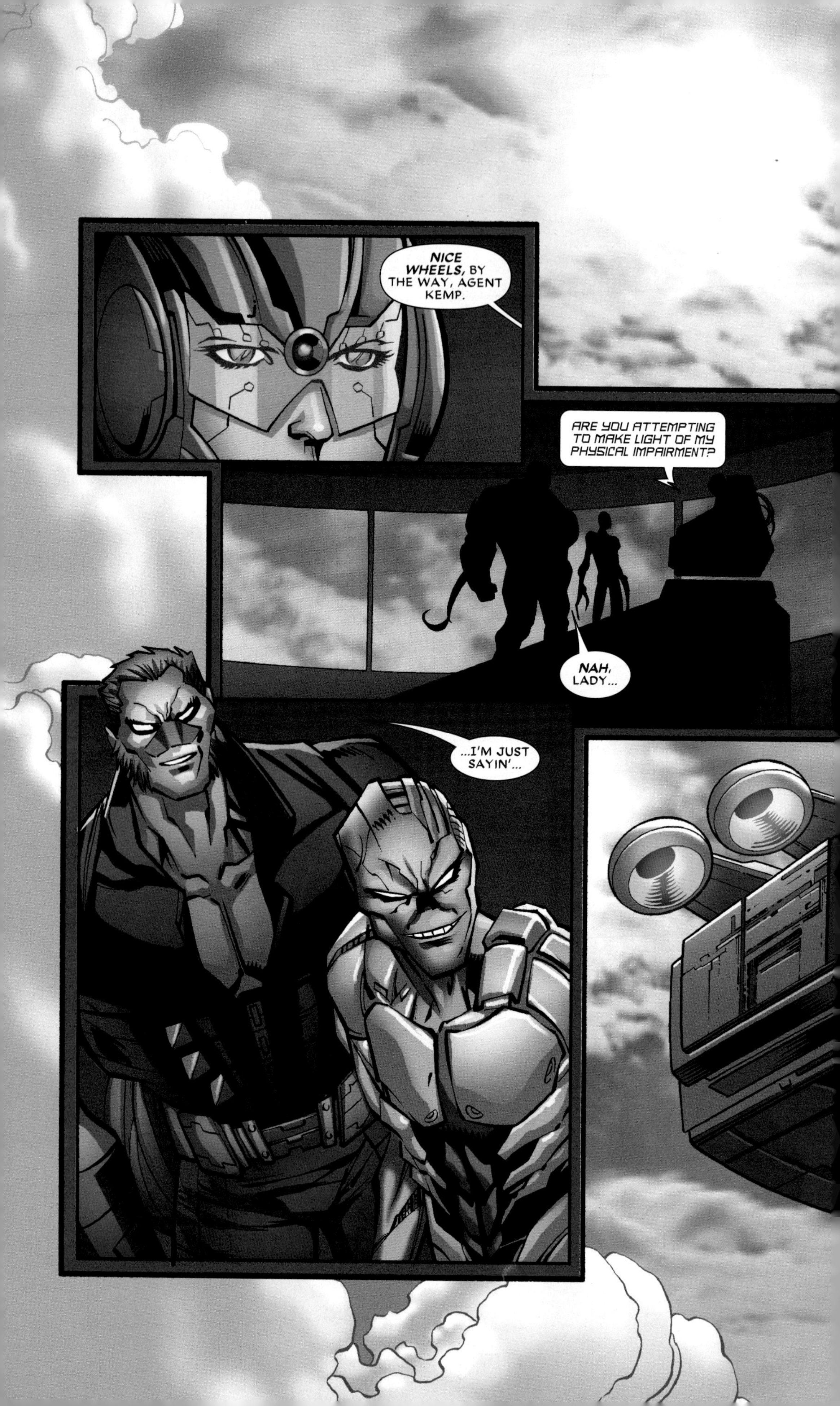
NICE WHEELS, BY THE WAY, AGENT KEMP.
ARE YOU ATTEMPTING TO MAKE LIGHT OF MY PHYSICAL IMPAIRMENT?
NAH, LADY...
...I'M JUST SAYIN'...

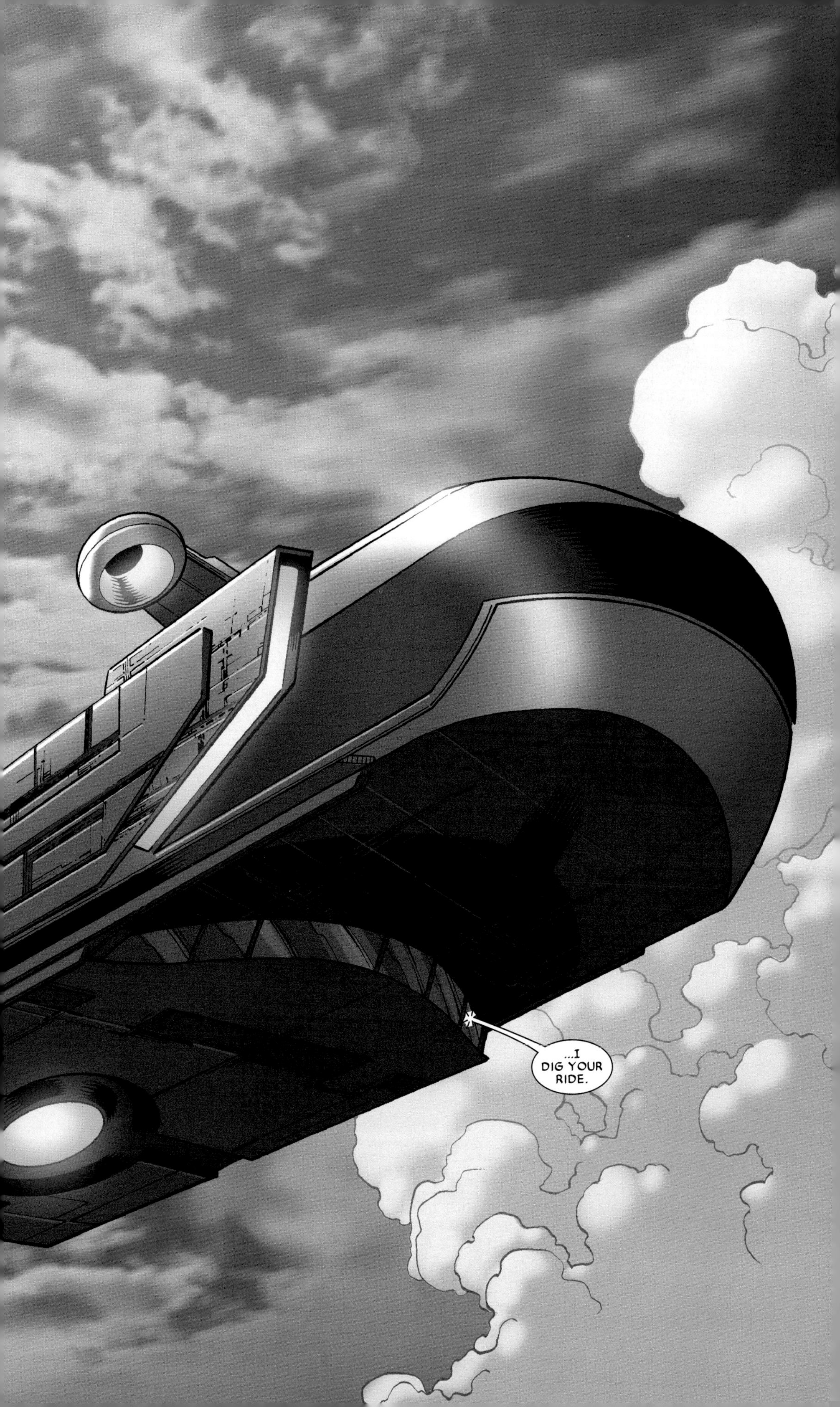
...I DIG YOUR RIDE.

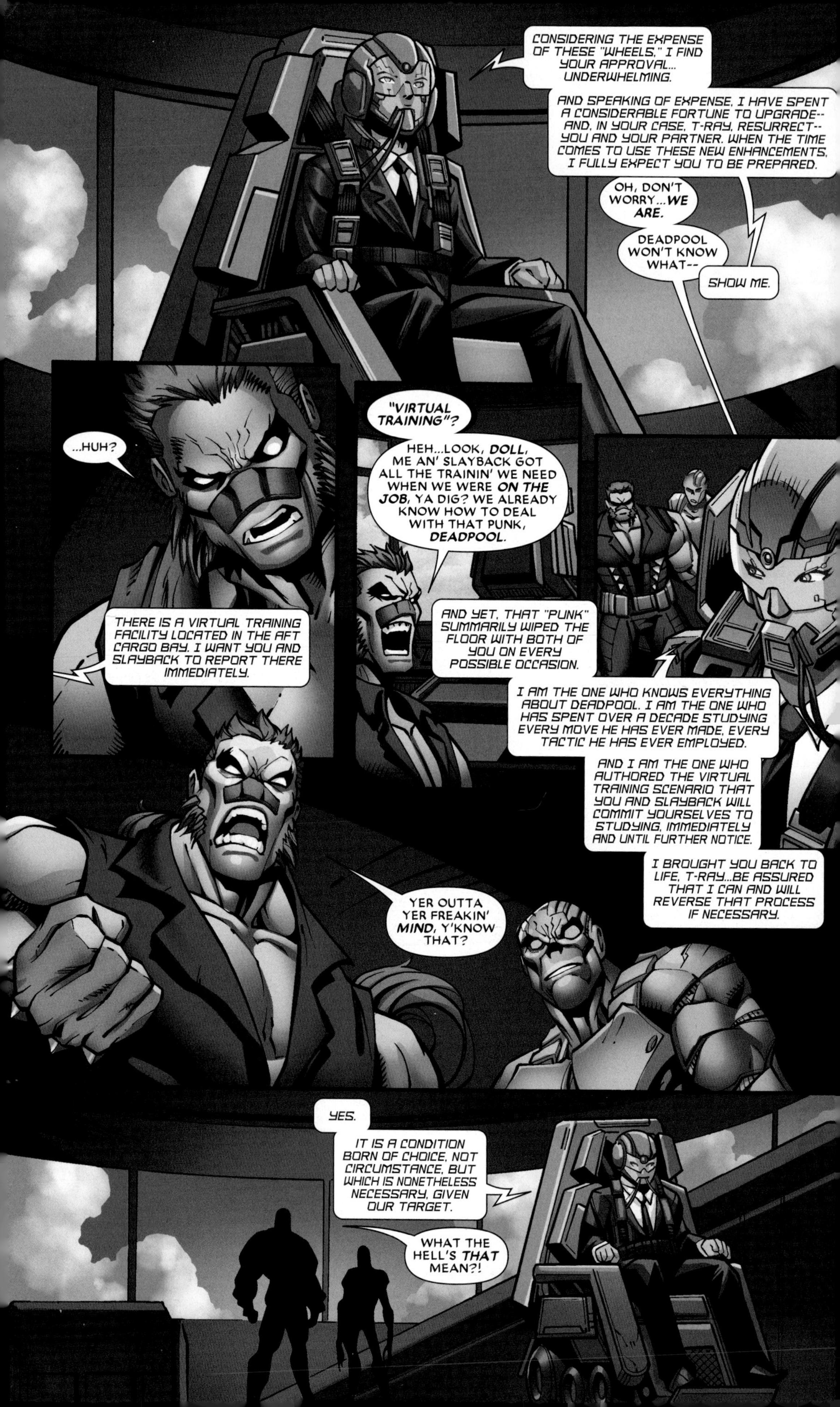
CONSIDERING THE EXPENSE OF THESE "WHEELS," I FIND YOUR APPROVAL... UNDERWHELMING.
AND SPEAKING OF EXPENSE, I HAVE SPENT A CONSIDERABLE FORTUNE TO UPGRADE-- AND, IN YOUR CASE, T-RAY, RESURRECT-- YOU AND YOUR PARTNER. WHEN THE TIME COMES TO USE THESE NEW ENHANCEMENTS, I FULLY EXPECT YOU TO BE PREPARED.
OH, DON'T WORRY...WE ARE.
DEADPOOL WON'T KNOW WHAT--
SHOW ME.
...HUH?
THERE IS A VIRTUAL TRAINING FACILITY LOCATED IN THE AFT CARGO BAY. I WANT YOU AND SLAYBACK TO REPORT THERE IMMEDIATELY.
"VIRTUAL TRAINING"?
HEH...LOOK, DOLL, ME AN' SLAYBACK GOT ALL THE TRAININ' WE NEED WHEN WE WERE ON THE JOB, YA DIG? WE ALREADY KNOW HOW TO DEAL WITH THAT PUNK, DEADPOOL.
AND YET, THAT "PUNK" SUMMARILY WIPED THE FLOOR WITH BOTH OF YOU ON EVERY POSSIBLE OCCASION.
I AM THE ONE WHO KNOWS EVERYTHING ABOUT DEADPOOL. I AM THE ONE WHO HAS SPENT OVER A DECADE STUDYING EVERY MOVE HE HAS EVER MADE, EVERY TACTIC HE HAS EVER EMPLOYED.
AND I AM THE ONE WHO AUTHORED THE VIRTUAL TRAINING SCENARIO THAT YOU AND SLAYBACK WILL COMMIT YOURSELVES TO STUDYING, IMMEDIATELY AND UNTIL FURTHER NOTICE.
I BROUGHT YOU BACK TO LIFE, T-RAY...BE ASSURED THAT I CAN AND WILL REVERSE THAT PROCESS IF NECESSARY.
YER OUTTA YER FREAKIN' MIND, Y'KNOW THAT?
YES.
IT IS A CONDITION BORN OF CHOICE, NOT CIRCUMSTANCE, BUT WHICH IS NONETHELESS NECESSARY, GIVEN OUR TARGET.
WHAT THE HELL'S THAT MEAN?!

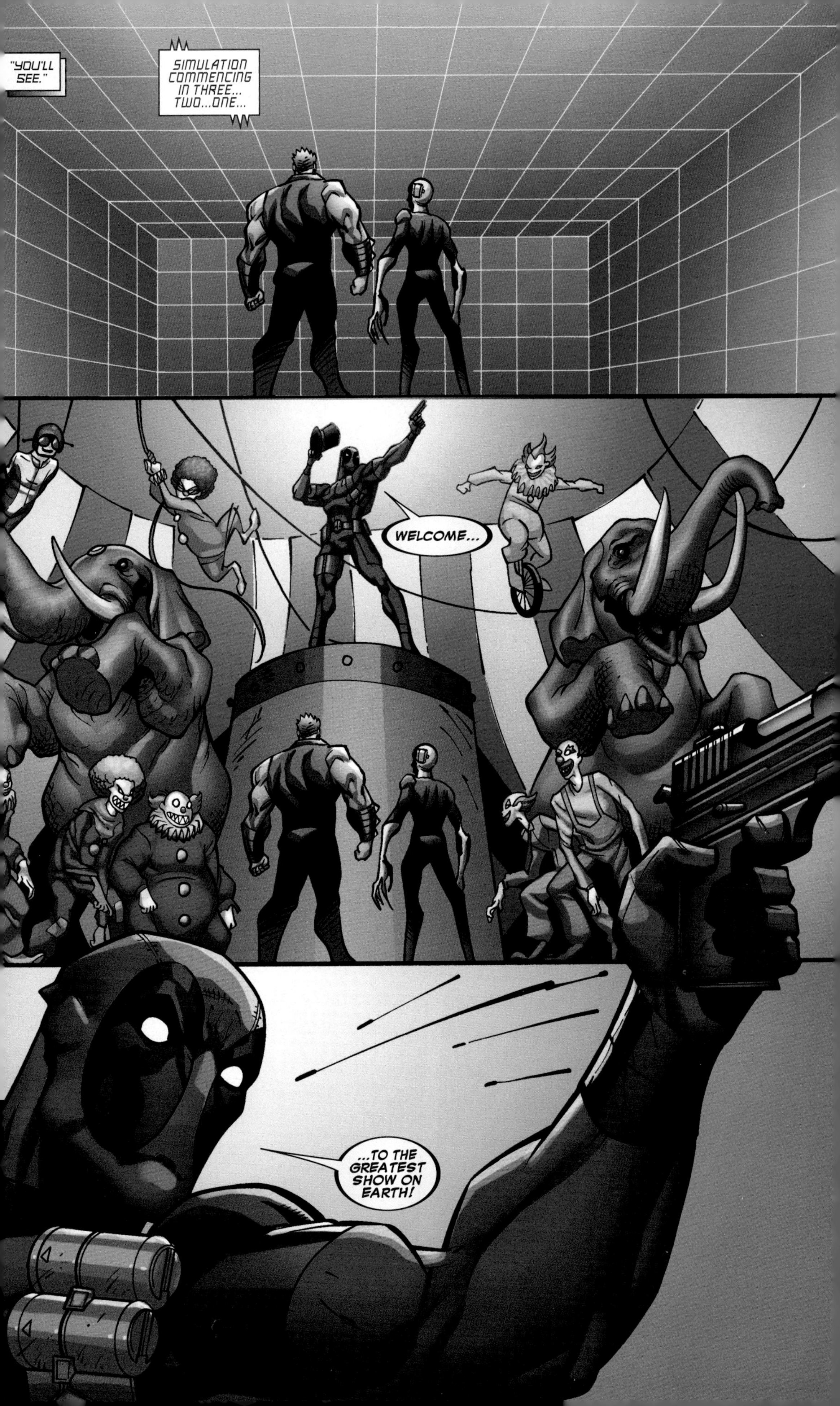

"YOU'LL SEE."
SIMULATION COMMENCING IN THREE... TWO...ONE...
WELCOME...
...TO THE GREATEST SHOW ON EARTH!

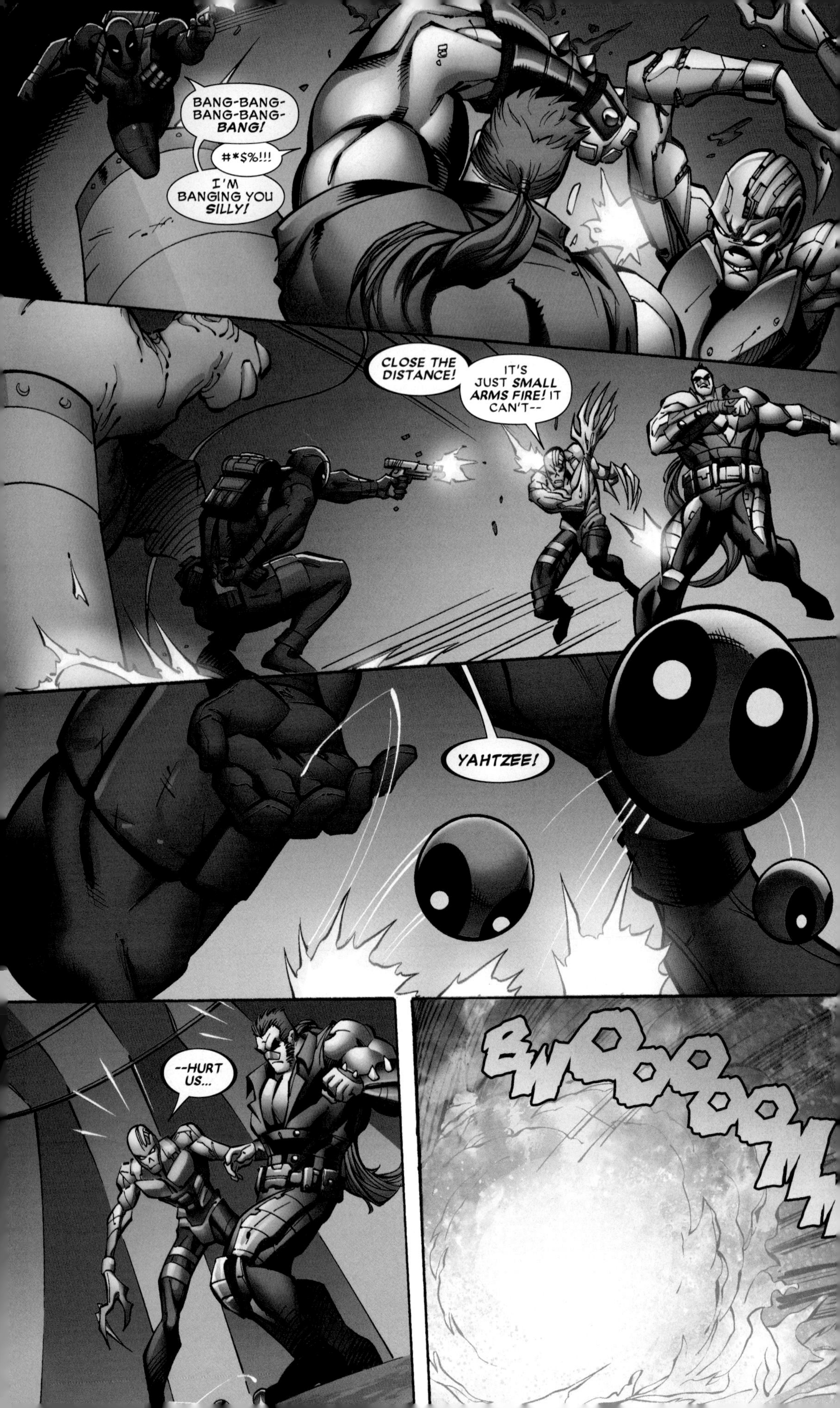

BANG-BANG-BANG-BANG-BANG!
#*$%!!!
I'M BANGING YOU SILLY!
CLOSE THE DISTANCE!
IT'S JUST SMALL ARMS FIRE! IT CAN'T--
YAHTZEE!
--HURT US...
BWOOOOOM

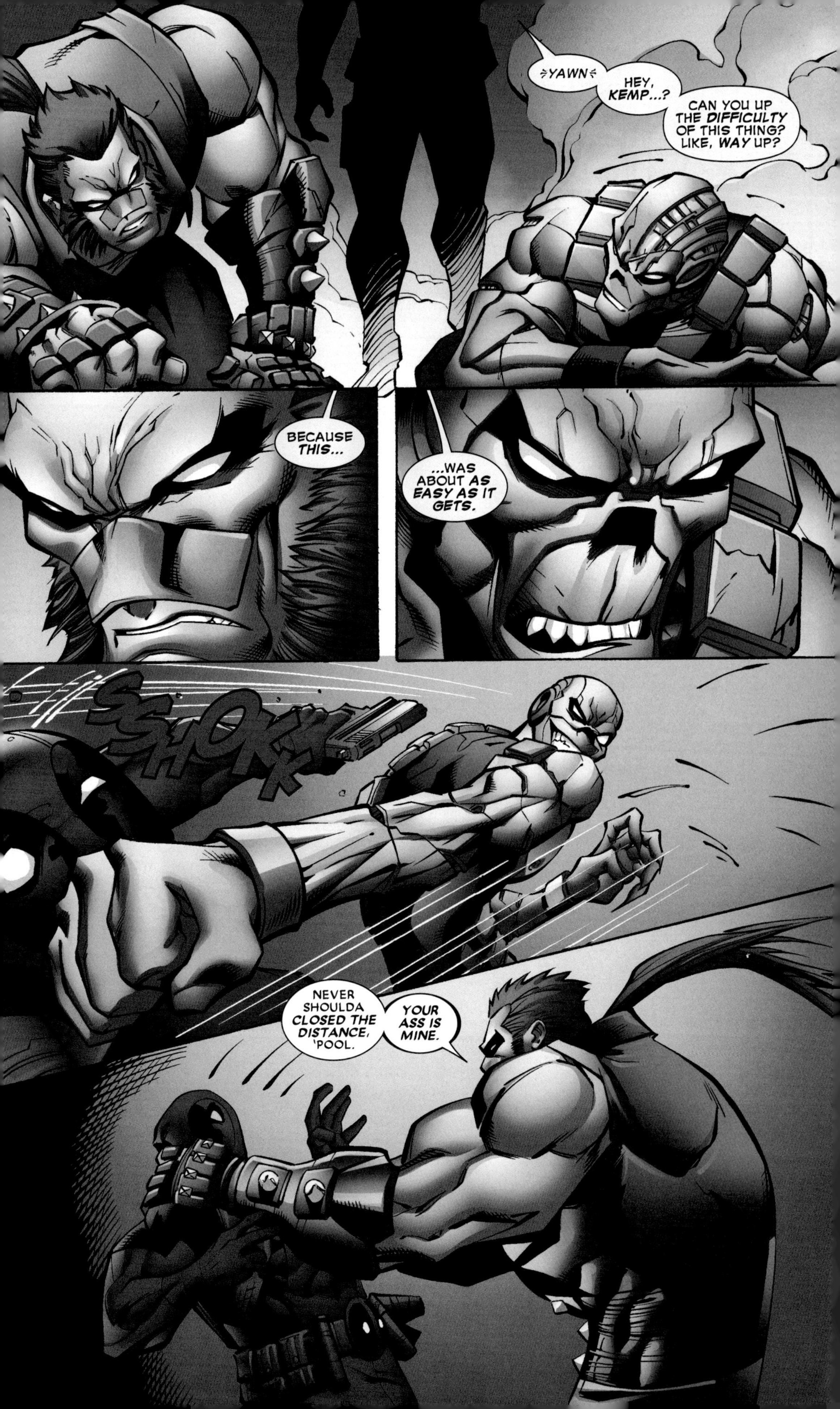
≈YAWN≈
HEY, KEMP...?
CAN YOU UP THE DIFFICULTY OF THIS THING? LIKE, WAY UP?
BECAUSE THIS...
...WAS ABOUT AS EASY AS IT GETS.
SSHOKK
NEVER SHOULDA CLOSED THE DISTANCE, 'POOL.
YOUR ASS IS MINE.

WAIT-- WHAT?

"YOUR GAS IS MINE"?!

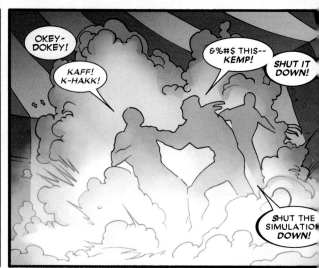

OKEY-DOKEY!

KAFF! K-HAKK!

&%#$ THIS-- KEMP!

SHUT IT DOWN!

SHUT THE SIMULATIO DOWN!

HOW'S THAT?

BETTER...?

BLAM BLAM BLAM

BLAM BLAM BLAM BLAM BLAM

BLAM

OR WORSE?

NO! IT'S HIM! HE'S REALLY--

FAILURE. TRY AGAIN.

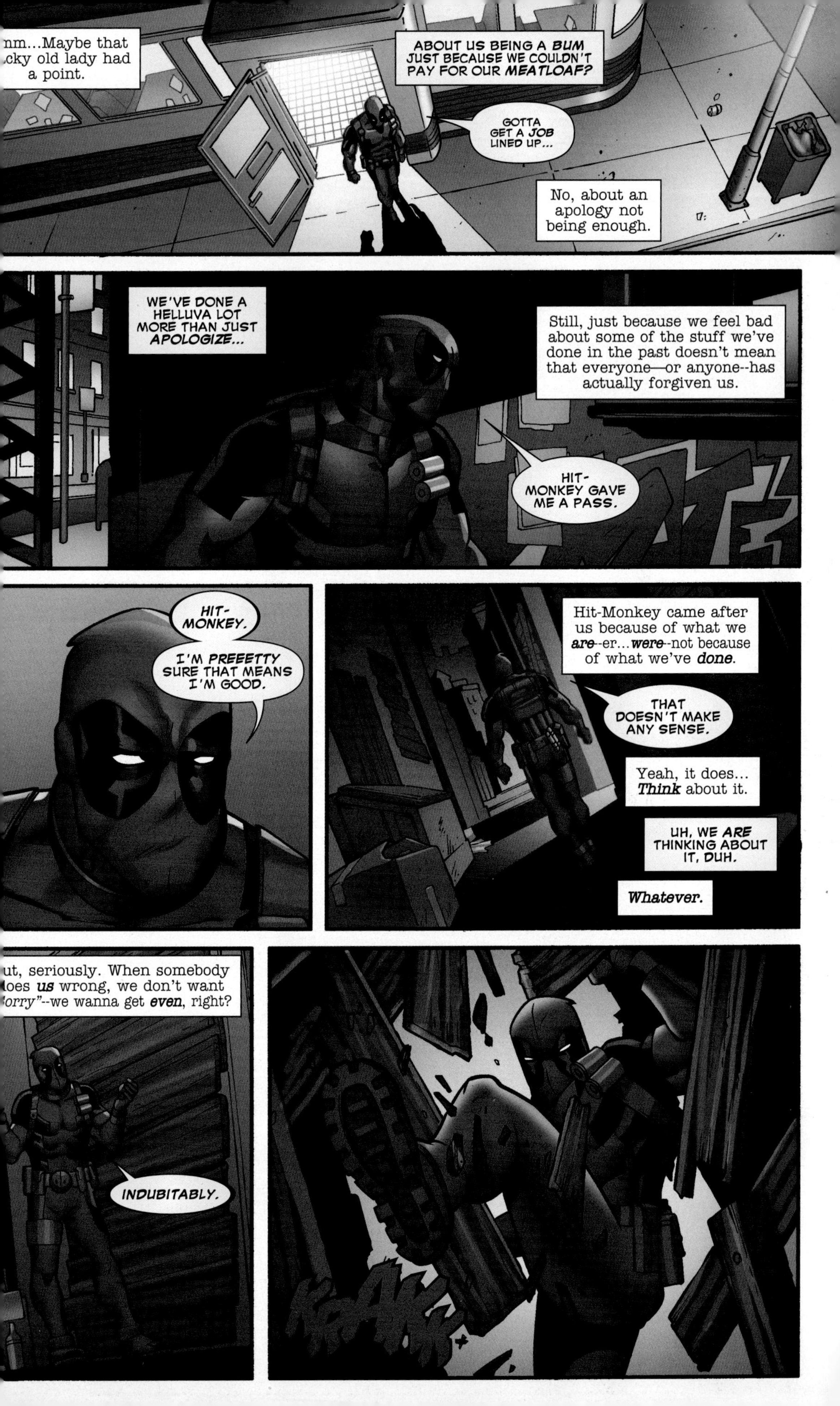

nm...Maybe that
cky old lady had
a point.
ABOUT US BEING A BUM JUST BECAUSE WE COULDN'T PAY FOR OUR MEATLOAF?
GOTTA GET A JOB LINED UP...
No, about an apology not being enough.
WE'VE DONE A HELLUVA LOT MORE THAN JUST APOLOGIZE...
Still, just because we feel bad about some of the stuff we've done in the past doesn't mean that everyone—or anyone--has actually forgiven us.
HIT-MONKEY GAVE ME A PASS.
HIT-MONKEY.
I'M PREEETTY SURE THAT MEANS I'M GOOD.
Hit-Monkey came after us because of what we are--er...were--not because of what we've done.
THAT DOESN'T MAKE ANY SENSE.
Yeah, it does... Think about it.
UH, WE ARE THINKING ABOUT IT, DUH.
Whatever.
ut, seriously. When somebody
loes us wrong, we don't want
orry"--we wanna get even, right?
INDUBITABLY.

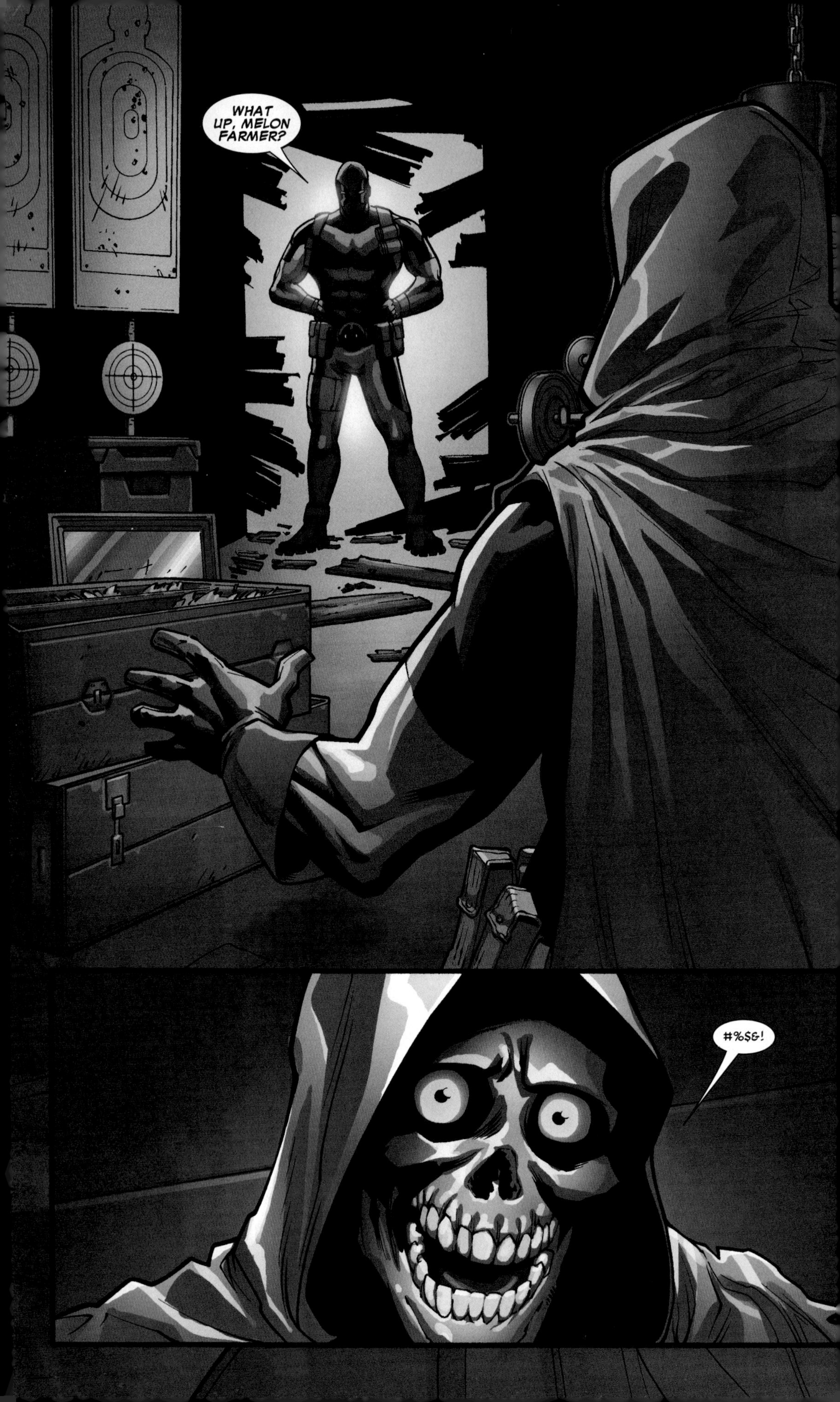
WHAT UP, MELON FARMER?
#%$&!

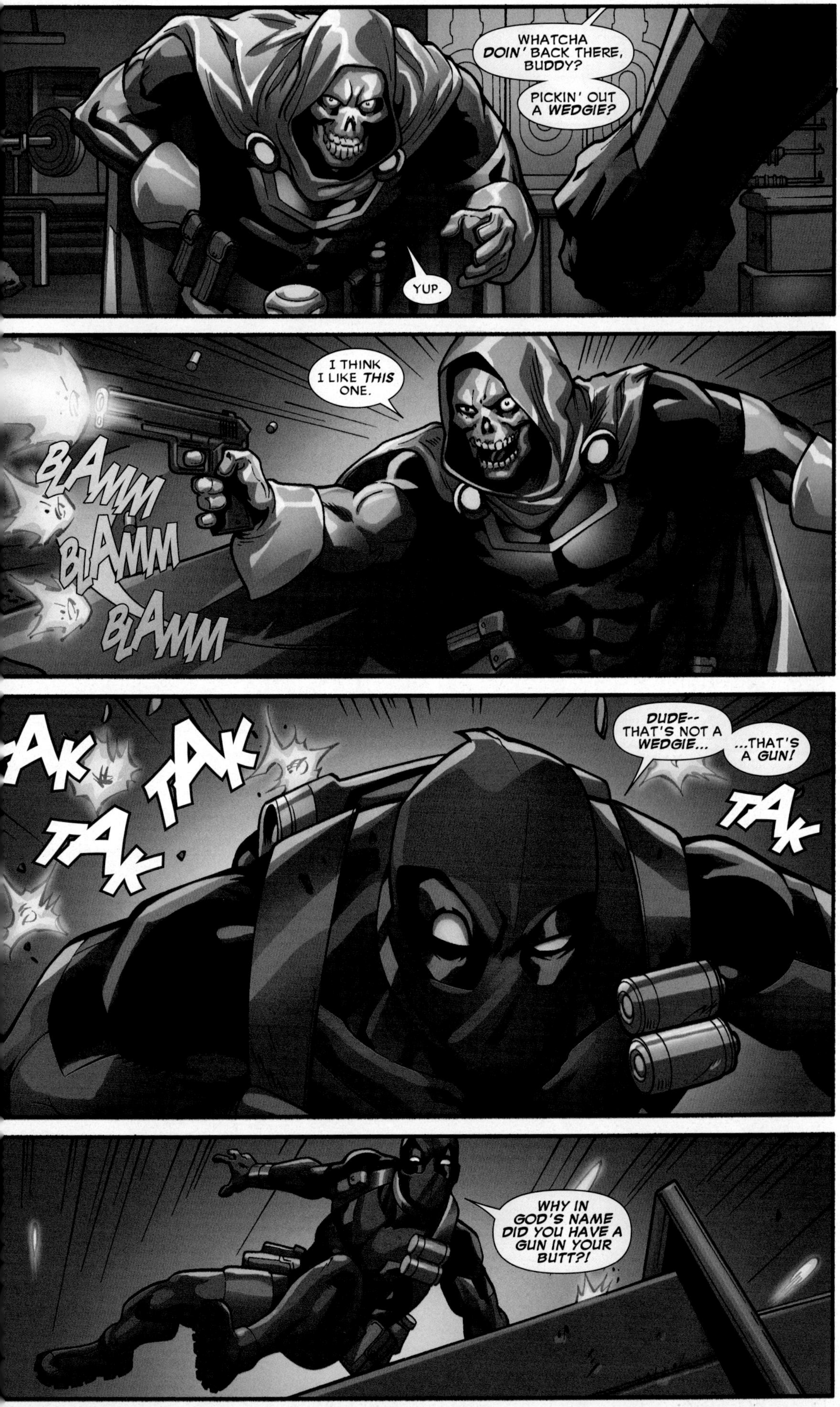
WHATCHA DOIN' BACK THERE, BUDDY?
PICKIN' OUT A WEDGIE?
YUP.
I THINK I LIKE THIS ONE.
BLAMM
BLAMM
BLAMM
TAK
TAK
TAK
DUDE-- THAT'S NOT A WEDGIE...
...THAT'S A GUN!
TAK
WHY IN GOD'S NAME DID YOU HAVE A GUN IN YOUR BUTT?!

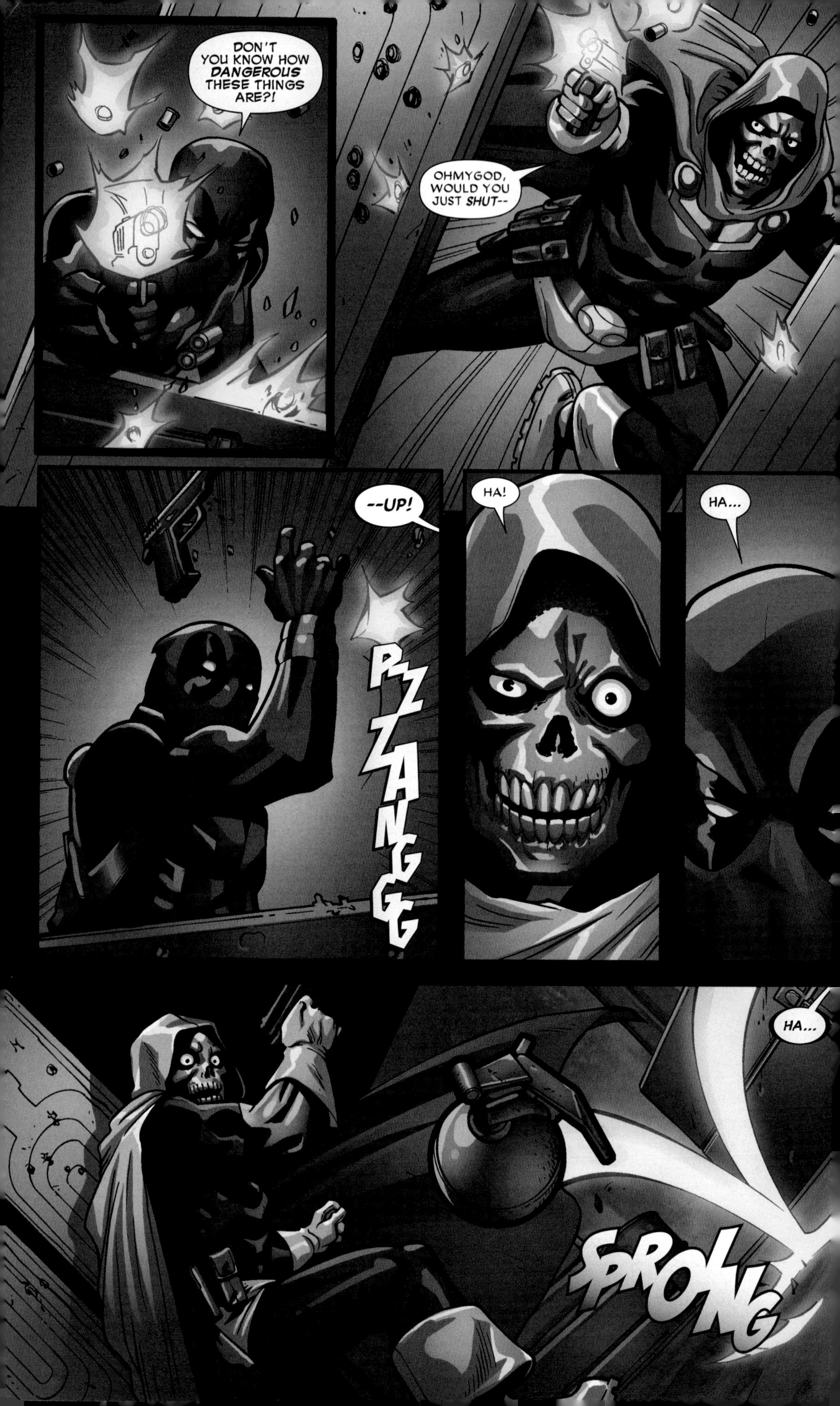
DON'T YOU KNOW HOW DANGEROUS THESE THINGS ARE?!
OHMYGOD, WOULD YOU JUST SHUT--
--UP!
PZZANGGG
HA!
HA...
HA...
SPROING

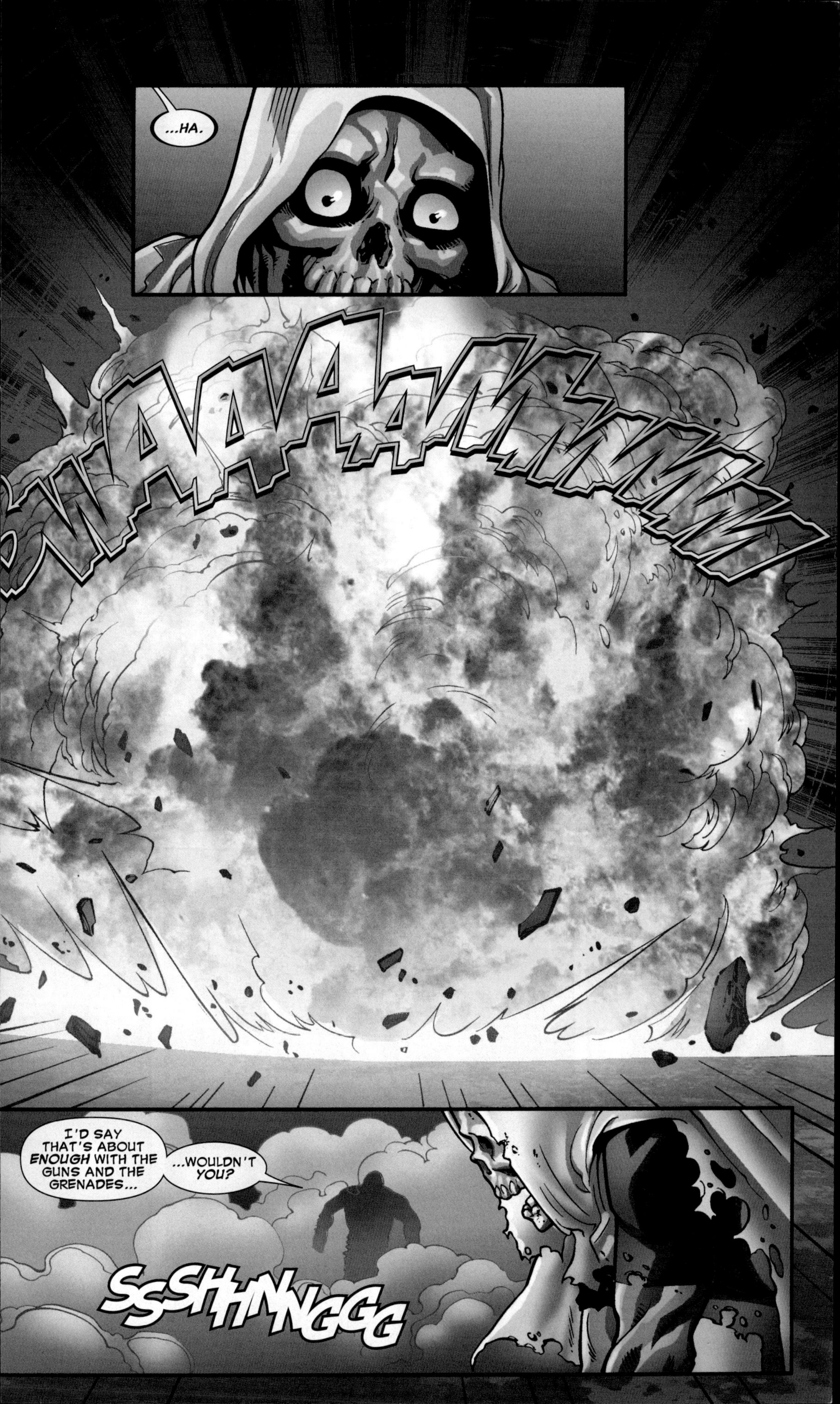

...HA.
BWAAAMMMM
I'D SAY THAT'S ABOUT *ENOUGH* WITH THE GUNS AND THE GRENADES...
...WOULDN'T *YOU?*
SSSHHNNGGG

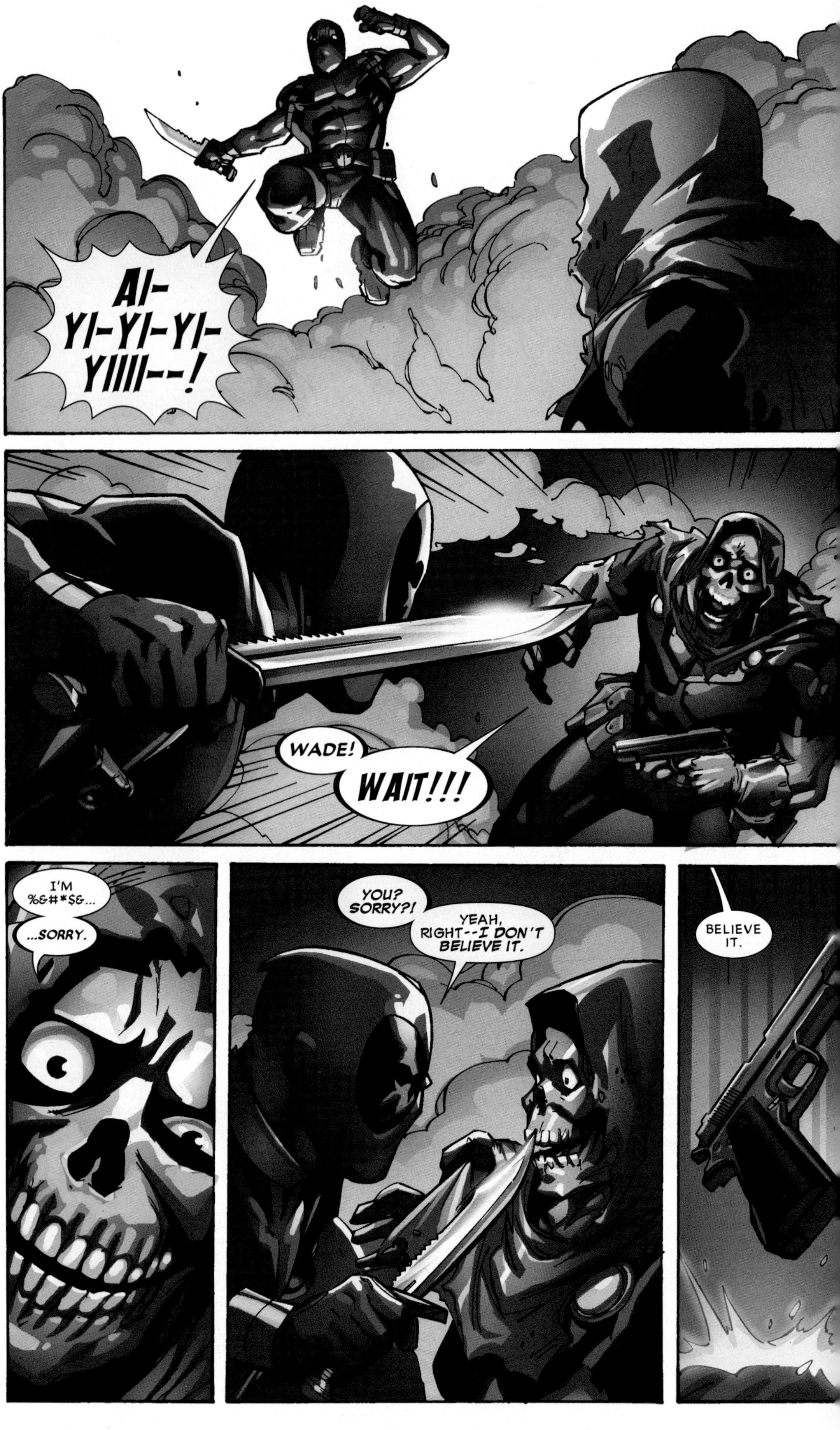
AI-
YI-YI-YI-
YIIII--!
WADE!
WAIT!!!
I'M
%&#*$&...
...SORRY.
YOU?
SORRY?!
YEAH,
RIGHT--I DON'T
BELIEVE IT.
BELIEVE
IT.

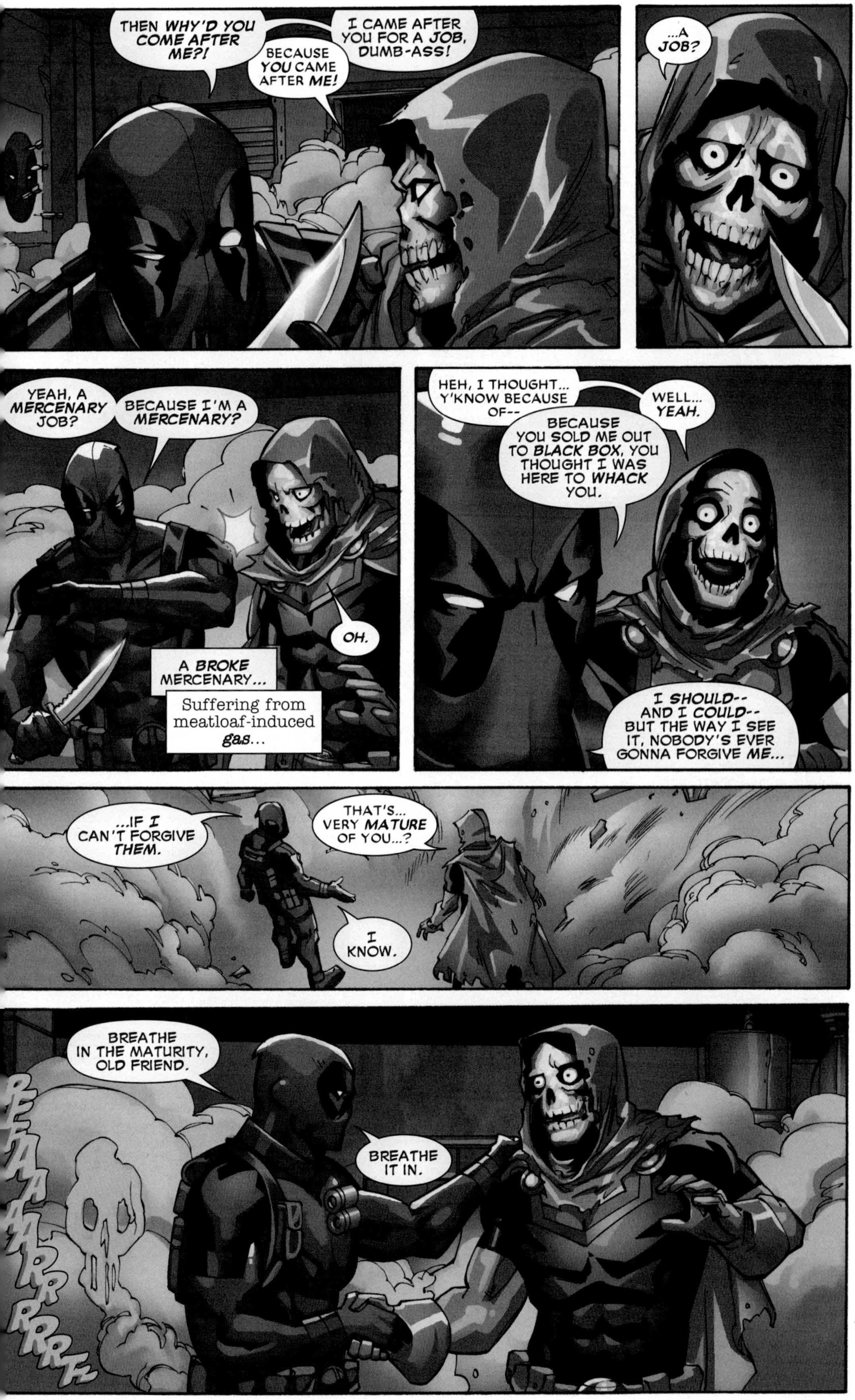

THEN WHY'D YOU COME AFTER ME?!
I CAME AFTER YOU FOR A JOB, DUMB-ASS!
BECAUSE YOU CAME AFTER ME!
...A JOB?
YEAH, A MERCENARY JOB?
BECAUSE I'M A MERCENARY?
A BROKE MERCENARY...
Suffering from meatloaf-induced gas...
OH.
HEH, I THOUGHT... Y'KNOW BECAUSE OF--
BECAUSE YOU SOLD ME OUT TO BLACK BOX, YOU THOUGHT I WAS HERE TO WHACK YOU.
WELL... YEAH.
I SHOULD-- AND I COULD-- BUT THE WAY I SEE IT, NOBODY'S EVER GONNA FORGIVE ME...
...IF I CAN'T FORGIVE THEM.
THAT'S... VERY MATURE OF YOU...?
I KNOW.
BREATHE IN THE MATURITY, OLD FRIEND.
BREATHE IT IN.
PFFAAAARRRRRF

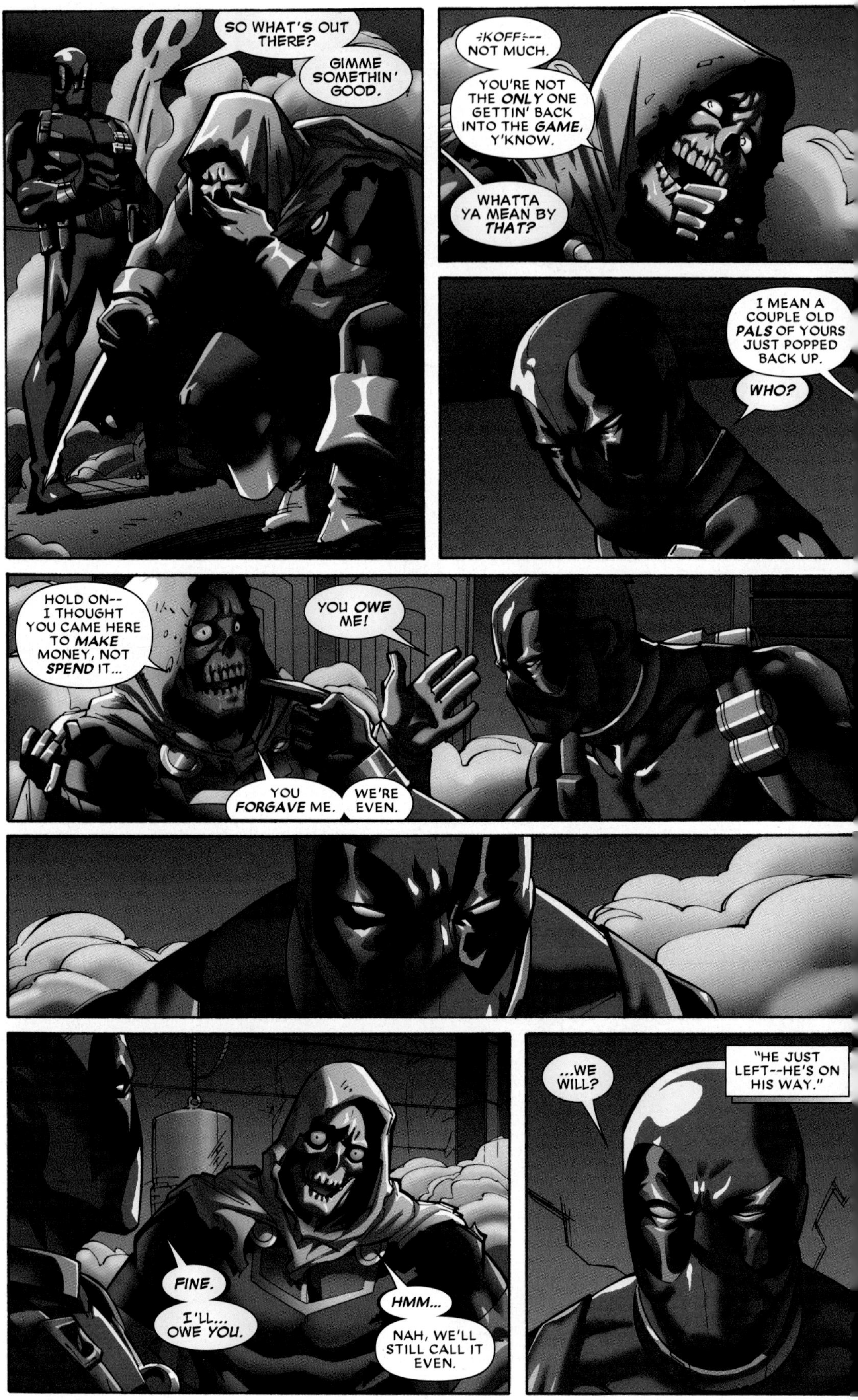

SO WHAT'S OUT THERE?
GIMME SOMETHIN' GOOD.
=KOFF=-- NOT MUCH.
YOU'RE NOT THE ONLY ONE GETTIN' BACK INTO THE GAME, Y'KNOW.
WHATTA YA MEAN BY THAT?
I MEAN A COUPLE OLD PALS OF YOURS JUST POPPED BACK UP.
WHO?
HOLD ON-- I THOUGHT YOU CAME HERE TO MAKE MONEY, NOT SPEND IT...
YOU OWE ME!
YOU FORGAVE ME.
WE'RE EVEN.
FINE.
I'LL... OWE YOU.
HMM...
NAH, WE'LL STILL CALL IT EVEN.
...WE WILL?
"HE JUST LEFT--HE'S ON HIS WAY."

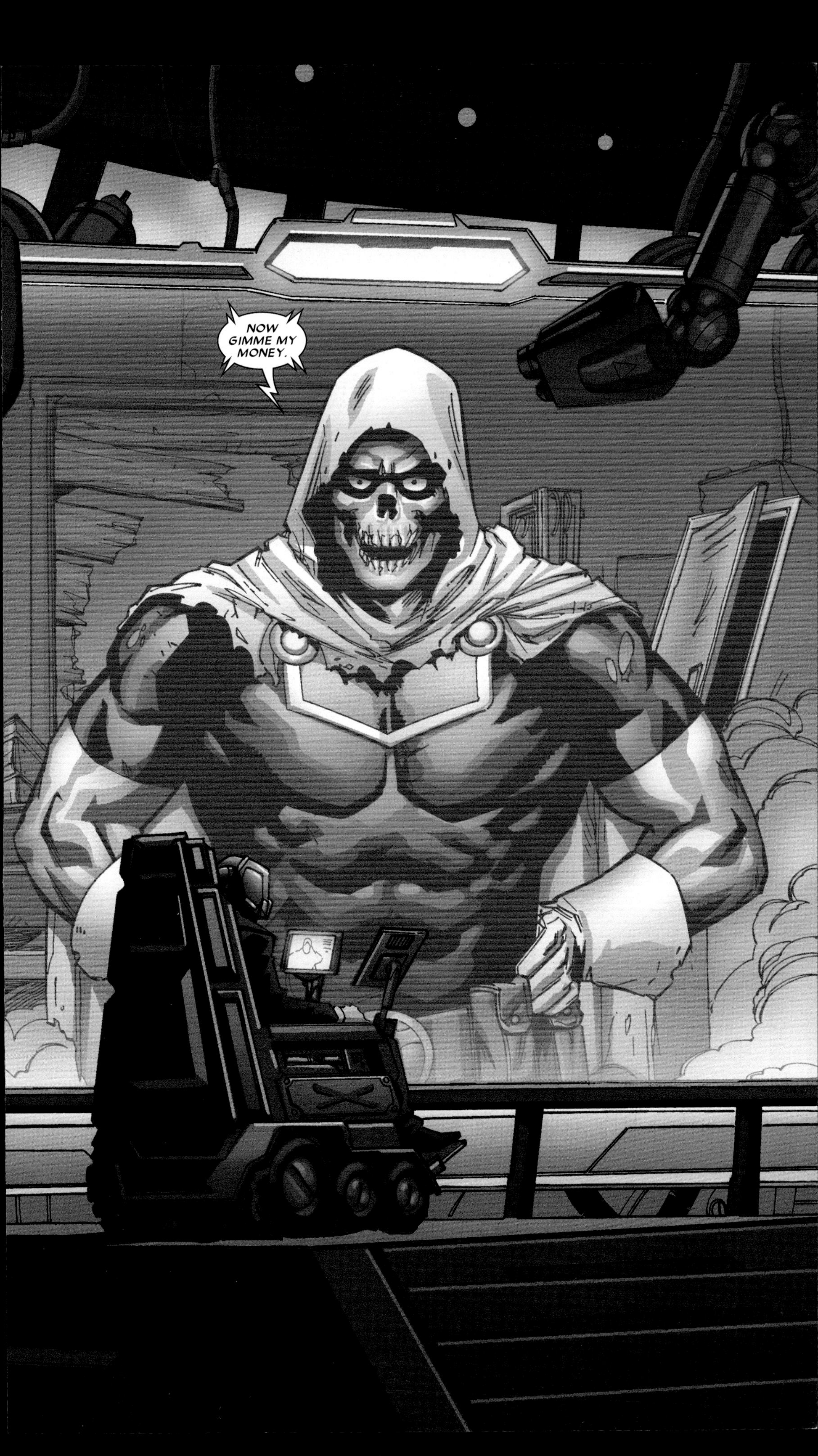
NOW GIMME MY MONEY.

63

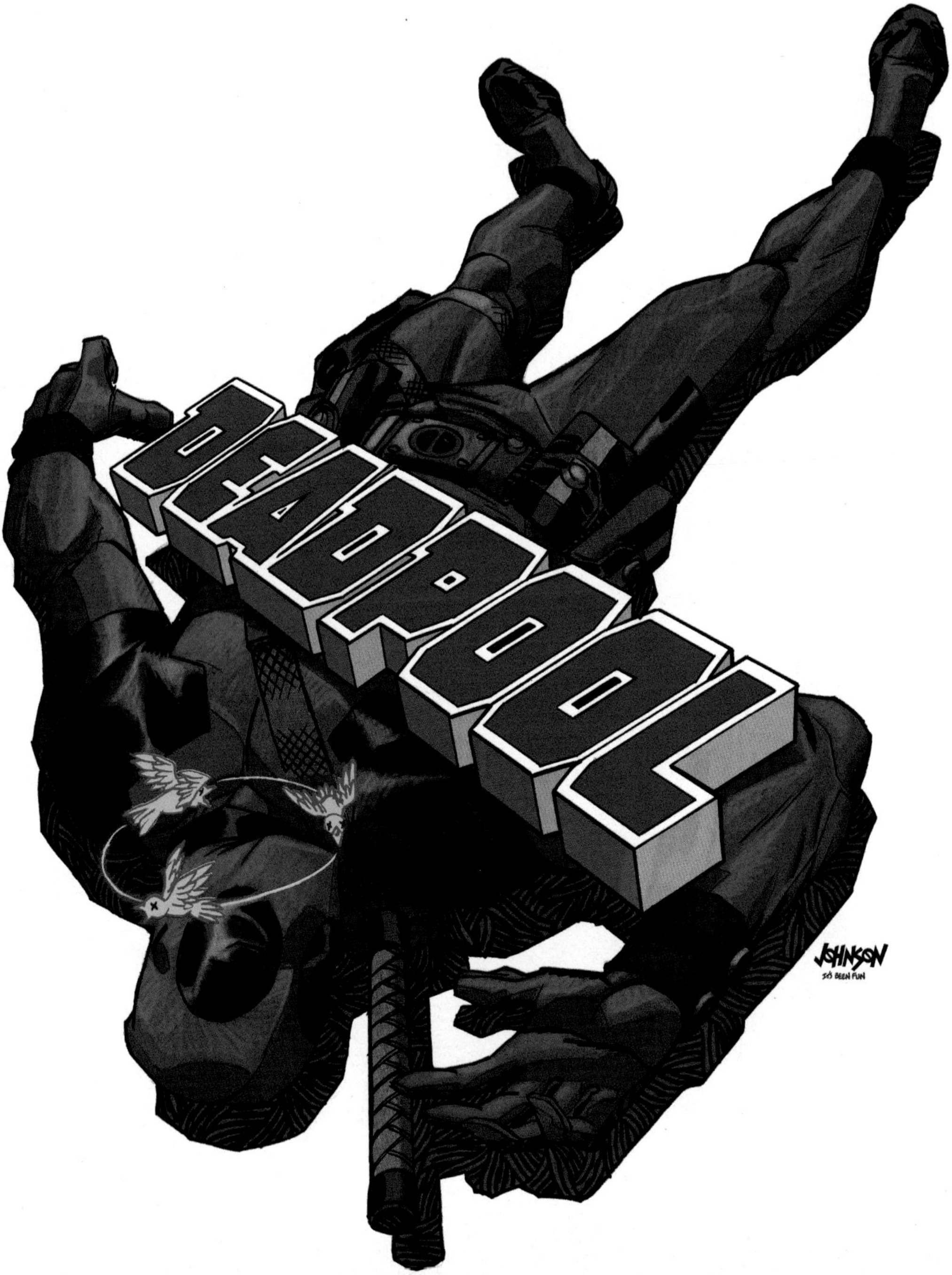
DEADPOOL
JOHNSON
IT'S BEEN FUN

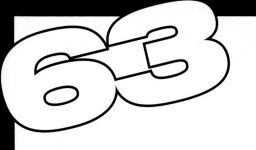

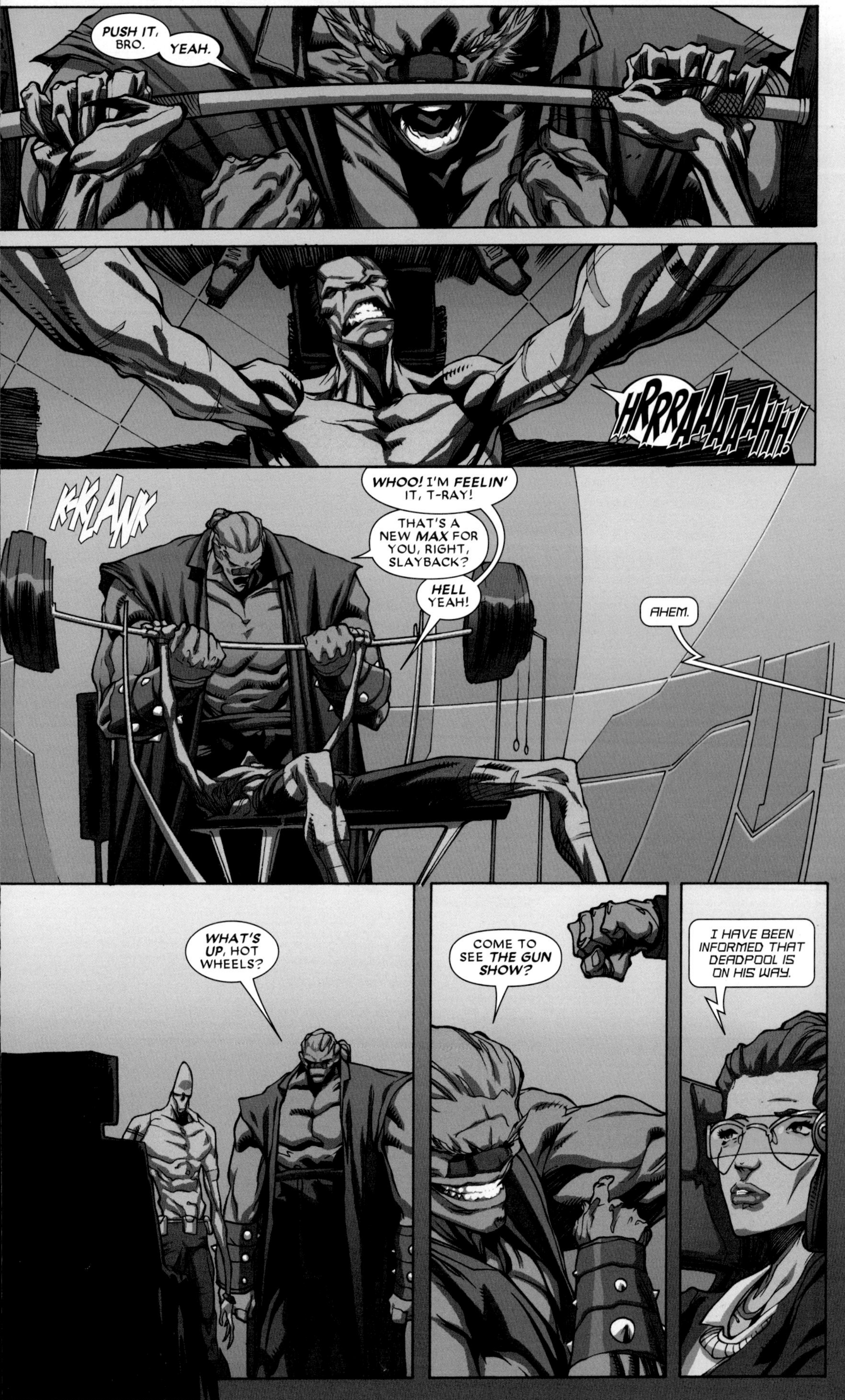
PUSH IT, BRO.
YEAH.
HRRRAAAAAHH!
K-KLANK
WHOO! I'M FEELIN' IT, T-RAY!
THAT'S A NEW MAX FOR YOU, RIGHT, SLAYBACK?
HELL YEAH!
AHEM.
WHAT'S UP, HOT WHEELS?
COME TO SEE THE GUN SHOW?
I HAVE BEEN INFORMED THAT DEADPOOL IS ON HIS WAY.

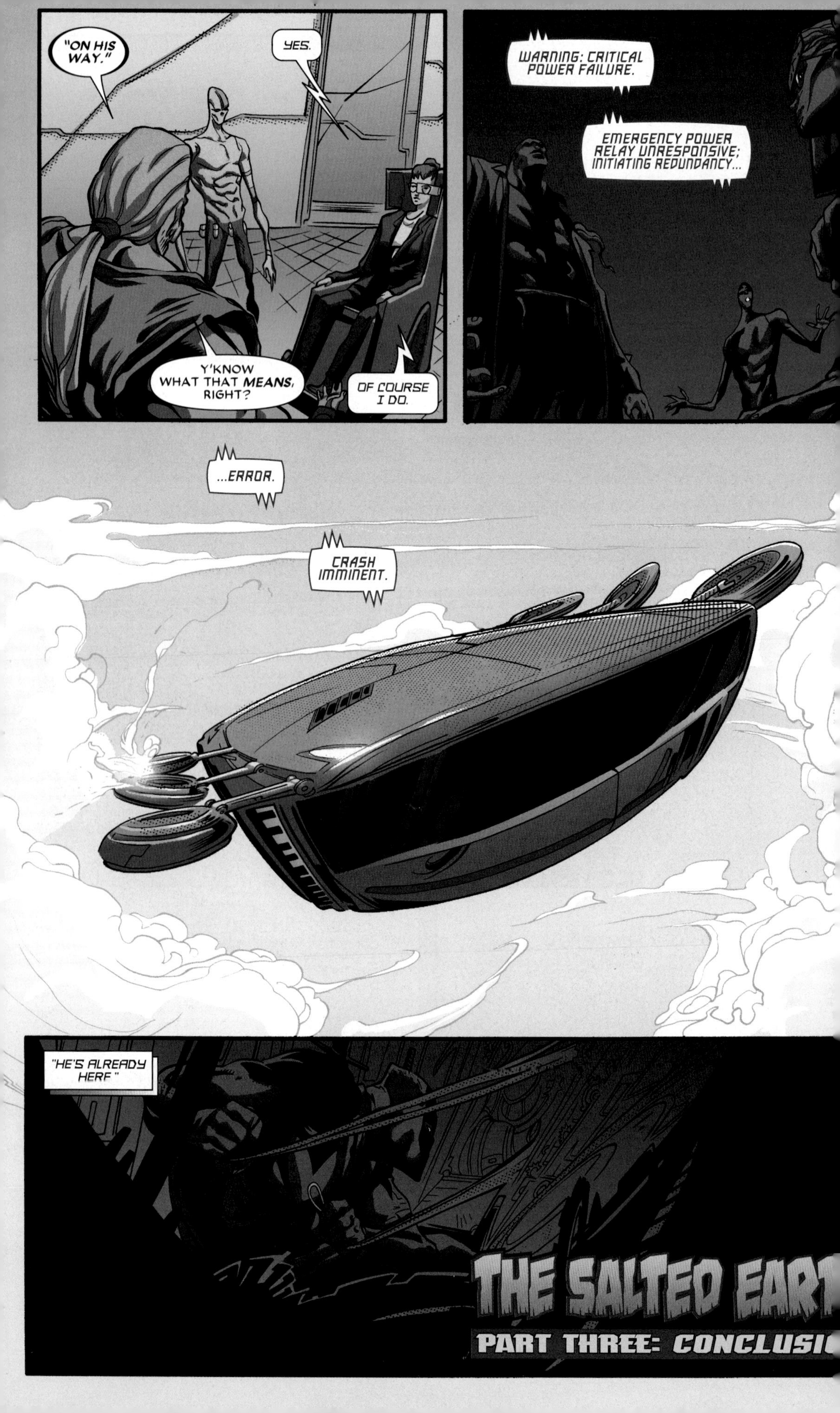
"ON HIS WAY."
YES.
Y'KNOW WHAT THAT MEANS, RIGHT?
OF COURSE I DO.
WARNING: CRITICAL POWER FAILURE.
EMERGENCY POWER RELAY UNRESPONSIVE; INITIATING REDUNDANCY...
...ERROR.
CRASH IMMINENT.
"HE'S ALREADY HERE"
THE SALTED EART
PART THREE: CONCLUSI

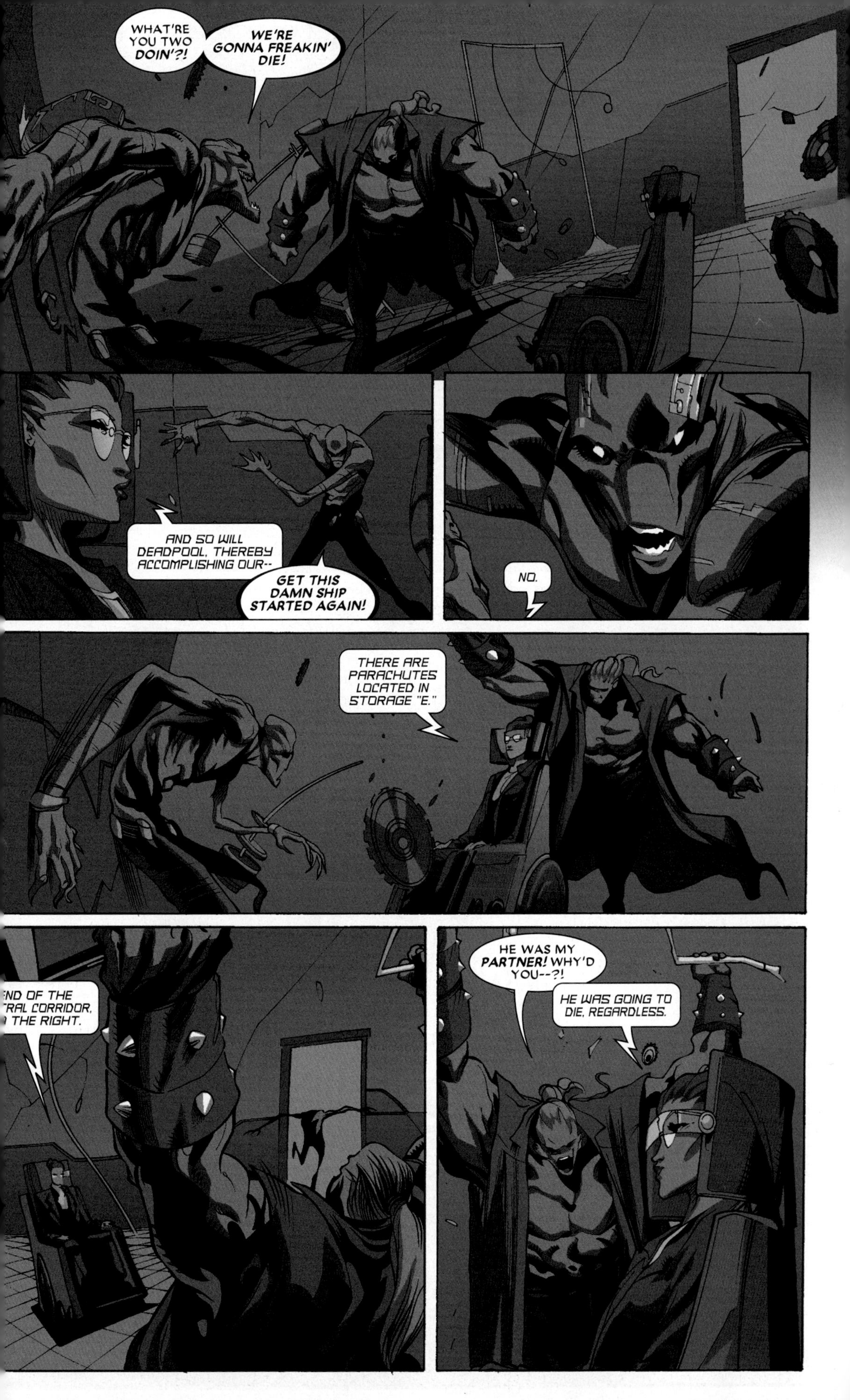
WHAT'RE YOU TWO DOIN'?!
WE'RE GONNA FREAKIN' DIE!
AND SO WILL DEADPOOL, THEREBY ACCOMPLISHING OUR--
GET THIS DAMN SHIP STARTED AGAIN!
NO.
THERE ARE PARACHUTES LOCATED IN STORAGE "E."
END OF THE TRAL CORRIDOR, THE RIGHT.
HE WAS MY PARTNER! WHY'D YOU--?!
HE WAS GOING TO DIE, REGARDLESS.

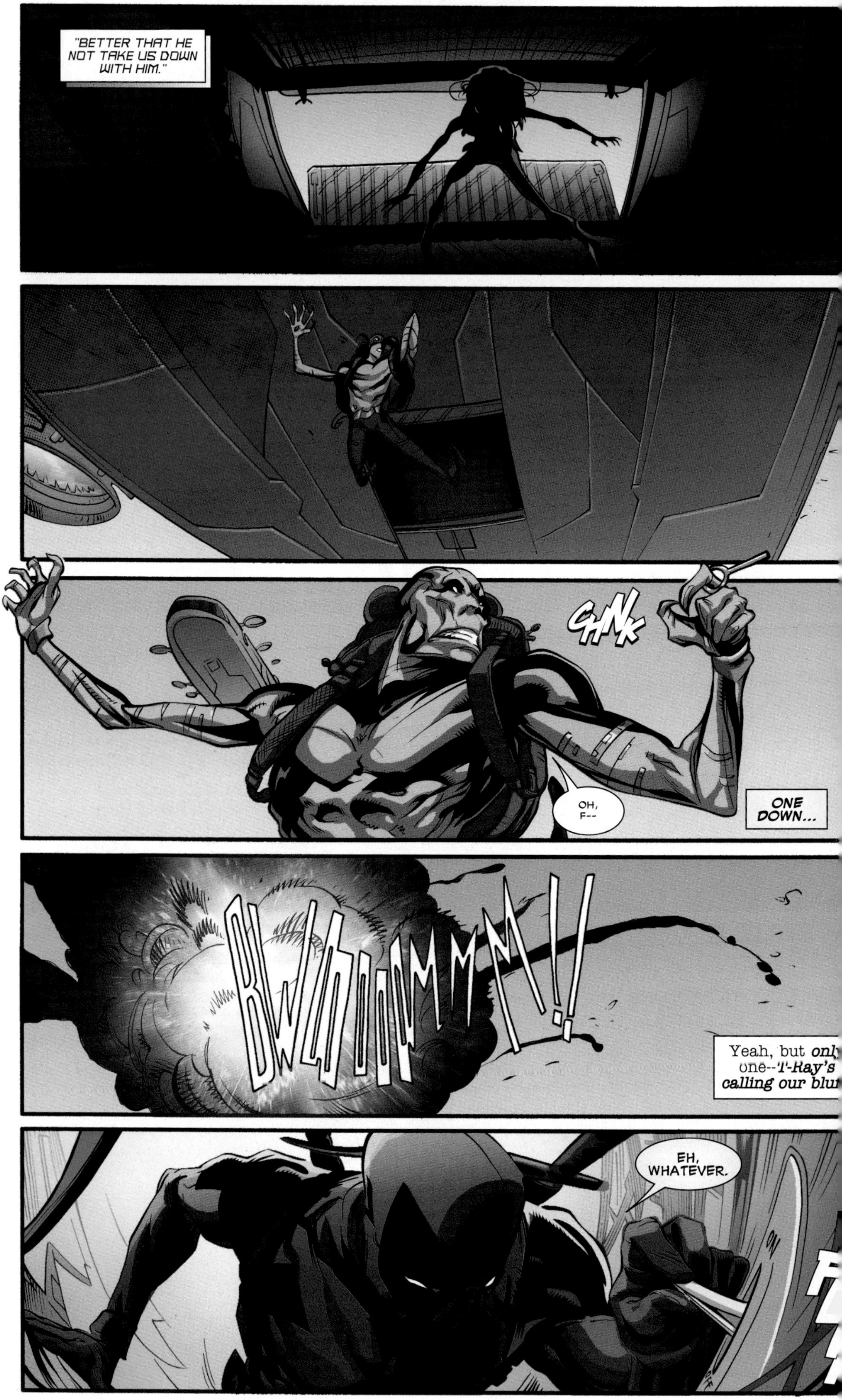

"BETTER THAT HE NOT TAKE US DOWN WITH HIM."
CHNK
OH, F--
ONE DOWN...
BWBOOMMM!!
Yeah, but
one--T-Ray's
calling our
EH, WHATEVER.

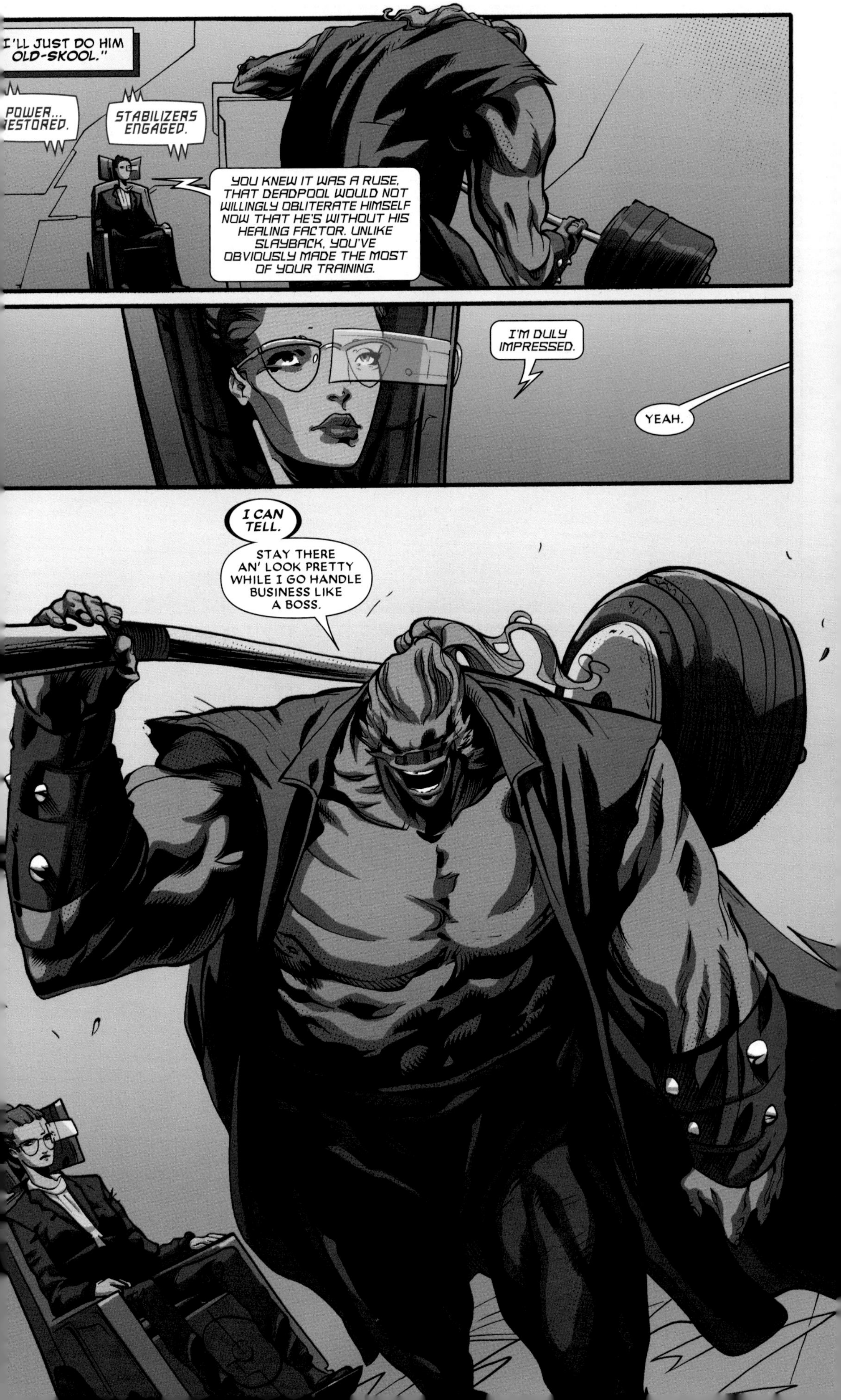

I'LL JUST DO HIM OLD-SKOOL."
POWER... RESTORED.
STABILIZERS ENGAGED.
YOU KNEW IT WAS A RUSE, THAT DEADPOOL WOULD NOT WILLINGLY OBLITERATE HIMSELF NOW THAT HE'S WITHOUT HIS HEALING FACTOR. UNLIKE SLAYBACK, YOU'VE OBVIOUSLY MADE THE MOST OF YOUR TRAINING.
I'M DULY IMPRESSED.
YEAH.
I CAN TELL.
STAY THERE AN' LOOK PRETTY WHILE I GO HANDLE BUSINESS LIKE A BOSS.

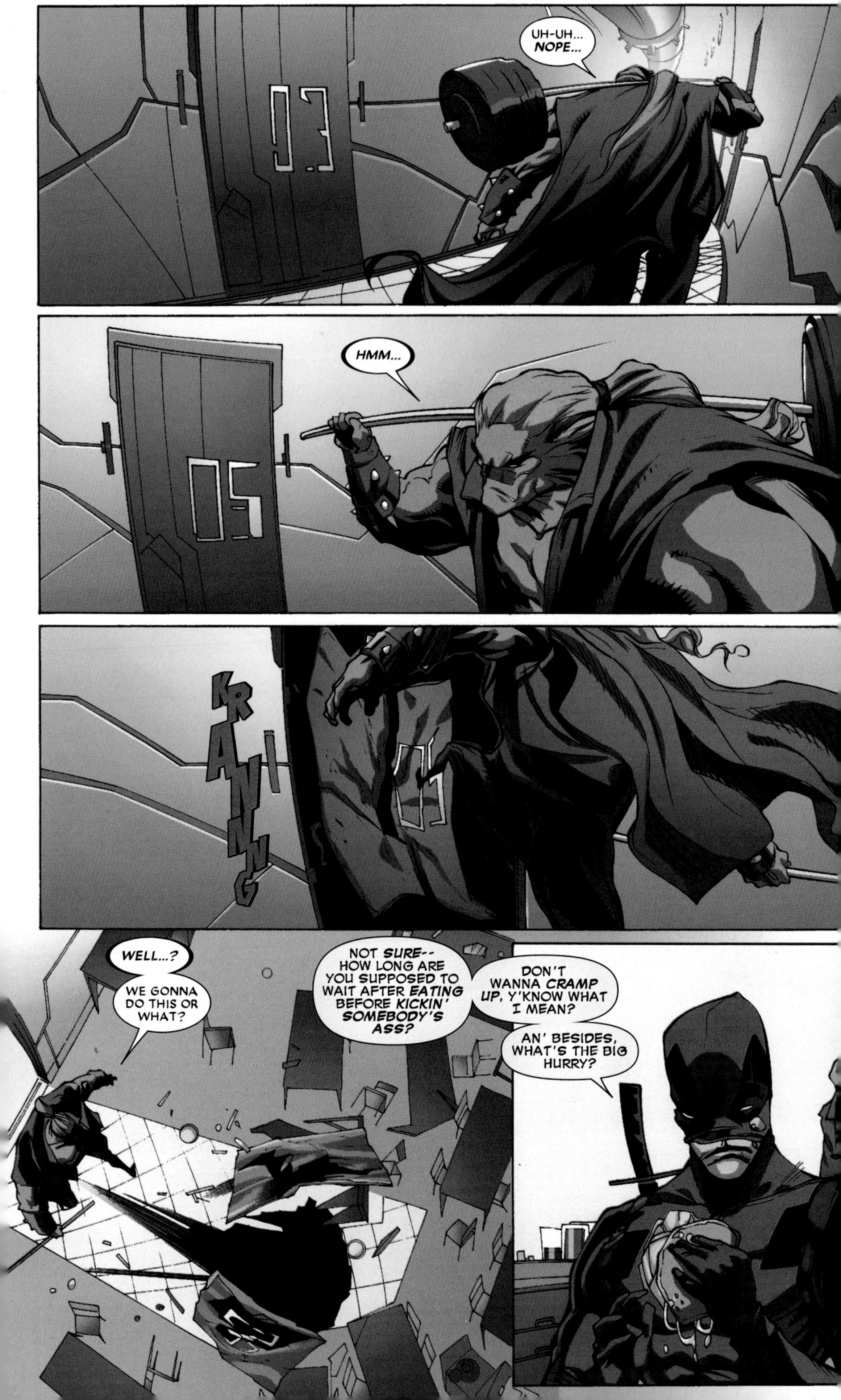

UH-UH... NOPE...
HMM...
KRANNNG
WELL...?
WE GONNA DO THIS OR WHAT?
NOT SURE-- HOW LONG ARE YOU SUPPOSED TO WAIT AFTER EATING BEFORE KICKIN' SOMEBODY'S ASS?
DON'T WANNA CRAMP UP, Y'KNOW WHAT I MEAN?
AN' BESIDES, WHAT'S THE BIG HURRY?

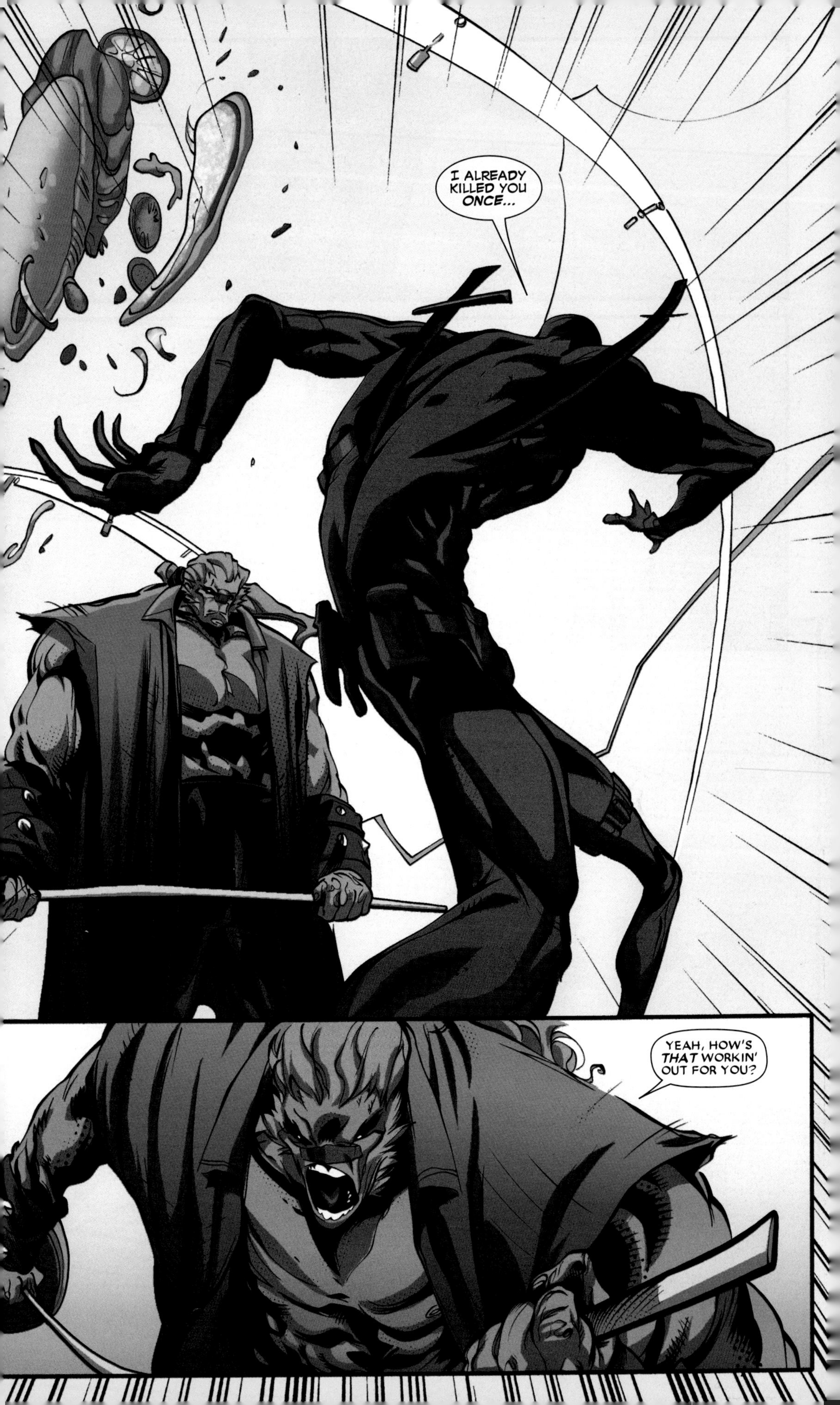
I ALREADY KILLED YOU ONCE...
YEAH, HOW'S THAT WORKIN' OUT FOR YOU?

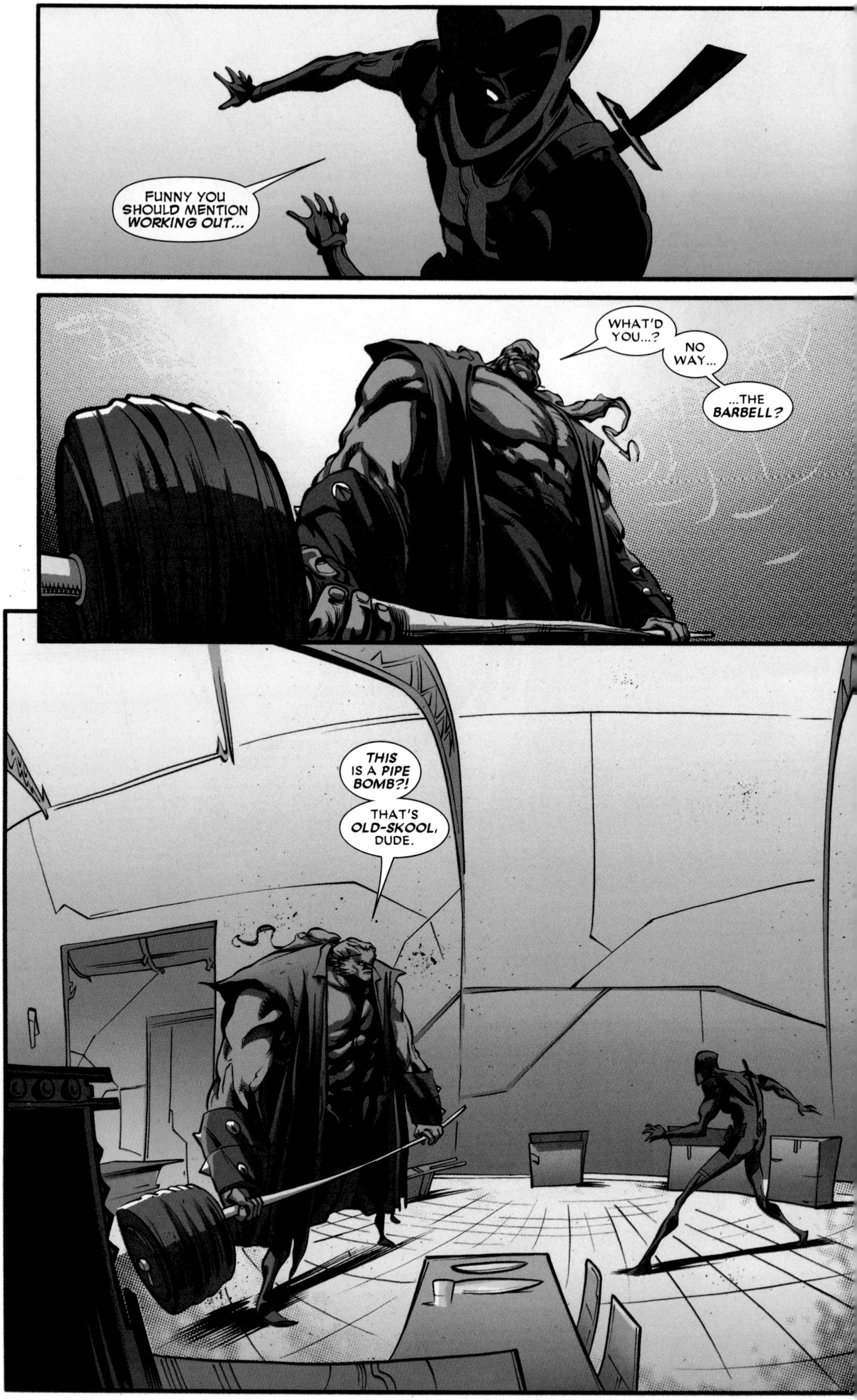
FUNNY YOU SHOULD MENTION *WORKING OUT...*
WHAT'D YOU...?
NO WAY...
...THE *BARBELL?*
THIS IS A *PIPE BOMB?!*
THAT'S *OLD-SKOOL,* DUDE.

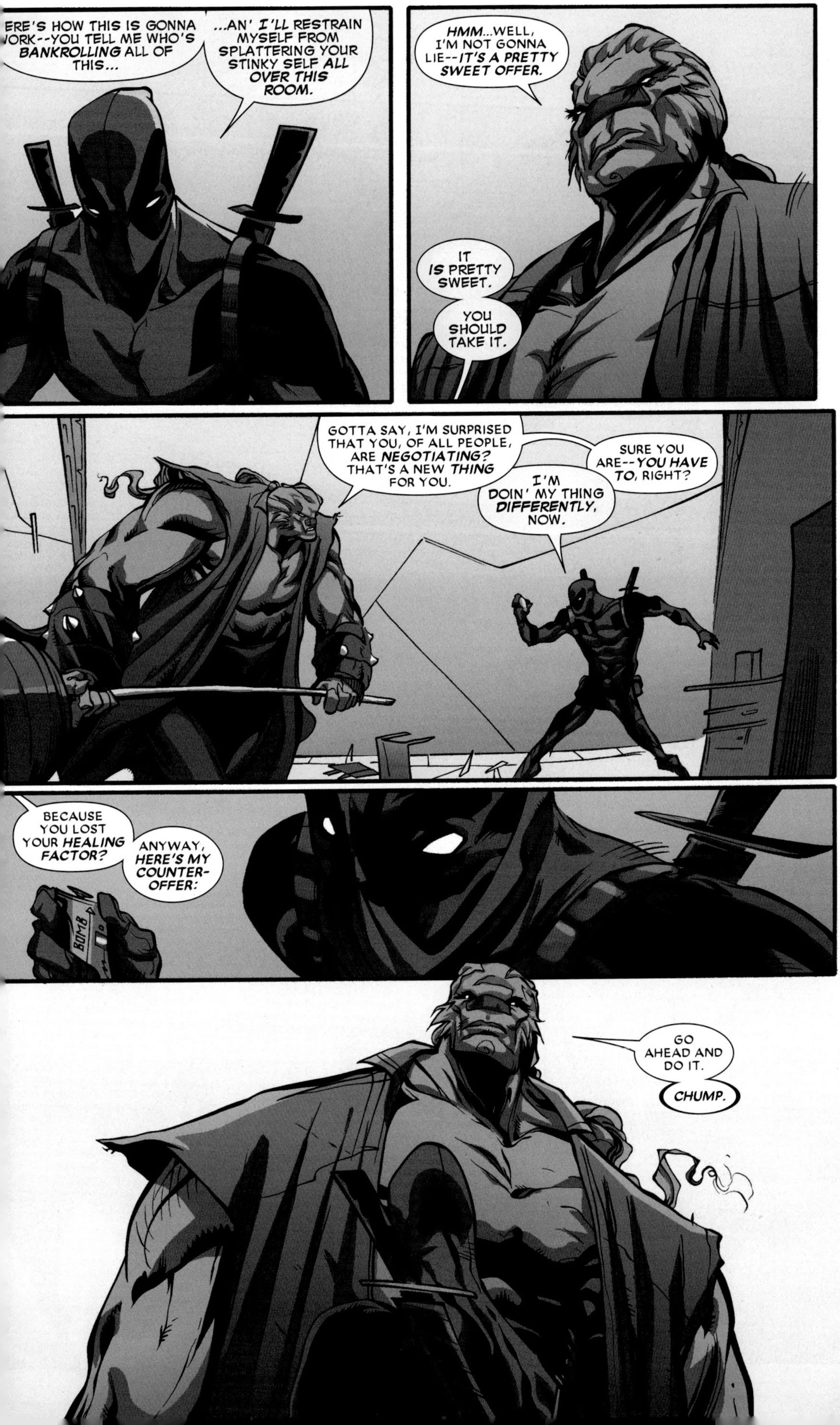
ERE'S HOW THIS IS GONNA VORK--YOU TELL ME WHO'S BANKROLLING ALL OF THIS...
...AN' I'LL RESTRAIN MYSELF FROM SPLATTERING YOUR STINKY SELF ALL OVER THIS ROOM.
HMM...WELL, I'M NOT GONNA LIE--IT'S A PRETTY SWEET OFFER.
IT IS PRETTY SWEET.
YOU SHOULD TAKE IT.
GOTTA SAY, I'M SURPRISED THAT YOU, OF ALL PEOPLE, ARE NEGOTIATING? THAT'S A NEW THING FOR YOU.
I'M DOIN' MY THING DIFFERENTLY, NOW.
SURE YOU ARE--YOU HAVE TO, RIGHT?
BECAUSE YOU LOST YOUR HEALING FACTOR?
ANYWAY, HERE'S MY COUNTER-OFFER:
BOMB
GO AHEAD AND DO IT.
CHUMP.

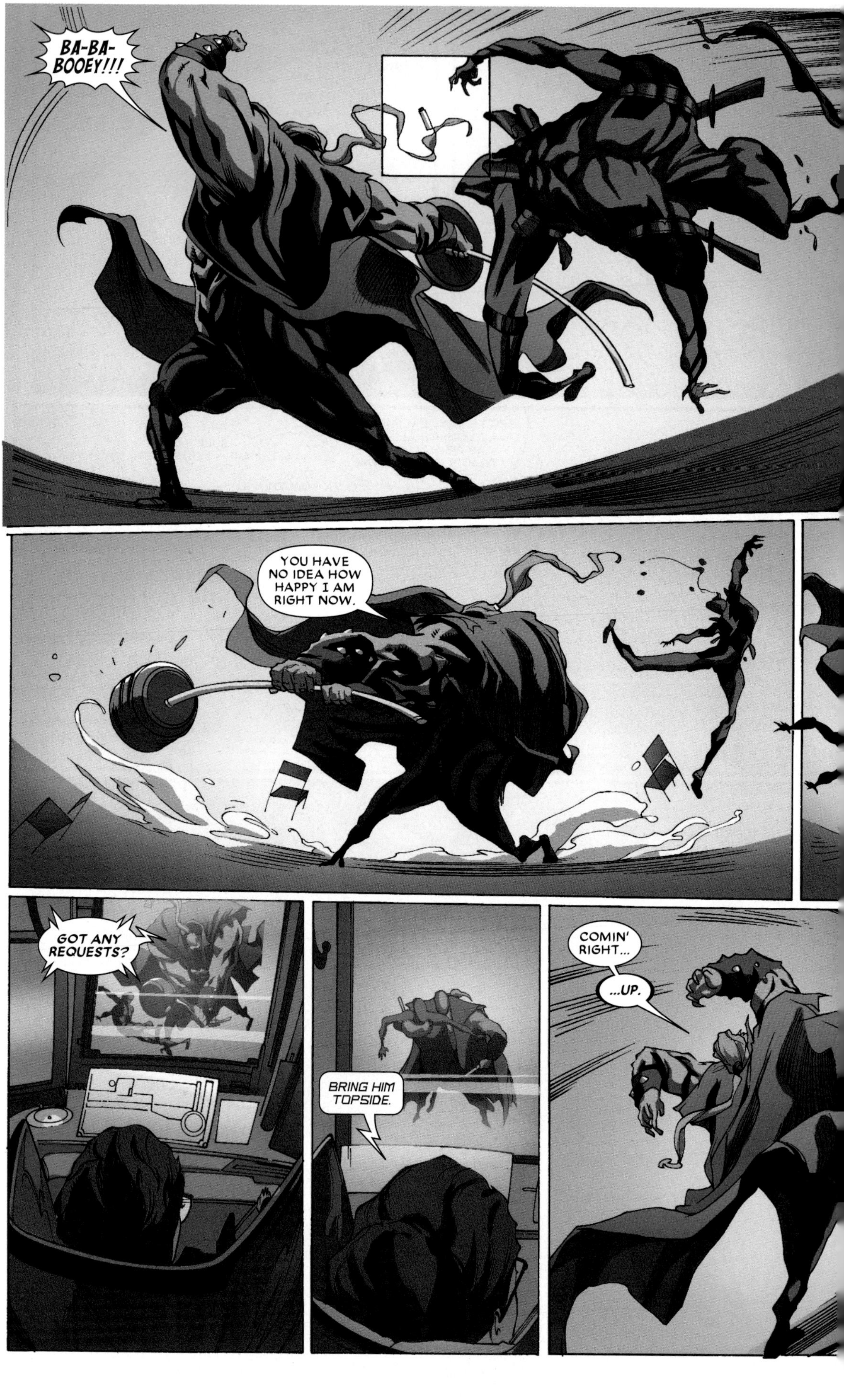
BA-BA-BOOEY!!!
YOU HAVE NO IDEA HOW HAPPY I AM RIGHT NOW.
GOT ANY REQUESTS?
BRING HIM TOPSIDE.
COMIN' RIGHT...
...UP.

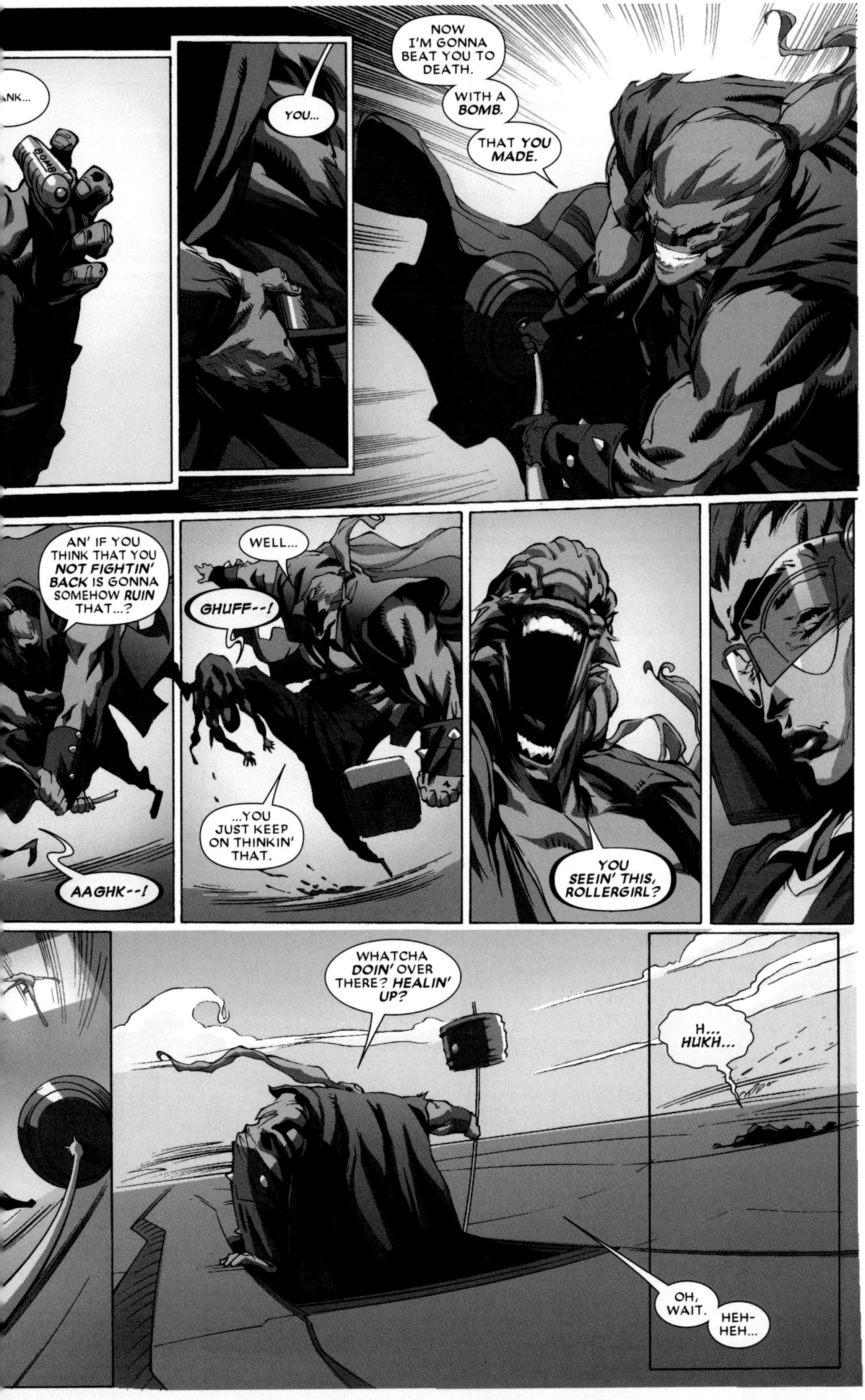

NK...
YOU...
NOW I'M GONNA BEAT YOU TO DEATH.
WITH A BOMB.
THAT YOU MADE.
AN' IF YOU THINK THAT YOU NOT FIGHTIN' BACK IS GONNA SOMEHOW RUIN THAT...?
AAGHK--!
WELL...
GHUFF--!
...YOU JUST KEEP ON THINKIN' THAT.
YOU SEEIN' THIS, ROLLERGIRL?
WHATCHA DOIN' OVER THERE? HEALIN' UP?
H... HUKH...
OH, WAIT.
HEH-HEH...

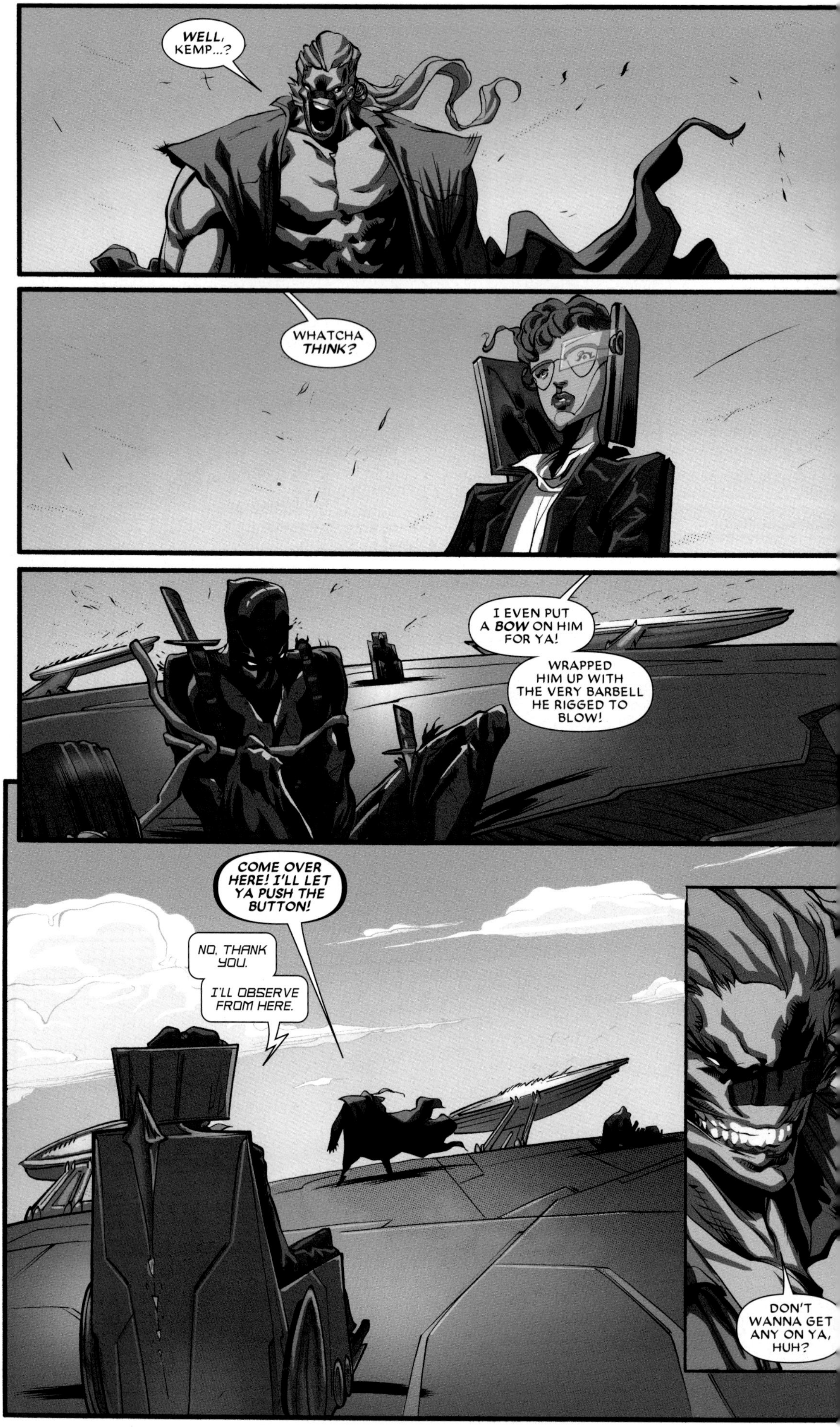
WELL, KEMP...?
WHATCHA THINK?
I EVEN PUT A BOW ON HIM FOR YA!
WRAPPED HIM UP WITH THE VERY BARBELL HE RIGGED TO BLOW!
COME OVER HERE! I'LL LET YA PUSH THE BUTTON!
NO, THANK YOU.
I'LL OBSERVE FROM HERE.
DON'T WANNA GET ANY ON YA, HUH?

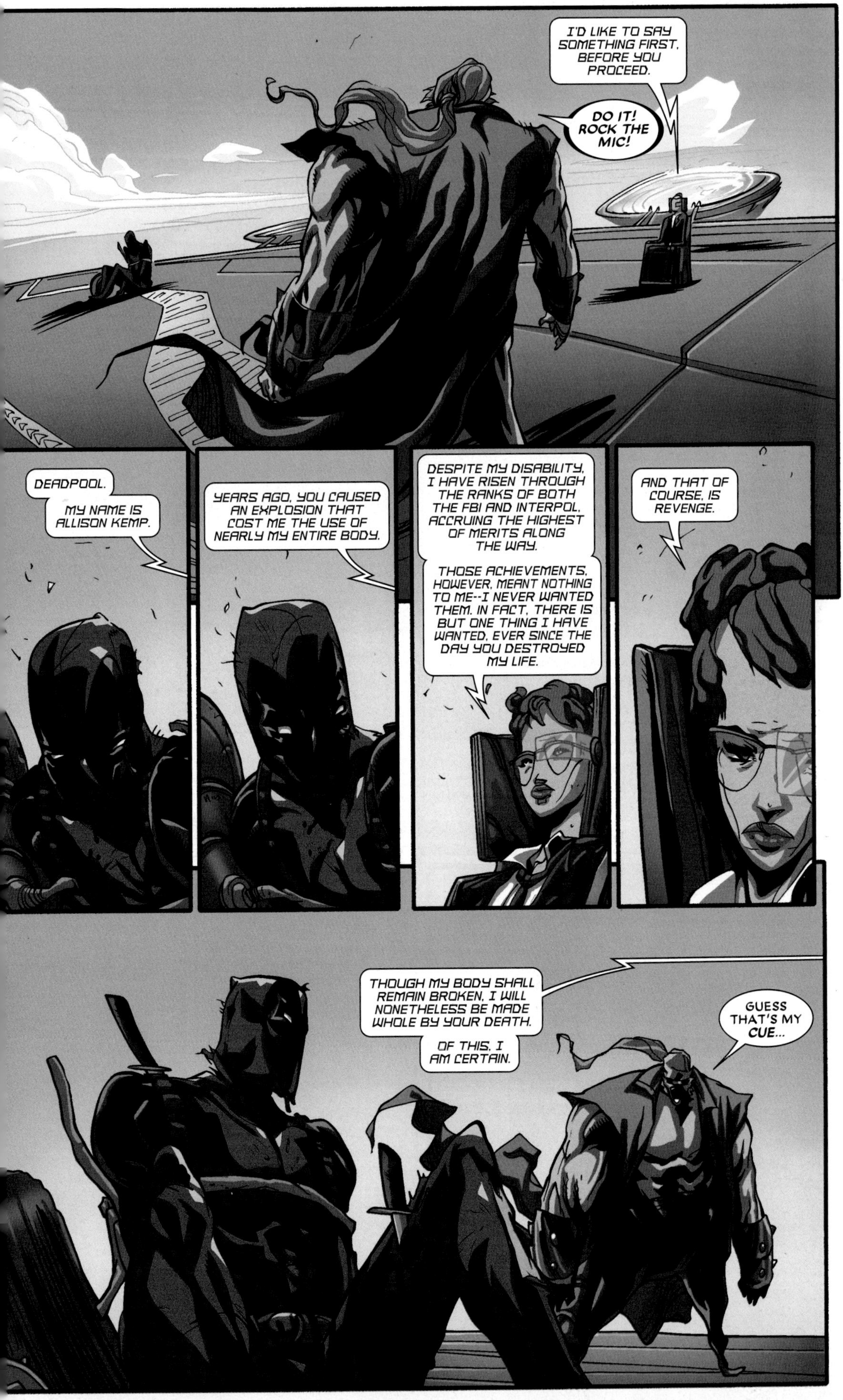
I'D LIKE TO SAY SOMETHING FIRST, BEFORE YOU PROCEED.
DO IT! ROCK THE MIC!
DEADPOOL.
MY NAME IS ALLISON KEMP.
YEARS AGO, YOU CAUSED AN EXPLOSION THAT COST ME THE USE OF NEARLY MY ENTIRE BODY.
DESPITE MY DISABILITY, I HAVE RISEN THROUGH THE RANKS OF BOTH THE FBI AND INTERPOL, ACCRUING THE HIGHEST OF MERITS ALONG THE WAY.
THOSE ACHIEVEMENTS, HOWEVER, MEANT NOTHING TO ME--I NEVER WANTED THEM. IN FACT, THERE IS BUT ONE THING I HAVE WANTED, EVER SINCE THE DAY YOU DESTROYED MY LIFE.
AND THAT OF COURSE, IS REVENGE.
THOUGH MY BODY SHALL REMAIN BROKEN, I WILL NONETHELESS BE MADE WHOLE BY YOUR DEATH.
OF THIS, I AM CERTAIN.
GUESS THAT'S MY CUE...

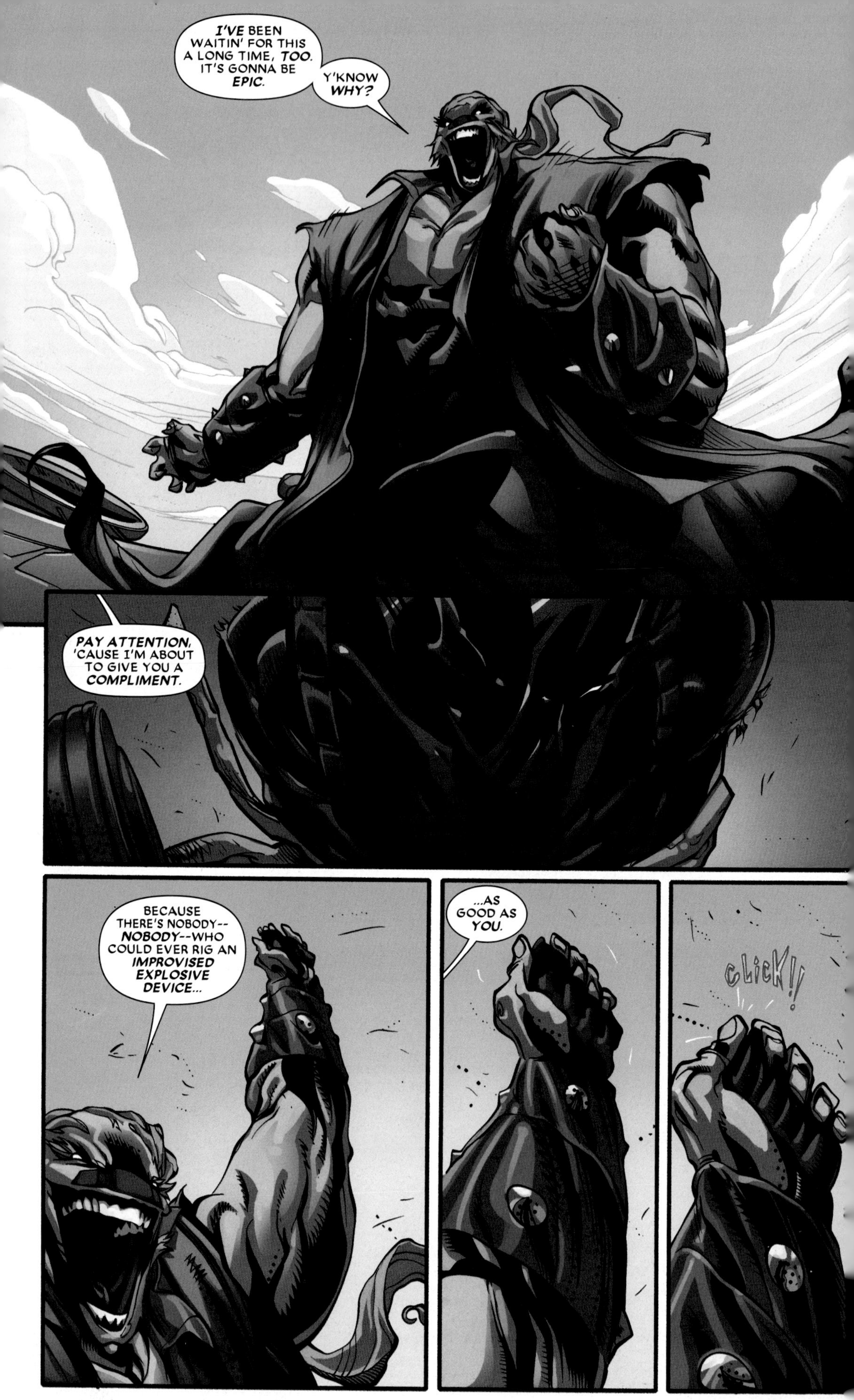

I'VE BEEN WAITIN' FOR THIS A LONG TIME, TOO. IT'S GONNA BE EPIC.
Y'KNOW WHY?
PAY ATTENTION, 'CAUSE I'M ABOUT TO GIVE YOU A COMPLIMENT.
BECAUSE THERE'S NOBODY-- NOBODY--WHO COULD EVER RIG AN IMPROVISED EXPLOSIVE DEVICE...
...AS GOOD AS YOU.
CLICK!!

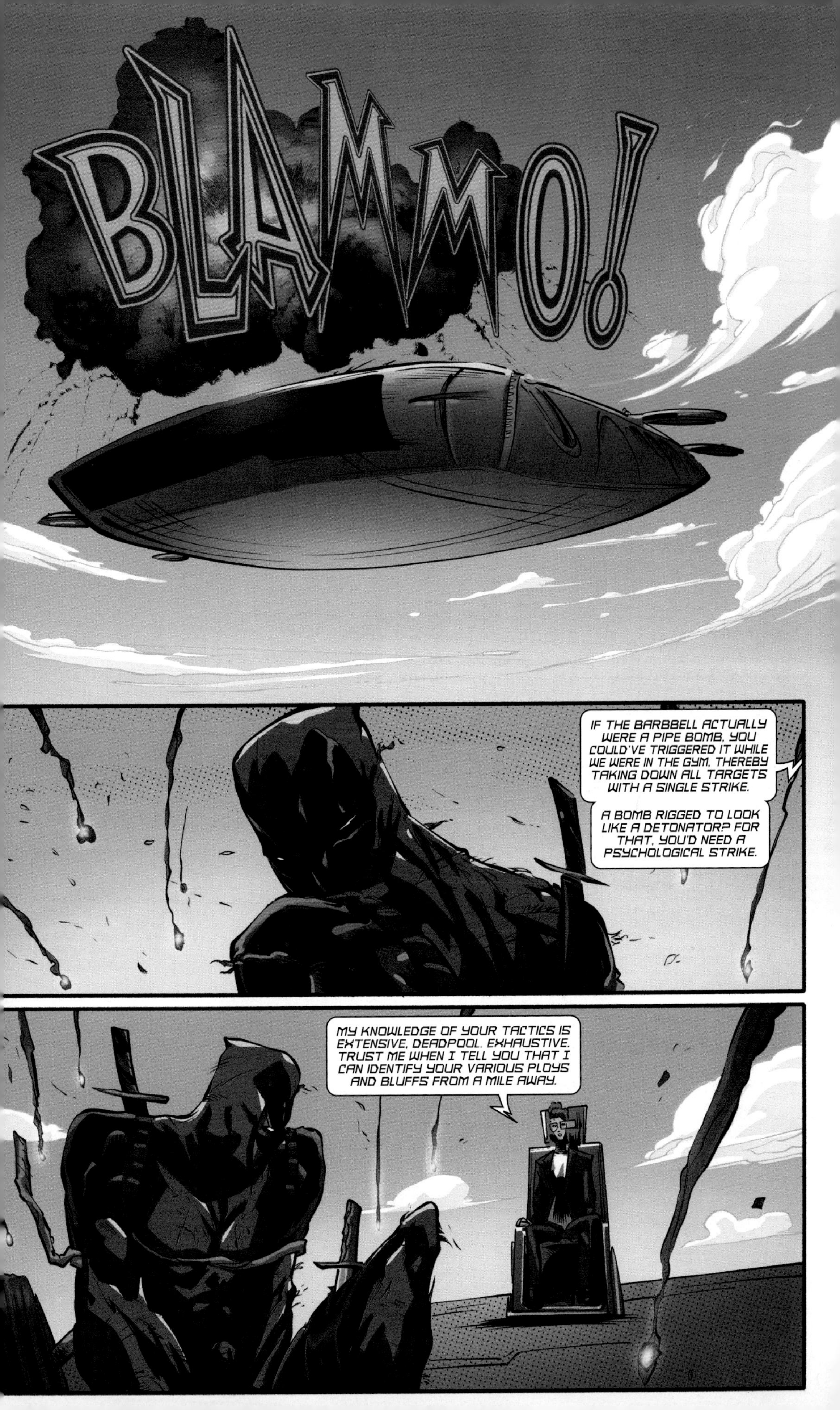
BLAMMO!
IF THE BARBBELL ACTUALLY WERE A PIPE BOMB, YOU COULD'VE TRIGGERED IT WHILE WE WERE IN THE GYM, THEREBY TAKING DOWN ALL TARGETS WITH A SINGLE STRIKE.
A BOMB RIGGED TO LOOK LIKE A DETONATOR? FOR THAT, YOU'D NEED A PSYCHOLOGICAL STRIKE.
MY KNOWLEDGE OF YOUR TACTICS IS EXTENSIVE, DEADPOOL. EXHAUSTIVE. TRUST ME WHEN I TELL YOU THAT I CAN IDENTIFY YOUR VARIOUS PLOYS AND BLUFFS FROM A MILE AWAY.

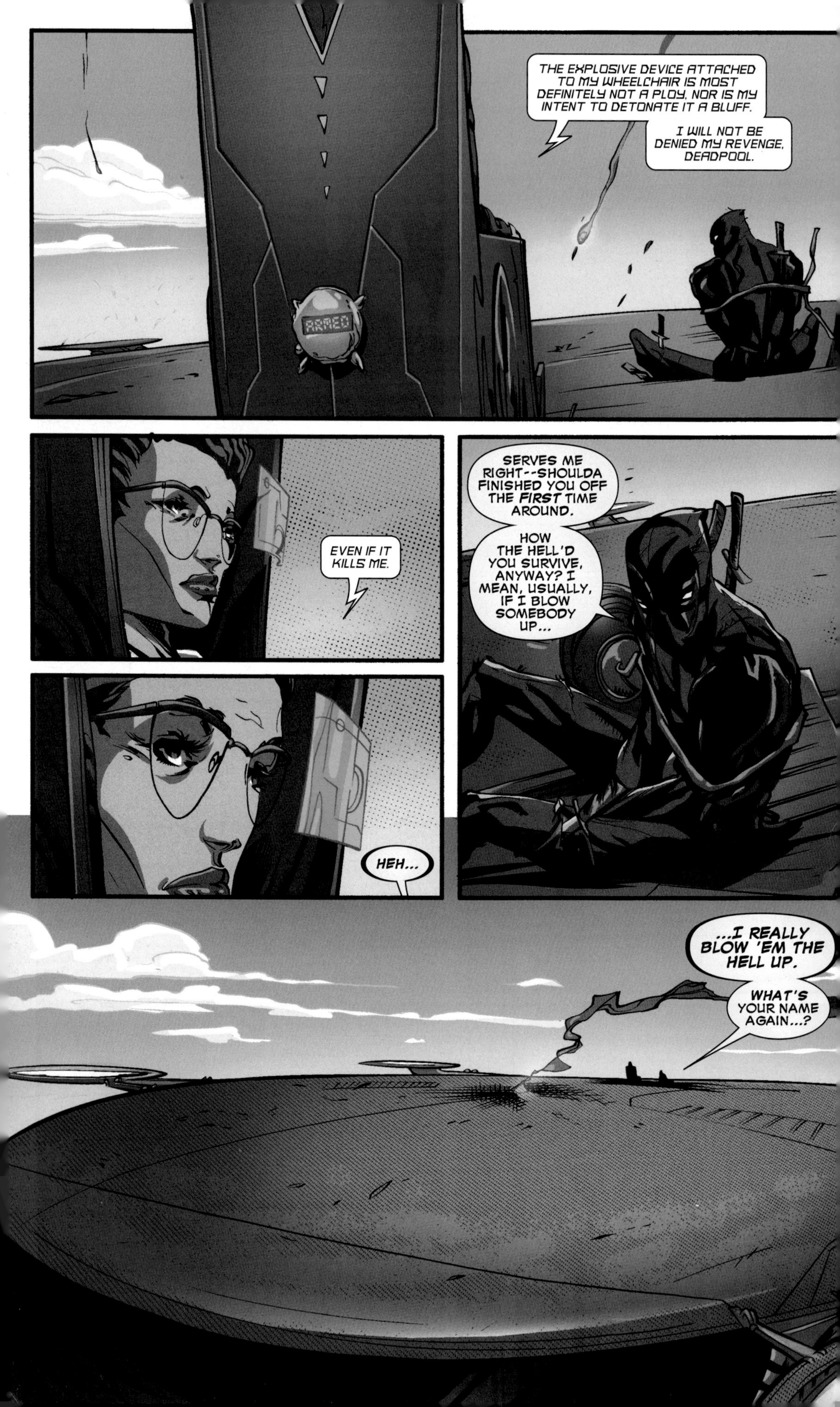

ARMED
THE EXPLOSIVE DEVICE ATTACHED TO MY WHEELCHAIR IS MOST DEFINITELY NOT A PLOY, NOR IS MY INTENT TO DETONATE IT A BLUFF.
I WILL NOT BE DENIED MY REVENGE, DEADPOOL.
EVEN IF IT KILLS ME.
SERVES ME RIGHT--SHOULDA FINISHED YOU OFF THE FIRST TIME AROUND.
HOW THE HELL'D YOU SURVIVE, ANYWAY? I MEAN, USUALLY, IF I BLOW SOMEBODY UP...
HEH...
...I REALLY BLOW 'EM THE HELL UP.
WHAT'S YOUR NAME AGAIN...?

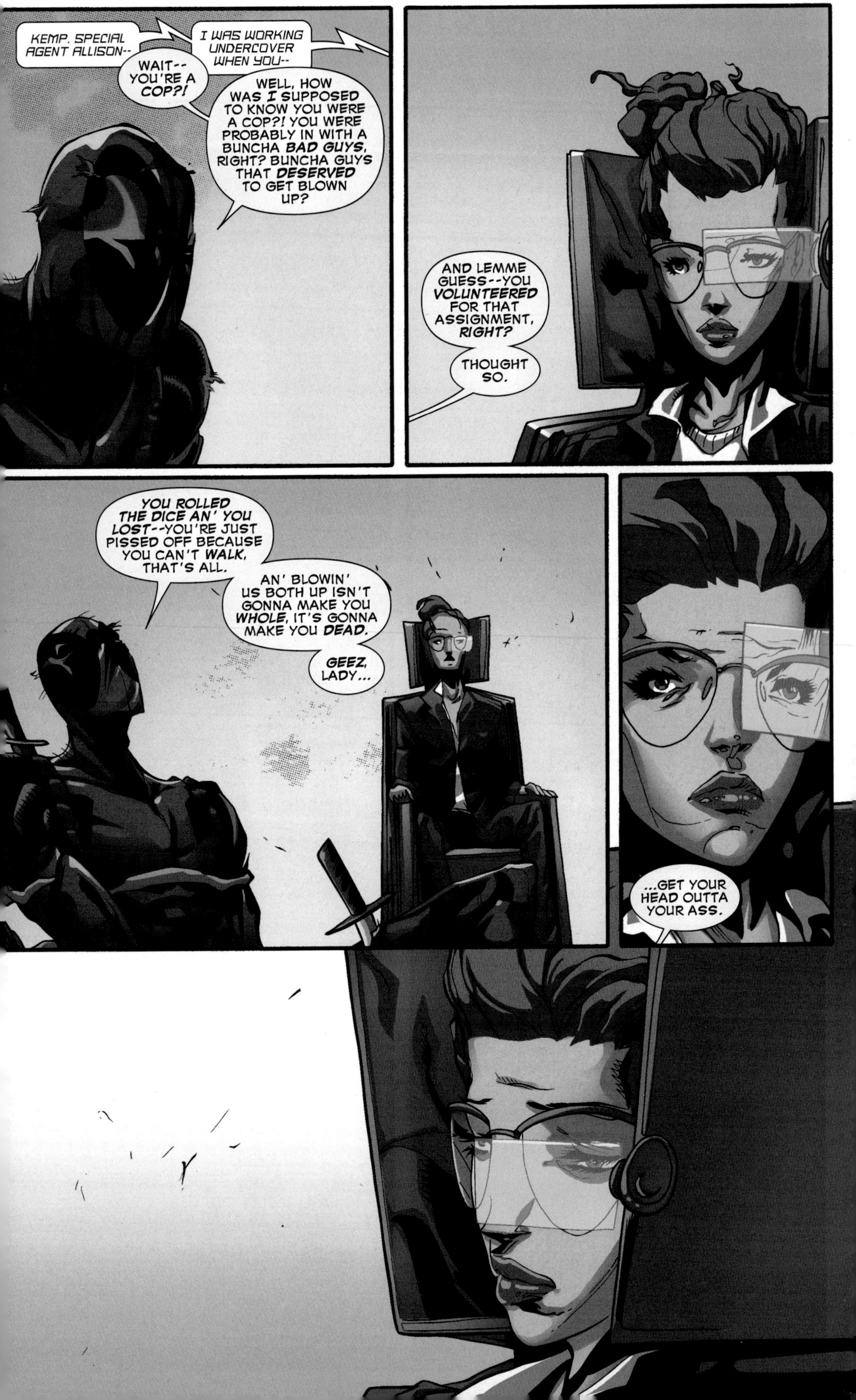
KEMP. SPECIAL AGENT ALLISON--
WAIT-- YOU'RE A COP?!
I WAS WORKING UNDERCOVER WHEN YOU--
WELL, HOW WAS I SUPPOSED TO KNOW YOU WERE A COP?! YOU WERE PROBABLY IN WITH A BUNCHA BAD GUYS, RIGHT? BUNCHA GUYS THAT DESERVED TO GET BLOWN UP?
AND LEMME GUESS--YOU VOLUNTEERED FOR THAT ASSIGNMENT, RIGHT?
THOUGHT SO.
YOU ROLLED THE DICE AN' YOU LOST--YOU'RE JUST PISSED OFF BECAUSE YOU CAN'T WALK, THAT'S ALL.
AN' BLOWIN' US BOTH UP ISN'T GONNA MAKE YOU WHOLE, IT'S GONNA MAKE YOU DEAD.
GEEZ, LADY...
...GET YOUR HEAD OUTTA YOUR ASS.

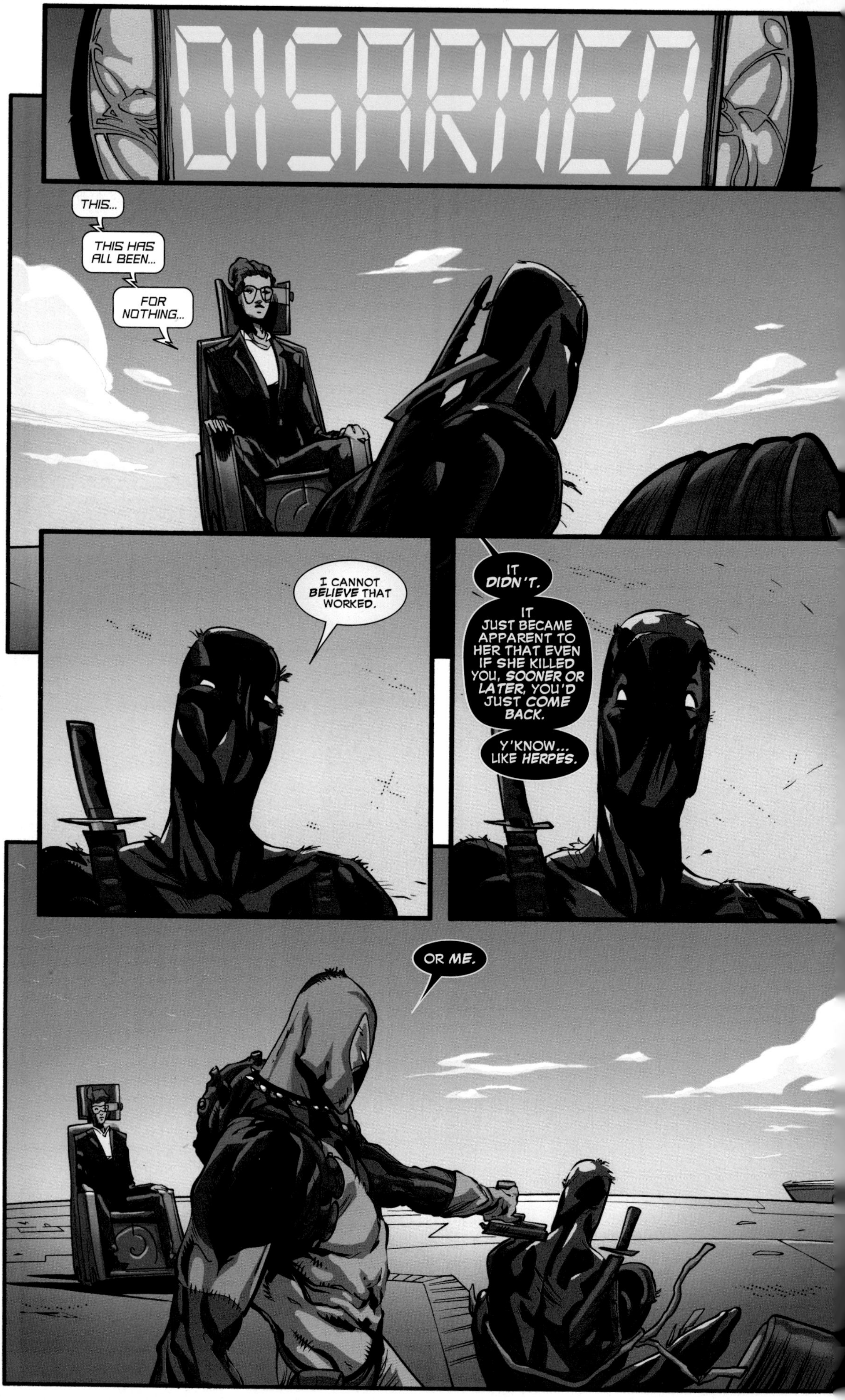
DISARMED
THIS...
THIS HAS ALL BEEN...
FOR NOTHING...
I CANNOT BELIEVE THAT WORKED.
IT DIDN'T.
IT JUST BECAME APPARENT TO HER THAT EVEN IF SHE KILLED YOU, SOONER OR LATER, YOU'D JUST COME BACK.
Y'KNOW... LIKE HERPES.
OR ME.

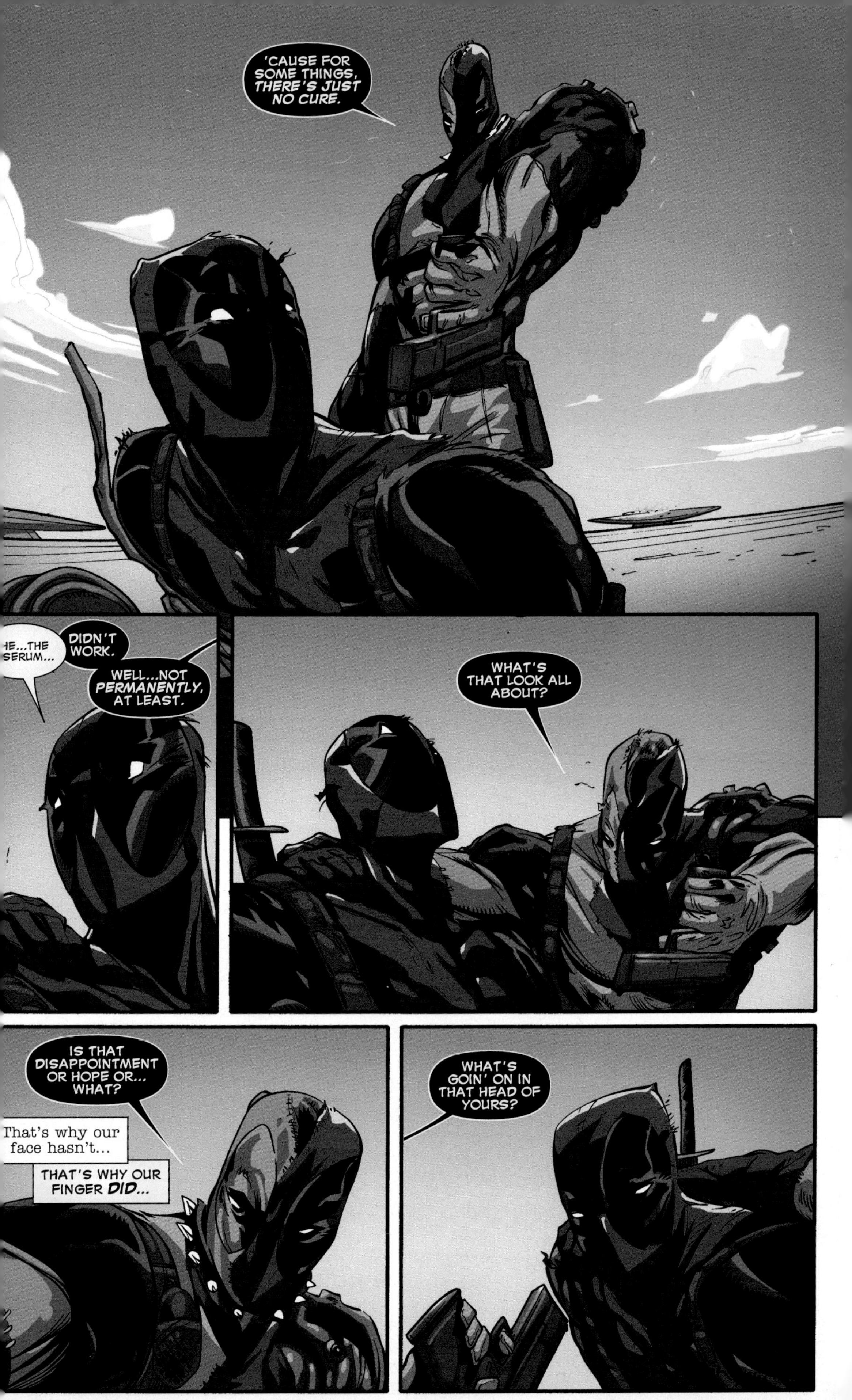
'CAUSE FOR SOME THINGS, THERE'S JUST NO CURE.
HE...THE SERUM...
DIDN'T WORK.
WELL...NOT PERMANENTLY, AT LEAST.
WHAT'S THAT LOOK ALL ABOUT?
IS THAT DISAPPOINTMENT OR HOPE OR... WHAT?
That's why our face hasn't...
THAT'S WHY OUR FINGER DID...
WHAT'S GOIN' ON IN THAT HEAD OF YOURS?

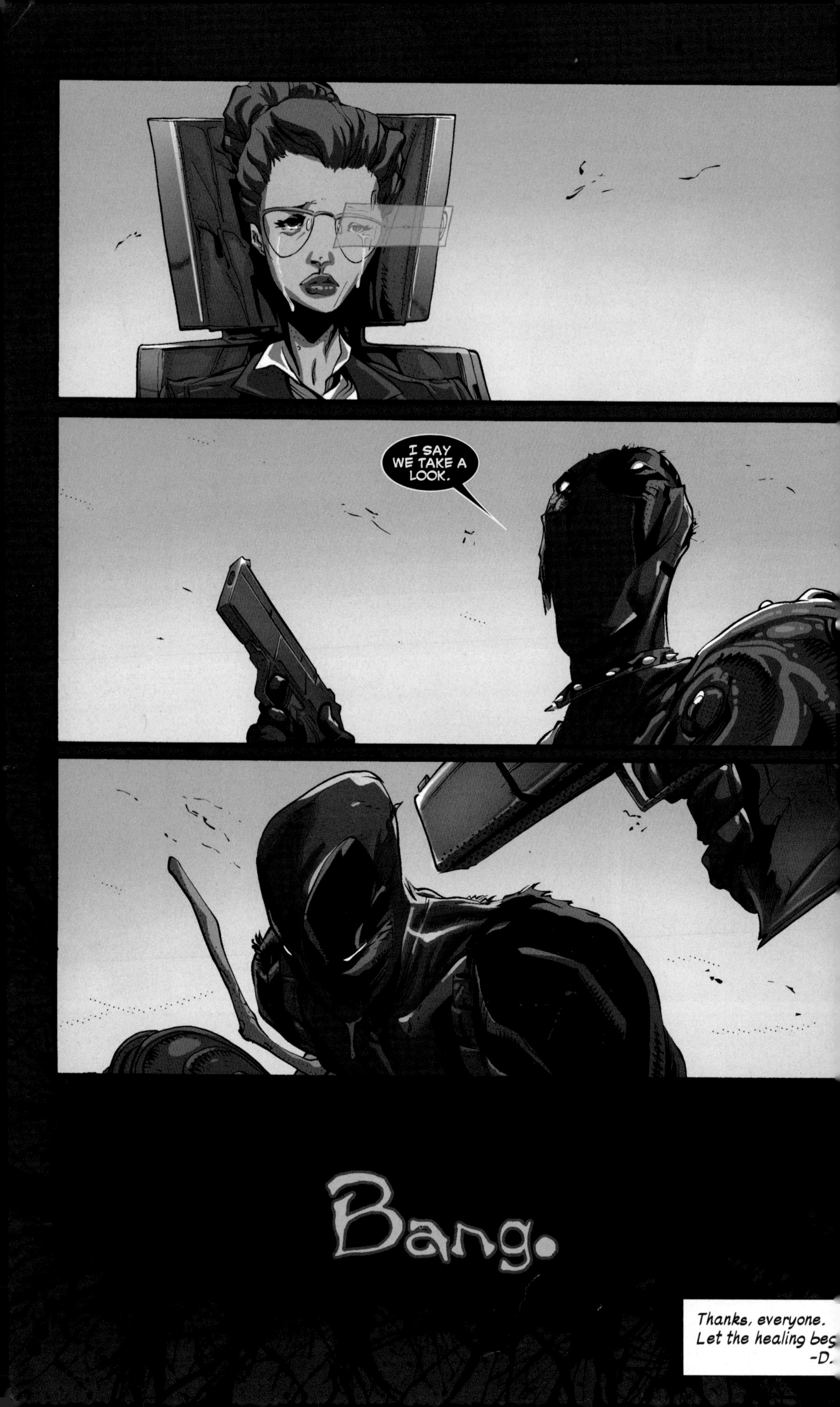
I SAY WE TAKE A LOOK.
Bang.
Thanks, everyone.
Let the healing beg
-D.

"Hey, man. So, ah, listen…Deadpool."

That's essentially [ho]w it started, with [Ax]el Alonso calling [m]e up and telling me [th]at the door was open [fo]r a new Deadpool [se]ries. Unfortunately, [it] was at a time when [th]e character's profile [ha]d dropped to a [re]cord low. Though [th]e character has [al]ways carried with it [a] small but intensely [lo]yal fanbase, it had [ne]ver before been [th]is small. This would [en]d up being, in my [hu]mble opinion, the [bi]ggest contributor to [th]is series' success.

No one was waiting [fo]r a new Deadpool [se]ries. Expectations [we]re zero. In other [wo]rds, I was free to do [an]ything I wanted… [be]cause no one really [ca]red. No one, that is, [ex]cept myself, Axel [an]d my first editor [on] the book, John [Ba]rber. We knew that [we] had something. [Th]e challenge was to [fi]gure out how to let [ev]eryone else know.

And that's when it [oc]curred to me that Deadpool and I had a common interest. As much as I wanted attention on this new series, Deadpool wanted it more. He'd been pushed to the margins of the Marvel Universe for long enough. It was time for everyone to get out of his way, hang back and just let him do his thing because a star's gonna shine no matter what.

Coincidentally, this is also when my already tenuous grasp on reality really began to slip.

From our soft opening in Wolverine: Origins to our grand entrance during Secret Invasion until now, 65 issues later (yes, 65—don't forget about our TWO "Point One" issues), the mission has remained the same: make as much noise as we can, cause as much chaos as possible, all with the simple intent of getting you, the readers, to look. Once we had that, all that was required was to swing the spotlight over to our boy Wade. Whether you were trying to make sense of what you were seeing or you were content to simply revel in the insanity of it all, the result was the same: We gotcha.

And you liked it. Admit it.

I know I did. Loved it, as a matter of fact. But now it's time for me to rejoin you, the fans. No one is looking forward to what Brian Posehn, Gerry Duggan and Tony Moore have coming up next more than I am. I cannot wait to once again pick up an issue of Deadpool and, just like you, have absolutely no idea what's going to happen. Guys? You have my attention.

Abuse it.

- Daniel Way
September 28,
2012

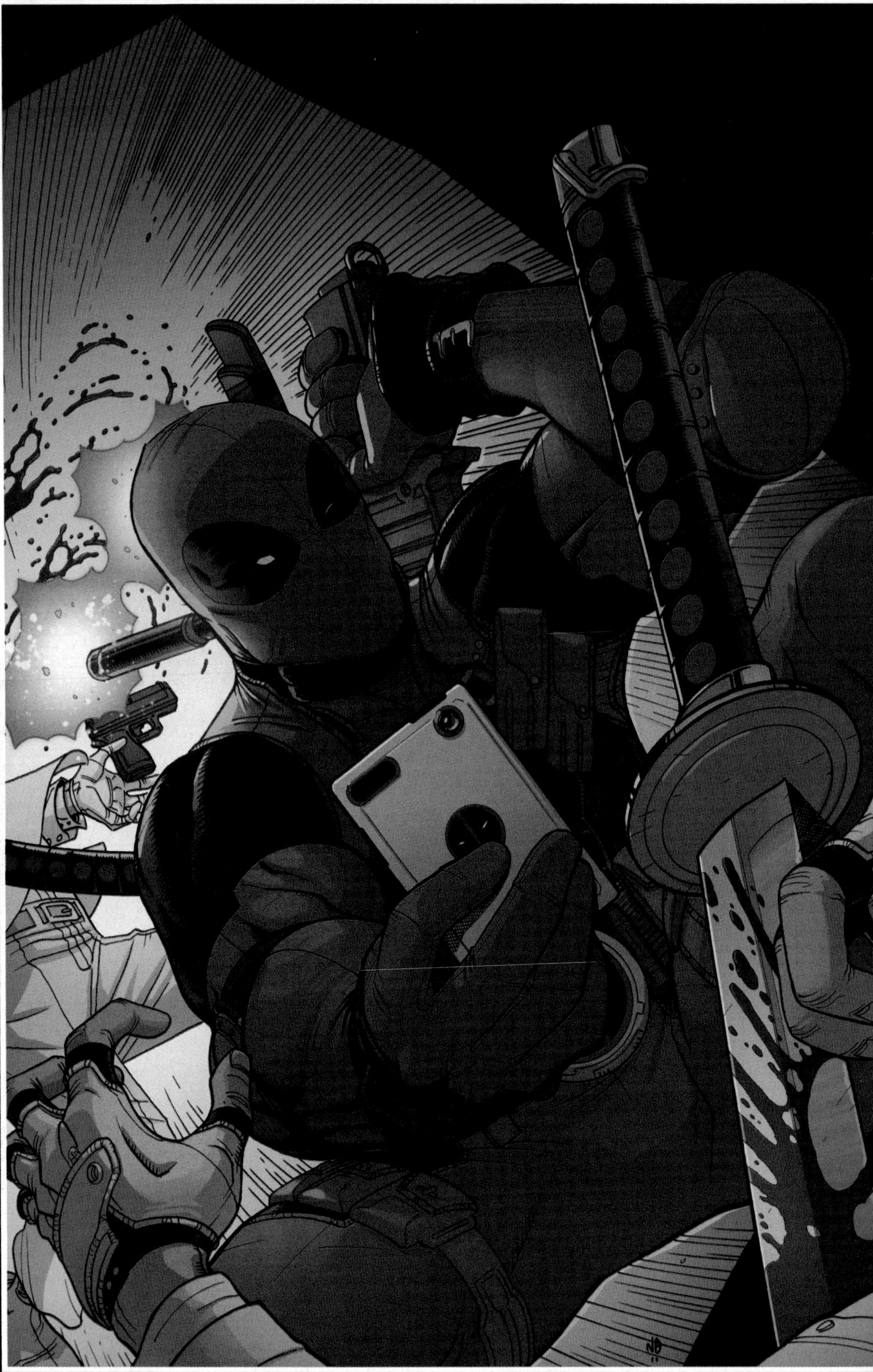

DEADPOOL #50 VARIANT
by Nick Bradshaw & Jim Charalampidis